Library Use Only

Encyclopedia of Domestic Violence and Abuse

Encyclopedia of Domestic Violence and Abuse

Volume 2: S–W and Primary Documents

LAURA L. FINLEY, EDITOR

Santa Barbara, California • Denver, Colorado • Oxford, England

Copyright 2013 by ABC-CLIO, LLC.

All rights reserved. No part of this publication may be reproduced, stored in a retrieval system, or transmitted, in any form or by any means, electronic, mechanical, photocopying, recording, or otherwise, except for the inclusion of brief quotations in a review, without prior permission in writing from the publisher.

Library of Congress Cataloging-in-Publication Data

Encyclopedia of domestic violence and abuse / Laura L. Finley, editor.
    volumes cm
Includes bibliographical references and index.
    ISBN 978–1–61069–001–0 (hard copy : alk. paper) — ISBN 978–1–61069–002–7 (ebook) 1. Family violence—Encyclopedias. 2. Abused women—Encyclopedias. 3. Older people—Abuse of—Encyclopedias. 4. Child abuse—Encyclopedias. 5. Family violence—United States—Encyclopedias. 6. Abused women—United States—Encyclopedias. 7. Older people—Abuse of—United States—Encyclopedias. 8. Child abuse—United States—Encyclopedias. I. Finley, Laura L., editor of compilation.
HV6626.E535   2013
362.82′9203—dc23   2012048843

ISBN: 978–1–61069–001–0
EISBN: 978–1–61069–002–7

17 16 15 14 13   1 2 3 4 5

This book is also available on the World Wide Web as an eBook.
Visit www.abc-clio.com for details.

ABC-CLIO, LLC
130 Cremona Drive, P.O. Box 1911
Santa Barbara, California 93116-1911

This book is printed on acid-free paper ∞

Manufactured in the United States of America

Contents

Alphabetical List of Entries	vii
Topical List of Entries	xi
Preface	xv
Acknowledgments	xvii
Introduction	xix
Timeline of Significant Events Related to Domestic Violence and Abuse	xxxiii
Encyclopedia Entries	1
Appendix 1: Primary Documents	571
1. Convention on the Elimination of All Forms of Discrimination Against Women	571
2. Report of the Inter-American Commission on Human Rights re: *Jessica Lenahan (Gonzales) et al. v. United States*	585
3. Trafficking Victims Protection Act of 2000	661
4. Violence Against Women Act	756
Appendix 2: State, National, and International Organizations Related to Domestic Abuse	815
Glossary	835
Recommended Resources: Books, Journals, Articles, and Videos	841
About the Editor and Contributors	851
Index	857

Alphabetical List of Entries

Acid Throwing
Africa and Domestic Abuse
AIDS and Domestic Violence
Alaska Natives and Domestic Abuse
Alcohol and Domestic Abuse
Ali, Somy
American Medical Association (AMA)
Amnesty International
Anger Management and Domestic Abuse
Animal Abuse and Domestic Abuse
Asia and Domestic Abuse
Athletes and Domestic Abuse
Avon Corporation

Battered Woman Syndrome
Batterer Intervention Programs
Beijing Declaration and Platform for Action
Biological and Psychological Theories about Domestic Abuse
The Body Shop
Break the Cycle
Brides Walk
Bullying and Domestic Abuse
Bystander Intervention Programs

The Caribbean and Domestic Abuse
Castle Rock v. Gonzales Case
Celebrities and Domestic Abuse
Centers for Disease Control and Prevention (CDC)
Child Abuse and Domestic Abuse
Children, Impact of Domestic Abuse on
Christianity and Domestic Abuse
College-Aged Victims
Convention on the Elimination of All Forms of Discrimination Against Women (CEDAW)
Courts and Domestic Abuse
Crisis Lines

Culturally Competent Services
Cycle of Violence

Demographic and Health Surveys
DeShaney v. Winnebago County Department of Social Services Case
Disabilities and Domestic Abuse
Disasters and Domestic Violence
Domestic Violence Prevention Enhancement and Leadership Through Alliances (DELTA) Program
Dowry Killings
Drugs and Domestic Abuse
Duluth Model

Economic Recession and Domestic Abuse
Educational Programs
Effects of Domestic Violence
Elder Abuse
End Violence Against Women (EVAW) International
Equality Now
Europe and Domestic Abuse

Failure to Protect
Family Structure and Domestic Abuse
Family Violence, Risk Factors for
Female Genital Mutilation (FGM)
Female Perpetrators
Feminism and Domestic Abuse
Films and Domestic Abuse
Financial Abuse
Forced Marriage and Domestic Abuse
Funding for Domestic Violence Services
Futures Without Violence

Gender-Related Theories
Global Fund for Women
Grassroots Movements

ALPHABETICAL LIST OF ENTRIES

Health Effects of Domestic Abuse
History of U.S. Domestic Violence before 1970
History of U.S. Domestic Violence Developments, 1970s
History of U.S. Domestic Violence Developments, 1980s
History of U.S. Domestic Violence Developments, 1990s
History of U.S. Domestic Violence Developments, 2000s
Honor Killings
Hospital and Medical Records and Domestic Abuse
Housing and Domestic Abuse
Hughes, Francine
Human Trafficking

Immigrant Victims of Domestic Abuse
Incite!
India and Domestic Abuse
International Violence Against Women Act (I-VAWA)
Islam and Domestic Abuse

Judaism and Domestic Abuse

Katz, Jackson
Kimmel, Michael
Kivel, Paul
Kristof, Nicholas and Sheryl WuDunn

Latin America and Domestic Abuse
Legislation and Policies, Dating Violence
Legislation and Policies, Domestic Abuse
Lesbian, Gay, Bisexual, and Transgendered (LGBT) Victims
Linguistic Analysis of Verbal Abuse
Liz Claiborne Inc.

Mai, Mukhtar
Male Victims of Domestic Abuse
Mam, Somaly
Mandatory Arrest Policies
Mary Kay Corporation
Mediation and Domestic Abuse
Men's Efforts against Domestic Abuse

Middle and Upper Classes and Domestic Abuse
The Middle East and Domestic Abuse
The Military and Domestic Violence
Minneapolis Domestic Violence Experiment
Mortality Review Boards and Domestic Abuse
Music and Domestic Abuse

National Coalition Against Domestic Violence (NCADV)
National Crime Victimization Survey (NCVS)
National Domestic Violence Hotline
National Family Violence Survey
National Network to End Domestic Violence (NNEDV)
National Organization for Men Against Sexism (NOMAS)
National Organization for Women (NOW)
National Teen Dating Abuse Helpline
Native Americans and Domestic Abuse
News Media and Domestic Abuse
Nongovernmental Organizations (NGOs) and Domestic Abuse
Nonprofit Organizations and Domestic Abuse
Nonviolence Theories and Domestic Abuse
North America and Domestic Abuse

Outreach Services

Patriarchy and Domestic Abuse
Personal Narrative: Kristin Franklin
Personal Narrative: Lauren Pilnick
Personal Narrative: Patricia
Personal Narrative: Sabrina
Physicians, Health-Care Providers, and Domestic Abuse
Pizzey, Erin
Policing Domestic Abuse
Pregnancy and Domestic Abuse
Prevention Institute
Prisons and Domestic Abuse
Psychological Effects of Domestic Abuse

Reproductive Coercion
Restraining Orders and Personal Protection Orders
Runaway and Homeless Youth

Schechter, Susan
Self-Defense, Homicides, and Domestic Abuse
Self-Defense, Legal Issues
Shelters for Domestic Abuse Victims
Simpson, O. J. Case
Social and Societal Effects of Domestic Abuse
Social Change Movements
Sociological Theories about Domestic Abuse
South America and Domestic Abuse
South and Southeast Asia and Domestic Abuse
Spiritual Abuse
Stalking
Straus, Murray
Support Groups for Victims of Domestic Abuse

Technology and Domestic Abuse
Teen Victims of Domestic Abuse
Therapy and Counseling for Domestic Abuse

Thurman, Tracey Case
Trafficking Victims Protection Act (TVPA)
Traumatic Brain Injury and Domestic Abuse
Tribal Law and Justice Act
Types of Domestic Abuse

UNIFEM and UN Women
Uniform Crime Reports
The United Nations and Domestic Abuse
U.S. Government Responses to Domestic Violence
United States v. Morrison Case

Verizon Foundation
Violence Against Women Act (VAWA)
Vital Voices

Walker, Lenore
War and Domestic Violence
Warning Signs of Abuse
Welfare and Domestic Abuse
White Ribbon Campaign
Women's Aid Federation of England
Women's Rights Movement
Women Thrive Worldwide
Workplace Violence and Domestic Abuse
World Health Organization (WHO)

Topical List of Entries

HISTORICAL INFORMATION

History of U.S. Domestic Violence before 1970
History of U.S. Domestic Violence Developments, 1970s
History of U.S. Domestic Violence Developments, 1980s
History of U.S. Domestic Violence Developments, 1990s
History of U.S. Domestic Violence Developments, 2000s
Women's Rights Movement

FORMS OF ABUSE

Acid Throwing
Christianity and Domestic Abuse
Dowry Killings
Female Genital Mutilation (FGM)
Financial Abuse
Forced Marriage and Domestic Abuse
Honor Killings
Human Trafficking
Islam and Domestic Abuse
Judaism and Domestic Abuse
Linguistic Analysis of Verbal Abuse
Reproductive Coercion
Spiritual Abuse
Stalking
Technology and Domestic Abuse
Types of Domestic Abuse
Workplace Violence and Domestic Abuse

VICTIMS AND OFFENDERS

Africa and Domestic Abuse
Alaska Natives and Domestic Abuse
Asia and Domestic Abuse
Athletes and Domestic Abuse
The Caribbean and Domestic Abuse
Celebrities and Domestic Abuse
Child Abuse and Domestic Abuse
College-Aged Victims
Disabilities and Domestic Abuse
Elder Abuse
Europe and Domestic Abuse
Female Perpetrators
Immigrant Victims of Domestic Abuse
India and Domestic Abuse
Latin America and Domestic Abuse
Lesbian, Gay, Bisexual, and Transgendered (LGBT) Victims
Male Victims of Domestic Abuse

MIDDLE AND UPPER CLASSES AND DOMESTIC ABUSE

The Middle East and Domestic Abuse
The Military and Domestic Violence
Native Americans and Domestic Abuse
North America and Domestic Abuse
Pregnancy and Domestic Abuse
Runaway and Homeless Youth

Self-Defense, Legal Issues
South America and Domestic Abuse
South and Southeast Asian and Domestic Abuse
Teen Victims of Domestic Abuse

UNDERSTANDING AND EXPLAINING ABUSE

Battered Woman Syndrome
Biological and Psychological Theories about Domestic Abuse
Cycle of Violence
Demographic and Health Surveys
Duluth Model
Family Structure and Domestic Abuse
Family Violence, Risk Factors for
Feminism and Domestic Abuse
Films and Domestic Abuse
Gender-Related Theories
Hospital and Medical Records and Domestic Abuse
Mortality Review Boards and Domestic Abuse
Music and Domestic Abuse
National Crime Victimization Survey (NCVS)
National Family Violence Survey
News Media and Domestic Abuse
Nonviolence Theories and Domestic Abuse
Patriarchy and Domestic Abuse
Psychological Effects of Domestic Abuse
Sociological Theories about Domestic Abuse
Uniform Crime Reports (UCR)
Warning Signs of Abuse

EFFECT OF ABUSE

Children, Impact of Domestic Abuse on
Effects of Domestic Violence
Health Effects of Domestic Abuse
Psychological Effects of Domestic Abuse
Self-Defense, Homicides, and Domestic Abuse
Social and Societal Effects of Domestic Abuse
Traumatic Brain Injury and Domestic Abuse
Welfare and Domestic Abuse

CORRELATES OF ABUSE

AIDS and Domestic Violence
Alcohol and Domestic Abuse
Animal Abuse and Domestic Abuse
Bullying and Domestic Abuse
Disasters and Domestic Violence
Drugs and Domestic Abuse
Economic Recession and Domestic Abuse
Housing and Domestic Abuse
Poverty and Domestic Abuse
Prisons and Domestic Abuse
War and Domestic Violence

KEY PEOPLE

Ali, Somy
Hughes, Francine
Katz, Jackson
Kimmel, Michael
Kivel, Paul
Kristof, Nicholas and Sheryl WuDunn
Mai, Mukhtar
Mam, Somaly
Personal Narrative: Kristin Franklin
Personal Narrative: Lauren Pilnick
Personal Narrative: Patricia
Personal Narrative: Sabrina
Pizzey, Erin
Schechter, Susan

TOPICAL LIST OF ENTRIES   xiii

Simpson, O. J. Case
Straus, Murray
Thurman, Tracey Case
Walker, Lenore

LAWS, COURT DECISIONS, AND POLICIES

Beijing Declaration and Platform for Action
Castle Rock v. Gonzales Case
Convention on the Elimination of All Forms of Discrimination Against Women (CEDAW)
DeShaney v. Winnebago County Department of Social Services Case
International Violence Against Women Act (I-VAWA)
Legislation and Policies, Dating Violence
Legislation and Policies, Domestic Abuse
Tribal Law and Justice Act
Trafficking Victims Protection Act (TVPA)
United States v. Morrison Case
Violence Against Women Act (VAWA)

INTERVENTIONS

Anger Management and Domestic Abuse
Batterer Intervention Programs
Bystander Intervention Programs
Courts and Domestic Abuse
Crisis Lines
Culturally Competent Services
Failure to Protect
Funding for Domestic Violence Services
Grassroots Movements
Mandatory Arrest Policies
Mediation and Domestic Abuse
Minneapolis Domestic Violence Experiment
National Domestic Violence Hotline
National Network to End Domestic Violence (NNEDV)
National Organization for Men Against Sexism (NOMAS)
National Organization for Women (NOW)
National Teen Dating Abuse Helpline
Outreach Services
Physicians, Health-Care Providers, and Domestic Abuse
Policing Domestic Abuse
Restraining Orders and Personal Protection Orders
Shelters for Domestic Abuse Victims
Support Groups for Victims of Domestic Abuse
Therapy and Counseling for Domestic Abuse
U.S. Government Responses to Domestic Violence

PREVENTION

Brides Walk
Domestic Violence Prevention Enhancement and Leadership Through Alliances (DELTA) Program
Educational Programs
Men's Efforts against Domestic Abuse
Social Change Movements

ORGANIZATIONS AND RESOURCES

American Medical Association (AMA)
Amnesty International
Avon Corporation
The Body Shop
Break the Cycle

TOPICAL LIST OF ENTRIES

Centers for Disease Control and Prevention (CDC)
End Violence Against Women (EVAW) International
Equality Now
Futures Without Violence
Global Fund for Women
Incite!
Liz Claiborne Inc.
Mary Kay Corporation
National Coalition Against Domestic Violence (NCADV)
Nongovernmental Organizations (NGOs) and Domestic Abuse
Nonprofit Organizations and Domestic Abuse
Prevention Institute
UNIFEM and UN Women
The United Nations and Domestic Abuse
Verizon Foundation
Vital Voices
White Ribbon Campaign
Women's Aid Federation of England
Women Thrive Worldwide
World Health Organization (WHO)

Preface

The *Encyclopedia of Domestic Violence and Abuse* is intended to be one component in the effort to prevent and educate about domestic violence, not only in the United States but worldwide. Providing information about abuse to scholars, practitioners, and students can help not just educate but hopefully inspire action to end the many forms of violence addressed herein.

These volumes, authored by 60 experts in the field, from scholars to practitioners to survivors of abuse, include 173 alphabetically arranged entries that describe the scope and extent of various forms of this abuse, occurring globally. The encyclopedia provides information about the people from the most vulnerable demographics and those who are most likely to perpetrate abuse. Entries are also included to help explain why abuse occurs and the impact it has, both on individuals and on society. Readers can find entries on global laws and policies devoted to addressing abuse; histories of the movement to end abuse; and information about groups, organizations, and corporations involved in those efforts. Key people and court cases are highlighted, as are important correlates, such as animal abuse and substance abuse.

Special Features

A timeline of important events related to domestic abuse, from ancient Rome to the present day, is featured at the beginning of the encyclopedia. At the end of volume two, following the entries, is Appendix 1, giving complete text of and introductions to primary source documents related to critical court decisions, legislation, and international treaties. Included are four documents: (1) Convention on the Elimination of All Forms of Discrimination Against Women (CEDAW), the international human rights treaty first adopted by the United Nations in 1979, which the United States has still not ratified; (2) the Report of the Inter-American Commission on Human Rights re: *Jessica Lenahan (Gonzales) et al. v. United States,* which was based on a U.S. court case where a woman sued a city in Colorado for not enforcing the order of protection against her husband, who subsequently murdered their three daughters; (3) the Trafficking Victims Protection Act of 2000 passed by the U.S. Congress; and (4) the Violence Against Women Act (VAWA) passed in Congress in 1994, which is up for reauthorization in 2012. Following that is Appendix 2, a list of recommended, helpful websites for state, national and international resources. After are is a glossary of key terms relating to domestic violence; a selected bibliography of recommended books, journals, journal articles, and multimedia sources; and brief contributor biographies. The comprehensive index will help readers navigate this timely and important volume, as will the lists of all entries at the beginning of the book, which are arranged both alphabetically and topically.

Acknowledgments

This project was truly a labor of love. Having worked in the field of domestic violence in some capacity for the last seven years, I am thrilled to have been able to share insights I have gained and to draw on the expertise of the many scholars, practitioners, and survivors whose work is included in this volume.

Tremendous thanks go to all the contributors whose entries will surely inform readers about the important topic of domestic abuse. It was a pleasure to work with such a diverse group of authors. Contributors to this volume include advocates, scholars of sociology, psychology, social work, women's issues, theology, and health care, as well as survivors themselves. To the survivors who shared their personal stories, I offer my deepest gratitude. Your courage and resilience are amazing.

Throughout the process of writing and editing, I was able to work with many great people at ABC-CLIO. First Sandy Towers and then Anne Thompson offered timely and useful suggestions and provided needed support. It was a pleasure to work with such professional editors.

I also want to thank my family for their continued support of my work. My husband Peter and daughter Anya also volunteer with a domestic violence center and are always helpful when mom needs her "writing time." I dedicate this volume to my amazing family and hope that it in some way helps ensure that when Anya is old enough to date, she is in nothing but healthy, happy relationships as she has witnessed with her parents.

Finally, I want to acknowledge the many people, including some close friends, who work daily to assist victims and to raise awareness about abuse. I am happy to devote 50 percent of royalties for this book to No More Tears, which offers assistance to victims. Led courageously and creatively by Somy Ali, one of my best friends, No More Tears truly is a model of what is best about humanity.

Introduction

Although this volume is focused on domestic abuse, entries cover topics relevant to broader human rights issues that disproportionately impact women. Examining the broader issues allows readers to attain a more thoughtful and critical understanding of domestic abuse, its causes, its impact, and possible solutions.

Domestic Abuse: A Global Human Rights Epidemic

Domestic abuse involves multiple types of violent and degrading behavior. Although any type of violence and humiliation is painful, domestic abuse is acutely so because it is perpetrated by someone who is supposed to provide love and respect. It is but one example of the many forms of violence women are most likely to endure across the globe. It is important to note, however, that men too are victims of abuse and that it is unacceptable in any form.

Scope and Extent of the Problem

Accurate statistics on domestic abuse are difficult to obtain because many victims never report the abuse. Victims do not report for many reasons, including shame, embarrassment, fear of retaliation, feeling as though the abuse is their fault, language barriers, the feeling that no one will believe them, lack of familiarity with laws and help services, distrust of authorities, and more.

It is estimated that one-third of the world's women will endure an abusive relationship during their lifetime. According to a major global study coordinated by the World Health Organization in 2005, 20 to 50 percent of the world's women had endured one or more form of gender-based violence, and 40 to 70 percent of the homicides of women across the world are committed by intimate partners. In 2005, Amnesty International reported that nearly one woman per hour is killed from domestic violence in the Russian Federation. This totals approximately 14,000 women annually. An estimated 70 percent of Russian women report being subjected to psychological, physical, sexual, or economic abuse. As of 2005, Russia had no law prohibiting domestic violence (Russia: One woman an hour being killed..., 2005).

In many South Asian countries, domestic violence is common and stems from traditional cultural beliefs that stress that women should be submissive to men. In Cambodia, for instance, women may still be encouraged to follow Chbab Srey, a code which teaches them to obey and respect their husbands and that, if he becomes violent, it is her fault because she failed in her wifely duties. Although Cambodia criminalized domestic violence in 2005, the law provides no specific penalty for violations. In China, domestic violence may be the result of women earning a higher level of education than men, Indian society remains quite patriarchal, with girls and women suffering numerous forms of oppression and violence. Even in Western Europe, generally a more developed region, the World Health Organization found in 2001 that between 20 and 50 percent of women have suffered from at least one form of abuse. In South Africa, Amnesty International reported that every six hours, a woman is killed by a husband or boyfriend (Amnesty International, 2005).

The 2005 World Health Organization study was the first major multicountry examination of domestic abuse. Researchers interviewed 24,000 women in 10 countries: Bangladesh, Brazil, Ethiopia, Japan, Namibia, Peru, Samoa, Serbia and Montenegro, Thailand, and the United Republic of Tanzania. In addition to identifying shockingly high rates of abuse all over, the study found specific risk factors. Individual factors placing women at risk included education, financial autonomy, previous victimization, social supports, and personal empowerment. Male partners' level of communication, substance use and abuse, employment status, and history of violence were risk factors. Socially, the degree of economic inequality between men and women, women's mobility and autonomy, attitudes about gender roles, level of male-to-male aggression, and family and community attitudes toward domestic violence were connected to rates of abuse. Twenty percent of the women interviewed had never spoken about the abuse before.

Risk Factor=Female

Anyone can be a victim of domestic abuse. Yet, as Heise (1989) explained, "This is not random violence; the risk factor is being female" (p. 13). That is, women and girls are at greatest risk. Typical estimates are that females constitute 85 percent of domestic violence victims in the United States. The remaining 15 percent of victims includes males being abused by females and males being abused by other males in gay relationships. In some years, domestic violence accounts for 20 percent of all nonfatal violent crime experienced by women in the United States. Rates of abuse are similar among homosexual relationships. Studies vary as to whether specific racial or ethnic groups are at greater risk to experience abuse, but it is clear that societal racism impacts victims' abilities to receive help. Victims of color may endure racism in the legal system, in health care, in education, and even in social services and shelters. They may fear that reporting the abuse will reinforce negative stereotypes about their racial or ethnic group. Some may endure additional pressure to keep their family together because of stereotypes about one-parent households. A historical lack of trust of authorities may increase the likelihood that victims of color will not report abuse to police. Similarly, classism affects the likelihood that victims will receive the support they need to remain safe from abuse. People making less money lack financial opportunities to leave abusers and support themselves. Studies have repeatedly shown that significant portions of women receiving welfare benefits have experienced abuse, with figures ranging from 19 to 33 percent. Affluent women may face very different but no less challenging barriers to reporting abuse and receiving help. Research has shown that this group is least likely to report abuse due to shame and embarrassment related to their position in society. Many blame themselves, asserting that abuse does not happen to people like them. Often, affluent victims are totally financially dependent on their partners. Negative stereotypes about the poor may result in heightened shame and self-blame, however, those with more resources may believe that it is only the poor who endure abuse.

Research has repeatedly shown that immigrants as a whole are at greater risk to endure abuse in intimate partner relationships, although data are not clear as to whether people from any particular region or country are more at risk. Immigrant victims may find it difficult to report abuse due to language barriers, financial instability, lack of knowledge of legal rights, fear of deportation, cultural values, and other reasons. Native Americans living on reservations are also at increased risk. Located largely in rural areas spread out over miles, victims may find reporting abuse and leaving abusers challenging due to lack of transportation, scarcity of resources, and complex jurisdictional issues.

Elder victims also suffer unique difficulties. Some were raised with the idea that abuse is normal and something people must learn to live with. They may have no financial resources of their own and may endure pressures from adult children to keep the relationship with an abusive spouse or partner together. Dating violence among young people, or abuse involving two people ages 14 to 22 in a dating relationship, is one of the fastest-growing types of abuse. Estimates are that 30 percent of teen relationships are abusive. Teenagers may not know that what they are experiencing is abuse, mistaking jealousy or even violence for love. A growing body of literature has documented the difficulties for victims with disabilities who have suffered domestic violence. Some may have a hard time communicating, and stereotypes about those with disabilities may make it difficult for victims to be believed. Shelters and other social services may not have made appropriate accommodations for victims with mental or physical disabilities.

Global Gender Inequalities

Far from just an individual or private matter, domestic abuse occurs within the context of a world in which women are still oppressed. Kirk and Okazawa-Rey (2007) explain that "macro-level inequalities are present in violence at the micro level" (p. 250). Violence against women begins before birth, as in the sex-selective abortions that are not uncommon (albeit illegal) in China, India, and the Republic of Korea. Female infanticide, emotional and physical abuse, and differential access to food, vaccinations, and medical care are another form of violence against women. Young girls suffer when they are forced into marriages or must undergo painful female genital mutilation, endure sexual or physical abuse by family members, or are sold or pushed into prostitution. In adolescence, girls suffer abuse, sexual violence, sexual harassment, forced prostitution, and are disproportionately the victims of human traffickers. Women of reproductive age (and increasingly, young girls) may endure marital rape, acid attacks, honor killings, dowry abuse, and more, while elderly women suffer from elder abuse and neglect.

Worldwide, women still lack equal rights and may be exploited in the home, workplace, schools, and in other institutions. Abuse of women by their husbands is usually deeply rooted in patriarchy. Men have traditionally been viewed as the rulers of their homes and women were to obey. It wasn't until the 1970s in the United States and the United Kingdom that activists were able to kick off a movement that began to counter the patriarchal norms and raise awareness about abuse. Yet societal patriarchy remains, to lesser and larger degrees, virtually everywhere across the globe. It manifests itself in many ways—gender inequalities in pay, access to work, political representation, educational opportunities, for instance—and is particularly acute in women's global access to justice, or at least, to justice that protects them and holds assailants and abusers accountable. Take this example: In 1992, an 18-year-old Italian woman alleged that a 45-year-old driving instructor took her to a remote location outside of Naples and raped her. According to the Third Division of the Italian Supreme Court, she could not actually have been raped because she was wearing blue jeans, which, according to the court "cannot be easily removed and certainly it is impossible to pull them off if the victim is fighting against her attacker with all her available force" (In Rowland, 2004, p. 596). And thus no justice for her; instead, like so many other women, she was blamed for her own assault.

Even before birth, females face tremendous discrimination. Globally, more than 100 million women are missing, according to Nobel Prize–winning economist Amartya Sen. Other studies put the number between 60 million and 101 million. That is, babies known to be females are never brought into the world. While females outnumber males in more developed nations because they tend to live longer, in poorer regions of the world males outnumber females by significant margins. For instance, China has 107 males for every 100 females. The ratio in India is 108 to 100 and in Pakistan, 111 to 100. These disparities are the result of several factors. Parents may be less likely to take infant daughters to doctors or for vaccinations. Sons are considered economically indispensable, while females are not. Since ultrasound technology has been available in these regions, women are finding out the sex of their babies and aborting girls. Sex-selective abortion is illegal, and laws in China and India prohibit doctors and ultrasound technicians from telling pregnant women the sex of their child, but some still do. In sum, more girls have been killed due to abortion and infanticide in the last 50 years simply because of their sex than all the men killed in all the battles of the twentieth century (Kristof & WuDunn, 2009).

Women suffer in childbirth, in part because in many regions of the world, they are left alone, with no prenatal or labor care, to endure the process. This, too, may result in fistulas that leave the women incontinent. Kristof and WuDunn (2009) tell the story of Mahabouba, who was just 14 when she was pregnant and couldn't afford a midwife and so tried to have her baby herself. Her pelvis was undeveloped, however, and after seven days of labor she was unconscious. The baby's head was stuck, and the result was that Mahabouba had lost circulation in her pelvis, a part of which had rotted. When she regained consciousness, Mahabouba found her baby was dead, and she had no control over her bladder or bowels. She was told by locals that she was cursed and was forced to live in a tent on the outside of the village, purposely left with the door off so the hyenas would eat her. She managed to crawl in the direction of a missionary village, and a day later was rushed to Addis Ababa's Fistula Hospital, where many other women waited for repair of the same problem. While it costs just $300 to repair a fistula, and about 90 percent are repairable, many women never see a doctor. Instead, these women find their lives basically over, as they are forced to live by themselves, ostracized because of their smell, and many die of infection or starve to death.

There are so many female circumcisions, that approximately every ten seconds, a different girl somewhere in the world endures this painful process. The girl is typically pinned down, her legs pulled apart, and someone with no training and no anesthetics uses a knife or razor blade to slice off a portion or all of her genitals. This practice is found in parts of Africa and is designed to minimize women's sexual pleasure, thus supposedly making her less promiscuous. In the late 1970s and 1980s, laws against female genital mutilation (FGM) were passed in 15 African countries. Yet, despite a law passed in Guinea in the 1960s, no one has ever been prosecuted for the offense, and some 99 percent of Guinean women have endured FGM. While Sudan prohibited the practice since 1946, more than 90 percent of Sudanese girls are estimated to have been cut (UNICEF, 2008).

In some parts of the world, rape and sexual assault are used as tools of control. Rape itself is widespread across the globe, with estimates that 21 percent of Ghanaian women's first introduction to sex was via rape. In Nigeria, 17 percent of women have endured rape or an attempted rape by the age of 19, while 21 percent of South African women have been raped by age 15. In Ethiopia, if a young man doesn't have a bride price (like a dowry paid by men) but is interested in a young girl, or if he thinks her family won't accept him, he and some friends might kidnap and rape her. She will be considered "ruined," which improves the young man's bargaining position, and the chance that he will suffer any legal consequences is minimal (Kristof & WuDunn, 2009).

In Darfur, the Janjaweed militias gang-raped women, then cut off their ears or otherwise mutilated them to mark them as rape victims. Women who report the rapes may suffer punishment, as in the cases when women are penalized for fornication because they engaged in sex before marriage and could not produce the required four eyewitnesses to testify they were raped. The United Nations estimates that 90 percent of girls over the age of three were sexually assaulted during the civil war in Liberia. Doctors who treat these women often advise them not to report to police, as the police are likely to rape them as well. Women in refugee camps in Rwanda, Darfur, and elsewhere fear being raped whenever they leave their camps, which they must do to get firewood and water. The Democratic Republic of Congo is perhaps the world capital of rape, as militias "discovered that the most cost-effective way to terrorize civilian populations is to conduct rapes of stunning brutality. Frequently the Congolese militias rape women with sticks or knives or bayonets, or else they fire their guns into the women's vaginas" (Kristof & WuDunn, 2009, p. 84). Among the many ways these victims suffer, they often endure painful and degrading fistulas, or tears in their bodies that leave them leaking urine and feces. As Kristof and WuDunn (2009) note, "Mass rape is as effective as slaughtering people, yet it doesn't leave corpses that lead to human rights prosecutions. And rape tends to undermine the victim groups' tribal structures, because leaders lose authority when they can't protect the women. In short, rape becomes a tool of war in conservative societies precisely because female sexuality is so sacred. Codes of sexual honor, in which women are valued based on their chastity, ostensibly protect women, but in fact they create an environment in which women are systematically dishonored" (p. 83). The threat of rape is also a tool of control. For example, in Kenya, women must pay for round-the-clock security because political enemies often have them raped.

Although honor killings are illegal, they are not uncommon in the Middle East, South, and Southeast Asia. The UN Population Fund has estimated some 5,000 honor killings occur each year, although it is likely much more because so many are considered suicides. Kristof and WuDunn (2009) offer the story of Du'a Aswad, a Kurdish girl from the north of Iraq. At age 17, she fell in love with a Sunni Arab boy. While no one knows if they slept together, her family assumed they did, and, with the encouragement of religious leaders, eight men stoned her to death in front of a large crowd that included security forces who did nothing to stop it. Honor rapes are also common. These are rapes intended to disgrace or demean the victim or as a way to punish entire families for real or perceived indiscretions, as in the case of Mukhtar Mai (included in this volume), who was gang-raped as a way to punish her brother.

The first documented acid attack occurred in Bangladesh in 1967, and while specific data documenting the frequency of such attacks is hard to find, it is by no means uncommon in South and Southeast Asia. Globally, the "cult of virginity" is widespread. Numerous religious texts advocate stoning girls to death if they fail to bleed on their wedding night or selling them into slavery if they lose their virginity.

It is not just men who are culpable for these forms of violence. In fact, research has shown that women may choose to have their female babies aborted out of fear their husbands will leave them or concern that baby girls are less prestigious. Women are the ones who make decisions about getting their daughters vaccinated. Women own or at least manage many brothels, and reports have shown women were involved in at least one-quarter of the gang rapes during the Sierra Leone civil war, typically luring women and girls to the rape site and restraining them during the act. Similar participation has been documented in Iraq and Haiti. Data have shown that in some places, women pledge support for domestic violence. One study found 62 percent of women in an Indian village supporting the practice. Globally, it is often mothers-in-law who use cruel corporal punishment against females and who participate in or even orchestrate honor killings and acid attacks. As Kristof and WuDunn (2009) pointed out, "women themselves absorb and transmit misogynistic values, just as men do. This is not a tidy world of tyrannical men and victimized women, but a messier realm of oppressive social customs adhered to by men and women alike" (p. 69).

Yet, as Kristof and WuDunn note, women are not the problem—they are the solution. Numerous studies show women to be the linchpins of economic development. When girls are educated and offered opportunities for work, it pays off. These girls delay marriage and pregnancy, resulting in lowered population. Since women tend to raise the children, more educated women do so in ways that are more progressive, resulting in offspring that are less likely to commit violent acts. And, importantly, they are less likely to be involved in abusive relationships.

Explaining Domestic Abuse

There are numerous explanations for abuse. Some focus on biological or psychological factors, while others address more sociological issues such as patriarchal systems and rigid gender roles. Most agree, however, that domestic abuse is generally the result of abusers' desire to obtain and maintain power and control over victims. Some have proposed that abusers suffer from certain types of personality disorders, such as borderline personality or antisocial personality disorders. Some studies have found almost 90 percent of batterers to have elevated scores on the Miller Clinical Multiaxial Inventory (MCMI), which indicates the likelihood that they suffer from a personality disorder, while others have found far lower rates. Dutton and Bodnarchuck (2005) contend that there is an "abusive personality," similar to borderline personality disorder, which is characterized by shame-based rage, a tendency to blame others, attachment anxiety, and sustained outbursts. They believe that abusers become violent when they fear abandonment, as they are excessively dependent on their partners for attention. Many have pointed to alcohol and drugs as a reason for abuse. Most experts recognize that there is a high correlation between abuse and alcohol, with alcohol being present in anywhere from 48 to 70 percent of cases. Rather than causal, however, researchers believe that abusers use the alcohol as an excuse. Alcohol may exacerbate the abuse, causing abusers to blow real or imagined problems out of proportion and lowering inhibitions. Because abuse is not caused by alcohol or drugs, though, it is incorrect to assume that sending abusers to rehabilitation or substance abuse interventions will stop it. Too often, however, courts do just that when sentencing abusers.

Social learning theories remain popular as a way of explaining abuse. According to these theories, males become abusers because they learned this behavior in their homes, while women seek out abusive partners because they learned the role of victim from their mothers. Social learning theories also emphasize that perpetrators and victims learn stereotypical gender roles and violence behavior from other sources, including media, athletic activities, and popular culture. There is no doubt that media plays a large role in perpetuating dangerous gender role stereotypes, as in advertisements that use images of beaten women to promote alcohol brands, video games in which the goal is to rape or murder, or music lyrics suggesting that "she had it coming." News media tends to describe abuse in passive terms and often uses language that blames victims for the abuse. Although experiencing abuse in the home does increase the risk that young people will later become involved in abusive relationships, many do not. Likewise, most people are exposed to similar media yet respond differently. Clearly, other explanations are required.

Other theories focus on biological explanations, asserting that abuse is either hereditary or the result of brain injuries. Genetic explanations have not been proven, but recent studies have found a difference between the brains of batterers who were abused as children and those who were not, suggesting that sustaining trauma as a child may alter the brain in ways that is connected to later violent behavior.

Family systems theory views the family as a dynamic organization made up of interdependent parts. Thus the behavior of one family member is affected by the response of other family members. According to this theory, the communication styles, conflict resolution techniques, and problem-solving skills of all family members must be addressed in order to truly understand why abuse occurs. Many feminists take issue with family systems theory, however, contending that it serves to blame victims. Feminists focus their explanation of domestic abuse on gender inequalities that occur in patriarchal cultures.

Forms of Abuse

Abuse can and does take many forms. In virtually all cases, abusers emotionally control their victims through such tactics as insults (at both the victim and loved ones), making hostile jokes, ignoring the victim's feelings, withholding approval, yelling, calling the victim derogatory names, blaming, minimizing, accusations, and more. Victims are typically isolated from family and friends. Abusers may isolate victims by literally imprisoning them in their homes, by moving them far away from supporters, by alienating those who might help the victim, and other tactics. Isolation is particularly acute for rural, Native American, and immigrant victims. Many victims endure sexual abuse, which can include but is not limited sexual assault, extreme criticism of sexual performance, constant demands for sexual activity, and chronic infidelity. In approximately 50 percent of abuse cases, victims endure physical abuse, which might include pinches, slaps, punches, bites, and more. Abusers may attempt to kill victims. In far too many cases, they succeed. Each year in the United States, an estimated 1,300 to 1,800 people are murdered as a result of domestic violence.

Who Are the Abusers?

Just as victims can be either female or male and come from any racial, ethnic, national, age, socioeconomic, religious, or educational group, so too can abusers. Most abusers do not have criminal records and may even be well liked and well established outside of the home. Common traits among male abusers include negative attitudes toward women, adherence to stereotypical gender roles, and a tendency to minimize or blame others for their violence. Research has shown that more patriarchal families experience more domestic abuse, whereas relationships that are more egalitarian in terms of power structure typically have the least.

Impact of Abuse

Victims of domestic abuse suffer in myriad ways. Psychologically, victims may experience lowered self-esteem and depression. Many develop unhealthy behaviors, such as substance abuse, unsafe sexual activity, and eating disorders. Physically, victims suffer from a host of problems, including ulcers, hypertension, skin disorders, chronic fatigue, back ailments, migraines, reproductive problems, and more. Some researchers, including psychologist Lenore Walker, believe victims suffer from learned helplessness. That is, victims feel helpless due to the repeated abuse and develop a distorted sense of reality that makes it difficult for them to leave abusers. In some cases, victims may suffer from post-traumatic stress disorder (PTSD), a condition characterized by feelings of reexperiencing a traumatic incident through recurrent dreams, recollections, or flashbacks. PTSD may involve sleep disturbances, outbursts of anger, difficulty concentrating, hypervigilance, exaggerated responses, and physiological reactions. Some believe that victims suffer from something like the Stockholm Syndrome, which is named after a situation in 1973 when four people who were held captive in a Stockholm bank vault for six days became attached to their captors and began to see them as friends. Yet others point out that abuse is far different from being held hostage, in that hostages tend not to have an intimate relationship with their captors and typically know that someone is helping advocate for them, trying to effect their release. In some cases, victims fight back. Occasionally, a victim kills his or her abuser. Although typically the victim is acting in self-defense, many are still arrested, prosecuted, and convicted. In about one-quarter of cases in which victims kill their abusers, they are in no imminent threat. This makes it difficult for legal professionals to believe they acted in self-defense. For instance, after years of enduring physical and verbal abuse, Judy Norman shot her husband while he was sleeping. Her lawyers argued she suffered from battered woman syndrome, but the judge refused to allow this defense, and Norman was convicted of manslaughter.

Domestic abuse impacts the entire community as well. It is the number one cause of women's homelessness. Victims use emergency health-care services eight times more often than do nonvictims, resulting in higher medical costs for everyone. Abuse breaks up families and disrupts communities. Children who witness or experience abuse are more likely to struggle in school and may eventually drop out. Those same children are at greater risk for involvement in delinquency. As Kristof and WuDunn (2009) point out, the failure to fully utilize half the world's skills and expertise because of global gender discrimination is, simply put, abominable.

Barriers to Leaving Abusers

One of the most frequently asked questions about abuse is why victims stay. In the 1920s, many people believed that only unintelligent victims stayed with abusers. In the 1930s and 1940s, it was believed that victims stayed because they were masochistic. Since the 1970s, most people have begun to realize that victims find it difficult to leave abusers and to remain free for many complex reasons, although simply asking the question puts the responsibility for ending abuse on the victim. Instead, we should be asking why abusers continue to beat, harass, and demean their victims.

Many victims fear retaliation by their abusers, a fear that is all too real given that the most dangerous time in an abusive relationship is when the victim is planning to leave, is leaving, or has just left the abuser. Abusers see this as a threat to the power and control they had maintained and may respond by increasing the frequency or severity of the abuse. It is at these times—for instance, when the abuser is served paperwork notifying him or her that the victim has a protection order, or when divorce papers are filed—that abusers may violently attack or even try to kill their victims.

Movement to End Abuse

Although women (and some men) had long spoken out about abuse and provided needed shelter and support to others who were enduring it, the battered women's movement gained steam in the 1970s in both the United Kingdom and the United States. An important part of the women's liberation movement, these women (and sometimes men) critiqued patriarchal systems that resulted in abuse of women. They called out law enforcement for their failure to respond to women, and they organized support systems. In the 1970s, 1980s, and 1990s, the world saw media attention to abuse; the development of crisis line, shelters, and other victim services; and the emergence of laws and training that helped police apprehend batterers and courts hold them accountable. More recent efforts have been made to address other forms of violence against women, including laws to prohibit female genital mutilation, human trafficking, acid attacks, honor killings, and more. As the movement has grown and evolved, greater effort has been placed on recognizing the unique needs of all types of victims, from children to elders, heterosexual to homosexual, poor to affluent, rural to urban, and more.

Although tragic, high-profile examples like the O. J. Simpson case in 1995 have called much-needed attention to the issue of domestic abuse. Simpson was acquitted of the June 13, 1994, murders of his former wife Nicole Brown Simpson and her friend Ronald Goldman, but the trial brought to light a lengthy history of domestic abuse. Nicole had made numerous calls to police, and O. J. was convicted and served two years' probation for a 1989 incident of abuse. In the week following Simpson's arrest for the murders, calls about domestic violence in Los Angeles increased 80 percent. States sought to enhance or add new legislation, such as New York's law that mandated arrest for persons committing domestic assault and required training for police. Colorado's new law, enacted in 1995, required police to take abusers into custody at the scene of violence and mandated arrest for the first violation of a restraining order, followed by jail time for subsequent violations. A bill that passed in California in 1995 increased by 10 times the funding for shelters and domestic abuse prosecutions.

One of the most celebrated pieces of legislation related to domestic abuse in the United States is the Violence Against Women Act (VAWA), which was initially signed into law by President Bill Clinton as part of the 1994 Crime Bill. One provision of VAWA is that women who are in the country illegally may self-petition for residency status or they can document a legitimate relationship and a history of abuse. This is essential for immigrant women, as many times abusers falsely promise to petition for their residency or use the threat of deportation as a tool of control. Passage of VAWA resulted in an almost immediate spike in calls from victims seeking help. The National Domestic Violence Hotline, which was established with VAWA, continues to receive some 22,000 calls per month (Strasser, 2012).

What More Is Needed?

Some 125 countries have enacted domestic violence laws, yet 603 million women live in the countries lacking legal protection from abuse. An average of 50 percent of surveyed men and women in countries without domestic violence legislation think it is sometimes justifiable for a man to beat his wife. In the countries that have laws, only 22 percent of people think it is acceptable. According to UN Women, 117 countries have equal pay laws, but on average, women are paid 10 to 30 percent less than men. There are 117 countries that outlaw sexual harassment in the workplace, yet 311 million women still work in places where there are no such protections. A third of women in the developing world are married or in some union by age 18, putting them at risk for early pregnancies and dangerous abuse. Only 52 countries have prohibited marital rape.

Although services for victims are far more extensive than they once were, many victims are still turned away from shelters or centers. Approximately 10 to 40 percent of those seeking assistance at a domestic violence shelter are turned away. Shelter staff believe that for every woman who calls a hotline or enters a shelter, 10 others are enduring abuse without seeking that help. Further, many shelters are not adequately prepared to deal with the unique needs of all victims. Elders, teens, persons with disabilities, LGBT persons, immigrants, and others might find that shelters do not make appropriate accommodations in regard to physical premises, training of staff, and/or services offered. There is still a huge shortage of shelters for male victims, which means that men suffering in abusive relationships either continue to suffer, find refuge with friends or family, or become homeless. Homeless shelters are not appropriate for victims of domestic violence in that they are open and well marked, not confidential, and not in secure, secret locations.

Victims in every state can obtain protective orders or restraining orders, although the process can be daunting. A 2005 study by the Department of Justice Bureau of Justice Statistics found that half of all protective orders are violated at least once, and many are violated routinely with no consequence.

Because many police agencies in the United States today use mandatory arrest policies, victims may be reluctant to call law enforcement out of fear that they too will be arrested. Despite decades of attention to these issues, it is still not uncommon to find police issuing minor warnings to abusers rather than taking abuse allegations seriously.

Although they can be a great place to identify abuse and to put victims in touch with needed support service, health-care providers still do not screen for abuse as often as they should. Courts sometimes fail to believe victims and thus do not hold abusers accountable. The entire legal process has often been said to revictimize.

Data from outside the United States is still inconsistent and insufficient, as many countries have yet to criminalize abuse or, if they have, do not enforce legislation. Many cultures still see abuse as a private matter, and thus victims are hesitant to report it. Research has shown abuse to be rampant in Latin America and the Caribbean, exacerbated by high rates of poverty, especially among indigenous women. Mexico only criminalized domestic violence in 2007, and significant gaps exist in much of the Latin American legislation. For instance, Peruvian law only covers those who are living together, and marital rape is not prohibited. Similarly, domestic abuse is a major problem in the Middle East and North Africa, where no country to date has criminalized all forms of domestic abuse. In some countries such as Iran, Syria, and Yemen, perpetrators of so-called honor crimes are treated leniently, if they are held accountable at all.

Since the mid-1980s, victim advocates have been emphasizing the need for coordinated community responses to abuse. Such responses accept that abuse is a community, not just personal, problem and thus requires a community-based intervention. Efforts involve bringing together key people and institutions with whom victims and abusers interact, including educators, law enforcement agencies, advocates, health-care providers, child protection services, social services, the business community, faith-based leaders, and more. In the 1990s and 2000s, efforts became more focused on prevention. There are three levels or tiers of prevention: (1) Primary prevention refers to stopping abuse before it occurs. This might include educational programs aimed at children to teach them about fair and healthy treatment of others, parenting support, and efforts to challenge gender role stereotypes. Primary prevention also includes advocacy and political action aimed at changing laws related to domestic abuse and promoting gender equality and human rights. (2) Secondary prevention involves targeting services to at-risk populations so as to reduce known risk factors. (3) Tertiary prevention, also known as intervention, involves minimizing the effects of abuse by supporting victims and their children and holding abusers accountable.

Increasingly, people are coming to see domestic violence as a human rights issue. States are required under international law to provide equal protection to all of their citizens. Domestic violence has also been viewed as a form of torture prohibited under international law. Specific treaties are applicable to domestic abuse. For instance, the International Covenant on Economic, Social, and Cultural Rights (ICESCR), passed by the UN General Assembly in 1966, prohibits sex discrimination, while the Convention on the Elimination of All Forms of Discrimination Against Women (CEDAW), adopted by the General Assembly in 1979, prohibits gender-based violence, including "physical, sexual and psychological violence occurring in the family, including battering, sexual abuse of female children in the household, dowry-related violence, marital rape, female genital mutilation and other traditional practices harmful to women." In 1994, the UN Commission on Human Rights appointed a special rapporteur on violence against women, its causes, and consequences. This special rapporteur is required to collect information about violence against women from multiple private and public sources, to disseminate that data, to make recommendations about measures and actions that can eliminate violence against women, and to work with other special rapporteurs, representatives, working groups, and independent experts of the UN Commission on Human Rights. In September 1995, the Fourth World Conference on Women adopted the Beijing Declaration and Platform of Action, which also addressed domestic abuse. The Beijing Platform has prompted some countries to make significant changes. For instance, Austria, Belarus, Bhutan, Hungary, Mexico, Portugal, and the Seychelles have all passed laws prohibiting marital rape, while Belarus, Russia, Poland and Zimbabwe have introduced shelters, refuges, and hotlines for victims. In April 1997, the UN Commission on Human Rights reiterated that governments cannot perpetrate any form of violence against women and have a duty to prevent, respond to, and punish perpetrators.

In their 2011–12 report, UN Women found 186 countries have ratified CEDAW to date, although 42 of them issued one or more reservation. Although the United States was actively involved in drafting CEDAW and President Jimmy Carter signed it on July 17, 1980, repeated attempts to ratify it have failed. A minimum of two-thirds of the Senate must vote to ratify for CEDAW to become binding on the United States. Opponents maintain that ratification would give the international community too much control over U.S. affairs. They maintain that CEDAW defines discrimination too broadly, which could result in frivolous lawsuits. Further, critics feel as though CEDAW would redefine "family," thus destroying the traditional family structure, and would interfere with parents' rights regarding how to raise their children. Proponents assert that CEDAW does none of these things but would instead be an important step, both in reality and symbolically, toward affirming gender equality.

In 2007, then-Senators Joseph Biden and Richard Lugar introduced into Congress the International Violence Against Women Act (IVAWA), which would provide funds for foreign aid devoted to preventing honor killings, bride burnings, acid attacks, mass rapes, genital cutting, and domestic violence. It would create an Office of Women's Global Initiatives within the Secretary of State's office in order to make gender violence a global priority.

Nonprofit organizations and nongovernmental organizations (NGOs) play a huge role in providing services to victims globally, as well as raising awareness through educational campaigns and outreach efforts. HEAL Africa, for instance, helps rape victims in the Congo. CARE fights FGM in Africa. While these efforts are both noble and important, sometimes they obscure the responsibility of governments to take action to end the many forms of violence, including domestic violence, that impact so many people across the globe. It is essential, then, that both efforts—the grassroots and the government-led—continue to occur and do so in ways that complement, not compete with, each other.

Kristof and WuDunn (2009) recommend that a modern movement for gender equality incorporate the following:

- Building a broad coalition that crosses liberal and conservative lines;
- Carefully and accurately publicizing results and challenges;
- Ensuring that helping women is not exclusive of helping men;
- Ensuring that American feminism focuses on these essential global human rights issues, not just civil rights concerns.

Taken seriously, these suggestions can improve the plight of not just women, but everyone.

Further Reading

Amnesty International. (2005). The impact of guns on women's lives. Retrieved September 17, 2012, from http://amnesty.ie/sites/default/files/report/2010/04/The%20Impact%20of%20Guns%20on%20Women%27s%20Lives.pdf

Dutton, D.G, & Bodnarchuk, M. (2005). Through a psychological lens: Personality disorder and spouse assault. In R. J. Gelles, D. R. Loseke, & M. Cavanaugh (Eds.), *Current controversies on family violence* (2nd ed., pp. 5–18). Newbury Park, CA: Sage.

Heise, L. (1989). International dimensions of violence against women. *Response, 12* (1), pp. 3–11

Kirk, G., & Okazawa-Rey, M. (2007). *Women's lives, multicultural perspectives* (4th ed.). New York: McGraw-Hill.

Kristof, N., & WuDunn, S. (2009). *Half the sky: Turning oppression into opportunity for women worldwide.* New York, NY: Alfred A. Knopf.

Russia: One woman an hour being killed through domestic violence—new report calls for action. *Amnesty International UK.* Retrieved September 17, 2012, from http://www.amnesty.org.uk/news_details.asp?NewsID=16671

Strasser, A-R. (2012, September 13). After 18 years, Violence Against Women Act has saved countless lives. Retrieved September 17, 2012, from http://thinkprogress.org/justice/2012/09/13/844011/vawa-18-anniversary/?mobile=nc

UN Women (2012). 2011-12 Progress of the World's Women: In Pursuit of Justice. Retrieved June 17, 2012, from http://progress.unwomen.org/wp-content/uploads/2011/06/EN-Factsheet-Global-Progress-of-the-Worlds-Women.pdf

UNICEF. (2008). *Changing a harmful social convention: Female genital mutilation/cutting.* Retrieved September 17, 2012, from http://www.unicef-irc.org/publications/pdf/fgm_eng.pdf

Timeline of Significant Events Related to Domestic Violence and Abuse

753 BCE	Romulus, founder of Rome, formalizes the first law of marriage requiring women to obey their husbands and husbands to rule their wives as possessions.
200 BCE	The end of the Punic Wars sees advances for wealthy women, who were able to pursue politics, study philosophy, and join new religious movements while men were away. Husbands cannot beat wives without sufficient evidence for divorce. Those convicted of striking without reason must provide their wives monetary compensation.
300 CE	The Church fathers reestablish the husband's patriarchal authority and the patriarchal values of Roman and Jewish law. The Roman Emperor, Constantine the Great, has his wife burned alive when she is no longer of use to him.
	Excessive violence from either marital partner is grounds for divorce in the Roman Empire, although women had to prove the charge. Women are not considered men's property if the behavior is sufficiently terrible.
900–1300	Women in Medieval Europe are viewed as subhuman. All classes of men regularly beat their wives, with the support of the Church, which advised men to castigate their wives and beat them if they need correction.
1400s	Numerous documents advise "chivalrous" men to brutally beat their wives for committing any offense, not out of rage but from concern for her.
1500s	Lord Hale, an English Jurist, sets the tradition of nonrecognition of marital rape. He states that when women married, they "gave themselves to their husbands in contract, and could not withdraw that consent until they divorced. The husband cannot be guilty of a rape committed by himself upon his lawful wife, for by their mutual matrimonial consent a contract with wife hath given herself in this

1500s *(cont.)*	kind unto her husband, which she cannot retract." This is the basis of the "contractual consent" theory. Lord Hale burned women at the stake as witches and has been characterized as a misogynist.
Late 1500s	During the reign of Ivan the Terrible in Russia, the State Church sanctions the oppression of women by issuing a Household Ordinance that describes when and how a man might most effectively beat his wife. He is allowed to kill a wife or serf for disciplinary purposes. A half a century later, many Russian women fight back. When they kill their husbands for all the injustices they have been forced to endure, their punishment is to be buried alive with only their heads above the ground and left to die. It is not against the law for a husband to kill his wife.
1531	European religious reformer Martin Luther described women's place as in the home. Because men have broad shoulders and more narrow hips, Luther declared they possess intelligence that women lack.
1609	King James I of England declares that kings are like fathers who must be obeyed.
1641	The Puritans in Massachusetts establish the code of law called the Body of Liberties, which denounced husbands beating their wives unless they were under attack. Divorce is allowed, but physical cruelty is not ample evidence. Women seeking divorce must show they were dutiful and have not provoked their husbands.
1740	Concerted efforts made in the American colonies to protect citizens from violent crime outside of the home. Concern about wife and child abuse recedes.
1760s	English jurist William Blackstone's *Commentaries on the Laws of England* declares crime an act that produces mischief in civil society and proclaims private acts as outside the domain of law. Blackstone specifically addresses wife-beating, referring to it as necessary for chastising women but recommending it be done in moderation.
1776	Abigail Adams tells her husband, President John Adams, to "remember the ladies."
1792	In *A Vindication of the Rights of Women,* Mary Wollstonecraft calls for more education and for improvements in the way men treat women.
1800s	Based partly on a belief that there is a connection between alcohol and wife-beating, the American temperance movement begins.

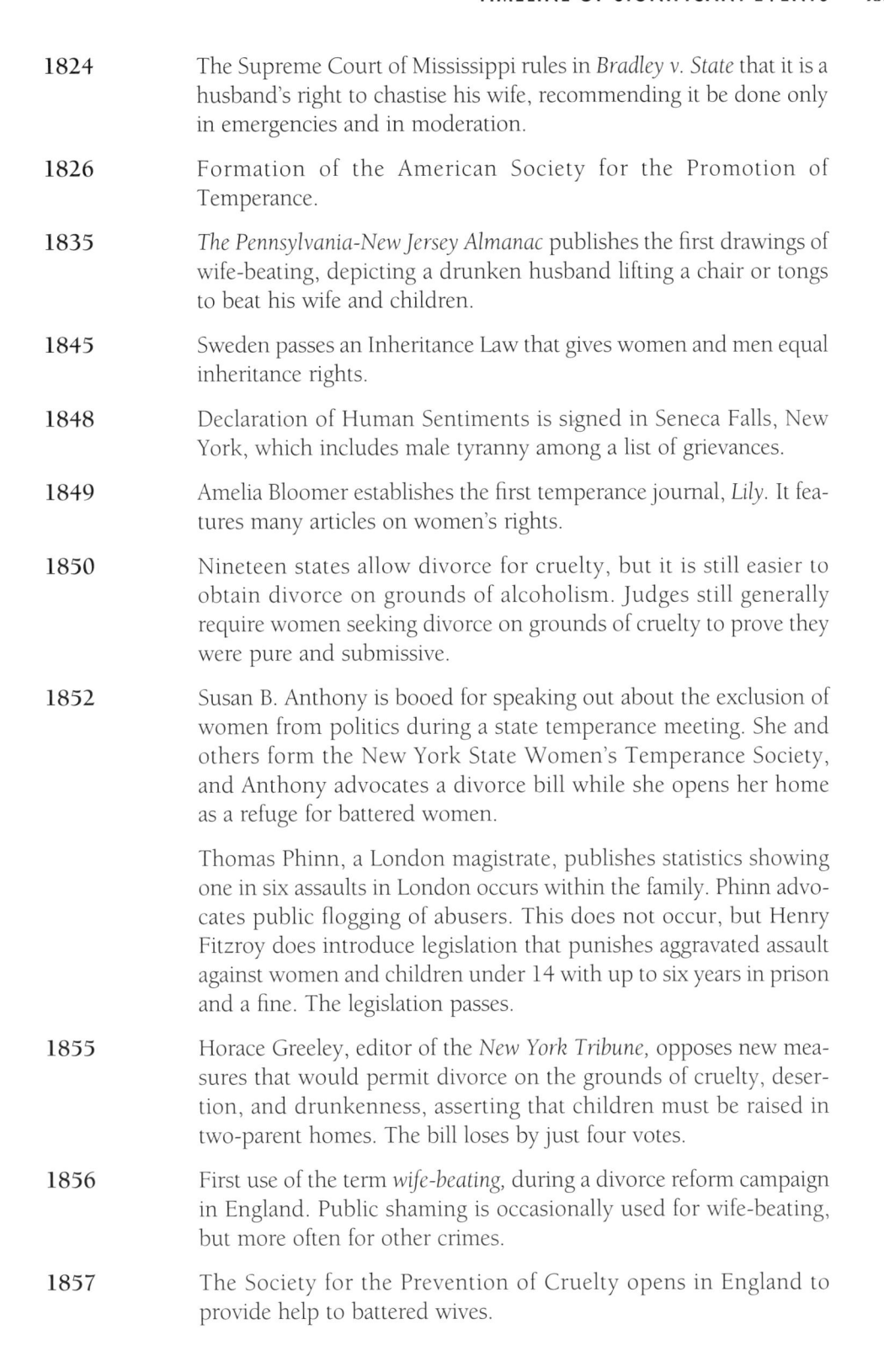

1824	The Supreme Court of Mississippi rules in *Bradley v. State* that it is a husband's right to chastise his wife, recommending it be done only in emergencies and in moderation.
1826	Formation of the American Society for the Promotion of Temperance.
1835	*The Pennsylvania-New Jersey Almanac* publishes the first drawings of wife-beating, depicting a drunken husband lifting a chair or tongs to beat his wife and children.
1845	Sweden passes an Inheritance Law that gives women and men equal inheritance rights.
1848	Declaration of Human Sentiments is signed in Seneca Falls, New York, which includes male tyranny among a list of grievances.
1849	Amelia Bloomer establishes the first temperance journal, *Lily*. It features many articles on women's rights.
1850	Nineteen states allow divorce for cruelty, but it is still easier to obtain divorce on grounds of alcoholism. Judges still generally require women seeking divorce on grounds of cruelty to prove they were pure and submissive.
1852	Susan B. Anthony is booed for speaking out about the exclusion of women from politics during a state temperance meeting. She and others form the New York State Women's Temperance Society, and Anthony advocates a divorce bill while she opens her home as a refuge for battered women.
	Thomas Phinn, a London magistrate, publishes statistics showing one in six assaults in London occurs within the family. Phinn advocates public flogging of abusers. This does not occur, but Henry Fitzroy does introduce legislation that punishes aggravated assault against women and children under 14 with up to six years in prison and a fine. The legislation passes.
1855	Horace Greeley, editor of the *New York Tribune*, opposes new measures that would permit divorce on the grounds of cruelty, desertion, and drunkenness, asserting that children must be raised in two-parent homes. The bill loses by just four votes.
1856	First use of the term *wife-beating*, during a divorce reform campaign in England. Public shaming is occasionally used for wife-beating, but more often for other crimes.
1857	The Society for the Prevention of Cruelty opens in England to provide help to battered wives.

1860	Susan B. Anthony helps the wife of a Massachusetts legislator escape abuse, which prompts Elizabeth Cady Stanton to introduce 10 new resolutions at the 1860 New York state convention in support of a new divorce bill. The onset of the Civil War in 1861 kills her proposals.
1864	A North Carolina court declares that a husband was allowed to choke his wife in order to make her behave, as no permanent damage was inflicted and the violence was not "excessive."
1866	A North Carolina court amends the law to allow a man to beat his wife with a stick as large as his finger but not larger than his thumb, which is promoted as progressive because it limits the violence a husband can perpetrate against his wife.
	The American Society for the Prevention of Cruelty to Animals is formed. It predates the founding of the Society for the Prevention of Cruelty to Children, established in 1875. Both predate any organization aimed at preventing cruelty to women.
1870	England's Married Women's Property Act allows women to keep their property when they divorce.
1871	Through a court decision, Alabama becomes the first state to rescind the legal right of men to beat their wives.
1874	A North Carolina court follows Alabama's lead but only allows courts to intervene when permanent injury has been inflicted.
1876	Lucy Stone, editor of *Woman's Journal,* a Boston newspaper, begins publishing a list of crimes against women and denouncing the leniency with which wife-beating is treated.
1878	In her article "Wife Torture in England," suffragist Frances Power Cobbe shocks readers with graphic depictions of wife-beating and lobbies for a bill allowing legal separation and child custody to women who have been beaten. The Matrimonial Causes Act passes but only allows divorce when the husband has been convicted of aggravated assault and the wife is considered to be in grave danger. Women who have committed adultery are not eligible for separation or child custody.
1880	Lucy Stone and her husband Henry Blackwell lobby for a bill similar to England's Matrimonial Causes Act. Stone and Blackwell join the movement for women's right to vote, believing that divorce reform and the reduction of abuse will occur when women vote off the bench those judges who treated abusers leniently.

1885	Founding of Chicago's Protective Agency for Women and Children, which provides legal and personal assistance to victims.
1896	Foundation of the National Association of Colored Women.
1900–1920	Establishment of family or domestic relations courts across the United States. Many see each partner as equally at fault in domestic abuse cases.
1911	The first family court is created in Buffalo, New York.
1912	Founding of U.S. Children's Bureau.
1919	U.S. women earn the right to vote with passage of the Nineteenth Amendment.
1921	In Sweden, marriage legislation gives women legal independence and equal rights as parents.
1923	England's Matrimonial Causes Act allows men and women to use the same grounds for divorce.
1930s	Beginning of era of influence of Freudian psychology. Helene Deutsch, a Freudian disciple, argues that women are masochistic, which explains that women secretly enjoy the pain of abuse and hence stay with violent husbands. Deutsch's views dominate the discourse about domestic abuse through the 1950s.
1931	Jane Addams wins the Nobel Peace Prize.
1945	Eleanor Roosevelt advocates for women's issues as part of the U.S. delegation to the United Nations.
1946	United Nations establishes the Commission on the Status of Women.
1960s	Pediatrician C. Henry Kempe and four colleagues publish "The Battered-Child Syndrome," which draws much attention to child abuse. Violence against wives is not addressed.
1960	*Palmer v. State* finds a woman responsible for involuntary manslaughter because she did not remove her toddler from an abusive domestic situation.
1961	Founding of human rights watchdog Amnesty International in London.
	President John F. Kennedy creates the President's Commission on the Status of Women. He appoints Eleanor Roosevelt as chair.

TIMELINE OF SIGNIFICANT EVENTS

1962 — New York State transfers domestic violence cases to civil court, where convicted wife-beaters receive shorter sentences than those assaulting strangers.

1963 — Foundation of Mary Kay Cosmetics Inc.

Congress passes Equal Pay Act.

1964 — John Snell, Richard Rosenwald, and Ames Robey's "The Wife-Beater's Wife: A Study of Family Interaction" calls women who claim to have been assaulted by their husbands "castrating," "masculine," "frigid," "passive," and "masochistic."

The first battered women's shelter in the world, Refuge House, opens in London.

Sex discrimination in employment is prohibited by the Civil Rights Act.

1966 — Formation of National Organization for Women (NOW).

1967 — Affirmative Action is expanded to include gender.

1969 — San Diego State offers the first BA program in women's studies.

California adopts "no fault" divorce.

1971 — Erin Pizzey establishes the Chiswick Centre in London, starting the shelter movement.

First *Ms.* magazine is published.

Copenhagen's first shelter, Kvindehuset (The Women's House), is opened by the Red Stockings, the Danish Women's Liberation organization.

1972 — Female activists from the United States visit the Chiswick Centre in London and establish Women's Advocates in St. Paul, Minnesota, as the first U.S. shelter for battered women.

Title IX prohibits gender discrimination in federally funded education programs.

1973 — A survivor of 10 years of marital abuse, Nancy Kirk-Gormley establishes the National Organization for Women (NOW) task force on battered women.

Rita Simon publishes her work about the Liberation Hypothesis, arguing women will become more criminal as they have greater opportunities in society.

Roe v. Wade decision ends prohibition on abortion.

1973–1976	Opening of shelters across the United States. Twenty battered women's shelters in operation by the end of 1976.
1974	With funds from the General Aid Office of the Netherlands, the first battered women's shelter is opened in Rotterdam.
	After two women refuse to stop squatting in two abandoned houses, Elsie is opened as the first battered women's shelter in Australia.
	Erin Pizzey publishes the first book about domestic abuse, *Scream Quietly or the Neighbours Will Hear*.
	Former prime minister of Japan Eisaku Sato wins the Nobel Peace Prize, despite his wife saying he beats her weekly.
1975	First National Family Violence Survey.
	Susan Brownmiller authors her book *Against Our Will: Men, Women, and Rape*.
	Brazil passes a penal code that prohibits husbands from selling, renting, or gambling away their wives.
1976	The first International Tribunal on Crimes Against Women convenes in Brussels, attracting 8,200 women from 33 countries.
	A series of lawsuits against police are filed, demanding police receive training specific to domestic violence.
	England's Domestic Violence and Matrimonial Proceedings Act gives women the right to obtain civil protection orders for domestic violence.
	Del Martin's *Battered Wives* attributes abuse to societal sexism, a position that is widely adopted by the battered women's movement.
	Pennsylvania establishes the first statewide domestic violence coalition.
	Nebraska passes first law prohibiting marital rape.
	La Casa de la Madres in San Francisco, California, is opened as the first battered women's shelter established by women of color.
1977	On March 9, after enduring more than 13 years of horrific abuse by husband Mickey, Francine Hughes sets fire to their bedroom while he sleeps. She is found not guilty by reason of temporary insanity. The story is later made into the film *The Burning Bed*, which aired on national television in 1987.
	The first rape crisis center opens in London.

1977 *(cont.)*	Oregon is the first state to mandate arrest for domestic violence through its Family Abuse Prevention Act. The Act also includes provisions for women to obtain restraining orders.
	In England, the Homeless Persons Act is passed, which gives a battered woman priority in obtaining housing. Many women live in refuges for up to nine months due to housing shortages.
1978	During the U.S Commission on Civil Rights' Consultation on Battered Women: Issues of Public Policy, the National Coalition Against Domestic Violence (NCADV) is organized with the goal of increasing financial aid to shelters, sharing information, and supporting research about abuse.
	Florida becomes the first state to levy a tax on marriage licenses to support battered women's shelters.
	Enactment of Pregnancy Protection Act.
	Foundation of the Women's Aid Federation of Northern Ireland.
	Captain Nancy Raiha and others start a domestic violence program at Fort Campbell, Kentucky, the first of its kind of a military facility.
	Minnesota is the first state to allow probable cause, or warrantless, arrest in cases of domestic abuse.
	John Rideout is the first person indicted for marital rape in Oregon. He is acquitted.
	Lenore Walker authors *The Battered Woman*.
1979	President Jimmy Carter establishes the Office of Domestic Violence, with a budget of $90,000 for grants, research, and dissemination of information.
	First U.S. Congressional hearings on domestic violence.
	UN General Assembly adopts the Convention on the Elimination of All Forms of Violence Against Women (CEDAW).
Late 1970s	By 1980, all but six states have laws addressing domestic violence.
1980	First NCADV national conference in Washington, D.C.
	Duluth, Minnesota, begins its Domestic Abuse Intervention Project, which involves a coordinated system of intervention including police, prosecutors, civil and criminal court judges, and probation officers. It also involves a batterer's intervention component and

parenting education programs. The Duluth program becomes a model for domestic violence intervention around the United States.

The Air Force establishes the Office on Family Matters to address domestic violence.

California becomes the first state to mandate treatment for convicted batterers.

1981 President Ronald Reagan cuts the Office of Domestic Violence due to budget cuts and a lack of support soon after taking office.

The first shelter for Asian women, Everywoman's Shelter, is established in Los Angeles by a Filipina victim, Nilda Rimote.

NCADV declares October 17 a Day of Unity on behalf of battered women, which eventually expands to Domestic Violence Awareness Month.

1981–82 Minneapolis domestic violence experiment finds that arrest is the best strategy in domestic violence cases.

1982 Founding of National Organization of Men Against Sexism (NOMAS).

1983 Federal funding for shelters is included in the Child Abuse and Prevention Treatment Act (CAPTA), but less than one-fourth of the original request is funded.

Publication of the Minneapolis Domestic Violence Experiment (MDVE), funded by the National institute of Justice, shows that arrest is more effective than other alternatives in reducing the likelihood of repeat violence. The study prompts many police departments to establish pro-arrest policies.

1984 Florida becomes the first state to mandate consideration of spousal abuse in child custody determinations.

The federal Family Violence Prevention and Services Act earmarks funding for domestic violence services.

1985 U.S. Surgeon General C. Everett Koop calls domestic violence a public health problem. His pronouncement and subsequent work prompt the Centers for Disease Control to include domestic violence research and eventually prevention in its body of work.

Tracey Thurman, who had called numerous times for help from the City of Torrington, Connecticut, police and who was left permanently disfigured and partially paralyzed by her ex-husband when he attacked her in the presence of police officers, wins a lawsuit that sparks more pro-arrest policies across the nation.

1985 *(cont.)*	The *Wall Street Journal* publishes a series of articles about the more than 19 years of abuse Charlotte Fedders experienced at the hands of her husband, John Fedders, Chief of the Enforcement Division of the Securities and Exchange Commission for the Reagan administration.
	First book about domestic violence and African American women, *Chain, Chain, Change,* is published by Evelyn White.
	In Seattle, the first support group for battered lesbians is started.
1986	India includes dowry killing as a form of domestic violence.
	Susan Schechter founds first program in the United States devoted to child abuse among families in which domestic violence occurs.
1987	NCADV established a national domestic violence hotline, using funds from Johnson & Johnson and from a national fund-raising effort called Shelter Aid.
	Naming the Violence by Kerry Lobel is the first book about lesbian battering.
	Expert testimony to explain the mental state and behavior of rape victims is allowed for the first time in *State v. Ciskie* to show why the victim did not call the police immediately. The defendant was convicted on four counts of rape.
	Founding of Global Fund for Women.
1988	Congress amends the Victims of Crime Act to require state victim compensation plans to include victims of domestic violence.
1989	Marc Lepine kills 14 women at Canada's Ecole Polytechnique.
1990	The U.S. Immigration and Naturalization Service first recognizes domestic violence as grounds for asylum.
	Democratic Governor Richard F. Celeste of Ohio grants clemency to 25 women who were convicted of killing or assaulting their abusive husbands or companions.
	Senator Joe Biden of Delaware and Representative Barbara Boxer introduced the Violence Against Women Act in the 101st Congress.
	The Cape Cod Women's Agenda hangs 31 painted t-shirts on a clothesline in Hyannis, Massachusetts, giving birth to the Clothesline Project.
1991	The American Medical Association (AMA) announces the beginning of its public health campaign addressing family violence.

Founding of White Ribbon Campaign in Canada.

In England, Southall Black Sisters launch the "Free Kiranjit Ahluwalia" campaign after she was given a life sentence for setting her abusive husband on fire. She is released in 1992 after her conviction is changed to manslaughter.

Liz Claiborne Inc. begins providing funding and support related to domestic violence.

Israel passes the Israeli Law for Prevention of Family Violence that allows for protection orders for physical, sexual, or psychological abuse.

Anita Hill testifies before Congress about the sexual harassment she endured from now Supreme Court Justice Clarence Thomas.

Israel is the first Middle Eastern country to enact domestic violence legislation by passing the Israeli Law for Prevention of Family Violence.

1992
Roman Catholic bishops in the United States issue the Church's first statement that the Bible does not condone spousal abuse.

The AMA's Council on Scientific Affairs recommends that physicians routinely screen female patients to identify abuse.

Domestic violence law enacted in the Cayman Islands.

Systematic rape of women used by Bosnian Serbs.

Belize passes law addressing domestic violence.

1993
Beginning July 5, all states now prohibit marital rape.

The United Nations issues the Declaration on the Elimination of Violence Against Women.

President Bill Clinton signs the Family Medical Leave Act (FMLA).

After a study by the Family Violence Prevention Fund finds that emergency department staff are not adequately trained regarding domestic violence screening and protocols, California passes AB 890 requiring training of health care providers.

Jackson Katz founds Mentors in Violence Prevention, a bystander empowerment program targeted at athletes but used with other populations to empower action to stop domestic violence.

1994
Defending Our Lives, a documentary about women who are in prison for killing their abusers, wins the Academy Award for best documentary.

1994 *(cont.)*	Nicole Brown Simpson and Ronald Goldman are murdered on June 13 in Brentwood, California.
	President Bill Clinton signs into law the Violence Against Women Act.
	England prohibits marital rape.
	The United Nations appoints a special rapporteur on Violence Against Women.
	International Criminal Tribunals in the former Yugoslavia and Rwanda are established and include sexual violence.
	Inter-American Convention on the Prevention, Punishment and Eradication of Violence against Women (known as the Convention of Belem do Para) is adopted.
	Chile adopts domestic violence law.
	Argentina prohibits domestic violence.
1995	President Clinton opens the Violence Against Women Office at the Department of Justice and appoints Bonnie Campbell as its first director.
	UN Fourth World Conference on Women in Beijing.
	Australia passes Family Law Reform Act.
	Bolivia passes law on domestic violence.
	Ecuador enacts legislation on domestic violence.
	Panama passes law defining crimes of intrafamily violence.
	O. J. Simpson is acquitted of the murders of Nicole Brown Simpson and Ronald Goldman.
	World Health Organization (WHO) establishes working group on female genital mutilation (FGM).
	National Alliance to End Sexual Violence forms.
1996	Congress passes the Personal Responsibility and Work Opportunity Reconciliation Act, reforming the "welfare" system. Provisions are included to allow flexibility for victims of domestic violence.
	Ireland adopts domestic violence legislation.
	Costa Rica adopts domestic violence legislation.
	Guatemala adopts domestic violence legislation.

El Salvador enacts legislation related to domestic violence.

Enactment of Austria's federal law on protection against family violence.

Two members of Congress propose legislation requiring professional athletes to lead a campaign against domestic violence. The legislation is not passed, in part due to opposition from the National Collegiate Athletic Association (NCAA).

Break the Cycle, focusing on teen dating violence awareness, education, prevention, and resources, is formed in Los Angeles.

1997 O. J. Simpson is found liable for the deaths of Nicole Brown Simpson and Ronald Goldman and ordered to pay $33 million to their families.

Belgium passes law addressing couples violence.

Bermuda passes law addressing domestic violence protection orders.

Honduras enacts legislation related to domestic violence.

President Clinton signs an antistalking law.

First Lady Hillary Clinton and Secretary of State Madeleine Albright found Vital Voices.

Founding of Prevention Institute.

Hong Kong adopts domestic violence legislation.

1998 Jordan is the first Arab nation to enact domestic violence legislation.

Taiwan adopts domestic violence legislation.

The International Criminal Court is established to prosecute sexual violence and gender crimes within the context of war crimes, crimes against humanity, and genocide and establishes a Gender and Children's Unit to improve investigation and prosecution of crimes related to gender inequality, including rape and other forms of sexual violence perpetrated against women and children.

1999 November 25th is designated as United Nations International Day for the elimination of violence against women.

Members of the National Task Force on Violence Against Women protest outside of Eric Clapton's Washington D.C. performance because of lyrics that glorify domestic violence.

TIMELINE OF SIGNIFICANT EVENTS

1999 *(cont.)*	Jessica Gonzales's abusive husband kidnaps and murders her three daughters. Police fail to respond to repeated attempts to get them to enforce the restraining order against her husband.
	Brunei passes Married Women Act.
2000	Beijing Plus Five conference held in New York to address domestic violence, trafficking, forced marriage, female circumcision, and honor killings.
	U.S. Supreme Court invalidates part of VAWA that gave victims the right to sue their attackers.
	Founding of Incite! Women of Color Against Violence.
	Colombia adopts a series of laws related to domestic violence.
	Commonwealth of the Northern Marianas adopts domestic violence laws.
	Passage of UN Security Council Resolution 1325, which calls for special protective measures for women and girls in armed conflict and emphasized the responsibility of all nations to put an end to impunity for perpetrators.
2001	China adopts domestic violence legislation.
	Germany enacts legislation providing civil law protection against domestic violence and harassment.
2002	President Clinton signs the 2000 Violence Against Women Act.
	The Office on Violence Against women becomes a unit separate from the Department of Justice, allowing higher priority and visibility.
	CDC issues its Costs of Intimate Partner Violence Against Women in the United States report.
	The U.S. Postal Service issues a Stop Family Violence Stamp to help raise funds for prevention.
	CDC's DELTA Project begins focusing on primary prevention of domestic violence.
	Bangladesh passes two laws addressing acid attacks.
	Chad passes a law on reproductive health that includes domestic violence.
2003	Establishment of End Violence Against Women (EVAW) International.
	England prohibits female genital mutilation.

Dominican Republic adopts legislation establishing shelters for men, women, children, and adolescent victims of domestic violence.

The World Health Organization releases the report *The Economic Dimensions of Interpersonal Violence,* finding, among other things, that in some countries, 70 percent of female murder victims were killed by a current or former husband or partner.

The New York Court of Appeals finds that the child welfare system cannot remove a child from the home simply because domestic violence is occurring.

Brazil law requires the establishment of domestic violence hotlines.

2004 Turkey mandates life sentences for those convicted of honor killings.

The Commission on Human Rights appoints a special rapporteur on trafficking in persons, focused largely on women and children.

2005 New CDC report finds that homicide is the second leading cause of traumatic death for pregnant and postpartum women.

U.S. Supreme Court rules in *Town of Castle Rock, Colorado v. Jessica Gonzales* that victims cannot sue police departments for failing to enforce restraining orders.

World Health Organization study documents widespread domestic violence globally.

U.S. Supreme Court rules that victims are not entitled to enforcement of their restraining orders.

Mexico passes legislation related to medical professionals' detection of domestic violence.

Bosnia and Herzegovina pass law on protection from domestic violence.

2006 President Bush signs the Violence Against Women Act of 2005 into law.

Congress declares the first full week in February Teen Dating Violence Awareness Week.

Albania passes legislation addressing family violence.

Greece passes legislation related to domestic violence.

Release of the UN Secretary-General's study on All Forms of Violence Against Women. It is the UN's first comprehensive report on the issue.

2008	Egypt prohibits female genital mutilation.
	Andorra amends its penal code to address domestic violence.
	The UN Secretary-General launches UNiTE to End Violence Against Women, a global campaign.
2009	East Timor's Penal Code addresses domestic violence.
	Hungary passes law on domestic violence.
	Obama administration creates "czar" of Violence Against Women.
2010	Congress declares February Teen Dating Violence Awareness Month.
	Obama administration grants asylum to a Mexican woman with a history of domestic violence from her common-law husband.
	Tribal Law and Justice Act enacted.
	The United Nations launches UN Women.
	The UN Secretary-General appoints a Special Representative on Sexual Violence in Conflict.
2011	Inter-American Commission on Human Rights determines the U.S. Supreme Court erred in stating there is no entitlement to enforcement of restraining orders.
	Affordable Care Act prohibits insurance companies from considering domestic violence a preexisting condition.
2012	Leaders in the European Union meet to create the Cadiz Declaration, which reiterated the commitment to enforce CEDAW.
	Congress debates reauthorization of VAWA.

SCHECHTER, SUSAN

Susan Schechter—social worker, writer, and leader in the domestic violence prevention movement—was one of the first to explore the intersection between domestic violence services and child protection efforts. She helped establish, along with others in the Abused Women's Coalition, the first domestic violence shelter in Chicago in 1976. In 1986, she founded the first program in the United States to address child abuse in families that were also affected by domestic violence, Advocacy for Women & Kids in Emergencies (AWAKE), at Children's Hospital in Boston. Schechter realized that the intersections of race and class were significant but often ignored factors in efforts designed to help women with violent partners, so she publicized this information. Aware that abused women and children reside in places that most battered women's movement efforts did not reach such as neighborhood clinics, hospitals, and schools, Schechter argued for multiple kinds of collaborations between systems and created curricula designed to train workers in organizations and agencies to provide adequate assistance to battered women and their families. She also suggested ways that women who choose to remain in violent relationships could do so with special assistance. Schechter's work impacted public policies and laws that currently protect battered women and their children.

Schechter, born and raised in Missouri, received a bachelor of arts degree from Washington University and a master's in social work from the University of Illinois at Chicago. Shortly after graduation, she began working as a social worker in Chicago, delivering speeches about domestic violence. From 1986 to 1993, Schechter founded AWAKE and served as its program coordinator and later contributed as a consultant. In *Expanding Solutions for Domestic Violence and Poverty: What Battered Women with Abused Children Need from Their Advocates* (2000), Schechter describes AWAKE's impact: "Although the hospital staff was initially skeptical, claiming that we would find few abused women in a children's hospital, we wrote a grant and hired our first battered women's advocate to join the child protection and family development clinic teams. Within two years, project staffs were helping hundreds of battered women." Today, AWAKE continues to identify and assist battered women who bring their abused children to Children's Hospital in Boston for treatment.

In 1991, Schechter began working as a clinical professor in the School of Social Work at the University of Iowa, where she partnered with several organizations, including the Edna McConnell Clark Foundation's Community Partnerships for Protecting Children (CPPC), where she tested an approach to improve the quality of support that families receive via the child protection system. She also served as a research associate at the university's Injury Prevention Research Center.

Schechter is the author of several books, monographs, and articles about domestic violence. Her first book, *Women and Male Violence: The Visions and Struggles of the Battered Women's Movement* (1982)—which documented the history of that movement, including causes of violence within families, strategies for helping battered women, and future steps for the movement—is a seminal work. In her reflections in *Women and Male Violence*, Schechter writes, "I hoped to tell a story about feminist, grassroots organizing and about the hard work required to build organizations, change law and social policy, and at the same time sustain a social movement. I wanted to brag about and document the accomplishments but also describe the hard, complicated work almost invisible underneath our new buildings and laws. It felt urgent to preserve this untouted knowledge that I could find nowhere else. I also wanted to extend a feminist exploration of theories about violence against women and open up debates about strategies, tactics, and future political directions."

As Schechter's work developed, she began to survey the movement and look for gaps in its efforts. In *Violence Against Women*, she explains, "The ensuing decades have introduced hundreds of new projects and taught many of us about our blind spots—for example, about our inability to respond to the needs of children and families living with poverty, multiple experiences of violence, and racism." Once these "blind spots" were illuminated, Schechter sought to eliminate them with books like the one she coauthored with Ann Jones in 1992, *When Love Goes Wrong: What to Do When You Can't Do Anything Right*. The book analyzes how control within relationships works, emphasizes the unique needs and concerns of women of color and poor women, offers personal stories about how some women maintain in violent relationships while others leave and manage without violent men, and suggests resources for women seeking assistance.

Another foundational work, *Effective Intervention in Domestic Violence and Child Maltreatment*, coauthored with Jeff L. Edleson in 1999, offers a set of guidelines and evaluative tools introduced to help assist those individuals in settings where dual types of abuse occur, such as spousal and child abuse. The resources and recommendations, endorsed by the National Council of Juvenile and Family Court Judges, have been used to help shape policy in areas involving child protection, domestic violence, and courts concerned with child maltreatment cases. It is reportedly one of the most important contributions to the battered women's movement of its kind.

Domestic Violence: A National Curriculum for Children's Protective Services (coauthored with Dr. Anne Ganley in 1996) puts forth a curriculum designed to train child protective services workers how to assist children in homes where domestic violence occurs. Throughout Schechter's career, she analyzed the link between domestic violence and poverty. Her many other publications—including one of her final projects, a coedited series with Jane Knitzer, *Early Childhood, Domestic Violence, and Poverty: Helping Young Children and Their Families*—continue to help shape current policy, practice, and public understanding regarding domestic violence, poverty, and children's well-being.

Because of her advocacy for a public child welfare system that supports battered women and their children, Schechter helped develop the Family Violence Prevention Fund's child welfare programming. In 2001, she began working as the director of *Building Comprehensive Solutions to Domestic Violence*, a project of the National Resource Center on Domestic Violence, designed to help domestic violence organizations collaborate in their work committed to helping battered women and their families, particularly poor families. She also served as chair of the Prevention and Early Intervention Task Force of the National Advisory Council on Violence Against Women.

Schechter received many awards and honors. In 2002, the University of Iowa Celebration of Excellence Among Women honored her with its Distinguished Achievement Award. The following year, she won the Leadership in Public Child Welfare Award from the National Association of Public Child Welfare for her work as an author and activist. She was appointed to the National Advisory Council on Violence Against Women by former Attorney General Janet Reno and former U.S. Secretary of Health and Human Services Donna Shalala. She was posthumously inducted into the Iowa Women's Hall of Fame in 2005.

According to Jill Davies and Jeff Edleson, "Susan changed how individuals thought about domestic violence, children, social work, and often even their careers by serving as their teacher and mentor. She had the ability to communicate the stories of battered women and their children to frontline workers as well as national policy makers and make new approaches seem both feasible and sensible." Fran S. Danis agrees. Danis called Schechter both a "historian and visionary" and highlighted "her ability to think critically about the responsibilities of the battered women's movement to listen to the voices of abused women and their children and to be responsive to their needs."

Awards and fellowships have been established in her honor. The Pennsylvania Coalition Against Domestic Violence developed the Susan Schechter Legacy Award in 2006. Similarly, the Family Violence Prevention Fund in San Francisco and CONNECT in New York City created the Susan Schechter Leadership Development Fellowship to honor Schechter and to support work designed to end violence in families.

Schechter is nationally recognized for working to build collaborations among domestic violence programs and organizations that focus on child welfare, early childhood education, and poverty. She argued that programs that help battered women and their husbands find jobs and housing should be a part of the services offered to families that experience violent relationships. She was particularly concerned about offering battered women and their children options that extend beyond Child Protective Services.

Schechter died at her home on February 3, 2004, of endometrial cancer. She was 57 years old. She is survived by her husband, Allen Steinberg, and their son Zachary.

See also: Children, Impact of Domestic Abuse on; Feminism and Domestic Abuse; History of U.S. Domestic Violence Developments, 1980s; Women's Rights Movement

Further Reading

Bergen, R., Edleson, J., & Renzetti, C. (Eds.) (2005). *Violence against women: Classic papers.* Boston, MA: Pearson/Allyn and Bacon.

Danis, F. (2006). A tribute to Susan Schechter: The visions and struggles of the battered women's movement. *Journal of Women and Social Work, 21*(3), 336–341.

Davies, J., & Edleson. J. (2004). In memoriam: Susan Schechter. *Violence Against Women,* 10, 955–957.

Schechter Fellowship: http://www.schechterfellowship.org

Schechter, S. (2000). *Expanding solutions for domestic violence and poverty: What battered women with abused children need from their advocates.* Harrisburg, PA: National Resource Center on Domestic Violence. Retrieved from http://www.mincava.umn.edu/documents/expandin/expandin.html

Schechter, S., & Knitzer, J. (2004). *Early childhood, domestic violence, and poverty: Helping young children and their families.* Ames: University of Iowa, School of Social Work. Retrieved January 31, 2013 from http://www.nccev.org/pdfs/series_all.pdf

Susan Schechter: http://www.mincava.umn.edu/classics/

KaaVonia Hinton-Johnson

SELF-DEFENSE, HOMICIDES, AND DOMESTIC ABUSE

Although many victims endure endless abuse without responding physically, some do take measures to defend themselves. Victims who use self-defense are sometimes acquitted in court hearings, but other times these victims are found guilty of various offenses and incarcerated.

Self-Defense and Types of Female Vicimization

Studies conducted on women's use of violence in relationships generally conclude that most women who use violence are either acting in self-defense or retaliating for abuse they have endured (Bair-Merritt et al., 2010). In essence, women's motives for being violent are typically reactions to the abuses they are suffering at the hands of their partners.

Much of the current literature in the field separates domestic violence into two categories: common couple violence and patriarchal terrorism. Common couple violence refers to occasional violent "outbursts" perpetrated by either the husband or wife. In comparison, patriarchal terrorism is when the male systematically terrorizes his family with violence and threats of violence. The types of abusive behaviors perpetrated by men against women in patriarchal terrorism include such acts as physical and sexual assaults, stalking, extreme jealousy, threatening behaviors, destruction of property, and harming pets. In domestic violence situations where there is violence perpetrated by both partners, research has found that women typically suffer more severe injuries due in part to their partners being physically larger and stronger, committing more dangerous behaviors, and repeating those behaviors more frequently (Gelles, 1974; Steinmetz, 1977; Straus, Gelles, & Steinmetz, 1980).

When battered women use force in an attempt to stop an attack, it is understandable that they might experience a mixture of complex emotional responses, such as fear in combination with anger due to previous victimizations. Therefore, self-defense and retaliation may become one in this situation. Even in instances where a battered wife kills her abusive husband, those murders are typically precipitated by frequent abuse, forced sex, severe injuries suffered by the woman, and the man's threats to kill his wife (Straus et al., 1980). This illustrates that battered women typically do not escalate their violent actions until the abuse they are suffering becomes more severe and sadistic.

Self-Defense and Theories

A battered woman who kills her offender has typically endured repeated, sometimes incremental acts of injury prior to self-defense, and she believes her actions will thwart death or serious injury. Having to risk death or serious injury by an intimate partner usually raises the question, "Why would she remain in an abusive relationship, especially to the point of lethal repercussions?" Researchers suggest a coarse, complicated mixture of concerns and realities for an abused woman, any of which can persuade against escape or hinder the removal of violation.

For example, psychologist Lenore Walker theorizes that battering comprises a cycle of three distinct phases (Walker, 1979). Stage one, the Tension-Building Stage, is typified by "minor" acts of physical violence (i.e., throwing objects, hitting, shoving, and grabbing), an escalation of emotional abuse (i.e., belittling, criticizing, verbally attacking the victim), and fear. During this phase, the woman may work hard to prevent further retaliation by complying with her offender. Although she is in the best position to determine when the next incident may occur, she may underestimate the severity of past abuse, and the effects of post-traumatic stress can numb her ability to respond against pending danger (Browne, 1987). Her anticipation of an impending assault is experienced at stage two, the Acute Battering Incident. Stage three, the Honeymoon Phase, depicts a calm respite in between battering incidents, if a successful intervention is not achieved. An abuser may try to soothe the victim with contrite, loving acts, or he may sincerely be aware that he went "too far" in the previous phase and ask for her forgiveness. Consequently, the victim may believe that her offender's actions were an aberration and reason that he and the relationship deserve another chance (Ferraro, 2003).

Critics of Walker's theory note that a cyclical expression of anger and frustration on the part of the abuser is not consistent with all violated women's experiences. Instead, these researchers and domestic violence interventionists view each battering incident as part of a spectrum of hostilities, which are intended to exert and maintain power and control over the victim. As an alternate framework, the "Power and Control Wheel" developed as part of the Duluth Model stresses such manipulation by offenders and centers their use of male privilege, social isolation, emotional abuse, economic deprivation, intimidation, and children or pets to control women's behavior.

A victimized woman may respond to mistreatment in various ways, either of which may require active, well-coordinated social support services for her coping and survival. Emotionally, for example, she may acquire depression or post-traumatic stress and experience a heightened sense of anxiety and fear over future victimization. She can develop difficulty in sleeping, concentrating, or performing everyday tasks. She may also become angry at the violence against her and physically aggress against her offender.

Self-Defense and Homicide

An estimated 1,300 people are killed from domestic violence annually in the United States. In other countries, death rates from domestic violence are far higher. For instance, approximately 14,000 women die each year from abusive relationships in Russia, and in India, an estimated 5,000 women are murdered each year from honor killings alone. Each day, more than a dozen women in India die from what are often called "kitchen fires" but are really homicides due to dowry disputes or some alleged dishonor (Murray, 2008). Risk factors that a victim will be murdered by her partner include stalking; estrangement (physical leaving, legal separation, etc.); strangulation (choking) during an assault; threats to kill; prior use of or access to weapons, especially firearms; forced sex; controlling, possessive, jealous behavior; drug and/or alcohol abuse; and, to lesser degrees, the presence in the household of children who are not the batterer's biological offspring; and unemployment of the batterer (Websdale, 2000).

Sometimes the psychological outcomes of domestic abuse victimization can result in women using violence as a way to defend themselves against the abuse (Ewing, 1990). There are occasions when the use of self-defense can end in homicide of the abuser. In 70–80 percent of intimate partner homicides, no matter which partner was killed, the man physically abused the woman before the murder (Campbell, Webster, Koziol-McLain, & Block, et al., 2003). Studies typically show that the most common scenario is men murdering their wives. For example, in 2007 in Virginia, female victims outnumbered male victims four to one (Bair-Merritt et al., 2010). Research has suggested that the type of abuse suffered by a victim may also be a predisposing factor for defending oneself with force. For example, earlier research on homicide cases found that rape and other severe sexual assaults toward the victim were more common in cases when homicide of the abuser occurred (Browne, 1987). In addition to homicide cases, self-defense is also found to be correlated with fighting back against the primary aggressor who is perpetrating the violence (Saunders, 1986). For example, a woman who is cornered physically may respond by striking her perpetrator with an object in an effort to escape the physical abuse.

The Legal System

In the legal system, when the concept of self-defense is used by a domestic abuse victim, it is often met with confusion and controversy. Victim's self-defense can be an issue in both criminal and civil court proceedings. Most jurisdictions offer victims of domestic abuse the option of obtaining civil protective orders in the legal system. These civil protective orders supply much-needed expeditious relief for victims of domestic abuse. In addition, the legal documentation of prior abuse has served as supporting evidence of domestic abuse in self-defense cases. Self-defense can also become an issue in divorce and child custody decisions by courts.

In criminal cases, legal definitions of self-defense vary slightly from state to state, but most criminal laws concur that physical force upon another person is justified when such force is necessary to protect oneself from imminent harm. The legal concept of self-defense also includes the element of proportionality, which basically mandates that force used during self-defense should not be out of proportion to the force necessary to protect oneself from imminent harm). Often the principle of proportionality creates problems for victims using self-defense in the legal system, due to deadly force being construed as "out of proportion" to protect self by judges and juries. However, in the modern variation, many states now instruct juries and judges to consider self-defense if the male partner has a history of abuse and if the female is in reasonable fear of imminent harm (Bergman & Berman-Barrett, 2000).

Generally, the prevalence of domestic abuse places great strain on law enforcement and the legal system, in terms of court cases, money, and time. Law enforcement is a critical agency in the investigation of domestic abuse cases and assessing the issue of self-defense. Law enforcement officers may be the first and most meaningful contact that domestic abuse victims have within the legal system and have not historically been perceived by some as responding adequately to meet victim needs. The Violence Against Women Act (1994) is an important federal legislative act that creates resources for victims and mandated a preferred arrest policy of the primary aggressor when sufficient evidence exists that domestic abuse has occurred. Law enforcement's ability to identify the primary aggressor is an important issue when determining self-defense in the legal system.

Additionally, victims of domestic abuse often attempt to maneuver their way through court systems that may not fully understand the complexities and dynamics of domestic abuse when the issue of self-defense is raised. In terms of prosecuting domestic abuse cases, typically prosecutors hold significant discretion in deciding who to charge and with what. Research has shown that criminal charges are more likely when the perpetrator is male; however, prosecutors are less likely to charge in cases characterized as "mutual assaults" (Worrall, Ross, & McCord, 2005). Cases labeled as mutual assault can create prosecutorial barriers due to the difficulty in determining a "true" victim and suspect. It is worth noting that victim's advocates from shelters or community agencies can also provide valuable assistance to domestic abuse victims and the legal system on many issues, including victim's self-defense.

Self-defense is sometimes used as a legal defense in cases where battered women kill their abusers. In these cases, expert testimony often centers on "battered woman syndrome." This term was originally coined by Lenore Walker to describe the phenomenon of common psychological effects often experienced by victims of domestic abuse. Battered women evidence offers a framework that speaks to the woman's mental state, why she may have perceived herself to be in danger at the time of the killing and why she did not leave the relationship earlier (Schuller & Hastings, 1996). Many experts in the field have critiqued battered woman syndrome due to it labeling the victim as if something is wrong or disordered about her rather than presenting each woman's situation from a unique individual perspective. The dialogue continues on the best approach to present evidence on victim's self-defense in the legal system.

One useful resource is the Women's Law Initiative (http://www.womenslaw.org), a national effort to provide legal information, help and support for women, teens, and girls living with or escaping domestic violence or sexual assault.

See also: Battered Woman Syndrome; Courts and Domestic Abuse; Self-Defense, Legal Issues; Violence Against Women Act (VAWA)

Further Reading

Bair-Merritt, M., Crowne, S., Thompson, D., Sibinga, E., Trent, M., & Campbell, J. (2010). Why do women use intimate partner violence? A systematic review of women's motivations. *Trauma Violence Abuse, 11*(4), 178–189.

Bergman, P., & Berman-Barrett, S.J. (2000). *The criminal law handbook: Know your rights, survive the system.* Berkeley, CA: Nolo Press.

Browne, A. (1987). *When battered women kill.* New York, NY: Free Press.

Campbell, J. C., Webster, D., Koziol-McLain, J., Block, C. R., et al. (2003). Assessing risk factors for intimate partner homicide. In Intimate partner homicide. *NIJ Journal, 250,* 14–19.

Ewing, C. P. (1990). Self-defense: A proposed justification for battered women who kill. *Law and Human Behavior, 14*(6), 579–594.

Ferraro, K. (2003). The words change, but the melody lingers: The persistence of the battered women syndrome in criminal cases involving battered women. *Violence Against Women, 9,* 110–129.

Gelles, R. J. (1974). *The violent home: A study of physical aggression between husbands and wives.* Beverly Hills, CA: Sage.

Murray, A. (2008). *From outrage to courage: Women taking action for health and justice.* Monroe, ME: Common Courage.

Saunders, D. (1986). When battered women use violence: Husband-abuse or self-defense? *Victims and Violence, 1*(1), 47–60.

Schuller, R. A., & Hastings, P. A. (1996). Trials of battered women who kill: The impact of alternative forms of expert evidence. *Law and Human Behavior, 20*(2), 167–187.

Steinmetz, S. (1977). The use of force for resolving family conflict: The training ground for abuse. *The Family Coordinator 26*(1), 19–26.

Straus, M., Gelles, R., & Steinmetz, S. (1980). *Behind closed doors: Violence in the American family.* New York, NY: Doubleday.

Walker, L. (1979). *The battered woman.* New York, NY: Harper & Row.

Websdale, N. (2000, February). *Lethality Assessment Tools: A critical analysis.* Harrisburg, PA: VAWnet, a project of the National Resource Center on Domestic Violence. Retrieved from http://www.vawnet.org/Assoc_Files_VAWnet/AR_lethality.pdf

Websdale, N. (1999). *Understanding domestic homicide.* Boston, MA: Northeastern University Press.

Worrall, J., Ross, J., & McCord, E. (2005). Modeling prosecutors' charging decisions in domestic violence cases. *Crime and Delinquency, 49*(10), 1–32.

Lynn Geurin, Shondrah Tarrezz Nash, and Elizabeth Biebel

SELF-DEFENSE, LEGAL ISSUES

Every American, including someone threatened by domestic abuse, has the legal right to defend herself when faced with a threat to her safety from another person. Therefore, domestic abuse victims may use a reasonable amount of force when it is necessary to repel a batterer's attack against them. They may produce evidence of this when charged with an assault or homicide in order to avoid a conviction. While abuse victims' advocates have called for expansion of the self-defense law, the rules historically require the threat of harm from a batterer to be imminent. Self-defense rules vary state by state on many issues, however, such as whether or not one must first attempt to retreat before using self-defense.

Normally, when a person physically harms another person, the act is against the law. It is a crime often called assault or battery. Even if not a crime, it still may be a civil wrong against the other person's rights, that is, a tort of assault or battery. However, an individual is sometimes legally permitted to strike or otherwise harm another person in order to protect herself or others nearby, such as her children. This defense to the alleged crime or tort is therefore known as "self-defense" in the former cases and "defense of others" in the latter. In such cases, the person's act of violence is seen as morally and legally justified, because people should have the right to protect themselves. We cannot always rely on the government to rescue us before harm occurs, so we permit this exception to the general rule against violence. The rules governing self-defense are generally the same for both criminal law and civil tort situations.

Where a domestic abuse victim physically acts out against his or her batterer, the victim may be charged with a crime and have to defend himself or herself in court. In order to use this defense to justify the act of violence, a person is required to bring forth some credible evidence that self-defense was necessary. Then the judge will permit the matter to be heard by the jury, and the jury will form its opinion of whether or not self-defense was in fact justified.

The jury will apply the law governing self-defense, as tendered by the judge, to facts of the case and make their judgment. The law that the judge will instruct the jury with regard to self-defense is found in case law and legislative statutes. American states inherited judicial case law, also called "common law," from England. Consequently, binding legal rules—that is, precedent—have come down from a long history of past cases. In addition, however, states have enacted codes of statutes that sometimes alter the historical rules of case law. Thus, statutes and, where no statutory rule exists, the historical case law provides the rules for whether or not self-defense may apply in a particular case. State law varies markedly in the area of criminal law, and self-defense is no exception. Because of this, one needs to be aware of the legal rules in one's particular state of residence to have a solid understanding of how self-defense may apply in that state.

In some states, once the person claiming self-defense brings forth some evidence to the fact, it remains that defendant's job to prove this to the jury by a "preponderance of evidence," meaning more likely than not. In other states, after the person's initial show of evidence, the burden switches and requires the state to prove that self-defense was not justified.

To claim self-defense, a domestic abuse victim must prove that her violent act toward her batterer was necessary and reasonable under the circumstances. First, the victim must not have physically provoked the attack. Such an "initial aggressor" loses the defense unless she has completely withdrawn or the batterer suddenly escalates the fight beyond the scope of her original attack. For example, even if a woman hits her husband with her hand without just cause, she may still claim self-defense if he returns the attack with a baseball bat or if he begins to assault her well after she has ceased.

Likewise, the victim may only defend herself against attacks that are unlawful. If a police officer is attempting to physically take a woman into custody to arrest her, she is not permitted to use self-defense against him, since police officers have lawful authority to make arrests. Of course, if an officer uses excessive force, then she would be justified in using self-defense against the officer because of the officer's illegal action.

Second, the victim must reasonably believe that force was necessary to repel the batterer. She (or he) must honestly believe it was necessary to use force, and that belief must have been a reasonable one. In other words, a reasonable woman in her shoes, a woman of the same age, size, and so on, would have felt the same way.

One may even use "deadly force" when it is reasonably necessary. Deadly force refers to force that is capable of causing serious injury or death. One is justified in using deadly force where the batterer is about to kill or about to cause serious bodily injury to the victim. Many states now also allow a victim to use deadly force where the batterer is about to commit a forcible felony against her, such as rape or kidnapping.

Finally, the last element to prove is that the level of force used was reasonable. If the victim's belief was reasonable about the need to act, her or his use of force must also have been proportional to the situation and not excessive. Similarly, if the attack is over and the batterer no longer poses any threat, the victim must cease the use of force. The right to self-defense ceases when the threat ceases.

Two issues have become central to the discussion of self-defense and domestic abuse. One involves the question of retreating, and the other the imminence of the threat. First, is the victim justified in using force where she or he instead could have retreated safely from the situation? Within the last decade, most states have adopted "stand your ground" laws that permit a person to use even deadly force without attempting to retreat. Only a minority of states retain the traditional rule that a person should try to retreat before taking advantage of self-defense, where the person can do so without serious danger. Even in states that require retreat, however, the "castle doctrine" provides an exception. It says that one is not required to retreat from one's home, one's place of sanctuary, one's "castle."

Despite the castle doctrine, courts have noticed the difficulty presented when both parties—a victim and a batterer, for example—reside in the same home. Most states now say that a co-occupant of a home may stand his or her ground against another co-occupant, maintaining a consistent "stand your ground" rule. The idea is that if a homeowner has the right to protect herself from an outside invader, then a co-occupant, and especially a victim of abuse, has the right to protect herself from an abuser within the home. A smaller group of states, however, have carved out an exception to the castle doctrine, requiring a co-occupant to attempt a retreat when feasible before using deadly force. These states fail to see the logic of encouraging, so to speak, lethal standoffs in the kitchen.

Another issue is the question of imminence of the threat. For force to be considered necessary, states traditionally require that it be immediately necessary or needed right at that moment. If the harm will not happen for a while, then force is not yet justified, since arguably it may never happen or may be avoided. This has presented special difficulties in cases of battered women. Oftentimes, victims are repeatedly abused in a cycle where further abuse is all but assured. In such cases, it has been argued by many scholars that a victim may have reasonably believed it was necessary to act, even if a response did not appear immediately necessary. In other words, it may be reasonable and necessary for a woman to act preemptively, before the batterer is once again poised to abuse her. By the time the batterer is poised to do so, it may be too late for the woman to effectively protective herself. Thus, in some cases her anticipatory strike should be justified. Other scholars, however, defend the imminence requirement as it stands.

Examples of such problematic cases include three major types of homicides that most often affect battered women. First, women may kill their batterer during one of their confrontations in which they are not in immediate fear for their lives. Second, women may do so while the batterer is asleep or otherwise being nonaggressive. Lastly, they may hire someone to take the batterer's life. In cases like these, it can be particularly difficult to tell when the use of force was necessary and to tell what level of force was reasonable to a battered woman. As noted above, however, such a victim historically would not be able to take advantage of self-defense law, because of the imminence requirement. Women are generally permitted to include expert testimony concerning battered woman syndrome in order to claim the defense. But homicides involving a sleeping batterer, for example, have rarely led to successful self-defense claims.

Where juries have accepted the evidence of battered woman syndrome in homicide or attempted homicide cases, it has generally served as an "imperfect" defense. This means that it did not remove the guilt but rather served as justification for a conviction under a lesser charge, for example, manslaughter rather than murder. Even where the conviction is not reduced, victims have sometimes been able to demonstrate that their sentences should be shorter or more lenient than others convicted of the same crime.

Many battered women, therefore, have spent or are spending time in prison for their acts of violence against a batterer. They have been convicted of crimes ranging from assault and battery to murder. Some of these victim offenders also send requests for pardons and clemency to state governors, in the hope that governors will commute their sentences or that parole boards will be receptive to their release.

Overall, battered woman syndrome has had a modest impact on the process and outcomes in the court system and among juries across the country. Practitioner and scholar advocates, including the American Law Institute, continue to call for change. Some scholars have even argued that defense claims outside of traditional self-defense may also justify the victim's act, such as the net benefit of the batterer's death in light of the gains to his victims and the view that the batterer has essentially forfeited his life due to his conduct.

Outside the legal question, some women have opted to obtain home defense products or training in self-defense techniques or firearms. However, women are advised that the safest course of action is to develop a safety plan to remove oneself from dangerous situations, rather than rely on physical forms of defense.

See also: Battered Woman Syndrome; Courts and Domestic Abuse; Self-Defense, Homicides, and Domestic Abuse; Walker, Lenore

Further Reading

Castle Rock v. Gonzales, 545 U.S. 748 (2005).
Chamelin, N. C., & Thomas, A. (2006). *Essentials of criminal law* (11th ed., pp. 81–84). Upper Saddle River, NJ: Pearson.
Dressler, J. (2009). *Understanding criminal law* (5th ed., pp. 223–257). Newark, NJ: Matthew Bender.
Erikson, P. E. (2007). Battered woman syndrome as a legal defense in cases of spousal homicide. In Nicky Ali Jackson (Ed.), *Encyclopedia of domestic violence* (pp. 70–76). New York, NY: Taylor & Francis Group.
Gardner T., & Anderson, T. (2012). *Criminal law* (11th ed., pp. 134–40). Belmont, CA: Cengage Learning.
People v. Goetz, 68 N.Y.2d 96 (N.Y. 1986).
Phelps, S., & Lehman, J. (Eds.). (2005). Self-defense. *West's encyclopedia of American law* (2nd ed., 9:89–91). Detroit, MI: Gale.
Samaha, J. (2011). *Criminal law* (10th ed., pp. 137–52). Belmont, CA: Cengage Learning.
The validity and use of evidence concerning battering and its effects in criminal trials. Retrieved from https://www.ncjrs.gov/pdffiles/batter.pdf
What can I do to be safe? http://www.domesticviolence.org/what-can-i-do-to-be-safe

W. Jesse Weins

SHELTERS FOR DOMESTIC ABUSE VICTIMS

In the earliest phase of the battered woman's movement, in the early 1970s, there were no shelters for victims. Instead, those in need sought refuge at homeless shelters, in their cars, or with family or friends. In 1971, British feminist and advocate Erin Pizzey started the first shelter for battered women in the United Kingdom. Her efforts were duplicated in Denmark, the United States, the Netherlands, and Australia in the 1970s. In 1981, the first shelter specifically designed for Asian American women, Everywoman's Shelter, was opened in Los Angeles. Many countries still lack adequate shelter space for victims. In July 2011, the region of Gaza opened its first shelter for abuse victims. In Russia, there are few domestic violence shelters, and the large city of Moscow still had not opened a shelter in 2005.

In 2011, the National Network to End Domestic Violence (NNEDV) commissioned their sixth annual 24-hour census of domestic violence services. On September 15, 2011, 89 percent of identified domestic violence programs in the United States participated in the National Census of Domestic Violence Services.

The results were published in the NNEDV report: *Domestic Violence Counts 2011. A 24-Hour Census of Domestic Violence Shelters and Services.* A total of 1,726 local domestic violence centers participated. Results showed that shelters served 67,399 victims in one day. Of those, 36,332 were provided emergency shelters or transitional housing. Another 31,007 adults and children were provided assistance by shelter staff for nonresidential needs, such as counselling, legal help, and support groups. Many victims are still turned away, as shelters are unable to accommodate all requests due to lack of staffing, inadequate specialized services, and limited funding. Some 64 percent of housing needs, 6,714 victims', went unmet in 2011.

In addition to sheltering survivors, most domestic violence centers operate crisis lines. In 2011, state and local centers received 21,748 calls, while the National Domestic Violence Hotline received 265,000 calls, or more than 22,000 per month. Many centers have also gotten involved in educational efforts, with 26,339 individuals in the United States and its territories receiving some form of training or education on the one-day survey.

In 2009, the first global shelter data count was initiated. Data for 2011 included Albania, Armenia, Australia, Austria, Azerbaijan, Canada, Chile, Cyprus, Denmark, England, Estonia, Georgia, Germany, Guatemala, Honduras, Hong Kong, Iceland, Israel, Italy, Liechtenstein, Luxembourg, Mexico, Netherlands, Nepal, Nicaragua, Pakistan, Peru, Portugal, Rwanda, Scotland, Slovenia, Spain, Sweden, the United States, and Vietnam. Participating were 2,636 shelters and 25 shelter networks. Results show that on just one day, 56,308 women and 39,130 children sought refuge from domestic violence. Another 7,608 women and 4,734 children had to be turned away.

Although women are more likely to be victims of domestic violence, men too can be abused. Most shelters have been established for women, however, and may prohibit male survivors or even male children of a certain age. According to one estimate, in the United Kingdom there are provisions for 7,500 refugee women but only 60 for men. Men's rights advocates maintain that shelters are increasingly including space for pets but still not for men. Oftentimes, male victims in need of safe housing end up in homeless shelters. These are not safe places, however, as their location should be known in the community (as opposed to domestic violence shelters, whose location should remain unknown).

Shelter staffs face numerous challenges in working with domestic violence victims. For one, it is essential that staff be trained to deliver services in ways that empower victims. Further, staff must do so in culturally competent ways. Shelter staff must also be ready to work with victims of all ages and both heterosexual and homosexual victims. Additionally, shelter staff must be trained in crisis management, proper documentation, and confidentially and privilege. State laws vary as to what point shelter staff might need to report certain things or in what instances they are required to provide specific information about survivors to various authorities, like police, Child Protective Services (CPS), and other court officials.

Not all victims will be "likable," nor will all those living in a communal shelter get along. Thus, shelter staff must make and enforce appropriate rules regarding sharing of space and resources, and so on. Most shelters also have rules about how victims interact with their children. While use of corporal punishment may be controversial, typically it is prohibited in shelters. Additionally, shelter staffs are mandatory reporters of child abuse. In the event that staffs reasonably believe a child may have been abused, they are required to report it to appropriate authorities. It is best to ensure that all women are aware of this upon entry to the shelter, and when a problem arises, the staff member should work with the victim to coordinate an investigation by Child Protective Services. Further, staff and volunteers should be trained in nonviolent conflict resolution. A series of tools for this purpose is available at http://www.vawnet.org/special-collections/ConflictRes.php.

Shelters must be prepared for emergencies and disasters, such as hurricanes, tornadoes, and earthquakes. Staff must be trained and protocols must be devised in the event that a shelter evacuation is required. Violence Against Women Network (VAWnet) features specialized resources for staff in addressing disasters at http://www.vawnet.org/special-collections/DisasterPrep.php.

One of the most challenging aspects of running a shelter is obtaining adequate funding. Today, many shelters seek government, foundation, or private grants to sustain their work. Albeit an important source of monies, oftentimes these funders require a narrowed or limited set of services, resulting in the domestic violence shelter having to refer victims to outside sources for legal, food, medical, child-care, educational, and other forms of assistance. In 1978, Florida became the first state to levy a tax on marriage licenses to support domestic violence shelters. In 1983, shelter funding was incorporated into the Child Abuse and Prevention Treatment Act (CAPTA), although less than one-fourth of the original request is funded. Important sources of shelter funding include the Mary Kay Foundation, Avon Foundation, as well as the Office of Violence Against Women and provisions of the Victims of Crime Act (VOCA) and the Violence Against Women Act (VAWA).

Since 2008, the NNEDV has sponsored the World Conference of Women's Shelters. The conference brings together scholars and shelter staff to further knowledge and action around assisting victims and ending abuse.

See also: Crisis Lines; Culturally Competent Services; National Network to End Domestic Violence (NNEDV); Outreach Services

Further Reading

Conflict resolution tools for domestic violence shelter staff. (n.d.). VAWnet. Retrieved June 23, 2012, from http://www.vawnet.org/special-collections/ConflictRes.php

Disaster and emergency preparedness and response. (n.d.). VAWnet. Retrieved June 23, 2012, from http://www.vawnet.org/special-collections/DisasterPrep.php

McLain, L. (2011). Women, disability and violence: Strategies to increase physical and programmatic access to victims' services for women with disabilities. *Center for Women Policy Studies.* Retrieved January 31, 2013 from http://www.centerwomenpolicy.org/programs/waxmanfiduccia/documents/BFWFP_WomenDisabilityandViolence_StrategietoIncreasePhysicalandProgrammaticAccesstoVictimsS.pdf

National Network to End Domestic Violence. (2012). Domestic violence counts 2011: A 24-hour census of domestic violence shelters and services. Retrieved June 11, 2012, from http://nnedv.org/docs/Census/DVCounts2011/DVCounts11_NatlReport_BW.pdf

Quinn, M. (2010). Open minds, open doors: Transforming domestic violence programs to include LGBTQ survivors. The Network La Red. Retrieved June 11, 2012, from http://www.ncall.us/sites/ncall.us/files/resources/GOLDEN%20VOICES%20REV%202011_0.pdf

Spangler, D., & Brandl, B. (2003). Golden voices: Support groups for older abused women. Violence Against Women Online Resources. Retrieved January 31, 2013 http://www.vaw.umn.edu/documents/goldenvoices/goldenvoices.html

Women with disabilities. Center for Women's Policy Studies. Retrieved June 11, 2012, from http://www.centerwomenpolicy.org/programs/waxmanfiduccia/documents/BFWFP_WomenDisabilityandViolence_StrategiestoIncreasePhysicalandProgrammaticAccesstoVictimsS.pdf

2011 global shelter data count. (2011). Global network of women's shelters. Retrieved January 31, 2013, from http://www.gnws.org/en/work/global-data-count.html

Laura L. Finley

SIMPSON, O. J. CASE

The 1995 criminal trial of celebrity football player Orenthal J. (O. J.) Simpson for the murder of his ex-wife Nicole Brown Simpson and her friend Ronald Goldman captured America's attention. Although the trial did little to directly change domestic violence law, it raised concerns regarding the ways in which domestic violence cases are frequently viewed in the legal and social realms. This entry will review the key details of the O. J. Simpson trial and recount the ways the trial highlighted issues surrounding the power and control of an abuser, the responses of police officers and judges, and the availability of community resources to victims and their family.

The Case

On Sunday night, June 12, 1994, Nicole Brown Simpson and Ronald Goldman were found dead in Nicole's Brentwood mansion. Over the next few days, police obtained a warrant for the arrest of the suspect, O. J. Simpson. The police spoke with Simpson's attorney, Robert Shapiro, and agreed that O. J. would report to police headquarters by 10:00 a.m. the morning of June 17th, the day after Nicole's funeral. However, the morning arrived and Simpson never showed. Officers arrived at O.J.'s house and found what appeared to be a suicide letter stating, "Don't feel sorry for me. I've had a great life, great friends. Please think of the real O. J. and not this lost person. Thanks for making my life special. I hope I helped yours. Peace and love, O. J." Around 6:20 p.m., a motorist in Orange County spotted Simpson riding in a white Bronco. Soon a dozen police cars were in pursuit of the Bronco as news helicopters flew overhead and broadcast the scene to 95 million viewers. The chase finally ended with Simpson's arrest in his own driveway. O. J.'s arraignment began on July 22, 1994, when he answered the question "How do you plead?" by answering, "Absolutely one hundred percent not guilty."

Six months later, on January 24, 1995, the murder trial began. Dominick Dunne, writer for *Vanity Fair*, described the trial as the "Super Bowl of murder trials." The trial lasted 133 days, presented 150 witnesses, and cost $15 million. The first group of witnesses included relatives and friends of Nicole and a 9-1-1 dispatcher who discussed O. J.'s history of domestic abuse toward Nicole. The 9-1-1 dispatcher reported receiving a call from Nicole in 1993 in which O. J. broke down the door at Nicole's house and could be heard screaming at Nicole in the background. Evidence was also presented regarding a domestic attack by O. J. on January 1, 1989. That night, the police arrived at the Simpson household to see Nicole running out of the bushes shouting, "He's going to kill me! He's going to kill me!" When the police informed O. J. that they were going to arrest him, he shouted, "The police have been out here eight times before and now you are going to arrest me for this! This is a family matter! Why do you want to make a big deal of it? We can handle it!" Four months later, O. J. pleaded no contest to the charge of spousal abuse. He was sentenced by a municipal judge to 120 hours of community service and two years' probation. He was also fined $200 and ordered to give $500 to a shelter for battered women.

The second group of witnesses for the prosecution established the possibility of the murder by O. J. Allan Park, O. J.'s limousine driver the night of Nicole's murder, testified that he arrived at O. J.'s house at 10:25 p.m. for O. J.'s scheduled flight to Chicago. Simpson, however, did not answer the door. Shortly before 11:00 p.m., Park said that he had seen someone black, tall, wearing dark clothes, weighing about 200 pounds entering the house. A few minutes later, Simpson emerged, telling Park he overslept. DNA experts then testified that the blood found at the crime scene matched O. J.'s blood. Furthermore, the blood could have come from only 1 out of 170 million sources of blood. In addition, the blood found on two black socks in O. J.'s bedroom matched Nicole's blood and could only fit 1 out of 6.8 billion sources of blood.

Next, the defense team, nicknamed "The Dream Team" by the media, took the stand. One of the most frequently discussed aspect of the defense case regarded Mark Fuhrman, the LAPD officer who found a bloody glove at O. J.'s house. Throughout his questioning on the stand, Fuhrman denied ever using the word "n*****." However, he was later proved to be lying when the defense played a tape of Fuhrman stating the derogatory term. This testimony opened the door for the defense to suggest that Furhman planted the evidence in O.J.'s home. The defense team brought 53 witnesses to testify for O. J. Simpson's innocence. Finally, in the turning point of the case, defense lawyer Johnnie Cochran had Simpson try on the bloodstained gloves to illustrate to the jury members that the gloves did not fit. To fasten the image in the jury's mind, Cochran concocted his infamous phrase, "If it doesn't fit, you must acquit."

On October 3, 1995, clerk, Deidre Robertson, announced, "We the jury in the above entitled action find the defendant, Orenthal James Simpson, not guilty of the crime of murder."

Society's Reaction

As the court's decision was publically aired on October 3, 1995, 150 million American viewers watched in awe, celebration, and despair. The court case was discussed for weeks as people argued over the final decision of the jury. Among domestic violence advocates, numerous concerns were brought to light, specifically the chilling details of the alleged acts of previous domestic violence attacks by O. J., the lack of response by police and court systems, and the lack of community resources utilized by Nicole.

Power and Control

In addition to the abuse incidences that were presented during the trial, there were numerous reported acts of domestic violence by O. J. In 1977, a neighbor reported hearing O. J. beating Nicole and claimed seeing Nicole with black eyes. In 1982, O. J. allegedly smashed photos of Nicole's family, threw her against a wall, and tossed her and her clothes out of the house. In 1985, Nicole called private security alleging that O. J. had bashed her car with a baseball bat. In 1987, O. J. allegedly struck Nicole and threw her to the ground. In 1989, O. J. allegedly slapped Nicole and pushed her from a slow-moving car. These events, if true, illustrate a typical story of a battered woman.

Batterers often utilize a variety of abusive behaviors, including coercion and threats, economic abuse, emotional abuse, intimidation, isolation, minimizing, denying and blaming, using children, and using male privilege. Batterers are often jealous, controlling and closed-minded. They typically blame others for their problems, minimize their abusive behaviors, and manipulate others through guilt. Many abusers are described by victims as having "Jekyll and Hyde" personalities. When initially involved with the abuser, victims often report that the abuser is charming. Many friends and families of victims will often say, "We would have never guessed he was abusive. He seemed so caring." Perpetrators are often able to present themselves in a positive light around others in order to conceal the abuse occurring at home.

Domestic violence is rarely a one-time act but rather a pattern of abuse that occurs repeatedly over a period of time. As the abuse continues, it frequently escalates in severity, and in severe cases, the escalation of violence leads to murder. In most family homicides, the murderer is the spouse and the crime occurs in the family home. Homicide frequently occurs after a series of assaultive incidents and most frequently when the victim is either attempting to leave or has left the relationship.

According to witnesses, O. J. allegedly utilized numerous abusive behaviors to gain power and control over Nicole. In addition, he spent time socializing with the local police officers, inviting them to his house and showing them his Heisman trophy. In fact, O. J. once appeared as the celebrity guest at the police department's Christmas party. One of the difficulties many victims face in attempting to escape abuse is the misconception of others that the abuse is not occurring.

Responses of Police and Judges

The O. J. Simpson case raised a multitude of questions regarding the ways in which the police and judges address domestic violence. For Nicole Brown Simpson, the system seemed to have failed at every step, from police not arresting O. J. to the court slapping him on the wrist with community service. Unfortunately, Nicole's story is not an uncommon example of a victim's experience with the legal system.

It has often been the view of our society that domestic violence is a family issue and therefore should remain out of the public realm. Police often responded to a domestic violence call and simply instructed the abuser to calm down and to then leave the scene, assuming the couple would work things out. In response to the lack of police enforcement of domestic violence laws, mandatory arrest laws have been enacted in all 50 states. Mandatory arrest laws require police officers to arrest the perpetrator when called to a domestic violence incident in which there is evidence that abuse has occurred. This minimizes the discretion of police officers among domestic violence arrests.

In addition to the lack of police response to Nicole's abuse, it also appeared that the legal system failed to hold O. J. accountable for his abusive acts. Despite the numerous reported acts of domestic violence, O. J. was found guilty only once in 1989 after pleading no contest to spousal abuse. He was sentenced by a municipal judge to 120 hours of community service and two years' probation. He was also fined $200 and ordered to give $500 to a shelter for battered women. It is a frequent complaint among domestic violence advocates that the American court system does not adequately punish perpetrators. It is not unusual for courts to reduce charges down to a misdemeanor or to offer pretrial interventions.

There is currently a push in the field of domestic violence to advocate for specialized domestic violence courts. Numerous recommendations to hold abusers accountable and protect victims have been suggested and implemented, including efficient case processing of domestic violence cases; coordinated networks of courts, victim service organizations and social service programs; informed decision-making among judges; enforced policies that hold perpetrators accountable for their actions; and available victim safety services.

Community Resources

It was rumored that five days before her murder, Nicole Brown Simpson called the Sojourner House for battered women. While there are numerous domestic violence hotlines and agencies that provide services for victims and their families, it is often difficult or near impossible for victims to access these services. Victims of abuse are often isolated and either unaware of available services or unable to access services due to lack of transportation, child care, finances, and/or time away from the abuser. Among many communities, domestic violence resources have long waiting lists, and services cannot be provided to everyone in need.

In response to the murder of Nicole Brown, her sister, Denise Brown, founded the Nicole Brown Charitable Foundation. The foundation was formed in 1994 as a campaign against domestic violence. In light of the Nicole Brown murder, and in memory of all the victims of domestic violence, we must focus on improving our system's response to domestic violence cases in order to protect victims from further harm. For additional information on the Nicole Brown Foundation, visit http://www.nicolebrown.org/index.html.

See also: Celebrities and Domestic Abuse; History of U.S. Domestic Violence Developments, 1990s; The Middle and Upper Classes and Domestic Abuse

Further Reading

Abramson, J. (Ed.). (1996). *Postmortem: The OJ Simpson case: Justice confronts race, domestic violence, lawyers, money, and the media*. New York, NY: Basic Books.

Barak, G. (2004). Representing O. J.: The trial of the twentieth century. In S. Chermak & F. Bailey (Eds.), *Crimes and trials of the century* (Vol. 2) (pp. 161–77). Westport, CT: Praeger.

Center for Court Innovation. (2009). Two decades of specialized domestic violence courts. http://www.vaw.umn.edu/documents/specializeddvcourts/specializeddvcourts.pdf

Edmonds, P. (1996, October 18). Messages mixed on domestic violence. *USA Today*. Retrieved June 4, 2012, from http://www.usatoday.com/news/index/nns091.htm

Finley, P., Finley, L., & Fountain, J. (2008). *Sports scandals*. Westport, CT: Praeger.

Resnick, F., & Walker, M. (1994). *Nicole Brown Simpson: The private diary of a life interrupted*. Vancouver, Canada: Newstar PR.

The People v. Simpson. (1994, October 10). *People*. Retrieved June 4, 2012, from http://www.people.com/people/archive/article/0,,20104089,00.html

Amanda Mathisen Stylianou

SOCIAL AND SOCIETAL EFFECTS OF DOMESTIC ABUSE

The impact of domestic violence does not end with the victims and perpetrators. Even though the actual acts of domestic violence are borne by individuals, the personal effects on the victims and perpetrators transcend the bearers and impact the entire society. Social effects refers to the ways that experiencing abuse impacts a person's later social interactions. Also of concern are the effects such violence has on one's social position. On the other hand, the societal effects of domestic violence refer to how acts of domestic violence affect the larger community.

The social effects of domestic violence include but are not limited to fear and anxiety, poor self-image or inferiority complex, poor educational and skill development ability, disruption of school lives and friendship, isolation, bullying and violent behaviors by children, and divorce/single parenthood. Victims may find engaging in subsequent healthy relationships to be challenging, as they may fear and mistrust others and are often cautious of being hurt again.

One of the social effects of domestic violence is fear and anxiety. According to Humphreys and Thiara (2003), of a group of women who had experienced domestic violence, 60 percent feared being killed by intimate partners or family members. Such fears could further degenerate into depression and isolation.

Domestic violence can also lead to a poor self-image. The form of domestic violence that most often results in this social effect is emotional or psychological abuse. Poor self image, in turn, may cause victims to develop psychological problems like eating disorders. It may also inhibit them from engaging in fulfilling, healthy relationships with others.

The consequences of this are often found in the poor educational and skill development ability of the victims. Victims who have a poor self-image may also find it difficult to cope in various educational and skill acquisitions and development programs because they already have a false belief that they are naturally unable to develop at the rate others do.

Another effect of domestic violence is the disruption of the school lives of children. When a series of abuses leads to divorce and primary caretakers relocate to new environment, the school programs of the children are truncated, their friendships lost, and employed caretakers may lose their jobs. And victims face further consequences such as depression and difficulty adjusting to a new environment. Some victims decide to remain in the relationship but with the possible consequence of not being productive both in the home and in the place of work because of post-traumatic stress disorder (PTSD). With PTSD, the victim has an overwhelming number of interpersonal, academic, and professional/occupational problems. Victims' loss of educational and economic opportunities is damaging not just to the individual and his or her family but also to the entire society. Displaying violent behaviors is another societal consequence of domestic violence. Victims may be angry and lash out at others, including their children, although it is important to note that most do not. Children who are products of violent homes are more likely to use violence with their peers, and as teens are at increased risk to engage in abusive and aggressive relationships.

Divorce as a result of domestic violence is another problematic factor both for those directly involved and for society. Children who have a single parent after a divorce inspired by abuse are less likely to have the parental care and guidance than their counterparts who are products of stable relationships. Lack of such parental responsibilities may result in children becoming delinquent. Victims of domestic violence are at increased risk for engaging in a host of risky behaviors that have both social and societal import. For example, victims may be more likely to use alcohol than nonvictims, resulting in additional need for substance abuse treatment and other family-level interventions (Brookoff, O'Brien, Cook, Thompson, & Williams, 1997).

Finally, suicide and murder are also societal effects of domestic violence. Both physical and emotional forms of violence can lead to suicide for victims who already feel devalued. Repeated abuse of individuals, after causing depression and isolation, may result in such individuals taking their lives since they believe they are of no value to themselves or to others. Experience has also shown that physical abuses have led to the death of victims. Both of these phenomena are antisocial and constitute crimes against society.

Societal Effects

One way domestic violence impacts entire communities is economic. Costs can be either direct or indirect. The resources required to respond to abuse—from those involving criminal justice to victim's services, help for children, medical needs, and beyond—are typically considered the direct costs. For instance, research shows that victims use health-care services more frequently than do nonvictims (Tjaden & Thoennes, 2000). A 2003 study by the Centers for Disease Control and Prevention (CDC) estimated the cost of health-care alone to be $4.1 billion, which was calculated based on 1995 cost figures. Additionally, research has repeatedly documented that domestic violence is one of the top causes for homelessness among women.

Indirect costs include the wages victims lose as a result of abuse. This is due to missed time, chronic tardiness, and loss of productivity that are associated with the abuse. The CDC (2003) estimated that victims miss almost eight million days of work annually. Clearly this is detrimental not just to the victims but to colleagues, who often must pick up the extra work, and for the employers as well.

Some measures suggested by scholars to deal with this problem include counseling for victims, couples counseling, conducting programs geared toward anger management and conflict resolution both for partners and for children in school, criminalizing acts of domestic violence, carrying out enlightenment programs highlighting the criminality in such acts, adequate and gender-neutral reportage of such acts, as well as addressing the patriarchal nature of society. It is clear that domestic violence is not just an individual problem but one that impacts entire communities. As such, it requires community solutions. Social change campaigns that help challenge societal norms that contribute to abuse are important, as is increased attention to the many ways abuse impacts everyone. Coordinated community responses (CCRs) can help link the various stakeholders in a community that must help address the problem.

See also: Children, Impact of Domestic Abuse on; Effects of Domestic Abuse; Health Effects of Domestic Abuse

Further Reading

Brookoff, D., O'Brien, K., Cook, C., Thompson, T., & Williams, C. (1997). Characteristics of participants in domestic violence: Assessment at the scene of domestic assault. *Journal of the American Medical Association, 277*(17), 1369–1373.

Centers for Disease Control and Prevention (CDC). (2003). *Costs of intimate partner violence against women in the United States.* Retrieved August 21, 2012, from http://www.cdc.gov/violenceprevention/pub/IPV_cost.html

Child Welfare: http://www.childwelfare.gov/can/impact

Community costs of domestic violence. (2011, July 19). The Advocates for Human Rights. Retrieved August 22, 2012, from http://stopvaw.org/Community_Costs_of_Domestic_Violence.html

Humphreys, C., & Thiara, R. (2003). Mental health and domestic violence: I call it symptoms of abuse. *British Journal of Social Work, 33,* 209–26.

McCue, M. (2008). *Domestic violence.* Santa Barbara, CA: ABC-CLIO.

Tjaden, P., & Thoennes, N. (2000). Full report of the prevalence, incidence, and consequences of violence against women: Findings from the National Violence Against Women Survey. Washington, DC: National Institute of Justice.

Mark Ikeke

SOCIAL CHANGE MOVEMENTS

Social change movements related to the area of domestic abuse have largely paralleled the feminist movement throughout history. In recent modernity, the process of social change was through the primary methods of public word-of-mouth and ever-advancing forms of media (pamphlets to newspapers to radio to television to

Internet). Social change movements consist of organized campaigns and various social involvements. They are usually collective in nature. Social movements are distinct, at least in their initial conception, from political parties and special interest groups and have as their goal changing some aspect of the status quo. Social change movements to end domestic abuse are plural in nature: to date, there has not existed one overarching movement with a clear goal, strategy, target, and scope for ending domestic abuse. As such, an important distinction exists between specific campaigns (one aspect of social change movements) and the larger social change movements from which they are derivative in their particular historical contexts.

Social change movements affiliated with ending domestic abuse have progressed from association with changing child labor/welfare laws (e.g., Society for the Prevention of Cruelty to Children) in Europe and the United States (late nineteenth century), to affiliations with feminist movements in Europe and the United States (first and second waves), to seeking government funding and mandates (e.g., Violence Against Women Act) in Western society (in the last half century), and finally to campaigning using new media (e.g., National Coalition on Domestic Violence) all over the globe (recently). In its varying applications, social change movements pertaining to domestic abuse have been *reformational*, desirous of changing both laws and norms of violence, and *radical* and *innovative*, seeking to change basic values (often associated with patriarchy), in scope. Although the ultimate emphasis is to change abuse outcomes for individuals (both causes and effects), the nature of these movements is often a peaceful, group-focused effort. Targets of domestic abuse social change movements are also diverse, with campaigns often targeting specific audiences (e.g., primary, secondary, and tertiary intervention models). Within the range of local movements, domestic abuse social change movements can be considered "old" in the West. As such, reviving the life (in the life cycle of movements' stages) and continuing membership of these movements is a constant struggle for domestic abuse organizations. However, with ever-evolving technology, some scholars classify specific domestic abuse campaigns and strategies as new social movements, particularly when conducted at the global level (e.g., World Health Organization funding of individual nations' change efforts). Perhaps because of their communal and largely feminist ties, domestic abuse social change movements often lack clear leadership; no one "owns" the movement to end domestic violence. Divergent targets (macro cultures or micro individuals), goals (raise awareness, punish offenders, or serve victims), and methods (political, religious, or corporate organizing and fear, guilt, or empathy appeals) have resulted from this lack of unifying focus.

Particularly in recent years, mediated technologies have been harnessed—to varying degrees with diverse levels of effectiveness—by most social change movements related to domestic abuse. As a result, otherwise waning older movements have been able to recruit new audiences they could not reach before due to resource or message limitations. However, new media's social change potential remains a controversial topic: Internet networking effectiveness is often overstated for specific goals such as behavior change (e.g., stopping physical violence), but broader goals such as raised awareness of the issue may be accomplished by a social campaign that goes *viral*. Especially today, campaigns modeled on social marketing approaches are implemented by specific groups. The most recent, thorough works on domestic abuse social change movements are provided by Lehrner and Allen (2008, 2009), who conclude that increased attention to the issue—as a social change movement (as opposed to mere service provision)—is necessary for its continued survival.

See also: Women's Rights Movement

Further Reading

Bennett, W. L. (2003). Communicating global activism: Strengths and vulnerabilities of networked politics. *Information, Communication & Society, 6*, 143–168.

Castells, M. (2007). Communication, power and counter-power in the network society. *International Journal of Communication, 1*, 238–266.

Cathcart, R. S. (1978). Movements: Confrontation as rhetorical form. *Southern Speech Communication Journal, 43*, 233–247.

Cismaru, M., & Lavack, A. M. (2011). Campaigns targeting perpetrators of intimate partner violence. *Trauma, Violence, & Abuse, 12*, 183–197.

Donovan, R. J., & Vlais, R. (2005). *VicHealth review of communication components of social marketing/public education campaigns focusing on violence against women*.Melbourne, Australia: Victorian Health Promotion Foundation. Retrieved January 31, 2013 from http://www.vichealth.vic.gov.au/Publications/Freedom-from-violence/Review-of-Public-Education-Campaigns-Focusing-on-Violence-Against-Women.aspx

Freeman, J. (1973). The origins of the women's liberation movement. *American Journal of Sociology, 78*, 792–811.

Lehrner, A., & Allen, N. E. (2008). Social change movements and the struggle over meaning-making: A case study of domestic violence narratives. *American Journal of Community Psychology, 42*, 220–234.

Lehrner, A., & Allen, N. E. (2009). Still a movement after all these years? Current tensions in the domestic violence movement. *Violence Against Women, 15*, 656–677.

Ryan, C., Carragee, K. M., & Schwerner, C. (1998). Media, movements, and the quest for social justice. *Journal of Applied Communication Research, 26*, 165–181.

The Ad Council Television Campaign for Domestic Violence Awareness: http://www.adcouncil.org/Our-Work/The-Classics/Domestic-Violence

Women and Social Movements Today: http://womhist.alexanderstreet.com/links/today.htm

Jessica J. Eckstein

SOCIOLOGICAL THEORIES ABOUT DOMESTIC ABUSE

Before the emergence of the broad social movements of the 1960s and 1970s, especially the women's movements that gave prominence to feminist theories, there existed what some call a "virtual conspiracy of silence" around issues of domestic violence (Clark and Lewis 1977, p. 26). Feminist sociology and criminology arose from social struggles that challenged social structure, norms, and beliefs about women's rights, opportunities, and positionality within society and that challenged the oppression of women through state practices, criminal justice system policies, and legislation.

Feminist theorists have pointed out that traditional or conventional sociological and criminological theories as well as mainstream legal definitions alike have approached and defined domestic violence (as well as other issues such as sex work, pornography, and sexual assault) from a male perspective. The experiences and insights of women, especially working-class, poor, and racialized women, have generally been overlooked until very recently.

Even otherwise critical theories of crime and punishment have tended to overlook or ignore issues of domestic violence. Marxist theories focused on broad political economic structures and the centrality of exploitation within the workplace have left the domestic realm and domestic labor issues largely untheorized. Anarchist theories, focused on condemnation of the state, have tended to view the domestic realm as a sphere of private affairs rather than a focus of political theory. Concern was instead placed in the public realm of state authority. In some anarchist theories, the family or community was presented uncritically as a realm of mutual aid and autonomy counterpoised to the state as the sphere of oppression and repression. At the same time, some early anarchists, notably the anarchist feminist Emma Goldman, did make connections between moral regulation through the state and religion and the oppression of women and domestic violence. Goldman, whose works influenced later generations of feminist theorists, also identified economic inequality for women and the dependence relations forged by marriage as important factors. These are political and economic issues related to social conditions rather than individual issues.

Contemporary critical theorists, building upon and developing the analyses of anarchism and socialism in association with feminist analyses, argue that violence against women, including violence within domestic relations, is related to the social and economic exclusion of women. They note also that the definition of abuse goes beyond physical acts to include economic abuse. This can involve not providing an economically dependent partner with proper funds to care for herself and/or children. These can have longer-term impacts.

Economic dependence can lead women to stay in abusive relationships or believe they have no options. This is related to other factors such as job training, labor market skills, or employment history. All of these can, in turn, be related to or exacerbated by abusive situations in which women are limited in or forbidden from outside work experiences. The shelter movement emerged as a response to this precarity, and most women who seek refuge in shelters are economically precarious. Socialist feminists ask why gendered roles are assigned to women in the first place. Women are exploited for sexuality and domestic labor as well as for paid labor.

Critical theorists suggest that the distinction between domestic and public is misleading, as patriarchal conditions provide male abusers with a sense of security in the home and outside it. They note too that domestic violence often spills over into the workplace as abusive male partners may visit workplaces and/or harass partners at work, either in person or over phone or e-mail.

Radical feminist theories focus on patriarchal social and ideological structures that reinforce male dominance throughout societal institutions, public and domestic. Radical feminism highlights the cultural and legislative construction of women as the property of men. Marriage, sexual assault, and domestic violence laws protect men's supposed property. At the same time, people who are structurally and socially unequal cannot be made equal through laws and punishment.

Recognizing the psychological as well as social aspects of domestic violence, social psychology theories have addressed issues associated with domestic violence. Social psychology theories propose conditions of learned helplessness to explain impacts of abuse and why some women stay in abusive relationships. This theory suggests that repeated abuse leaves victims with a sense that they cannot control or change events in their lives. Abuse leads to depression, low self-esteem, and passivity in which attempts to change or leave abusive conditions are viewed as doomed to fail. This theory does not explain why most women in North America actually do leave abusive domestic situations.

Among more conservative approaches to explain domestic violence is rational choice theory. Using a market model of human behavior, rational choice theory explains criminal events as outcomes of conscious decision making by people involving estimates of the cost, opportunity, and perceived success of engaging in criminal activity. Influenced by classical liberal theories, for rational choice theories people are rational calculating actors who weigh costs and benefits of engaging in activities, including considerations of the likelihood of punishment.

Research in the 1980s, during the height of influence of rational choice theory, claimed to support theoretical positions of rational choice, suggesting that men engage in rational choice calculations in domestic conflicts. The conclusion was that threats of legal sanctions would deter men from committing potential offences. This research had a direct impact on policy, leading to mandatory arrest laws in 15 states in the United States. Later studies in the United States contradicted the initial findings. Sherman (1992) concluded that arrests had no impact on reducing crime in repeat domestic offences. In some cases, among unemployed and/or unmarried offenders, arrests increased incidences of reoffending.

Overall, rational choice theory has been less effective in explaining expressive rather than instrumental offenses. Emotional or impulsive offenses are such that offenders are less likely to weigh costs and benefits or to consider impacts somewhere in the future, as might be the case for planned or instrumental offenses such as theft or break and enter.

Feminist theory has also contributed to research in victimology, examining the impacts of domestic violence on women and the disproportionate harm done to women in domestic violence. While both men and women are victims of domestic violence, victimology research shows that women are subjected to greater brutality and are more often victimized. Women are more likely to be injured or killed and are more likely to require medical or social assistance. Similarly, while domestic violence occurs within same-sex relationships, women are most often and most brutally subjected to domestic violence within heterosexual relationships.

In addition to changing perspectives on domestic violence, feminist criminologists have played important parts in changing legislation and social policy. Feminist criminologists were active in mobilizing for legislative changes that require police and prosecutors to charge and prosecute cases of domestic violence where there are probable grounds for commission of an offense. Radical, anarchist, and socialist feminists have been instrumental in mobilizing to build networks of shelters and support services for women.

See also: Feminism and Domestic Abuse; Gender-Related Theories

Further Reading

Clark, L., & Lewis, D. (1977). *Rape: The price of coercive sexuality.* Toronto, ON: Women's Press.

Johnson, H., & Pottie Bunge, V. (2001). Prevalence and consequences of spousal violence in Canada. *Canadian Journal of Criminology, 43*(1), 27–45.

O'Grady, W. (2007). *Crime in Canadian context: Debates and controversies.* Toronto, ON: Oxford University Press.

Shantz, J. (2012). *Crime/punishment/power: Sociological explanations.* Dubuque, IA: Kendall Hunt.

Sherman, L. (1992). *Policing domestic violence.* New York, NY: Free Press.

Sherman, L., & Bark, R. (1984). The specific deterrent effects of arrest for domestic assault. *American Sociological Review, 49*, 261–272.

Walker, L. (1979). *The battered woman.* New York, NY: Harper and Row.

Jeff Shantz

SOUTH AMERICA AND DOMESTIC ABUSE

Many studies have shown that domestic abuse is prevalent in South American counties. Gender role norms, economics, education and other factors all play a role in explaining abuse. The United Nations has established programs in the region and many nongovernmental organizations (NGOs) help educate the public and provide services to victims.

Introduction

The Economic Commission for Latin America and the Caribbean (ECLAC) indicated in 2009 that the few studies conducted in Latin and South America have shown that different forms of domestic violence occur in all social classes. However, women who have fewer economic resources and lower levels of education are more vulnerable to become victims.

The progress and recognition of the problem of domestic violence in the public sphere are seen in the ratification of international treaties related to the fight against gender violence. The Inter-American Convention of Belém do Pará (1992) to prevent, punish, and eradicate violence against women led to legislative changes in almost all South American and Latin American countries. In 2005, a second generation of laws was created to address the issue of gender violence.

Despite these advances, it is important to note that a study involving eight South American countries (Argentina, Chile, Colombia, Ecuador, Paraguay, Peru, Uruguay, and Venezuela) about NGOs' perception of the application of the laws concluded that the governments have not covered all aspects necessary to reduce such violence. Moreover, the majority (83.78 percent) of NGOs considers that the implementation mechanisms are insufficient, and 89.19 percent considers that the funds established for their application are insufficient.

A regional report shows that in 2007, approximately 32.6 percent of urban women and 34.1 percent of rural women over 15 years old do not study or earn their own income. In addition, women over the age of 25 perform housework and in most cases without compensation (ECLAC, 2007). In the same vein, there are still social problems such as social inequality, poverty, institutional weakness, delinquency, crime, and armed violence.

It is also important to recognize the cultural differences and nuances of each country that affect the level of development and welfare of its residents. Some specific problems, such as armed conflict, continue to be experienced in countries such as Colombia, while in countries such as Peru, this problem has been eliminated.

Other characteristics continue to differentiate the various countries. For example, according to the World Bank (2011), Bolivia does not apply the concept of ethnic minorities in its own country because most of its inhabitants are indigenous (62 percent).

According to Ellner (2003), Venezuela presents political polarization with the aftereffects of nongovernability and institutional weakness. Brazil, despite being the most developed country in the region, suffers high levels of social crime.

Given the cultural diversity and social situation in South American countries, common patterns are highlighted that influence the perception and tolerance of domestic violence. For example, some countries consider domestic violence a mechanism of discipline.

The study of the World Health Organization (WHO) developed by Garcia-Moreno, Jansen, Ellsberg, Heise, and Watts (2006) noted how the social context influences the tolerance of domestic violence, especially sexual violence, which is ignored or justified in some countries. For example, when a large percentage of women in Peru were asked for reasons to refuse sex with their partner, they stated that they felt they had no right to refuse sex under any circumstances.

Women are also exposed to complex violence in the context of the family, occurring together with domestic violence. For example, Cáceres (2011) noted that most Colombian women (70.2 percent) have complex violence, and 29.8 percent suffer only partner violence. Women during their lifetime were victims of child abuse, sexual abuse, and partner violence among parents, displacements, and natural disasters.

Prevalence

In a study conducted by the WHO in 2006, Brazil and Peru were selected to represent the South American region. This study took into account the lifetime prevalence of physical violence, sexual violence, and the combination of the two. Psychological violence was not considered. Results indicated that Peru has the highest percentage of severe physical violence (49 percent), ranks second in the combination of physical and sexual violence (47 percent), and third in sexual violence (47 percent). Differences were observed between the provinces and the city. There was a higher percentage of severe physical violence in the province (62 percent) than in the capital (50 percent). The same phenomenon occurs in regard to sexual violence: 47 percent in the province and 23 percent in the city. The combination of physical and sexual violence yielded 69 percent in the province and 52 percent in the city.

Brazil also registered a higher prevalence in the province compared to the capital: physical violence in the province (34 percent) as opposed to (27 percent) in the capital, sexual violence (14 percent) in the province compared to (10 percent) in the capital, and the combination of physical and sexual violence (37 percent) in the province as opposed to (29 percent) in the city. In general, the WHO study (2006) notes that between 66.6 percent and 50 percent of women in the cities who participated in the study have experienced physical violence and are likely to have experienced severe physical violence.

Lary and Garcia-Moreno (2009) reviewed several studies about the prevalence of domestic violence internationally. For example, the Worldsafe Study included Chile as a South American country and found that 25 percent of women aged 15 and 49 suffer physical violence. Another study, the Democratic and Health Surveys (2004), included Colombia, noting that 40 percent of women suffer physical violence and 11 percent sexual violence.

In its 2009 report on domestic violence, ECLAC stated that in the Plurinational State of Bolivia (2008), almost 40 percent of women between 15 and 49 suffered emotional violence. In Colombia (2005) and Peru (2004), over 60 percent of women suffer such violence.

Characteristics of Domestic Abuse

Cultural norms that relate to men and women, especially those that relate to submission, control, and enforcement of the customs of traditional institutions that maintain the male hierarchy, aid in propagating domestic violence. According to the National Demographic and Health Survey carried out by Profamilia (2005) in Colombia, 78.8 percent of women do not seek help, and when they do, it is to buy and renegotiate power within the relationship, to press for the violence to stop and for the abuser to change.

Femicide

The prevalence of femicides in Central and South American countries is 45.39 per every million women. In comparison, the prevalence of femicides in North America is 18.67 per million women (San Martin et al., 2010). Colombia is in the top 5 world rankings, with an incidence of 1,091 and prevalence of 49.64 femicides per million. Also above the global mean are Bolivia (165 in 34.17 in incidence and prevalence) and Paraguay (71 of incidence and prevalence 27.54). Argentina ranks in 16th place, just below the average of the 44 countries, with an incidence of 302 and a prevalence of 15.19 (per million).

Achievements and Challenges

In South America, the UN presence is coordinated by UN-Women Andean region, which covers 11 countries and is responsible for ensuring that the objectives of the millennium are followed. Those objectives are fighting poverty, inequality, and violence against women.

The achievement-oriented services to victims highlighted the progress in most countries. For example, Brazil created family police stations starting in 1985 and today has 450 nationwide. Argentina created an integrated system between different institutions of government and UNICEF in favor of gender equality.

Another example of good practice can be found in Uruguay's education network for women in Latin America and the Caribbean, and in Chile the creation in 2009 of 59 battered women shelters. However, the striking decline in international agency support of NGOs in Argentina and Chile has caused a shortfall in resources.

Further research should be conducted in Latin and South American countries to facilitate the understanding of the problem. The results of future studies about domestic violence in the region may help guide the development and implementation of more effective policies.

See also: Demographic and Health Surveys; Latin America and Domestic Abuse; The United Nations and Domestic Abuse; World Health Organization (WHO)

Further Reading

Alhabib, S., Nur, U., & Jones, R. (2010). Domestic violence against women: Systematic review of prevalence studies. *Journal Family and Violence*, 25(4), 369–382 doi:10.1007/s10896-009-9298-4

Cáceres, E. (2011). Tratamiento psicológico centrado en el trauma en mujeres víctimas de violencia de pareja. Tesis doctoral, Universidad Complutense de Madrid. Madrid: Spain.

Economic Commision for Latin America and Caribbean (ECLAC). (CEPAL, 2007). Objetivos de desarrollo del Milenio. Informe 2006: Una Mirada a la igualdad entre sexos y la autonomía de la mujer en América Latina y el Caribe, Santiago de Chile (LC/G.2352).

Economic Commision for Latin America and Caribbean (ECLAC). (CEPAL, 2009). ¡Ni una más! Del dicho al hecho: ¿Cuánto falta por recorrer? Únete para poner fin a la violencia contra las mujeres. Retrieved from http://www.eclac.org/mujer/noticias/noticias/2/37892/Niunamas2009.pdf

Ellner, S. (2003). Introduction: The search for explanations. In E. Steven & H. Daniel (Eds.), *Venezuelan politics in the Chavez era*. Boulder, CO: Lynne Rienner, 7–26.

Garcia-Moreno, C. G., Jansen, H., Ellsberg, M., Heise, L., & Watts, C. H. (2006). On behalf of the WHO Multi-country Study on Women's Health and Domestic Violence against Women Study Team. Prevalence of intimate partner violence: Findings from the WHO multi-country study on women's health and domestic violence. *The Lancet*, 368 (9543), 1260–269. doi: 10.1016/S0140-6736(06)69523-8

Lary, H., & Garcia-Moreno, C. (2009). Partner aggression across cultures. In O. Daniel & M. W. Erica (Eds.), *Psychological and physical aggression in couples: Causes and interventions* (pp. 59–75). Washington, DC: American Psychological Association Press.

Profamilia. (2005). Violencia contra las mujeres y niños. En la Encuesta Nacional de Demografía y Salud (Ende). Bogotá, Colombia. Retrieved from http://www.profamilia.org.co/encuestas/Profamilia/Profamilia/images/stories/ENDS-2005/general/capitulo_XIII.pdf

Rioseco, L. (CEPAL, 2005). Buenas prácticas para la erradicación de la violencia domestica en la region de América Latina y el Caribe. Unidad Mujer y Desarrollo. Santiago de Chile. http://www.eclac.org/publicaciones/xml/4/22824/lcl2391e.pdf

San Martín, J., Iborra, I., García, Y., & Martínez, P. (2010). III Informe Internacional Violencia contra la mujer en las relaciones de pareja. *Serie documentos 16*. Centro Reina Sofía [CRS]. Valencia: Spain. Retrieved from http://www.eclac.org/mujer/noticias/noticias/2/37892/Niunamas2009.pdf

The World Bank (2011). Pueblos indígenas, pobreza y desarrollo humano en América. Retrieved from http://web.worldbank.org/WBSITE/EXTERNAL/BANCOMUNDIAL/EXTSPPAISES/LACINSPANISHEXT/0,,contentMDK:20505826~menuPK:508626~pagePK:146736~piPK:226340~theSitePK:489669~isCURL:Y,00.html

Eduin Caceres-Ortiz

SOUTH AND SOUTHEAST ASIA AND DOMESTIC ABUSE

Domestic abuse is a significant problem in South and Southeast Asian families, as well as among immigrant groups who come to the US from the countries in this region. Cultural issues may make it difficult for victims to report abuse and to receive help. There are, however, many organizations devoted to assisting South and Southeast Asian victims.

Scope and Extent of the Problem

Although women across the globe experience domestic violence at shocking rates, some groups are uniquely vulnerable. Most research finds that violence against women is one of the most common victimizations experienced by immigrants, and immigrants are at greater risk for domestic violence homicide. Yoshihama and Dabby (2009) found that immigrants of Hispanic and Asian descent experience a higher risk of homicide in general than persons born in the United States. A study of femicide in New York found immigrants constituted 51 percent of intimate partner homicide victims between 1995 and 2002.

Data on domestic violence among South Asian immigrants is limited. While it is always difficult to obtain precise figures on domestic violence, unique cultural issues may prevent Asian immigrants from reporting abuse. Further, studies vary as to what countries they include as "Asian." Some data sources include India, Pakistan, Bangladesh, Bhutan, Nepal, Maldives, Afghanistan, Iran, and Sri Lanka, while others include only a portion of those countries or exclude them altogether.

Nonetheless, data seems clear that victims of Asian descent suffer abuse at high rates. Raj and Silverman (2002) surveyed women living in the greater Boston area. They found that more than 40 percent of the 160 South Asian women indicated that they were victims of intimate partner violence. Importantly, only half of the women who experienced intimate partner violence were aware of services available to help.

Dabby, Patel, and Poore (2010) analyzed data from a total of 160 cases of domestic violence–related homicides occurring between 2000 and 2005 in 23 states among Asian and Pacific Islander families. They found that 72 percent of homicides involved intimate partners. Another 16 percent involved nonintimate partner family killings. The most frequent scenario was that a wife was killed by her husband (40 percent) or an ex-wife killed by her ex-husband (17 percent). A total of 86 percent of the intimate partner murder victims were females, and 86 percent of the perpetrators were men.

Much of the data about Asian immigrants and domestic violence comes from domestic violence organizations. Sakhi for South Asian Women is a domestic violence organization in New York City. Between January 1 and December 31, 2009, the organization received 673 crisis calls or e-mails. Of those, 35 percent were from people of Indian origin, 19 percent from people of Bangladeshi origin, 12 percent from people of Pakistani origin, and 16 percent whose country of origin was unavailable. In Houston, DAYA serves South Asian victims. Between 2003 and 2009, DAYA saw a dramatic increase in calls for help, from 189 to 3,847. The organization noted a 27 percent increase in calls between 2007 and 2009. No More Tears serves domestic violence victims in South Florida. Of the 50 women served between 2007 and 2010, five (10 percent) have been South Asian: two from Pakistan, two from India, and one from Bangladesh. All had experienced verbal, physical, and sexual forms of abuse.

Forms of Abuse

Globally, abuse takes many forms. Women endure physical and sexual abuse, verbal and emotional abuse, financial control, and much more. In some regions, women suffer in different ways. So-called honor killings, referred to by the United Nations Commission on Human Rights as "one of society's oldest gender-based crimes," are unfortunately common in parts of Asia. In India, an estimated 5,000 women are killed each year from such killings. These crimes are generally perpetrated by a girl's father, brother, or spouse because she is perceived to have dishonored the family, either through adultery or some other behavior considered inappropriate for women in these cultures. Another form of abuse that occurs across the globe but is found in many Asian countries is acid attacks. Perpetrators, typically male, permanently disfigure, and in some cases kill, their victims by throwing acid on them. Despite new laws criminalizing acid attacks in 2002, more than 2,600 cases have been reported in Bangladesh since 1989. *New York Times* reporter and author Nicholas Kristof (2008) investigated acid attacks in the large area from Asia to Afghanistan. He described them as "a kind of terrorism that becomes accepted as part of the background noise in the region."

Barriers to Leaving Abusers

Victims of domestic violence face tremendous barriers in leaving abusive partners. Asian women face some of the same barriers to getting safe as do other victims, but they may also face unique challenges. In many Asian countries, privacy, loyalty, and shame are important values. To tell others what is considered personal family business is unacceptable. An unsuccessful marriage is shameful, and women must be loyal to their husband and to their families, who may have helped select their spouses.

The involvement of in-laws or other extended family members often makes it more difficult for Asian women to leave abusers. Family members may discourage women from disclosing abuse or seeking help. In many cases, family members are part of the problem. That is, in-laws may join in the abuse. Divorce is still taboo in many Asian communities.

Abuse is viewed as normal in some Asian cultures—as something women must endure. Some countries still lack appropriate laws to protect victims and hold batterers accountable. Only 89 countries have legislation officially prohibiting domestic violence. Other countries have appropriate legislation but fail to enforce it.

Some Asians are Muslim. In some situations, abusers misinterpret the Quran, saying it condones physical abuse of their wives. Women tell of seeking assistance from imams, who tell them Allah wants them to stay together.

Resources

In the United States, some services have been developed to assist immigrant victims of domestic violence and Asian immigrant victims, specifically. A part of the Violence Against Women Act (VAWA), first passed in 2000, provides legal reforms to address some of the legal and economic dependencies imposed on battered immigrant women. Abused spouses may self-petition for a green card on his or her own, rather than through the spouse. Another provision is cancellation of removal, which lets an abused spouse who has already been subjected to removal proceedings based on their immigration status to request to remain in the United States. The U-visa lets a victim of crime, including domestic violence, who has been helpful to its investigation or prosecution of the offender(s) apply for a nonimmigrant visa and work permit. Finally, VAWA allows immigrant victims access to public benefits such as food stamps. There are, however, several significant obstacles to these well-intentioned legal reforms for immigrant battered women. Legal help is expensive, and the VAWA application requires documentation that immigrants may not have access to. An additional difficulty lies in outreach. Many victims have no idea they are eligible to file a VAWA petition. Some of the biggest difficulties in assisting immigrant victims, including South Asians, relate to the scarcity of culturally appropriate services. Many domestic violence agencies are unprepared to translate for South Asian victims and do not always respect different ethnic or racial groups' religious and cultural needs, including food preferences and difficulties living in communal shelters. If victims are not assured that someone on staff will speak their language and work hard to meet their specific needs, they may leave and end up returning to abusers.

Many domestic violence organizations have been created to specifically address the needs of Asian victims. Asian-specific organizations have helped domestic violence victims obtain shelter, legal counsel, health care, and other necessary services. Given their specialized focus, agencies like Sakhi in New York, Sahara in Miami, and DAYA in Houston have been able to provide culturally appropriate therapy and group services as well.

Many of these organizations also advocate for women's rights, particularly domestic violence and immigrant women's rights. They attempt to bring about legislative and public policy reform and to sensitize law enforcement and healthcare providers, as well as other social service providers, about the unique issues faced by Asian women. The South Asian Women's Network features a list of resources on their website, http://www.sawnet.org.

See also: Acid Attacks; Asia and Domestic Abuse; Dowry Killings; Forced Marriage and Domestic Abuse; Honor Killings

Further Reading

Abraham, M. (1995). Ethnicity, gender, and marital violence: South Asian women's organizations in the United States. *Gender & Society, 9*(4), 450–468.

Abraham, M. (2000). Isolation as a form of marital violence: The South Asian immigrant experience. *Journal of Social Distress and the Homeless, 9*(3), 221–236.

Bangladesh: Acid attacks continue despite new laws. (2009, January 5). Retrieved December 10, 2009, from http://alertnet.org/thenews/newsdesk/IRIN/7c05353a22b4bcd12cffcb51cfe65c38.htm

Bhuyan, R., Mell, M., Senturia, K., Sullivan, M., & Shiu-Thornton, S. (2005). "Women must endure according to their karma": Cambodian immigrant women talk about domestic violence. *Journal of Interpersonal Violence, 20*(8), 902–921.

Bui, H. N. (2003). Help-seeking behavior among abused immigrant women. *Violence Against Women, 9*(2), 207–239.

Dabby, C., Patel, H., and Poore, G. (2010, February). Shattered lives: Homicide, domestic violence, and Asian families. *Asian and Pacific Islander Health Forum*. Retrieved October 17, 2010, from http://www.apiahf.org/images/stories/Documents/publications_database/dv_execsum_ho micide.pdf

Dasgupta, S. (2000). Charting the course: An overview of domestic violence in the South Asian community in the United States. *Journal of Social Distress and the Homeless, 9*(3), 173–185.

Dasgupta, S., & Warrier, S. (1996). "In the footsteps of 'Arundhati' ": Asian Indian women's experiences of domestic violence in the United States. *Violence Against Women, 2*(3), 238–259.

Kim, J., & Sung, K. (2000). Conjugal violence in Korean American families: A residue of the cultural tradition. *Journal of Family Violence, 15*(4), 331–345.

Kristof, N. (2008, November 30). Terrorism that's personal. *New York Times*. Retrieved January 7, 2010, from http://www.nytimes.com/2008/11/30/opinion/30kristof.html

Lee, E. (2007). Domestic violence and risk factors among Korean immigrant women in the United States. *Journal of Family Violence, 22*, 141–149.

Liao, M. S. (2006). Domestic violence among Asian Indian immigrant women: Risk factors, acculturation, and intervention. *Women & Therapy, 29*(1/2), 23–39.

McDonnell, K., & Abdulla, S. E. (2001). Project AWARE. Asian/Pacific Islander Resource Project.

Police Violence & Domestic Violence. (n.d.). *Incite! Women of Color Against Violence*. Retrieved January 7, 2010, from http://www.incite-national.org/media/docs/2883_toolkitrev-domesticviolence.pdf

Raj, A., & Silverman, J. (2002). Violence against immigrant women. *Violence Against Women, 8*(3), 367–398.

Raj, A., & Silverman, J. (2007). Domestic violence help-seeking behaviors of South Asian battered women residing in the United States. *International Review of Victimology, 14*, 143–170.

Sakhi: http://www.sakhi.org

Shiu-Thornton, S., Senturia, K., & Sullivan, M. (2005). "Like a bird in a cage": Vietnamese women survivors talk about domestic violence. *Journal of Interpersonal Violence, 20*(8), 959–976.

Yoshihama, M., & Dabby, C. (2009, September). Domestic violence in Asian, Native Hawaiian, and Pacific Islander homes. Retrieved October 20, 2010, from http://www.vaw.umn.edu/documents/factsandstats/factsandstats.pdf

Laura L. Finley

SPIRITUAL ABUSE

There are various kinds of domestic abuses, ranging from physical, emotional, social, sexual, and economic to spiritual abuse. With the exception of spiritual abuse, all the others have enjoyed an overwhelming acceptance as constituting domestic violence. A small number of scholars, however, have raised questions about whether spiritual abuse constitutes domestic violence. Since spiritual abuse has the same effects as every other kinds of domestic abuse, it should also be given attention so that its debilitating effects can be properly handled.

What Is Spiritual Abuse?

Spiritual abuse might be called misapplication of religion for the purpose of oppressing the victim. Although there may not be physical violence involved, a nonviolent act intended to harm or injure, whether emotionally, psychologically, or physically, constitutes abuse.

Yehuda, Friedman, Rosenbaum, Labinsky, and Schmeidler (2007) found that abuse is more common among very devout Jews and occurs more frequently among those who adopted religion later in life (as opposed to those who were raised to be observant). Alkhateeb (1999) asserts that abuse occurs in approximately 10 percent of Muslim families in the United States.

One of the trickiest things about spiritual abuse, however, is that those who oppress others spiritually often cite scripture that supports their actions and truly believe that they are helping or "saving" the other, not harming them. The following examples highlight the ways abusers of various faiths misuse scriptural texts.

Islamic abusers of their wives have misrepresented Surah 4, Ayah 34 of the Quran, which reads: "Men are the protectors and maintainers of women because Allah gave them more to the one than to the other, and because they support them from their means. So devout women are extremely careful and attentive in guarding. Concerning women who are rebellious (*nushooz*) you fear, admonish them, then refuse to share their beds, then hit them; but if they become obedient, do not show means of annoyance against them. For Allah is most High, Great." This verse has been interpreted to mean that men should take economic and physical control over their wives because Allah has made it so, given that most men are physically stronger and were historically the breadwinners for their families. Women are to show absolute respect for their husbands and abstain from infidelity. Yet many imams and other Islamic religious teachers frown at this overt distortion of the Quran and point out that the Prophet never hit his wife all through his lifetime and even made an express statement, "Never hit the handmaid of Allah," in the collection of the hadith. So he could not have approved of that. The last sermon of the Prophet, according to opponents of abuse, instructed men to treat their wives well.

A similar situation is found in Christianity. Some men have (mis)read verses of the Bible as meaning that women should be absolutely submissive to the husband. Take a look at the following Bible verses: "Wives, submit to your own husbands as to the Lord, for the husband is the head of the wife as also Christ is the head of the church" (Eph. 5:22–23) and "A man ... is God's image and glory, but woman is man's glory. For man did not come from woman but woman came from man; and man was not created for woman but woman for man" (1 Cor. 11:7–9).

Christian spiritual abusers have misunderstood the essence of biblical passages like these. They continue their acts of abuse unapologetically, claiming approval of a patriarchal family structure by the Holy Scripture. But they have lost sight of the biblical admonition that says that "woman is not independent of man, and man is not independent of woman" (1 Cor. 11:11). Further, the above is a quote from Paul, not from Jesus.

Similarly, Jewish abusers have misinterpreted scripture to justify abuse. Some cite a proclamation from Maimonides that they say authorizes beating your wife if she fails to complete housework. Again, Jewish scholars and others note that this interpretation takes the proclamation out of context and that no Jewish scripture advocates wife-beating.

Another form of spiritual abuse is the denial of religious freedom. Abusers might not allow a devout partner to attend services, or might coerce him or her to follow a different faith. Spiritual abuse can also come in the form of a partner ridiculing the religious and moral beliefs of the victim. The perpetrator of this kind of abuse subjects the values of the victim to absurd tests with the intention of seeing the victim fail. Once the perpetrator gets this result, he or she mocks the victim about the claims of his or her religious sincerity, which can erode the confidence and faith of the victim.

Additionally, abusers might manipulate the spirituality of children as a tool to control their victim.

Many victims turn to their religious leaders for assistance. In particular, African American women have been found to reach out to faith leaders to assist them in abusive situations (Bent-Goodley & Fowler, 2006). Unfortunately, some of these leaders are not very helpful. Instead of sharing more accurate interpretations of scripture and assisting victims in escaping abuse or in seeking the help they seek, some religious leaders revictimize them by citing the same misinterpretations, insisting they stay with dangerous abusers, and promoting couples counseling where it is inappropriate (Bent-Goodley & Fowler, 2006).

On the other hand, many faith leaders have made great efforts to learn more about abuse so that they can better assist those in need. Below is a sample of some groups and organizations that address spiritual abuse.

Solutions

Scholars, counselors, ministers, pastors, priests, rabbis, imams, and other religious leaders have urged practical solutions in coercive spiritual situations.

Founded in 1977, the Faith Trust Institute "is a national, multifaith, multicultural training and education organization with global reach working to end sexual and domestic violence." It provides training, consultation, and resources at http://www.faithtrustinstitute.org.

The Peaceful Family Project is a Muslim organization devoted to assisting Muslim victims and sharing the true meaning of the Quran's teachings. It provides awareness workshops for communities as well as Muslim leaders, conducts research, and shares resources with victims and allies. Additional information is available at http://www.peacefulfamilies.org.

The Christian Coalition Against Domestic Abuse (CCADA) helps correct misconceptions about abuse among Christian couples and provides resources and training for Christian faith leaders. More information is available at its website, http://www.ccada.org

Jewish Women International (JWI) provides prevention training, resources to victims and advocates, and advocacy for legislation like the Violence Against Women Act (VAWA). It also offers several downloadable toolkits for faith leaders. These are available at the organization's website, http://www.jwi.org.

One way of handling this problem is for the victim to build his or her self-confidence. And this can only come through studying and understanding one's religious texts and teachings such that no one make you doubt or question your faith. With such unwavering confidence, the victim is better able to cope with the attendant emotional problems.

Religious bodies should also organize programs and workshops where abuse and domestic violence are freely discussed. The target audience should be all families, not just those who have experienced abuse.

Communication in a family or relationship is also necessary. This should also carry with it a better understanding of the patriarchal structures of the family and most societies in general. Here it is important to stress that being the head of a family does not grant man the power of an absolute ruler.

It is clear that the nature of spiritual abuse is markedly different from most other kinds of domestic violence. This is because of the damaging effects on not just the victim's emotions but also, and more uniquely, on his/her spirit. In spite of the effects, religious leaders are urged to partner with some other organizations (as some are already doing) to provide not only spiritual solutions but also social services to victims.

See also: Christianity and Domestic Abuse; Islam and Domestic Abuse; Judaism and Domestic Abuse; Types of Domestic Abuse

Further Reading

Alkhateeb, S. (1999). Ending domestic violence in Muslim families. *Journal of Religion and Abuse*, 1(44), 49–59.

Bent-Goodley, T., & Fowler, D. (2006). Spiritual and religious abuse: Expanding what is known about domestic violence. *Affilia, 21*(3), 282–295.
Faith Trust Institute: http://www.faithtrustinstitute.org
The Professional Education Taskforce on Family Violence (1991). *Family violence: Everybody's business, somebody's life.* Sydney, Australia: Federation Press.
Safe Place Ministries: http://www.safeplaceministries.com
Yehuda, R., Friedman, M, Rosenbaum, T., Labinsky, E., & Schmeidler, J. (2007). History of past sexual abuse among married observant Jewish women. *American Journal of Psychiatry, 164*(11), 1700–1706.

Mark Ikeke

STALKING

Stalking is a form of unwanted attention by an individual or group of persons aimed at an individual that produces the effect of harassment, threat to, or intimidation of the person being stalked and that would cause a reasonable person to feel fear. Stalking also involves repeated attempts to create fear in the person who is the victim of the attacks. Generally, similar behaviors that might be perpetrated but do not cause fear for one's safety or the safety of one's family are classified as harassment. Stalking is more often a crime perpetrated by a person known to the victim, although a variety of stalker profiles exist.

Although stalking is usually not perpetrated by members living with the victim, it is a form of violence against women (or men), more often of the psychological or emotional type than of the purely violent type.

Behaviors associated with stalking include following victims; sending unwanted text messages, e-mails, or calling the victim; sending gifts or leaving items for the victim; vandalizing property and making threats against the safety of the victim, the victim's dependent children, pets, or extended family members; loitering near the victim's workplace, home, or other places where the stalker might run into the victim; and, in extreme cases, physical or sexual assault upon the victim.

All 50 states, the District of Columbia, and the U.S. overseas territories have all passed legislation defining stalking as a crime, although the definitions of what constitutes stalking both in terms of actions and repetition vary by locality. The first legislation was passed by the State of California in 1990. Just prior to the passing of the California law, the widely publicized case of the young actress Rebecca Schaeffer, who was murdered by a stalker in 1989, brought attention to cases of stalking. Within the next three years, all states had passed similar legislation against stalking.

There has been much revision to stalking legislation as the psychology of stalkers becomes better understood and as stalking has come to be seen more often as perpetrated by persons known by the victims. Also, legislative revisions have sought to clarify the laws and close loopholes. As part of this process, the U.S. Department of Justice created a model antistalking law for states to use as a basis in 1993. Since this was a model and states still develop laws on their own, often in response to locally publicized attacks, there is not complete uniformity on the definitions of

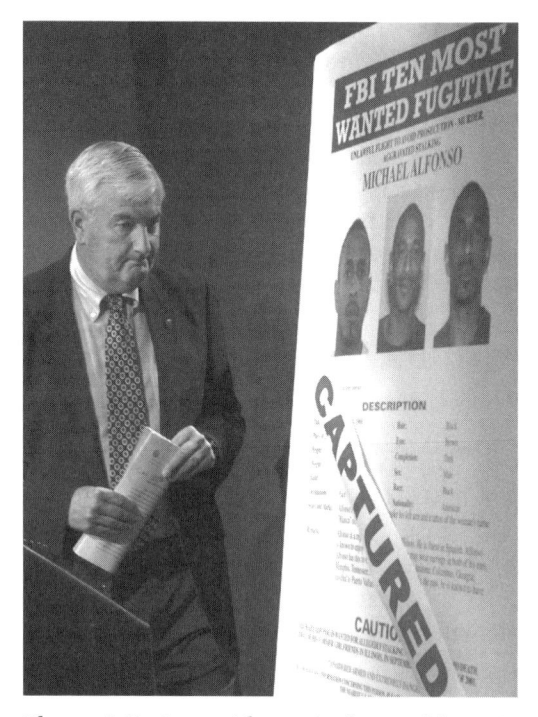

Thomas J. Kneir, special agent in charge of the FBI's Chicago office, walks past the wanted poster of Michael Alfonso, after a news conference Friday, July 16, 2004. Alfonso, listed on FBI's 10 most wanted list, was captured by Mexican Federal Investigative Police and Mexican Immigration Service in Vera Cruz, Mexico the previous day. Alfonso is accused of stalking and then killing two former girlfriends in Illinois, one in September 1992 and the other in June 2001. (AP Photo/M. Spencer Green)

stalking, on the penalties, or on evidentiary issues. The growth of new forms of technology has also added complexity to legislation about stalking in recent years as cyberstalking has become a new form of stalking behavior.

There are a number of shared components of the laws. For instance, most states require proof that the stalking behavior is a pattern of repetition. Most also require that the threat be credible, although not all stalking behaviors, such as sending gifts, make this explicit. In place of the threat language, some states use another commonality in requiring that the person feel fear, or that a reasonable person in the victim's situation would feel fear. Another common feature is that states require the intent of the perpetrator must be to put the victim in fear. States vary as to exactly what type of fear (of harm, of death, etc.) this might be. Finally, states also generally consider stalking to be a misdemeanor, which means that offenses involve fines, or occasionally short jail sentences. Some states do allow for felony stalking charges to be brought in certain circumstance, often in combination with other crimes such as breaking and entering.

The definitions of stalking vary slightly over different fields from psychology to criminology. The initial use of the word was derived in the sixteenth century from the stalking of prey, and in most instances, the idea of a person hunting a prey still underlies the concept. Since stalking can include a complex of behaviors most of which are not illegal in and of themselves—such as the sending of texts and e-mails, sending of gifts, calling on the phone, talking in person, appearing on the same street or in the same location—legal definitions often states that the behaviors must be at least twice or must repeat despite stated resistance to contact.

Current Bureau of Justice statistics for the United States suggest that about 14 out of 1,000 adults experience stalking behavior each year, with half of those reporting weekly contact, and 11 percent reporting that the behavior has happened for five or more years. And while males and females experience harassment in the same numbers, three times as many women were reported to be victims of stalking. Male victims of stalking are equally likely to be stalked by men and women, whereas women are overwhelmingly likely to be stalked by males. Most stalking victims also report that they perceive their stalkers to be roughly the same age and the same race as themselves.

According to the Bureau of Justice, the most common behaviors for stalking victims to report are unwanted phone calls and messages. Other common behaviors included the stalker showing up at places without a legitimate reason, spying behaviors, and waiting inside or outside places where the victim would be expected to show up (such as work, home, or near family members).

There are many different typologies of stalkers, and many studies have attempted to classify stalkers according to their modes of choosing a victim, their sense of a relationship to the victim, or the underlying behaviors exhibited during stalking behavior.

Although stalkers are often portrayed in the media as being persons out of touch with reality who believe the object of their attentions to be enamored of them, in reality, most stalkers are ex-partners of the persons they stalk. Stalkers typically fall into one of three categories: simple obsessional, love obsessional, or erotomaniac. In the majority of cases, the stalker is of the simple obsessional type; in these cases, the stalker has a prior relationship with the stalker, and the victim has attempted to break off a relationship, and the stalker is attempting to continue the relationship or seeks reconciliation through continued contact with the other party. Typical relationships include former romantic partners, neighbors, coworkers, teachers, or students. Typically, these stalkers approach their victims in order to gain some amount of control over the victim. A second type of stalker, much less common, does seek out connections and relationship with victims he or she does not know. The stalker has typically just fixated on the victim without having had previous contact. These stalkers typically act under the belief that if they can just have contact with the victim, they will manage to win over the victim to fall in love with them and see how much the stalker really cares for the victim. The third grouping is the erotomaniac category. These stalkers also have not had any previous contact with their victims. Typically, they believe the victim is deeply in love with them. Due to mental health issues or delusions, they fixate on the victim based on the fantasy that the victim is in love with them. The final large grouping of stalkers involves people who stalk their victims out of anger or revenge of some sort. In this case, stalkers do know their victims, but the intent is most clearly intimidation or harm. Regarding all these types of stalkers, studies done of victims suggest that perceived reasons why stalking may have begun tend to emphasize anger, retaliation, spite, or a desire to control the victim.

One of the newest areas of stalking that legislation is still trying to catch up with is cyberstalking. This involves the sending of e-mails, text messages, or contact through social networking sites. Sometimes, as stalking becomes more invasive, it can include attempts to load software onto a victim's computer to capture information or hack into her or his computer. Other types of cyberstalking can include identity theft and pretending to be the victim online or spreading fake information posing as the victim.

Stalking violence tends to occur more often when the stalking has continued for longer periods of time and when there has been an escalation of stalking behaviors from nonaggressive to more aggressive behaviors during the time. About 50 percent of stalking victims receive threats of physical violence against themselves, and about a third will actually be victims of violence. Homicide itself is exceedingly rare in stalking cases, with only about 1 in 400 victims being killed by their stalkers. The chances of a stalking victim actually being physically hurt by her or his stalker is more likely to occur if they had a past intimate connection, and the second most common group are those who casually knew their stalkers.

Victim responses typically change as the length of stalking increases or the severity of the threats or actions increase. Typically, victims begin by changing their routines. Especially for victims who previously knew their stalkers, this may involve changing their living situation, varying their routes to work, changing places they visit for shopping or recreational activities, or even changing their socializing patterns. Physical effects can also be seen. The most common effect is anxiety, and it can lead to weight loss, insomnia, headaches, nausea, general ill-being. In longer-term cases, the effects of stalking can lead to a diagnosis of post-traumatic stress disorder. The victim's psychological response also goes through a range of emotions, from fear and anxiety to annoyance and anger.

Among stalking victims, the greatest fears that were reported included a fear of bodily harm and worries that they could not guess what would happen next. Other fears included a fear that the stalking would not end and of death. The psychological effects of stalking can be quite severe. Stalking has been described as a form of mental attack on a person. The most common effects are intimidation and a feeling of lack of safety, hypervigilance, insomnia, and isolation. Stalking can, in more extreme cases, lead to those being stalked changing jobs, moving to new cities, or becoming recluses.

In dealing with stalkers, the law enforcement course of action is generally to provide short-term crisis intervention for the survivor and criminal prosecution for the offender. Although many stalking incidents go unreported, victims are encouraged to keep logs of all stalking activity and to file police reports, even when police might suggest there are reasons for the unwanted contact. After a pattern is established or a threat seems potential, law enforcement often suggests that victims place a restraining order against the offender, which attempts to limit the offender's physical proximity as well as limit other types of communication between the parties.

In less than one-third of states is first-time stalking a felony offense, although second-time stalking is a felony in the majority of states. Factors that may aggravate charges include the possession of weapons, violation of parole or other pending charges, and if the victim is under 16 years of age.

See also: Restraining Orders and Personal Protection Orders; Technology and Domestic Abuse; Types of Domestic Abuse

Further Reading

Baum, K., Catalano, S., Rand, M., & Rose, K. (2009, January). *Stalking victimization in the United States. Bureau of Justice Statistics Special Report.* Washington, DC.

Burgess, A., Baker, T., Greening, D. et al. (1997, December). Stalking behaviors within family violence. *Journal of Family Violence, 27*(4), 398–403.

Logan, T. K., Cole, J., Shannon, L., & Walker, R. (2006). *Partner stalking: How women respond, cope, and survive (Springer Series on Family Violence)*. New York, NY: Springer.

Pinals, D. (2007). *Stalking: Psychiatric perspectives and practical approaches*. New York, NY: Oxford University Press.

Stalking Behavior Website: http://www.stalkingbehavior.com/interventions.htm Stalking Victims Sanctuary: http://stalkingvictims.com/

Andrea Dickens

STRAUS, MURRAY

Murray Straus is professor of sociology at the University of New Hampshire. In 1968, he founded and continues to serve as co-director of the Family Research Laboratory. Dr. Straus received his PhD in 1956 from the University of Wisconsin, Madison. He is the founding editor of *Teaching Sociology* and *Journal of Family Issues*, and the author or coauthor of over 250 articles and over 20 books on crime, corporal punishment, aggression, partner violence, and measurement of conflict tactics in family relationships. His work, controversial in some academic circles, is yet renowned for its cross-national and -cultural applications. Best known for his studies of aggression, corporal punishment, and domestic abuse in families, Dr. Straus and his colleagues have consistently researched provocative areas with methods subject to scrutiny in many disciplines.

Classified within the "family violence perspective" of domestic abuse research, Dr. Straus created the Conflict Tactics Scales (CTS) in the early 1970s. The CTS are typically used to measure conflict and individuals' potential for violence in interpersonal relationships. The CTS, whether in its original or revised CTS2 form, has been implemented in over 1,000 studies. Originally created to measure three categories of conflict resolution—Reasoning, Verbal Aggression, and Violence—the CTS2, in response to many criticisms, relabeled the items in these categories; the revision included Physical Assault (formerly Violence), Physical Injury (added), Psychological Aggression (formerly Verbal Aggression), Sexual Coercion (added), and Negotiation (formerly Reasoning). The CTS, most commonly used to assess abuse by family violence researchers, is also the source of the most debate in the domestic abuse literature. Criticisms focus on failures of the CTS and family violence researchers to assess context, injury, fear, coercion, and control or to accurately reflect victims' experiences in the form of specific violent relationships.

Straus and colleagues reported that abuse may occur in 60 percent of all marriages (Straus & Gelles, 1990). Although prevalence of domestic abuse in the United States was initially tracked in the late 1960s, the emergence of Straus's work with the CTS marked the point at which prevalence findings became controversial. A second controversy surrounding family violence perspectives—and Straus's work in particular—is the consistent finding that men and women report similar frequencies of victimization. The finding that women perpetrate abuse as often as or more than men, reported by family violence researchers using both the CTS and other measures, has been documented in over 200 individual studies. However, critics of the CTS and the family violence perspective discount these findings, arguing the research fails to account for context, injury, and relationship types.

Another controversy sparked by research from Straus and colleagues, using the Parent-Child version of the CTS (CTSPC), was the finding that parental use of corporal punishment may increase children's likelihood of a lowered IQ and increased antisocial behavior, read by some as abuse perpetration, later in life (Straus, Sugarman, & Giles-Sims, 1997). To date, the CTS, in all its versions, is the most frequently used assessment of abusive tactics in family relationships. As a result, the research of Dr. Straus remains the most referenced—both critically and positively regarded—in the field of domestic abuse research and applied professions.

See also: Child Abuse and Domestic Abuse; Children, Impact of Domestic Abuse on; Female Perpetrators; Male Victims of Domestic Abuse

Further Reading

Family Research Laboratory: http://www.unh.edu/frl/

Fiebert, M. S. (2011). *References examining assaults by women on their spouses or male partners: An annotated bibliography*. Retrieved from California State University, Psychology Department website: http://www.csulb.edu/~mfiebert/assault.htm

National Institute of Justice on Measuring Domestic Abuse: http://www.nij.gov/topics/crime/intimate-partner-violence/measuring.htm

Straus, M. A. (2004). Cross-cultural reliability and validity of the Revised Conflict Tactics Scales: A study of university student dating couples in 17 nations. *Cross-Cultural Research, 38*, 407–432.

Straus, M. A., & Gelles, R. J. (1986). Societal change and change in family violence from 1975 to 1985 as revealed by two national surveys. *Journal of Marriage and the Family, 48*, 465–479.

Straus, M. A., & Gelles, R. J. (1990). *Physical violence in American families: Risk factors and adaptations to violence in 8,145 families*. New Brunswick, NJ: Transaction.

Straus, M. A., Hamby, S. L., & Warren, W. L. (2003). *The Conflict Tactics Scales handbook: Revised Conflict Tactics Scales (CTS2), CTS: Parent-Child Version (CTSPC)*. Los Angeles, CA: Western Psychological Services.

Straus, M. A., Sugarman, D., & Giles-Sims, J. (1997). Corporal punishment by parents and subsequent anti-social behavior of children. *Archives of Pediatrics & Adolescent Medicine, 151*, 761–767.

Jessica J. Eckstein

SUPPORT GROUPS FOR VICTIMS OF DOMESTIC ABUSE

Support groups are one of the important forms of self-help for survivors of domestic violence and abuse. Participation decreases the long-term impact of trauma and abuse, provides members with understanding and a safe environment, and offers the chance to explore issues affected by violent relationships. Support groups provide an opportunity to examine cultural identity, gain support with mental health issues, build support network, and increase understanding of their experiences.

A variety of services are available to the victims of domestic abuse. They can be accessed via domestic violence shelters at secret locations, community services, hospitals, clergy, and via the Internet. Some of the most common available services to survivors of domestic abuse are individual and group counseling, family and couple counseling, and placement in support and psychoeducational groups. Such services assist survivors with needs related to abuse including safety, recovery from trauma, emotional and financial support, access to health and legal services, and career support and development.

If counseling groups come as a predetermined packet of services for those who suffer from domestic violence and sexual assault, it is assumed that support groups are the treatment of choice. If counseling, therapy, and education are provided by mental health practitioners such as social workers and counselors, support groups may be facilitated by professionals or by volunteer group members who themselves are survivors of trauma and abuse. Consequently, participation in support groups brings significant gains in self-esteem and self-efficacy; in locus of control and improved health; changed attitudes toward family, marriage, and marital functioning; and decreased violence among spouses if they remain in a relationship.

Available research literature states that support groups are less educational, less structured, and often focused on emotions that group members experience after surviving trauma and abuse. Initially, support groups were developed in shelters for women who required a refuge from an abusive relationship and were in need of emotional and financial support. The available body of research and best practices literature defines several common focuses for the work of support groups with domestic abuse survivors. First, the future safety of the women and their children and a more promising view of the future: often battered women chose to return to their homes and stay in the relationship that caused them pain and danger. This happens when they experience economic dependency and feel they have to save the relationship or family. Such decisions are influenced by personal and cultural beliefs and often limited financial means.

The second focus is to assist survivors in admitting and recognizing abuse without minimization or denial. Based on cultural values and observed generational abuse in their own families, battered women may also have a sense of responsibility for the abuse and violence in their relationships. Thus, in support groups, survivors provide mutual personal and interpersonal safety through exploring and sharing their stories, expressing hurt feelings, and gaining understanding of their experiences. Sharing their stories allows survivors to know that they are not alone; also, such experiences greatly empower women. It gives them a feeling of being able to contribute to the well-being of others. Consequently, sharing personal stories promotes healing and recovery.

Third, because of the controlling and abusive relationship, women often find themselves socially isolated, misunderstood, and victimized by their own family members and friends. As such, support groups can provide a safe and trusting environment where victims can address without judgment a plethora of emotions such as self-blame, anger, feeling of guilt, low self-esteem and learned helplessness, depressive symptoms, and perceived health status. Fourthly, members of support groups gain understanding of how and why violence happens. Members learn about survivors' beliefs regarding male-female roles and sexism. Learning to rebuild trusting relationships in a supportive atmosphere of such groups, members gain an opportunity for a safe self-exploration and relational self-examination.

Considering the cultural background of group members is essential. When talking about Latina, black, or Asian women, one should remember that each cultural group consists of many different ethnic and racial representatives. Latina women, for example, can be Mexican, Cuban, Colombian, Brazilian, Argentinean, or Chilean. Black women can be of African, Haitian, or Bahamian decent. Asian women can be with Pacific Islander, Asian American, Japanese, Chinese, or other background.

While recovering from abusive relationships, group members rebuild and develop a support system and support network. This helps women to develop coping skills, strengthen resilience, and make changes in their lives. Through the positive experience in the group, women begin to develop and extend new healthy relationships outside of the group. Such support groups are particularly essential for divorced Latina immigrant women whose friends and families are left in their country of origin. Immigrant women may experience different forms of psychological abuse than women who have a status of a permanent residency or U.S. citizenship. Financial dependence (e.g., forced to work illegally), immigrant status (e.g., threat to take children or refusal to file papers), limited language, and limited transportation are the points of forcing dominance and isolation associated with less self-help. Additionally, knowing the fact that Latina women tend to go back to their abusive relationships more frequently than non-Latina white ones, support groups become an especially valuable source of support.

Women's race, ethnicity, age, and socioeconomic status play a significant role in the decision-making process regarding which support group to attend. These factors often determine the "sense of belonging and comfort level" within the group. Additionally, differences in behavioral norms, beliefs, and values are determined by culture and have to be accounted for in choosing interventions while working with survivors.

Even though there is limited research available about working specifically with African American women abuse survivors and how they heal and recover, some culture-specific findings are available. Existing literature states that the ethnic and cultural makeup of a support group is an important factor for African American women in the decision-making process. Group homogeneity by culture, race, and socioeconomic status allows survivors of violence to explore cultural identity and provide them with understanding and acceptance. This in turn promotes an open dialogue and the sharing of personal stories, and brings healing, recovery, and a decreased sense of isolation.

It is important to keep a facilitator and group members culturally congruent. Group members who are representative of a minority group stress that they feel more understood when their group leader is the same race and culture. It allows women to more freely explore the issues of their cultural identity, abuse and trauma, oppression, and personal values.

There are similar findings for groups whose members are Asian women. It is important to note that while forming groups of women with Asian heritage, facilitators should be careful defining "Asian" because of its diverse ethnic and cultural representation. These may include language, level of acculturation (e.g., where the person was born and raised), values, and religious and/or spiritual orientation. Based on the above factors, facilitators have to be sensitive to specific aspects of the many contributing cultural characteristcs victims may hold in order to accommodate group members and provide emotional comfort, a feeling of safety, and belonging to promote recovery and healing.

Age is another culture-specific factor in providing support to abuse survivors. Unfortunately, it often happens that older abused women are a minority in battered women's support groups. Because the issues presented by younger members differ from those who are older, older victims may not always fully benefit from traditional support groups. Some women have been in long-lasting abusive relationships, while others experienced violence after divorce or the death of their previous partner later in their lives. Some older women report being abused by their adult children, grandchildren, or other family members due to medical or mental health conditions. Thus, most commonly presented problems are health concerns, relationship with adult children, grief, and long-term-relationships.

For many older abuse survivors, support groups are a refuge for finding understanding, support, peace and hope, decreasing isolation, and improving physical and mental health. Groups foster personal growth, and one of the outcomes of attending support groups is that some women leave long-lasting abusive relationships and even begin dating.

In order for abuse survivors to feel safe and comfortable, support groups can be offered in different locations. These may include senior and aging centers, churches and faith-based organizations, health-care settings, or libraries. There are some difficulties associated with starting support groups for older abused women, and these may be based on participation, location, and transportation. Thus, participation may be determined by the cultural beliefs regarding the secrecy and feeling of privacy about family-related problems. Choice of words describing abuse, domestic violence, and sexual assault must be carefully considered, because many women do not identify with such terms. Transportation and freedom to leave the house can be difficult based on location, medical and psychological conditions, as well as employment conditions of an abusive spouse or a caregiver and the physical location of the support group.

Another factor to consider is the time frame for groups. Some groups are ongoing; others are limited in duration. This is determined by the location of the meetings and facilitators and whether they are professionals or volunteers. This factor may become a limiting issue for survivors seeking a support group and related services.

With the increasing use of computer-mediated communications, numerous support groups may be found online via newsgroups and chat rooms for those uncomfortable or unable to seek help from a local domestic violence service provider. A simple Google search reveals numerous support groups as well. Locating well-established counseling and self-help services through the Internet amplifies the availability for violence survivors to get connected with other victims of abuse and thus acquire and maintain help, support, and build networks. Virtual support groups are cost-effective and can be conveniently accessed at any time of day; one can control how long he or she may be there and determine "selective self-presentation." Also, for online group members, it is easier to define one's own activity level in the group that may provide a sense of control and safety.

See also: Crisis Lines; Shelters for Domestic Abuse Victims; Therapy and Counseling for Domestic Abuse

Further Reading

Brandl, B., Hebert, M., Rozwadowski, J., & Spangler, D. (2003). Feeling safe, feeling strong: Support groups for older abused women. *Violence Against Women, 9*(12), 1490–1503. doi: 10.1177/1077801203259288

Hurley, A., Sullivan, P., & McCarthy, J. (2007). The construction of self in online support groups for victims of domestic violence. *British Journal of Social Psychology, 46*, 859–874. doi: 10.1348/014466606X171521

Larance, L., & Porter, M. (2004). Observations from practice: Support group members as a process of social capital formation among female survivors of domestic violence. *Journal of Interpersonal Violence, 19*(6), 676–690. doi: 101177/0886260504263875

Liu, L., Tsong, Y., & Hayashino, D. (2007). Group counseling with Asian American women: Reflections and effective practices. *Women and Therapy, 30*(3–4), 193–208. doi: 10.1300/J015v30n03_14

Molina, O., Lawrence, S., & Azhar-Miller, A. (2009). Divorcing abused Latina immigrant women's experiences with domestic violence support groups. *Journal of Divorce and Remarriage, 50*, 459–471. doi: 10.1080/10502550902970561

Taylor, J. (2000). Sisters of the Yam: African American women's healing and self-recovery from intimate male partner violence. *Issues in Mental Health Nursing, 21*, 515–531.

Tutty, L., Bidgood, B., & Rothery, M. (1993). Support groups for battered women: Research on their efficacy. *Journal of Family Violence, 8*(4), 325–343.

Tatyana Cottle

TECHNOLOGY AND DOMESTIC ABUSE

Technology and abuse as concurrent phenomena have increased exponentially over the last two decades, largely due to the increase in easily accessible forms of technology, including cellular telephones (calling, texting, imaging, and tracking capabilities) and Internet technologies (e-mail; instant messaging; public message forums; identity theft of financial, personal, and private information; and tracking of browsing histories) used to facilitate domestic abuse.

In the past 20 years, technology has served as both bane and boon to victims of domestic abuse. In the 1990s, society commenced widespread use of the Internet and digital mobile telephones. With more than 80 percent of Americans using the Internet in 2011 and 96 percent of U.S. citizens using cellular phones (CTIA, 2011), new media forms have been used to exacerbate and abet perpetrators who can now abuse through a variety of methods.

In the realm of Internet behaviors, cyberbullying has been studied extensively in terms of peer relationships. However, the use of technological resources to psychologically abuse a domestic victim has not received comparable attention from domestic abuse researchers. Cyberstalking, also primarily studied in nondomestic contexts, is typically perpetrated against ex-intimates. To increase coercive control and harassment over victims, abusers can increase the immediacy of their abusive behavior through e-mail, instant messaging, chat room conversations, and by constant monitoring of webpage histories or using keyloggers (keystroke tracking software). While in or out of domestic relationships with their victim, abusive partners can send harmful e-mail messages to a victim and access passwords in order to send e-mail messages on behalf of victims (e.g., inappropriate messages to their colleagues, family, and friends sent from the victim's e-mail accounts). Social networking sites such as Facebook, organizational intranets, YouTube, and LinkedIn can be used to publically humiliate victims.

Cellular telephones are another primary technology used by domestic abusers. The most common form of abuse committed in this context is that of texting intimates–to maintain a constant psychological presence in their lives; to send hurtful messages, images, or videos; and to habitually interrupt the day-to-day life of the victim. In addition to simply calling or leaving voice messages for their victims, abusers also use cellular telephones in domestic abuse by tracking via global positioning systems; monitoring by accessing the call histories of particular accounts;

relabeling, changing, and deleting victims' saved contact information; and altering account access and calling plans without their knowledge.

Recent studies of technological domestic abuse perpetration indicate not only that victims consistently report experiencing this means of abuse, but also that current instruments used to assess abusive behaviors have not adapted to include technological methods of abuse. Initial work in this area supports the idea of technology use as a generational phenomenon, with higher prevalence of abuse-via-technology being reported more by younger victims than by their older counterparts—a finding not maintained outside this context, in cases of abuse without technological means.

To date, Internet services and cellular telephones are the primary methods of abuse-via-technology. Further, technological innovations have merged the power of these tools, with recent abilities to access the Internet from a cellular telephone, or smartphone. Most domestic abuse research on this phenomenon has focused on teenage relationships. The use of technology for abusive means in adult partner and family relationships has yet to be thoroughly examined.

See also: Stalking; Types of Domestic Abuse

Further Reading

Cellular Telecommunications Industry Association (CTIA). (2011). *Wireless industry indices: Semi-annual data survey results: A comprehensive report from CTIA analyzing the U.S. wireless industry, year-end 2010.* Retrieved from http://www.ctia.org/advocacy/research/index.cfm/AID/10316

Complete Online Safety Resources from the BC Rural Women's Network: http://www.onlinesafetytoolkit.com/

Eckstein, J. J., & Lever-Mazzuto, K. (2011, October). *Connections between intimate partner violence (IPV) and technologically-mediated communication: Construct explication and creation of a measure.* Paper presented at the meeting of New York State Communication Association, Ellenville, NY.

SafetyNet Project from the National Network to End Domestic Violence: http://www.nnedv.org/projects/safetynet.html

Sheridan, L. P., & Grant, T. (2007). Is cyberstalking different? *Psychology, Crime & Law, 13,* 627–640.

Short, E., & McMurray, I. (2009). Mobile phone harassment: An exploration of students' perceptions of intrusive texting behavior. *Human Technology, 5,* 163–180.

Southworth, C., Dawson, S., Fraser, C., & Tucker, S. (2005, June). *A high-tech twist on abuse: Technology, intimate partner stalking, and advocacy.* Safety Net: Safe & Strategic Technology Project at the National Network to End Domestic Violence Fund. Retrieved from http://www.nnedv.org

Spence-Diehl, E. (2003). Stalking and technology: The double-edged sword. *Journal of Technology in Human Services, 22,* 5–18.

United States Census Bureau. (2011). *Statistical abstract of the United States: 2012* (131st ed.). Washington, DC. Retrieved from http://www.census.gov/compendia/statab/

Westbrook, L. (2007). Digital information support for domestic violence victims. *Journal of the American Society for Information Science and Technology, 58,* 420–432.

Jessica J. Eckstein

TEEN VICTIMS OF DOMESTIC ABUSE

Teenagers can become victims of domestic abuse by witnessing intimate partner violence between their caregivers, by being abused by their caregivers, or by being abused by their own romantic partners. Intimate partner violence among teenagers is a growing problem in the United States. For many years, studies about intimate partner violence reflected adult cases without taking into account teenage victims. Furthermore, a number of researchers who began to dedicate their efforts to study teen dating violence failed to recognize significant differences between adult relationships and teenage relationships. Moreover, the lack of emphasis on adolescent characteristics is also noticeable in legislation regarding intimate partner violence.

Domestic Violence

It has been estimated that every year 3 million children and 10 million teenagers witness domestic violence in their homes. Witnessing domestic violence can increase youngsters' risk of developing academic, social, and psychological problems. Indeed, these children report high rates of depression, anxiety, post-traumatic stress disorder, delinquency, substance abuse, interpersonal difficulties, violence, and low self-esteem. Many teenagers who observe violence between their parents run away from their homes or engage in violent relationship themselves.

Women who were exposed to domestic violence growing up report higher rates of being victims of intimate partner violence themselves than women who had never seen their parents become violent against one another. Research has found that men who witnessed intimate partner violence during childhood are significantly more likely than others to abuse their romantic partners later in life.

Abuse by Caregivers

Approximately 50 percent of men who abuse their intimate partners also abuse the children living in their homes. A study conducted by Tyler, Brownridge, and Melander (2011) suggested that the abuse rate against teenagers may be as high as 66 percent in households where intimate partner abuse is present. The authors indicated that adolescents who are physically abused or who do not receive parental warmth are more likely to abuse substances and involve themselves in delinquent acts. Moreover, teenagers who are neglected, denied parental warmth, and who commit delinquent acts are more likely to become perpetrators of dating violence. On the other hand, the risk factors for becoming a victim of dating violence include being subjected to more parental physical violence, being neglected, and having been involved in delinquent activities.

The U.S. Department of Justice reported in 1993 that children who reside with caregivers who engage in domestic violence are 1,500 times more likely to suffer from abuse than children who live in households where their caregivers do not engage in intimate partner violence. Research has found that 40 to 60 percent of mothers of child victims of abuse were being victimized themselves by their husbands or boyfriends compared to 13 percent of mothers whose children denied ever being abused.

Teen Dating Violence

Nearly 10 percent of teenagers in the United States report being subjected to physical violence by their intimate partner at least once during the previous 12 months. Results from the National Longitudinal Study of Adolescent Health indicated that between 20 and 30 percent of American teenagers report being abused verbally or psychologically during the previous 12 months.

Some studies suggest that teenage boys and girls use violence in their relationships at similar rates. However, other studies indicate that females are the primary victims of violence and that males are more likely to use severe forms of physical and sexual violence. Further, a study conducted by Molidor and Tolman (1998) indicated that 90 percent of abused boys reported feeling minimal pain or no pain at all during the worst abusive episode, while only 8.7 percent of the abused girls reported minimal suffering or no suffering at all. A total of 47.8 percent of abused girls indicated severe pain and bodily injuries as a result of the worst abusive episode. In the same study, Molidor pointed out several gender differences regarding the reasons for using violence and regarding who initiates the violence. For instance, 70 percent of the girls in the sample compared to 27 percent of boys stated that their romantic partners were the ones initiating the violence.

Teenagers' motivations to commit violent acts against intimate partners differ according to gender. Even though males and females indicate that they behave aggressively out of anger, girls are more likely to report that they use violence to defend themselves. Indeed, a total of 36 percent of the females in Molidor's sample stated they were trying to defend themselves when they used violence toward their partners. On the other hand, boys are more likely to state that they use aggression with the objective of taking control in the relationship.

Teenagers' reactions to their intimate partners' use of aggression also varies according to gender. Teenage males tend to laugh at girls who attempt to use violence against them, while girls tend to report higher rates of depressive symptoms, suicide attempts, and substance abuse. Studies about adolescents' interpretation of the use of violence revealed that girls seemed to view violence as a way to intimidate the other, and boys seemed to justify the use of violence if they felt they were provoked by girls first. Further, females tend to define abuse according to the consequences of the act (e.g., if it causes pain is abuse), and males tend to define abuse depending on the intention behind the act (e.g., if the intention was to inflict pain is abuse).

Several differences exist between abusive adult relationships and abusive teenage relationships. First, female teenagers are less likely than adult females to depend on their intimate partners for economic support, to share a residence, to be married, and to have children with their abusers. The aforementioned factors can diminish the power dynamics that play a role in adult relationships where women may stay in the relationship due to their sense of powerlessness.

Second, teenagers' attitudes are deeply influenced by the support or the rejection of peers. It is expected that teenagers who surround themselves with peers who condone intimate partner violence will be more likely to use or accept the use of violence in their relationships. Moreover, teenagers' behavior in intimate settings is expected to differ significantly from teenage behaviors in group settings. Indeed, research shows that boys report being more likely to hit a girl back if she acts aggressively toward them in front of others than if she uses violence when the two of them are alone.

Third, when faced with relationship conflicts, teenagers are less likely than adults to use effective communication and coping mechanisms. This issue can lead teenagers to use or expect to be subjected to verbal, emotional, or physical violence in romantic relationships. Moreover, due to their lack of dating experience, teenagers may hold distorted beliefs about their roles in relationships.

Fourth, adolescents' general desire to become independent from their parents may lead them to tolerate abuse from their romantic partners. This situation may get exacerbated if their living conditions at home are not ideal. Children who are being abused, rejected, or neglected in their households are more likely to stay in abusive intimate relationships. In some cases, these children may even run away with an abusive partner to escape from the mistreatment they are being subjected to at home.

Lastly, the law does not always offer protection to teenage victims of dating violence. The organization Break the Cycle studied the state laws in the United States regarding domestic violence and dating violence and found that only seven states in the country have proper legislation in place to protect young victims. For example, California is one of the states that received an A under Break the Cycle's grading system. California allows underage victims of intimate partner violence over the age of 12 to request restraining orders against their abusers even if the abusers are minors and even if the victim and the perpetrator are not legally married.

On the other hand, Kentucky and Missouri were among the states that received a failing grade in offering protection to teenagers. Kentucky does not allow individuals in dating relationships to obtain protective orders against their abusers. If married, teenagers can access protective orders, but the law does not specify if a protective order can be issued against another minor. It is also unclear to whether or not underage victims can request a protective order on their own behalf.

In Missouri, minors cannot request protection orders against their abusers, and protection orders cannot be taken against underage abusers. Moreover, Missouri does not recognize stalking as a form of abuse, and it does not have an established procedure that schools can use to respond to dating violence.

Human Trafficking

Human trafficking has been defined by Congress as "modern day slavery." The Trafficking Victims Protection Act of 2000 (TVPA) states that "severe forms of trafficking in persons" means "sex trafficking in which a commercial sex act is induced by force, fraud, or coercion, or in which the person induced to perform such act has not attained 18 years of age."

It has been estimated that 325,000 American children are currently at risk of sexual exploitation. Teenagers who are being neglected or abused in their own homes or who run away from their homes are at a very high risk of being sexually exploited by their intimate partners. Traffickers may pose as boyfriends and groom teenagers for a certain period of time with the objective of forcing them or coercing them into prostitution. Research has shown that traffickers purposely identify teenagers who are perceived as vulnerable due to poverty, minority status, lack of family support, homelessness, and a history of child abuse. Once they identify their victims, traffickers who pose as boyfriends lead the teenagers to believe that they care for them by buying them gifts, offering them money, or a place to stay. They later start using psychological manipulation to coerce them into selling their bodies. If the children refuse, traffickers use physical violence, sexual violence, or death threats toward them or their families.

Teen Dating Violence Month

In 2006, both Chambers of the U.S. Congress declared that the first week of February would be designated Teen Violence Awareness Week. In 2010, members of Congress decided to dedicate the full month of February to raise awareness about teen dating violence and to promote prevention and intervention efforts.

Protective Factors and Prevention Efforts

Certain protective factors can reduce adolescents' risk of being subjected to dating violence. These protective factors include having social skills, conflict resolution skills, communication skills, effective coping mechanisms, emotional regulation, and having a strong bond with their caregivers. Thus, preventive efforts that can help adolescents develop these protective factors can increase their chances of engaging in relationships free of violence.

See also: Break the Cycle; Educational Programs; Human Trafficking; Legislation and Policies, Dating Violence; Runaway and Homeless Youth

Further Reading

Break the Cycle: http://www.breakthecycle.org

Carlson, B. E. (1984). Children's observations of interparental violence. In A. R. Roberts (Ed.), *Battered women and their families* (pp. 147–167). New York, NY: Springer.

Centers for Disease Control and Prevention: http://www.cdc.gov/violenceprevention/intimatepartnerviolence/teen_dating_violence.html

Eaton, D. K., Kann, L., Kinchen, S., Shanklin, S., Ross, J., Hawkins, J., Harris, W. A., Lowry, R., McManus, T., Chyen, D., Lim, C., Brener, N. D., & Wechsler, H. (2008). *Youth risk behavior surveillance: United States, 2007*. Washington, DC: U.S. Department of Health and Human Services.

McKibben, L., DeVos, E., & Newberger, E. (1989). Victimization of mothers of abused children: A controlled study. *Pediatrics, 84*, 531–535.

Molidor, C., & Tolman, R. M. (1998). Gender and contextual factors in adolescent dating violence. *Violence Against Women, 4*(2), 180–194.

Roberts, T. A., & Klein, J. (2003). Intimate partner abuse and high-risk behavior in adolescents. *Archives of Pediatrics and Adolescent Medicine, 157*, 375–380.

Straus, M.A. (1992). Children as witnesses to marital violence: A risk factor for lifelong problems among a nationally representative sample of American men and women. In *Report of the Twenty-Third Ross Roundtable*. Columbus, OH: Ross Laboratories.

Tyler, K. A., Brownridge, D. A., & Melander, L. A. (2011). The effect of poor parenting on the male and female dating violence perpetration and victimization. *Violence and Victims 26*(2), 218–230.

U.S. Department of Justice. (1993). *Family violence: Interventions for the justice system*. Washington DC: U.S. Government Printing Office.

Maria F. Espinola

THERAPY AND COUNSELING FOR DOMESTIC ABUSE

A variety of services is available to the survivors of domestic violence. Victims can access help though domestic violence shelters, community mental health services, hospitals, and clergy. Individual and group counseling, family and couple counseling, psychoeducational and support groups can be accessed to reduce the effects of abuse.

Victims of domestic violence can access a variety of services that assist in reducing the effects of abuse. Some of the most commonly available services provide individual and group counseling, family and couple counseling, placement in support groups and psychoeducation. Such assistance can be accessed through a wide range of placements: for example, domestic violence shelters at secret locations, agencies, hospitals, churches, and some may even be accessed via the Internet. Mental health counselors and psychologists, marriage and family therapists, and social workers are common providers of such services.

Domestic violence shelters and agencies specializing in the treatment of domestic abuse may offer services rather comprehensive but short in duration. Besides crisis counseling, individual and/or group counseling, couple and family therapy, support and psychoeducational groups, there are groups for batterers providing education and skills training related to anger management, addictions, communication skills, stress management, assertiveness training, and conflict resolution and mediation skills. Additionally, career and vocational counseling are especially beneficial to those who are left with little or no financial means and very limited support after separation from an abusive partner.

Repeated abuse is most frequently perpetrated by husbands against their wives and children. As a result, children witness the violence between their parents or become physically and/or emotionally abused themselves. Children and adolescents who experienced abuse should be receiving counseling and therapeutic help to overcome post-traumatic syndrome disorder that may have an immediate or delayed onset. Such first steps will allow healthier personal growth and emotional development, prevent depression and anxiety, improve self-esteem and feelings of safety and confidence, as well as promoting resilience.

In terms of assessment, clinicians should consider numerous factors while working within the victim's identified culture. These can include age, ethnicity, socioeconomic status, level of acculturation, cultural coping strategies, the partner's occupational status, prior exposure to violence, family structure, and normative approval of violence. It is also important to understand the similarities and differences of form and pattern between heterosexual partner abuse and same-sex partner abuse.

There are some issues that clinicians often face when working with victims of domestic abuse. These are manipulation, expressions of anger, dissociation, denial, and minimization of violence, and compliance. According to Roberts (2002), clinicians should address these by doing the following:

1. Develop trusting and supportive relationships through empathic listening, validation of victim's experience, feelings and thoughts, realistic reassurance, planning and advocacy.
2. Clinicians should provide a safe environment and allow the client to establish the tone and pace of treatment.
3. Respond to immediate physical and emotional needs by teaching coping strategies and techniques such as relaxation, self-care and physical exercise, guided imagery exercises, and role playing.

When working with victims of abuse one should validate painful experiences and strong feelings of shame, fear, and confusion, and provide positive and supportive messages that can be powerful and reassuring as well as offer hope and safety. In working with victims of domestic violence, it is also important to identify potential barriers for the abused to develop ways of more independent thinking and self-sufficient behavior in order to better care for themselves and children.

Because of an abusive relationship, victims tend to develop mistaken beliefs about themselves and others, which hinders their ability to feel worthy, confident, and hopeful and to manage their lives effectively. According to Douglas and Strom (1988), patterns of mistaken beliefs that battered women develop can be put in three categories. First, distorted thinking develops as a result of childhood experiences observing their mothers being abused. It creates the idea of a male or one family member being an authority figure and in control of the household. Such beliefs support the notion of subordination in the family and contribute to the abusive relationship. A second category of beliefs develop as a result of abusive experience where one person holds power and control via physical and emotional abuse, using corporal force, emotional and financial isolation and control, and intimidation. A third category of thinking patterns is developed because of the negative psychological effects of violence. As a result of abuse, a victim may suffer from depression, anxiety, and other mood distortions as well as low self-esteem and feelings of worthlessness, hopelessness, and confusion: this can be generalized about all adult victims of domestic violence. Challenging distorted thinking through thought restructuring, information, and support, victims of domestic abuse learn to modify their thinking in order to change feelings and responding behaviors.

The first goal during the period of crisis is to create a safe atmosphere for the clients through refuge and developing a safety plan or contract, and to focus on stabilization and restoring emotional well-being. Clinicians then need to assist clients to identify and meet all basic needs in order for them to prepare a successful getaway from an abusive situation. Consequently, a step-by-step behavior plan may be developed in case of the need for escape: whom to call, when and how children will get out, and so on. Additionally, there are some issues that clinicians often face when working with victims of domestic abuse. These are manipulation, expression of anger, dissociation, denial, compliance, and minimization of violence.

Individual Counseling and Therapy

Short-term counseling or crisis interventions are often provided to victims entering a shelter or a facility that assists with domestic violence situation. This can be in an individual or a group setting. The focus of intervention is on regaining control and autonomy over one's own life, developing choice-making skills and symptom relief strategies, stress management, and distorted thinking. It is important to assist a victim in identifying her own strengths and resilience as well as focus on the idea of becoming a survivor rather than a victim.

Children and adolescents often experience abuse if they live in a family where violent behavior is a part of family system functioning. While working with abused and traumatized children and adolescents, therapists often use play and art therapy approaches that are developmentally and age appropriate with the variety of materials. Similar goals are established when working with this age group as with adults: safety and trust have to be restored, along with anger and stress management as a part of coping and interpersonal skills. Children may have difficulty accepting a crisis, and therefore avoid coping with the situation. When counseling children, it is important to work on feelings about the crisis and defining support systems. When working with adolescents, concentrating on solution-focused activities as well as establishing reasonable expectations may be an appropriate direction of the treatment.

McDonald, Jouriles, and Skopp (2006) in their research about long-term effects of Project SUPPORT, a study of long-term effects on conduct problems among children experiencing domestic violence in the family conducted by Renee McDonald and Ernest N. Jouriles from Southern Methodist University and Nancy Skopp from University of Houston, suggested an additional goal while working with children and mothers who come to shelters. Mothers with maltreated children should be provided with continuous emotional support and a set of tools to promote healthier child management and nurturing skills. Furthermore, as a further preventive matter McDonald et al. (2006) state that home visits by various professionals tend to decrease child maltreatment.

Based on the developmental and emotional levels of a child or adolescent, the therapy modality may be individual and/or in small group. Both children and adolescents find social support in such groups that let them know that they are not alone.

Emerging research shows that yoga and mindfulness practice appear to be very effective in working with the difficult emotions, stress reduction, depression, anxiety, and chronic pain often associated with domestic abuse. Mindfulness practice and yoga are not considered traditional therapeutic approaches but can be effective when used consistently and with appropriate support from a clinician. People of all ages may respond to this approach with equal success, and additional research suggests a long-lasting positive effect of such interventions.

Other therapeutic approaches include feminist-oriented, solution-focused therapies and Eye Movement Desensitization and Reprocessing (EMDR). Feminist-oriented therapy comes out of the consciousness-raising groups women activists held in the 1960s and 1970s. The idea is to create nonhierarchical, empowerment-based therapeutic settings that address not only the individual's concerns but also the broader societal marginalization of women. According to the Institute for Solution-Focused Therapy, it "is future-focused, goal-directed, and focuses on solutions, rather than on the problems that brought clients to seek therapy." EMDR was developed by Francine Shapiro in 1987 and is used for treatment of post-traumatic stress disorder (PTSD).

Group Therapy

Currently, there are two main modalities of group therapy available to both victims of abuse and perpetrators. These are gender-specific and mixed-gender or conjoint treatment approaches. Gender-specific groups, available to both victims of abuse and perpetrators, are considered the dominant approach to treating domestic violence and are organized separately for men and women. Such an approach is taken for several reasons. One is that a described setting provides a greater sense of safety for victims.

Batterer intervention programs are for those who are physically abusive with their partners and spouses, and focus on accountability and learning nonviolent ways to communicate. Some programs attempt to address issues of domestic violence holistically by attending to problems of personal history of victimization and its relationship with their current conduct as adults, and to tie in mental health and developmental distortions, addiction problems, attachment issues, and violent behavior. Other programs use culturally based approaches by correlating ethnicity and race, manhood, class, and life context issues. Typically, such groups follow a psychoeducational approach geared toward cognitive restructuring, anger management, and interpersonal skills. Most programs do not have a clinical orientation.

Working with families is important in looking at the context of the relationship in which violence happens. It is crucial to assess and deal with what was happening before the abuse started and to know how long abuse has been going on. It is also important to know if it was for the first time or not. Domestic violence–focused couple therapy (DVFCT) is a safety-focused approach that has been developed and changed over 15 years by Stith, McCollum, and Rosen, Marriage and Family faculty at Virginia Tech University. DVFCT is used as a primary treatment model with couples who opt to stay together after episodes of violence between the partners. It can also be used as an intervention model for couples with a high risk level for conflict and no criminal justice system involvement.

Practitioners have been debating about the effectiveness of conjoint couple treatment and the safety of involving previously victimized and abused spouses as a part of the topics discussed in the sessions. However, research literature supports the benefits of conjoint couple treatment; to be specific, participants report reduction of marital violence and overall improvement in marital relationships.

See also: Crisis Lines; Culturally Competent Services; Psychological Effects of Domestic Abuse; Shelters for Domestic Abuse Victims

Further Reading

Aldarondo, E., & Mederos, F. (Eds.). (2002). *Programs for men who batter*. Kingston, NJ: Civic Research Institute.

Douglas, M., & Strom, J. (1988). Cognitive therapy with battered women. Special Issue: Cognitive-behavior therapy with women. *Journal of Rational Emotive Cognitive Behavior Therapy, 6*(1–2), 33–49.

McDonald, R., Jouriles, E., & Skopp, N. (2006). Reducing conduct problems among children brought to women's shelters: Intervention effects 24 months following termination of services. *Journal of Family Psychology, 20*(1), 127–136.

Roberts, A. (2002). *Handbook of domestic violence intervention strategies: Policies, programs, and legal remedies*. New York: Oxford University Press.

Stith, S., McCollum, E., & Rosen, K. (2011). *Couples therapy for domestic violence: Finding safe solutions*. Washington, DC: American Psychological Association.

Tatyana Cottle

THURMAN, TRACEY CASE

Tracey Thurman, who was stabbed repeatedly in the head, neck, and chest by her estranged husband Charles J. "Buck" Thurman, Jr., was awarded $1.9 million in 1985 due to the court's finding that the City of Torrington, Connecticut, police had failed to protect her from Buck's known violence. Her attorneys claimed the inadequate attention to Tracey, and the many other women suffering in abusive homes, failed to provide equal protection under the law. Police had ignored his growing violence and were dismissive of Tracey's restraining order. The case helped prompt changes in domestic violence laws, including the "Thurman Law" passed in Connecticut. The law required police to arrest perpetrators in cases of domestic violence, even if the victim does not want to do so. Known as mandatory arrest policies, they remain controversial in that research is unclear whether this is the best approach.

Tracey met Buck in 1979, at age 18. She had dropped out of high school in Torrington and moved to Florida after her mother had died of lung cancer. Buck was working for a construction crew at a site near where Tracey worked as a maid. The two moved in together within two weeks and moved often. It wasn't long before he began beating her. At first she would slap him back, but the abuse worsened. Tracey left him and returned to Torrington when she found out she was pregnant, but Buck chased her and apologized. He talked Tracey, who wanted her child to grow up with two parents, into getting married. They moved some more. Tracey lived in constant fear, never knowing when or why Buck would attack her. She left him several times, only to return when he apologized. She recalled one time when

Buck returned home from being out with some friends and, "in the middle of my sleep, he choked me. My tongue was hanging out of my mouth, and I was gasping for air. If I didn't kick him, he would have killed me. The look on his face—it was like a blank look. I knew I had to get out" (Park, Schindehette, & Speidel, 1989). In October 1982, she again fled to Torrington and Buck again followed her there. He began stalking her, showing up where she was and calling her sometimes more than 25 times per day.

Also in October 1982, Buck attacked Tracey at the home of Judy Bentley and Richard St. Hilaire. Mr. St. Hilaire and Ms. Bentley made a formal complaint of the attack and requested that Buck be prohibited from their property. He returned in early November and was forcibly removed from the premises. Tracey Thurman and Mr. St. Hilaire went to the Torrington police headquarters to make a formal complaint, but the police refused to accept it. A few days later, Buck threatened Tracey while she was in her car. Police Officer Neil Gemelli watched as Buck broke Tracey's windshield while she sat in the car. He was arrested and convicted the following day for breaching the peace. Buck received a suspended sentence of six months and a two-year "conditional discharge," during which he was ordered to stay completely away from Tracey Thurman and from the Bentley-St. Hilaire residence and was ordered to commit no further crimes.

Buck did not comply. On New Year's Eve, 1982, he returned to the Bentley-St. Hilaire residence and threatened Tracey. She called the Torrington Police Department, but no action was taken despite the violation of the restraining order. Tracey Thurman reported many other violations and threats between January 1, 1983, and May 4, 1983. On May 4 and 5, 1982, Tracey and Ms. Bentley both reported that Buck had threatened to kill them. Tracey wanted him arrested, but Detective Storrs of the Torrington Police refused to take Ms. Bentley's complaint. Tracey was told to return three weeks later. She returned several times seeking arrest warrants and was put off repeatedly by police.

She had been separated from Buck for eight months when she obtained a restraining order against him on May 6, 1983. Tracey recalls begging the Torrington, Connecticut, police force for protection, but they kept telling her they needed "proof." On June 10, 1983, Buck showed up at the home of a friend Tracey was visiting. He demanded to speak to Tracey. Her son was napping at the time. When the police did not respond after about 15 minutes, Tracey went outside to speak to Buck to dissuade him from hurting their son. She called the police to report the violation of the restraining order, but by the time an officer arrived on the scene 25 minutes later, Buck had stabbed his wife 13 times in the face, neck, and shoulders. Police found Tracey on the ground, bleeding profusely. Buck stood nearby, holding a bloodied knife. Still, the responding officer did not move to arrest Buck. Buck even kicked Tracey in the head, breaking her neck in front of the officer. According to Park, Schindehette, and Speidel, M. (1989), he "ran inside and grabbed his young son, C. J., and screamed, 'I killed your f—ing mother.' Not until Tracey's limp body was lifted into an ambulance was Buck finally arrested—more than 45 minutes after her desperate telephone plea."

Tracey was left paralyzed on the right side of her body. Her left side was numb. She was hospitalized for seven months. Tracey testified against Buck, who was convicted and served a 14-year sentence. She then filed a lawsuit against the Torrington City Police. Mahlon Sabo, Chief of Police, even admitted that they trained officers to avoid making arrests in cases involving husbands and wives. Buck was allowed to stay in Torrington until his trial and to work as a short-order cook. He allegedly served many police officers and has boasted that he told police officers he would kill his wife.

In 1989, the Tracey Thurman story was made into a television movie called *A Cry for Help*. Nancy McKeon starred as Tracey. Tracey's son C. J was arrested for drug, violence, and weapons charges in 1999 and in 2010 was convicted of possession with intent to sell. He was sentenced to seven years in prison.

See also: Castle Rock v. Gonzales Case; Mandatory Arrest Policies; Policing Domestic Abuse; Restraining Orders and Personal Protection Orders

Further Reading

Park, J., Schindehette, S., & Speidel, M. (1989, October 9). Thousands of women, fearing for their lives, hear a scary echo in Tracey Thurman's cry for help. *People*. Retrieved June 29, 2012, from http://www.people.com/people/archive/article/0,,20121378,00.html

Thurman v. City of Torrington. (1984, October 23). Available at 595 F.Supp. 1521: http://cyber.law.harvard.edu/vaw00/thurmanexcerpt.html

Laura L. Finley

TRAFFICKING VICTIMS PROTECTION ACT (TVPA)

"The Trafficking Victims Protection Act (TVPA) of 2000 was and still is the largest piece of human rights legislation in U.S. history. The TVPA created the first comprehensive federal law to address human trafficking and modern-day slavery, targeting both domestic and international dimensions of this crime" (World Vision, n.d.).

The TVPA "is arguably the most important anti-trafficking law ever passed. Its main purpose is to eradicate human trafficking, and it is a seminal piece of law in that it defines 'human trafficking,' thus providing the framework by which the government comprehends and combats this growing scourge" (Klarevas & Buckley, 2009). Prior to the TVPA's October 2000 enactment, "no comprehensive Federal law existed to protect victims of trafficking or to prosecute their traffickers" (ACF, n.d., p. 1).

In the mid-1990s, then-First Lady Hillary Rodham Clinton brought focus to the issue of human trafficking. At the time, reports were emerging about women and even young girls being sold into prostitution, largely in the former Soviet Union, Eastern Europe, and South Asia. With Attorney General Janet Reno and Secretary of State Madeleine Albright, Clinton elevated the issue in Washington D.C., and suggested legislation to provide resources for victims and to prosecute perpetrators. The original TVPA had broad bipartisan support. Although many believe that the

Rachel Lloyd, founder of Girls Education and Mentoring Services (GEMS), mentors a victim of sex trafficking. (AP Photo/Mary Altaffer)

TVPA focuses only on sex trafficking, it provides protection for all trafficked persons, including those who are forced or bonded into labor (CdeBaca, 2010). The TVPA involves a three-pronged approach called the "three P's": Prevent human trafficking overseas; Protect victims and help them rebuild their lives in the U.S. with Federal and state support; and Prosecute traffickers of persons under stiff Federal penalties.

The U.S. Department of State is responsible for monitoring the implementation of the TVPA. It provides funds to international organizations assisting victims and to training and education of law enforcement and other first responders. Further, the TVPA also authorizes the U.S. Department of State to produce a report in which they rank countries regarding their progress toward eradicating trafficking, assisting victims, and prosecuting offenders. The annual report assesses 184 countries, ranking them into three tiers based on the scope of trafficking in each country and each country's progress toward combating it. Those countries that are consistently ranked as Tier Three because they have large amounts of trafficking and are doing little to address it can be sanctioned by the U.S government. In 2011, Tier Three Countries included: Burma, Central African Republic, the Democratic Republic of Congo, Cuba, Equatorial Guinea, Eritrea, Micronesia, Mauritania, Madagascar, Libya, Lebanon, Kuwait, North Korea, Guinea Bissau, Iran, Papua New Guinea, Saudi Arabia, Sudan, Turkmenistan, Venezuela, Yemen, and Zimbabwe.

The TVPA authorizes housing, educational, health care, job training and other state and federal assistance to victims, as long as they go through a process called "certification," which is administered by the U.S. Department of Health and Human Services. Additionally, the TVPA created the T visa, allowing trafficking victims to become temporary U.S. residents. Trafficking victims are also eligible for the Witness Protection Program.

The TVPA made human trafficking a felony with severe penalties. Moreover, the law addresses the subtle means of coercion used by traffickers to bind their victims in to servitude, including: psychological coercion, trickery, and the seizure of documents [like passports], activities which were difficult to prosecute under preexisting involuntary servitude statutes and case law" (ACF, n.d., p. 2). In other words, the TVPA "[c]reates new crimes of forced labor; trafficking with respect to involuntary servitude or forced labor; sex trafficking by force, fraud or coercion ... [It also] mandates that restitution be paid to victims" (World Vision, n.d.). With a victim-centered approach, the TVPA follows "the proposition that ignorance is not an excuse. The strip club owner who looks the other way as so-called talent agents enslave women: that's not a bystander; that's an accomplice. The landlord who turns a blind eye and collects rent from "massage parlors" where foreign women are held for forced prostitution: that's not rent; that's complicity ... [T]he updated law puts down a marker: whether you partake or profit, you're accountable" (CdeBaca, 2010).

Every few years, the TVPA must be renewed. It was first reauthorized in 2003, followed by reauthorizations in 2005, 2008, and 2011. Congress failed to vote in time to authorize the TVPRA of 2011. As of the time of this writing, Congress has still not reauthorized TVPA. One of the concerns about the reauthorization is that gave a grant to the U.S. Conference of Catholic Bishops. The Obama administration withdrew the grant, however, because the Conference, consistent with the religious views of many Catholics, refused to "refer trafficking survivors to a 'full range of obstetric care'"—i.e., access to birth control and abortions. Thus, partisan issues have prevented the reauthorization, so U.S. efforts to combat trafficking, according to Eaves (2012), are essentially on hold.

See also: Human Trafficking; Kristof, Nicholas and Sheryl WuDunn; Mam, Somaly

Further Reading

ACF (Administration for Children and Families). (n.d.). Trafficking Victims Protection Act of 2000: Fact Sheet. U.S. Dept. of Health and Human Services. Retrieved at: http://www.acf.hhs.gov/trafficking/about/TVPA_2000.pdf

ATEST (The Alliance to End Slavery & Trafficking). (n.d.). ATEST Proposals for the 2011 Trafficking Victims Protection Reauthorization Act. Retrieved at: http://www.endslaveryandtrafficking.org/news/atest-proposals-2011-trafficking-victims-protection-reauthorization-act

CdeBaca, L. (2010, May 3). Trafficking Victims Protection Act: Progress and Promise. U.S. Dept. of Justice's National Human Trafficking Conference, Washington, DC. Retrieved at: http://www.state.gov/g/tip/rls/rm/2010/141446.htm

CTS. (n.d.) Trafficking Victims Protection Act. World Vision. Retrieved at: http://www.worldvisionacts.org/latest_bill_to_fight_child_slavery

Eaves, J. (2012, January 30). Congress: Don't play politics with child slavery. Retrieved from http://blog.worldvision.org/advocacy/congress-dont-play-politics-with-child-slavery/

IJM (International Justice Mission). (2011). Spotlight: The Office to Monitor and Combat Trafficking in Persons. Retrieved from http://www.ijm.org/justice-campaigns/tip

Klarevas, L., & Buckley, C. (2009, July 15). Human Trafficking and the Child Protection Compact Act of 2009. Human Trafficking and the Trafficking Victims Protection Act section. Retrieved at: http://writ.news.findlaw.com/commentary/20090715_klarevas_buckley.html

O'Brien, C. (2008/2009, Winter). An analysis of global sex trafficking. *Indiana Journal of Political Science,* 6-18. http://www.indianapsa.org/?page_id=6

World Vision. (n.d.). The Trafficking Victims Protection Act. Retrieved at: http://www
.worldvision.org/resources.nsf/main/lobbying-resources/$file/trafficking-victims
-protection-act.pdf

Cheryl O'Brien

TRAUMATIC BRAIN INJURY AND DOMESTIC ABUSE

A traumatic brain injury (TBI) refers to a specific type of damage to the brain that is not present at birth nor degenerative but rather is caused by external physical force. TBI is typically the result of a blow or repeated blows to the head, shaking of the brain, penetration of the brain by an object like a gun or knife, loss of oxygen, or colliding with a stationary object. Further, a person can suffer from a TBI based on the cumulative effect of a combination of traumas to the brain. Annually, an estimated 1.7 million Americans suffer from TBI. Some three-quarters of these are mild forms, generally resulting in concussions. According to the U.S. Department of Health and Human Services (2006), annually "50,000 die; 235,000 are hospitalized with TBI and survive; and 1.1 million people are treated and released from hospital emergency departments."

The most vulnerable groups are children under the age of four, the elderly, and people in their late teens and twenties: children and the elderly because of falls, and teens and early adults because of car crashes, sports, and other risk-taking behaviors. Military personnel engaged in violent conflicts are also susceptible. Estimates are that some 20 percent of veterans from the wars in Iraq and Afghanistan have a TBI. While TBI itself is not equivalent to permanent brain damage, it can lead to that end. Approximately 26.5 percent of TBIs are caused when the victim's head is struck by or against something, and another 10 percent are caused by assaults.

Domestic violence—specifically, physical force—can also be the cause of a TBI. Corrigan, Wolfe, Mysiw, Jackson, and Bogner (2003) found that 30 percent of domestic violence survivors reported a loss of consciousness at least once, while 67 percent reported long-term effects that may have been related to a head injury. Of domestic violence victims presenting to emergency rooms, 30 percent reported losing consciousness because of a physical assault at least once.

Oftentimes, TBI goes undiagnosed for victims of domestic violence. TBIs are hard to diagnose in general. One study found that trauma centers failed to identify mild TBIs in more than half of patients. Additionally, the symptoms of TBI are sometimes slow to develop. Domestic violence survivors may exhibit symptoms that appear to be some form of mental illness, like depression, anxiety, tension, and/or inability to adapt to changing situations, thus masking the fact that the true problem is a TBI. Some domestic violence victims suffering from TBI exhibit behavioral issues like failure to follow through and missing appointments, which are either considered personal problems or simply effects of their trauma, rather than signs of TBI.

In general, research supports that persons with disabilities are at greater risk for abuse. An abuser living with someone with a preexisting TBI may find it very challenging and stressful. Persons who have a TBI, diagnosed or not, may not be able to perceive, remember, or understand risky situations or relationships. Further, persons suffering from TBI may engage in risk-taking behaviors, such as drinking or drug use, that put them at increased risk for abuse.

According to experts, the following are common signs of TBI:

- Balance and visual difficulties
- Slurring of speech
- Fatigue
- Sleep
- Short-term memory loss
- Difficulty with concentration and attention
- Difficulty with abstraction and conceptualization
- Heightened distractibility
- Problems with long-term goal setting
- Difficulty with task completion
- Issues with long-term planning
- Problems with self-monitoring
- Increased impulsivity
- Increased tension and anxiety
- Depression
- Decreased frustration tolerance
- Educational/vocational problems
- Interpersonal difficulties, such as lack of intimacy and substance abuse

Survivors suffering from TBI may endure revictimization from courts and Child Protective Services (CPS), as they are not knowledgeable about the issue or the TBI may be undiagnosed. For instance, survivors with TBI may forget to pick up children from school, resulting in a call to CPS. Some victims tell of being removed from domestic violence shelters because they had difficulty following rules—a characteristic of TBI.

There is some research to suggest that head injuries, and perhaps TBIs, are related to why abusers behaving the way they do. For instance, the same groups that are overrepresented as batterers—military and athletes—are at great risk for suffering a TBI. Perhaps head trauma leads to impulse control problems, distorted judgment, communication difficulties, and hypersensitivity to alcohol, as well as increased stress among families, which all result in increased likelihood of abuse.

As the Avner and Deward (n.d.) explained, "Batterers will use every life circumstance to their advantage to further manipulate and control victims. The presence of a brain injury provides new opportunities for tactics of power and control. For example, new forms of manipulation may include making the victim doubt her own perceptions and memory of the abuse, using statements such as: 'That never happened,' or 'You're crazy.' The BI may also be used as a further tool of isolation, explaining away her accounts of abuse and subsequent need for support and help as a symptom of the brain injury." Additionally, as with any medical issue, batterers may withhold treatment or therapy as another way to control victims.

The New York State Coalition Against Domestic Violence has provided a guide for service providers working with victims of domestic violence to help them identify TBI and better support those in need. Recommendations include not presuming a survivor is free of a TBI simply because no diagnosis has been made, reevaluating adherence to shelter rules that might be challenging for victims of TBI, ensuring staff and volunteers are trained about TBI, developing community connections to better serve victims who are suffering from TBI, and reformatting safety plans to take into account the effects of a TBI. Additionally, the National Center for Victims of Crime (NCVC) provides information about working with domestic violence victims suffering from TBI at http://www.ncvc.org/ncvc/AGP.Net/Components/documentViewer/Download.aspxnz?DocumentID=47764. One recommendation is to keep meetings brief, as victims may suffer from attention and memory problems. To protect victims' physical safety, NCVC recommends:

- Removing tripping hazards such as throw rugs
- Keeping hallways, stairs, and doorways free of clutter
- Putting a nonslip mat in the bathtub or shower floor.
- Installing grab bars next to the toilet and in the tub or shower
- Installing handrails on both sides of stairways
- Improving lighting inside and outside the home

It is also recommended that health-care professionals screen for domestic violence and in doing so identify if the survivor is suffering from TBI. For instance, the HELPS tool is useful for screening. It involves a few simple questions:

H- Were you ever HIT on the head?
E- Did you ever seek EMERGENCY room treatment?
L- Did you ever LOSE consciousness?
P- Are you having PROBLEMS with concentration or memory?
S- Did you experience SICKNESS or other problems following the injury?

The Department of Health and Human Services (DHHS) (Traumatic brain injury screening, 2006) offers a useful list of screening instruments at https://tbitac.norc.org/download/screeninginstruments.pdf. DHHS cautions that screening may be challenging "due to cognitive challenges that can affect insight, memory, and ability to concentrate. Some individuals may be unable to accurately report information or details surrounding their injury. Individuals with TBI often experience fatigue, which may affect their ability to sit through a lengthy questionnaire."

The Violence Against Women Network (VAWnet) has an entire collection on the intersection of domestic violence and TBI. It is available at http://www.vawnet.org/special-collections/DVBrainInjury.php.

See also: Biological and Psychological Theories about Domestic Abuse; Effects of Domestic Abuse; The Military and Domestic Violence; Psychological Effects of Domestic Abuse

Further Reading

Avner, J., & DeWard, S. (n.d.). Domestic violence and traumatic brain injury: Understanding the intersections. *National Council on Domestic and Sexual Violence*. Retrieved January 31, 2013 from http://www.ncdsv.org/images/TBIandDVWebinarSlides.pdf

Brain Injury Association of America: http://www.biausa.org

Clemmitt, M. (2012, June 1). Traumatic brain injury. *CQ Researcher,* 22(20), 477–500.

The intersection of brain injury and domestic violence. (n.d.). New York State Coalition Against Domestic Violence. Retrieved June 23, 2012, from http://www.vawnet.org/Assoc_Files_VAWnet/IntersectionBrainInjuryDV.pdf

Corrigan, J. D., Wolfe, M., Mysiw, J., Jackson, R. D. & Bogner, J. A. (2003). Early identification of mild traumatic brain injury in female victims of domestic violence. *American Journal of Obstetrics and Gynecology,* 188, S71–S76.

Jackson, H., Philp, E., Nuttall, R. L., & Diller, L. (2002). Traumatic brain injury: A hidden consequence for battered women. *Professional Psychology: Research & Practice,* 33(1), 39–45.

Mechanic, M. B., Weaver, T. L., & Resick, P. A. (2008). Risk factors for physical injury among help-seeking battered women. *Violence Against Women,* 14(10), 1148–1165.

Monahan, K., & O'Leary, K. D. (1999). Head injury and battered women: An initial inquiry. *Health and Social Work,* 24(4), 269–278.

Traumatic brain injury screening: An introduction. (2006, August). Department of Health and Human Services. Retrieved June 23, 2012, from https://tbitac.norc.org/download/screeninginstruments.pdf

Laura L. Finley

TRIBAL LAW AND JUSTICE ACT

Signed into law by President Barack Obama on July 29, 2010, the Tribal Law and Justice Act (TLOA) is a comprehensive, multifaceted federal law designed to improve the government's ability to work with Native American tribes in the investigation and prosecution of crimes impacting tribal communities, including crimes against Native American women.

According to the U.S. Census Bureau, in 2010, 2.78 million people identified themselves as Native American, based on 565 federally recognized tribes. Approximately 1.9 million live on 314 reservations throughout the United States, commonly referred to as "Indian Country." Native Americans have some of the highest rates of poverty, unemployment, disease, substandard housing, lack of health care, and high school dropout in the United States. The Centers for Disease Control and Prevention reported in 2009 that Native Americans have the highest rate of alcohol-related deaths in America, at almost 12 percent, four times higher than the national average. As well, Native Americans have the highest rate of mental health disorders and suicide rates in the United States, with 25 suicides per 100,000.

Issues of law, crime, and justice have taken center stage for Native American communities that last several decades. The U.S. Department of Justice Bureau of Statistics reported in 2004 that Native Americans experience a per capita rate of violence twice that of the U.S. resident population. On average, Native Americans experienced an estimated one violent crime for every 10 residents age 12 or older. Statistics from the Southwest Center for Law and Policy (2008) indicate that 92 percent of Native American girls who have had sexual intercourse reported having been forced to have sex against their will. Over 67 percent of those girls reported to have been pregnant by the end of the 12th grade. According to the National Center for Victims of Crime (2009), 83 percent of Native American women had experienced physical or sexual intimate partner violence in their lifetimes, and one in three will be victims of rape in their lifetimes. In fact, 44 percent of Indian Health Service emergency rooms reported not having an accessible protocol, or trained personnel in place for sexual assault investigations. Approximately 68 percent of Native American women reported severe forms of domestic violence and/or suffered injuries from domestic violence, and 73 percent reported moderate or severe injuries, with nearly one in four (22 percent) reporting more than 20 different domestic violent injury incidents. In fact, in 2005, Native American women had the highest rate of intimate partner victimization (18.2 per 1,000) in the United States, compared to African American women (8.2), white women (6.3), and Asian American women (1.5).

One of the most difficult aspects of addressing the rising rates of victimization among Native America women are issues related to tribal criminal law and jurisprudence. Enforcing tribal criminal law in and adjacent to Indian Country is often a complex and, at times, confusing jurisdictional quagmire. Factors such as whether the crime is a felony or misdemeanor, whether the criminal perpetrators and/or victims are Native Americans, and whether the crime violates tribal, state, or federal law complicates the process. For example, tribal courts have limited powers when it comes to sentencing some of their own members for felony crimes. The maximum a tribe can sentence a Native American who commits a felony offense is one year in jail. Thus, tribal courts only focus on misdemeanor crimes. Additionally, more than 50 percent of Native American women have husbands or boyfriends of other races living with them on reservations; thus, tribal prosecutors often are unable to act in many cases of domestic violence. Domestic violence enforcement is complicated by jurisdictional problems as well. Tribal courts have little or no authority over non-Native Americans, and often tribal law enforcement officers are confused about whether or not they are able to arrest anyone who is not a Native American. There also is confusion over whether tribes have civil jurisdiction over protection orders relating to non-Native Americans. In fact, the U.S. Attorney's Office has declined to prosecute over 50 percent of violent crimes committed within the jurisdiction of Indian Country: 42 percent of the rejections were attributed to weak or insufficient admissible evidence; 18 percent to "no federal offense evident"; and another 12 percent to witness problems. The result has led to rising violent crime rates and the widespread victimization of Indian American women.

The TLOA was designed to address this issue and improve public safety in tribal communities. The law gives tribes greater sentencing authority, improves defendants' rights, establishes new guidelines and training for officers handling domestic violence and sex crimes, strengthens services to victims, helps combat alcohol and drug abuse and helps at-risk youth, expands recruitment and retention of Bureau of Indian Affairs and tribal officers, and gives them better access to criminal databases. Specifically, the TLOA addresses the following:

- Creates a nine-member Indian Law and Order Commission to conduct a comprehensive study of law enforcement and criminal justice in tribal communities, including

jurisdiction issues and jail systems. The commission must report their findings to Congress and the president in 2012.
- Requires federal prosecutors to maintain data on criminal declinations in Indian Country and to share evidence to support tribal court prosecutions.
- Increases tribal court authority from one to three years' imprisonment where certain constitutional protections are met.
- Improves transparency in public safety spending.
- Requires federal officials to testify in tribal court to support prosecution in that court.
- Increases sexual assault training.
- Requires the Bureau of Prisons to notify tribal authorities when releasing sex offenders who will work or live in Indian Country.
- Creates standardized protocols on the handling of all aspects of sex assault cases by the Indian Health Service, the Justice Department, tribes, and organizations.
- Expands tribal law enforcement officers' training on interviewing domestic and sexual violence victims, and on collecting and preserving evidence.
- Directs the U.S. Comptroller General to do a study on the abilities of IHS facilities to collect, maintain, and secure evidence of sex assaults and domestic violence. Findings and recommendations must be reported to Congress.
- Authorizes deputization of special assistant U.S. attorneys and encourages federal courts to hold cases in Indian Country.
- Requires each U.S. attorney's office with Indian Country jurisdiction to appoint at least one assistant U.S. attorney to serve as a tribal liaison. The liaison's duties will include addressing any backlog in the prosecution of major crimes and providing tribal law enforcement with technical assistance and training on evidence-gathering and interviewing techniques.
- Authorizes deputization of tribal officers to enforce federal law.
- Increases recruitment and retention efforts of tribal and BIA officers.
- Expands training for BIA and tribal officers.
- Provides access to criminal records to tribal police.

See also: Alaska Natives and Domestic Abuse; Native Americans and Domestic Abuse; U.S. Government Responses to Domestic Violence; Violence Against Women Act (VAWA)

Further Reading

Bhungalia, L. (2001). Native American women and violence. Retrieved August 7, 2011, from http://www.now.org/nnt/spring-2001/nativeamerican.html

The Centers for Disease Control and Prevention. (2009). Suicide. Retrieved August 14, 2011, from http://www.cdc.gov/violenceprevention/suicide/

The National Center for Victims of Crime. (2009). Domestic violence. Retrieved on August 8, 2011, from http://www.ncvc.org/ncvc/main.aspx?dbName=DocumentViewer&DocumentID=38711

The Southwest Center for Law and Policy. (2008). Domestic violence. Retrieved August 7, 2011, from http://www.swclap.org/

Tribal Court Clearing House. (n.d.). Tribal codes or statutes. Retrieved August 7, 2011, from http://www.tribal-institute.org/lists/codes.htm

U.S. Census Bureau. (2010). Native American population. Retrieved August 8, 2011, from http://2010.census.gov/2010census/data/index.php

U.S. Department of Interior. (2011). Indian affairs. Retrieved August 8, 2011, from http://www.bia.gov/index.htm

U.S. Department of Justice, Office of Justice Programs, Bureau of Justice Statistics. (2004). American Indians and Crime. Retrieved August 7, 2011, from http://bjs.ojp.usdoj.gov/content/pub/pdf/aic02.pdf

The White House. (2010, July 29). Remarks by the President before signing the Tribal Law and Order Act. Retrieved August 7, 2011, from http://www.whitehouse.gov/the-press-office/remarks-president-signing-tribal-law-and-order-act

Tony Gaskew

TYPES OF DOMESTIC ABUSE

Although when people hear the term domestic violence they often think of physical abuse, perpetrators use many other strategies to control their victims. De Benedictis, Jaffe, and Segal (2006) provide a thorough list of questions to determine if one or someone one knows is experiencing any of the types of domestic abuse. These include but are not limited to questions about fear of a partner, fear that a partner will take children away, avoiding topics that seem to aggravate a partner, believing one deserves to be mistreated, feeling as though one is crazy or overreacting to a partner's behaviors, constant accusations, financial control, isolation from family and friends, verbal humiliation, and unwanted sexual behavior. Additionally, victims should pay close attention to threats made by abusers, against themselves, children, others, or even family pets, as such threats tend to be predictive of later violence.

According to de Benedictis, Jaffe, and Segal (2006), the main types of domestic abuse are physical abuse; verbal or nonverbal abuse (which includes psychological, mental, and emotional abuse); sexual abuse; stalking or cyberstalking; economic or financial abuse; and spiritual abuse. Most others—and in particular, the Duluth Model's Power and Control wheel—include isolation, intimidation, use of male privilege, using of children, and minimizing, denying, and blaming. Batterers are typically abusing their partners with many of these types simultaneously. Most research shows that abusive situations start out more subtly, with abusers using emotional and verbal tactics first. Abuse almost always involves some type of isolation, as it is to a batterer's advantage if the victim does not have a strong support network to help her. Approximately half of all abusive situations involve physical violence.

De Benedictis, Jaffe, and Segal (2006) define physical abuse as "the use of physical force against another person in a way that ends up injuring the person, or puts the person at risk of being injured. Physical abuse ranges from physical restraint to murder." Laws in every state prohibit physical abuse and victims in all 50 states can obtain restraining or personal protection orders against abusers who have physically assaulted them. Common forms of physical abuse include but are not limited to pushing, slapping, hitting, punching, choking, pinching, biting, and burning. Such physical abuse often results in significant short- and long-term injury to victims. According to the Centers for Disease Control and Prevention (CDC), an estimated 552,000 women each year require medical treatment for injuries by abusers.

Emotional abuses can be verbal or nonverbal. Victims report that, although they do not have physical scars or wounds from these types of abuse, the effects are often longer-lasting and healing is more difficult. Common types of emotional or verbal abuse, according to de Benedictis et al. (2006), include threats, intimidation, destruction of property, humiliation, name-calling, public criticism, and constant accusations or checking up on the victim.

Sexual abuse includes sexual assault, sexual exploitation, and sexual harassment. Sexual assault occurs when someone is forced or coerced to participate in unwanted, unsafe or degrading sexual activity. Sexual exploitation might include forcing someone to look at pornography or to participate in taking pornographic pictures or filming. Sexual harassment involves ridiculing another or making harmful remarks about one's sexuality. Victims have the most difficulty discussing sexual forms of abuse; thus, it is estimated to be the most underreported type of abuse.

According to de de Benedictis et al. (2006), "stalking is harassment of or threatening another person, especially in a way that haunts the person physically or emotionally in a repetitive and devious manner. Stalking of an intimate partner can take place during the relationship, with intense monitoring of the partner's activities. Or stalking can take place after a partner or spouse has left the relationship. The stalker may be trying to get their partner back, or they may wish to harm their partner as punishment for their departure. Regardless of the fine details, the victim fears for their safety."

Victims may be stalked at or near their homes, at work, in other daily patterns, or via the Internet or phone. The latter is referred to as cyberstalking. Common forms include but are not limited to following or tracking someone, often with a global positioning device; hiring or asking someone else to track the victim; repeated calls, text messages, or e-mails; recording the victim with hidden cameras; utilizing public records to find someone; going through someone's trash; and contacting family, friends, and colleagues to keep tabs on someone.

Stalking is very dangerous. Experts consider it to be one of the strongest predictors of potentially lethal violence. In 85 percent of domestic violence homicides, the victim was previously stalked by the abuser. Despite laws prohibiting stalking in all 50 states, Klein, Salomon, Huntington, DuBois, and Lang (2009) found that police response to it still needs improvement, as officers still fail to identify it accurately and thus are not providing the necessary legal support.

Economic or financial abuse occurs when a person controls the financial access or well-being of another against the person's best interests or wishes. Financial abuse includes stealing money or assets, withholding access to funds, sabotaging a victim's credit, and preventing the victim from working, among other things. Although this type of abuse occurs in many abusive relationships, it is particularly common with elderly victims (Branigan, 2004).

Spiritual abuse involves controlling of the victim's access to and free will to practice the religion of his or her choice, including the right not to practice a religion at all. De Benedictis et al. (2006) list the following as common forms of spiritual abuse:

- using the spouse's or intimate partner's religious or spiritual beliefs to manipulate them
- preventing the partner from practicing their religious or spiritual beliefs

- ridiculing the other person's religious or spiritual beliefs
- forcing the children to be reared in a faith that the partner has not agreed to

The Duluth Model was developed in the 1980s as a way to hold batterers accountable and ensure victims' safety. It privileges the voices and experiences of victims and calls for coordinated community responses that challenge societal norms and revamp institutions that perpetuate abuse. The Power and Control Wheel was developed based on victims' experiences. As the title suggests, power and control are at the center of the wheel, as it is this that is the cause of abuse. Around the outside of the wheel are the various types of abuse, including specific strategies abusers might use. The basic Power and Control Wheel includes using coercion and threats; using intimidation; using emotional abuse; using isolation; minimizing, denying and blaming; using children; using male privilege; and using economic abuse.

Coercion might include making actual threats, constant threats to leave the victim, threats to commit suicide, to report her to child protective or welfare services, or threats of deportation, as well as coercing her to do illegal things or making her drop charges. Intimidation involves inducing fear through looks, comments, and gestures. It can also include destruction of property, animal or pet abuse, and displaying of weapons in threatening ways. Isolation involves controlling what the victim does, who she sees, and when she can go out. Abusers minimize, deny, and blame by telling victims they are overreacting, that the abuse didn't really happen, or that it is really their own fault. Children are manipulated by abusers who might use them to relay messages, threaten to get custody, or even threaten to kill the kids. Male privilege involves treating victims like servants and making all the important household decisions.

Other versions of the Power and Control Wheel have been created to focus on specific victim groups. Specific wheels address abuse of children, immigrants, people with disabilities, teens, and more.

See also: Child Abuse; Children, Impact of Domestic Abuse on; Duluth Model; Financial Abuse; Spiritual Abuse; Stalking; Warning Signs of Abuse

Further Reading

Branigan, E. (2004). *His money or our money: Financial abuse of women in intimate partner relationships.* Coburg, VIC: The Coburg Brunswick Community Legal and Financial Counseling Centre, Inc.

de Benedictis, T., Jaffe, J., & Segal, J. (2006). Domestic violence and abuse: Types, signs, symptoms, causes, and effects. American Academy of Experts in Traumatic Stress. Retrieved June 29, 2012, from http://www.aaets.org/article144.htm

The Duluth Model Wheel Gallery. (2011). Domestic abuse intervention programs. Available at http://www.theduluthmodel.org/training/wheels.html

Klein, A., Salomon, A., Huntington, N. DuBois, J., & Lang, D. (2009). A statewide study of stalking and its criminal justice response. Sudbury, MA: Advocates for Human Potential. Retrieved August 20, 2012, from https://www.ncjrs.gov/pdffiles1/nij/grants/228354.pdf

Meyers, R. (2010, August 6). Warning signs of domestic violence. *Huffington Post*. Retrieved August 18, 2012, from http://www.huffingtonpost.com/randy-susan-meyers/warning-signs-of-domestic_b_671321.html

What is the Duluth Model? (2011). Domestic Abuse Intervention Programs. Retrieved June 29, 2012, from http://www.theduluthmodel.org/about/index.html

Violence Against Women Network: http://www.vawnet.org/domestic-violence/intervention.php

Laura L. Finley

UNIFEM AND UN WOMEN

UN Women, which includes the United Nations Development Fund for Women (UNIFEM), is an important international organization for addressing domestic abuse across the globe. Working toward improving gender equality worldwide, UN Women's focus areas include, among others, violence against women (which includes violence against girls based on their female gender). The overarching issue of gender equality is critical to decreasing domestic abuse and other forms of violence against women. Violence against women is recognized in the international community as a human rights violation, and UNIFEM (a part of UN Women) has worked for many years to address such violence.

UNIFEM was established in 1976. UNIFEM

> is the women's fund at the United Nations, dedicated to advancing women's rights and achieving gender equality ... [It] maintains strong ties to both women's organizations and governments, linking them with the UN system to join national and international political action, and to create momentum for change.... Active in all regions and at different levels, UNIFEM works with countries to formulate and implement laws and policies to eliminate discrimination and promote gender equality ... UNIFEM also aims to transform institutions to make them more accountable to gender equality and women's rights, to strengthen the capacity and voice of women's rights advocates, and to change harmful and discriminatory practices in society. Two international agreements frame UNIFEM's work: the Beijing Platform for Action resulting from the Fourth World Conference on Women in 1995, and the Convention on the Elimination of All Forms of Discrimination against Women (CEDAW), known as the women's bill of rights that includes a commitment to prevent, eradicate and punish violence against women and girls. (UN Women, n.d.a)

UNIFEM (along with three other previously distinct parts of the UN system) is now part of UN Women. "In July 2010, the United Nations General Assembly created UN Women, the United Nations Entity for Gender Equality and the Empowerment of Women ... It merges and builds on the important work of four previously distinct parts of the UN system, which focused exclusively on gender equality and women's empowerment" (UN Women, 2011a). Created to streamline UN efforts to promote gender equality worldwide, UN Women has three main roles: (1) "To support inter-governmental bodies, such as the Commission on the Status of Women, in their formulation of policies, global standards and norms"; (2) To help member nations "to implement these standards, ... to provide suitable technical and financial support to those countries that request it, and to forge effective partnerships with civil society";

and (3) "To hold the UN system accountable for its own commitments on gender equality" by monitoring the United Nations' progress (UN Women, 2011a).

UN Women offers capacity development and training to countries seeking assistance on gender equality; it holds expert group meetings to analyze research and assess practices that aim to promote gender equality; it produces reports for the United Nations and countries about incorporating gender equality across policy areas and departments. For

> countries that request its assistance, UN Women works with government and nongovernmental partners to help them put in place the policies, laws, services and resources that women require to move towards equality ... UN Women provides grants to fuel innovative, high-impact programmes by government agencies and civil society groups through two funds—the Fund for Gender Equality and the UN Trust Fund to End Violence against Women ... UN Women offers regular information on women's rights issues to the General Assembly, the Economic and Social Council, and the Security Council. It maintains the UN Secretary-General's database on violence against women, which tracks measures to end violence taken by UN Member States and UN organizations. UN Women also backs efforts to advance international commitments to gender equality at intergovernmental negotiations around specific development issues such as migration and climate change ... As the chair of the UN Inter-Agency Network on Women and Gender Equality, UN Women helps orchestrate the efforts of 25 UN organizations to promote gender equality across the UN system. (UN Women, 2011b)

UNIFEM goodwill ambassador Nicole Kidman takes part in a press conference to announce the results of UNIFEM's "Say No to Violence against Women" campaign at UN headquarters in New York on November 25, 2008. (AP Photo/Henny Ray Abrams)

"Voluntary financial contributions sustain UN Women's programmes and affirm support for gender equality goals. Funding comes from governments, foundations, corporations, organizations and individuals ... National Committees are active in 18 countries as independent, nongovernmental organizations that support the mission of UN Women. They conduct membership programmes, advocacy, public education about UN Women and global women's issues, and fundraising for UN Women's programmes around the world" (UN Women, 2011c).

UN Women works on several fronts towards ending violence against women and girls. This includes tackling its main root: gender inequality. Efforts are multiplied through advocacy campaigns and partnerships with governments, civil society and the UN system. Initiatives range from working to establish legal frameworks and specific national actions, to supporting prevention at the grassroots level, including in conflict and post-conflict situations. UN Women has also supported data collection on violence against women, facilitating new learning on the issue. UN Women plays an active role in supporting the UN Secretary-General's multi-year *UNiTE to End Violence against Women* campaign, launched in 2008 ... UN Women's *Say NO to Violence against Women* initiative advances the objectives of the *UNiTE* campaign through social mobilization ... On behalf of the UN system, UN Women manages the UN Trust Fund to End Violence against Women and it offers various resources, tools, and publications for free online. (UN Women, n.d.b)

See also: Beijing Declaration and Platform for Action; Social Change Campaigns; The United Nations and Domestic Abuse

Further Reading

UN Women. (n.d.a). About UNIFEM section. Retrieved from http://www.unifem.org/about/

UN Women. (n.d.b). Violence against women section. Retrieved from http://www.unifem.org/gender_issues/violence_against_women/

UN Women. (2011). Handbook for national action plans on violence against women. Retrieved from http://www.unwomen.org/publications/handbook-for-national-action-plans-on-violence-against-women/

UN Women. (2011). The United Nations Trust Fund to End Violence against Women: Annual report 2010. Retrieved from http://www.unwomen.org/publications/the-united-nations-trust-fund-to-end-violence-against-women-annual-report-2010/

UN Women. (2011a). About UN Women section. Retrieved from http://www.unwomen.org/about-us/about-un-women/

UN Women. (2011b). How We Work section. Retrieved from http://www.unwomen.org/how-we-work/?show=Programme_and_Technical_Assistance

UN Women. (2011c). Donors and national committees sections. Retrieved from http://www.unwomen.org/partnerships/

UNIFEM. (2010). Ending violence against women and girls: UNIFEM Strategy and Information Kit. Retrieved from http://www.unifem.org/materials/item_detail.php?ProductID=185

Cheryl O'Brien

UNIFORM CRIME REPORTS

Created in 1929 by the International Association of Chiefs of Police and overseen by the Federal Bureau of Investigations (FBI), the Uniform Crime Reports (UCR) are the nation's most frequently used reports on crime rates. The UCR was created because at the time, there was no uniform, centralized source of crime statistics. Although not without flaws, the UCR has allowed practitioners, researchers, and the general public to measure changes in crime rates over time.

Each year, the FBI collects, publishes, and archives data obtained through the UCR. The original data comes in the form of reports to police, which are then collected at the precinct level and passed along. Annually, the FBI reports crime statistics in general, as well as hate crimes, and the number of law enforcement officers who were assaulted or killed. These are available at the website http://www.fbi.gov/about-us/cjis/ucr/ucr.

The UCR does not include all crimes. Instead, it divides crimes into two parts. Part 1 offenses include criminal homicide, forcible rape, robbery aggravated assault, burglary, larceny, motor vehicle theft, and larceny. Part 1 crimes are known, collectively, as Index Crimes. Part 2 offenses include simple assault, curfew offenses and loitering, embezzlement, forgery and counterfeiting, disorderly conduct, driving under the influence, drug offenses, fraud, gambling, liquor offenses, offenses against the family, prostitution, public drunkenness, runaways, sex offenses, stolen property, vandalism, vagrancy, and weapons offenses.

One of the limitations of the UCR is that, since it only counts crimes reported to police, it misses the many incidents that occur but are not reported. There are many reasons why people do not report crime to police, including but not limited to lack of awareness about the system and how to report (particularly true for immigrants), distrust of police, belief that law enforcement cannot solve the crime, hope that the crime can be addressed by other means, and others. The crime that is undoubtedly occurring but is not counted in official measures like the UCR is often referred to by criminologists as the "dark figure of crime."

Additionally, the UCR utilizes the hierarchy rule, which means that when multiple offenses can be recorded during a specific criminal incident, only the most serious offense is counted. For instance, if a woman is killed by her husband during his attempt to steal her car, only the murder would be counted, not the motor vehicle theft. Further, critics note that the UCR focuses only on "street" crimes, not white-collar crime, often referred to as "crime in the suites."

Despite the limitations listed above, the UCR is a valuable tool for measuring crime, especially when used in conjunction with other measures, such as the National Crime Victimization Survey (NCVS).

Each state has its own directions related to capturing domestic violence data, as each state's laws read somewhat differently. For instance, New York counts the following relationship categories: Wife by husband (including wife, ex-wife, husband, and ex-husband), husband by wife (including husband, ex-husband, wife, and ex-wife), child by parent (any age), parent by child (any age), other family relation (aunts, uncles, grandparents, sisters-in-law, cousins, and other blood relatives), and intimate partners (current and former intimate partners who were never married).

See also: National Crime Victimization Survey (NCVS)

Further Reading

Uniform Crime Reports: http://www.fbi.gov/about-us/cjis/ucr/ucr

Laura L. Finley

THE UNITED NATIONS AND DOMESTIC ABUSE

The United Nations (UN), an international body with representation from 192 nations, has contributed much toward understanding and responding to domestic abuse.

The United Nations has coordinated a series of conferences on women's rights since the mid-1970s. The first conference was held in Mexico in 1975, then Copenhagen in 1980, Nairobi in 1985, followed by the Beijing Conference in 1995. These conferences were sponsored by the UN Commission on the Status of Women (CSW). CSW was established by the United Nations Economic and Social Council (ECOSOC) in 1946. Its goal is to prepare reports and recommendations to ECOSOC related to the promotion of women's political, economic, civil, social and educational rights. The Commission also makes recommendations to the Council on problems requiring immediate attention in the field of women's rights.

The Beijing Conference was considered a turning point for global women's rights, as it resulted in what is known as the Beijing Declaration and Platform for Action that has influenced numerous policy and practical changes across the globe. It provided a framework for addressing a variety of issues, including: (1) women and poverty; (2) education and training of women; (3) women and health; (4) violence against women; (5) women and armed conflict; (6) women and the economy; (7) women in power and decision making; (8) institutional mechanisms for the advancement of women; (9) human rights of women; (10) women and media; (11) women and the environment; and (12) the girl-child. The drafting of the Convention on the Elimination of All Forms of Discrimination Against Women (CEDAW) also represented a huge step toward enacting basic human rights for women across the globe.

According to the United Nations, the most common form of violence against women is violence by an intimate partner. Women across the globe endure domestic violence at tremendously high rates, ranging from 6 percent of women in China to 48 percent in Zambia, Ethiopia and Peru. One-third of women murdered each year in the United States suffered at the hands of an intimate partner, while in Australia, Canada, and Israel, between 40 and 70 percent of women's murders are due to domestic violence.

The United Nations recognizes the tremendous costs of violence against women. They include not just the direct costs of services for victims and their children and to bring perpetrators to justice, but also the indirect costs, such as loss of employment and productivity. In the United States, the Centers for Disease Control and Prevention (CDC) estimate that domestic violence costs more than $5.8 billion per year, with $4.1 billion alone for direct medical and health-care services, while in Canada the direct costs have been estimated at more than $1 billion Canadian annually.

Given that domestic abuse is a severe and pervasive problem across the globe, the United Nations has called for strengthening data collection in order to inform and influence policy. Further, while the data presented above is disturbing, it is surely an underestimate of the scope of the problem, given that many victims do not report abuse. A 2005 WHO study based on data from 24,000 women in 10 countries noted that 55 to 95 percent of women who had been physically abused by their partners had never contacted the police, NGOs, or shelters for help (Garcia-Moreno et al., 2005).

Many countries still lack adequate legislation to address all forms of violence against women. The lack of effective laws, or the failure to implement such laws where they exist, prohibits both justice and healing. Many states have no specific legal provisions against domestic violence. Marital rape is not a prosecutable offense in more than 50 countries. In many places, laws contain loopholes that allow perpetrators to act with impunity, for instance, letting a rapist go free under the penal code if he marries the victim.

The United Nations encouraged countries to develop comprehensive laws specific to violence against women. The 1994 Violence Against Women Act in the United States, which authorized a multifaceted approach to the problem—including federal support for training for police, prosecutors, and judges, shelters and rape prevention programs, and a national telephone hotline, among other things—is held up as an example of such comprehensive laws. Review and reform of laws have brought significant advances. For example, psychological and economic violence are now incorporated in the legal definition of domestic violence in a number of countries, including Costa Rica, Guatemala, Honduras, and South Africa.

The United Nations also tries to compile and acknowledge the many nonlegal efforts taken across the globe to address domestic abuse. Activities range from government campaigns to let women know which laws exist to prevent and punish violence, to global petitions, to community and village meetings on the adverse effects of female genital mutilation, to projects to engage men and boys in preventing violence against women. There is still a lack of systemic evaluation of measures that are being taken, and thus little is known about the effectiveness of these interventions. In addition to data collection and evaluation, the United Nations advocates for increasing awareness about domestic abuse in order to change attitudes and influence behavior among all demographic groups.

The United Nations has also noted that many countries do not undertake systematic data collection on all forms of violence against women. Consequently, little is known about the ways various forms of violence affect different groups of women. The United Nations calls for increased data collection that can be used to devise meaningful strategies to address such violence.

UN Women

In July 2010, the United Nations launched UN Women, the organization's only entity to specifically address gender-related issues. Prior to the launch of UN Women, there were four separate entities that addressed gender-related issues: the United Nations Development Fund for Women (UNIFEM), the Division for the Advancement of Women (DAW), the International Research and Training Institute for the Advancement of Women (INSTRAW), and the Office of the Special Adviser on Gender Issues and Advancement of Women (OSAGI).

UN Women's primary functions are:

- To support intergovernmental bodies, such as the Commission on the Status of Women, in their formulation of policies, global standards, and norms.
- To help member states to implement these standards, standing ready to provide suitable technical and financial support to those countries that request it and to forge effective partnerships with civil society.
- To hold the UN system accountable for its own commitments on gender equality, including regular monitoring of system-wide progress.

The UN Women website features news and updates specifically related to violence against women.

Further, the UN Women website features a compilation of publications to women's empowerment and gender equality. In 2006, the Secretary General published a study entitled "Ending Violence against Women: From Words to Action." Another featured publication is the *Handbook for Legislation on Violence against Women*, which was created in 2009. It is available in English, Arabic, Chinese, French, Russian, and Spanish. The 68-page document is available is a CD-Rom that provides an analysis of the state of gender equality 25 years after the passage of CEDAW.

Successes

The United Nations cites numerous successes related to reducing violence against women on their website. These are changes implemented due at least in part to the agency's efforts and include but are not limited to:

- The adoption of laws against domestic and sexual violence, and rape and family law provisions in Colombia, Sierra Leone, Vietnam, Zimbabwe, and others;
- Support for legislation in Rwanda that criminalizes gender-based violence;
- Collection of survey data on violence against women in South Africa, Tanzania, Kenya, Cameroon, and Papua New Guinea;
- Providing access to legal and counseling services for women in the Syrian Arab Republic;
- Integration of UNDP research on gender violence into Jamaica's national action plan;
- Development of the *Handbook for Legislation on Violence against Women* by UN Women.
- Creation of the Global Virtual Knowledge Centre to End Violence against Women and Girls (http://www.endvawnow.org), which provides more than 700 practical tools in over 50 languages to assist legislators, policy makers, and practitioners in their work to end violence against women and girls;
- Development by UN Women of *The Handbook for National Action Plans on Violence against Women*;
- Through a joint effort of several UN agencies, the launching of Stop Rape Now (http://stoprapenow.org/get-cross/) to prevent the use of rape as a tactic of war and respond effectively to the needs of survivors;
- Established the Partners for Prevention: Working with Boys and Men to Prevent Gender-Based Violence in Asia and the Pacific;
- Development of a sensitivity training program for medical professionals in Ecuador, Lebanon, Nepal, Russia, and Sri Lanka, among others;

- Through UNICEF (the UN Children's Fund), developed a manual for football coaches to help them talk to boys about violence against women and girls;
- Utilized the 2010 FIFA World Cup in South Africa as a vehicle to raise awareness, including a mass-media campaign and the development of a video game called Breakaway (http://www.breakawaygame.com).

Current Efforts

In 2008, the United Nations, under Secretary General Ban Ki-moon, launched the campaign UNiTE to End Violence Against Women. The campaign is designed to bring together a variety of UN offices and agencies, along with individuals and non-governmental groups, to galvanize efforts to prevent violence against women and girls around the world. Agencies involved include United Nations Entity for Gender Equality and the Empowerment of Women (UN Women); Inter-agency Network on Women and Gender Equality (IANWGE); Office for the High Commissioner for Human Rights (OHCHR); United Nations Action Against Sexual Violence (UN Action); United Nations Children's Fund (UNICEF); United Nations Development Programme (UNDP); United Nations Population Fund (UNPF); United Nations High Commission for Refugees (UNHCR); and the World Health Organization (WHO).

Explaining that violence against women takes many forms, all of which not only harm women and girls but are devastating for whole communities, UNiTE acknowledges that states are failing to meet their responsibility. UNiTE works to influence laws and policies, mobilize the public, and strategically partner with organizations, businesses, and institutions to effect social change.

UNiTE aims to achieve the following five goals in all countries by 2015:

- Adopt and enforce national laws to address and punish all forms of violence against women and girls
- Adopt and implement multisectoral national action plans
- Strengthen data collection on the prevalence of violence against women and girls
- Increase public awareness and social mobilization
- Address sexual violence in conflicts

The UNiTE web site includes a toolkit of actions for governments and local authorities, Schools and universities, civil society, and businesses. In 2011, the UNiTE campaign held a worldwide t-shirt design competition for men aged 18 to 25 years old. The competition invited men and boys to stand up to violence by creating designs that demonstrated equality and respect for women and girls. Say NO—UNiTE to End Violence against Women (http://www.saynotoviolence.org) is the social mobilization platform for the UNiTE campaign. Say NO—UNiTE counts, showcases and facilitates local and national advocacy efforts toward ending violence against women and girls by individuals, governments, civil society and UN partners. Through an interactive and social media–friendly website, Say NO—UNiTE engages people from all walks of life and links local actions to an expanding global network. In September 2011, the UNiTE campaign in Latin

America and the Caribbean organized a three-day workshop in Panama City for 26 musical, visual, and performing arts artists in the region. At the workshop, the artists learned more about the issue of violence against women and girls and used their creativity to generate ideas, messages, and initiatives to raise public awareness.

In March 2009, UN Deputy Secretary-General Asha-Rose Migiro launched the Secretary-General's database on violence against women, the first global "one-stop shop" for information on measures undertaken by UN member states to address violence against women, as well as available data and statistics. It contains information on services for victims and survivors, and relevant data on capacity-building and awareness-raising activities for public officials, and on the prevalence of violence and the criminal justice sector response to it. The database is available at http://webapps01.un.org/vawdatabase/home.action.

As part of the growing effort to include men as part of the solution to ending violence against women, UN Secretary-General Ban Ki-moon launched his Network of Men Leaders. The network supports the work of women around the world to defy destructive stereotypes, embrace equality, and inspire men and boys everywhere to speak out against violence. The leaders in this expanding network—current and former politicians, civil society and youth activists, religious and community leaders, cultural figures, and other prominent individuals—work in their spheres of influence to undertake specific actions to end violence against women, from raising public awareness, to advocating for adequate laws, to meeting with young men and boys, to holding governments accountable.

See also: Educational Programs; Men's Efforts against Domestic Abuse; Social Change Campaigns; UNIFEM and UN Women

Further Reading

Garcia-Moreno, C., Jansen, H., Ellsberg, M., Heise, L, & Watts, C. (2005). WHO Multi-Country Study on Women's Health and Domestic Violence against Women. Geneva: World Health Organization.

UN Women. (n.d.). Violence against women section. Retrieved from http://www.unifem.org/gender_issues/violence_against_women/

UN Women. (2011). Handbook for national action plans on violence against women. Retrieved from http://www.unwomen.org/publications/handbook-for-national-action-plans-on-violence-against-women/

UN Women. (2012, February). Inventory of United Nations system activities to prevent and eliminate violence against women. Retrieved August 20, 2012, from http://www.un.org/womenwatch/daw/vaw/inventory/inventory-2012.pdf

UN Women. (2012). 2011–12 Progress of the world's women: In pursuit of justice. Retrieved June 17, 2012, from http://progress.unwomen.org/wp-content/uploads/2011/06/EN-Factsheet-Global-Progress-of-the-Worlds-Women.pdf

Women and Violence. (1996). United Nations. Retrieved August 20, 2012, from http://www.un.org/rights/dpi1772e.htm

Laura L. Finley

U.S. GOVERNMENT RESPONSES TO DOMESTIC VIOLENCE

Since the 1970s, the U.S. government has addressed domestic violence through research, policies, and legislation. In 1979, President Jimmy Carter established the Office of Domestic Violence, with a budget of $90,000 for grants, research, and dissemination of information. President Ronald Reagan dismantled the office in 1981, citing budget woes and lack of support.

In 1994, Congress enacted the Violence Against Women Act (VAWA) under President Bill Clinton, who had grown up with an abusive stepfather. VAWA was the first federal legislation intended to hold batterers accountable and keep victims safe. VAWA also provided funding and support for coordinated community responses to domestic violence. Additionally, VAWA authorized self-petition for residency status for victims of domestic violence, thereby offering victims of abuse who are undocumented to obtain permission to reside in the United States to work and to drive. VAWA was proposed by then-Senator Joe Biden. One provision of the 1994 Act, which authorized federal civil remedy for victims of gender-based violence, was considered unconstitutional by the U.S. Supreme Court in 2000 in *U.S. v. Morrison*.

In 2000 and again in 2005, President George W. Bush signed reauthorizations of VAWA. According to the National Domestic Violence Hotline, the 2000 reauthorization included:

- Identifying the additional related crimes of dating violence and stalking
- The creation of a much-needed legal assistance program for victims of domestic violence and sexual assault
- Promoting supervised visitation programs for families experiencing violence
- Further protecting immigrants experiencing domestic violence, dating violence, sexual assault or stalking, by establishing U- and T-visas and by focusing on trafficking of persons

The 2005 reauthorization included the following:

- Containing provisions that exclusively serve to protect immigrant victims of domestic violence but also include immigration protections to alleviate violence against immigrant women that previous legislation had tried, but failed to alleviate
- Developing prevention strategies to stop violence before it starts
- Protecting individuals from unfair eviction due to their status as victims of domestic violence or stalking
- Creating the first federal funding stream to support rape crisis centers
- Developing culturally and linguistically specific services for communities
- Enhancing programs and services for victims with disabilities
- Broadening VAWA service provisions to include children and teenagers

Another reauthorization was debated in summer, 2012 and approved in 2013. Despite the title, men also qualify for relief under VAWA.

In 2000, Congress enacted the Trafficking Victims Protection Act (TVPA). It is aimed at punishing traffickers, helping victims, and preventing trafficking through educational and outreach efforts. The TVPA authorizes the State Department to issue an annual report that classifies countries based on their efforts to address trafficking.

In 2003, President Bush announced the creation of the Family Justice Center Initiative, which was intended to help coordinate efforts to achieve justice for victims.

In 2010, President Obama signed the Tribal Law and Justice Act. It is intended to help coordinate efforts to address abuse and assault in Indian country.

The Office of Violence Against Women (OVW) is part of the U.S. Department of Justice. Its mission, according to its website, is "to provide federal leadership in developing the nation's capacity to reduce violence against women and administer justice for and strengthen services to victims of domestic violence, dating violence, sexual assault, and stalking." The OVW funds 21 programs, which include the Children and Youth Exposed to Violence Program; Grant to Encourage Arrest Policies and Enforcement of Protection Orders Program; Court Training and Improvements Program; Culturally and Linguistically Specific Services for Victims of Domestic Violence, Dating Violence, Sexual Assault and Stalking; Education, Training, and Enhanced Services to End Violence Against and Abuse of Women with Disabilities Grant Program; Engaging Men and Youth Program; Enhanced Training and Services to End Violence Against and Abuse of Women Later in Life Program; Grants to Reduce Sexual Assault, Domestic Violence, and Stalking on Campus Program; Legal Assistance for Victims Grant Program; Rural Domestic Violence, Dating Violence, Sexual Assault and Stalking Assistance Program; Services to Advocate for and Respond to Youth Program; Sexual Assault Service Program; Tribal s=Sexual Assault Service Program; State Sexual Assault and Domestic Violence Coalitions Program; Services, Training, Education and Policies (STEP) to Reduce Domestic Violence, Dating Violence, Sexual Assault and Stalking in Secondary Schools Grant Program; STOP Violence Against Women Formula Grant Program; Transitional Housing Assistance Grants for Victims of Domestic Violence, Dating Violence, Stalking or Sexual Assault Program; Tribal Governments Program; and the Tribal Domestic Violence and Sexual Assault Coalitions Grant Program. Since its inception, the OVW has awarded over $4.7 billion in grants to help implement VAWA. More information is available at http://www.ovw.usdoj.gov/.

In 2009, President Obama created a "czar" position for Violence Against Women. In 2010, he instituted a multifaceted effort to address domestic violence. It included the following, according to Henderson (2010):

- Defending childhood initiative: launched by the attorney general and aimed at protecting children from the harmful consequences of witnessing violence.
- Civil protection orders: The Department of Justice will release new tools and guidance for communities to improve issuance and enforcement of protective orders.
- Forums on sexual assault: The White House Council on Women and Girls, which is headed by senior adviser Valerie Jarrett, and the Department of Justice will hold regional forums across the country in the next six months aimed at reducing sexual assault.
- Legal access: The Department of Justice will launch pilot projects in New Orleans and Baltimore to provide pro bono legal services to victims of domestic violence.

- Maternal, infant and early childhood home visits: Funded by a $1.5 billion health-care legislation set aside over the next five years, it provides for home visitation services and early intervention in domestic violence and child abuse cases.
- Housing assistance: The Department of Housing and Urban Development will release rules to housing authorities and landlords to ensure that victims of abuse do not lose their housing because of crimes committed against them.
- Financial literacy: The FDIC will release Friday an updated version of its Money Smart curriculum that will include information for victims of domestic violence.

In 2012, President Obama's Affordable Care Act, which prohibited insurance companies from treating domestic violence as a preexisting condition and thereby denying insurance or increasing rates for women is upheld as constitutional by the U.S. Supreme Court. In April 2012, President Obama issued an executive order requiring federal agencies to adopt policies to prevent or punish acts of domestic violence.

The White House has also elevated the issue of domestic violence by proclaiming February Teen Dating Violence Awareness Month.

One remarkable omission is that the U.S. government has never ratified the Convention on the Elimination of All Forms of Violence Against Women (CEDAW). Signed by President Carter in 1979, numerous ratification attempts have failed. President Obama has pledged to push Congress to ratify CEDAW, as it is the only international human rights treaty specifically addressing gender inequalities.

See also: Convention on the Elimination of All Forms of Violence Against Women (CEDAW); Funding for Domestic Violence Services; Legislation and Policies, Dating Violence; Legislation and Policies, Domestic Abuse; Violence Against Women Act (VAWA)

Further Reading

Council on Women and Girls: http://www.whitehouse.gov/administration/eop/cwg

Domestic violence. (n.d.). U.S. Department of Justice. Retrieved from http://www.justice.gov/archive/fbci/progmenu_domv.html

Henderson, N. (2010, October 27). Obama launches initiatives to fight domestic violence. *Washington Post.* Retrieved June 29, 2010, from http://www.washingtonpost.com/wp-dyn/content/article/2010/10/27/AR2010102705307.html

Office on Violence Against Women: http://www.ovw.usdoj.gov/

Smith. T. (2012, April 19). Obama seeks federal guidelines to prevent or punish acts of domestic violence. *Washington Post.* Retrieved June 29, 2012, from http://www.washingtonpost.com/blogs/federal-eye/post/obama-seeks-federal-guidelines-to-prevent-or-punish-acts-of-domestic-violence/2012/04/19/gIQA9yqcTT_blog.html

VAWA laws for abuse victims. (2011, November 11). *WomensLaw.org.* Retrieved June 29, 2012, from http://www.womenslaw.org/laws_state_type.php?id=10270&state_code=US

Violence Against Women Act. (n.d.). *National Domestic Violence Hotline.* Retrieved June 29, 2012, from http://www.thehotline.org/get-educated/violence-against-women-act-vawa/

Laura L. Finley

UNITED STATES V. MORRISON CASE

Decided by the U.S. Supreme Court on May 15, 2000, *United States v. Morrison* centered on a challenge to a part of the Violence Against Women Act of 1994 (VAWA), 42 USC section 13981, which provided for a federal civil remedy for victims of gender-motivated violence. The court determined in a 5-4 decision that Congress had overstepped its authority in enacting this provision, and thus the victim was due no civil remedy. The ruling invalidated that provision of VAWA. It did not prevent victims from suing their attackers at all, but instead said those cases should be heard in state courts. Victims of domestic abuse and sexual assault often choose not to file suits, however, because of the trauma involved in seeing, often repeatedly, their assailant in court hearings.

The case began when, in 1994, Christy Brzonkala, then a student at Virginia Tech, accused football players James Crawford and Antonio Morrison of raping her. She sued Morrison and the school under VAWA's new civil rights remedy, which authorized federal lawsuits against persons who perpetrated gender-based violence.

The civil remedy provision was considered part of the Commerce Clause. Congress had been presented extensive evidence that violence against women was an issue of interstate commerce, such as when victims are denied the opportunity to travel or work. The court rejected that this was something Congress could regulate through the Commerce Clause. Following other decisions like *DeShaney v. Winnebago County*, the court also held that the Equal Protections Clause of the Fourteenth Amendment only applies to state action. The National Organization for Women's Legal Defense and Education Fund helped bolster that argument, obtaining support from 35 states but to no avail.

Ten years later, more women had taken sexual violence lawsuits to state supreme courts. One report by University of Arizona law school professor Ellen Bublick found more than 100 such lawsuits between 2000 and 2005, compared to less than 10 between 1970 and 1975. Clearly even more lawsuits, then, are heard in lower courts. Most of these lawsuits, however, are not directed at the assailants but instead at a third party, typically an organization or entity that has more assets. Attorneys often don't take the cases when they are against individuals because the payout won't be large enough. VAWA's civil remedy would have addressed those issues, as it encouraged courts to award attorney's fees to successful plaintiffs, thereby making the case more appealing for an attorney. It also extended the statute of limitations to four years, allowing victims more time to determine if they wanted to file such a suit. Goldscheid (2003) maintained that the civil legal remedy in general has been an important element of advancing gender equality, as it linked gender-based crime to hate crime. Then-Senator Joe Biden made this point when he introduced VAWA in 1990, arguing that just as attacks aimed at blacks or Hispanics are considered civil rights crimes, so too should sexual assault, 90 percent of which is perpetrated against women.

Since criminal courts often do not provide the redress that victims are seeking, many advocates see being able to file a lawsuit against the attacker and/or third parties as essential. A 2004 study in Philadelphia and Kansas City, Missouri, found prosecutions in only half of the cases in which a sexual assault perpetrator was arrested. Prosecutors may not be willing to go forward because they doubt the victim or because they lack evidence. In civil courts, however, the burden of proof is lower; as opposed to "beyond a reasonable doubt," civil courts use the "preponderance of evidence standard." Advocates maintain that receiving damages helps victims recuperate from lost income and medical expenses.

Brzonkala won a Woman of Courage Award from the National Organization for Women in 2000.

Sexual assault and domestic violence remain significant problems on college campus. Leonard, Quigley, and Collins (2002) found that approximately 30–40 percent of both male and female college students had experienced some form of abuse with a dating partner. Mustaine and Tewksbury (1999) found 10 percent of women attending nine colleges had been stalked in the previous six months. The Feminist Majority Foundation reported in 2005 that 32 percent of college students are domestic violence victims. Fisher, Cullen, and Turner (2000) state that one-third of college women experience sexual assault by their male partners. As in Brzonkala's case, athletes are overrepresented as perpetrators of sexual assaults on campuses. One study found athletes were accused in 20 percent of sexual assault cases but were just 3 percent of the student body. A study surveying college police departments found that athletes were 40 percent more likely to be accused of sexual assault than other students.

See also: College-Aged Victims; Courts and Domestic Abuse; Violence Against Women Act (VAWA)

Further Reading

Benedict, J. (1998). *Athletes and acquaintance rape*. Thousand Oaks, CA: Sage.
Bushey, C. (2010, May 26). Why don't more women sue their rapists? *Slate*. Retrieved June 29, 2012, from http://www.slate.com/articles/double_x/doublex/2010/05/why_dont_more_women_sue_their_rapists.html
Fisher, S., Cullen, F., & Turner, M. (2000). *The sexual victimization of college women*. Washington, DC: U.S. Department of Justice.
Goldscheid, J. (2003). Advancing equality in domestic violence law reform. *Journal of Gender, Social Policy, & the Law, 11*(2), 417–426.
Leonard, K., Quigley, B., & Collins, R. (2002). Physical aggression in the lives of young adults: Prevalence, location, and severity among college and community samples. *Journal of Interpersonal Violence, 17*, 533–550.
Liu, L. (2000). Supreme Court shows vulnerability with close decisions. *National Organization for Women*. Retrieved June 20, 2012, from http://www.now.org/nnt/summer-2000/supreme.html
Mustaine, E., & Tewksbury, R. (1999). A routine activity theory explanation for women's stalking victimizations. *Violence Against Women, 5*(1), 43–62.
Schwartz, M., & DeKeseredy, W. (1997). *Sexual assault on college campus*. Thousand Oaks, CA: Sage.
Schwartz, M., & Leggett, M. (1999). Bad dates or emotional trauma? The aftermath of campus sexual assault. *Violence Against Women, 5*, 251–271.

Snyder, E., & Morgan, L. (2005, August). Domestic violence ten years later. *American Bar Association Law Trends and News.* Retrieved June 29, 2012, from http://www.americanbar.org/newsletter/publications/law_trends_news_practice_area_e_newsletter_home/domviolence.html

United States v. Morrison (2000). Available at http://www.oyez.org/cases/1990-1999/1999/1999_99_5/

Violence Against Women Act. (n.d.). *National Domestic Violence Hotline.* Retrieved June 29, 2012, from http://www.thehotline.org/get-educated/violence-against-women-act-vawa/

Laura L. Finley

VERIZON FOUNDATION

The Verizon Foundation, part of Verizon Communications Inc., was created because domestic violence affects many aspects of society, including absence from work and health-care costs. The company also knows the effect of domestic violence on the individual victims, who are usually women and children. The Verizon Foundation tries to use its resources to prevent domestic violence and to provide support to victims of it, through technical support, human expertise, and financial support to organizations that fight for this cause.

Verizon Communications Inc. is a wireless and wireline communications company, providing services such as wireless cellphone service and broadband Internet service. The Verizon Foundation is a part of this company that focuses on various social issues, including domestic violence. Verizon explains that its foundation uses the partnerships it maintains, as well as its financial resources and technological expertise, to focus on these causes. On its website, the foundation states: "We hope our investment will help prevent domestic violence, improve victims' quality of life and enable them to become productive members of society, reduce workplace absence, decrease medical and mental healthcare costs, and provide children with safe home environments" (Verizon Foundation, "Domestic Violence," 2011a).

Verizon's principal way of helping women affected by domestic abuse is to provide support for already established organizations. It provides support in three different ways: financial donations, technical support, and human expertise. This support goes to organizations that work to counteract domestic violence by providing one or more of the following types of aid: prevention, education, relief to victims, and empowerment.

Verizon has provided support for many organizations since the inception of its foundation. Some of the causes it has helped include Dove's campaign to empower young women and the Family Violence Prevention Fund's program to teach high school male athletes moral and ethical behaviors. It helped set up an online database for Dress for Success Worldwide, a program that provides professional clothing and additional resources. It also sponsors a National Domestic Violence Pro Bono Directory of free legal help for victims, through the American Bar Association Commission on Domestic Violence.

Verizon donates money to many different organizations and programs related to the cause of domestic abuse. In 2008, the company donated $4.7 million to this cause, according to its website. As of a press release dated September 29, 2011, the company stated it has financed over $28 million toward the prevention of domestic violence.

The company encourages its employees to volunteer for local nonprofits, including organizations that focus on domestic violence prevention and education. Its website shows that in 2010, Verizon employees volunteered over 730,000 hours to nonprofit organizations and schools; some of this time was donated to domestic violence organizations. Further, a Verizon volunteer who donates 50 hours or more in one year can apply for a $750 grant for the nonprofit organization. Through this Volunteer Incentive Program, Verizon donated over $5.5 million in 2010.

Verizon educates and works with other organizations on the topic of how technology can both prevent domestic violence and contribute to it. Verizon works with the Safety Net Project, which educates on this topic. For instance, those who carry out domestic abuse often control and monitor Internet and phone use. The Safety Net Project advocates using caution with technology that might be watched. For example, a victim should continue to use a watched computer for simple searches to avoid suspicion, but should find an unmonitored one, such as at a library, at work, or at a friend's house, to look for help and resources related to domestic abuse. At the same time, victims can use technology for help. For instance, a victim can have a donated cell phone that is unknown to the abuser to use for help.

Since 2006, Verizon has consistently partnered with other organizations to host a yearly National Domestic Violence Summit. The summits offer an opportunity for organizations and individuals to come together to share information and learn more about domestic violence. Although the topics change each year, they include various strategies for law enforcement, educators, nonprofits, and programs to work to overcome domestic violence. The first summit in 2006 included three different topics: figuring out ways to use technology to help victims of domestic abuse and organizations that support them, working together to increase education and knowledge, and coming up with ways to start new programs or expand already established programs that support this cause.

Although much of Verizon's efforts against domestic abuse involve providing support for or partnering with other organizations, Verizon also has its own program called the Verizon Wireless Hope Line. This program collects used cell phones and gives them with service to nonprofit organizations to provide to those affected by domestic abuse. Those who have Verizon Wireless service can dial #HOPE on their phones to reach the National Domestic Violence Hotline, which provides around-the-clock confidential support. Verizon has also donated money to this organization.

Verizon sponsors many events throughout each year on the issue of domestic abuse. For instance, in September 2011, Verizon showed "Monsters," a video it produced and funded on domestic violence from the viewpoint of a child, and used the screening event to educate victims on how to get support and to educate the community on how to offer support.

See also: Funding for Domestic Violence Services; Technology and Domestic Abuse

Further Reading
National Network to End Domestic Violence. (2011). Internet and computer safety. Retrieved on September 24, 2011, from http://nnedv.org/internetsafety.html

Verizon. (2011). Verizon and National Domestic Violence Hotline launch "Monsters." Retrieved on October 4, 2011, from http://newscenter.verizon.com/press-releases/verizon/2011/verizon-and-national-domestic.html

Verizon Foundation. (2011a). Domestic violence. Retrieved September 16, 2011, from http://foundation.verizon.com/core/domestic.shtml

Verizon Foundation. (2011b). Verizon volunteer programs. Retrieved on January 31, 2013, from http://www.verizonfoundation.org/employee-retiree/verizon-volunteers-program/

Sharon Thiel

VIOLENCE AGAINST WOMEN ACT (VAWA)

Following a four-year effort by women's rights activists and supportive legislators, in 1994, the Violence Against Women Act (VAWA) was passed within an omnibus crime bill and signed by President Bill Clinton. VAWA is landmark legislation to improve criminal justice and community-based responses to domestic violence, dating violence, sexual assault, and stalking in the United States. According to the National Network to End Domestic Violence (NNEDV), "VAWA created the first U.S. federal legislation acknowledging domestic violence and sexual assault as crimes, and provided federal resources to encourage community-coordinated responses to combating violence." VAWA programs serve women, men, and children.

Women's rights organizations were critical to VAWA's drafting and 1994 passage. Pat Reuss, VAWA's lead lobbyist, recalls:

> The feat began in 1990, when [then] Sen. Joe Biden, D-Del., and then Rep. Barbara Boxer, D-Calif. . . .pulled together the anti-violence community's 15-year efforts with hopes a national conversation about violence prevention and services would begin. Advocates led by NOW [National Organization for Women] and NOW Legal Defense Fund pulled together a working group and began the daunting task of helping draft the proposal. More than 2,000 field experts, state and national organizations came together in what is now known as The National Task Force to End Sexual and Domestic Violence. The task force had no money at its disposal and few staff members to work on the bill. Without email or cell phones, curly-paper fax machines allowed us to trade ideas and successes . . . After completing the process of drafting the bill, the largest obstacle—getting VAWA passed—still lay before us. To do so, the innovative, comprehensive legislation needed a large grassroots movement pushing it forward. We reached out to every progressive organization on the books that focused on target issues from women's rights to civil rights, anti-poverty to unionization. We also called in help from experts in medicine, law enforcement and public policy to secure passage of VAWA. (Reuss 2004)

Administered by the federal government, VAWA programs have been essential to enacting funding and legal reforms that have changed federal, tribal, state, and local responses to domestic violence. VAWA 1994 helped create community-coordinated responses, bringing criminal justice, social service practitioners, nonprofit organizations, community organizations, and activists together to better address domestic violence locally. Further, VAWA helped give much-needed recognition and support

Democratic Representative Gwen Moore, from Wisconsin, accompanied by Representative John Conyers pauses during a news conference on Capitol Hill in Washington on May 16, 2012. She spoke in support of the unrestricted reauthorization of the Violence Against Women Act. (AP Photo/J. Scott Appelwhite)

for the local efforts being coordinated by domestic violence shelters, rape crisis centers, and other community organizations nationwide. VAWA also enhanced federal prosecution of interstate domestic violence and sexual assault crimes and provided federal guarantees of interstate enforcement of protection orders.

The Office on Violence Against Women (OVW) was created within the Department of Justice to administer VAWA grants for programs to communities across the United States. Annually, VAWA-funded services reach hundreds of thousands of victims. For example, in the six-month reporting period from January to June 2009 alone, OVW grantees reported that more than 125,300 victims were served; over 253,000 services (including shelter, civil legal assistance, and crisis intervention) were provided to victims; more than 3,400 individuals were arrested for violation of protection orders; and 261,622 protection orders were granted in jurisdictions that receive funding from VAWA to enforce protection orders. OVW's technical assistance funding supports: (1) developing resources to support the issuance and enforcement of protection orders; (2) improving judicial response to violence against women through judicial institutes; (3) supporting the work of victim advocates; (4) improving the response of prosecutors to sexual and domestic violence; and (5) legal assistance for victims. VAWA grants assist victims in a variety of ways, as through Transitional Housing Grants, which help meet victims' ongoing need for safe, affordable housing after leaving emergency shelter.

Through VAWA grants, recipients fund many full-time job positions required for a community response to violence. For example, the State of Alabama reported that VAWA's STOP Recovery Act funds support 31 full-time employees, "including court personnel, sheriffs' deputies, victim service officers, intake advocates, prosecutors, court advocates, sexual assault nurse examiners, crisis line coordinators, counselors, and shelter managers" (Carbon 2010, p. 4). Among other things, VAWA grants also support training programs. For example, between January 2005 and June 2009, more than 1,161,000 individuals received domestic violence training, including 191,330 law enforcement officers, 21,649 prosecutors, and 32,265 court personnel. Those numbers do not include the subgrantees who receive VAWA funding from the states for training purposes.

VAWA's effects have been very positive. "Hundreds of companies ... have created Employee Assistance Programs that help victims of domestic violence," according to NDVH.

> More victims are coming forward and receiving lifesaving services to help them move from crisis to stability, and the criminal justice system has improved its ability to keep victims safe and hold perpetrators accountable. Since VAWA was first passed in 1994: There has been as much as a 51% increase in reporting by women and a 37% increase in reporting by men. The number of individuals killed by an intimate partner has decreased by 34% for women and 57% for men, and the rate of non-fatal intimate partner violence against women has decreased 53%. VAWA not only saves lives, [but according to some] it also saves money. In its first six years alone, VAWA saved taxpayers at least $14.8 billion in net averted social costs ... [C]ivil protection orders saved one state (Kentucky) on average $85 million in a single year. States have passed more than 660 laws to combat domestic violence, sexual assault and stalking. All states have passed laws making stalking a crime and strengthened laws addressing date rape and spousal rape. (Sullivan & McLaughlin, n.d.)

Susan Carbon, Director of the OVW, testified on VAWA's benefits:

> One of the signature achievements of VAWA is the development of the concept of a coordinated community response ... VAWA encourages jurisdictions to bring together stakeholders from diverse backgrounds to share information and to use their distinct roles to improve community responses to violence against women. These players include, but are not limited to: victim advocates, police officers, prosecutors, judges, probation and corrections officials, health care professionals, leaders within faith communities, and survivors of violence against women ... VAWA and subsequent legislation created new federal interstate domestic violence, stalking and firearms possession crimes, strengthened penalties for repeat sex offenders and repeat domestic abusers, addressed prosecution of violations of protection orders, and required states, tribes, and territories to give full faith and credit to protection orders issued by other states, tribes and territories. VAWA encourages federal prosecutors to work closely with state, local and tribal prosecutors to ensure that batterers, stalkers, and rapists are held accountable for their crimes. Since the enactment of

VAWA, the Justice Department has prosecuted more than 2,600 cases under both the criminal interstate provisions and the Gun Control Act provisions that target domestic violence abusers. Often these cases involve the most aggressive and violent abusers who cross state lines to pursue their victims. In addition, strengthening of the cyberstalking laws has allowed the Department of Justice to prosecute cases using the latest technology in a way that would be difficult for the states to pursue. (Carbon, 2010, pp. 1–2)

VAWA initially passed in 1994, but, periodically, it must be reauthorized. During each reauthorization, VAWA has been improved based on victims' needs. For instance, VAWA's first reauthorization in 2000 created a legal assistance program for victims and expanded the definition of crime to include dating violence and stalking. It also included provisions for supervised visitation programs for families experiencing domestic violence, as well as improved protections for immigrant victims by establishing U- and T-visas and by focusing on trafficking of persons.

NDVH notes that VAWA's next reauthorization in 2005 further improved protections for immigrant victims. "Specifically, VAWA provides relief by enabling battered immigrants to attain lawful permanent residence ... without having to depend on the cooperation or participation of their batterers" (Shetty & Kaguyutan, 2002). VAWA 2005 offered a more holistic approach to addressing violence. "In addition to enhancing criminal and civil justice and community-based responses to violence, VAWA 2005 created notable new focus areas, according to NNEDV [National Network to End Domestic Violence]. These include: Developing prevention strategies to stop violence before it starts; Protecting individuals from unfair eviction due to their status as victims of domestic violence or stalking; Creating the first federal funding stream to support rape crisis centers; Developing culturally- and linguistically-specific services for communities; Enhancing programs and services for victims with disabilities; and Broadening VAWA service provisions to include children and teenagers." Finally, "VAWA 2005 included for the first time provisions specifically aimed at ending violence against American Indian and Alaska Native women" (Carbon, 2010, p. 7).

As with VAWA's 1994 passage and subsequent reauthorizations, advocacy organizations like NNEDV were at the forefront of promoting the 2011 reauthorization. Government officials are also calling for VAWA's reauthorization. Susan B. Carbon, Director of the OVW, states:

> The resources authorized by VAWA and subsequent legislation have never been more important than they are today. In the best of economic times, a victim worries about finding a job and housing and providing for her children; these problems intensify during a recession. During an economic downturn, a victim of domestic violence faces additional obstacles to leaving her abuser: Shelters and service providers that serve victims have been facing economic crises of their own: State funding cuts and declining charitable donations threaten their ability to survive and serve. As documented in a national census of domestic violence services conducted by the National Network to End Domestic Violence on one day in September 2008, 8,927 requests for services went unmet due to lack of resources. When the census was re-conducted in September 2009, that number had risen to 9,280 unmet requests. (Carbon, 2010, p. 3)

Advocates and others are calling for improvement programs in these areas: prevention; sexual assault; rural areas; women of color; homicide prevention; bystander intervention training; medical interventions; housing, workplace, and military protections; research; teen dating violence; children exposed to violence; and domestic violence and child custody. Notably, "the Department of Justice, after consultation with Indian tribes," seeks to "expand protections to address the epidemic of domestic violence against Native women" and address jurisdictional problems that have made it difficult to prosecute perpetrators of violence against Native women (Carbon, 2011). NNEDV notes that victims' rights organizations are also "working with state coalitions, national organizations, and Congress to ensure ... targeted investments in VAWA grant programs through the appropriations process," which allocates funding. Thus, VAWA supporters not only mobilize for reauthorization, but also to pressure Congress to fund VAWA programs through the appropriations process.

VAWA was again considered for reauthorization in 2012. Congress was in heated partisan debate over the provisions related to assisting immigrant and LGBT victims in particular but approved VAWA in 2013.

See also: Immigrants and Domestic Abuse; Legislation and Polices, Domestic Abuse; Lesbian, Gay, Bisexual and Transgendered (LGBT) Victims; U.S. Government Responses to Domestic Violence; *United States v. Morrison* Case

Further Reading

Carbon, S. (2010, May 5). The increased importance of the Violence Against Women Act in times of economic crisis. Statement to the Committee on the Judiciary. Retrieved from http://www.ovw.usdoj.gov/docs/statement-impt-economic-crisis.pdf

Carbon, S. (2011, August). Messages from the director, Office on Violence Against Women, Retrieved from http://www.ovw.usdoj.gov/director-august2011msg.html

Futures Without Violence. (2011). Key Senate committee considers VAWA. Retrieved from http://www.futureswithoutviolence.org/content/features/detail/1286/

NDVH (National Domestic Violence Hotline). (n.d.). 10 years of progress and moving forward. Retrieved from http://www.thehotline.org/get-educated/violence-against-women-act-vawa/

NNEDV (National Network to End Domestic Violence). (2007–2011). Violence Against Women Act section. Retrieved from http://www.nnedv.org/policy/issues/vawa.html

NOW. (1995–2011). Violence against Women in the United States. Legislation section. Retrieved from http://www.now.org/issues/violence/stats.html#endref15

Reuss, P. (2004, Fall). The Violence Against Women Act: Celebrating 10 years of prevention. Retrieved from http://www.now.org/nnt/fall-2004/vawa.html

Shetty, S., & Kaguyutan, J. (2002, February). Immigrant victims of domestic violence: Cultural challenges and available legal protections. Harrisburg, PA: VAWnet. Retrieved from http://www.vawnet.org/applied-research-papers/print-document.php?doc_id=384

Sullivan, P., & McLaughlin, M. (n.d.). Reauthorization of the Violence Against Women Act (VAWA). VAWA Saves Lives and Saves Money section. Retrieved from http://www.nnedv.org/docs/Policy/VAWA_Reauthorization_Fact_Sheet.pdf

USDOJ (U.S. Department of Justice). (2011, February). FY 2012 Performance budget: Office on Violence Against Women. Retrieved from http://www.justice.gov/jmd/2012justification/pdf/fy12-ovw-justification.pdf

Cheryl O'Brien

VITAL VOICES

Vital Voices (VV) is a nongovernmental organization (NGO) that identifies, trains, and empowers emerging women leaders and social entrepreneurs around the globe, enabling them to create a better world.

History

The Vital Voices Global Partnership (VVGP) grew out of the U.S. government's successful Vital Voices Democracy Initiative (VVDI). VVDI was established in 1997 by First Lady Hillary Rodham Clinton and former Secretary of State Madeleine Albright to promote the advancement of women as a U.S. foreign policy goal. Through the VVDI, the U.S. government, the Inter-American Development Bank, the United Nations, the World Bank, the Nordic Council of Ministers, the European Union, and other governments coordinated VV conferences throughout the world, bringing together thousands of emerging women leaders from more than 80 countries. As a result of these conferences, regional VV initiatives were launched that continue to give women the skills and resources they need to improve themselves, their communities, and their countries. The positive response to the VVDI led to the creation of VVGP as a nonprofit NGO in June 2000.

First Lady Hillary Rodham Clinton speaks at the Vienna Conference Center at the "Vital Voices: Women in Democracy" conference on July 11, 1997. (AP Photo/ Martin Gnedt)

Mission and Model

The mission of VV is to "identify, invest in, and bring visibility to extraordinary women around the world by unleashing their leadership potential to transform lives and accelerate peace and prosperity in their communities." The first step of their model is to identify a leader. This leader may be established, or she may be a novice, but either way, she has identified a problem in her community and is committed to solving it. VV observes how this woman is committed to making her community and country a better place to live and work. The organization invests time, training, resources, and mentorship in this leader. Through training and mentoring, VV offers new skills and knowledge to help this woman gain visibility and have a greater impact. VV also connects her to other female leaders in similar fields, and to an international community where ideas can be shared, and encouragement and support are provided to help reach her goals. The women VV invests in take the new knowledge, expertise, and access to networks that they've gained and "pay it forward" to the next wave of female leaders. This ripple effect triggers new progress toward greater political participation, economic empowerment, and human rights. By drawing attention to these women, the issues they work on, and their achievements, VV creates a more enabling environment for sustaining their progress. The power of VV lies in finding extraordinary women leaders, maximizing their impact, and extending their reach to make the world a safer place for everyone.

The VV international staff and team includes over 1,000 partners, pro bono experts, and leaders, including senior government, and corporate and NGO executives. VV has trained and mentored more than 10,000 emerging women leaders from over 127 countries in Africa, Asia, Eurasia, Latin America and the Caribbean, and the Middle East since it began in 1997. In turn, these women have returned home to train and mentor more than 500,000 additional females in their communities, making them the vital voices of our time. Research has shown that investments in women are directly related to a country's greater prosperity, poverty alleviation, and reduction in corruption.

Projects

VV works in three main areas: human rights, economic empowerment, and political participation. Women all over the world experience various forms of violence, including human trafficking, domestic violence, sexual violence, and harmful traditional practices. VV views women's rights as human rights: as long as violence against women continues, their human rights are limited. The organization's human rights work is centered around three goals. They seek to raise issues of concern through international public awareness campaigns; collaborate with civil society, government, and business to address violence through a multistakeholder approach; and promote effective policies by connecting practitioners and policy makers to ensure the full protection of women's rights. VV human rights projects include initiatives to combat human trafficking in the United States and Cameroon, and a global partnership of experts working to end violence against women.

Globally, women account for 10 percent of income, 66 percent of the workforce, 50 percent of food production, and 1 percent of property ownership. VV recognizes the relationships between investment in women and poverty alleviation, less government corruption, and greater general prosperity. They view women as powerful instruments of economic growth and change, and therefore invest in leadership and skills training for entrepreneurs and business leaders. Their programs for economic empowerment include Vital Voices Global Businesswomen's Network, which links local women's business associations and VV chapters to build a means for connecting businesswomen worldwide; Entrepreneurs in Handcrafts, in which women business leaders who manage small-to-medium size enterprises in the creative industry focus on advancing their businesses to make positive change in their communities; and the Global Women's Mentoring Partnership, in which aspiring female professionals from around the world are linked with and mentored by one of *Fortune* magazine's Most Powerful Women.

A growing body of research is finding that women's increased presence in politics is associated with more education reforms, social development, and achieving gender equality across all sectors. However, worldwide, women hold only 19.1 percent of seats in national parliaments, with the other 81.9 percent being held by men. Without positions of political and public leadership, women's voices are not heard in regard to important political issues. VV operates under the principle that equal representation of women in politics can contribute to a more peaceful and prosperous world. Their projects in political and public leadership include the Emerging Pacific Women's Leadership Program, which provides female leaders from 11 Pacific Island countries with training to advocate for women's economic opportunities and leadership in civil society throughout the Pacific Island region. In 2012, VV will launch the Global Women's Leadership and Public Policy Program to strengthen the abilities of women government officials, establish a transnational network of women government officials to mentor and share best practices, and to support women government officials' capacity to build robust relationships with civil society organizations.

See also: Nongovernmental Organizations

Further Reading

Albright, M. K., & Clinton, H. R. (2000). *America's commitment: Women 2000*. President's Interagency Council on Women. Retrieved from http://secretary.state.gov/www/picw/2000commitment/index.html

Coonan, T., & Thompson, R. (2005). Ancient evil, modern face: The fight against human trafficking. *Georgetown Journal of International Affairs, 6*, 43–52.

Vital Voices: http://www.vitalvoices.org/

Kristin A. Bell

WALKER, LENORE

Lenore E. A. Walker, EdD, developed the term battered woman syndrome (BWS) in 1977 as part of her research concerning the effects of physical, sexual, and/or psychological abuse on women in intimate relationships. Her research has assisted in educating people about the dynamics of interpersonal violence, prevention, and the psychological and legal implications of abuse. She has provided expert testimony in criminal and civil cases involving battered women who commit violent acts in self-defense against their abusive partners. She provides training workshops, lectures, and has appeared on numerous television programs, including *Good Morning America*, the *Oprah Winfrey Show*, and the *CBS Morning News*. She has authored numerous publications and 15 books including *The Battered Woman* (1979), *The Battered Woman Syndrome* (1984/2000), *Terrifying Love: Why Battered Women Kill and How Society Responds* (1989), and *Abused Women and Survivor Therapy* (1994). Dr. Walker has served as chair on various task forces and committees including the American Psychological Association President's Task Force on Violence and the Board of Director's Task Force in Child Abuse Policy and the Committee on International Relations in Psychology. She has also received several awards for her work including the Distinguished Woman Psychologist Leader Award and the award for Distinguished Professional Contributions to Psychology in the Public Interest.

Dr. Walker earned her undergraduate psychology degree in 1962 from Hunter College of the City University of NewYork and a master's of science in clinical school psychology in 1967 from City College of the City University of New York. In 1972, she earned her EdD in school psychology from Rutgers State University of New Jersey, and she completed her postdoctoral master's degree in clinical psychopharmacology in 2004 from Nova Southeastern University. Dr. Walker is a licensed psychologist in Florida, New Jersey, and Colorado and serves as the executive director of the Domestic Violence Institute. She is the president and CEO of Walker and Associates Ltd., which provides psychological assessments for individuals with trauma symptomatology resulting from domestic violence. She also works on forensic cases involving sexual abuse, discrimination, and other issues resulting from abuse. She is a professor in the clinical and forensic concentration at Nova Southeastern University and a diplomat of Family and Clinical Psychology.

Dr. Walker began her work with battered women in the 1970s as a feminist therapist working with abused children and their families. "I was teaching at Rutgers Medical School and mothers would bring in their children and talk about how they were being beaten in order to protect their child from the abuse"

(Dr. Walker, personal communication, October 18, 2011). This led her to develop a research proposal called "The Battered Woman Syndrome," which was funded by the National Institute of Mental Health and included data collection from over 400 battered women from 1977 to 1981.

In 1998, she picked up the research on BWS and began revising questionnaires and looking more specifically at BWS, developing a more comprehensive definition of BWS, and including research samples from prison populations, and women from different countries and various cultures. Her renewed research efforts continue today. In addition, Dr. Walker has created the Survivor Therapy Empowerment Program, a group psychoeducational program that "helps women to better understand how the violence they have experienced has impacted their lives and what they can do about it" (Walker, 2009, p. 389). Walker has been and remains one of the most vocal advocates for the need for psychotherapeutic services for victims.

> There has been controversy throughout the years about how to work with battered women to help them heal ... should you just provide safety and support or professional services as well? I have always taken the side that should they need professional services, it should be available and it should be the best professional services (including psychotherapy and assessment), not because they're mentally ill but because mentally ill women do get battered and it's across all demographic groups and for some people it does cause mental illness. Some people it does not. I have one foot, a stronger foot, in the psychology community to make sure that they have the tools to provide the right services for victims of violence and that is very important for me to be able to do that. (Dr. Walker, personal communication, October 18, 2011)

See also: Battered Woman Syndrome; Psychological Effects of Domestic Abuse; Self-Defense, Homicides, and Domestic Abuse; Self-Defense, Legal Issues

Further Reading

Walker & Associates, LLC, a member of the Forensic Psychology Group. (2005). Retrieved from http://www.drlenorewalker.com/
Walker, L. E. (1979). *The battered woman*. New York: NY: Harper and Row.
Walker, L. E. A. (2009). *The battered woman syndrome* (3rd ed.). New York, NY: Springer.

Kathryn Goesel

WAR AND DOMESTIC VIOLENCE

The costs of war can be calculated in terms of the economic, social, political, and psychological loss or gain, as well as loss of human lives and the devastation of the environment. Some of the often neglected costs of war are the effects it has on women. Women are often the targets of violence by an enemy force. For example, in the Great Lakes region of Africa, specifically in the Democratic Republic of the Congo, rape has been used as a weapon of war in order to intimidate the population and to destroy its culture and ethnicity. In war zones, women are often the victims of kidnappings and forced into prostitution, sold as sex slaves, or forced into other forms of slavery. However, war also has staggering effects on women, men, and children who reside far from the combat arena.

Many studies have been done that focus on the correlation between war and domestic violence. In a six-week period, in 2002, four U.S. soldiers from Fort Bragg in North Carolina killed their wives after returning from Afghanistan. Moreover, in the summer of 2009, a *CBS News* report found that "more than 25,000 spouses and domestic partners have been attacked over the past decade. Nearly 90 spouses have died" (Couric, 2009). While numbers regarding domestic violence are never concrete due to underreporting in the civilian population, the problem can be worse in the military possibly due to its culture. Victims want the violence to stop, but they often do not want to get the perpetrator in trouble. In the military this might have significant resonance because getting in trouble might be a loss of a pay grade or loss of a job. Moreover, the fear of retribution coupled with firearms might be enough to silence most victims.

Some argue that the high rate of domestic violence among current and former members of the military is due to the horrors and atrocities committed and witnessed while in active combat. In addition, those in this camp argue that domestic violence is an indirect result of post-traumatic stress disorder (PTSD). Others warn that substance abuse might be the trigger that leads one into a violent rage. Yet others argue that the culture of the military might be the driving force behind the pervasiveness of domestic abuse. A UN organization for women contends, "It is not the experience of conflict but the culture of violence and masculinity that permeates military forces that causes soldiers to be violent in civilian life" (UNIFEM, n.d.).

A 2002 study by researchers from Yale University and Veterans Affairs Medical Center in West Haven, Connecticut, examined the association between exposure to combat and spousal abuse and other social ills found in former combat veterans with a diagnosis of PTSD. The researchers studied Vietnam veterans and concluded that with no combat exposure "21% of *current* abuse of one's partner or spouse would probably not have occurred" (Prigerson, Maciejewski, & Rosenheck, 2002, p. 61). The study contends that combat exposure leads to PTSD and that PTSD indirectly results in spousal abuse. However, the study does not analyze the potential role that the culture of the military might play in adding to such a higher prevalence of domestic violence in the military than in the civilian population. The study recommends effective PTSD treatment in order to reduce domestic violence in the military family.

According to data from the Department of Defense Advocacy Program for fiscal year 2010, the rates of spouse abuse increased by 1.2 percent from 2009 and declined by 9.7 percent from 2001. The DOD contends that the decline could be a result of the "effectiveness of military prevention and early intervention programs, decline in the number of spouse abuse reported incidents unrelated to the effectiveness of the program, a reluctance of victims to report abuse, the ongoing impact of deployment of military personnel or some combination of the factors" (Department of Defense, 2010). The DOD also states that the number of incidents reported increased., explaining that this might be due to changes in the criteria. In 2010, 16 victims died due to domestic violence. Ninety-four percent of the perpetrators of domestic violence were men, and 81 percent were active duty members of the military.

According to the National Domestic Violence Hotline (n.d.), calls from members of the military have increased by more than half. In 2010, calls nearly doubled. The Department of Defense argues that increased advertising and awareness have led to a rise in calls, while others believe that domestic violence is increasing in the military. The Domestic Violence Hotline (n.d.) reports that 92 percent of the callers were female and 8 percent were male. Forty-two percent were between the ages of 25 and 35, while 27 percent were under 25. In 73 percent of the cases, the callers reported emotional abuse, in 61 percent reported physical abuse, and in 7 percent reported sexual abuse. These numbers demonstrate the same cases had two or three types of abuse.

In 2010, the National Domestic Violence Hotline reports that 1,200 callers found obtaining adequate service problematic. The barriers to direct service from the most significant to the least are unavailability of services, transportation issues, mental health, gender, and disabilities. The barriers to legal services are finances, unavailability of services, transportation issues, cultural barriers, and language barriers.

According to the *Army Times*, drug abuse, suicides, child abuse, and domestic violence are all on the rise. Domestic spousal abuse went up by 33 percent between 2006 and 2011. Research demonstrates that PTSD increases domestic violence. General Chiralli added that "A person diagnosed with post-traumatic stress is three times more likely to participate in some kind of partner aggression. That is why it is so critical to eliminate the stigma associated with post-traumatic stress and get people in for treatment to deal with their alcohol problem, their drug abuse problem, their prescription drug abuse problem, or anger management problems, spouse abuse or child abuse" (Tan, 2012).

The general's statements were based on research conducted by the army and published in *Army 2020: Generating Health and Discipline in the Force Ahead of the Strategic Reset: Report 2012*. The army reports that cases of domestic violence increased by 85 percent from 1,459 to 2,699. The army argues that the high increase is due to a lower rate in 2006, yet it adds that the low numbers might be due to a large number of soldiers on deployment.

However, it is not only soldiers fighting in a foreign land, but also people living in conflict zones that are susceptible to increased rates of domestic violence. Research has shown that married couples residing in conflict zones are victims of domestic violence more often than those residing in relatively peaceful and nonviolent areas are. In fact, according to domestic violence statistics from the Gaza Strip, "husbands exposed to political violence are nearly twice as likely to be physically violent and more than twice as likely to be sexually violent toward their wives" (Stone, 2010).

The frustration and humiliation spurred on by economic and psycho/social factors including trauma and PTSD have been argued to lead men "to violently reassert their position of power in the only situation that remains under their control: the domestic sphere" (Stone, 2010). Prior to UNIFEM merging into UN Women, the organization released a report outlining violence against women. According to UNIFEM (n.d.), the correlation between war and the increased prevalence of domestic violence is due to "the availability of weapons, the violence male family members have experienced or meted out, the lack of jobs, shelter, and basic services." The research demonstrates that participants in war struggle to return to nonviolent peacetime conduct.

According to UNIFEM (n.d.), "Only 45 countries have legislation protecting women against domestic violence, but many of these laws are not regularly enforced, especially during periods of conflict." Many nations, including the United States, and the United Nations argue that everyone should be saved from the scourge of domestic violence. However, safety, security, and support for survivors often fail to protect victims. "The upheaval of war itself makes it nearly impossible for women to seek redress from government entities. But cultural and social stigmas, as well as a woman's status in society, also affect her ability to protect herself or seek protection."

Experts argue that because of the prevalence of domestic violence in conflict zones, postconflict zones, and among those that have exposed to conflict, domestic violence must be acknowledged and "addressed in humanitarian, legal and security responses and training in emergencies and post-conflict reconstruction" (UNIFEM, n.d.). Moreover, all members of militaries, civilians in conflict zones, and survivors must have the financial, legal, psychosocial, and health services to aid in resetting back to what should be a nonviolent peaceful society.

See also: Disasters and Domestic Abuse; The Military and Domestic Abuse; Traumatic Brain Injury and Domestic Abuse

Further Reading

Beckham, J. C., Feldman, M. E., & Kirby, A. C. (1998). Atrocities exposure in Vietnam combat veterans with chronic posttraumatic stress disorder: Relationship to combat exposure, symptom severity, guilt and interpersonal violence. *Journal of Trauma Stress, 11*, 777–785.

Campbell, J. C., Garza, M. A., Gielen, A. C., O'Campo, P., Kub, J., Dienemann, J., Snow Jones, A., & Jafar, E. (2003). Intimate partner violence and abuse among active duty military women. *Violence Against Women, 9*(9), 1072–1092. doi:10.1177/1077801203255291

Collins, D. (2009). 4 wives slain in 6 weeks at Fort Bragg. *CBS News*. Retrieved from http://www.cbsnews.com/2100-201_162-517033.html

Cotter, J. (2002). War and domestic violence. *The Red Critique*. Retrieved from http://redcritique.org/SeptOct02/waranddomesticviolence.htm

Couric, K. (2009). The hidden casualties of war. *CBS News*. Retrieved from http://www.cbsnews.com/stories/2009/01/28/eveningnews/main4761199.shtml

Department of Defense (2010). Department of Defense Advocacy Program for fiscal year 2010. Retrieved from http://www.ncdsv.org/images/DoD_FAPSpouseAndChildAbuseData_2010.pdf

Martin, S. L., Gibbs, D. A., Johnson, R. E., Sullivan, K., Clinton-Sherrod, M., Hardison Walters, J. L., & Rentz, E. D. (2010). Substance use by soldiers who abuse their spouses. *Violence Against Women, 16*(11), 1295–1310. doi:10.1177/1077801210387038

Miles, D. (2010). Military launches domestic violence awareness campaign. *American Forces Press Service*. Retrieved from http://www.defense.gov/news/newsarticle.aspx?id=61131

National Domestic Violence Hotline. (n.d.). Military calls: 2006 through 2010. *National Center on Domestic and Sexual Violence*. Retrieved from http://www.ncdsv.org/images/NDVH_MilitaryCalls2006Through2010.pdf

Prigerson, H., Maciejewski, P., & Rosenheck, R. (2002). Population attributable fractions of psychiatric disorders and behavioral outcomes associated with combat exposure among US men. *American Journal of Public Health, 92*(1), 59–63.

Sertori, T. (2010). Domestic violence is a war zone. *Jakarta Times*. Retrieved from http://www.thejakartapost.com/news/2010/03/09/domestic-violence-a-war-zone.html

Stone, J. L. (2010). War zone life breeds violence. *Harvard Crimson*. Retrieved from http://www.thecrimson.com/article/2010/2/10/violence-political-domestic-nbsp/

Tan, M. (2012). Overall suicides down 10 percent for 2011. *Army Times*. Retrieved from http://www.armytimes.com/news/2012/01/army-overall-suicides-drop-goldbook-unveiled-013012w/

Trauma Foundation. (2002). The war at home: Domestic violence and war. *Trauma Foundation*. Retrieved from http://www.traumaf.org/featured/10-11-02domesticviolence.html

United States Army. (2012). Army 2020: Generating health and discipline in the force ahead of the strategic reset: Report 2012. *Army Times*. Retrieved from http://militarytimes.com/static/projects/pages/army-goldbook.pdf

UNIFEM. (n.d.). Violence against women. Retrieved from http://www.unifem.org/attachments/products/213_chapter01.pdf

Chuck Goesel

WARNING SIGNS OF ABUSE

Abuse is a cycle that one learns from watching others or being the object of abuse. Therefore it is a pattern of behavior, *not* a single action of abuse that is likely to stop after one incident. Abusers are often apologetic and regret their actions, and so it is easy to fall back into normal activity. Days, weeks, or even months later, the abuser is extremely likely to strike again, and typically the violence begins to occur more frequently and with greater severity. Abuse affects all races, ethnic backgrounds, religions, social class, economic status, and educational level and can be of any age. Every 15 seconds someone is slapped, throttled, thrown, pushed, kicked and beaten at the hands of someone they know.

There are several warning signs that indicate a potentially abusive relationship or person. At first, the abuser might seem charming, sweet, warm, or polite. He or she might say all the right things, do the things one would hope a partner would do; and perhaps be romantic. Then the abuser starts to use persuasion in small, unnoticeable ways and to slowly change from requests to stronger and stronger commands. Little by little an abusive person's attitudes and behavior start to change and morph into a manner that is unlike the original person. These changes may even be unrecognizable to someone in the relationship, as this seeming spell of persuasion and manipulation transforms into the truth and reality of the person gradually taking control of another person's life. People outside of this relationship may notice these gradual or rapid changes, but it is much harder to recognize and acknowledge the abuse while *in* the relationship. Often the excuse for abusers' harsh treatment toward others is because they claim to love them or want to teach them the "right way." People caught in this situation may deny they are experiencing abuse, as they have been repeatedly told by the abusers that everything is their own fault. More often than not, the abuser and the abused appear to be the perfect couple to outsiders.

Abusers, often having well-established skills in these areas, tend to be very good at lying, manipulation, and controlling other people without it being obvious to the person in the relationship. It is a misconception that in order to be in an abusive situation, one has to be physically hit. Abuse comes in many forms, and while some abused people might not have bruises on their faces, they are comparable to victims of physical abuse, such as those who have been pushed, shoved, choked, kicked, bitten, had limbs twisted, hair pulled, vigorously shaken, or slapped. People who are emotionally, verbally, psychologically, and financially abused should not be discounted or be told they are not suffering the same as a physical abuse victim. Abuse is abuse, regardless of how it is categorized. On average, it takes a woman seven attempts to leave her abuser before she is successful. A person's psychological chains are just as strong as or stronger than physical chains.

Warning Signs of a Controlling Person

- Creates many excuses for behavior
- Tells inconsistent lies that do not add up
- Is isolated from friends and family
- Takes away personal items such as a cell phone and car keys
- Checks a partner's phone records
- Monitors the miles on a vehicle
- Times the distance it takes from point A to point B
- Keeps tabs on money the partner spends

Signs of an Emotionally Abusive Situation

- Belittling or bullying behavior
- Yelling derogatory slurs
- Taunting and name-calling (such as stupid, worthless, and an abomination)
- Humiliating one in public and private
- Finding pleasure in making someone cry
- Stripping away one's layers of reserve and self-respect
- Using angry hand gestures
- Accusing the partner of cheating
- Isolating the partner from things once loved
- Separating the partner from contacting friends and family
- Threatening to leave
- Using the excuse that the abuser loves the partner
- Ignoring partner's feelings
- Asking the same antagonizing questions
- Questioning partner's decisions and reasoning

WARNING SIGNS OF ABUSE

Warning Signs of an Abusive Person

- Very clingy
- Constantly wanting to call
- Excessively questioning one's actions and whereabouts
- Randomly showing up at partner's places of work or school
- Surprising one in a way that feels like stalking
- Insisting that things should be done a certain way
- Unpredictable behavior
- Short temper or snapping at the slightest thing
- Wanting to have sex for the wrong reasons
- Threatening to commit suicide if the partner leaves
- Increased use of drugs and/or alcohol

More Serious Signs Are When an Abuser Threatens the Following:

- To have the partner institutionalized
- Telling the partner that no one will believe their story
- Saying that the abuser will not let them go
- There is nowhere the partner can escape, or that the abuser will find them
- To kill the partner
- Teaching them a lesson
- Teaching them to respect the abuser
- Wanting the partner to fear the abuser as a way of showing respect
- Blaming the partner for things out of their control
- Threatening that the partner could disappear with no one to question the abuser's actions

Women (or men) may rationalize that their partner just gets a little angry, controlling, or obsessive and that they do not mean it. At first, the abuser may make a suggestion that steadily leads to a constant correction of how something should be done, which can then lead to lectures on how incompetent the partner is, because the partner is not doing what she or he was told to do. The more the partner may try to comply with the abuser, the worse the situation gets.

If an abusive person makes the person he is dating constantly uncomfortable, not at ease, or unsafe around him, then the situation is more than likely unsafe, and the partner hould take serious inventory of this potentially harmful relationship.

Women are more likely to stay in an abusive relationship if there are children involved. Once an abuser is arrested, he or she has the option of paying bail, using a bail bond person, or having a family member or friend pay bail. Times have changed in the sense that a women does not need to press charges against her attacker, as a police officer can and will arrest the abusive partner once the officer witnesses signs of abuse. Once the abuser is arrested, a bail hearing will be set where an amount of money will be negotiated for this person's release, at which point the woman will not need to attend or voice her opinion, if she chooses not to. It will then be up to the state's attorney's office to press charges and prosecute the accused. The more proof of abuse—for example, doctor and hospital records, photographs, neighbor's testimony, and such—the stronger the case will be against this person.

Many scholars have argued that the lack of swift prosecution of abusers and the lax laws against domestic abuse have been two of the reasons why domestic abuse has been widely accepted and practiced.

If there is a child/children involved, the family courts will have to decide the matter. Typically, there has to be evidence that the child is in danger from the accused abusive parent; otherwise, the parent cannot be legally barred from accessing the child/children, if there is no evidence of abuse toward them.

Remedies

A support system is crucial. A support system consists of a person or persons who can give advice, guidance, help, or assist someone in a negative or abusive situation. This can be friends or family members, coworkers, fellow students, neighbors, or even strangers if the situation presents itself.

An emergency plan is also important. This is a plan of escape if one finds herself in an undesirable, harmful, or potentially dangerous situation. It is recommended that victims plan a list of actions to be taken in order to leave quickly and safely; think critically about how to escape, what obstacles might be presented, and solutions to any foreseeable events. Victims should: carry a passport, driver's license, and/or birth certificate to travel; a large sum of cash, *not* credit cards or checks (nothing traceable); pick a secure location or shelter; have a backup plan or two in case the location is uninhabitable. Buy an on-the-go cell phone, or a cheap cell phone that you can load minutes on without having to have a paper bill (this also eliminates having to have a physical address), and change passwords and/or create a new e-mail account, as well as other accounts. A person may want to change her appearance by changing her hair color and cut (or wearing a wig), attire, in addition to using colored contact lenses among other things. Keep a spare set of car keys to an automobile, having already packed a set of clean clothes in the truck; then rent or purchase another car in the future. Establish a post office box instead of a street address, and be very careful not to fill out surveys or let people know the address of a new location.

Additionally, it is recommended that victims keep a secret bank account for an emergency. Many people who are abusive tend to control financial information such as credit cards, bank accounts, and joint savings. Do not be afraid to go to a shelter or ask for help.

Other important things to carry:

- Medication
- Marriage certificate
- Medical and dental records
- Insurance policies
- Prescription glasses
- Hearing aids
- Children's vaccination records
- School records
- Social Security card

- Title to the car
- Phone book
- Recent credit report

Collect these items slowly and cautiously so as to not raise any suspicion. Perhaps the most important tip for anyone in an abusive relationship is to tell someone what is going on, despite how angry an abusive partner might become if he were to find out. It is perhaps the most important risk to let someone know of an abusive situation, rather than suffering silently, which may later result in irreversible bodily harm or death. Learning self-defense can be another important tool to surviving an abusive relationship. Local community centers may offer classes at little or no cost, such as a rape self-defense class.

The following is a list of hotline numbers for people in need of help.

National Clearinghouse on Marital and Date Rape
(510) 524-1582
National Coalition for Victim Assistance
(800) 879-6682
Parents Without Partners
(800) 637 7974
CDC National AIDS Hotline
(800) 342-2437
National Women's Health Network
(202) 347-1140 (lesbian heath issues)
National Resource Center on Child Abuse and Neglect
(800) 227-5242
Resource Center on Child Custody and Child Protection
(800) 527-3223 (not a crisis service)
Committee for Mother and Child Rights, Inc.
(703) 722-3652 (guidance on custody)
Child Help USA
(800) 422-4453 (for abusive parents)

See also: Cycle of Violence; Types of Domestic Abuse

Further Reading

Meyers, R. (2010, August 6). Warning signs of domestic violence. *Huffington Post.* Retrieved June 29, 2012, from http://www.huffingtonpost.com/randy-susan-meyers/warning-signs-of-domestic_b_671321.html

Signs of domestic violence. (n.d.). *Livestrong.* Retrieved September 17, 2012, from http://www.livestrong.com/signs-of-domestic-violence/

Warning signs of domestic violence. (n.d.). An Abuse, Rape, and Domestic Violence Aid and Resource Collection (AADVARC), Retrieved September 17, 2012, from http://www.aardvarc.org/dv/signs.shtml

Natasha A. Abdin

WELFARE AND DOMESTIC ABUSE

Research has repeatedly shown that economic factors can exacerbate domestic abuse. A 2004 study by the National Institute of Justice (NIJ), for instance, found that domestic violence is more common and more severe in economically disadvantaged neighborhoods, with women residing in those locations twice as likely to report abuse as those in more advantaged neighborhoods. Living with abusers who are unemployed or underemployed, as well as worrying about finances, increases the risk of violence against women. Women whose male partners experienced two or more stretches of unemployment during the five-year study were nearly three times as likely to be victimized. Further, studies have documented that domestic violence is a significant contributor to homelessness. A study by the U.S. Conference of Mayors in 2007 found 39 percent of cities cited domestic violence as the primary cause of homelessness among families. A study by the ACLU in 2003 found that 25 percent of homeless mothers had experienced physical abuse the year prior.

It follows, then, that victims of domestic violence will be disproportionately represented on welfare case rolls. Research bears that out. In the later 1990s, studies estimated that 50 to 60 percent of women receiving welfare benefits had experienced violence from a current or former intimate partner. Another study found that 38 percent of domestic violence victims become homeless at some point in their lives. Although often victims are homeless because they are fleeing the abuse and have nowhere specific to go, in some cases they are kicked out by landlords. For instance, a woman in North Carolina was evicted because she was reportedly too loud when she jumped from her second-story balcony as her ex-boyfriend shot at her, while a Michigan woman was evicted because her ex-boyfriend attacked her in their apartment (the landlord called this criminal activity).

Temporary Assistance to Needy Families (TANF) is what most people mean when they say welfare. TANF is administered through the Office of Family Assistance. It provides assistance and work training and opportunities for needy families through block grants to states and tribes that are then used to develop the specific parameters of their programs. TANF was developed in 1996 as part of a comprehensive welfare reform effort. It replaced Aid to Families with Dependent Children (AFDC), the Job Opportunities and Basic Skills Training (JOBS) program, and the Emergency Assistance (EA) program. The four main goals of TANF are: (1) assisting needy families so that children can be cared for in their own homes; (2) reducing the dependency of needy parents by promoting job preparation, work, and marriage; (3) preventing out-of-wedlock pregnancies; and (4) encouraging the formation and maintenance of two-parent families. Recipients of TANF are required, with a few exceptions, to work as soon as possible and no later than two years after beginning to collect assistance. Single parents must either work or continue their education for at least 30 hours per week. Two-parent families must participate in work or educational activities for 35 to 55 hours per week, depending on circumstances. Failure to comply with work or education requirements can result in a reduction or elimination of benefits. States are not allowed to penalize families with children under the age of six if their failure to work or go to school is due to lack of child care. States with less than 50 percent of single-parent and less than 90 percent of two-parent families participating in work or education will receive less federal funding. Additionally, there is a five-year cumulative limit for anyone receiving TANF.

On October 1, 2008, a provision was added to address work requirements for victims of domestic violence. States electing the Family Violence Option under section 402(a)(7) of the Social Security Act are obliged to screen and identify victims of domestic violence, refer victims to services, and, if needed, waive work or educational requirements as long as needed to escape abuse. States are given flexibility in determining which requirements to waive and for how long.

Advocates applauded the exceptions for victims of domestic violence, noting that obtaining work or going to school is challenging for anyone who is struggling but more so for domestic violence victims, who need support and often simply time to get free from abuse and back on their feet. Domestic violence often follows women to the workplace, as abusers may stalk them, call or show up repeatedly, or otherwise sabotage the victim's work. Victims tell of abusers turning off alarm clocks so they oversleep and miss training or work. Without an exception, women might feel they cannot quit or change jobs, even if it is the safest move, because they would fear loss of benefits.

The exception is not flawless, however. A major challenge remains in how to identify victims. Most people don't go to the welfare office and announce themselves as victims, so caseworkers must ask questions to help identify eligible persons. Thus it is imperative that caseworkers be trained on domestic violence and how to ask these questions in a sensitive manner. Dellasega (2007), for instance, has documented the frequency of dominator-style methods, what she and others call relational aggression, among and between females employed at domestic violence and other social service agencies. Traditional welfare agencies have been criticized for promoting discourses and practices that reinforce the dominance of white, masculine, and middle-class society (Jurik, Cavendar, & Cowgill, 2009). Victims often report that their interactions with caseworkers were stressful and that they felt verbally harassed. They tell of waiting in long lines just for a five-minute conversation with a rude caseworker who didn't seem to care about them. Many find it difficult to even get to the welfare office, as they lack reliable transportation and often must take time off of work for meetings or struggle with how to care for their children while they meet with a caseworker.

Critics have maintained that the welfare law already had provisions for women who need more time to get off of welfare. Some believe the exception will encourage people to lie or to turn every disagreement into an act of abuse. Further, Satel (2000) argued that "the amendment puts abused women at even greater risk by turning these women into cash cows for their deadbeat lovers. Consider: a mother and her children are living with a shiftless lout who sponges off her government check, food stamps, and Section 8 apartment. He learns that battered women can keep getting their benefits. If keeping his partner brutalized means a regular check for him, some men will do just that" (in Roleff, 2000, pp. 161–62).

Another concern is that the dismantling of the former welfare system, even with the domestic violence exception, has driven more and more victims away from state and federal agencies and to nonprofits for help. This, then, seems to imply that the government has little or no responsibility to victims, and it serves to overwhelm the nonprofits in a community.

See also: Economic Recession and Domestic Abuse; Housing and Domestic Abuse; Workplace Violence and Domestic Abuse

Further Reading

Crook, W. (2001). Trickle-down bureaucracy: Does the organization affect client responses to programs? *Administration in Social Work, 26*(1), 27–59.
Dellasega, C. (2007). *Mean girls grown up.* New York: Wiley.
Finley, L. (2010). Where's the peace in this movement? A domestic violence advocates reflections on the movement. *Contemporary Justice Review, 13*(1), 57–69.
Gonnerman, J. (1997, March 10). Welfare's domestic violence. *The Nation.*
James, S., Johnson, J., Raghavan, C., Lemos, T., Barakett, M., & Woolis, D. (2003). The violent matrix: A study of structural, interpersonal, and intrapersonal violence among a sample of poor women. *American Journal of Community Psychology, 31*(1/2), 129–141.
Jurik, N., Cavendar, G., & Cowgill, G. (2009). Resistance and accommodation in a post-welfare social service agency. *Journal of Contemporary Ethnography, 38*(1), 25–51.
Prah, P. (2006, January 6). Domestic violence. *CQ Researcher, 16*(1), 1–24.
Roleff, T. (2000). *Domestic violence: Opposing viewpoints.* San Diego, CA: Greenhaven.
Rose, N. (1995). Gender, race, and the welfare state: Government work programs from the 1930s to the present. *Feminist Studies, 19*(2), 318–343.
Satel, S. (2000). Welfare reform should not include an exemption for victims of domestic violence. In T. Roleff (Ed.), *Domestic violence: Opposing viewpoints* (pp. 160–163). San Diego, CA: Greenhaven.

Laura L. Finley

WHITE RIBBON CAMPAIGN

The White Ribbon Campaign is an awareness raising effort organized primarily by men and boys to educate men and boys to be active in working to end violence against women. The white ribbon became a grassroots symbol of opposition to violence against women following the mass murder of 14 women by an avowed anti-feminist at the École Poytechnique in Montreal in 1989. In response to the massacre, and as an expression of outrage at the levels of violence against women in Canadian society, some men began wearing white ribbons. The Campaign began in Canada in 1991 as part of an effort to mobilize men and boys to address the role of males in perpetuating violence against women in order to halt violence against women. The wearing of a white ribbon would symbolize publicly opposition to violence against women and a commitment to end violence. The first campaign succeeded in distributing over 100,000 white ribbons and served to generate substantial public debate and discussion. Prominent founders of the campaign included educator Michael Kaufman and Toronto politician Jack Layton, who would later become leader of the New Democratic Party and the Leader of the Official Opposition in the Canadian Parliament.

White Ribbon Campaign groups do educational outreach work in schools, postsecondary campuses, and workplaces. They also work with mass media to promote the campaign events and goals. Campaign events are geared toward educating men and boys about occurrences of violence against women and means for ending violence within their own communities. Broader education raises awareness about male violence against women within the specific society in which participants live. Campaign organizers view the wearing of the white ribbon as a pledge by the wearer to never commit or condone violence against women as well as being a pledge never to stay silent about violence against women and girls.

The central organizing principle of the White Ribbon Campaign is that men must have an active role in striving to end violence against women. Rather than being an issue for women to address through women's movements and awareness raising campaigns, men must take responsibility for violence against women domestically and socially. Toward this end men must make a commitment to promote and defend gender equality as well as addressing the harmful impacts of masculinity and male privilege in contemporary contexts. At the same time women are involved in campaigns in specific locations and the White Ribbon Campaign explicitly supports the work of women's organizations.

From its local origin, the White Ribbon Campaign has grown to become globally the largest campaign of men and boys working to halt violence against women and girls. Campaign events are now held in more than 60 countries. Numerous governments as well as the United Nations have recognized the activities of the White Ribbon Campaign. Campaigns are run every year for around 16 days beginning November 25 and lasting until December 16. Some male feminists in Canada have taken up wearing the white ribbon as a broader sign of support for women's movements and national efforts to end domestic violence.

See also: Men's Efforts Against Domestic Abuse; National Organization for Men Against Sexism (NOMAS); North America and Domestic Abuse

Further Reading

Connell, R. (2005). *Masculinities*. Berkeley: University of California Press.
Kaufman, M., & Kimmel, M. (2011). *The guy's guide to feminism*. Berkeley: Seal Press.
Tarrant, S. (2009). *Men and feminism*. Berkeley: Seal Press.
Wood, J. T. (2010). *Gendered lives: Communication, gender, and culture*. New York: Wadsworth.

Jeff Shantz

WOMEN'S AID FEDERATION OF ENGLAND

Women's Aid Federation of England is a coalition of charities that work against domestic violence of women and children in England. It is one of four national parts of the Women's Aid Federation, the other three covering Scotland, Northern

Ireland, and Wales. The coalition works at both the local and national levels to promote practices to prevent domestic violence as well as to establish opportunities for victims of domestic violence to find support and aid. The scope of its activities includes educational outreach, refuges for women and children in danger, campaigns for better legal protection, advocacy, and a Freephone 24-hour hotline.

The first Women's Aid refuge was founded by Erin Pizzey in Chiswick, a borough of London, in 1971. It was the first domestic violence shelter in the world. Initially, the group that met was not focused on domestic violence, but on women's issues more generally; they met in order to exchange ideas on how to work at the local level. The group's focus took shape after a bruised woman pleaded for help from the group, stating that no one else would listen to her. From there, the idea of creating safe shelter for women and children escaping domestic violence began to emerge.

It was the group's policy that no one should be turned away, leading to many of the shelters becoming overwhelmed with the help they tried to offer. The group also began to support research into domestic violence and its prevalence.

The National Women's Aid became an official national organization in 1974. At the time, it united 40 various agencies and refuges. One of the early goals of the group was to highlight the problems that women who were the victims of domestic violence faced, being passed from government agency to agency without clear guidelines on how the government could assist them. As a unified organization, the agencies were better able to advocate for change and push for the first legislation dealing with domestic violence, the Domestic Violence and Matrimonial Proceedings Act, which was passed in 1976.

Throughout its history, Women's Aid has helped to put forward new attention and research to highlight types of abuse and neglect that were previously unnoticed in general society. Much of the progress that has been made in providing shelter, education, and in helping women and children in abusive situations has been as a result of this research highlighting problems that had simply never been noticed by the media or government before.

In 1977, the Housing Act 1977 declared that women and dependent children who were at risk of domestic violence were to be legally recognized as homeless and therefore were eligible for assistance. By the late '70s, in part because of the attention the group had placed on the issue of domestic violence, a Scottish Research survey highlighted that one in four violent crimes was a case of "wife assault."

Following this research, Women's Aid advocated for domestic violence to be considered both a criminal and civil matter, and pushed for police and criminal justice to investigate and prosecute such crimes.

In the Family Act, Part IV in 1996, this would be more systematically realized. The protections this law offered included automatic powers of arrest to the police when there was a threat of violence in domestic situations.

In recent years, campaigns have been launched geared toward teenagers and toward strategizing with corporations and celebrities to bring greater attention and support to their causes. Celebrity patrons and ambassadors include names such as

Sarah Brown (wife of former prime minister Gordon Brown), BBC radio host and journalist Dame Jenni Murray, UK television personality Charlie Webster, and Tana and Gordon Ramsay (chef).

Women's Aid itself, because it coordinates between activities, has a small board and a paid staff of about 35 members; most of the work done and services provided are by various charities, local organizations and councils, and individual groups and refuges. The agency particularly works to determine areas of need and find existing or new ways to close these gaps. It also coordinates efforts between widely divergent groups that work on the national, regional, and local levels as well as working with government, local council, private charitable, and religious groups together.

Current projects and campaigns include "Real Men," which is aimed toward men, stating that real men do not commit acts of domestic violence; a campaign focused on teenage girls to instill in them the idea that they should "Expect Respect"; a legislative campaign objecting to proposed cuts to legal aid that could leave more survivors of domestic violence at risk of not receiving such aid; and a set of "Empowering Women Awards" to honor and celebrate the work of women who have either survived domestic violence or who have helped others who were victims of domestic violence.

See also: Europe and Domestic Abuse; Pizzey, Erin

Further Reading

Dobash, R., & Dobash, R. (1992). *Women, violence and social change*. London, England: Routledge,

Gilroy, R., & Woods, R. (1994). *Housing women*. London, England: Routledge.

Mullender, A. (1996). *Rethinking domestic violence: The social work and probation response*. London, England: Routledge.

National Centre for Domestic Violence: http://www.ncdv.org.uk/

Richards, L., Letchford, S., & Stratton, S. (2008). *Policing domestic violence (Blackstone's Practical Policing)*. Oxford, England: Blackstone Press.

Women's Aid Federation website: http://www.womensaid.org.uk/

Andrea J. Dickens

WOMEN'S RIGHTS MOVEMENT

Although women and some male allies were involved with some efforts to address domestic violence in earlier decades, it was the feminist movement of the 1960s and 1970s that brought significant attention to the issue. Feminist activists today are still advocating for more education about abuse, for additional services for victims, and for increased efforts to hold abusers accountable.

Overview of Women's Rights Movements

Feminists and historians typically trace three distinct periods or waves of women's rights activism in the United States. While there were small pockets of activism for women's equality before this time, the first wave is generally thought to have started during the Civil War era. Drawing on writings from French Revolution–era authors like Mary Wollstonecraft, Harriet Taylor, and John Stuart Mill, activists began to challenge the idea that women were to be held exclusively to a domestic ideal that relegated them largely to the home or to low-paid domestic labor. Activists argued for property and voting rights for women. In England and the United States, people like Benjamin Rush, a well-known physician, promoted the idea that a more broadly educated female populace would be good for democracy. This advocacy, however, was almost exclusively on behalf of middle-class white women.

Many of the female activists were also involved in the temperance movement. Some believed it was drunken husbands who were responsible for the violence women endured in the home. Women also held leadership roles within the labor movement. Mary Harris Jones, known as Mother Jones, is perhaps the most widely known female activist for improving working conditions for both men and women.

In the early 1900s, women's activism for control over their bodies grew in strength and influence. As early as 1836, Sarah Grimke authored a pamphlet that provided advice on contraception. Watching women suffer through countless pregnancies due to flawed contraceptive methods and then line up for $5, often-botched abortions, Margaret Sanger challenged the 1873 Comstock Laws that made it a crime to send any obscene, lewd, or lascivious material through the mail and that banned the distribution of educational information about abortion.

Women also played a central role in the abolition movement. One of the first antislavery books was authored by Lydia Maria Child in 1833, and it was Harriet Beecher Stowe's classic *Uncle Tom's Cabin* that mobilized the north to oppose slavery. On July 19, 1848, more than 200 women met in Seneca Falls, New York, to call for universal suffrage for women. Modeled after the Declaration of Independence, the Declaration of Sentiment called for full rights for women under the law. Women did not get the right to vote with the passage of the post–Civil War constitutional amendments, as the Fifteenth Amendment only applied to black males. Women's rights groups continued to meet, with the emphasis largely on obtaining the right to vote, a dream that was enacted at the federal level (the state of Wyoming already provided women's suffrage) with the ratification of the Nineteenth Amendment.

What is known as the second wave of feminist activism began in the 1950s. Some women were inspired to challenge traditional gender roles after their experience working in traditionally male fields during World War II. This wave, which is what most people think of when they are discussing the women's rights movement, emphasized gender equality in the workplace, access to reproductive health care, increasing women's political participation, and civil rights legislation. Drawing on their slogan "the personal is political," activists in the decades between 1950 and the later 1970s also took on issues that were once considered private, including legalized abortion and domestic abuse. Women's rights activists achieved much, including but not limited to the Equal Pay Act of 1963; Title VII of the Civil Rights Act (which forbids workplace discrimination); creation of the Equal Employment Opportunity Commission (EEOC) and the extension of Affirmative Action to women; and Title IX of the Education Act of 1972 (prohibiting gender discrimination in schools and universities).

By most accounts, it was popular books that helped usher in the second wave. Helen Gurley Brown's (1962) *Sex and the Single Girl*, a bestseller, urged women to view sex as something enjoyable. Betty Friedan's (1963) *The Feminine Mystique* critiqued the cult of domesticity, prompting women to question whether the home was where they must remain.

Activists of the second wave gained tactics and strategies from the civil rights movement, and some (albeit far from all) supported it. In 1966, after seeing the successes of the National Association for the Advancement of Colored People (NAACP), a group of 300 women convened to form the National Organization for Women (NOW).

Over time, the women's rights movement splintered. The liberal branch stayed focused on antidiscrimination legislation, emphasizing equal pay and promotions for female workers. Radical feminists maintained that the legal system could never adequately address gender discrimination until patriarchy was completely eliminated. They denounced traditional gender roles in many cases, even motherhood. Smaller splinter groups included socialist feminists, who saw the roots of gender equality in capitalism. A growing gay activism also challenged the white, heterosexual emphasis held by many feminist activists.

Second-wave activists were successful at raising awareness about gender inequalities. Further, they helped establish the first women's studies programs at universities. One of the most divisive efforts of the second wave was the promotion of the Equal Rights Amendment (ERA). The ERA made it through Congress with little opposition in 1971, but when it was sent to the states for ratification in 1972, the furor began. It was not just conservative males that opposed the ERA; some women's groups did as well, fearing it would jeopardize some of the achievements that had already been made for women. The ERA was not ratified. By the mid-1980s, the second wave was largely over.

The third wave started in the 1980s and continues today. Third-wave feminists are challenging gender inequalities using different tools and tactics and are far more inclusive than the earlier movements, which tended to include largely middle-class white women. Third-wave feminists are reaching out to men as allies and using today's technologies and art forms to address gender inequalities. It is a movement focused largely on female empowerment and less on male's oppression.

Women's Rights Movement and Domestic Violence

In regard to domestic violence, the second wave not only did much to raise awareness about what had previously been considered a "private" matter, it also ushered in new laws criminalizing abuse and established shelters and other resources for victims. At first a grassroots effort, the movement today is far more formalized, even bureaucratic, by some definitions. Some of the important seeds of the domestic violence efforts were planted in England, when Erin Pizzey opened the first domestic violence shelter in Chiswick in 1971. Four years later, her *Scream Quietly or the Neighbors Will Hear* was the first book about domestic violence written from a battered woman's perspective. Her influential work gave voice to survivors and prompted others to speak or write about their trauma. In 1976, *Ms.* became the first national magazine to put a battered woman on the cover and helped ignite the U.S. movement. These efforts helped lead to the establishment of Women's Aid in 1974 and England's Domestic Violence Bill in 1976, which provided for civil protection orders for domestic violence victims.

The first U.S.-based shelter was opened by the Women's Advocates in 1973 in St. Paul, Minnesota, and by 1982, there were more than 300 shelters across the U.S. Women's Advocates and some other shelters were organized around a radical feminist ideology, with the goal of creating an egalitarian space for women. Most were communal structures modeled on the ideal home that rejected the hierarchies of the outside sphere.

In 1976, Pennsylvania established the first state coalition against domestic violence and became the first state to pass legislation providing for orders of protection for battered women. Oregon was the first state to legislate mandated arrest in domestic violence cases, in 1977, although by 1978, only nine states had legislation specifically prohibiting domestic violence. In 1977, Lenore Walker originated the concept of battered woman syndrome, followed by the publication of her book *The Battered Woman* in 1979. While it did much to draw additional attention to the issue and assisted in the defense of women who had fought back against their abusive spouses, critics note that Walker's work ushered in an era in which the focus was on individual victims, rather than on challenging deeper gender inequalities that impacted all women. States also began to take action on sexual assault. In 1971, the first rape crisis center was opened in the United States by the Bay Area Women Against Rape. Oregon became the first state to criminalize marital rape in 1977, and by 1980, every state had some type of rape shield law to protect rape victims from being revictimized during prosecution of perpetrators. The 1970s saw the beginning of help programs for batterers as well. In 1977, Emerge, the first counseling program for men who batter, was founded in Boston, Massachusetts.

The U.S. Commission on Civil Rights sponsored the Consultation on Battered Women: Issues of Public Policy in Washington, D.C., in 1978. More than 100 nationally represented women come together to organize around the needs of the newly formed battered women's movement. It is during this hearing that the National Coalition Against Domestic Violence (NCADV) was formed. Lisa Leghorn promoted the feminist position, arguing that it was fundamental gender inequalities that needed changing, at the U.S. Commission on Civil Rights consultation. "That the nuclear family is not working in this culture can no longer be questioned. Changes in the law can be used to help protect women from flagrant abuses of power by men as well as private and public institutions. Yet these very abuses cannot be prevented through changes in the law, but only by changes in the culture which sustains them" (U.S. Commission on Civil Rights, 1978, pp. 140–141). In 1979, President Carter established the Office on Domestic Violence.

Two important court cases in 1976, *Scott v. Hart* and *Bruno v. Codd*, inspired battered women to file lawsuits nationwide against police departments, departments of probation, and the Family Court system. In *Scott v. Hart*, police were told they had to respond to domestic violence calls seriously and must work with advocates to pass out resource cards to victims. *Bruno v. Codd* also required police to take abuse far more seriously by making arrests in felony assault cases and in many misdemeanors as well as enforcing protection orders.

Domestic violence discourse and advocacy took a different direction in the United States during the 1980s. The focus became treating domestic violence as a crime. Law enforcement officers, then, were key, and efforts were made to encourage police to make arrests and hold batterers accountable. The 1980s saw the first scientific study testing the effects of arrest in misdemeanor cases of domestic violence. In 1981–82, researchers Lawrence Sherman and Richard Berk tested three different police responses to domestic violence over an 18-month period: arrest, separation, and mediation. Their goal was to determine what works best in reducing repeat incidents of physical violence. The results, released in 1984, revealed that arrest was the most effective strategy. This research helped fuel the call for mandatory arrest policies. In 1985, *Thurman v. Torrington* is the first federal case in which a battered woman sued a city because police failed to protect her from her husband's violence. Tracey Thurman won a $2 million judgment against the city. The suit prompted Connecticut's passage of a mandatory arrest law. By the mid-1990s, 15 states plus Washington, D.C., had adopted mandatory arrest laws for domestic violence. Such laws require officers to arrest someone when there is probable cause, regardless of whether the victim wants an arrest made. Before such laws, victims were often asked whether they wanted their perpetrator arrested.

While many applauded the efforts to hold batterers accountable, today there remains skepticism and even criticism about mandatory arrests. Some advocates see them as disempowering victims, and research to replicate MDVE has not necessarily shown arrest to always be the best practice. Further, many have noted the loss of feminist perspective that highlights the role that broader gender inequalities play in abusive relationships. "The transformation of domestic violence, from a liberation to a crime discourse, was one of the more insidious processes which developed during the Reagan years. Feminist discussions and demands for equal protection were utilized as grounds for legitimating of a crime control model" (Ferraro, 1996, p. 81). Similarly, the 1980s saw shelter advocates shift their emphasis from empowerment of battered women to a more individualistic emphasis on treating "clients." The federal funds that were available were designated for services and not community education, and thus advocates gave more attention to individual counseling for women than to addressing gender inequalities and public education. To receive public contracts, shelters had to begin employing more credentialed staff and move toward more widely recognized social service models that were less radical and more bureaucratic.

Despite the concern that the movement has lost its feminist roots, the 1980s did usher in some important public attention to the issue of abuse. In 1980, the first National Day of Unity was held in October. Established by the National Coalition Against Domestic Violence, it was intended as a way to mourn battered women who were murdered, to celebrate survivors, and to honor advocates and activists. The day turned into a week and, in 1987, expanded to become Domestic Violence Awareness Month, commemorated still in October. In 1982, *60 Minutes* aired a program, *A Place to Go*, describing the work of battered women's shelters in Texas. It was the most highly viewed television program that season and served to raise awareness among the general public. In 1985, U.S. Surgeon General C. Everett Koop issued an influential report identifying domestic violence as a major health problem. In 1989, the National Coalition Against Domestic Violence followed the lead of Women's Aid in the United Kingdom and established the first national toll-free domestic violence hotline.

See also: Europe and Domestic Abuse; Feminism and Domestic Abuse; North America and Domestic Abuse; Patriarchy and Domestic Abuse

Further Reading

Danis, F. (2006). A tribute to Susan Schechter: The visions and struggles of the battered women's movement. *Affilia, 21*(3), 336–341.

Enke, A. (2003). Taking over domestic space: The battered women's movement and public protest. In V. Gosse & R. Moser (Eds.), *The world the sixties made: Politics and culture in recent America* (pp. 162–190). Philadelphia, PA: Temple University Press.

Evans, S. (2004). *Tidal wave: How women changed America at century's end.* New York, NY: Free Press.

Ferraro, K. (1996, fall). The dance of dependency: A genealogy of domestic violence discourse. *Hypatia, 11*(4), 77–92.

Lerner, A., & Allen, N. (2009). Still a movement after all these years? Current tensions in the domestic violence movement. *Violence Against Women, 15*(6), 656–677.

McGregor, H. (1989). *Working for change: Movement against domestic violence.* Concord, MA: Paul and Co.

Morrison, A. (n.d.). Changing the domestic violence (dis)course: Moving from white victim to multicultural survivor. *UC Davis Law Review.* Retrieved June 11, 2012, from http://lawreview.law.ucdavis.edu/issues/39/3/deconstructing-image-repertoire-women-of-color/DavisVol39No3_MORRISON.pdf

Pleck, E. (1987). *Domestic tyranny.* New York, NY: Oxford University Press.

Pyles, L., & Postmus, J. (2004). Addressing the problem of domestic violence: How far have we come? *Affilia, 19*(4), 376–388.

Rothenburg, B. (2003). "We don't have time for social change": Cultural compromise and the battered woman syndrome. *Gender & Society, 17*(5), 771–787.

Spalter-Roth, R., & Schrieber, R. (1995). Outsider issues and insider tactics: Strategic tensions in the women's policy network during the 1980s. In M. M. Ferree & P. Y. Martin (Eds.), *Feminist organizations: Harvest of the new women's movement* (pp. 105–127). Philadelphia, PA: Temple University Press.

U.S. Commission on Civil Rights. (1978). Battered women: Issues of public policy. Consultation sponsored by the U.S. Commission on Civil Rights, Washington, D.C, January 30–31

Laura L. Finley

WOMEN THRIVE WORLDWIDE

Women Thrive Worldwide is a nonprofit organization based in Washington, D.C., whose goal is to help facilitate "U.S. policies that help women lift themselves and their families out of poverty." Originally called the Women's Edge Coalition, it was founded in 1998 to help advocate, craft, and form policies that create financially viable opportunities for women who live in poverty, primarily focusing in the United

Representatives renew commitment to fast in solidarity with poor women around the world. (PRNewsFoto/Women Thrive Worldwide)

States, taking an active role in helping other countries and trade programs that put women in the forefront. Their hope is to give power back to women by combining their efforts by networking with 40,000 individuals and more than 50 different coalitions (in the United States).

Women Thrive Worldwide has teamed up with a variety of partners, such as local women's groups, the Women, Faith, and Development Alliance (WFDA) formed in 2006, and the Modernizing Foreign Assistance Network, better known as MFAN, established two years after WFDA.

The focus of this organization is on women, because women have a much higher risk of living in poverty than their male counterparts. In fact, sociologists have found that single women in the United States are 10 times more likely to live in poverty than men; one part of this multifaceted reason is the unequal paid wages in labor (Cawthorne, 2008). Women not only in the United States but around the world are more often associated with sharing their scarce resources with their children and their community at large. Due to economic and social barriers that hold back women around the world, they constantly face discrimination that prevents them from having enough money to survive, let alone being able to support their family, as studies have shown that a women's income (in third-world countries) is spent on food, health care, and whatever education is being offered to their children. Research has shown that girls who are educated have a greater chance of survival and are three times less likely to contract AIDS (Cawthorne, 2008). Most unindustrialized countries do not offer free education to children, so it is pressed upon the family to try and afford this privilege.

The organization listens to the voices of both sexes and explains why it is important to invest in women. By listening to these individuals, one can learn how to help and teach women new things, not simply by ordering women to do a task. It is important to understand that women often put themselves last as they prefer to feed their children and starve themselves if there is not enough food for both. Women account for 829 million persons out of the 1 billion-plus living in extreme forms of poverty (Cawthorne, 2008).

Women Thrive Worldwide has raised the question that if one is unaware of the burdens that these women face, how are we able to help them without first understanding what their needs are? While this organization has made significant changes in the lives of countless women, they are a small group of dedicated humanitarians that function on a tight budget. They work to spread their ideas to leaders in Washington, D.C., in an effort to rally support for foreign aid. They are actually able to create solutions to problems that so many women face on a daily basis with hard facts and evidence that their methods work; in return they empower not only women, but their surrounding communities as well. Women help to educate and encourage others to become involved in their own governmental systems and be aware of U.S. aid programs that are accessible in their country. This organization understands how to partner with others, build a coalition, and has a passion to achieve their goal in helping women worldwide, which will then lead to ending the fight on world poverty.

The organization also stresses the fact that as Americans, citizens have a powerful voice to help change and make the U.S. Congress sit up and take notice. We have the power to influence and pressure our government to do more, as the United States only spends 1 percent of its federal budget to help those internationally. Americans have this leverage, but this advantage largely goes unrecognized.

One example of this organization's action took place in 2005, where it helped women receive small loans to build back their businesses after the tsunami in Sri Lanka. The organization visited this place that was struck with disaster the year before to make sure the funds were received and used properly. What followed was a tremendous rise in prosperity due to their action to help women.

The website explains in detail the five main issues that face women. They are Economic Opportunity, Violence, Food Security, International Assistance, and Fair Trade. On the topic of food, the organization's Food Security Campaign called Help Women Feed the World challenges its readers to create a meal on $2, a daily budget that 2.5 billion people live on in some parts of the world (nearly a billion people manage to live on a $1 or less). Another interesting feature on their website under the tab of "Press Room" are various videos that portray a wide variety of issues covered by the organization.

The organization has received numerous awards and has been cited as a worthwhile charity from rating agencies, winning 4 stars in 2010 from the Charity Navigator Organization, and is recognized by the Catalogue for Philanthropy in greater Washington, D.C. On Women Thrive Worldwide's website, under the "Get Involved" tab, they list three fair-trade companies that offer eco-friendly, recycled, handmade gifts that help support the women who craft these items, with a portion of the purchase price going to the Women Thrive Worldwide Organization.

See also: Nongovernmental Organizations (NGOs)

Further Reading

CAMFED Organization: http://US.camfed.org
Cawthorne, A. (2008). The straight facts on women in poverty. *Center for American Progress.* Retrieved September 17, 2012, from http://www.americanprogress.org/issues/women/report/2008/10/08/5103/the-straight-facts-on-women-in-poverty/
Women Thrive Worldwide: http://www.womenthrive.org

Natasha A. Abdin

WORKPLACE VIOLENCE AND DOMESTIC ABUSE

Workplace violence involves violent acts, including physical assaults and threats of assaults, directed toward persons at work or on duty, according to the National Institute for Occupational Safety (NIOSH) (2001). Examples of workplace violence range from verbally offensive or threatening language to sexual harassment or assault and stalking. Domestic violence is another example of workplace violence and is one of the more common forms. According to a 2006 study from the U.S. Bureau of Labor Statistics, almost one-quarter of private industry establishments with more than 1,000 employees reported at least one incidence of domestic violence in 2005.

The Centers for Disease Control and Prevention (CDC), NIOSH, and the Occupational Safety and Health Administration (OSHA) typically classify workplace violence into four types: (1) criminal intent; (2) customer/client; (3) worker-on-worker; and (4) personal relationship.

Governmental data has shown that approximately 24 percent of workplace violence is related to personal relationships. This most often includes instances when someone who is not an employee gains access to and commits a crime at a specified work site against an employer or customer/client who is a current or former intimate partner. For example, a survivor of domestic violence may be stalked at the workplace by her abuser, or the abuser may constantly issue threats while at work via phone or e-mail. The same behaviors might occur between two employees who formerly had a relationship. In the worst cases, abusers injure or even kill victims at workplaces, and sometimes target others who are on site as well. Stalking is perhaps the most worrisome behavior, in that studies repeatedly have verified that stalking is a predictor of lethal domestic violence. In 85 percent of cases in which a victim is murdered by an abuser, s/he had been stalked prior.

A 1998 study of domestic violence survivors found that 74 percent of employed battered women were harassed by their partner while they were at work. In 2005, the U.S. Department of Labor conducted a national telephone survey of 1,200 full-time employees, finding that 21 percent had experienced domestic violence and 44 percent had experienced some impact of domestic violence at their workplace. One study found 44 percent of female victims were left without transportation when an abuser disabled their car or hid their keys, prohibiting them from going to work. Seventy-five percent of abusers use workplace resources to control their victims.

They may use company phones, e-mails, and vehicles, and may use paid work time to attend court.

According to the U.S. Department of Labor Bureau of Labor Statistics, between 1997 and 2009 spouses, boyfriends/girlfriends and ex-boyfriends/ex-girlfriends were responsible for a total of 369 on-the-job deaths. Women are at much greater risk of being killed by an intimate partner at the workplace (321 deaths to 38 for men). Tiesman, Gurka, Konda, Coben, and Amandus (2012) found that the perpetrator was a current or former intimate partner in almost one-third of all the cases in which a woman was killed in U.S. workplaces between 2003 and 2009.

Signs that an employee may be experiencing domestic violence include:

- Arriving to work late or very early
- Unplanned or increased use of earned time or paid time off
- Decreased productivity
- Tension around receiving repeated personal phone calls
- Wearing long sleeves on a hot day or sunglasses inside
- Difficulty making decisions alone
- Avoiding windows
- Repeated discussion of marital or relationship problems
- Flowers or gifts sent to work for no apparent reason
- Vague, nonspecific medical complaints

Workplace domestic violence takes a toll on productivity. Arias and Corso (2005) conducted a telephone survey of 8,000 women and found that those involved in abusive relationships lost an average of 7.2 days of work-related productivity. Domestic violence impacts victims' concentration, ability to perform job duties, punctuality, and attendance. A 2005 study in Maine found that 60 percent of victims had lost their jobs to domestic abuse. The impact of domestic violence in the workplace is felt not just by victims but by the entire society. Domestic violence results in, on the whole, the loss of more than 7.9 million workdays annually, which is the equivalent of 32,000 full-time jobs, according to the CDC. The CDC has estimated in 1995 that intimate partner rape, physical assault, and stalking cost a total of $5.8 billion each year for direct medical and mental health care services and lost productivity from paid work and household chores. Updated in 2003, the cost was estimated at $8.3 billion and is surely far higher in 2012. According to the Bureau of Labor Statistics in 2008, Americans suffer 2.2 million medically treated injuries due to interpersonal violence annually, at a cost of $37 billion ($33 billion in productivity losses, $4 billion in medical treatment).

In the 1990s, corporations began to pay more attention to workplace domestic violence. A 2007 survey by Safe Horizon, the Corporate Alliance to End Partner Violence, and Liz Claiborne Inc. found 63 percent of corporate executives believe domestic violence is a major societal problem and 55 percent believe it to impact their companies' productivity. Despite understanding of the seriousness of the problem, only 13 percent said they think their company has a role in addressing domestic violence. Further, less than 30 percent of U.S. workplaces have a formal policy or program to address workplace domestic violence. Employers should care, though, as they may be held liable in certain cases. In one case, a wrongful death action against an employer who failed to respond to an employee's risk of domestic violence on the job cost the employer $850,000.

Victims can obtain protection orders that can be applied to the workplace. Such orders list places the abuser must stay a specified distance from, which can include the work site. Employees who obtain such orders must inform relevant staff, such as Human Resources, to ensure all key people are aware of the order and a protocol is developed should the abuser show up. In some places, an employer can seek a restraining order against someone who has disrupted or harassed employees. In Arizona, Arkansas, and California, an employer can petition for a restraining order on behalf of someone else. Experts recommend, however, that employers do this only in consultation with the victim, as proceeding against his or her wishes may increase the risk. In North Carolina and Nevada, the law requires consultation with the victim before a petition can be filed. Whether it is the victim or employer who applies for the order, it is imperative that safety plans be developed, as victims are at increased risk when separating from abusers. Numerous studies have found that more than 70 percent of women who are injured from domestic violence sustained their injuries after separation.

Aside from seeking or supporting victims in obtaining protection orders, employers can play an important role for victims by simply listening and expressing support. Employers can discuss what the victim needs and identify a personalized plan to ensure everyone's safety. In some cases, it might be appropriate to temporarily reassign job duties for the victim. For instance, if his/her work is generally in a very public area of the work site, perhaps a move to a less open space would be helpful. Work hours can be changed, and in some cases an employee could be allowed to temporarily complete work assignments remotely. Phone numbers can be changed, as can e-mail addresses, and receptionists can be cautioned not to forward calls from the abuser. Direct deposits of paychecks can be adjusted so the abuser no longer has access. Another employee or a security guard could be asked or assigned to accompany the victim to his or her vehicle after work. Consistent with federal legislation, all employee information must remain confidential and secure. Additionally, employers can assist victims with developing safety plans or can make appropriate referrals to agencies that can help. Family and medical leave laws may require employers to allow leave for employees enduring domestic violence. Twenty-one states have this type of legislation

Employers can also help obtain important documentation of the abuse. Helping victims save voice mails and e-mails, documenting frequency of contact via phone or in person, and any violations of protection orders can be incredibly helpful. In the case of Susan Stills of New York, it was, in part, her employers' records of Susan's bruises and other injuries, harassing phone calls, and missed time that resulted in her husband's conviction for domestic violence. Because the records showed numerous violent incidents, Susan's abuser was given a 36-year sentence, the longest ever in New York state in a case that did not result in a homicide.

The Corporate Alliance to End Partner Abuse has identified several companies as having best practices when it comes to preventing and responding to domestic violence. At the top of the list is Allstate Insurance Company, the nation's largest publicly held personal insurer.

Allstate Insurance Company is committed to empowering victims of domestic violence. Allstate's SAFE HANDS program provides support to victims by developing programming and funding financial empowerment curricula and training materials and offering grants for service providers. Allstate also encourages its employees to volunteer with local domestic violence centers. The Allstate Foundation Domestic Violence program also coordinates a national conference and annual research poll to address awareness and perceptions of abuse. The Allstate Foundation is also working with the National Network to End Domestic Violence (NNEDV) to develop public awareness campaigns.

In addition, Allstate has repeatedly been acknowledged for being a great place to work, in particular for females. *Chicago* magazine named Allstate on the top five places to work in 2005, and Diversity Inc. called Allstate a "Top 10" company for its commitment to diversity. It was named a top company for executive women by the National Association of Female Executives (NAFE) in 2006. In September 2005, Allstate was named one of the 100 Best Companies for Working Mothers by *Working Mother* magazine. This was Allstate's 15th time being selected as such. In May 2005, Allstate was one of only eight companies named "Best Companies for Women of Color" by *Working Mother*.

On April 18, 2012, President Obama signed a memorandum requiring federal agencies to develop policies to address the workplace effects of domestic violence and provide assistance to employees who are victims. Workplaces Respond to Domestic & Sexual Violence provides a useful tool for employers seeking to develop such policies. It is available at http://www.workplacesrespond.org/policy_tool/begin. The Corporate Alliance to End Partner Abuse also has a variety of useful tools (http://www.caepv.org), as does the Safe at Work Coalition (http://www.safeatworkcoalition.org).

See also: Financial Abuse; Technology and Domestic Abuse; Types of Domestic Abuse; Verizon Foundation

Further Reading

Arias I., & Corso P. (2005). Average cost per person victimized by an intimate partner of the opposite gender: A comparison of men and women. *Violence and Victims, 20*(4), 379–391.

CAEPV National Benchmark Telephone Survey. (2005). Corporate Alliance to End Partner Violence. Retrieved from http://www.caepv.org/getinfo/facts_stats.php?factsec=3

Corporate Alliance to End Partner Abuse: http://www.caepv.org/

Corporate Leaders and America's Workforce on Domestic Violence Survey. (2007). Safe Horizon, the Corporate Alliance to End Partner Violence, and Liz Claiborne Inc. Retrieved from http://www.caepv.org/about/program_detail.php?refID=34

Costs of intimate partner violence against women in the United States. (2003). Centers for Disease Control and Prevention, National Center for Injury Prevention and Control. Retrieved from http://www.cdc.gov/violenceprevention/pdf/IPVBook-a.pdf

The Facts on Workplace and Domestic Violence: http://www.futureswithoutviolence.org/userfiles/file/Workplace/Workplace.pdf

Max, W., Rice, D., Finkelstein, E., Bardwell, R., & Leadbetter, S. (2004). The economic toll of intimate partner violence against women in the United States. *Violence and Victims*, *19*(3), 259–272.

Ridley, E., Rioux, J., Lim, K., Mason, D., Houghton, K., Luppi, F., & Melody, T. (2005). Domestic violence survivors at work: How perpetrators impact employment. Maine Department of Labor and Family Crisis Services Retrieved from Safe at Work Coalition: http://www.safeatworkcoalition.org/whatisdv.htm

Tiesman, H., Gurka, K., Konda, S., Coben, J., & Amandus, H. (2012). Workplace homicides among U.S. women: The role of intimate partner violence. *Annals of Epidemiology*, 22, 277–284.

U.S. Department of Labor, Bureau of Labor Statistics. (2010). Occupational Homicides by Selected Characteristics, 1997–2009. Retrieved from http://www.bls.gov/iif/oshwc/cfoi/work_hom.pdf

U.S. Department of Labor, Bureau of Labor Statistics. (2006). *Survey of workplace violence prevention*, 2005. Washington, DC. Retrieved from http://www.bls.gov/iif/oshwc/osnr0026.pdf

Workplaces Respond to Domestic and Sexual Violence: A National Resource Center: http://www.workplacesrespond.org/

Laura L. Finley

WORLD HEALTH ORGANIZATION (WHO)

The World Health Organization (WHO), in addition to seeing to its mandate of eliminating disease, dealing with global health issues, and attaining the highest level of health for all people, has taken up the issue of domestic abuse seriously. Its 2005 landmark study based on interviews with more than 24,000 women from rural and urban areas in 10 countries—Bangladesh, Brazil, Ethiopia, Japan, Namibia, Peru, Samoa, Serbia and Montenegro, Thailand, and the United Republic of Tanzania—revealed that women are more at risk at home than on the streets. One Peruvian woman interviewed is reported as saying: "He hit me in the belly and made me miscarry two babies—identical or fraternal twins, I don't know. I went to the Loayza hospital with heavy bleeding and they cleaned me up" (WHO, 2005). With this report and since the establishment of the Department of Gender, Women and Health (GWH), the WHO has continually been at the forefront of issues of domestic abuse as it has troubling repercussions on women's health.

The origin of WHO dates back to the United Nations Conference on International Organization, which took place in San Francisco in 1945. But it was the International Health Conference, organized from June 19 to July 22, 1946, that adopted the constitution of what will become the "World Health Organization," thereby crystallizing the need to have a single international entity to oversee global public health issues. The WHO was formally established on April 7, 1948, as a specialized arm of the United Nations (UN). This organization, formed right after the two world wars, took over the public health functions of the Health Organization of the erstwhile League of Nations.

The work of the organization is conducted by the World Health Assembly, the Executive Board, and the Secretariat with funding from member states and donors. The World Health Assembly, made up of delegates from all 194 member states of the United Nations, is the supreme governing body of WHO, which meets at its headquarters in Geneva each year (in May) to decide on the organization's policies and programs. The Assembly appoints the 34-member Board taking into account equitable geographical distribution. The Secretariat is made up of the Director-General and other technical and administrative staff as required. Dr. Margaret Chan is the current Director-General of WHO; she was appointed by the World Health Assembly on November 9, 2006, having worked previously in the capacity of Assistant Director-General for Communicable Diseases as well as Representative of the Director-General for Pandemic Influenza. WHO has regional offices in the six main regions of the world, including country offices that deal with specific and context-specific health challenges. Since 1995, the *World Health Report*, which is WHO's major annual publication, has been giving regular reports on global health issues affecting its member states. This has been a key health policy document for governments, donors, and other health stakeholders.

The WHO's mandate is fulfilled through its core functions, which include providing leadership on matters critical to health and engaging in partnerships where joint action is needed; shaping the research agenda and stimulating the generation, translation, and dissemination of valuable knowledge; setting norms and standards and promoting and monitoring their implementation; articulating ethical and evidence-based policy options; providing technical support, catalyzing change, and building sustainable institutional capacity; and monitoring the health situation and assessing health trends.

On the specific issue of domestic abuse, the United Nations defines violence against women as "any act of gender-based violence that results in, or is likely to result in, physical, sexual or mental harm or suffering to women, including threats of such acts, coercion or arbitrary deprivation of liberty, whether occurring in public or in private life" (WHO, 2011). An additional principle in WHO's Constitution considers health to be a state of complete well-being, socially, mentally, and physically. Thus, being in good health does not merely suggest the absence of disease or infirmity. It is in line with this definition and the organization's mandate to eradicate all forms of gender-based violence and harm that the UN General Assembly in 1999 designated November 25 as the International Day for the Elimination of Violence against Women. Other days recognized and sanctioned by the WHO include the World Health Day, which falls on April 7 of each year; World AIDS Day; and World Mental Health Day.

In recent years, the WHO's Department of Gender, Women and Health (GWH), which seeks to draw attention to the ways in which biological and sociocultural factors affect the health of women and men, boys and girls, has been committed to Millennium Development Goal 3—gender equality and empowerment of women. To GWH, as expressed by many other gender-oriented groups, the achievement of the MDGs by 2015 is highly incumbent on the achievement of Goal 3. Global health concerns continue to grow, and the controversy surrounding some of them, including the politicization of health policy, cannot go unnoticed. However, the WHO has been committed to dealing with these issues and is therefore fully ensnared in world health politics through public research, advocacy, and several other campaign activities. Through these initiatives, the WHO, in conjunction with other human rights organizations, has been able to bring the issue of domestic abuse into the limelight.

See also: Nongovernmental Organizations; The United Nations and Domestic Abuse

Further Reading

Burci, G. L., & Vignes, C-H. (2004). *World Health Organization.* The Hague, the Netherlands: Kluwer Law International.

Department of Gender, Women and Health—WHO. http://www.who.int/gender/en/

Ellsberg, M., & Heise, L. (2005). *Researching violence against women: A practical guide for researchers and activists.* World Health Organization (Dept. of Gender, Women and Health).

Lee, K. (2009). *The World Health Organization (WHO).* Oxon, England, and New York, NY: Routledge.

The World Health Organization. (2005). WHO multi-country study on women's health and domestic violence against women. Geneva, Switzerland: WHO. http://www.who.int/gender/violence/who_multicountry_study/en/

The World Health Organization. (2007). Working for health: An introduction to the World Health Organization. Geneva, Switzerland: WHO. http://www.who.int/about/brochure_en.pdf

The World Health Organization. (2011). Violence against women factsheet, http://www.who.int/mediacentre/factsheets/fs239/en/index.html

Nathan Andrews

Appendix 1: Primary Documents

1. Convention on the Elimination of All Forms of Discrimination Against Women

In Brief:
CEDAW is the only international human rights treaty that specifically addresses gender equality. To date, 187 countries have ratified CEDAW. The United States has not. (For more information, see entry on **Convention on the Elimination of All Forms of Discrimination against Women (CEDAW)** *in the encyclopedia.)*

INTRODUCTION

On 18 December 1979, the Convention on the Elimination of All Forms of Discrimination against Women was adopted by the United Nations General Assembly. It entered into force as an international treaty on 3 September 1981 after the twentieth country had ratified it. By the tenth anniversary of the Convention in 1989, almost one hundred nations have agreed to be bound by its provisions.

The Convention was the culmination of more than thirty years of work by the United Nations Commission on the Status of Women, a body established in 1946 to monitor the situation of women and to promote women's rights. The Commission's work has been instrumental in bringing to light all the areas in which women are denied equality with men. These efforts for the advancement of women have resulted in several declarations and conventions, of which the Convention on the Elimination of All Forms of Discrimination against Women is the central and most comprehensive document.

Among the international human rights treaties, the Convention takes an important place in bringing the female half of humanity into the focus of human rights concerns. The spirit of the Convention is rooted in the goals of the United Nations: to reaffirm faith in fundamental human rights, in the dignity and worth of the human person, in the equal rights of men and women. The present document spells out the meaning of equality and how it can be achieved. In so doing, the Convention establishes not only an international bill of rights for women, but also an agenda for action by countries to guarantee the enjoyment of those rights.

In its preamble, the Convention explicitly acknowledges that "extensive discrimination against women continues to exist," and emphasizes that such discrimination "violates the principles of equality of rights and respect for human dignity." As defined in article 1, discrimination is understood as "any distinction, exclusion or restriction made o.1 the basis of sex ... in the political, economic, social, cultural, civil or any other field." The Convention gives positive affirmation to the principle of equality by requiring States parties to take "all appropriate measures, including legislation, to ensure the full development and advancement of women, for the purpose of guaranteeing them the exercise and enjoyment of human rights and fundamental freedoms on a basis of equality with men" (article 3).

The agenda for equality is specified in fourteen subsequent articles. In its approach, the Convention covers three dimensions of the situation of women. Civil rights and the legal status of women are dealt with in great detail. In addition, and unlike other human rights treaties, the Convention is also concerned with the dimension of human reproduction as well as with the impact of cultural factors on gender relations.

The legal status of women receives the broadest attention. Concern over the basic rights of political participation has not diminished since the adoption of the Convention on the Political Rights of Women in 1952. Its provisions, therefore, are restated in article 7 of the present document, whereby women are guaranteed the rights to vote, to hold public office and to exercise public functions. This includes equal rights for women to represent their countries at the international level (article 8). The Convention on the Nationality of Married Women—adopted in 1957—is integrated under article 9 providing for the statehood of women, irrespective of their marital status. The Convention, thereby, draws attention to the fact that often women's legal status has been linked to marriage, making them dependent on their husband's nationality rather than individuals in their own right. Articles 10, 11 and 13, respectively, affirm women's rights to non-discrimination in education, employment and economic and social activities. These demands are given special emphasis with regard to the situation of rural women, whose particular struggles and vital economic contributions, as noted in article 14, warrant more attention in policy planning. Article 15 asserts the full equality of women in civil and business matters, demanding that all instruments directed at restricting women's legal capacity "shall be deemed null and void." Finally, in article 16, the Convention returns to the issue of marriage and family relations, asserting the equal rights and obligations of women and men with regard to choice of spouse, parenthood, personal rights and command over property.

Aside from civil rights issues, the Convention also devotes major attention to a most vital concern of women, namely their reproductive rights. The preamble sets the tone by stating that "the role of women in procreation should not be a basis for discrimination." The link between discrimination and women's reproductive role is a matter of recurrent concern in the Convention. For example, it advocates, in article 5, "a proper understanding of maternity as a social function," demanding fully shared responsibility for child-rearing by both sexes. Accordingly, provisions for maternity protection and child-care are proclaimed as essential rights and are incorporated into all areas of the Convention, whether dealing with employment, family law, health care or education. Society's obligation extends to offering social services, especially child-care facilities, that allow individuals to combine family responsibilities with work and participation in public life. Special measures for maternity protection are recommended and "shall not be considered discriminatory." (article 4). "The Convention also affirms women's right to reproductive choice. Notably, it is the only human rights treaty to mention family planning. States parties are obliged to include advice on family planning in the education process (article l O.h) and to develop family codes that guarantee women's rights "to decide freely and responsibly on the number and spacing of their children and to have access to the information, education and means to enable them to exercise these rights" (article 16.e).

The third general thrust of the Convention aims at enlarging our understanding of the concept of human rights, as it gives formal recognition to the influence of culture and tradition on restricting women's enjoyment of their fundamental rights. These forces take shape in stereotypes, customs and norms which give rise to the multitude of legal, political and economic constraints on the advancement of women. Noting this interrelationship, the preamble of the Convention stresses "that a change in the traditional role of men as well as the role of women in society and in the family is needed to achieve full equality of men and women." States parties are therefore obliged to work towards the modification of social and cultural patterns of individual conduct in order to eliminate "prejudices and customary and all other practices which are based on the idea of the inferiority or the superiority of either of the sexes or on stereotyped roles for men and women" (article 5). And Article 1O.c. mandates the revision of textbooks, school programmes and teaching methods with a view to eliminating stereotyped concepts in the field of education. Finally, cultural patterns which define the public realm as a man's world and the domestic sphere as women's domain are strongly targeted in all of the Convention's provisions that affirm the equal responsibilities of both sexes in family life and their equal rights with regard to education and employment. Altogether, the Convention provides a comprehensive framework for challenging the various forces that have created and sustained discrimination based upon sex.

The implementation of the Convention is monitored by the Committee on the Elimination of Discrimination against Women (CEDAW). The Committee's mandate and the administration of the treaty are defined in the Articles 17 to 30 of the Convention. The Committee is composed of 23 experts nominated by their Governments and elected by the States parties as individuals "of high moral standing and competence in the field covered by the Convention."

At least every four years, the States parties are expected to submit a national report to the Committee, indicating the measures they have adopted to give effect to the provisions of the Convention. During its annual session, the Committee members discuss these reports with the Government representatives and explore with them areas for further action by the specific country. The Committee also makes general recommendations to the States parties on matters concerning the elimination of discrimination against women.

The full text of the Convention is set out herein.

CONVENTION ON THE ELIMINATION OF ALL FORMS OF DISCRIMINATION AGAINST WOMEN

The States Parties to the present Convention,

Noting that the Charter of the United Nations reaffirms faith in fundamental human rights, in the dignity and worth of the human person and in the equal rights of men and women,

Noting that the Universal Declaration of Human Rights affirms the principle of the inadmissibility of discrimination and proclaims that all human beings are born free and equal in dignity and rights and that everyone is entitled to all the rights and freedoms set forth therein, without distinction of any kind, including distinction based on sex,

Noting that the States Parties to the International Covenants on Human Rights have the obligation to ensure the equal rights of men and women to enjoy all economic, social, cultural, civil and political rights,

Considering the international conventions concluded under the auspices of the United Nations and the specialized agencies promoting equality of rights of men and women,

Noting also the resolutions, declarations and recommendations adopted by the United Nations and the specialized agencies promoting equality of rights of men and women,

Concerned, however, that despite these various instruments extensive discrimination against women continues to exist,

Recalling that discrimination against women violates the principles of equality of rights and respect for human dignity, is an obstacle to the participation of women, on equal terms with men, in the political, social, economic and cultural life of their countries, hampers the growth of the prosperity of society and the family and makes more difficult the full development of the potentialities of women in the service of their countries and of humanity,

Concerned that in situations of poverty women have the least access to food, health, education, training and opportunities for employment and other needs,

Convinced that the establishment of the new international economic order based on equity and justice will contribute significantly towards the promotion of equality between men and women,

Emphasizing that the eradication of apartheid, all forms of racism, racial discrimination, colonialism, neo-colonialism, aggression, foreign occupation and domination and interference in the internal affairs of States is essential to the full enjoyment of the rights of men and women,

Affirming that the strengthening of international peace and security, the relaxation of international tension, mutual co-operation among all States irrespective of their social and economic systems, general and complete disarmament, in particular nuclear disarmament under strict and effective international control, the affirmation of the principles of justice, equality and mutual benefit in relations among countries and the realization of the right of peoples under alien and colonial domination and foreign occupation to self-determination and independence, as well as respect for national sovereignty and territorial integrity, will promote social progress and development and as a consequence will contribute to the attainment of full equality between men and women,

Convinced that the full and complete development of a country, the welfare of the world and the cause of peace require the maximum participation of women on equal terms with men in all fields,

Bearing in mind the great contribution of women to the welfare of the family and to the development of society, so far not fully recognized, the social significance of maternity and the role of both parents in the family and in the upbringing of children, and aware that the role of women in procreation should not be a basis for discrimination but that the upbringing of children requires a sharing of responsibility between men and women and society as a whole,

Aware that a change in the traditional role of men as well as the role of women in society and in the family is needed to achieve full equality between men and women,

Determined to implement the principles set forth in the Declaration on the Elimination of Discrimination against Women and, for that purpose, to adopt the measures required for the elimination of such discrimination in all its forms and manifestations,

Have agreed on the following:

PART I

Article 1
For the purposes of the present Convention, the term "discrimination against women" shall mean any distinction, exclusion or restriction made on the basis of sex which has the effect or purpose of impairing or nullifying the recognition, enjoyment or exercise by women, irrespective of their marital status, on a basis of equality of men and women, of human rights and fundamental freedoms in the political, economic, social, cultural, civil or any other field.

Article 2
States Parties condemn discrimination against women in all its forms, agree to pursue by all appropriate means and without delay a policy of eliminating discrimination against women and, to this end, undertake:

(a) To embody the principle of the equality of men and women in their national constitutions or other appropriate legislation if not yet incorporated therein and to ensure, through law and other appropriate means, the practical realization of this principle;

(b) To adopt appropriate legislative and other measures, including sanctions where appropriate, prohibiting all discrimination against women;

(c) To establish legal protection of the rights of women on an equal basis with men and to ensure through competent national tribunals and other public institutions the effective protection of women against any act of discrimination;

(d) To refrain from engaging in any act or practice of discrimination against women and to ensure that public authorities and institutions shall act in conformity with this obligation;

(e) To take all appropriate measures to eliminate discrimination against women by any person, organization or enterprise;

(f) To take all appropriate measures, including legislation, to modify or abolish existing laws, regulations, customs and practices which constitute discrimination against women;

(g) To repeal all national penal provisions which constitute discrimination against women.

Article 3
States Parties shall take in all fields, in particular in the political, social, economic and cultural fields, all appropriate measures, including legislation, to en sure the full development and advancement of women , for the purpose of guaranteeing them the exercise and enjoyment of human rights and fundamental freedoms on a basis of equality with men.

Article 4
1. Adoption by States Parties of temporary special measures aimed at accelerating de facto equality between men and women shall not be considered discrimination as defined in the present Convention, but shall in no way entail as a consequence the maintenance of unequal or separate standards; these measures shall be discontinued when the objectives of equality of opportunity and treatment have been achieved.

2. Adoption by States Parties of special measures, including those measures contained in the present Convention, aimed at protecting maternity shall not be considered discriminatory.

Article 5
States Parties shall take all appropriate measures:

(a) To modify the social and cultural patterns of conduct of men and women, with a view to achieving the elimination of prejudices and customary and all other practices which are based on the idea of the inferiority or the superiority of either of the sexes or on stereotyped roles for men and women;

(b) To ensure that family education includes a proper understanding of maternity as a social function and the recognition of the common responsibility of men and women in the upbringing and development of their children, it being understood that the interest of the children is the primordial consideration in all cases.

Article 6
States Parties shall take all appropriate measures, including legislation, to suppress all forms of traffic in women and exploitation of prostitution of women.

PART II

Article 7
States Parties shall take all appropriate measures to eliminate discrimination against women in the political and public life of the country and, in particular, shall ensure to women, on equal terms with men, the right:

(a) To vote in all elections and public referenda and to be eligible for election to all publicly elected bodies;

(b) To participate in the formulation of government policy and the implementation thereof and to hold public office and perform all public functions at all levels of government;

(c) To participate in non-governmental organizations and associations concerned with the public and political life of the country.

Article 8
States Parties shall take all appropriate measures to ensure to women, on equal terms with men and without any discrimination, the opportunity to represent their Governments at the international level and to participate in the work of international organizations.

Article 9
1. States Parties shall grant women equal rights with men to acquire, change or retain their nationality. They shall ensure in particular that neither marriage to an alien nor change of nationality by the husband during marriage shall automatically change the nationality of the wife, render her stateless or force upon her the nationality of the husband.

2. States Parties shall grant women equal rights with men with respect to the nationality of their children.

PART III

Article 10
States Parties shall take all appropriate measures to eliminate discrimination against women in order to ensure to them equal rights with men in the field of education and in particular to ensure, on a basis of equality of men and women:

(a) The same conditions for career and vocational guidance, for access to studies and for the achievement of diplomas in educational establishments of all categories in rural as well as in urban areas; this equality shall be ensured in pre-school, general, technical, professional and higher technical education, as well as in all types of vocational training;

(b) Access to the same curricula, the same examinations, teaching staff with qualifications of the same standard and school premises and equipment of the same quality;

(c) The elimination of any stereotyped concept of the roles of men and women at all levels and in all forms of education by encouraging coeducation and other types of education which will help to achieve this aim and, in particular, by the revision of textbooks and school programmes and the adaptation of teaching methods;

(d) The same opportunities to benefit from scholarships and other study grants;

(e) The same opportunities for access to programmes of continuing education, including adult and functional literacy programmes, particularly those aimed at reducing, at the earliest possible time, any gap in education existing between men and women;

(f) The reduction of female student drop-out rates and the organization of programmes for girls and women who have left school prematurely;

(g) The same Opportunities to participate actively in sports and physical education;

(h) Access to specific educational information to help to ensure the health and well-being of families, including information and advice on family planning.

Article 11

1. States Parties shall take all appropriate measures to eliminate discrimination against women in the field of employment in order to ensure, on a basis of equality of men and women, the same rights, in particular:

(a) The right to work as an inalienable right of all human beings;

(b) The right to the same employment opportunities, including the application of the same criteria for selection in matters of employment;

(c) The right to free choice of profession and employment, the right to promotion, job security and all benefits and conditions of service and the right to receive vocational training and retraining, including apprenticeships, advanced vocational training and recurrent training;

(d) The right to equal remuneration, including benefits, and to equal treatment in respect of work of equal value, as well as equality of treatment in the evaluation of the quality of work;

(e) The right to social security, particularly in cases of retirement, unemployment, sickness, invalidity and old age and other incapacity to work, as well as the right to paid leave;

(f) The right to protection of health and to safety in working conditions, including the safeguarding of the function of reproduction.

2. In order to prevent discrimination against women on the grounds of marriage or maternity and to ensure their effective right to work, States Parties shall take appropriate measures:

(a) To prohibit, subject to the imposition of sanctions, dismissal on the grounds of pregnancy or of maternity leave and discrimination in dismissals on the basis of marital status;

(b) To introduce maternity leave with pay or with comparable social benefits without loss of former employment, seniority or social allowances;

(c) To encourage the provision of the necessary supporting social services to enable parents to combine family obligations with work responsibilities and participation in public life, in particular through promoting the establishment and development of a network of child-care facilities;

(d) To provide special protection to women during pregnancy in types of work proved to be harmful to them.

3. Protective legislation relating to matters covered in this article shall be reviewed periodically in the light of scientific and technological knowledge and shall be revised, repealed or extended as necessary.

Article 12

1. States Parties shall take all appropriate measures to eliminate discrimination against women in the field of health care in order to ensure, on a basis of equality of men and women, access to health care services, including those related to family planning.

2. Notwithstanding the provisions of paragraph 1 of this article, States Parties shall ensure to women appropriate services in connection with pregnancy, confinement and the post-natal period, granting free services where necessary, as well as adequate nutrition during pregnancy and lactation.

Article 13

States Parties shall take all appropriate measures to eliminate discrimination against women in other areas of economic and social life in order to ensure, on a basis of equality of men and women, the same rights, in particular:

(a) The right to family benefits;

(b) The right to bank loans, mortgages and other forms of financial credit;

(c) The right to participate in recreational activities, sports and all aspects of cultural life.

Article 14

1. States Parties shall take into account the particular problems faced by rural women and the significant roles which rural women play in the economic survival of their families, including their work in the non-monetized sectors of the economy, and shall take all appropriate measures to ensure the application of the provisions of the present Convention to women in rural areas.

2. States Parties shall take all appropriate measures to eliminate discrimination against women in rural areas in order to ensure, on a basis of equality of men and

women, that they participate in and benefit from rural development and, in particular, shall ensure to such women the right:

(a) To participate in the elaboration and implementation of development planning at all levels;

(b) To have access to adequate health care facilities, including information, counseling and services in family planning;

(c) To benefit directly from social security programmes;

(d) To obtain all types of training and education, formal and non-formal, including that relating to functional literacy, as well as, inter alia, the benefit of all community and extension services, in order to increase their technical proficiency;

(e) To organize self-help groups and co-operatives in order to obtain equal access to economic opportunities through employment or self-employment;

(f) To participate in all community activities;

(g) To have access to agricultural credit and loans, marketing facilities, appropriate technology and equal treatment in land and agrarian reform as well as in land resettlement schemes;

(h) To enjoy adequate living conditions, particularly in relation to housing, sanitation, electricity and water supply, transport and communications.

PART IV

Article 15

1. States Parties shall accord to women equality with men before the law.

2. States Parties shall accord to women, in civil matters, a legal capacity identical to that of men and the same opportunities to exercise that capacity. In particular, they shall give women equal rights to conclude contracts and to administer property and shall treat them equally in all stages of procedure in courts and tribunals.

3. States Parties agree that all contracts and all other private instruments of any kind with a legal effect which is directed at restricting the legal capacity of women shall be deemed null and void.

4. States Parties shall accord to men and women the same rights with regard to the law relating to the movement of persons and the freedom to choose their residence and domicile.

Article 16

1. States Parties shall take all appropriate measures to eliminate discrimination against women in all matters relating to marriage and family relations and in particular shall ensure, on a basis of equality of men and women:

(a) The same right to enter into marriage;

(b) The same right freely to choose a spouse and to enter into marriage only with their free and full consent;

(c) The same rights and responsibilities during marriage and at its dissolution;

(d) The same rights and responsibilities as parents, irrespective of their marital status, in matters relating to their children; in all cases the interests of the children shall be paramount;

(e) The same rights to decide freely and responsibly on the number and spacing of their children and to have access to the information, education and means to enable them to exercise these rights;

(f) The same rights and responsibilities with regard to guardianship, wardship, trusteeship and adoption of children, or similar institutions where these concepts exist in national legislation; in all cases the interests of the children shall be paramount;

(g) The same personal rights as husband and wife, including the right to choose a family name, a profession and an occupation;

(h) The same rights for both spouses in respect of the ownership, acquisition, management, administration, enjoyment and disposition of property, whether free of charge or for a valuable consideration.

2. The betrothal and the marriage of a child shall have no legal effect, and all necessary action, including legislation, shall be taken to specify a minimum age for marriage and to make the registration of marriages in an official registry compulsory.

PART V

Article 17

1. For the purpose of considering the progress made in the implementation of the present Convention, there shall be established a Committee on the Elimination of Discrimination against Women (hereinafter referred to as the Committee) consisting, at the time of entry into force of the Convention, of eighteen and, after ratification of or accession to the Convention by the thirty-fifth State Party, of twenty-three experts of high moral standing and competence in the field covered by the Convention. The experts shall be elected by States Parties from among their nationals and shall serve in their personal capacity, consideration being given to equitable geographical distribution and to the representation of the different forms of civilization as well as the principal legal systems.

2. The members of the Committee shall be elected by secret ballot from a list of persons nominated by States Parties. Each State Party may nominate one person from among its own nationals.

3. The initial election shall be held six months after the date of the entry into force of the present Convention. At least three months before the date of each election the Secretary-General of the United Nations shall address a letter to the States Parties inviting them to submit their nominations within two months. The Secretary-General shall prepare a list in alphabetical order of all persons thus nominated, indicating the States Parties which have nominated them, and shall submit it to the States Parties.

4. Elections of the members of the Committee shall be held at a meeting of States Parties convened by the Secretary-General at United Nations Headquarters. At that meeting, for which two thirds of the States Parties shall constitute a quorum, the persons elected to the Committee shall be those nominees who obtain the largest number of votes and an absolute majority of the votes of the representatives of States Parties present and voting.

5. The members of the Committee shall be elected for a term of four years. However, the terms of nine of the members elected at the first election shall expire at the end of two years; immediately after the first election the names of these nine members shall be chosen by lot by the Chairman of the Committee.

6. The election of the five additional members of the Committee shall be held in accordance with the provisions of paragraphs 2, 3 and 4 of this article, following the thirty-fifth ratification or accession. The terms of two of the additional members elected on this occasion shall expire at the end of two years, the names of these two members having been chosen by lot by the Chairman of the Committee.

7. For the filling of casual vacancies, the State Party whose expert has ceased to function as a member of the Committee shall appoint another expert from among its nationals, subject to the approval of the Committee.

8. The members of the Committee shall, with the approval of the General Assembly, receive emoluments from United Nations resources on such terms and conditions as the Assembly may decide, having regard to the importance of the Committee's responsibilities.

9. The Secretary-General of the United Nations shall provide the necessary staff and facilities for the effective performance of the functions of the Committee under the present Convention.

Article 18
1. States Parties undertake to submit to the Secretary-General of the United Nations, for consideration by the Committee, a report on the legislative, judicial, administrative or other measures which they have adopted to give effect to the provisions of the present Convention and on the progress made in this respect:

(a) Within one year after the entry into force for the State concerned;

(b) Thereafter at least every four years and further whenever the Committee so requests.

2. Reports may indicate factors and difficulties affecting the degree of fulfillment of obligations under the present Convention.

Article 19
1. The Committee shall adopt its own rules of procedure.
2. The Committee shall elect its officers for a term of two years.

Article 20

1. The Committee shall normally meet for a period of not more than two weeks annually in order to consider the reports submitted in accordance with article 18 of the present Convention.

2. The meetings of the Committee shall normally be held at United Nations Headquarters or at any other convenient place as determined by the Committee.

Article 21

1. The Committee shall, through the Economic and Social Council, report annually to the General Assembly of the United Nations on its activities and may make suggestions and general recommendations based on the examination of reports and information received from the States Parties. Such suggestions and general recommendations shall be included in the report of the Committee together with comments, if any, from States Parties.

2. The Secretary-General of the United Nations shall transmit the reports of the Committee to the Commission on the Status of Women for its information.

Article 22

The specialized agencies shall be entitled to be represented at the consideration of the implementation of such provisions of the present Convention as fall within the scope of their activities. The Committee may invite the specialized agencies to submit reports on the implementation of the Convention in areas falling within the scope of their activities.

PART VI

Article 23

Nothing in the present Convention shall affect any provisions that are more conducive to the achievement of equality between men and women which may be contained:

(a) In the legislation of a State Party; or

(b) In any other international convention, treaty or agreement in force for that State.

Article 24

States Parties undertake to adopt all necessary measures at the national level aimed at achieving the full realization of the rights recognized in the present Convention.

Article 25

1. The present Convention shall be open for signature by all States.

2. The Secretary-General of the United Nations is designated as the depositary of the present Convention.

3. The present Convention is subject to ratification. Instruments of ratification shall be deposited with the Secretary-General of the United Nations.

4. The present Convention shall be open to accession by all States. Accession shall be effected by the deposit of an instrument of accession with the Secretary-General of the United Nations.

Article 26
1. A request for the revision of the present Convention may be made at any time by any State Party by means of a notification in writing addressed to the Secretary-General of the United Nations.

2. The General Assembly of the United Nations shall decide upon the steps, if any, to be taken in respect of such a request.

Article 27
1. The present Convention shall enter into force on the thirtieth day after the date of deposit with the Secretary-General of the United Nations of the twentieth instrument of ratification or accession.

2. For each State ratifying the present Convention or acceding to it after the deposit of the twentieth instrument of ratification or accession, the Convention shall enter into force on the thirtieth day after the date of the deposit of its own instrument of ratification or accession.

Article 28
1. The Secretary-General of the United Nations shall receive and circulate to all States the text of reservations made by States at the time of ratification or accession.

2. A reservation incompatible with the object and purpose of the present Convention shall not be permitted.

3. Reservations may be withdrawn at any time by notification to this effect addressed to the Secretary-General of the United Nations, who shall then inform all States thereof. Such notification shall take effect on the date on which it is received.

Article 29
1. Any dispute between two or more States Parties concerning the interpretation or application of the present Convention which is not settled by negotiation shall, at the request of one of them, be submitted to arbitration. If within six months from the date of the request for arbitration the parties are unable to agree on the organization of the arbitration, any one of those parties may refer the dispute to the International Court of Justice by request in conformity with the Statute of the Court.

2. Each State Party may at the time of signature or ratification of the present Convention or accession thereto declare that it does not consider itself bound by paragraph I of this article. The other States Parties shall not be bound by that paragraph with respect to any State Party which has made such a reservation.

3. Any State Party which has made a reservation in accordance with paragraph 2 of this article may at any time withdraw that reservation by notification to the Secretary-General of the United Nations.

Article 30
The present Convention, the Arabic, Chinese, English, French, Russian and Spanish texts of which are equally authentic, shall be deposited with the Secretary-General of the United Nations.

IN WITNESS WHEREOF the undersigned, duly authorized, have signed the present Convention.

Source: Convention on the Elimination of All Forms of Discrimination against Women. Text. 1979. Available at http://www.un.org/womenwatch/daw/cedaw/cedaw.htm

2. Report of the Inter-American Commission on Human Rights re: *Jessica Lenahan (Gonzales) et al. v. United States*

In Brief:

Jessica Gonzales's (now Lenahan) husband kidnapped her three daughters in 1999, in violation of a restraining order. Gonzales contacted the Castle Rock, Colorado, police multiple times to report the violation and in fear for the safety of her daughters. Police failed to respond, at one point even telling Gonzales to leave them alone. Simon Gonzales subsequently murdered the three girls before being killed by police. After the U.S. Supreme Court ruled that victims in the United States are not entitled to enforcement of their protection orders, Gonzales and her team of lawyers submitted the case to the Inter-American Commission on Human Rights for their consideration. This court determined that enforcement of a protection order is a fundamental human right. For more information, see entry in encyclopedia on **Castle Rock v. Gonzales Case.**

REPORT No. 80/11
CASE 12.626
MERITS
JESSICA LENAHAN (GONZALES) ET AL.
UNITED STATES (*)
July 21, 2011

I. SUMMARY

1. This report concerns a petition presented to the Inter-American Commission on Human Rights (hereinafter the "Commission" or "IACHR") against the Government of the United States (hereinafter the "State" or the "United States") on December 27, 2005, by Caroline Bettinger-Lopez, Emily J. Martin, Lenora Lapidus, Stephen Mcpherson Watt, and Ann Beeson, attorneys-at-law with

---

*Commission Member Dinah L. Shelton did not take part in the discussion and voting on this case, pursuant to Article 17(2) of the Commission's Rules of Procedure.

the American Civil Liberties Union.[1] The petition was presented on behalf of Ms. Jessica Lenahan, formerly Jessica Gonzales,[2] and her deceased daughters Leslie (7), Katheryn (8) and Rebecca (10) Gonzales.

2. The claimants assert in their petition that the United States violated Articles I, II, V, VI, VII, IX, XVIII and XXIV of the American Declaration by failing to exercise due diligence to protect Jessica Lenahan and her daughters from acts of domestic violence perpetrated by the ex-husband of the former and the father of the latter, even though Ms. Lenahan held a restraining order against him. They specifically allege that the police failed to adequately respond to Jessica Lenahan's repeated and urgent calls over several hours reporting that her estranged husband had taken their three minor daughters (ages 7, 8 and 10) in violation of the restraining order, and asking for help. The three girls were found shot to death in the back of their father's truck after the exchange of gunfire that resulted in the death of their father. The petitioners further contend that the State never duly investigated and clarified the circumstances of the death of Jessica Lenahan's daughters, and never provided her with an adequate remedy for the failures of the police. According to the petition, eleven years have passed and Jessica Lenahan still does not know the cause, time and place of her daughters' death.

3. The United States recognizes that the murders of Jessica Lenahan's daughters are "unmistakable tragedies."[3] The State, however, asserts that any petition must be assessed on its merits, based on the evidentiary record and a cognizable basis in the American Declaration. The State claims that its authorities responded as required by law, and that the facts alleged by the petitioners are not supported by the evidentiary record and the information available to the Castle Rock Police Department at the time the events occurred. The State moreover claims that the petitioners cite no provision of the American Declaration that imposes on the United States an affirmative duty, such as the exercise of due diligence, to prevent the commission of individual crimes by private actors, such as the tragic and criminal murders of Jessica Lenahan's daughters.

4. In Report N° 52/07, adopted on July 24, 2007 during its 128th regular period of sessions, the Commission decided to admit the claims advanced by the petitioners under Articles I, II, V, VI, VII, XVIII and XXIV of the American Declaration, and to proceed with consideration of the merits of the petition. At the merits stage, the

---

[1] By note dated October 26, 2006, the Human Rights Clinic of Columbia University Law School was accredited as a co-petitioner, and on July 6, 2011 Peter Rosenblum was accredited as co-counsel and Director of said Clinic. By note dated October 15, 2007, Ms. Araceli Martínez-Olguín, from the Women's Rights Project of the American Civil Liberties Union, was also accredited as a representative. The University of Miami School of Law Human Rights Clinic was later added as co-petitioner, with Caroline Bettinger-Lopez as a representative of the Human Rights Clinic and lead counsel in the case. Sandra Park from the Women's Rights Project of the American Civil Liberties Union was also accredited later as co-counsel in the case.
[2] The Commission will refer throughout the report to the presumed victim as Jessica Lenahan, which she has indicated is the name she currently uses. See, December 11, 2006 Observations from Petitioners, Ex. E: Declaration of Jessica Ruth Lenahan (Gonzales).
[3] Reply by the Government of the United States of America to the Final Observations Regarding the Merits of the Case by the Petitioners, October 17, 2008, p. 1.

petitioners added to their allegations that the failures of the United States to conduct a thorough investigation into the circumstances surrounding Leslie, Katheryn and Rebecca's deaths also breached Jessica Lenahan's and her family's right to truth in violation of Article IV of the American Declaration.

5. In the present report, having examined the evidence and arguments presented by the parties during the proceedings, the Commission concludes that the State failed to act with due diligence to protect Jessica Lenahan and Leslie, Katheryn and Rebecca Gonzales from domestic violence, which violated the State's obligation not to discriminate and to provide for equal protection before the law under Article II of the American Declaration. The State also failed to undertake reasonable measures to protect the life of Leslie, Katheryn and Rebecca Gonzales in violation of their right to life under Article I of the American Declaration, in conjunction with their right to special protection as girl-children under Article VII of the American Declaration. Finally, the Commission finds that the State violated the right to judicial protection of Jessica Lenahan and her next-of kin, under Article XVIII of the American Declaration. The Commission does not consider that it has sufficient information to find violations of articles V and VI of the American Declaration. As to Articles XXIV and IV of the American Declaration, it considers the claims related to these articles to have been addressed under Article XVIII of the American Declaration.

II. PROCEEDINGS SUBSEQUENT TO ADMISSIBILITY REPORT N° 52/07

6. In Report No. 52/07, adopted on July 24, 2007, the Commission declared Ms. Lenahan's petition admissible in respect of Articles I, II, V, VI, VII, XVIII and XXIV of the American Declaration and decided to proceed with the analysis of the merits of the case.

7. Report N° 52/07 was forwarded to the State and to the Petitioners by notes dated October 4, 2007. In the note to the petitioners, the Commission requested that they provide any additional observations they had within a period of two months, in accordance with Article 38(1) of the Commission's Rules of Procedure. In both notes, the Commission placed itself at the disposal of the parties with a view to reaching a friendly settlement of the matter in accordance with Article 38(4) of its Rules, and requested that the parties inform the Commission as soon as possible whether they were interested in this offer. In a communication dated October 12, 2007, the petitioners informed the Commission that they were amenable to engaging in friendly settlement discussions with the United States, which the Commission forwarded to the State on January 30, 2008. By letter dated October 15, 2007, Ms. Araceli Martínez-Olguín from the American Civil Liberties Union requested that all communications from the Commission pertaining to this matter be sent to her as well as to Mr. Watt and Ms. Bettinger-Lopez at their respective addresses.

8. In a communication dated March 24, 2008, the petitioners submitted to the Commission their final observations on the merits of the matter. The Commission forwarded to the State these observations by letter dated March 26, 2008, with a request pursuant to Article 38 (1) of its Rules to present any additional observations

regarding the merits within two months. In a communication dated March 24, 2008, the petitioners also requested a merits hearing before the Commission during its 132° period of sessions. By letter dated August 4, 2008, the petitioners reiterated their request for a merits hearing during the 133° period of sessions, which was granted by the Commission on September 22, 2008. In a communication dated October 16, 2008, the State forwarded to the Commission its merits observations on this matter, which were transmitted to the petitioners on October 21, 2008.

9. The petitioners submitted additional observations and documentation to the Commission on October 21 and 22, 2008; March 12 and July 16, 2009; and January 11, February 20, and June 5, 2010; communications which were all duly forwarded to the State.

10. On August 3, 2009, the Commission requested the State to submit the complete investigation files and all related documentation in reference to the death of Simon Gonzales and of Leslie, Katheryn and Rebecca Gonzales, within a period of one month.

11. The State submitted additional observations to the Commission on April 9, 2010, which were duly forwarded to the petitioners.

12. The Commission convened a merits hearing pertaining to this case during its 133° ordinary period of sessions on October 22, 2008 with the presence of both parties.

13. During the processing of this case, the IACHR has received several *amicus curiae* briefs, which were all duly forwarded to the parties. In a communication dated July 6, 2007, Katherine Caldwell and Andrew Rhys Davies, attorneys for the firm Allen & Overy LLP, submitted an *amici curiae* brief, on behalf of several organizations, entities and international and national networks dedicated to the protection of the rights of women and children.[4] In a communication dated January 4, 2008,

---

[4] The *amicus curiae* brief was also presented by the Center for Justice and International Law (CEJIL); The Latin American and Caribbean Committee for the Defense of Women's Rights (CLADEM); *Asociación Civil por la Igualdad y la Justicia* (ACIJ), Argentina; *Asociación por los Derechos Civiles* (ADC), Argentina; *Centro de Estudios Legales y Sociales* (CELS), Argentina; *Fundación Mujeres en Igualdad*, Argentina; *Fundación para Estudio e Investigación de la Mujer*, Argentina; *Instituto de Derechos Humanos, Facultad de Ciencias Jurídicas y Sociales, Universidad Nacional de La Plata*, Argentina; Tracy Robinson, Faculty of Law, University of the West Indies, Barbados; *La Oficina Jurídica Para la Mujer*, Cochabamba, Bolivia; Constance Backhouse, Professor of Law and University Research Chair, University of Ottawa, Canada; Canadian Association of Sexual Assault Centres, British Columbia, Canada; Harmony House, Ottawa, Ontario, Canada; Professor Elizabeth Sheehy, University of Ottawa Faculty of Law, Canada; *Centro de Derechos Humanos y Litigio Internacional* (CEDHUL), Colombia; *Corporación Sisma - Mujer*, Colombia; *Liga de Mujeres Desplazadas*, Colombia; *Fundación Paniamor*, Costa Rica; *La Fundación PROCAL (Promoción, Capacitación y Acción Alternativa)*, Costa Rica; *Centro de Apoyo Aquelarre* (CEAPA), Dominican Republic; *Movimiento de Mujeres Dominico - Haitiana* (MUDHA), Dominican Republic; *Núcleo de Apoyo a la Mujer* (NAM), Dominican Republic; Jacqueline Sealy-Burke, Director, Legal Aid and Counseling Clinic (LACC), Grenada; *Comisión Mexicana de Defensa y Promoción de los Derechos Humanos, A.C.* (CMDPDH), México; *Organización Popular Independiente, A.C.*, Ciudad Juárez, México; *Organización Red de Mujeres Contra la Violencia*, Nicaragua; *Centro de la Mujer Panameña* (CEMP), Panamá; *Asociación Pro Derechos Humanos* (APRODEH), Lima, Perú; *Red Nacional de Casas de Refugio para Mujeres y Niñas Víctimas de Violencia Familiar y Sexual*, Perú.

Jennifer Brown and Maya Raghu from Legal Momentum; David S. Ettinger and Mary-Christine Sungaila from Horvitz & Levy LLP; and various local, national and international women's rights and human rights organizations,[5] presented an *amicus curiae* brief. On October 15, 2008, the Commission received a supplemental *amicus curiae* brief by Maya Raghu from Legal Momentum; David S. Ettinger and Mary-Christine Sungaila from Horvitz & Levy LLP; and various local, national and international women's rights and human rights organizations.[6]

14. By letter dated October 20, 2008, Professor Rhonda Copelon presented an *amicus curiae* brief on behalf of the International Women's Human Rights Law Clinic of the City University of New York School of Law, the Center for Constitutional Rights and Ms. Ayumi Kusafaka, Prof. Vahida Nainar, Andrew Fields and Jennifer Green. By letter dated October 17, 2008, William W. Oxley, Christopher Chaudoir, Phylipp Smaylovsly, Melanie D. Phillips, and Jonathan Roheim from Orrick, Herrington & Sutcliffe, LLP presented an *amicus curiae* brief with various local, national and international women's rights and human rights organizations as signatories.[7]

15. By communication dated October 17, 2008, Amy Myers, Elizabeth Keyes, and Morgan Lynn from Women Empowered against Violence (WEAVE) presented an

---

[5] The *amicus curiae* brief was also presented by Legal Momentum; World Organization for Human Rights USA; Break the Cycle; Harriet Buhai Center for Family Law; California Women's Law Center; The Feminist Majority Foundation; the Allard K. Lowenstein International Human Rights Clinic; National Center for Women & Policing; The National Congress of Black Women, Inc.; National Organization for Women Foundation, Inc.; National Women's Law Center; and Women Lawyers Association of Los Angeles.

[6] The *amicus curiae* brief was also presented by the *Asociación para el Desarrollo Integral de Personas Violadas*, (ADIVAC); Break the Cycle; Harriett Buhai Center for Family Law; California Women's Law Center; Center for Gender & Refugee Studies; Central American Resource Center; Professor John Cerone; Monica Ghosh Driggers, Esq., Honorable Marjory D. Fields; The Feminist Majority Foundation; Harvard Law School Gender Violence Clinic; Professor Dina Francesca Haynes; Human Rights Watch; The Immigration Law Clinic at the University of Detroit Mercy; The International Women's Human Rights Clinic; The International Committee of the National Lawyers Guild; The Leitner Center for International Law and Justice at Fordham Law School; The Walter Leitner International Human Rights Clinic; Los Angeles Chapter of the National Lawyers Guild; The Allard K. Lowenstein International Human Rights Clinic; National Center for Women & Policing; The National Congress of Black Women, Inc.; National Organization for Women Foundation, Inc.; National Women's Law Center; Professor Sarah Paoletti; Professor Susan Deller Ross; Seton Hall University School of Law Center for Social Justice; Professor Deborah M. Weissman; Women Lawyers Association of Los Angeles; and World Organization for Human Rights USA.

[7] The *amicus curiae* brief was also presented by Break the Cycle; The Children's Rights Project of Public Counsel Law Center; Coalition Against Child Abuse and Neglect (CCAN); Domestic Violence Legal Empowerment Appeals Project (DV LEAP); Family Violence Prevention Fund; Human Rights Watch; Illinois Clemency Project for Battered Women; In Motion; Justice for Children; Men Stopping Violence; The Nassau County Coalition Against Domestic Violence; Pace Women's Justice Center; Rockland Family Shelter; Safe House Center; South Carolina Coalition Against Domestic Violence and Sexual Abuse (SCCADV ASA); Willamette University College of Law, Child and Family Advocacy Clinic.

amicus curiae brief. By communication dated October 17, 2008, Cristina Brandt-Young, Amanda Beltz, and Yisroel Schulman from the Domestic Violence Clinical Center of the New York Legal Assistance Group and Sarah M. Buel, Clinical Professor of Law of the University of Texas School of Law presented an *amicus curiae* brief with various local, national and international women's rights and human rights organizations.[8]

16. By communication dated October 10, 2008, the National Centre for Domestic Violence, Baker & McKenzie (Sydney), Freehills Foundation (Australia) and the Equal Justice Project (Auckland), represented by Lovells LLP, presented an *amicus curiae* brief in support of the petitioner's arguments. By communication dated November 13, 2008, Lucy Simpson and Kirsten Matoy Carlson from the Indian Law Resource Center and Jacqueline Agtuca and Terri Henry from the Sacred Circle National Resource Center to End Violence Against Native Women[9] presented an *amicus curiae* brief.

17. On April 11, 2011, the Commission also received a communication accrediting the University of Miami School of Law Human Rights Clinic as a co-petitioner, and Caroline Bettinger-Lopez as a representative of the Human Rights Clinic and lead counsel in the case. By communication dated April 18, 2011, Sandra Park from the Women's Rights Project of the American Civil Liberties Union was also accredited as co-counsel in the case. On July 6, 2011, the Commission received an additional communication accrediting Peter Rosenblum as co-counsel in the case and as Director of the Human Rights Clinic of Columbia Law School.

III. POSITIONS OF THE PARTIES

A. Position of the Petitioners

18. The petitioners allege that Jessica Lenahan, of Native-American and Latin-American descent, lived in Castle Rock, Colorado and married Simon Gonzales in 1990.[10] In 1996, Simon Gonzales allegedly began adopting abusive behavior

---

[8] The *amicus curiae* brief was also presented by The New York Legal Assistance Group; the University of Texas School of Law Domestic Violence Clinic; the California Partnership to End Domestic Violence; the Domestic Violence Report; the National Association of Women Lawyers; the Sanctuary for Families; Professor Elizabeth Schneider; University of Baltimore Family Law Clinic; University of California at Berkeley Law School (Boalt Hall) Domestic Violence Practicum; University of Cincinnati College of Law Domestic Violence and Civil Protection Order Clinic; University of Toledo College of Law Domestic Violence Clinic; and the Victims Rights Law Center.

[9] The *amicus curiae* brief was also presented on behalf of the Alaska Native Women's Coalition (ANWC); Battered Women's Justice Project (BWJP); Cangleska, Inc., Clan Star, Inc.; La Jolla Indian Tribe (the "Tribe"); Legal Momentum; Mending the Sacred Hoop, Inc. (MSH); National Center on Domestic and Sexual Violence; National Congress of American Indians (NCAI); National Organization of Sisters of Color Ending Sexual Assault (SCESA); Ohitika Najin Win Oti; Our Sister's Keeper Coalition (OSKC); Pauma Band of Mission Indians (the "Tribe"); Qualla Women's Justice Alliance; Shelter of Safety (SOS); Tribal Law and Policy Institute (TLPI); White Buffalo Calf Woman Society, Inc. (WBCWS); Women Spirit Coaltion (WSC); and YMCA Clark County.

[10] Hearing on the matter of *Jessica Gonzales v. United States* at the 127th Ordinary Period of Sessions of the Inter-American Commission on Human Rights, March 2, 2007.

towards Jessica Lenahan and their three daughters Leslie, Katheryn and Rebecca (ages 7, 8 and 10). In 1999, after he attempted to commit suicide, Jessica Lenahan filed for divorce and started living separately from him.

19. They allege that after Jessica Lenahan separated from Simon Gonzales, he continued displaying erratic and unpredictable behavior that harmed her and their daughters. Between January and May, 1999, Simon Gonzales had several run-ins with the Castle Rock Police Department (hereinafter "CRPD"), among these, for road rage while driving with his daughters, for two break-ins to Jessica Lenahan's house, and for trespassing on private property and obstructing public officials at the CRPD station. The petitioners allege that by June 22, 1999, Simon Gonzales was a name that "the CRPD—a small police department in a small town—knew or should have known to be associated with domestic violence and erratic and reckless behavior."[11]

20. Jessica Lenahan requested and obtained a restraining order from the Colorado Courts on May 21, 1999.[12] The petitioners indicate that the temporary restraining order directed Simon Gonzales not to "molest or disturb the peace" of Jessica Lenahan or their children; excluded Simon Gonzales from the family home; and ordered him to "remain at least 100 yards away from this location at all times."[13] The petitioners affirm that the front page of the temporary restraining order noted in capital letters that the reserve side contained "important notices for restrained parties and law enforcement officials."[14] The reverse side of the temporary restraining order allegedly directed law enforcement officials as follows: "You shall use every reasonable means to enforce this restraining order . . . .," according to the requirements of Colorado's mandatory arrest law.[15] When the order was issued, the petitioners report that it was entered into the Colorado Bureau of Investigation's central registry of restraining orders, which is a computerized central database registry that is accessible to any state or local enforcement agency connected to the Bureau, including the Castle Rock Police Department.[16]

21. Jessica Lenahan alleges that, despite the issuance of the temporary order, her former husband continued to terrorize her and the children. She called the CRPD to report this and other violations of the restraining order, but the police ignored most

---

[11] Final Observations Regarding the Merits of the Case submitted by the petitioners, March 24, 2008, p. 9.
[12] See Petitioners' petition dated December 27, 2005, Exhibit A: Temporary Restraining Order dated May 21, 1999 and Petitioners' petition dated December 27, 2005, Exhibit B: Decision of District Court, County of Douglas, State of Colorado making temporary restraining order permanent.
[13] See Petitioners' petition dated December 27, 2005, Exhibit A: Temporary Restraining Order dated May 21, 1999.
[14] See Petitioners' petition dated December 27, 2005, Exhibit A: Temporary Restraining Order dated May 21, 1999.
[15] See Petitioners' petition dated December 27, 2005, Exhibit A: Temporary Restraining Order dated May 21, 1999.
[16] See C.R.S. § 18-6-803.7 (Colorado's Central Registry Statute), Petitioners' petition dated December 27, 2005.

of her calls and in her words: "they would be dismissive of me, and they scolded me for calling them and asking for help."[17]

22. On June 4, 1999, the state court made permanent the temporary restraining order, including slight changes such as granting Jessica Lenahan sole physical custody of the three girls and allowing Simon Gonzales occasional visitation or "parenting time."[18] The petitioners claim that, upon Jessica Lenahan's request, the judge restricted Simon Gonzales' weekly contact with the girls to one "mid-week dinner visit," that Simon and Jessica Lenahan would previously arrange.[19]

23. The petitioners allege that, in Colorado, as in other states, a restraining order represents a judicial determination that any violation of its terms threatens the safety of the domestic violence victim. As with Colorado's mandatory arrest law mentioned previously, restraining orders "are specifically meant to cabin police discretion in determining whether a threat exists in the face of evidence of such a violation."[20]

24. Despite the existence of the restraining order, the petitioners claim that on Tuesday, June 22, 1999, Simon Gonzales abducted his three daughters and their friend from the street in front of Jessica Lenahan's home. Simon Gonzales allegedly abducted his daughters in violation of the restraining order, since time for visitation had not been previously arranged with Jessica Lenahan. In response, over the next ten hours, Jessica Lenahan repeatedly contacted the CRPD to report the children missing, and to request the enforcement of her restraining order. According to the petition, the police continuously ignored her cries for help. During her conversations with various police officers from the CRPD, Jessica Lenahan clearly communicated that Simon Gonzales had abducted the children, in violation of a valid restraining order, that there was no pre-arranged dinner visit, and that she was concerned for the safety of her missing children.

25. The petition relates that Jessica Lenahan first called the police department on June 22nd, 1999, approximately at 5:50 p.m. seeking advice. During this conversation she communicated to the dispatcher that she did not know where her children were, that she thought perhaps her daughters had been taken by her ex-husband, and that this visit had not been pre-arranged as required by the restraining order. She also informed them that their friend Rebecca Robinson had also been taken. Around 7:40 p.m., Jessica Lenahan called the police department a second time

---

[17] Hearing on the matter of *Jessica Gonzales v. United States* at the 127th Ordinary Period of Sessions of the Inter-American Commission on Human Rights, March 2, 2007.
[18] See Petitioners' petition dated December 27, 2005, Exhibit: B, Decision of District Court, County of Douglas, State of Colorado making temporary restraining order permanent.
[19] The exact language of the order was "Respondent, upon reasonable notice, shall be entitled to a mid-week dinner visit with the minor children. Said visit shall be arranged by the parties." See Exhibit B, Petitioners' petition dated December 27, 2005, Decision of District Court, County of Douglas, State of Colorado making temporary restraining order permanent.
[20] Final Observations Regarding the Merits of the Case submitted by the petitioners, March 24, 2008, p. 8.

noting that she held a restraining order against Simon Gonzales and that she was concerned over her children's safety.

26. The petitioners claim that at approximately 7:50 p.m., two hours after Jessica Lenahan first called the Castle Rock Police Department, Officer Brink and Sergeant Ruisi arrived at her house. Jessica Lenahan allegedly showed both officers a copy of the restraining order, which expressly directed them to arrest Simon Gonzales upon violation of the order. Jessica Lenahan explained to the officers that the judge had specifically noted in the order that the dinner visit was to be "pre-arranged" by the parties, that Simon Gonzales's normal visitation night was on Wednesday evenings, and that she had communicated to her former husband that he could not switch nights that week, since the girls had plans for their friend to sleep over.[21] Officer Brink allegedly held the restraining order in his hands and glanced at it briefly, and then communicated to Jessica Lenahan that there was nothing he could do because the children were with their father. The Officers promised Jessica Lenahan that they would drive by Simon Gonzales' apartment to see if he and the girls were there.

27. The petitioners claim that shortly after 8:30 p.m., Jessica Lenahan was able to reach Simon Gonzales by phone and learned that he was with the girls at an amusement park in Denver, approximately 40 minutes from Castle Rock. She also received an alarming call from Simon Gonzales' girlfriend, Rosemary Young, asking questions about his mental health history, his capacity for harming himself or the children, and his access to firearms. Ms. Young also communicated that Simon Gonzales had threatened to drive off a cliff earlier that day.

28. After these calls, Jessica Lenahan became more alarmed and called the CRPD for a third time to communicate her concerns. The dispatcher allegedly communicated to Jessica Lenahan that an officer would be sent to her house, but the officer never arrived. Officer Brink did telephone Jessica Lenahan shortly thereafter, and she explained to him again that she had a restraining order, that it was "highly unusual," "really weird," and "wrong" for Simon Gonzales to have taken the girls to Denver on a weeknight, and that she was "so worried," particularly because it was almost bedtime and the girls were still not home.

29. Jessica Lenahan allegedly called the CRPD a fourth and a fifth time before 10:00 p.m., and requested several actions from Officer Brink including a) that an officer be dispatched to locate Simon Gonzales and the children in Denver, and to call the Denver police; b) to put on a statewide All Points Bulletin[22] for Simon Gonzales and the missing children; and c) to contact Rosemary Young. Officer Brink allegedly refused to perform any of these three actions and asked Jessica Lenahan to wait until

---

[21]December 11, 2006 Observations from Petitioners, Ex. F: Progress Report CR #99-26856, p. 3 (containing statement from Jessica Lenahan's best friend, who was with her when the girls disappeared and who remained with her throughout the course of the evening, stating that "Simon normally has the children on Wednesday nights").
[22]An All Points Bulletin is an electronic dissemination of wanted-person information, known as "APB."

10:00 p.m. to see whether Simon Gonzales returned with the children. In light of police inaction in the face of her concerns, Jessica Lenahan alleges that:

> I was shocked when they responded that there was nothing they could do because Denver was outside of their jurisdiction. I called back and begged them to put out a missing children alert or contact the Denver police, but they refused. The officer told me I needed to take this matter to divorce court and told me to call back if the children were not back home in a few hours. The officer said to me: "at least you know where the children are, they are with their father." I felt totally confused and humiliated. I called the police again and again that night.[23]

30. Jessica Lenahan allegedly called the police department a sixth time around 10:00 p.m. to report that her children were still not home and again informed them about the restraining order. During the call, the dispatcher asked Jessica Lenahan to call back on a non-emergency line and scolded her stating that it was "a little ridiculous making us freak out and thinking the kids are gone."[24] Jessica Lenahan called again a seventh time at midnight to inform the CRPD that she was at her husband's apartment, that no one was home and she feared that her husband had "run off with my girls."[25] The dispatcher told her that she would send an officer, but the officer never arrived.

31. Shortly thereafter, Jessica Lenahan drove to the CRPD where she met with Detective Ahlfinger, to whom she communicated again that she had a restraining order against Simon Gonzales, that she was afraid he had "lost it," and that he might be suicidal. According to the petitioners, inaction and indifference persisted in the response of the police even after Jessica Lenahan went to the Castle Rock Police Department and filed an incident report. The police simply replied that the father of the children had the right to spend time with them, even though she repeatedly mentioned the restraining order against him and that no visitation time had been agreed upon. She was only advised to wait until 10:00 p.m., and when she called at that time, her pleas were dismissed, and she was again told to wait, until 12:00 a.m.

32. The petitioners allege that approximately ten hours after Jessica Lenahan's first call to the police, Simon Gonzales drove up to and parked outside the police station at 3:15 a.m. on June 23, 1999, waited approximately 10-15 minutes, and then

---

[23] Hearing on the matter of *Jessica Gonzales v. United States* at the 127th Ordinary Period of Sessions of the Inter-American Commission on Human Rights, March 2, 2007.

[24] U.S. Response to the Petition Alleging Violations of the Human Rights of Jessica Gonzales by the United States of America and the State of Colorado, September 22, 2006, Tab D: Investigator's Progress Report, CRPD, Castle Rock, Colorado, Third Call at 12:57 hrs., CR #99-3226.

[25] December 11, 2006 Observations from the petitioners, citing U.S. Response to the Petition Alleging Violations of the Human Rights of Jessica Gonzales by the United States of America and the State of Colorado, September 22, 2006, Tab E: Office of the District Attorney, Eighteenth Judicial District. Report Date: 7/1/99, Report by Karen Meskis, Date of offense: 6/23/99 (statement from Dispatcher Lisk noting that "on June 23, 1999 at 0034 hours....Jessica Gonzales called dispatch and stated that she was at her husband's residence in her maroon Explorer and her ex-husband picked up their three kids and had not returned them. She was told to wait for an officer at his location").

began shooting at the station. The police returned fire and shot and killed Simon Gonzales, and then discovered the bodies of Leslie, Katheryn and Rebecca in the back of Simon Gonzales' truck, apparently having been shot to death. The petitioners indicate that Jessica Lenahan trusted that the police would take action, and had she known the police would not do anything to locate her daughters, she would have undertaken steps to find them herself and avoid the tragedy.

33. After hearing about the shooting from Rosemary Young, Jessica Lenahan drove to the police station.[26] The petitioners allege that the officers refused to offer Jessica Lenahan any information on whether the girls were alive or not, and ignored her pleas to see the girls and identify them for about twelve hours. According to the petition, despite repeated pleas from the family, the deaths of Leslie, Katheryn and Rebecca Gonzales were never duly investigated by the State. Jessica Lenahan allegedly never learned any details of how, when and where her daughters died, their death certificates do not state this information, and therefore, she is still unable to include this information on their grave stones.[27]

34. The petitioners claim that, to this day, Jessica Lenahan does not know whether the numerous bullets found inside of their bodies came from Simon Gonzales' gun or the guns of the police officers who fired upon the truck. She also alleges that she has never received any information as to why Simon Gonzales was approved to purchase a gun that night by the Federal Bureau of Investigations, since gun dealers cannot sell guns to individuals who are subject to a restraining order in the United States.

35. The petitioners claim that the investigations conducted by the authorities solely related to the shooting death of Simon Gonzales. According to them, these investigations summarily conclude that Simon Gonzales had murdered his children before the shootout at the CRPD station, yet provide little evidence to substantiate this conclusion. They claim that the evidence in these documents is insufficient to determine which bullets killed the Jessica Lenahan's daughters; those of the CRPD, or those of Simon Gonzales.

36. The petitioners allege that Jessica Lenahan and her family remain deeply traumatized by the deaths of Leslie, Katheryn and Rebecca Gonzales. The petitioners indicate that their sense of loss has been aggravated by the failure of Colorado and federal authorities to adequately investigate these deaths and respond with the information the family seeks. As set forth in the declaration of Jessica Gonzales' mother, Tina Rivera, the entire family has experienced great trauma and feels that closure to their tragedy will only come once questions surrounding the girls' deaths are answered.[28]

---

[26]Hearing on the matter of *Jessica Gonzales v. United States* at the 127th Ordinary Period of Sessions of the Inter-American Commission on Human Rights, March 2, 2007.
[27]Hearing on the matter of *Jessica Gonzales v. United States* at the 127th Ordinary Period of Sessions of the Inter-American Commission on Human Rights, March 2, 2007.
[28]Final Observations Regarding the Merits of the Case submitted by the petitioners, March 24, 2008, Exhibit A: Declaration of Tina Rivera, March 17, 2008.

37. The petitioners indicate that Jessica Lenahan filed suit in the United States District Court for the District of Colorado, a court of federal jurisdiction, alleging that the City of Castle Rock and several police officers had violated her rights under the Due Process Clause of the Fourteenth Amendment, claiming both substantive and procedural due process challenges. Firstly, in the realm of substantive due process, Jessica Lenahan argued that she and her daughters had a right to police protection against harm from her husband. In the realm of procedural due process, she argued that she possessed a protected property interest in the enforcement of the terms of her restraining order and that the Castle Rock police officers' arbitrary denial of that entitlement without due process violated her rights. Jessica Lenahan also claimed that the City had failed to properly train its police officers in relation to the enforcement of restraining orders, and had a policy of "recklessly" disregarding the right to police protection created by such orders.

38. The District Court dismissed Jessica Lenahan's case, and on appeal a panel of judges of the Third Circuit Court of Appeals affirmed in part and reserved in part. This finding was then affirmed in a rehearing before all of the judges of the appellate court ("*en banc*" review).

39. Jessica Lenahan's case reached the Supreme Court, the highest court in the United States. On June 27, 2005, the Supreme Court rejected all of the claims presented by Jessica Lenahan, holding that her due process rights had not been violated. The Supreme Court held that despite Colorado's mandatory arrest law and the express and mandatory terms of her restraining order, Jessica Lenahan had no personal entitlement to police enforcement of the order under the due process clause.

40. The petitioners claim that, under the American Declaration, the judiciary had the obligation to provide a remedy for the police officers' failure to enforce the restraining order issued in favor of Jessica Lenahan in violation of state law and principles of international human rights law, which it failed to do. Moreover, the petitioners claim that the United States Supreme Court's decision in *Town of Castle Rock v. Gonzales* leaves Jessica Lenahan and countless other domestic violence victims in the United States without a judicial remedy by which to hold the police accountable for their failures to protect domestic violence victims and their children.

41. Regarding federal avenues, the petitioners mention two previous decisions from the United States Supreme Court, which read together with *Town of Castle Rock v. Gonzales*, allegedly severely limit access to such avenues for victims of domestic violence perpetrated by private actors.[29] In regards to potential state remedies and due

---

[29] The petition refers to the case of *United States v. Morrison*, 529 U.S. 598 (2000), according to which the United States Supreme Court struck down a federal law which created a cause of action to sue perpetrators for domestic violence by holding that Congress did not have the constitutional authority to adopt such law. The petition also refers to the case of *DeShaney v. Winnebago County Department of Social Services*, 489 U.S. 189 (1989) where the Supreme Court allegedly held that the government is under no substantive obligation to protect an individual from violence committed by a non-State actor.

process for domestic violence victims, the petitioners argue that a civil tort suit under Colorado law against either the Town of Castle Rock or the individual officers involved, although technically available to Jessica Lenehan, would have had no possibility of success due to the doctrine of sovereign immunity. In regards to administrative channels, the petitioners claim that they have thoroughly reviewed a variety of Castle Rock sources, but have not located any information pointing to mechanisms available to file administrative complaints against the CRPD or the Town of Castle Rock.

42. The petitioners finally highlight that domestic violence is a widespread and tolerated phenomenon in the United States that has a disproportionate impact on women and negative repercussions on their children. They maintain that the failings of the Castle Rock Police Department in this case are representative of a larger failure by the United States to exercise due diligence in response to the country's domestic violence epidemic.[30] The petitioners contend that Jessica Lenanan's claims are paradigmatic of those of numerous domestic violence victims in the United States, the majority of which are women and children, who pertain disproportionately to racial and ethnic minorities and to low-income groups. Even though the prevalence, persistence and gravity of the issue are recognized at the state and federal levels, and certain legislative measures have been adopted to confront the problem, the historical response of police officers has been to treat it as a family and private matter of low priority, as compared to other crimes. According to the petitioners, the present case demonstrates that police departments and governments still regularly breach their duties to protect domestic violence victims by failing to enforce restraining orders.

43. The petitioners also recently presented information to the Commission pertaining to two legal developments that they consider pertinent to the Commission's decision in this case. They highlight the 2009 sentence of the Inter-American Court of Human Rights in the case of *Claudia Ivette González and Others v. Mexico*,[31] as a source of key principles of state responsibility in the context of violence against women.[32] They particularly underscore the emphasis of this judgment on the obligation of States to act with due diligence towards acts of violence against women perpetrated by private actors. They also highlight that in April of 2009, the United States Department of Homeland Security articulated a new position recognizing the eligibility of foreign domestic violence victims for asylum in certain circumstances, thereby recognizing state responsibility to protect those victims.

44. The petitioners have presented their legal allegations under Articles I, II, IV, V, VI, VII, XVIII and XXIV of the American Declaration focusing on three main

---

[30]Final Observations Regarding the Merits of the Case submitted by the petitioners, March 24, 2008, page 2.
[31]I/A Court H.R., *Case of González et al. ("Cotton Field") v. Mexico*. Preliminary Objection, Merits, Reparations and Costs. Judgment of November 16, 2009. Series C No. 205.
[32]Petitioners' observations presented on February 19, 2010 and June 5, 2010.

issues.[33] First, they claim this case is about the United States' affirmative obligations under the American Declaration to exercise due diligence to protect domestic violence victims who are beneficiaries of court issued restraining orders when the government has knowledge that those victims, and their children, are in danger. Second, they affirm that this case is about the government's obligation to provide a remedy when it does not comply with its duty to protect. Third, they argue that this case is about a mother's right to truth, information and answers from the State as to when, where and how her daughters died after they were abducted in violation of a domestic violence restraining order, and the police ignored her calls for help.

B. Position of the State

45. The United States recognizes that the murders of Leslie, Katheryn and Rebecca Gonzales are "unmistakable tragedies."[34] The State, however, underscores that any petition must be assessed on its merits, based on the evidentiary record and a cognizable basis in the American Declaration. The State claims that the facts alleged by the petitioners are not supported by the evidentiary record and that the petition has not demonstrated a breach of duty by the United States under the American Declaration. The State claims that the evidentiary record demonstrates that throughout the evening of June 22, 1999 and the early hours of June 23, 1999, the Castle Rock Police Department responded professionally and reasonably to the information Jessica Lenahan provided and that the information available at the time revealed no indication that Simon Gonzales was likely to commit a crime against his own children.

46. In response to the petitioners' overall description of the facts, the State argues that the petitioners' filings in this case present a "misleading, and in some instances, manifestly inaccurate portrayal of the facts."[35] The State identifies three fundamental differences between the petitioners' claims and the actual record in this case.

47. The State first alleges that, contrary to the petitioners' allegations, the record does not support the proposition that the restraining order was actually violated on the evening of June 22, 1999 and that Jessica Lenahan ever conveyed to the CRPD that it had been violated. During Jessica Lenahan's first call to the CRPD, she communicated that she had granted Simon Gonzales permission to see the children that evening for a mid-week dinner visit and that she had discussed with him the logistics for picking up the girls. Furthermore, the State claims that the restraining order granted Simon Gonzales "parenting time with the minor children on alternating weekends commencing after work on Friday evening and continuing through 7:00 p.m. Sunday evening," a "mid-week dinner visit" to

---

[33]Hearing on the matter of *Jessica Gonzales v. United States* at the 133th Ordinary Period of Sessions of the Inter-American Commission on Human Rights, October 22, 2008.

[34]Reply by the Government of the United States of America to the Final Observations Regarding the Merits of the Case by the Petitioners, October 17, 2008, p. 1.

[35]Reply by the Government of the United States of America to the Final Observations Regarding the Merits of the Case by the Petitioners, October 17, 2008, p. 14.

be "arranged by the parties," and two weeks of "extended parenting time during the summer."[36] The State recognizes that the evidentiary record shows that Jessica Lenahan informed the police of the existence of the restraining order during her calls, but maintains that she never conveyed to the police that the restraining order had been violated. Therefore, the State claims that there was no probable cause for the CRPD to believe that the restraining order had been violated and the circumstances did not trigger Colorado's mandatory arrest statute, as petitioners claim.

48. The second difference is that the State denies that Leslie, Katheryn and Rebecca Gonzales were ever abducted by their father. The transcripts of Jessica Lenahan's calls to the CRPD do not reveal any indication that she believed, or that she conveyed to the police, that her daughters had been abducted. She initially sought assistance and advice to determine whether her daughters were with Simon Gonzales or not. The record shows that Jessica Lenahan did not characterize the situation as an "abduction" to the police until after midnight. It was at this point that the CRPD took steps to enter an Attempt to Locate BOLO[37] into the system.

49. The third difference that the State highlights is that it rejects the notion advanced by the petitioners that the police "should have known" that Jessica Lehanan [sic] and her daughters faced a "real and immediate risk." According to the State, Jessica Lenahan never conveyed such a concern to the police during the evening of June 22 of 1999, and Simon Gonzales was not known by the CRPD to be a dangerous individual capable of committing violent crimes. The State recognizes that available information does suggest that Simon Gonzales was emotionally unstable and had been displaying erratic behavior before the murder of the girls, but there is very little in the evidentiary record to suggest that Simon Gonzales was prone to physical violence. The fact that the restraining order granted regular and substantial parenting time to Simon Gonzales outside of the family home would lead a reasonable person to conclude that neither Jessica Lenahan nor the Court considered Simon Gonzales to pose a physical threat to his children.

50. The United States also notes the following about the Commission and its fact-finding capacity:

> .... with due respect to the Commission, it is not a formal judicial body that is fully equipped with a strong set of fact-finding authorities and tools. The Commission's petition and hearing process does not involve a discovery procedure, nor does it have formal rules of evidence or provisions for witness examination and cross-examination. In this context, we urge the Commission to exercise prudence

---

[36]Reply by the Government of the United States of America to the Final Observations Regarding the Merits of the Case by the Petitioners, October 17, 2008, pp. 14-15, citing Petitioners' petition dated December 27, 2005, Exhibit B: Decision of District Court, County of Douglas, State of Colorado making temporary restraining order permanent on June 4, 1999.

[37]BOLO is an acronym for "Be On The Look Out." An Attempt to Locate BOLO is directed to other jurisdictions so that they may notify the requesting police department if they locate the individual in question. Reply by the Government of the United States of America to the Final Observations Regarding the Merits of the Case by the Petitioners, October 17, 2008, p. 9.

and caution with respect to its examination of the facts, and consider that the Petitioners bear the burden of establishing facts that constitute a breach of the Declaration.[38]

51. The State claims that, in the wake of the tragedy, two investigations were undertaken by the Colorado Bureau of Investigations and by the Critical Incident Team (hereinafter "CIT") of the 18th Judicial District which were prompt, extensive and thorough. Moreover, a supplemental report was prepared by one of the investigators called to the scene. The State expresses surprise that the petitioners now argue that, because there was no adequate investigation, the actual cause of the death of the children is unknown. The State considers that the petitioners' suggestion that the gunfire originating from the CRPD officers may have killed the children is contradictory to their original petition and to the evidence amassed in the investigative reports mentioned by the State, which indicate that Simon Gonzales murdered the children.

52. The State moreover sustains that the United States' judicial system, at both the state and federal level, was available to Jessica Lenahan. With respect to the sole legal action initiated by Jessica Lenahan, the judicial process was efficient and fairly considered her claims at every stage of the litigation and the case rose to the United States Supreme Court. That Jessica Lenahan did not ultimately prevail in the particular suit she filed in federal court does not mean that she was denied access to the right to a fair trial or due process under Articles XVIII and XXIV of the American Declaration. The State also affirms that domestic violence victims do have recourses available to them at the state and local level, and that protection orders can effectively safeguard their beneficiaries.

53. The State contends that Ms. Lenahan had access to remedies and that the case she filed was decided on the merits. Other valid legal claims, at the state and administrative level, may have been available to Jessica Lenahan, but she chose not to pursue them, and therefore, there is no way of knowing whether other legal theories she could have asserted would have resulted in an eventual adjudication of the facts.[39] In response to the petitioners' argument that the failure to adequately enforce a

---

[38] Reply by the Government of the United States of America to the Final Observations Regarding the Merits of the Case by the Petitioners, October 17, 2008, p. 60.

[39] For example, the State alleges that Jessica Lenahan never filed a complaint with the Castle Rock Police Department or with the Town of Castle Rock which would have prompted an investigation of her complaint by either entity. In addition, although Jessica Lenahan chose not to pursue a claim under Colorado law, such as a civil suit in State court against the police officers under State tort law, the State alleges that "had she been able to establish that the Castle Rock police officers acted 'willfully and wantonly' outside the scope of their employment, she should have filed a civil suit against them in state court." Furthermore, the State argues that the Colorado Governmental Immunity Statute would have permitted such a suit had she been able to meet this standard. The State also alleges that, had Simon Gonzales survived, an additional range of remedies such as criminal prosecution and criminal or civil contempt proceedings would have been available to Jessica Gonzales.

restraining order must give rise to a cause of action, the State finds this argument unsustainable from a factual and legal perspective.

54. The State also describes a series of additional remedies and protections for victims of domestic violence at the national and state levels, entailing billions of dollars devoted to implementing programs related to domestic violence, as well as diverse laws that have been designed to improve the investigation of domestic violence cases. The State alleges that, at the national level, Congress has adopted three major pieces of legislation that recognize the seriousness of domestic violence and the importance of a nationwide response: the Violence against Women Act of 1994 (hereinafter "VAWA 1994"), the Violence against Women Act of 2000 (hereinafter "VAWA 2000"), and the Violence against Women and Department of Justice Reauthorization Act of 2005 (hereinafter "VAWA 2005").

55. The State alleges that the petitioners cite no provision of the American Declaration that imposes on the United States an affirmative duty, such as the exercise of due diligence, to prevent the commission of individual crimes by private parties. The petitioners cite case law of the Inter-American Court of Human Rights and of the Inter-American Commission on Human Rights, but these precedents cannot be interpreted to impose such a broad affirmative obligation upon the United States to prevent private crimes, such as the tragic and criminal murders of Leslie, Katheryn and Rebecca Gonzalez [sic]. The State moreover claims that the petitioners attempt unsuccessfully to argue that the entire corpus of international human right law and non-binding views of international bodies are embodied in obligations contained in the American Declaration, which in turn, are binding upon the United States. As a legal matter, the United States maintains that it is not bound by obligations contained in human rights treaties it has not joined and the substantive obligations enshrined in these instruments cannot be imported into the American Declaration.

56. In this regard, the State considers that the sentence of the Inter-American Court of Human Rights in the case of *Campo Algodonero* is based in very different legal and factual circumstances from those present in the case of Jessica Lenahan and her daughters.[40] The State alleges that the facts driving this Court sentence centered on the systematic and consistent failure of the Mexican authorities to address the murders and disappearances of hundreds of women in Ciudad Juarez due to an official culture of discrimination and stereotyping; claims that are different from what has been presented in this case. Unlike the police in the case of *Campo Algodonero*, the CRPD officers had no reason to believe that any prevention measures where necessary in this case since Jessica Lenahan did not demonstrate concern for the physical safety of her children throughout her calls. The State also clarifies that the U.S. Department of Homeland Security's position is that under some circumstances, victims of domestic violence may satisfy all of the generally applicable requirements of asylum law; a position which does not translate into a general State recognition of responsibility related to human rights obligations pertaining to this issue.

---

[40] State Observations presented on April 2, 2010.

57. The State emphasizes that "all States owe a moral and political responsibility to their populations to prevent and protect them from acts of abuse by private individuals."[41] States around the world routinely prohibit and sanction such acts under their criminal laws, and the United States' commitment to preventing domestic violence and protecting victims is shown by the steps taken at the state and federal level to respond to domestic violence. For purposes of interpreting the United States' legal obligations, however, the State notes that "it is essential to bear in mind that the judging of governmental action such as in this case has been and will remain a matter of domestic law in the fulfillment of a state's general responsibilities incident to ordered government, rather than a matter of international human rights law to be second-guessed by international bodies." [42]

58. The State moreover alleges that the content of the due diligence standard that the petitioners would like the Commission to apply is substantively unclear. The content of the due diligence standard does not provide guidance to the State with respect to its "putative" duties to prevent private violence other than the need to be "effective," which is the objective of all crime prevention measures. In the same vein, the State claims that even if the Commission applies the "due diligence" or a similar duty, the United States has met this standard.

IV. ANALYSIS

59. In this section, the Commission sets forth its findings of fact and law pertaining to the allegations advanced by the petitioners and the State. In its analysis and in accordance with article 43(1) of its Rules of Procedure, the Commission bases its findings on the arguments and evidence submitted by the parties, the information obtained during the two hearings before the IACHR related to this case,[43] and information that is a matter of public knowledge.[44]

60. First, the Commission proceeds to set forth the facts that it considers proven. Second, the Commission moves on to analyze whether the United States incurred international responsibility under Articles I, II, IV, V, VI, VII, XVIII and XXIV of the American Declaration, based on these facts.

---

[41] Reply by the Government of the United States of America to the Final Observations Regarding the Merits of the Case by the Petitioners, October 17, 2008, p. 41.

[42] Reply by the Government of the United States of America to the Final Observations Regarding the Merits of the Case by the Petitioners, October 17, 2008, p. 41.

[43] Hearing on the matter of *Jessica Gonzales v. United States* at the 133th Ordinary Period of Sessions of the Inter-American Commission on Human Rights, October 22, 2008; Hearing on the matter of *Jessica Gonzales v. United States* at the 127th Ordinary Period of Sessions of the Inter-American Commission on Human Rights, March 2, 2007.

[44] Article 43(1) of the Rules of Procedure of the Inter-American Commission on Human Rights provides that: "The Commission shall deliberate on the merits of the case, to which end it shall prepare a report in which it will examine the arguments, the evidence presented by the parties, and the information obtained during hearings and on-site observations. In addition, the Commission may take into account other information that is a matter of public knowledge."

A. Findings of Fact

61. After a comprehensive review of the arguments and evidence presented by the parties, the Commission concludes that the following facts have been proven:

1. The Existence of a Restraining Order against Simon Gonzales

62. The evidence presented to the Commission shows that at the time of the events subject to this petition, Jessica Lenahan possessed a valid restraining order against Simon Gonzales, initially granted on a temporary basis on May 21, 1999[45] and then rendered permanent on June 4, 1999.[46] The initial order directed Simon Gonzales "not to molest or disturb the peace of the other party or any child;" excluded him from the family home; and ordered Simon Gonzales to remain at least 100 yards away from this location at all times.[47] The Court further found that "physical or emotional harm" would result if Simon Gonzales were not excluded from the "home of the other party."[48] The reserve side of the temporary restraining order reiterated the requirements of Colorado's mandatory arrest law,[49] and contained important instructions for the restrained party and law enforcement officials which are discussed in detail *infra* in paras. 139-140.

63. When rendered permanent on June 4, 1999, the order granted Jessica Lenahan temporary sole physical custody of her three daughters.[50] The order restricted Simon Gonzales' time with his daughters during the week to a "mid-week dinner visit" that Simon Gonzales and Jessica Lenahan had to previously arrange "upon reasonable notice."[51] Simon Gonzales was also authorized parenting time with his daughters on alternating weekends starting after work on Friday evening and continuing through 7:00 p.m. on Sunday evening, and was entitled to two weeks of extended parenting time during the summer.[52] After the order was rendered permanent, Jessica Lenahan and Simon Gonzales would normally arrange for him to have the children on Wednesday nights.[53]

---

[45] See Petitioners' petition dated December 27, 2005, Exhibit A: Temporary Restraining Order dated May 21, 1999.
[46] See Petitioners' petition dated December 27, 2005, Exhibit B: Decision of District Court, County of Douglas, State of Colorado making temporary restraining order permanent on June 4, 1999.
[47] See Petitioners' petition dated December 27, 2005, Exhibit A: Temporary Restraining Order dated May 21, 1999.
[48] See Petitioners' petition dated December 27, 2005, Exhibit A: Temporary Restraining Order dated May 21, 1999.
[49] See C.R.S. § 18-6-803.5 (3), Colorado's Mandatory Arrest Statute, Petitioners' petition dated December 27, 2005.
[50] See Petitioners' petition dated December 27, 2005, Exhibit B: Decision of District Court, County of Douglas, State of Colorado making temporary restraining order permanent.
[51] See Petitioners' petition dated December 27, 2005, Exhibit B: Decision of District Court, County of Douglas, State of Colorado making temporary restraining order permanent.
[52] See Petitioners' petition dated December 27, 2005, Exhibit B: Decision of District Court, County of Douglas, State of Colorado making temporary restraining order permanent.
[53] December 11, 2006 Observations from Petitioners, Tab F: Progress Report, CR #99-26856, Report by Investigator Rick Fahlstedt, Dated July 1, 1999 (Interview with Heather Edmuson, Jessica Gonzales' best friend).

64. When the order was issued, it was entered into the Colorado Bureau of Investigation's central registry of restraining orders, which is a computerized central database registry that is accessible to any state or local enforcement agency connected to the Bureau, including the Castle Rock Police Department.[54] In Colorado, like in other states, a restraining order represents a judicial determination that any violation of its terms threatens the safety of the domestic violence victim. When the Colorado General Assembly passed mandatory arrest legislation in 1994, it held that "the issuance and enforcement of protection orders are of paramount importance in the state of Colorado because protection orders promote safety, reduce violence, and prevent serious harm and death."[55]

2. Simon Gonzales' Family and Criminal History prior to June 22, 1999

65. Throughout Jessica Lenahan's relationship with Simon Gonzales he demonstrated "erratic and emotionally" abusive behavior towards her and her daughters.[56] Jessica Lenahan has described how "he would break our children's toys and other belongings, impose harsh discipline on the children and threaten to kidnap them, drive recklessly, exhibit suicidal behavior, and act verbally, physically, and sexually abusive to me."[57] Simon Gonzales' frightening and destructive behavior continued despite Jessica Lenahan's efforts to separate from him, including forcing Jessica Lenahan to perform sexual favors for clothing and other necessities.[58] He would also stalk her outside of her house, her job and on the phone "at all hours of the day and night," often while high on drugs, and break into her house.[59]

66. Jessica Lenahan initially requested a restraining order from the District Court of Douglas County in Colorado, on May 21, 1999, due to Simon Gonzales' increasingly erratic and unpredictable behavior over the years.[60] As justification, she indicated that Simon Gonzales had committed several incidents of violence against herself and her daughters, including trying to hang himself in the garage in the presence of his daughters and purposely breaking the children's belongings.[61] She expressly indicated that she and her daughters were in imminent danger of "harm to my/our emotional health or welfare if the defendant is not excluded from the

---

[54]See C.R.S. § 18-6-803.7 (Colorado's Central Registry Statute), Petitioners' petition dated December 27, 2005.
[55]See C.R.S. § 13-14-102 (1)(a) *Civil Protection Orders—Legislative Declaration*.
[56]December 11, 2006 Observations from Petitioners, Ex E: Declaration of Jessica Ruth Lehahan [sic] (Gonzales), Dated December 6, 2006, para. 5.
[57]December 11, 2006 Observations from Petitioners, Ex E: Declaration of Jessica Ruth Lehahan [sic] (Gonzales), Dated December 6, 2006, para. 5.
[58]December 11, 2006 Observations from Petitioners, Ex E: Declaration of Jessica Ruth Lehahan [sic] (Gonzales), Dated December 6, 2006, para. 9.
[59]Hearing on the matter of *Jessica Gonzales v. United States* at the 127th Ordinary Period of Sessions of the Inter-American Commission on Human Rights, March 2, 2007.
[60]December 11, 2006 Observations from Petitioners, Ex. A: Jessica Gonzales, Verified Complaint for Restraining Order, May 21, 1999; Ex. E: Declaration of Jessica Ruth Lenahan [sic] (Gonzales), Dated December 6, 2006.
[61]December 11, 2006 Observations from Petitioners, Ex. A: Jessica Gonzales, Verified Complaint for Restraining Order, May 21, 1999.

family home or the home of another."[62] She requested to the Court that Simon Gonzales be allowed only limited contact with her to discuss "alteration of visits or matters concerning the children."[63]

67. Simon Gonzales' criminal history shows that he had several run-ins with the police in the three months preceding June 22, 1999.[64] Jessica Lenahan called the Castle Rock Police Department on at least four occasions during those months to report domestic violence incidents. She reported that Simon Gonzales was stalking her,[65] that he had broken into her house and stolen her wedding rings,[66] that he had entered into her house unlawfully to change the locks on the doors,[67] and that he had loosened the water valves on the sprinklers outside her house so that water flooded her yard and the surrounding neighborhood.[68] Simon Gonzales also received a citation for road rage on April 18, 1999, while his daughters were in his car without seatbelts,[69] and his drivers' license had been suspended by June 23, 1999.[70]

68. When Jessica Lenahan called the CRPD police on May 30, 1999 to report a break-in of her house perpetrated by Simon Gonzales, a CRPD officer was

---

[62] December 11, 2006 Observations from Petitioners, Ex. A: Jessica Gonzales, Verified Complaint for Restraining Order, May 21, 1999.
[63] December 11, 2006 Observations from Petitioners, Ex. A: Jessica Gonzales, Verified Complaint for Restraining Order, May 21, 1999.
[64] December 11, 2006 Observations from Petitioners, Ex. H: Castle Rock Police Department Individual Inquiry on Simon Gonzales, Dated June 23, 1999.
[65] December 11, 2006 Observations from Petitioners, Ex. E: Declaration of Jessica Ruth Lenahan [sic] (Gonzales), Dated December 6, 2006, para. 13.
[66] December 11, 2006 Observations from Petitioners, Ex. E: Declaration of Jessica Ruth Lenahan [sic] (Gonzales), Dated December 6, 2006.
[67] December 11, 2006 Observations from Petitioners, Ex. Q: Castle Rock Police Department Offense Report (Violation of a Restraining Order, Domestic Violence), Dated May 30, 1999.
[68] December 11, 2006 Observations from Petitioners; Ex. I: Critical Incident Team Report, Dated June 23, 1999, R. E. Garrett, Detective, Declaration of Josey Ranson, baby-sitter for the girls and family friend (indicating that "Jessica Ruth made previous police reports noting: Simon deliberately broke the sprinklers while Jessica and the girls were at church. Simon changed the locks on the house after he had moved out, causing Jessica and the girls to be locked out for several hours. The police found Simon in the bedroom after a restraining order had been issued ordering Simon to stay away from the home . . . . Simon had 'lost' control"); Ex. F: Progress Report, CR #99-26856, Report by Investigator Rick Fahlstedt, Dated July 1, 1999, Interview with Ernestine Rivera, Jessica Gonzales' mother (indicating that "Simon had been driving around the house, stalking her [Jessica Gonzales]. That Simon had moved out of the house, but still snuck into the house and hid so he could jump out and scare Jessica or the kids. . . .That Jessica had the locks changed on her house as soon as Simon moved out. That Jessica believes that Simon stole a key from one of the kids. That several weeks ago, Jessica found Simon in her room smoking cigarettes and drinking beer. That Simon was very compulsive and possessive").
[69] December 11, 2006 Observations from Petitioners, Exhibit S: Castle Rock Police Department Municipal Summons, Dated April 18, 1999.
[70] U.S. Response to the Petition Alleging Violations of the Human Rights of Jessica Gonzales by the United States of America and the State of Colorado, September 22, 2006, Tab G: Statement Signed by Cpl. Patricia A. Lisk.

dispatched to her house.[71] At this time, she showed the officer the restraining order and the CRPD later requested that Simon Gonzales come to the police station to discuss the violation of the restraining order.[72] During the CRPD contact with Simon Gonzales, they described him in a police report as "uncooperative" and "initially refused to respond to the Police Department for questioning."[73] When Simon Gonzales did go to the CRPD that day, he entered a restricted area, and was charged with trespass and with the obstruction of public officials.[74] When he was asked by the officer to sign the summons, he "refused," and began to walk out of the lobby in an attempt to keep the officer from serving him the summons.[75]

69. Prior to 1999, the Denver Police had taken Simon Gonzales to a hospital psychiatric facility in 1996 after he attempted suicide in front of Jessica Gonzales and their daughters.[76] A non-extraditable warrant for Mr. Gonzales' arrest had also been issued in Larimer County by June 23, 1999.[77]

---

[71] December 11, 2006 Observations from Petitioners, Ex. Q: Castle Rock Police Department Offense Report (Violation of a Restraining Order, Domestic Violence), Dated May 30, 1999.

[72] December 11, 2006 Observations from Petitioners, Exhibit R: Castle Rock Police Department Offense Report (Trespass on Private Property; Obstruction of Duties of Public Official), Dated May 30, 1999.

[73] December 11, 2006 Observations from Petitioners, Exhibit R: Castle Rock Police Department Offense Report (Trespass on Private Property; Obstruction of Duties of Public Official), Dated May 30, 1999.

[74] December 11, 2006 Observations from Petitioners, Exhibit R: Castle Rock Police Department Offense Report (Trespass on Private Property; Obstruction of Duties of Public Official), Dated May 30, 1999.

[75] Since Simon Gonzales did not listen to the officer, the officer describes how "I placed my right hand on the rear of his neck and my left hand on his left elbow. I turned him around and escorted him to a chair where he was told to sit" and two other officers responded to the lobby to assist with the situation. December 11, 2006 Observations from Petitioners, Exhibit R: Castle Rock Police Department Offense Report (Trespass on Private Property; Obstruction of Duties of Public Official), Dated May 30, 1999.

[76] December 11, 2006 Observations from Petitioners, Ex. E: Declaration of Jessica Ruth Lenahan (Gonzales), Dated December 6, 2006; Ex. F: Progress report, CR #99-26856, Report by Investigator Rick Fahlstedt, Dated July 1, 1999 (including statement from Jessica Gonzales' mother, Ernestine Rivera, "That around January 1997, Simon Gonzales attempted to hang himself in the garage. That Denver police department should have a report on this incident"); Ex. J : Police Emergency Mental Illness Report, June 16, 1996.

[77] U.S. Response to the Petition Alleging Violations of the Human Rights of Jessica Gonzales by the United States of America and the State of Colorado, September 22, 2006, Tab G: Statement signed by Cpl. Patricia A. Lisk, p. 7.

The report including the investigation by the 18th Judicial Critical Incident Team of the shooting death of Simon Gonzales found that records indicated that Simon Gonzales had been contacted by the police prior to June 22, 1999 for the following incidents, among others: on November 7, 1986, Simon Gonzales was arrested for driving under the influence in Pueblo, Colorado; on September 23, 1989, he was arrested for driving under the influence in Denver, Colorado; on April 18, 1999, he was contacted by the CRPD for a traffic altercation; on May 30, 1999, he was contacted by the CRPD for allegedly violating a restraining order issued by Jessica Lenahan; and on May 30, 1999, he was arrested for trespassing in a restricted area of the police building without permission. See, Final Observations Regarding the Merits of the Case submitted by the petitioners, March 24, 2008, Ex. C, 18th Judicial Critical Incident Team Shooting of Simon Gonzalez [sic] Castle Rock PD Case #99-3226.

70. On Tuesday June 22, 1999 in the evening, Simon Gonzales purchased a Taurus 9mm handgun with 9 mm ammunition, from William George Palsulich, who held a Federal Firearms License since 1992.[78] Simon Gonzales went to Palsulich's house at 7:10 p.m on June 22, 1999 with Leslie, Katheryn and Rebecca Gonzales.[79] Simon Gonzales successfully passed a background check processed through the Federal Bureau of Investigations the evening of June 22nd, 1999, which was required to purchase the gun.[80]

3. Jessica Lenahan's Contacts with the Castle Rock Police Department during the Evening of June 22, 1999 and the Morning of June 23, 1999

71. At the time of the events, Jessica Lenahan worked as a janitor at a private cleaning business that serviced the CRPD and knew most of the officers, dispatchers and employees there.[81] Not knowing the whereabouts of her daughters, the record before the Commission shows that Jessica Lenahan had eight contacts with the CRPD during the evening of June 22, 1999 and the morning of June 23, 1999.[82] The eight contacts included four telephone calls she placed to the CRPD emergency line; one telephone call she placed to the CRPD non-emergency line at the request of a dispatcher; one phone call from a CRPD officer; a visit by two CRPD officers to her

---

[78] December 11, 2006 Observations from Petitioners, Tab N: Interview with William George Palsulich by the 18th Judicial District Critical Incident Team Detectives Bobbie Garret and Christian Contos, June 23, 1999, 7:04 p.m; Investigation by the Critical Incident Team (CIT) of 18th Judicial District. See, Exhibit C of the Final Observations Regarding the Merits of the Case submitted by the petitioners, March 24, 2008, p. 32.

[79] December 11, 2006 Observations from Petitioners, Tab N: Interview with William George Palsulich by the 18th Judicial District Critical Incident Team Detectives Bobbie Garret and Christian Contos, June 23, 1999, 7:04 p.m.; Investigation by the Critical Incident Team (CIT) of 18th Judicial District. See, Exhibit C of the Final Observations Regarding the Merits of the Case submitted by the petitioners, March 24, 2008, p. 32.

[80] December 11, 2006 Observations from Petitioners, Tab N: Interview with William George Palsulich by the 18th Judicial District Critical Incident Team Detectives Bobbie Garret and Christian Contos, June 23, 1999, 7:04 p.m.

[81] December 11, 2006 Observations from Petitioners, Ex E: Declaration of Jessica Ruth Lenahan (Gonzales), Dated December 6, 2006.

[82] U.S. Response to the Petition Alleging Violations of the Human Rights of Jessica Gonzales by the United States of America and the State of Colorado, September 22, 2006, Tab A: Jessica Gonzales/Dispatch, Tape Transcription; Tab B: CRPD Incident Report 06/22/99, 19:42 hrs; Tab E: Office of the District Attorney, Eighteenth Judicial District, Report Date: 07/01/99. Report by Karen Meskis, Date of Offense 06/23/99, p. 7 (Statement from Dispatcher Lisk that: At 20:43 Jessica Lenahan called back on a 911 line and stated her children were at Elitches Park with their father); Tab C: Investigator's Progress Report, Castle Rock Police Department, Castle Rock, Colorado, CR# 99-3226, Call from Officer Brink to Jessica Gonzales; Tab D: Investigator's Progress Report, Castle Rock Police Department, Castle Rock, Colorado, Third Call at 21:57 hrs., CR# 99-3226; and Tab F: Castle Rock Police Department Incident Report 90623004, 06/23/99, 00:06 hrs. See also, December 11, 2006 Observations from Petitioners, Ex. B: Jessica Gonzales/Dispatch, Tape Transcription, CR# 99-3223.

house after the first call; and a visit by her to the CRPD station.[83] During each of these contacts, she reported to the police dispatchers that she held a restraining order against Simon Gonzales, that she did not know where her daughters were, that they were children, and that perhaps they could be with their father.[84]

72. Jessica Lenahan first called the Castle Rock Police Station at 7:42 p.m.[85] on the evening of June 22, 1999, to seek advice.[86] During this call, Jessica Lenahan reported to the dispatcher the following:

> I filed a Restraining Order against my husband and we had agreed that whatever night was best, I would let him have the dinner hour .... and I don't know whether he picked them up today or not.... We're leaving but tonight there was no sign of him around or anything and the girls are gone and I don't know if I should go search through town for them.[87]

73. During this call, Jessica Lenahan also communicated to the dispatcher that "the scary part"[88] is that she did not know where her children were, that she was very

---

[83] U.S. Response to the Petition Alleging Violations of the Human Rights of Jessica Gonzales by the United States of America and the State of Colorado, September 22, 2006, Tab A: Jessica Gonzales/Dispatch, Tape Transcription; Tab B: CRPD Incident Report 06/22/99, 19:42 hrs; Tab E: Office of the District Attorney, Eighteenth Judicial District, Report Date: 07/01/99. Report by Karen Meskis, Date of Offense 06/23/99, p. 7 (Statement from Dispatcher Lisk that: At 20:43 Jessica Lenahan called back on a 911 line and stated her children were at Elitches Park with their father); Tab C: Investigator's Progress Report, Castle Rock Police Department, Castle Rock, Colorado, CR# 99-3226, Call from Officer Brink to Jessica Gonzales; Tab D: Investigator's Progress Report, Castle Rock Police Department, Castle Rock, Colorado, Third Call at 21:57 hrs., CR# 99-3226; and Tab F: Castle Rock Police Department Incident Report 90623004, 06/23/99, 00:06 hrs. See also, December 11, 2006 Observations from Petitioners, Ex. B: Jessica Gonzales/Dispatch, Tape Transcription, CR# 99-3223.

[84] U.S. Response to the Petition Alleging Violations of the Human Rights of Jessica Gonzales by the United States of America and the State of Colorado, September 22, 2006, Tab B: CRPD Incident Report 06/22/99, 19:42 hrs.

[85] Petitioner's Observations concerning the September 22, 2006 Response of the United States Government, December 11, 2006, Exhibit G, Castle Rock Police Department Dispatch Log June 22 and June 23, 1999; U.S. Response to the Petition Alleging Violations of the Human Rights of Jessica Gonzales by the United States of America and the State of Colorado, September 22, 2006, Tab A: Jessica Gonzales/Dispatch, Tape Transcription.

[86] U.S. Response to the Petition Alleging Violations of the Human Rights of Jessica Gonzales by the United States of America and the State of Colorado, September 22, 2006, Tab A: Jessica Gonzales/Dispatch, Tape Transcription.

[87] Final Observations Regarding the Merits of the Case submitted by the petitioners, March 24, 2008, p. 10, citing U.S. Response to the Petition Alleging Violations of the Human Rights of Jessica Gonzales by the United States of America and the State of Colorado, September 22, 2006, Tab A: Jessica Gonzales/Dispatch, Tape Transcription.

[88] Final Observations Regarding the Merits of the Case submitted by the petitioners, March 24, 2008, p. 10, citing U.S. Response to the Petition Alleging Violations of the Human Rights of Jessica Gonzales by the United States of America and the State of Colorado, September 22, 2006, Tab A: Jessica Gonzales/Dispatch, Tape Transcription, at 1.

upset[89] and "I just don't know what to do."[90] She indicated that she had last seen them at 5:30 p.m. and that the girls had a friend with them. As a response to this phone call, two officers were dispatched to Jessica Lenahan and Simon Gonzales' houses and drove around Castle Rock looking for his pick-up truck.[91] During the visit of the officers, Jessica Lenahan explained that Simon Gonzales usually communicated with her when he picked up their daughters, but that he had not contacted her that night.[92]

74. When Jessica Lenahan called the police station for a second time at 8:43 p.m., she informed them that she had learned that her husband had taken their daughters to Denver, outside of the Castle Rock police department jurisdiction, without her knowledge.[93] CRPD Officer Brink returned Jessica Lenahan's telephone call,[94] where she communicated that the girls were at Elitches Park in Denver with their father, that she did not consider this "cool" because two of the girls had school the next day, and that she considered this "highly unusual," "wrong," and "weird."[95] Officer Brink in response advised her to inform the Court that her husband had violated their divorce decree, because based on the information she was offering he did not consider the restraining order violated. He closed the conversation by communicating to her that "at least you know where the kids are right now."[96]

---

[89] Final Observations Regarding the Merits of the Case submitted by the petitioners, March 24, 2008.
[90] Final Observations Regarding the Merits of the Case submitted by the petitioners, March 24, 2008, p. 10, citing U.S. Response to the Petition Alleging Violations of the Human Rights of Jessica Gonzales by the United States of America and the State of Colorado, September 22, 2006, Tab A: Jessica Gonzales/Dispatch, Tape Transcription.
[91] U.S. Response to the Petition Alleging Violations of the Human Rights of Jessica Gonzales by the United States of America and the State of Colorado, September 22, 2006, Tab B: CRPD Incident Report 06/22/99, 19:42 hrs; Tab E: Office of the District Attorney, Eighteenth Judicial District. Report Date: 7/01/99, Report by Karen Meskis, Date of offense: 6/23/99, p. 10.
[92] U.S. Response to the Petition Alleging Violations of the Human Rights of Jessica Gonzales by the United States of America and the State of Colorado, September 22, 2006, Tab B: CRPD Incident Report 06/22/99, 19:42 hrs; December 11, 2006 Observations from Petitioners, Tab E: Declaration of Jessica Ruth Lenahan (Gonzalez) [sic], dated December 6, 2006.
[93] U.S. Response to the Petition Alleging Violations of the Human Rights of Jessica Gonzales by the United States of America and the State of Colorado, September 22, 2006, Tab E: Office of the District Attorney, Eighteenth Judicial District. Report Date: 7/01/99, Report by Karen Meskis, Date of offense: 6/23/99.
[94] U.S. Response to the Petition Alleging Violations of the Human Rights of Jessica Gonzales by the United States of America and the State of Colorado, September 22, 2006, Tab C: Investigator's Progress Report, Castle Rock Police Department, Castle Rock, Colorado, Cr #99-3226, Call from Officer Brink to Jessica Gonzales.
[95] U.S. Response to the Petition Alleging Violations of the Human Rights of Jessica Gonzales by the United States of America and the State of Colorado, September 22, 2006, Tab D: Investigator's Progress Report, Castle Rock Police Department, Castle Rock, Colorado, Cr #99-3226, Third Call at 21:57 hours.
[96] U.S. Response to the Petition Alleging Violations of the Human Rights of Jessica Gonzales by the United States of America and the State of Colorado, September 22, 2006, Tab C: Investigator's Progress Report, Castle Rock Police Department, Castle Rock, Colorado, Cr #99-3226, Call from Officer Brink to Jessica Gonzales.

At 8:49 p.m. an entry was made in the CRPD dispatch log of telephone calls reflecting Jessica Lenahan's children had been found as reported by her.[97]

75. Jessica Lenahan called the CRPD a third time at 9:57 p.m. that evening.[98] During this call, she informed the dispatcher that her kids were still not home, that she was upset, and that she "did not know what to do."[99] She related to the dispatcher a conversation she had with Simon Gonzales that evening:

> I, I just told him [Simon Gonzales], I said, you know I would really like to call the cops cause they're looking for you cause we didn't know ...... And he said, we're at Elitches, we're fine. And I'm like, well why didn't you tell me. And he said, well 'cause I thought I had 'em overnight and I said, no, you know you didn't.[100]

76. During the call, the dispatcher asked Jessica Lenahan to call her back on a "non-emergency line."[101] In response to Jessica Lenahan's concerns, the dispatcher communicated to her the following:

> I don't know what else to say, I mean ...... I wish you guys uh, I wish you would have asked or had made some sort of arrangements. I mean that's a little ridiculous making us freak out and thinking the kids are gone ...[102]

---

[97] Petitioner's Observations concerning the September 22, 2006 Response of the United States Government, December 11, 2006, Exhibit G, Castle Rock Police Department Dispatch Log June 22 and June 23, 1999; Final Observations Regarding the Merits of the Case submitted by the petitioners, March 24, 2008, p. 10, citing U.S. Response to the Petition Alleging Violations of the Human Rights of Jessica Gonzales by the United States of America and the State of Colorado, September 22, 2006, Tab E: Office of the District Attorney, Eighteenth Judicial District. Report Date: 7/01/99, Report by Karen Meskis, Date of Offense: 6/23/99, p. 7.

[98] U.S. Response to the Petition Alleging Violations of the Human Rights of Jessica Gonzales by the United States of America and the State of Colorado, September 22, 2006, Tab D: Investigator's Progress Report, Castle Rock Police Department, Castle Rock, Colorado, Cr #99-3226, Third Call at 21:57 hours.

[99] U.S. Response to the Petition Alleging Violations of the Human Rights of Jessica Gonzales by the United States of America and the State of Colorado, September 22, 2006, Tab D: Investigator's Progress Report, Castle Rock Police Department, Castle Rock, Colorado, Cr #99-3226, Third Call at 21:57 hours.

[100] U.S. Response to the Petition Alleging Violations of the Human Rights of Jessica Gonzales by the United States of America and the State of Colorado, September 22, 2006, Tab D: Investigator's Progress Report, Castle Rock Police Department, Castle Rock, Colorado, Cr #99-3226, Third Call at 21:57 hours.

[101] U.S. Response to the Petition Alleging Violations of the Human Rights of Jessica Gonzales by the United States of America and the State of Colorado, September 22, 2006, Tab D: Investigator's Progress Report, Castle Rock Police Department, Castle Rock, Colorado, Cr #99-3226, Third Call at 21:57 hours.

[102] U.S. Response to the Petition Alleging Violations of the Human Rights of Jessica Gonzales by the United States of America and the State of Colorado, September 22, 2006, Tab D: Investigator's Progress Report, Castle Rock Police Department, Castle Rock, Colorado, Cr #99-3226, Third Call at 21:57 hours.

77. To these comments from the dispatcher, Jessica Lenahan answered "well, I mean, I really thought the kids were gone too," that she was a "mess" and that she was "freaking out."[103] The Dispatcher on duty encouraged Jessica Lenahan to try to call the suspect and then also to return a call to the police department.[104] The same Dispatcher later reported that she "could tell [Jessica] Gonzales was nervous."[105] The Dispatcher reported to investigators subsequently her belief that Simon Gonzales had a wish for a vengeance against the police department because of the contact he had with them recently, where he was charged with trespassing.[106]

78. Another dispatcher reported to the state investigators after the shooting death of Simon Gonzales, that Jessica Lenahan also called around midnight to report that her daughters, ages 7, 8, and 10 were still not home.[107] Dispatcher O'Neill indicates in the report that she detected from her conversations with Jessica Lenahan that "she was very worried about her children" and that "she wanted an officer to meet her" at her husband's apartment.[108] Jessica Lenahan informed the dispatcher that Simon Gonzales had run off with the girls.[109] Dispatcher O'Neill advised Jessica Lenahan that an officer would be dispatched and the officer was dispatched by Cpl. Patricia Lisk, but three other calls were pending and the officer was unable to respond.

---

[103] U.S. Response to the Petition Alleging Violations of the Human Rights of Jessica Gonzales by the United States of America and the State of Colorado, September 22, 2006, Tab D: Investigator's Progress Report, Castle Rock Police Department, Castle Rock, Colorado, Cr #99-3226, Third Call at 21:57 hours.

[104] U.S. Response to the Petition Alleging Violations of the Human Rights of Jessica Gonzales by the United States of America and the State of Colorado, September 22, 2006, Tab D: Investigator's Progress Report, Castle Rock Police Department, Castle Rock, Colorado, Cr #99-3226, Third Call at 21:57 hours.

[105] Final Observations Regarding the Merits of the Case submitted by the petitioners, March 24, 2008, p. 10 citing U.S. Response to the Petition Alleging Violations of the Human Rights of Jessica Gonzales by the United States of America and the State of Colorado, September 22, 2006, Tab E: Office of the District Attorney, Eighteenth Judicial District. Report Date: 7/01/99, Report by Karen Meskis, Date of offense: 6/23/99, p. 10.

[106] Final Observations Regarding the Merits of the Case submitted by the petitioners, March 24, 2008, p. 10 citing U.S. Response to the Petition Alleging Violations of the Human Rights of Jessica Gonzales by the United States of America and the State of Colorado, September 22, 2006, Tab E: Office of the District Attorney, Eighteenth Judicial District. Report Date: 7/01/99, Report by Karen Meskis, Date of offense: 6/23/99, p. 10.

[107] December 11, 2006 Observations from Petitioners, Ex. B: Jessica Gonzales/Dispatch, Tape Transcription, CR# 99-3223; U.S. Response to the Petition Alleging Violations of the Human Rights of Jessica Gonzales by the United States of America and the State of Colorado, September 22, 2006, Tab E: Office of the District Attorney, Eighteenth Judicial District. Report Date: 7/01/99, Report by Karen Meskis, Date of offense: 6/23/99, p. 2.

[108] U.S. Response to the Petition Alleging Violations of the Human Rights of Jessica Gonzales by the United States of America and the State of Colorado, September 22, 2006, Tab E: Office of the District Attorney, Eighteenth Judicial District. Report Date: 7/01/99, Report by Karen Meskis, Date of offense: 6/23/99, p. 2.

[109] December 11, 2006 Observations from Petitioners, Ex. B: Jessica Gonzales/Dispatch, Tape Transcription, CR# 99-3223.

79. Jessica Lenahan arrived at the police department at about 12:30 a.m, with her 13-year old son and "was crying."[110] Jessica Lenahan spoke to the dispatchers telling them that "she didn't know what to do" about her children and that she was "scared for them."[111] In response, Officer Aaron Ahlfinger was dispatched to the CRPD to speak to Jessica Lenahan and filed a missing person's report on the children and the truck.[112] She reported to the Officer again that she had a restraining order against Simon Gonzales, that he had picked up their three daughters from her residence around 5:30 p.m that day, that she was afraid he had "lost it," and that he might be suicidal. She was worried that Simon Gonzales had abducted the children, but said "no" when the Officer asked her whether she believed Simon Gonzales would harm them.[113] She informed the Officer that he might have taken the children to the Pueblo Area and that she had tried to reach him via his home and cell phone since 8:00 p.m., but that he was not answering, and that she was getting a message that the lines were disconnected.[114] After Officer Ahlfinger left the station, he drove through Simon Gonzales' neighborhood, but did not see his vehicle in front of the residence and also called him on his home and cell phone.[115]

80. An hour after Jessica Lenahan visited the CRPD station, at 1:40 a.m, Officer Ahlfinger requested that Dispatcher Lisk send an "Attempt to Locate BOLO" for Mr. Gonzales and his vehicle.[116] After Officer Ahlfinger left, Dispatcher Lisk began investigating how to send the bulletin on the "attempt to locate" based on the information she had, but was unable to do so by the time Simon Gonzales arrived at the

---

[110] U.S. Response to the Petition Alleging Violations of the Human Rights of Jessica Gonzales by the United States of America and the State of Colorado, September 22, 2006, Tab E: Office of the District Attorney, Eighteenth Judicial District. Report Date: 07/01/99. Report by Karen Meskis, Date of Offense: 06/23/99, p. 3; See also, Tab F, Castle Rock Police Department Incident Report 90623004, 06/23/99, 00:06 hrs.

[111] U.S. Response to the Petition Alleging Violations of the Human Rights of Jessica Gonzales by the United States of America and the State of Colorado, September 22, 2006, Tab E: Office of the District Attorney, Eighteenth Judicial District. Report Date: 07/01/99. Report by Karen Meskis, Date of Offense: 06/23/99, p. 3; See also, Tab F: Castle Rock Police Department Incident Report 90623004, 06/23/99, 00:06 hrs.

[112] U.S. Response to the Petition Alleging Violations of the Human Rights of Jessica Gonzales by the United States of America and the State of Colorado, September 22, 2006, Tab F, Castle Rock Police Department Incident Report 90623004, 06/23/99, 00:06 hrs.

[113] U.S. Response to the Petition Alleging Violations of the Human Rights of Jessica Gonzales by the United States of America and the State of Colorado, September 22, 2006, Tab F, Castle Rock Police Department Incident Report 90623004, 06/23/99, 00:06 hrs.

[114] U.S. Response to the Petition Alleging Violations of the Human Rights of Jessica Gonzales by the United States of America and the State of Colorado, September 22, 2006, Tab F, Castle Rock Police Department Incident Report 90623004, 06/23/99, 00:06 hrs.

[115] U.S. Response to the Petition Alleging Violations of the Human Rights of Jessica Gonzales by the United States of America and the State of Colorado, September 22, 2006, Tab F, Castle Rock Police Department Incident Report 90623004, 06/23/99, 00:06 hrs.

[116] U.S. Response to the Petition Alleging Violations of the Human Rights of Jessica Gonzales by the United States of America and the State of Colorado, September 22, 2006, Tab G: Statement signed by Cpl. Patricia A. Lisk.

CRPD approximately at 3:25 a.m.[117] In a declaration after the shooting death of Simon Gonzales, she stated that between 2:15—2:45 a.m. she attempted to find the guidelines in the three books pertaining to Attempt to Locates.[118] She also tried to locate information on Simon Gonzales' driver's license and a valid license plate number for the truck he was driving through the Colorado Department of Motor Vehicles.[119] Cpl. Lisk reported to one of the investigators after Simon Gonzales' shooting death that "she had other problems entering information into the screens for the attempt to locate, i.e., no physical descriptions on the children. Dispatcher Lisk reports that she spent a considerable time looking at CBI manuals and trying to determine how to enter the information while dispatching and answering other calls."[120]

81. At approximately 3:25 a.m. Simon Gonzales drove his pick-up truck to the CRPD and fired shots through the window.[121] There was an exchange of gunfire with officers from the station. In the course of this shooting, he was fatally wounded and killed, and when the officers approached the truck they discovered the bodies of three young girls subsequently identified as Leslie, Katheryn, and Rebecca Gonzales.[122]

4. The Investigation of Leslie, Katheryn and Rebecca Gonzales' Deaths by the Authorities

82. The Colorado Bureau of Investigations (hereinafter "CBI") undertook a detailed investigation of the crime scene.[123] The investigation report contains: 1) descriptions

---

[117]U.S. Response to the Petition Alleging Violations of the Human Rights of Jessica Gonzales by the United States of America and the State of Colorado, September 22, 2006, Tab E: Office of the District Attorney, Eighteenth Judicial District. Report Date: 07/01/99. Report by Karen Meskis, Date of Offense: 06/23/99, p. 6.

[118]U.S. Response to the Petition Alleging Violations of the Human Rights of Jessica Gonzales by the United States of America and the State of Colorado, September 22, 2006, Tab G: Statement signed by Cpl. Patricia A. Lisk.

[119]U.S. Response to the Petition Alleging Violations of the Human Rights of Jessica Gonzales by the United States of America and the State of Colorado, September 22, 2006, Tab E: Office of the District Attorney, Eighteenth Judicial District. Report Date: 07/01/99. Report by Karen Meskis, Date of Offense: 06/23/99, p. 6.

[120]U.S. Response to the Petition Alleging Violations of the Human Rights of Jessica Gonzales by the United States of America and the State of Colorado, September 22, 2006, Tab E: Office of the District Attorney, Eighteenth Judicial District. Report Date: 07/01/99. Report by Karen Meskis, Date of Offense: 06/23/99, p. 6.

[121]U.S. Response to the Petition Alleging Violations of the Human Rights of Jessica Gonzales by the United States of America and the State of Colorado, September 22, 2006, Tab E: Office of the District Attorney, Eighteenth Judicial District. Report Date: 07/01/99. Report by Karen Meskis, Date of Offense: 06/23/99.

[122]U.S. Response to the Petition Alleging Violations of the Human Rights of Jessica Gonzales by the United States of America and the State of Colorado, September 22, 2006, Tab E: Office of the District Attorney, Eighteenth Judicial District. Report Date: 07/01/99. Report by Karen Meskis, Date of Offense: 06/23/99, pp. 6-7.

[123]Reply by the Government of the United States of America to the Final Observations Regarding the Merits of the Case by the Petitioners, October 17, 2008, p. 11, mentioning detailed investigation undertaken by the Colorado Bureau of Investigation (CBI), dated July 19, 1999, which can be found at Exhibit B of Final Observations Regarding the Merits of the Case submitted by the petitioners, March 24, 2008.

of the crime scene and how the integrity of the scene was protected by personnel on site, 2) the evidence collected at the crime scene, including evidence relating to the weapons used, and 3) descriptions of the bodies and physical locations of the victims inside the truck. The investigation was undertaken with the involvement of eight CBI crime scene agents, and other personnel on the scene within hours of the shooting.[124] The report of this investigation does not contain any conclusions as to which bullets struck Leslie, Katheryn and Rebecca Gonzales or the time and place of their deaths.

83. A second investigation was undertaken at about 4:30 a.m. on June 23rd by the Critical Incident Team (hereinafter "CIT") of the 18th Judicial District, involving 18 members of the CIT, as well as a number of additional investigators.[125] This report includes descriptions of the interviews with the five officers involved in the shooting death of Simon Gonzales; interviews of 12 witnesses; an interview with Jessica Lenahan; an interview with Simon Gonzales' ex-girlfriend, Rosemary Young; and interviews with other relatives and acquaintances of Simon and Jessica Lenahan.[126] The final report also includes a statement of Simon Gonzales' history; information regarding the autopsies of Simon Gonzales and his daughters; information regarding additional evidence secured from the homes of Simon Gonzales, Jessica Lenahan and Rosemary Young; a description of the physical evidence recovered from the crime scene; and a discussion of Simon Gonzales' possible motives for the shooting at the CRPD.[127]

84. In its "summary of investigation" section, the CIT report states that as a result of the exchange of gunfire between the police officers and Simon Gonzales, "the 18th Judicial District Critical Incident Team was called out to investigate the circumstances surrounding the shooting."[128] Regarding the death of Leslie, Katheryn and

---

[124] Reply by the Government of the United States of America to the Final Observations Regarding the Merits of the Case by the Petitioners, October 17, 2008, p. 11, mentioning detailed investigation undertaken by the Colorado Bureau of Investigation (CBI), dated July 19, 1999, which can be found at Exhibit B of Final Observations Regarding the Merits of the Case submitted by the petitioners, March 24, 2008.

[125] Reply by the Government of the United States of America to the Final Observations Regarding the Merits of the Case by the Petitioners, October 17, 2008, p. 11, mentioning detailed investigation undertaken by the Critical Incident Team (CIT) of the 18th Judicial District, which can be found at Exhibit C of Final Observations Regarding the Merits of the Case submitted by the petitioners, March 24, 2008.

[126] Reply by the Government of the United States of America to the Final Observations Regarding the Merits of the Case by the Petitioners, October 17, 2008, p. 11, mentioning detailed investigation undertaken by the Critical Incident Team (CIT) of the 18th Judicial District, which can be found at Exhibit C of Final Observations Regarding the Merits of the Case submitted by the petitioners, March 24, 2008.

[127] Reply by the Government of the United States of America to the Final Observations Regarding the Merits of the Case by the Petitioners, October 17, 2008, p. 11, mentioning detailed investigation undertaken by the Critical Incident Team (CIT) of the 18th Judicial District, which can be found at Exhibit C of Final Observations Regarding the Merits of the Case submitted by the petitioners, March 24, 2008.

[128] Reply by the Government of the United States of America to the Final Observations Regarding the Merits of the Case by the Petitioners, October 17, 2008, p. 11, mentioning detailed investigation undertaken by the Critical Incident Team (CIT) of the 18th Judicial District, which can be found at Exhibit C of Final Observations Regarding the Merits of the Case submitted by the petitioners, March 24, 2008.

Rebecca Gonzales, the CIT report solely concludes that the "autopsies revealed that the three girls were shot at extremely close range and were not struck by any rounds fired by the officers. The exact location of the homicides of the children has not been determined. There were no injuries to any police officers, bystanders or witnesses. There is no information to indicate that there were any other suspects involved besides Simon James Gonzales." [129]

85. The autopsy reports of Leslie, Katheryn and Rebecca before the Commission only confirm about Rebecca Gonzales that her cause of death was determined to be "brain injuries due to a through and through large caliber gunshot to the right side of the head;"[130] and for both Katheryn and Leslie "brain injuries due to a through and through large caliber gunshot to the left side of the head."[131] The autopsy reports do not identify which bullets, those of the CRPD or Simon Gonzales, struck Leslie, Katheryn and Rebecca Gonzales.[132]

5. Legal Process for Jessica Lenahan's Claims in the United States

86. Jessica Lenahan filed suit on January 23, 2001, in the United States District Court for the District of Colorado, a court of federal jurisdiction, alleging that the City of Castle Rock and several police officers had violated her rights under the Due Process Clause of the Fourteenth Amendment, presenting both substantive and procedural challenges as described *supra* para. 37.

87. Accepting her allegations as true, the District Court dismissed her case regarding both claims. The Court held that "[w]hile the State may have been aware of the dangers that [the children] faced in the free world, it played no part in their creation, nor did it do anything to render [them] any more vulnerable to them," since Jessica Lenahan's daughters were not in the State's custody, but their father's.[133] Therefore, the Court found that the plaintiffs had failed to state a claim since solely proving "inaction" from the police officers does not rise to the level of "conscience-shocking affirmative conduct or indifference," which is needed to support a violation of substantive due process.[134] In the realm of procedural due process, the District Court held that the regulatory language of the mandatory arrest statute

---

[129] Report of investigation undertaken by the Critical Incident Team (CIT) of the 18th Judicial District, which can be found at Exhibit C of Final Observations Regarding the Merits of the Case submitted by the petitioners, March 24, 2008.

[130] Final Observations Regarding the Merits of the Case submitted by the petitioners, March 24, 2008; Exhibit E: Douglas County Coroner's Report for Rebecca Gonzales.

[131] Final Observations Regarding the Merits of the Case submitted by the petitioners, March 24, 2008; Exhibit F: Douglas County Coroner's Report: Katheryn Gonzales, and Exhibit G: Douglas County Coroner's Report: Leslie Gonzales.

[132] Final Observations Regarding the Merits of the Case submitted by the petitioners, March 24, 2008; Exhibits E, F, and G: Douglas County Coroner's Reports for Rebecca, Katheryn and Leslie Gonzales.

[133] See Petitioners' petition dated December 27, 2005, Exhibit C: District Court Order, Gonzales v. City of Castle Rock et Al., January 23, 2001, citing *DeShaney v. Winnebago*, 489 U.S. 189, 201 (1989).

[134] See Petitioners' petition dated December 27, 2005, Exhibit C: District Court Order, Gonzales v. City of Castle Rock et Al., January 23, 2001, p. 69.

was not truly "mandatory," since it offered police officers discretion to determine whether probable cause exists, therefore, it considered that Jessica Lenahan did not have a protectable property interest in the enforcement of the order.

88. Thereafter, a panel of judges of the Tenth Circuit Court of Appeals affirmed in part and reversed in part the District Court decision.[135] In regards to Jessica Lenahan's substantive due process challenge, the Court considered that Jessica Lenahan had failed to show that any affirmative actions by the defendants created or increased the danger to the victims; a requirement that the Court considered necessary to succeed on a substantive due process claim.[136] The Tenth Circuit Court however reached a different conclusion in regards to Jessica Lenahan's procedural process claim, interpreting the Colorado Mandatory Arrest Statute as containing a mandatory duty to arrest, based on the use of the word "shall," when an officer has information amounting to probable clause that the order has been violated. The Court considered that the complaint in this case, viewed most favorably to Jessica Lenahan, indicated that defendant police officers used no reasonable means to enforce the restraining order, even though she communicated to the authorities that she held one, and that Simon Gonzales had taken his daughters in violation of this order. Therefore, under these circumstances, the Court concluded that Jessica Lenahan had effectively alleged a procedural due process claim with respect "to her entitlement to enforcement of the restraining order by every reasonable means."[137]

89. This finding was then affirmed in a rehearing before all the judges of the court ("*en banc*" review).[138] The Court underscored that Jessica Lenahan's entitlement to police enforcement of the restraining order arose when the order was issued by the state court, since it was granted based on the court's finding that "irreparable injury would result to the moving party if no order was issued."[139] The Court considered that not only the order itself mandated that it be enforced, but the Colorado legislature had also passed a series of statutes to ensure its enforcement. It found that there was no question in this case that the restraining order mandated the arrest of Simon Gonzales under specified circumstances, or at a minimum required the use of reasonable means to enforce the order, which limited the police officers' discretion in its implementation. Among other findings, the Court ruled that "the statute

---

[135] See Petitioners' petition dated December 27, 2005, Exhibit D: 10th Circuit Panel Decision, Gonzales v. City of Castle Rock, et. Al., October 15, 2002.

[136] The Tenth Circuit held that a substantive due process argument fails when the plaintiffs are unable to "point to any affirmative actions by the defendants that created or increased the danger to the victims." See Petitioners' petition dated December 27, 2005, Exhibit D: 10th Circuit Panel Decision, Gonzales v. City of Castle Rock, et. Al., October 15, 2002, p. 6.

[137] See Petitioners' petition dated December 27, 2005, Exhibit D: 10th Circuit Panel Decision, Gonzales v. City of Castle Rock, et. Al., October 15, 2002, p. 6.

[138] See Petitioners' petition dated December 27, 2005, Exhibit E: 10th Circuit Court En Banc Decision, Gonzales v. City of Castle Rock, et. Al., April 29, 2004.

[139] See Petitioners' petition dated December 27, 2005, Exhibit E: 10th Circuit Court En Banc Decision, Gonzales v. City of Castle Rock, et. Al., April 29, 2004.

promised a process by which [Jessica Lenahan's] restraining order would be given vitality through careful and prompt consideration of an enforcement request, and the constitution requires no less. Denial of that process drained all of the value from her property interest in the restraining order."[140]

90. Jessica Lenahan's claims at the national level reached the United States Supreme Court, the highest judicial and appellate court in the United States. On June 27, 2005,[141] the Supreme Court rejected all of Jessica Lenahan's claims by holding that under the Due Process Clause of the 14th Amendment of the U.S. Constitution, Colorado's law on the police enforcement of restraining orders did not give Jessica Lenahan a property interest in the enforcement of the restraining order against her former husband. In its analysis, the Supreme Court considered the Colorado Statute in question and the pre-printed notice to law enforcement officers on the restraining order, holding that a "well-established tradition of police discretion has long coexisted with apparently mandatory arrest statutes,"[142] and that the "deep-rooted nature of law-enforcement discretion, even in the presence of seemingly mandatory legislative commands,"[143] had been previously recognized by the United States Supreme Court.

91. The Supreme Court specifically noted that:

> It is hard to imagine that a Colorado police officer would not have some discretion to determine that—despite probable cause to believe a restraining order has been violated—the circumstances of the violation or the competing duties of that officer or his agency counsel decisively against enforcement in a particular instance. The practical necessity for discretion is particularly apparent in a case such as this one, where the suspected violator is not actually present and his whereabouts are unknown.[144]

6. Problem of Domestic Violence in the United States and Colorado

92. Throughout the processing of this case before the Commission, both parties have presented information related to the situation of domestic violence in the United States and the quality of the state response, as context to their claims.

93. Both parties recognize the gravity and prevalence of the problem of domestic violence in the United States, at the time of the events and the present. The petitioners highlight that in the United States between one and five million women

---

[140]See Petitioners' petition dated December 27, 2005, Exhibit E: 10th Circuit Court En Banc Decision, Gonzales v. City of Castle Rock, et. Al., April 29, 2004.
[141]See Petitioners' petition dated December 27, 2005, Exhibit F: U.S. Supreme Court Decision, Town of Castle Rock v. Gonzales, 545 U.S. 748 (2005), 125 S. Ct. 2796.
[142]See Petitioners' petition dated December 27, 2005, Exhibit F: U.S. Supreme Court Decision, Town of Castle Rock v. Gonzales, 545 U.S. 748 (2005), 125 S. Ct. 2796, 2805-2806.
[143]See Petitioners' petition dated December 27, 2005, Exhibit F: U.S. Supreme Court Decision, Town of Castle Rock v. Gonzales, 545 U.S. 748 (2005), 125 S. Ct. 2796, 2806.
[144]See Petitioners' petition dated December 27, 2005, Exhibit F: U.S. Supreme Court Decision, Town of Castle Rock v. Gonzales, 545 U.S. 748 (2005), 125 S. Ct. 2796, 2806.

suffer non-fatal violence at the hands of an intimate partner each year.[145] The United States Government characterizes the problem as "acute" and "significant," and acknowledges that there were at least 3.5 million incidents of domestic violence in a four-year period, contemporary with the facts pertaining to this case.[146] Available estimates only display part of the reality, since reports indicate that only about half of the domestic violence that occurs in the United States is actually reported to the police.[147]

94. Studies and investigations presented by the parties reveal that women constitute the majority of domestic violence victims in the United States.[148] Some sectors of the United States female population are at a particular risk to domestic violence acts,

---

[145] Petitioners' petition dated December 27, 2005 and Final Observations Regarding the Merits of the Case submitted by the petitioners, March 24, 2008, citing statistics from Center for Disease Control and Prevention, *Costs of Intimate Partner Violence against Women in the United States* 18 (2003) (estimating 5.3 million intimate partner assaults against women in the United States each year); Patricia Tjaden and Nancy Thoennes, U.S. Department of Justice, Office of Justice Programs, National Institute of Justice, *Extent, Nature and Consequences of Intimate Partner Violence*, July 2000.

[146] U.S. Response to the Petition Alleging Violations of the Human Rights of Jessica Gonzales by the United States of America and the State of Colorado, September 22, 2006, p. 12.

[147] Feminist Majority Foundation, Domestic Violence Information Center, Domestic Violence Facts, http://www.feminist.org/other/dv/dvfact.html cited in Amicus Curiae Presented in Favor of Petitioner by William W. Oxley and others, October 17, 2008, p. 4; Callie Marie Rennison, U.S. Department of Justice, Bureau of Justice Statistics, NCJ 197838, *Intimate Partner Violence, 1993-2001*, 1 [Feb. 2003]. See also, U.S. Response to the Petition Alleging Violations of the Human Rights of Jessica Gonzales by the United States of America and the State of Colorado, September 22, 2006, p. 12 citing U.S. Department of Justice, Bureau of Justice Statistics, *Family Violence Statistics*, Mathew Durose and Others (June 2005); Final Observations Regarding the Merits of the Case submitted by the petitioners, March 24, 2008, citing Lawrence A. Greenfield et al., U.S. Department of Justice, *Violence by Intimates* 38 (1998).

[148] A United States Department of Justice report on family violence statistics discussed by both parties in their pleadings, found that family violence accounted for 11% of all reported and unreported violence between 1998 and 2002, and that the majority of the victims—73%—were female. In regards to fatal family violence, the same report indicates that about 22% of the murders in 2002 were family murders and 58% of those victims were female. See, U.S. Response to the Petition Alleging Violations of the Human Rights of Jessica Gonzales by the United States of America and the State of Colorado, September 22, 2006, p. 12, citing U.S. Department of Justice, Bureau of Justice Statistics, *Family Violence Statistics*, Mathew Durose and Others (June 2005).

The United States Department of Justice has also previously indicated that women are five to eight times more likely to be victims of domestic violence than men. See, Final Observations Regarding the Merits of the Case submitted by the petitioners, March 24, 2008, citing Lawrence A. Greenfield et al., U.S. Department of Justice, *Violence by Intimates* 38 (1998).

Other studies have found that domestic abuse is the leading cause of injury to American women; that at least one in three American women experience physical abuse by a partner; and that approximately one-third of the women murdered in the United States each year are killed by an intimate partner. See, C.J. Newton, Domestic Violence: An Overview, FINDCOUNSELING.COM Mental Health Journal, February 2001, http://www.findcounseling.com/journal/domestic-violence/; Montana State University-Northern, *Statistics*, http://www.msun.edu/stuaffairs/response/stats/stats/html, cited in Amicus Curiae Brief presented in favor of petitioners by Women Empowered against Violence (WEAVE) before the IACHR, October 17, 2008.

such as Native American women and those pertaining to low-income groups.[149] Children are also frequently exposed to domestic violence in the United States, although definitive numbers are scarce.[150]

95. Empirical research presented to the Commission also confirms that in order to regain control over departing spouses and children, batterers will escalate violence after the battered spouse attempts to separate from her abuser.[151] In many cases and as part of the escalation of violence, the abduction of the children is a means to coerce the resumption of the marital relationship and/or reestablish the batterer's control.[152] Therefore, when a battered parent seeks to leave an abusive relationship, this is the time where the children are more at risk and more in need of legal protections and interventions from law enforcement agencies.[153]

---

[149]A 2000 national domestic violence survey identified several groups of women that are at a particular risk of domestic violence acts, including women pertaining to lower-income groups and women pertaining to minority groups. See, Patricia Tjaden and Nancy Thoennes, U.S. Department of Justice, Office of Justice Programs, National Institute of Justice, *Extent, Nature and Consequences of Intimate Partner Violence*, July 2000, p. 33 (The survey consists of telephone interviews with a nationally representative sample of 8,000 U.S. women and 8,000 U.S. men about their experiences with intimate partner violence. The survey compares victimization rates among women and men, specific racial groups, Hispanics and non-Hispanics, and same-sex and opposite-sex cohabitants. It also examines risk factors associated with intimate partner violence, the rate of injury among rape and physical assault victims, injured victims' use of medical services, and victims' involvement with the justice system).

The United States Congress identified Native American women as a group at particular risk of domestic violence by including a specific title within the VAWA 2005 geared towards the "Safety of Indian Women." VAWA 2005 indicates that Indian women experience the violent crime of battering at a rate of 23.2 per 1,000, compared with 8 per 1,000 among Caucasian women. *See*, Violence against Women and Department of Justice Reauthorization Act of 2005, P.L. No. 109—162 § 901 (2) (2006), Title XI—Safety for Indian Women; Amicus Curiae Brief of November 13, 2008, submitted by Lucy Simpson and Kirsten Matoy Carlson from the Indian Law Resource Center and Jacqueline Agtuca and Terri Henry from the Sacred Circle National Resource Center to End Violence Against Native Women.

Native American women are also the most likely to report experiencing domestic violence, followed by African American women, Caucasian women, and Latina women. *See*, Matthew R. Durose et al., U.S. Department of Justice, Bureau of Justice Statistics, *Family violence Statistics: Including Statistics on Strangers and Acquaintances*, 10 NCJ 207846 (June 2005), available at http://www.ojp.usdoj.gov.bjs/pub/pdf/fvs.pdf, cited in Amicus Curiae Brief presented in favor of petitioners by Women Empowered Against Violence (WEAVE) before the IACHR, October 17, 2008, p. 9.

[150]National Center for Children Exposed to Violence, *Domestic Violence* (2007); Bonnie E. Carlson, *Children Exposed to Intimate Partner Violence: Research Findings and Implications for Intervention* 1 Trauma, Violence & Abuse 321, 323 (2000), cited in Amicus Curiae Brief presented in favor of petitioners by William W. Oxley, and others before IACHR, on October 17, 2008, p. 5.

[151]Barbara J. Hart, Minnesota Center against Violence & Abuse, *Parental Abduction and Domestic Violence* (1992), http://www.mincava.umn.edu/documents/hart/hart.html, cited in, Amicus Curiae Brief presented in favor of petitioners by William W. Oxley and others before IACHR on October 17, 2008, p. 4, note 10.

[152]Barbara J. Hart, Minnesota Center Against Violence & Abuse, *Parental Abduction and Domestic Violence* (1992), http://www.mincava.umn.edu/documents/hart/hart.html cited in Amicus Curiae Brief presented in favor of petitioners by William W. Oxley, and others before IACHR, October 17, 2008, para. 32, p. 8.

[153]Barbara J. Hart, Minnesota Center Against Violence & Abuse, *Parental Abduction and Domestic Violence* (1992), http://www.mincava.umn.edu/documents/hart/hart.html cited in Amicus Curiae Brief Presented in Favor of Petitioner by William W. Oxley, and others before IACHR, October 17, 2008, para. 32, p. 8.

96. The Commission has also received information in the context of this case indicating that the problem of domestic violence in the United States was considered a "private matter," and therefore, undeserving of protection measures by law enforcement agencies and the justice system.[154] Once domestic violence was finally recognized as a crime, women were still very unlikely to gain protection in the United States because of law enforcement's widespread under-enforcement of domestic violence laws.[155] Very often, the police responded to domestic violence calls either by not taking any action, by purposefully delaying their response in the hope of avoiding confrontation, or, by merely attempting to mediate the situation and separate the parties so they could "cool off."[156]

97. Therefore, the creation of the restraining order[157] is widely considered an achievement in the field of domestic violence in the United States, since it was an attempt at the state level to ensure domestic violence would be treated seriously.[158] A 2002 national survey found that female victims of intimate partner violence are significantly more likely than their male counterparts to obtain a protective or restraining order against their assailants.[159] However, one of the most serious historical limitations of civil restraining orders has been their widespread lack of

---

[154] For example, the United States Attorney General documented in 1984 that the law enforcement's perception of the problem as a "private matter" translated into inaction from the police and law enforcement agencies in general to domestic violence reports. See, U.S. Department of Justice, *Final Report: Attorney General's Task Force on Family Violence* 3 (1984).

[155] See, e.g., Thurman v. City of Torrington, 595 F. Supp. 1521 (D. Conn. 1984) (Case where police refused to respond to woman's repeated requests for protection. Police watched as estranged husband stabbed and kicked victim in her neck, throat, and chest, paralyzing her from the neck down and causing permanent disfigurement.), cited in, Supplemental Amicus Curiae Brief submitted by Maya Raghu from Legal Momentum and others on behalf of petitioners on October 15, 2008, p. 40, note 22.

[156] Michaela M. Hoctor, Comment, *Domestic Violence as a Crime Against the State: The Need for Mandatory Arrest in California*, 85 Ca. L. Rev. 643, 649 (1997); Daniel D. Polsby, *Suppressing Domestic Violence with Law Reforms*, 83 J. Crim. L. & Criminology 250, 250-251 (1992); Dennis P. Saccuzzo, *How Should the Police Respond to Domestic Violence: A Therapeutic Jurisprudence Analysis of Mandatory Arrest*, 39 Santa Clara L. Re. 765, 767 (1999) cited in, Supplemental Amicus Curiae Brief submitted by Maya Raghu from Legal Momentum and others on behalf of petitioners on October 15, 2008, pp. 41–42.

[157] A restraining order can include provisions restricting contact; prohibiting abusive behavior; determining child custody and visitation issues; mandating offender counseling; and even forbidding firearm possession. By 1989, all 50 states and the District of Columbia had enacted statutes authorizing civil restraining orders as a means of protecting victims of domestic violence and preventing further abuse.

[158] David M. Zlotnick, *Empowering the Battered Woman: The Use of Criminal Contempt Sanctions to Enforce Civil Protection Orders*, 56 Ohio Street L.J. 1153, 1170 (1995) cited in, Supplemental Amicus Curiae Brief submitted by Maya Raghu from Legal Momentum and others on behalf of petitioners on October 15, 2008, p. 46.

[159] This national survey also showed that approximately one million victims of violence against women obtain protective or restraining orders against their attackers annually and approximately 60% of these orders are violated by the assailants. *See*, Patricia Tjaden and Nancy Thoennes, U.S. Department of Justice, Office of Justice Programs, National Institute of Justice,*Extent, Nature and Consequences of Intimate Partner Violence*, July 2000, pp. 52–53.

enforcement by the police.[160] Police officers still tend to support "traditional patriarchal gender roles, making it difficult for them to identify with and help female victims."[161]

98. To effectively address the problem of domestic violence, at the federal level, Congress has adopted three major pieces of legislation that recognize the seriousness of domestic violence and the importance of a nationwide response: the Violence against Women Act of 1994 (hereinafter "VAWA 1994"), the Violence against Women Act of 2000 (hereinafter "VAWA 2000") and the Violence against Women and Department of Justice Reauthorization Act of 2005 (hereinafter "VAWA 2005"). VAWA is a comprehensive legislative package including the requirement for states and territories to enforce protection orders issued by other states, tribes and territories. However, most laws that protect persons in the United States from domestic violence and provide civil remedies against perpetrators and other responsible parties are state and local laws and ordinances. Over the past two decades, states have adopted a host of new laws to improve the ways that the criminal and civil justice systems respond to domestic violence.

99. Finally, the petitioners have presented a series of available statistics pointing to the alarming rates of domestic violence in the State of Colorado, uncontested by the State. Approximately half of the murders in Colorado are committed by an intimate or former partner and the victims are disproportionately female.[162] On average over a period of three years, 45 percent of female homicide victims statewide were killed by an intimate partner.[163] The Denver Metro Domestic Violence Fatality Committee ("the Denver Committee") identified 54 domestic violence-related fatalities in Colorado for 1996; 52 for 1997; 55 for 1998; and 69 for 1999.[164] Between

---

[160]U.S. Department of Justice, National Institute of Justice, *Research Preview: Civil Protection Orders: Victims' Views on Effectiveness*, January 1998, http:/.www.ncjrs.gov/pdffiles/fs000191.pdf.

[161]Martha Smithey, Susanne Green, & Andrew Giacomazzi, National Criminal Justice Reference Service, *Collaborative Effort and the Effectiveness of Law Enforcement Training Toward Resolving Domestic Violence* 19 (Jan. 14, 2002), *available at* http://www.ncjrs.gov/pdffiles1/nij/grants/191840.pdf., cited in, Amicus Curiae Brief presented in favor of petitioners by Women Empowered Against Violence (WEAVE) before the IACHR, October 17, 2008, p. 6.

[162]December 11, 2006 Observations from Petitioners, Tab P: Declaration of Randy James Saucedo, Advocacy and Audit Director of the Colorado Coalition Against Domestic Violence, Dated December 6, 2006, citing as sources Project Safeguard, Fatality Review Project, Colorado 2005.

[163]Margaret L. Abrams, Joanne Belknap & Heather C. Melton, Project Safeguard, *When Domestic Violence Kills: The Formation and Finding of the Denver Metro Domestic Violence Fatality Review Committee* 13 (2001), available at http://www.members.aol.com/projectsafeguard/fremanual.pdf, discussed by petitioners in their Observations Concerning the March 2, 2007, Hearing Before the Commission, May 14, 2007.

[164]Margaret L. Abrams, Joanne Belknap & Heather C. Melton, Project Safeguard, *When Domestic Violence Kills: The Formation and finding of the Denver Metro Domestic Violence Fatality Review Committee* 13 (2001), available at http://www.members.aol.com/projectsafeguard/fremanual.pdf, discussed by petitioners in their Observations Concerning the March 2, 2007, Hearing Before the Commission, May 14, 2007.

2000 and 2005, 17 children were killed during incidents related to domestic violence.[165] In 2005, approximately 7,478 civil protection orders to protect from domestic violence were filed in the Colorado civil court system, and approximately 14,726 domestic violence cases were filed in Colorado county courts, constituting more than 20% of all the criminal cases filed.[166]

100. The petitioners also presented evidence of newspaper coverage indicating that domestic violence-related fatalities continue to rise in Colorado with alarming frequency since the murder of Leslie, Katheryn and Rebecca Gonzales. Between December 2005 and September 2006, five domestic violence-related murders were reported in the state of Colorado, two of which occurred in Castle Rock. In December 2005, a woman was stabbed to death in Denver, Colorado by her ex-boyfriend.[167] More specifically, on April 2006, another woman was found shot dead by her boyfriend in Pueblo, Colorado, who had been previously arrested twice for domestic violence and aggravated assault, and had four restraining orders against him.[168] In September 2006, a woman and her daughter were killed by the husband of the former and the stepfather of the latter in Castle Rock, Colorado; and another woman was killed when her boyfriend dragged her behind a vehicle for more than a mile.[169]

B. Considerations of Law

101. The Commission now presents its conclusions as to the human rights violations claimed in this case under Articles I, II, IV, V, VI, VII, XVIII and XXIV of the American Declaration, based on the proven facts and the additional considerations advanced in this section.

---

[165] December 11, 2006 Observations from Petitioners, Tab P: Declaration of Randy James Saucedo, Advocacy and Audit Director of the Colorado Coalition Against Domestic Violence, Dated December 6, 2006, citing as sources Project Safeguard, Fatality Review Project, Colorado 2005.

[166] December 11, 2006 Observations from Petitioners, Tab P: Declaration of Randy James Saucedo, Advocacy and Audit Director of the Colorado Coalition Against Domestic Violence, Dated December 6, 2006, citing as source State of Colorado Court Administration Office Website, County Court Civil Filings by Type, FY 2005.

[167] *Scorned Czech Boyfriend Confesses Killing Brazilian Au Pair Ex-Girlfriend in US*, Associated Press, December 15, 2005, discussed by petitioners in their Observations Concerning the March 2, 2007, Hearing Before the Commission, May 14, 2007, p. 22, note 79.

[168] Nick Bonham, *Police Label Homicide "Fatal-Attraction Killing,"* The Pueblo Chieftain, April 4, 2006, discussed by petitioners in their Observations Concerning the March 2, 2007, Hearing Before the Commission, May 14, 2007. p. 22, note 80.

[169] John C. Esslin & Tillie Fong, *Police Think Man Killed Spouse, Stepdaughter*, Rocky Mountain News, Sep. 14, 2006, and Don Mitchell, *Murder, Kidnap Charges Filed in Colorado Dragging Death, Suspect Accused of Killing Girlfriend*, Associated Press, September 26, 2006, discussed by petitioners in their Observations Concerning the March 2, 2007, Hearing Before the Commission, May 14, 2007, page 22, notes 81 and 83.

1. The Right to Equality before the Law and the Obligation not to Discriminate (Article II), the Right to Life (Article I), and the Right to Special Protection (Article VII), established in the American Declaration

102. Article II of the American Declaration provides that:

All persons are equal before the law and have the rights and duties established in this Declaration, without distinction as to race, sex, language, creed or any other factor.

103. Article I of the American Declaration provides that:

Every human being has the right to life, liberty and the security of his person.

104. Article VII of the American Declaration, in turn, establishes that:

All women, during pregnancy and the nursing period, and all children, have the right to special protection, care and aid.

105. The petitioners argue that discrimination in violation of Article II of the American Declaration was the common thread in all of the State presumed failures to guarantee the rights of Jessica Lenahan and her daughters enumerated in said instrument. They contend that the State's failure to adequately respond to Jessica Lenahan's calls regarding the restraining order, to conduct an investigation into the death of Leslie, Katheryn and Rebecca Gonzales, and to offer her an appropriate remedy for the police failure to enforce this order, all constituted acts of discrimination and breaches to their right to equality before the law and non-discrimination under Article II of the American Declaration. They also contend that the State's duty to protect these victims from domestic violence was of broad reach, also implicating their right to life and their right to special protection under Articles I and VII of the American Declaration, given the factual circumstances of this case. The petitioners allege that the American Declaration imposes a duty on State parties to adopt measures to respect and ensure the full and free exercise of the human rights enumerated therein; a duty which under certain circumstances requires State action to prevent and respond to the conduct of private persons. They furthermore invoke the due diligence principle to interpret the scope of State obligations under the American Declaration in cases of violence against women; obligations they consider the State failed to discharge in this case.

106. The State, for its part rejects the petitioners' arguments by claiming that the tragic murders of Leslie, Katheryn and Rebecca Gonzales were not foreseen by anyone, and therefore, the State did act diligently to protect their lives, based on the information that the CRPD had available at the time of the events. The State also alleges that the state authorities adequately investigated the death of Leslie, Katheryn and Rebecca Gonzales, and therefore, did not incur in any discrimination. The State rejects the arguments presented by the parties related to the American Declaration and the applicability of the due diligence principle to the facts of this case by claiming that: a) the American Declaration is a non-binding instrument and its provisions are aspirational; b) that the American Declaration is devoid of

any provision that imposes an affirmative duty on States to take action to prevent the commission of crimes by private actors; and that b) even though the due diligence principle has found expression in several international instruments related to the problem of violence against women, its content is still unclear.

107. The Commission has repeatedly established that the right to equality and non-discrimination contained in Article II of the American Declaration is a fundamental principle of the inter-American system of human rights.[170] The principle of non-discrimination is the backbone of the universal and regional systems for the protection of human rights.[171]

108. As with all fundamental rights and freedoms, the Commission has observed that States are not only obligated to provide for equal protection of the law.[172] They must also adopt the legislative, policy and other measures necessary to guarantee the effective enjoyment of the rights protected under Article II of the American Declaration.[173]

109. The Commission has clarified that the right to equality before the law does not mean that the substantive provisions of the law have to be the same for everyone, but that the application of the law should be equal for all without discrimination.[174] In practice this means that States have the obligation to adopt the measures necessary to recognize and guarantee the effective equality of all persons before the law; to abstain from introducing in their legal framework regulations that are discriminatory towards certain groups either in their face or in practice; and to combat discriminatory practices.[175] The Commission has underscored that laws and policies should be examined to ensure that they comply with the principles of equality and non-discrimination; an analysis that should assess their potential discriminatory impact, even when their formulation or wording appears neutral, or they apply without textual distinctions.[176]

---

[170] See, IACHR Report 40/04, Case 12.053, *Maya Indigenous Community* (Belize), October 12, 2004, para. 163; IACHR Report 67/06, Case 12.476, *Oscar Elías Bicet et al.* (Cuba), October 21, 2006, para. 228; IACHR, *Report on Terrorism and Human Rights*, Doc. OEA/Ser.L./V/II.116 Doc. 5 rev. 1 corr. , 22 October 2002, para. 335.

[171] See, e.g., International Covenant on Civil and Political Rights (Articles 2 and 26); International Covenant on Economic, Social and Cultural Rights (Articles 2.2 and 3); European Convention on Human Rights (Article 14); African Charter on Human and People's Rights (Article 2).

[172] IACHR, Report N° 40/04, Case 12.053, *Maya Indigenous Community* (Belize), October 12, 2004, para. 162.

[173] IACHR, Report N°40/04, Case 12.053, *Maya Indigenous Community* (Belize), October 12, 2004, para. 162.

[174] IACHR, Report N° 57/96, Case 11.139, *William Andrews* (United States), December 6, 1996, para. 173.

[175] IACHR, Report N° 67/06, Case 12.476, *Oscar Elías Bicet et al.* (Cuba), October 21, 2006, paras. 228–231; IACHR Report N° 40/04, Case 12.053, *Maya Indigenous Community* (Belize), October 12, 2004, paras. 162 and 166.

[176] IACHR, *Access to Justice for Women Victims of Violence in the Americas*, OEA/Ser. L/V/II. doc.68, January 20, 2007, para. 90.

110. Gender-based violence is one of the most extreme and pervasive forms of discrimination, severely impairing and nullifying the enforcement of women's rights.[177] The inter-American system as well has consistently highlighted the strong connection between the problems of discrimination and violence against women.[178]

111. In the same vein, the international and regional systems have pronounced on the strong link between discrimination, violence and due diligence, emphasizing that a State's failure to act with due diligence to protect women from violence constitutes a form of discrimination, and denies women their right to equality before the law.[179] These principles have also been applied to hold States responsible for failures to protect women from domestic violence acts perpetrated by private actors.[180] Domestic violence, for its part, has been recognized at the international level as a human rights violation and one of the most pervasive forms of discrimination, affecting women of all ages, ethnicities, races and social classes.[181]

112. Various international human rights bodies have moreover considered State failures in the realm of domestic violence not only discriminatory, but also violations to the right to life of women.[182] The Commission has described the right to life "as the supreme right of the human being, respect for which the enjoyment of all other rights depends."[183] The importance of the right to life is reflected in its

---

[177] See, e.g., United Nations General Assembly Resolution, Human Rights Council, *Accelerating efforts to eliminate all forms of violence against women: ensuring due diligence in prevention*, A/HRC/14/L.9/Rev.1, 16 June 2010; United Nations Declaration on the Elimination of Violence against Women, General Assembly Resolution 48/104, December 20, 1993, A/RES/48/104, February 23, 1994; United Nations, *Beijing Declaration and Platform for Action*, Fourth World Conference on Women, September 15, 1995, A/CONF.177/20 (1995) and A/CONF.177/20/Add.1 (1995); CEDAW Committee,*General Recommendation 19: Violence against Women*, (11th Session 1992), U.N. Doc.A/47/38 at 1 (1993).

[178] See generally, IACHR, Report N° 28/07, Cases 12.496-12.498, *Claudia Ivette González and Others*, (Mexico), March 9, 2007; IACHR, Report N° 54/01, Case 12.051, *Maria Da Penha Maia Fernandes* (Brazil), Annual Report of the IACHR 2001; IACHR, *Access to Justice for Women Victims of Violence in the Americas*, Inter-Am. C.H.R., OEA/Ser.L/V/II, Doc. 68 (January 20, 2007); I/A Court H.R., *Case of González et al. ("Cotton Field") v. Mexico*, Judgment of November 16, 2009.

[179] See generally, CEDAW Committee, Communication 2/2003, *Ms. A.T. v. Hungary*, 26 January 2005; European Court of Human Rights, *Case of Opuz v. Turkey*, Application No. 33401/02, 9 June 2009; IACHR, Report N° 28/07, Cases 12.496-12.498, *Claudia Ivette González and Others* (Mexico), March 9, 2007; I/A Court H.R., *Case of González et al. ("Cotton Field") v. Mexico*, Judgment of November 16, 2009.

[180] See generally, IACHR, Report N° 54/01, Case 12.051, *Maria Da Penha Maia Fernandes* (Brazil), April 16, 2001; European Court of Human Rights, *Case of Opuz v. Turkey*, Application No. 33401/02, 9 June 2009.

[181] United Nations General Assembly, *Elimination of Domestic Violence against Women*, U.N. Doc. A/Res/58/147 (February 19, 2004).

[182] See generally, European Court of Human Rights, *Case of Opuz v. Turkey*, Application No. 33401/02, 9 June 2009; European Court of Human Rights, *Kontrová v. Slovakia*, no. 7510/04, ECHR 2007-VI (extracts); CEDAW Committee, Views on Communication No. 5/2005, *Sahide Goekce v. Austria*, July 21, 2004.

[183] IACHR, Report 97/03, Case 11.193, *Gary T. Graham (Shaka Sankofa) v. United States*, December 29, 2003, para. 26; IACHR, Report 62/02, Case 12.285, *Michael Domingues* (United States), October 22, 2002, para. 38.

incorporation into every key international human rights instrument.[184] The right to life is one of the core rights protected by the American Declaration which has undoubtedly attained the status of customary international law.[185]

113. The Commission has also recognized that certain groups of women face discrimination on the basis of more than one factor during their lifetime, based on their young age, race and ethnic origin, among others, which increases their exposure to acts of violence.[186] Protection measures are considered particularly critical in the case of girl-children, for example, since they may be at a greater risk of human rights violations based on two factors, their sex and age. This principle of special protection is contained in Article VII of the American Declaration.

114. In light of the parties' arguments and submissions, there are three questions before the Commission under Articles I, II and VII of the American Declaration that it will review in the following section. The first is whether the obligation not to discriminate contained in Article II of the American Declaration requires member States to act to protect women from domestic violence; understanding domestic violence as an extreme form of discrimination. The second question pertains to the content and scope of this legal obligation under the American Declaration in light of the internationally recognized due diligence principle, and when analyzed in conjunction with the obligations to protect the right to life and to provide special protection contained in Articles I and VII of the American Declaration. The third is whether this obligation was met by the authorities in this case.

a. Legal obligation to protect women from domestic violence under Article II of the American Declaration

115. The Commission begins analyzing this first question by underscoring its holding at the admissibility stage,[187] that according to the well-established and long-standing jurisprudence and practice of the inter-American human rights system, the American Declaration is recognized as constituting a source of legal obligation for OAS member states, including those States that are not parties to the American

---

[184]*See, e.g.,* Universal Declaration of Human Rights, article 3; International Covenant on Civil and Political Rights, article 6; European Convention on Human Rights, article 2; African Charter on Human Rights and Peoples' Rights, article 4, among others.
[185]IACHR, *Report on Terrorism and Human Rights*, Doc. OEA/Ser.L./V/II.116 Doc. 5 rev. 1 corr., 22 October 2002, para. para. 38, note 103.
[186]IACHR, Report Nº 28/07, Cases 12.496-12.498, *Claudia Ivette González and Others* (Mexico), March 9, 2007, paras. 251-252; IACHR, *Access to Justice for Women Victims of Violence in the Americas,* OEA/Ser. L/V/II. doc.68, January 20, 2007, paras. 195-197; IACHR, *Violence and Discrimination against Women in the Armed Conflict in Colombia*, OEA/Ser/L/V/II. 124/Doc.6, October 18, 2006, paras. 102-106; IACHR, *Report on the Rights of Women in Haiti to be Free from Violence and Discrimination*, OEA/Ser.L/V/II, Doc. 64, March 10, 2009, para. 90.
[187]IACHR, Report on Admissibility Nº 52/07, Petition 1490-05, *Jessica Gonzales and Others (United States)*, July 24, 2007, para. 56.

Convention on Human Rights.[188] These obligations are considered to flow from the human rights obligations of Member States under the OAS Charter.[189] Member States have agreed that the content of the general principles of the OAS Charter is contained in and defined by the American Declaration,[190] as well as the customary legal status of the rights protected under many of the Declaration's core provisions.[191]

116. The inter-American system has moreover held that the Declaration is a source of international obligation for all OAS member states, including those that have ratified the American Convention.[192] The American Declaration is part of the human rights framework established by the OAS member states, one that refers to the obligations and responsibilities of States and mandates them to refrain from supporting, tolerating or acquiescing in acts or omissions that contravene their human rights commitments.

117. As a source of legal obligation, States must implement the rights established in the American Declaration in practice within their jurisdiction.[193] The Commission has indicated that the obligation to respect and ensure human rights is specifically set forth in certain provisions of the American Declaration.[194] International

---

[188] See I/A Court H.R., *Advisory Opinion OC-10/89 "Interpretation of the Declaration of the Rights and Duties of Man within the Framework of Article 64 of the American Convention on Human Rights,"* July 14, 1989, Ser. A N° 10 (1989), paras. 35–45; *James Terry Roach and Jay Pinkerton v. United States*, Case 9647, Res. 3/87, 22 September 1987, Annual Report of the IACHR 1986-87, paras. 46–49.

[189] Charter of the Organization of American States, Arts. 3, 16, 51.

[190] See, e.g., OAS General Assembly Resolution 314, AG/RES. 314 (VII-O/77), June 22, 1977 (entrusting the Inter-American Commission with the preparation of a study to "set forth their obligations to carry out the commitments assumed in the American Declaration of the Rights and Duties of Man"); OAS General Assembly Resolution 371, AG/RES (VIII-O/78), July 1, 1978 (reaffirming its commitment to "promote the observance of the American Declaration of the Rights and Duties of Man"); OAS General Assembly Resolution 370, AG/RES. 370 (VIII-O/78), July 1, 1978 (referring to the "international commitments" of OAS member states to respect the rights recognized in the American Declaration of the Rights and Duties of Man).

[191] IACHR, Report N° 19/02, Case 12.379, *Lare-Reyes et al.* (United States), February 27, 2002, para. 46.

[192] See I/A Court H.R., *Advisory Opinion OC-10/89 "Interpretation of the Declaration of the Rights and Duties of Man within the Framework of Article 64 of the American Convention on Human Rights,"* July 14, 1989, Ser. A N° 10 (1989), para. 45 (The Court held that "for the member states of the Organization, the Declaration is the text that defines the human rights referred to in the Charter").

[193] *See, as reference,* Statute of the Inter-American Commission on Human Rights (1979), article 1, providing that the Commission was created "to promote the observance and defense of human rights" and defining human rights as those rights set forth both in the American Declaration and the American Convention. *See also*, American Convention on Human Rights, article 29 (d), stating that no provision of the Convention should be interpreted "excluding or limiting the effect that the American Declaration of the Rights and Duties of Man and other international acts of the same nature may have;" *See also*, Rules of Procedure of the Inter-American Commission of Human Rights (2009), articles 51 and 52, empowering the Commission to receive and examine petitions that allege violations of the rights contained in the American Declaration in relation to OAS members states that are not parties to the American Convention.

[194] Inter-American Commission on Human Rights, Report on Terrorism and Human Rights, OEA/Ser.L/V/II.116 Doc. 5 rev. 1 corr. 22 October 2002, para. 339. The report cites as examples Articles XVIII and XXIV of the American Declaration.

instruments in general require State parties not only to respect the rights enumerated therein, but also to ensure that individuals within their jurisdictions also exercise those rights. The continuum of human rights obligations is not only negative in nature; it also requires positive action from States.

118. Consonant with this principle, the Commission in its decisions has repeatedly interpreted the American Declaration as requiring States to adopt measures to give legal effect to the rights contained in the American Declaration, including cases alleging violations under Article II.[195] The Commission has not only required States to refrain from committing human rights violations contrary to the provisions of the American Declaration,[196] but also to adopt affirmative measures to guarantee that the individuals subject to their jurisdiction can exercise and enjoy the rights contained in the American Declaration.[197] The Commission has traditionally interpreted the scope of the obligations established under the American Declaration in the context of the international and inter-American human rights systems more broadly, in light of developments in the field of international human rights law since the instrument was first adopted, and with due regard to other rules of international law applicable to members states.[198]

119. In its analysis of the legal obligations contained in the American Declaration, the Commission has also noted that a State can be held responsible for the conduct of non-State actors in certain circumstances.[199] It has moreover held that the rights

---

[195] IACHR, Report N° 40/04, Case 12.053, *Maya Indigenous Community* (Belize), October 12, 2004, para. 162; IACHR Report N° 67/06, Case 12.476, *Oscar Elías Bicet et al.* (Cuba), October 21, 2006, paras. 227–231.

[196] See, e.g., IACHR, Report 63/08, Case 12.534, *Andrea Mortlock* (United States), July 25, 2008, paras. 75-95; IACHR, Report 62/02, Case 12.285, *Michael Domingues* (United States), October 22, 2002, paras. 84–87.

[197] See, e.g., IACHR, Report N° 81/10, Case 12.562, *Wayne Smith, Hugo Armendariz, et al.* (United States), July 12, 2010 paras. 61-65; IACHR, Report N° 40/04, Case 12.053, *Maya Indigenous Community* (Belize), October 12, 2004, paras. 122-135, 162, and 193-196; IACHR, Report N° 75/02, Case 11.140, *Mary and Carrie Dann* (United States, December 27, 2002, paras. 124-145.

[198] See, generally, IACHR, Report N° 81/10, Case 12.562, *Wayne Smith, Hugo Armendariz, et al.* (United States), July 12, 2010; IACHR, Report N° 63/08, Case 12.534, *Andrea Mortlock (United States),* July 25, 2008; IACHR, Report N° 40/04, Case 12.053, Maya Indigenous Community (Belize), October 12, 2004; IACHR, Report N° 75/02, Case 11.140, *Mary and Carrie Dann* (United States, December 27, 2002; IACHR, Report N° 62/02, Case 12.285, *Michael Domingues* (United States), October 22, 2002.

[199] IACHR, Report N° 40/04, Case 12.053, *Maya Indigenous Community* (Belize), October 12, 2004, paras. 136-156 (The Commission found the State of Belize responsible under the American Declaration when it granted logging and oil concessions to third parties to utilize the land occupied by the Maya people, without the effective consultation and the informed consent of this indigenous community, resulting in significant environmental damage); IACHR, Resolution 12/85, Case 7615 (Brazil), March 5, 1985 (The Commission found the State of Brazil responsible under the American Declaration when it failed to undertake timely and effective measures to protect the Yanomami indigenous community from the acts of private individuals settling in their territory—due to the construction of a highway—which resulted in the widespread influx of epidemics and disease).

contained in the American Declaration may be implicated when a State fails to prevent, prosecute and sanction acts of domestic violence perpetrated by private individuals.[200] Furthermore, the Commission notes that both the universal system of human rights and the inter-American system of human rights—referring to the International Covenant on Civil and Political Rights, the American Convention, and other international instruments—have underscored that the duty of the State to implement human rights obligations in practice can extend to the prevention and response to the acts of private actors.[201]

120. In light of these considerations, the Commission observes that States are obligated under the American Declaration to give legal effect to the obligations contained in Article II of the American Declaration. The obligations established in Article II extend to the prevention and eradication of violence against women, as a crucial component of the State's duty to eliminate both direct and indirect forms of discrimination. In accordance with this duty, State responsibility may be incurred for failures to protect women from domestic violence perpetrated by private actors in certain circumstances.

121. The Commission also underscores that a State's breach of its obligation to protect women from domestic violence under Article II may also give rise to violations of the right to life established in Article I of the American Declaration, and the duty to provide special protection under Article VII of the American Declaration in given cases. These principles will be reviewed in the following section.

b. The American Declaration, the Due Diligence Principle and Domestic Violence

122. The Commission notes that the principle of due diligence has a long history in the international legal system and its standards on state responsibility. It has been applied in a range of circumstances to mandate States to prevent, punish, and provide remedies for acts of violence, when these are committed by either State or non-State actors.[202]

---

[200]See, Report N° 54/01, Case 12.051, *Maria Da Penha Maia Fernandes* (Brazil), Annual Report of the IACHR 2001, paras. 3, 37-44.
[201]See, e.g., Human Rights Committee, General Comment No. 31, The Nature of the General Legal Obligation Imposed on States Parties to the Covenant, CCPR/C/21/Rev.1/Add. 13, May 26, 2004; I/A Court H.R., Velásquez Rodríguez Case, Judgment of July 29, 1988, Series C No. 4.
[202]For a more detailed discussion, see generally J. Hessbruegge. 2004. "The Historical development of the doctrines of attribution and due diligence in international law," New York University Journal of International Law, vol. 36; Robert P. Barnidge, Jr., The Due Diligence Principle under International Law, International Community Law Review (2006); Johanna Bourke-Martignoni,*The History and Development of the Due Diligence Standard in International Law and its Role in the Protection of Women against Violence*, Due Diligence and its Application to Protect Women from Violence (2008); Report from Special Rapporteur on violence against women, its causes and consequences, Yakin Ertürk, *The Due Diligence Standard as a Tool for the Elimination of Violence against Women*, E/CN.4/2006/61.

123. The Commission moreover observes that there is a broad international consensus over the use of the due diligence principle to interpret the content of State legal obligations towards the problem of violence against women; a consensus that extends to the problem of domestic violence. This consensus is a reflection of the international community's growing recognition of violence against women as a human rights problem requiring State action.[203]

124. This consensus has found expression in a diversity of international instruments, including General Assembly resolutions adopted by consensus,[204] broadly-approved declarations and platforms,[205] treaties,[206] views from treaty bodies,[207] custom,[208] jurisprudence from the universal and regional systems,[209] and other sources of international law. For example, the United Nations Human Rights Council, has underscored this year that States must exercise due diligence to prevent, investigate, prosecute and punish the perpetrators of violence against women and girl-children, and that the failure to do so "violates and impairs or nullifies the enjoyment of their human rights and fundamental freedoms."[210]

---

[203] See, e.g., *Vienna Declaration and Programme of Action*, A/CONF.157/23, 12 July 1993, paras. 18 and 38.

[204] See, e.g., United Nations General Assembly Resolution, Human Rights Council, *Accelerating efforts to eliminate all forms of violence against women: ensuring due diligence in prevention*, A/HRC/14/L.9/Rev.1, 16 June 2010 (adopted without a vote); United Nations General Assembly Resolution, *Intensification of efforts to eliminate all forms of violence against women*, A/RES/64/137, 11 February 2010 (adopted without a vote); United Nations, *Declaration on the Elimination of Violence against Women,* General Assembly resolution 48/104, December 20, 1993, A/RES/48/104, February 23, 1994 (adopted without a vote). See also,*Elimination of Domestic Violence against Women*, G.A. Res. 58/147, U.N. GAOR, 58th Sess., U.N. Doc. A/Res/58/147 (February 19, 2004) (adopted without a vote).

[205] See, e.g., United Nations, *Beijing Declaration and Platform for Action,* Fourth World Conference on Women, September 15, 1995, A/CONF.177/20 (1995) and A/CONF.177/20/Add.1 (1995), paras. 112-126.

[206] See, e.g., Inter-American Convention on the Prevention, Punishment and Eradication of Violence against Women (hereinafter "Convention of Belém do Pará"), Article 7(b).

[207] See, e.g., United Nations, Committee on the Elimination of Discrimination against Women, *General Recommendation 19, Violence against women*, U.N. Doc. HRI/GEN/1//Rev.1 (1994), para. 11.

[208] Report of the Special Rapporteur on violence against women, its causes and consequences, *The Due Diligence Standard as a Tool for the Elimination of Violence against Women,* Commission on Human Rights, Sixty-second session, E/CN.4/2006/61, January 20, 2006, para. 29 (The United Nations Special Rapporteur on Violence against Women therein established that the duty of due diligence has attained the status of a norm of customary international law, which obligates States to prevent and respond with due diligence to acts of violence against women).

[209] See, e.g., European Court of Human Rights, *Case of Opuz v. Turkey*, Application No. 33401/02, 9 June 2009, para. 246; Committee on the Elimination of Discrimination against Women, Views on Communication No. 6/2005, *Fatma Yildrim v. Austria*, July 21, 2004, para. 12.1.1; Committee on the Elimination of Discrimination against Women, Views on Communication No. No. 2/2003, *A.T. v. Hungary*, January 26, 2003, para. 9.2.

[210] United Nations General Assembly Resolution, Human Rights Council, *Accelerating efforts to eliminate all forms of violence against women: ensuring due diligence in prevention*, A/HRC/14/L.9/Rev.1, 16 June 2010.

125. The international community has consistently referenced the due diligence standard as a way of understanding what State's human rights obligations mean in practice when it comes to violence perpetrated against women of varying ages and in different contexts, including domestic violence. This principle has also been crucial in defining the circumstances under which a State may be obligated to prevent and respond to the acts or omissions of private actors. This duty encompasses the organization of the entire state structure—including the State's legislative framework, public policies, law enforcement machinery and judicial system—to adequately and effectively prevent and respond to these problems.[211] Both the Inter-American Commission and the Court have invoked the due diligence principle as a benchmark to rule on cases and situations of violence against women perpetrated by private actors, including those pertaining to girl-children.[212]

126. The evolving law and practice related to the application of the due diligence standard in cases of violence against women highlights in particular four principles. First, international bodies have consistently established that a State may incur international responsibility for failing to act with due diligence to prevent, investigate, sanction and offer reparations for acts of violence against women; a duty which

---

[211]*See, e.g.*, United Nations General Assembly Resolution, Human Rights Council, *Accelerating efforts to eliminate all forms of violence against women: ensuring due diligence in prevention*, A/HRC/14/L.9/Rev.1, 16 June 2010, paras. 1-16; United Nations, *Declaration on the Elimination of Violence against Women*, General Assembly resolution 48/104, December 20, 1993, A/RES/48/104, February 23, 1994, Article 4; United Nations General Assembly Resolution, *Intensification of efforts to eliminate all forms of violence against women*, A/RES/63/155, January 30, 2009, paras. 8-16; CEDAW, General Recommendation 19: *Violence against Women*, (11th Session 1992), U.N. Doc.A/47/38 at 1 (1993), paras. 1–23.
See also, IACHR, Report 28/07, Cases 12.496-12.498, *Claudia Ivette González and Others*, March 9, 2007; IACHR, Report N° 54/01, Case 12.051, *Maria Da Penha Maia Fernandes* (Brazil), April 16, 2001; IACHR, *Access to Justice for Women Victims of Violence in the Americas*, OEA/Ser. L/V/II. doc.68, January 20, 2007; I/A Court H.R., *Case of González et al. ("Cotton Field") v. Mexico*, Judgment of November 16, 2009.
For references to the European and African systems of human rights see, European Court of Human Rights, *Case of Opuz v. Turkey*, Application No. 33401/02, 9 June 2009; Protocol to the African Charter on Human and Peoples' Rights on the Rights of Women in Africa, Adopted by the 2nd Ordinary Session of the Assembly of the Union, Maputo, 11 July 2003, Article 4.

[212]*See, e.g.*, IACHR, Report N° 28/07, Cases 12.496-12.498, *Claudia Ivette Gonzalez and Others* (Mexico), March 9, 2007, paras. 160–255; IACHR, Report N° 54/01, Case 12.051, *Maria Da Penha Maia Fernandes* (Brazil), April 16, 2001, paras. 55–58; IACHR, *Access to Justice for Women Victims of Violence in the Americas*, OEA/Ser. L/V/II. doc.68, January 20, 2007, paras. 26-58; IACHR, *The Situation of the Rights of Women in Ciudad Juárez, Mexico: The Right to be Free from Violence and Discrimination*, OEA/Ser.L/V/II.117, Doc. 44, March 7, 2003, para. 104; IACHR, *Violence and Discrimination against Women in the Armed Conflict in Colombia*, OEA/Ser/L/V/II. 124/Doc.6, October 18, 2006, para. 24; IACHR, *Report on the Rights of Women in Chile: Equality in the Family, Labor and Political Spheres*, OEA/Ser.L/V/II.134, Doc. 63, March 10, 2009, para. 44; IACHR, *Report on the Rights of Women in Haiti to be Free from Violence and Discrimination*, OEA/Ser.L/V/II, Doc. 64, March 10, 2009, para. 80. See also generally, I/A Court H.R., *Case of González et al. ("Cotton Field") v. Mexico*. Preliminary Objection, Merits, Reparations and Costs. Judgment of November 16, 2009. Series C No. 205.

may apply to actions committed by private actors in certain circumstances.[213] Second, they underscore the link between discrimination, violence against women and due diligence, highlighting that the States' duty to address violence against women also involves measures to prevent and respond to the discrimination that perpetuates this problem.[214] States must adopt the required measures to modify the social and cultural patterns of conduct of men and women and to eliminate prejudices, customary practices and other practices based on the idea of the inferiority or superiority of either of the sexes, and on stereotyped roles for men and women.

127. Third, they emphasize the link between the duty to act with due diligence and the obligation of States to guarantee access to adequate and effective judicial remedies for victims and their family members when they suffer acts of violence.[215] Fourth, the international and regional systems have identified certain groups of women as being at particular risk for acts of violence due to having been subjected to discrimination based on more than one factor, among these girl-children, and women pertaining to ethnic, racial, and minority groups; a factor which must be considered by States in the adoption of measures to prevent all forms of violence.[216]

128. The protection of the right to life is a critical component of a State's due diligence obligation to protect women from acts of violence. This legal obligation pertains to the entire state institution, including the actions of those entrusted with safeguarding the security of the State, such as the police forces.[217] It also extends

---

[213] *See generally*, IACHR, Report N° 28/07, Cases 12.496-12.498, *Claudia Ivette González and Others* (Mexico), March 9, 2007; European Court of Human Rights, *Case of Opuz v. Turkey*, Application No. 33401/02, 9 June 2009; CEDAW Committee, Views on Communication 6/2005, *Fatma Yildirim v. Austria* (July 21, 2004).

[214] *See, e.g.*, United Nations, *Declaration on the Elimination of Violence against Women*, General Assembly resolution 48/104, December 20, 1993, A/RES/48/104, February 23, 1994, articles 3 and 4; United Nations, Committee on the Elimination of Discrimination against Women, General Recommendation 19, *Violence against women*, U.N. Doc. HRI/GEN/1//Rev.1 (1994), paras. 1, 11, and 23; IACHR, Report N° 4/01, *Maria Eugenia Morales de Sierra* (Guatemala), January 19, 2001, para. 44.

[215] *See, e.g.*, United Nations General Assembly Resolution, *Intensification of efforts to eliminate all forms of violence against women*, A/RES/63/155, January 30, 2009, paras. 11, 14, 15 and 16; IACHR, *Access to Justice for Women Victims of Violence in the Americas*, Inter-Am. C.H.R., OEA/Ser.L/V/II, Doc. 68 (January 20, 2007), paras. 123-216; IACHR, Report N° 54/01, Case 12.051, *Maria Da Penha Maia Fernandes* (Brazil), Annual Report of the IACHR 2001, paras. 36-44.

[216] United Nations General Assembly Resolution, Human Rights Council, *Accelerating efforts to eliminate all forms of violence against women: ensuring due diligence in prevention*, A/HRC/14/L.9/Rev.1, 16 June 2010, para. 10; IACHR, *Violence and Discrimination against Women in the Armed Conflict in Colombia*, OEA/Ser/L/V/II.124/Doc.6, October 18, 2006, para. 140; IACHR, *Access to Justice for Women Victims of Violence in the Americas*, Inter-Am. C.H.R., OEA/Ser.L/V/II, Doc. 68 (January 20, 2007), para. 272; CEDAW Committee, General Recommendation 25, on*Temporary Special Measures*, U.N. Doc./CEDAW/C/2004/I/WP.1/Rev.1 (2004), section II, para. 12.

[217] See, IACHR, Report N° 28/07, Cases 12.496-12.498, *Claudia Ivette Gonzalez and Others* (Mexico), March 9, 2007, paras. 247-255; I/A Court H.R., *Case of González et al. ("Cotton Field") v. Mexico*. Preliminary Objection, Merits, Reparations and Costs. Judgment of November 16, 2009. Series C No. 205, para. 245.

to the obligations a State may have to prevent and respond to the actions of non-state actors and private persons. [218]

129. The duty of protection related to the right to life is considered especially rigorous in the case of girl-children. [219] This stems, on the one hand, from the broadly-recognized international obligation to provide special protection to children, due to their physical and emotional development.[220] On the other, it is linked to the international recognition that the due diligence duty of States to protect and prevent violence has special connotations in the case of women, due to the historical discrimination they have faced as a group.[221]

130. In light of these considerations, the Commission observes that the evolving standards related to the due diligence principle are relevant to interpret the scope and reach of States' legal obligations under Articles I, II, and VII of the American Declaration in cases of violence against women and girl-children taking place in the domestic context. Cases of violence against women perpetrated by private actors require an integrated analysis of the State's legal obligations under the American Declaration to act with due diligence to prevent, investigate, sanction and offer remedies.

131. International and regional human rights bodies have also applied the due diligence principle to individual cases of domestic violence. The Inter-American Commission, for its part, established in the case of *Maria Da Penha Maia Fernandes v. Brazil* that the obligation of States to act with the due diligence necessary to investigate and sanction human rights violations applies to cases of domestic violence.[222] The Commission interpreted the duty to act with due diligence towards

---

[218] See, IACHR, Report N° 28/07, Cases 12.496-12.498, *Claudia Ivette Gonzalez and Others* (Mexico), March 9, 2007, paras. 247-255.
[219] See, IACHR, Report N° 28/07, Cases 12.496-12.498, *Claudia Ivette Gonzalez and Others* (Mexico), March 9, 2007, paras. 247-255; I/A Court H.R., *Case of González et al. ("Cotton Field") v. Mexico*. Preliminary Objection, Merits, Reparations and Costs. Judgment of November 16, 2009. Series C No. 205, para. 245.
[220] See, IACHR, Report N° 62/02, Case 12.285, *Michael Domingues* (United States), October 22, 2002, para. 83.
[221] See, e.g., United Nations General Assembly Resolution, Human Rights Council, *Accelerating efforts to eliminate all forms of violence against women: ensuring due diligence in prevention*, A/HRC/14/L.9/Rev.1, 16 June 2010; United Nations General Assembly Resolution, *Intensification of efforts to eliminate all forms of violence against women*, A/RES/64/137, 11 February 2010 and A/RES/63/155, January 30, 2009; United Nations, *Declaration on the Elimination of Violence against Women*, General Assembly resolution 48/104, December 20, 1993, A/RES/48/104, February 23, 1994; United Nations, *Beijing Declaration and Platform for Action, Fourth World Conference on Women*, September 15, 1995, A/CONF.177/20 (1995) and A/CONF.177/20/Add.1 (1995); CEDAW, General Recommendation 19: *Violence against Women*, (11th Session 1992), U.N. Doc.A/47/38 (1993).
[222] In this case, the Commission noted that more than 17 years had passed since the launching of the investigation into the attacks suffered by the victim and to date the case against the accused remained opened without a final ruling.

domestic violence broadly, encompassing not only the prompt investigation, prosecution, and sanction of these acts, but also the obligation "to prevent these degrading practices."[223] Furthermore, it found the existence of a general pattern of State tolerance and judicial inefficiency towards cases of domestic violence, which promoted their repetition, and reaffirmed the inextricable link between the problem of violence against women and discrimination in the domestic setting. [224]

132. In the realm of prevention, the European Court of Human Rights and the CEDAW Committee have also issued a number of rulings finding States responsible for failures to protect victims from imminent acts of domestic violence when they have considered that the authorities knew of a situation of real and immediate risk to the wife, her children, and/or other family members, created by the estranged husband, and the authorities failed to undertake reasonable measures to protect them from harm. In determining the question of knowledge, one common feature of these rulings is that the State authorities had already recognized a risk of harm to the victim and/or her family members, but had failed to act diligently to protect them. The recognition of risk was reflected in the issuance of protection orders,[225] the detention of the aggressor,[226] assistance to the victim and/or her family members in the filing of complaints,[227] and the institution of criminal proceedings,[228] in response to the victim's and/or her family members repeated contacts with the authorities. This line of reasoning has also been followed by the European Court in cases where social services had already recognized a risk of harm to children who were abused in the home setting, and failed to adopt positive measures to prevent further abuse from taking place.[229]

133. In several of these cases, the States have been held responsible for violations to the right to life when their authorities failed to undertake reasonable measures to protect children from domestic violence resulting in their death even though they knew or should have known of a situation of risk.[230] Among these are cases where

---

[223]IACHR, Report N° 54/01, Case 12.051, *Maria Da Penha Maia Fernandes* (Brazil), April 16, 2001, para. 56.
[224]IACHR, Report N° 54/01, Case 12.051, *Maria Da Penha Maia Fernandes* (Brazil), April 16, 2001, para. 55.
[225]*See* CEDAW Committee, Views on Communication No. 5/2005, *Sahide Goekce v. Austria*, July 21, 2004; CEDAW Committee, Views on Communication No. 6/2005, *Fatma Yildrim v. Austria*, July 21, 2004.
[226]See, European Court of Human Rights, *Branko Tomasic and Others v. Croatia,* Application No. 46598/06, 15 January 2009.
[227]See, European Court of Human Rights, *Kontrová v. Slovakia*, Application No. 7510/04, ECHR 2007-VI (extracts).
[228]*See*, European Court of Human Rights, *Case of Opuz v. Turkey*, Application No. 33401/02, 9 June 2009.
[229]European Court of Human Rights, *Case of E. and Others v. the United Kingdom*, Application No. 33218/96; *Z and Others v. the United Kingdom* [GC], Application no. 29392/95 ECHR 2001-V.
[230]See, European Court of Human Rights, *Kontrová v. Slovakia*, Application No. 7510/04, ECHR 2007-VI (extracts); European Court of Human Rights, *Branko Tomasic and Others v. Croatia*, Application No. 46598/06, 15 January 2009; see also I/A Court H.R., *Case of González et al. ("Cotton Field") v. Mexico*. Preliminary Objection, Merits, Reparations and Costs. Judgment of November 16, 2009. Series C No. 205.

children were murdered by a parent in a domestic violence situation, and the authorities had already recognized the risk involved after one of their parents had filed complaints related to domestic violence.[231]

134. In the analysis of the cases referred to, the European Court of Human Rights has advanced important principles related to the scope and content of the State's obligation to prevent acts of domestic violence. The European Court has considered the obligation to protect as one of reasonable means, and not results, holding the State responsible when it failed to take reasonable measures that had a real prospect of altering the outcome or mitigating the harm.[232] The Court has established that authorities should consider the prevalence of domestic violence, its hidden nature and the casualties of this phenomenon in the adoption of protection measures; an obligation which may be applicable even in cases where victims have withdrawn their complaints.[233] Given the nature of domestic violence, under certain circumstances authorities may have reason to know that the withdrawal of a complaint may signify a situation of threats on the part of the aggressor, or the State may at a minimum be required to investigate that possibility.[234] Lastly, the Court has ruled that a State's failure to protect women from domestic violence breaches their right to equal protection of the law and that this failure does not need to be intentional.[235]

135. As the Commission has previously held in cases involving the American Declaration, while the organs of the Inter-American System are not bound to follow the judgments of international supervisory bodies, their jurisprudence can provide constructive insights into the interpretation and application of rights that are common to regional and international human rights systems.[236]

136. In the following section, the Commission will apply these considerations to the specific case of Jessica Lenahan and Leslie, Katheryn and Rebecca Gonzales.

c. Analysis of the response of the authorities in this case

137. Considering the specific circumstances of this case, the Commission proceeds to review: i) whether the state authorities at issue should have known that the

---

[231] See, European Court of Human Rights, *Kontrová v. Slovakia*, Application No. 7510/04, ECHR 2007-VI (extracts); European Court of Human Rights, *Branko Tomasic and Others v. Croatia*, Application No. 46598/06, 15 January 2009.
[232] European Court of Human Rights, *Case of Opuz v. Turkey*, Application No. 33401/02, 9 June 2009, para. 136; *E. and Others v. the United Kingdom*, no. 33218/96, para. 99.
[233] European Court of Human Rights, *Case of Opuz v. Turkey*, Application No. 33401/02, 9 June 2009, para. 132.
[234] *See, generally,* European Court of Human Rights, *Case of Opuz v. Turkey*, Application No. 33401/02, 9 June 2009.
[235] European Court of Human Rights, *Case of Opuz v. Turkey*, Application No. 33401/02, 9 June 2009, para. 191.
[236] IACHR, Report 63/08, Case 12.534, *Andrea Mortlock* (United States), July 25, 2008, para. 80; IACHR, Report 98/03, *Statehood Solidarity Committee* (United States), December 29, 2003, paras. 91–93.

victims were in a situation of imminent risk of domestic violence; and ii) whether the authorities undertook reasonable measures to protect them from these acts. The Commission's examination in this case will not be limited to the actions of just the Castle Rock Police Department, since the State's due diligence obligation requires the organization and coordination of the work of the entire State structure to protect domestic violence victims from imminent harm.

i. The authorities' knowledge that victims were in a situation of risk

138. The undisputed facts of this case show that Jessica Lenahan possessed a valid restraining order at the time of the events, initially granted by the justice system on a temporary basis on May 21, 1999,[237] and then rendered permanent on June 4, 1999.[238] The terms of the temporary order included both Jessica Lenahan and her daughters as beneficiaries and indicated expressly that "physical or emotional harm" would result if Simon Gonzales was not excluded from their home. When the order was rendered permanent, Jessica Lenahan was granted temporary sole physical custody of her three daughters. Simon Gonzales was also granted parenting time under the terms of the protection order, under certain conditions. Simon Gonzales' time with his daughters during the week was restricted to a "mid-week dinner visit" that Simon Gonzales and Jessica Lenahan had to previously arrange "upon reasonable notice."

139. The reverse side of the temporary order contained important notices for the restrained party and for law enforcement officials.[239] The order indicated to the restrained party the following:

> .... IF YOU VIOLATE THIS ORDER THINKING THAT THE OTHER PARTY OR A CHILD NAMED IN THIS ORDER HAS GIVEN YOU PERMISSION **YOU ARE WRONG**, AND CAN BE ARRESTED AND PROSECUTED ...
>
> THE TERMS OF THE ORDER CANNOT BE CHANGED BY AGREEMENT OF THE OTHER PARTY OR THE CHILD(REN). ONLY THE COURT CAN CHANGE THIS ORDER ...

140. For law enforcement officials, the order stated the following, mirroring the terms of the Colorado Mandatory Arrest Statute[240] in force at the time of the events:

> YOU SHALL USE EVERY REASONABLE MEANS TO ENFORCE THE RESTRAINING ORDER.

---

[237] See Petitioners' petition dated December 27, 2005, Exhibit A: Temporary Restraining Order dated May 21, 1999.
[238] See Petitioners' petition dated December 27, 2005: Exhibit B: Decision of District Court, County of Douglas, State of Colorado making temporary restraining order permanent on June 4, 1999.
[239] See Petitioners' petition dated December 27, 2005, Exhibit A: Temporary Restraining Order dated May 21, 1999.
[240] See C.R.S. § 18-6-803.5 (3), *Colorado's Mandatory Arrest Statute*, Petitioners' petition dated December 27, 2005.

YOU SHALL ARREST OR, IF AN ARREST WOULD BE IMPRACTICAL UNDER THE CIRCUMSTANCES, SEEK A WARRANT FOR THE ARREST OF THE RESTRAINED PERSON WHEN YOU HAVE INFORMATION AMOUNTING TO PROBABLE CAUSE THAT THE RESTRAINED PERSON HAS VIOLATED OR ATTEMPTED TO VIOLATE ANY PROVISION OF THIS ORDER.

YOU SHALL ENFORCE THIS ORDER EVEN IF THERE IS NO RECORD OF IT IN THE CENTRAL REGISTRY.

YOU ARE AUTHORIZED TO USE EVERY REASONABLE EFFORT TO PROTECT THE ALLEGED VICTIM AND THE ALLEGED VICTIM'S CHILDREN TO PREVENT FURTHER VIOLENCE.

141. The Commission considers that the issuance of this restraining order and its terms reflect that the judicial authorities knew that Jessica Lenahan and her daughters were at risk of harm by Simon Gonzales. The petitioners have construed this order before the Commission as a judicial determination of that risk upon breach of its terms; an allegation uncontested by the State. The order precludes even the parties from changing the terms by agreement, since only the relevant Court can change this order.

142. The Commission considers that the issuance of a restraining order signals a State's recognition of risk that the beneficiaries would suffer harm from domestic violence on the part of the restrained party, and need State protection. This recognition is typically the product of a determination from a judicial authority that a beneficiary—a woman, her children and/or other family members—will suffer harm without police protection. The United States itself acknowledges in its pleadings that it has adopted a series of measures at the federal and state levels to ensure that protection orders are effectively implemented by the police, since they represent an assessment of risk and a form of State protection.[241]

143. Therefore, the Commission considers that the State's recognition of risk in this domestic violence situation through the issuance of a restraining order—and the terms of said order—is a relevant element in assessing the human rights implications of the State's action or inaction in responding to the facts presented in this case. It is a key component in determining whether the State authorities should have known that the victims were in a situation of imminent risk of domestic violence upon breach of the terms of the order. It is also an indicator of which actions could have been reasonably expected from the authorities.

144. With respect to the question of which actions could have reasonably been expected, the justice system included language in this order indicating that its enforcement terms were strict; and that law enforcement authorities were responsible for implementing this order when needed. The order expressly mandates law enforcement officials—by employing the word "shall"—to act diligently to either

---

[241] See, Reply by the Government of the United States of America to the Final Observations Regarding the Merits of the Case by the Petitioners, October 17, 2008, pages 25-34.

arrest or to seek a warrant for the arrest of the aggressor in the presence of information amounting to probable cause of a violation. The order authorizes and requires law enforcement officials to use every reasonable effort to protect the alleged victim and her children from violence.

145. In light of this judicial recognition of risk, and the corresponding need for protection, the State was obligated to ensure that its apparatus responded effectively and in a coordinated fashion to enforce the terms of this order to protect the victims from harm. This required that the authorities entrusted with the enforcement of the restraining order were aware of its existence and its terms; that they understood that a protection order represents a judicial determination of risk and what their responsibilities were in light of this determination; that they understood the characteristics of the problem of domestic violence; and were trained to respond to reports of potential violations. A proper response would have required the existence of protocols or directives and training on how to implement restraining orders, and how to respond to calls such as those placed by Jessica Lenahan.

ii. Measures undertaken to protect the victims

146. In this case, it is undisputed that Jessica Lenahan had eight contacts with the Castle Rock Police Department throughout the evening of June 22nd and the morning of June 23rd of 1999, and that during each of these contacts she informed the Castle Rock Police Department that she held this restraining order. She also informed them that she did not know the whereabouts of her daughters, that they were very young girls, and that she was afraid they had been picked up by their father without notice, along with their friend.

147. Therefore, in this case the CRPD was made aware that a restraining order existed. Knowing that this restraining order existed, they would have reasonably been expected to thoroughly review the terms of the order to understand the risk involved, and their obligations towards this risk. According to the requirements of the order itself, the CRPD should have promptly investigated whether its terms had been violated. If in the presence of probable cause of a violation, they should have arrested or sought a warrant for the arrest of Simon Gonzales as the order itself directed. This would have been part of a coordinated protection approach by the State, involving the actions of its justice and law enforcement authorities.

148. National law enforcement guidelines provided by the parties concerning the enforcement of restraining orders are instructive on the minimum measures that police authorities should have adopted to determine whether the order at issue had been violated. Guidelines from the International Association of Chiefs of Police,[242] presented by the petitioners, provide that an officer must read an order

---

[242] International Association of Chiefs of Police, *A Law Enforcement Officer's Guide to Enforcing Orders of Protection Nationwide* (2006), presented as Exhibit K of December 11, 2006 Observations from Petitioners.

in its entirety in determining its potential violation; that when a victim does not have a copy of her order, police officers should attempt to verify its existence; and that when missing, officers should attempt to locate and arrest the abuser and seize firearms subject to state, territorial, local or tribal prohibitions. There are some factors that police officers can weigh to determine the potential risk due to a restraining order violation, including threats of suicide from the aggressor; a history of domestic violence and violent criminal conduct; the separation of the parties; depression or other mental illness; obsessive attachment to the victim; and possession or access to weapons, among others. When an abuser has fled the scene, the guidelines instruct police officers to: determine whether the abuser's actions warrant arrest; and to follow departmental procedure for dealing with a criminal suspect who has fled the scene.

149. The Law Enforcement Training Manual published by the Colorado Coalition against Domestic Violence,[243] mentioned by the State,[244] offers similar guidelines to law enforcement officials when responding to potential restraining order violations in compliance with the Colorado Mandatory Arrest Statute. The Manual underscores as critical that the police should be trained on the complex dynamics of the problem of domestic violence in order to appropriately respond to victims' calls. For example, an aggressor's control tactics over the victim may include abusing the children, since they are often what is most important to the victim. The manual identifies red flags that indicate that life-threatening violence against the victim or her family members is more likely to occur: the separation or divorce of the parties; the obsessive possessiveness on the part of the aggressor; threats to commit suicide; the issuance of protection or restraining orders; depression on the part of the abuser; a prior history of criminal behavior on the part of the abuser; incidents related to stalking; and an aggressor's access to weapons. The manual indicates that police officers should not base their assessment of potential lethality on the victim's tone or demeanor, since it may not correspond to the seriousness of the situation,

---

[243]Colorado Coalition Against Domestic Violence, Law Enforcement Training Manual, 2nd Edition (October 2003), mentioned in Reply by the Government of the United States of America to the Final Observations Regarding the Merits of the Case by the Petitioners, October 17, 2008, p. 32.

[244]The State mentions this manual as an example of positive steps taken at the state level to respond to domestic violence and to provide adequate training to police officers. The State claims that aside from mandatory training programs, there are several elective training programs that many police departments in Colorado provide as additional training to police officers. One example is the training provided by the Colorado Coalition against Domestic Violence (CCADV), a non-profit organization, with this law enforcement manual, which the State describes as "comprehensive." The State also claims that this manual "explores in depth the dynamics of domestic violence and the legislative history of Colorado statutory provisions on domestic violence, the law enforcement response, domestic violence risk factors, restraining and protection orders, full faith and credit, violation of protection orders, other Colorado statutes governing protection orders, and the procedure of enforcement of protection orders and other considerations." See Reply by the Government of the United States of America to the Final Observations Regarding the Merits of the Case by the Petitioners, October 17, 2008, pp. 24, 32–33.

and may be the product of the unequal power relations inherent to domestic violence.

150. Based on a thorough review of the record, the Commission considers that the CRPD failed to undertake the mentioned investigation actions with the required diligence and without delay. Its response can be at best characterized as fragmented, uncoordinated and unprepared; consisting of actions that did not produce a thorough determination of whether the terms of the restraining order at issue had been violated.

151. The Commission presents below some observations concerning the CRPD response from the evidence presented by the parties.

152. First, the Commission does not have any information indicating that the police officers who responded to Jessica Lenahan's calls and those who visited her house ever thoroughly reviewed the permanent restraining order to ascertain its terms and their enforcement obligations. Available information indicates that they took note of the existence of the order based on the information that Jessica Lenahan provided throughout the evening, and their conclusions and biases regarding this information, and not on the actual terms of the order. For example, as soon as they heard from Jessica Lenahan that the protection order provided Simon Gonzales with parenting time, there was no follow-up to determine whether the terms of the order limited this parenting time. Jessica Lenahan told dispatchers and officers consistently, and repeatedly, throughout the evening of June 22nd and the morning of June 23rd that she was concerned over the whereabouts of her daughters. While Jessica Lenahan did indicate at a point in the evening that she did not think Simon Gonzalez [sic] would harm his daughters,[245] the dispatchers and officers apparently applied only their personal perceptions in determining that the girls were safe because they were with their father. From the record, it is also evident that information pertaining to the existence of the restraining order was not adequately communicated between the dispatchers and police officers throughout the evening, and that Jessica Lenahan was consistently asked the same questions during each of her calls.[246]

153. Second, by 8:49 p.m in the evening of June 22nd, Jessica Lenahan had informed the police that Simon Gonzales had taken the girls to another jurisdiction in Colorado without notice. However, the police officers' actions to locate Katheryn, Leslie and Rebecca were limited to Castle Rock until their bodies were found early the next morning. The police officers should have called the Denver police department to alert them of the situation, but they failed to do so. They knew by midnight

---

[245]U.S. Response to the Petition Alleging Violations of the Human Rights of Jessica Gonzales by the United States of America and the State of Colorado, September 22, 2006, Tab F, Castle Rock Police Department Incident Report 90623004, 06/23/99, 00:06 hrs.

[246]See, for example, U.S. Response to petition alleging violations of the human rights of Jessica Gonzales by the United States of America and the State of Colorado, September 22, 2006, Tab G: Statement Signed by Cpl. Patricia Lisk.

that Simon Gonzales might have taken them to the Pueblo Area, but they failed to perform any actions to search for them there.

154. Third, the file before the Commission also shows that the police officers never did a thorough check of Simon Gonzales' previous criminal background and contacts with the police. This history displayed a pattern of emotional issues, and unpredictable behavior that would have been important in understanding the risk of a violation of the protection order.

155. Fourth, the information before the Commission indicates there were apparently no protocols or directives in place guiding police officers on how to respond to reports of potential restraining order violations involving missing children, which contributed to delays in their response. For example, the undisputed facts show that it took a dispatcher an hour—between 2:15–3:25 a.m.—to find the guidelines to enter an "Attempt to Locate BOLO" for Simon Gonzales and his vehicle.[247] She also reported having problems entering information into the screens for the "Attempt to Locate" because she was missing crucial information such as the physical descriptions of the children. This information was never requested from Jessica Lenahan despite her eight contacts with the police during that evening.

156. Fifth, the lack of training of the Castle Rock police officers throughout the evening of June 22nd and the morning of June 23rd was evident. The response of the Castle Rock police officers, when assessed as a whole throughout this time period, displays misunderstandings and misinformation regarding the problem of domestic violence. Even the State concedes in its pleadings that, from the point of view of the CRPD, this situation appeared to be a "misunderstanding" between Mr. and Ms. Gonzales, and the officers had a sense of relief that the children were at least in a known location with their father, even though he was subject to a restraining order.[248]

157. Some statements display that police officers did not understand the urgency or seriousness of the situation. When Jessica Lenahan called the CPRD for a third time at 9:57 p.m. to report that her children were still not home, the dispatcher asked her to call back on a "non-emergency line," and told her she wished that she and Simon Gonzales had made some arrangements since "that's a little ridiculous making us freak out and thinking the kids are gone."[249]

158. Sixth, the Commission notes that the police officers throughout the evening evidence that they did not understand that they were the ones responsible for ascertaining

---

[247] U.S. Response to the Petition Alleging Violations of the Human Rights of Jessica Gonzales by the United States of America and the State of Colorado, September 22, 2006, Tab G: Statement signed by Cpl. Patricia A. Lisk.

[248] Reply by the Government of the United States of America to the Final Observations Regarding the Merits of the Case by the Petitioners, October 17, 2008, p. 7.

[249] U.S. Response to the Petition Alleging Violations of the Human Rights of Jessica Gonzales by the United States of America and the State of Colorado, September 22, 2006, Tab D: Investigator's Progress Report, Castle Rock Police Department, Castle Rock, Colorado, Cr #99-3226, Third Call at 21:57 hours.

whether the restraining order had been violated. They kept on asking Jessica Lenahan to call them back throughout the evening, and to contact Simon Gonzalez [sic] herself, even though they were aware that this was a domestic violence situation. The State itself in its pleadings has presented as a defense that Jessica Lenahan never reported to the police officers that the restraining order had been violated. The Commission has manifested its concern on how States mistakenly take the position that victims are themselves responsible for monitoring the preventive measures, which leaves them defenseless and in danger of becoming the victims of the assailant's reprisals.[250]

159. Seventh, the established facts also show systemic failures not only from the CRPD, but from the Federal Bureau of Investigations. On June 22, 1999, Simon Gonzales purchased a Taurus 9mm handgun with 9 mm ammunition, from William George Palsulich, who held a Federal Firearms License since 1992.[251] Simon Gonzales contacted Palsulich at 6:00 p.m on June 22, 1999, in response to an advertisement Palsulich had placed in the newspaper concerning the sale of the gun, asking whether he could purchase the gun and ammunition.[252] Simon Gonzales went to Palsulich's house at 7:10 p.m on June 22, 1999 with Leslie, Katheryn and Rebecca Gonzales to purchase this gun.[253] The record before the Commission indicates that the seller processed a background check through the Federal Bureau of Investigations in order to make the sale to Simon Gonzalez [sic].[254] Palsulich initially had to decline the sale since the FBI refused the background check, but the FBI later called and informed Palsulich that the transaction had been approved.[255] The State has not

---

[250] IACHR, *Access to Justice for Women Victims of Violence in the Americas*, OEA/Ser. L/V/II. doc. 68, January 20, 2007, para. 170.

[251] December 11, 2006 Observations from Petitioners, Tab N: Interview with William George Palsulich by 18th Judicial District Critical Incident Team Detectives Bobbie Garret and Christian Contos, June 23, 1999, 7:04 p.m; Final Observations Regarding the Merits of the Case submitted by the petitioners, March 24, 2008, Ex. C: 18th Judicial Critical Incident Team Shooting of Simon Gonzales Castle Rock PD Case #99-3226, p. 32.

[252] December 11, 2006 Observations from Petitioners, Tab N: Interview with William George Palsulich by the 18th Judicial District Critical Incident Team Detectives Bobbie Garret and Christian Contos, June 23, 1999, 7:04 p.m.

[253] December 11, 2006 Observations from Petitioners, Tab N: Interview with William George Palsulich by 18th Judicial District Critical Incident Team Detectives Bobbie Garret and Christian Contos, June 23, 1999, 7:04 p.m; Final Observations Regarding the Merits of the Case submitted by the petitioners, March 24, 2008, Ex. C: 18th Judicial Critical Incident Team Shooting of Simon Gonzales Castle Rock PD Case #99-3226, p. 32.

[254] December 11, 2006 Observations from Petitioners, Tab N: Interview with William George Palsulich by 18th Judicial District Critical Incident Team Detectives Bobbie Garret and Christian Contos, June 23, 1999, 7:04 p.m; Final Observations Regarding the Merits of the Case submitted by the petitioners, March 24, 2008, Ex. C: 18th Judicial Critical Incident Team Shooting of Simon Gonzales Castle Rock PD Case #99-3226, p. 32.

[255] December 11, 2006 Observations from Petitioners, Tab N: Interview with William George Palsulich by 18th Judicial District Critical Incident Team Detectives Bobbie Garret and Christian Contos, June 23, 1999, 7:04 p.m; Final Observations Regarding the Merits of the Case submitted by the petitioners, March 24, 2008, Ex. C: 18th Judicial Critical Incident Team Shooting of Simon Gonzales Castle Rock PD Case #99-3226, p. 32.

contested this point, nor it has indicated how the background check of a person, such as Simon Gonzales, subject to a restraining order and having a criminal history, could have been approved. The State has not explained either why the restraining order apparently did not show up in the review of data performed as part of the background check.

iii. Conclusions

160. Based on these considerations, the Commission concludes that even though the State recognized the necessity to protect Jessica Lenahan and Leslie, Katheryn and Rebecca Gonzales from domestic violence, it failed to meet this duty with due diligence. The state apparatus was not duly organized, coordinated, and ready to protect these victims from domestic violence by adequately and effectively implementing the restraining order at issue; failures to protect which constituted a form of discrimination in violation of Article II of the American Declaration.

161. These systemic failures are particularly serious since they took place in a context where there has been a historical problem with the enforcement of protection orders;[256] a problem that has disproportionately affected women—especially those pertaining to ethnic and racial minorities and to low-income groups—since they constitute the majority of the restraining order holders.[257] Within this context, there is also a high correlation between the problem of wife battering and child abuse, exacerbated when the parties in a marriage separate. Even though the Commission recognizes the legislation and programmatic efforts of the United States to address the problem of domestic violence, these measures had not been sufficiently put into practice in the present case.[258]

162. The Commission underscores that all States have a legal obligation to protect women from domestic violence: a problem widely recognized by the international community as a serious human rights violation and an extreme form of discrimination. This is part of their legal obligation to respect and ensure the right not to discriminate and to equal protection of the law. This due diligence obligation in principle applies to all OAS Member States.

---

[256] See U.S. Department of Justice, Attorney General's Task Force on Domestic Violence: Final Report, pages. 18-19 (1984). For a more detailed review of this issue, see section on "findings of fact" *supra* paras. 91-99.

[257] See, U.S. Department of Justice, Bureau of Justice Statistics, National Crime Victimization Survey (2007); Centers for Disease Control and Prevention (CDC), Costs of Intimate Partner Violence in the United States (2003); Patricia Tjaden and Nancy Thoennes, U.S. Department of Justice, Office of Justice Programs, National Institute of Justice, *Extent, Nature and Consequences of Intimate Partner Violence*, July 2000; Lawrence A. Greenfield et al., U.S. Department of Justice, *Violence by Intimates* 38 (1998). For a more detailed review of this issue, see section on "findings of fact" *supra* paras. 91–99.

[258] IACHR, Report Nº 54/01, Case 12.051, *Maria Da Penha Maia Fernandes* (Brazil), April 16, 2001, para. 57.

163. The States' duties to protect and guarantee the rights of domestic violence victims must also be implemented in practice. As the Commission has established in the past, in the discharge of their duties, States must take into account that domestic violence is a problem that disproportionately affects women, since they constitute the majority of the victims.[259] Children are also often common witnesses, victims, and casualties of this phenomenon.[260] Restraining orders are critical in the guarantee of the due diligence obligation in cases of domestic violence.[261] They are often the only remedy available to women victims and their children to protect them from imminent harm. They are only effective, however, if they are diligently enforced.

164. In the case of Leslie, Katheryn and Rebecca Gonzales, the Commission also establishes that the failure of the United States to adequately organize its state structure to protect them from domestic violence not only was discriminatory, but also constituted a violation of their right to life under Article I and their right to special protection as girl-children under Article VII of the American Declaration. As with other obligations under the American Declaration, States are not only required to guarantee that no person is arbitrarily deprived or his or her life. They are also under a positive obligation to protect and prevent violations to this right, through the creation of the conditions that may be required for its protection. In the case of Leslie, Katheryn and Rebecca Gonzales, the State had a reinforced duty of due diligence to protect them from harm and from deprivations of their life due to their age and sex, with special measures of care, prevention and guarantee. The State's recognition of the risk of harm and the need for protection—through the issuance of a protection order which included them as beneficiaries—made the adequate implementation of this protection measure even more critical.

165. The State's duty to apply due diligence to act expeditiously to protect girl-children from right to life violations requires that the authorities in charge of receiving reports of missing persons have the capacity to understand the seriousness of the phenomenon of violence perpetrated against them, and to act immediately.[262] In this case, the police appear to have assumed that Jessica Lenahan's daughters and their friend would be safe with Simon Gonzales because he was Leslie, Katheryn and Rebecca's father. There is broad international recognition of the connection

---

[259]IACHR, Report N° 54/01, Case 12.051, *Maria Da Penha Maia Fernandes* (Brazil), April 16, 2001, para. 47.

[260]*See,* Study of Dr. Paulo Sergio Pinheiro as Independent Expert for the United Nations Study on Violence against Children pursuant to General Assembly Resolution 60/231, 29 August 2006, paras. 38–47.

[261]United Nations, Report of the Special Rapporteur on violence against women, its causes and consequences, Yakin Ertürk, *The Due Diligence Standard as a tool for the Elimination of Violence against Women,* E/CN.4/2006/61, para. 49; IACHR, *Access to Justice for Women Victims of Violence in the Americas,* OEA/Ser. L/V/II. doc. 68, January 20, 2007, para. 53.

[262]See generally, IACHR, Report N° 28/07, Cases 12.496-12.498, *Claudia Ivette Gonzalez and Others* (Mexico), March 9, 2007, paras. 247–255; I/A Court H.R., *Case of González et al. ("Cotton Field") v. Mexico.* Preliminary Objection, Merits, Reparations and Costs. Judgment of November 16, 2009. Series C No. 205, para. 285.

between domestic violence and fatal violence against children perpetrated by parents, and the CRPD officers should have been trained regarding this link.[263] The police officers should also have been aware that the children were at an increased risk of violence due to the separation of their parents, Simon Gonzales' efforts to maintain contact with Jessica Lenahan, and his criminal background. Moreover, the Commission knows of no protocols and/or directives that were in place to guide the police officers at hand on how to respond to reports of missing children in the context of domestic violence and protection orders.[264] The police officers' response throughout the evening was uncoordinated, and not conducive to ascertaining whether the terms of the order had been violated by Simon Gonzales.

166. As part of its conclusions, the Commission notes that when a State issues a protection order, this has safety implications for the women who requested the protection order, her children and her family members. Restraining orders may aggravate the problem of separation violence, resulting in reprisals from the aggressor directed towards the woman and her children, a problem which increases the need of victims to receive legal protection from the State after an order of this kind has been issued. Jessica Lenahan has declared before the Commission how she desisted from taking more actions to find her daughters that evening thinking that the State would do more to protect them, since she held a restraining order.[265]

167. The Commission notes with particular concern the insensitive nature of some of the CRPD comments to Jessica Lenahan's calls, considering that in her contacts she demonstrated that she was concerned for the well-being of her daughters. For example, and as noted earlier, when Jessica Lenahan called the CPRD for a third time at 9:57 p.m. to report that her children were still not home, the dispatcher told her she wished that she and Simon Gonzales had made some arrangements since "that's a little ridiculous making us freak out and thinking the kids are gone."[266]

---

[263] The recent United Nations Study on Violence against Children confirms that the majority of violent acts experienced by children are perpetrated by people who are part of their lives, including parents, and that intimate partner violence heavily affects children. See, Study of Paulo Sergio Pinheiro as Independent Expert for the United Nations Study on Violence against Children, pursuant to General Assembly Resolution 60/231, 29 August 2005, para. 28. A recent United Nations Study on Violence against Women has highlights that "[c]hildren are often present during episodes of domestic violence" and that "[d]omestic or intimate partner violence can....be fatal for children." See, United Nations, Report of the Secretary-General, *In Depth Study on All Forms of Violence against Women*, A/61/122/Add.1, July 6, 2006, para. 169.

[264] See, e.g., National Center for Missing and Exploited Children, Missing and Abducted Children, *A Law Enforcement Guide to Case Investigation and Case Management*, Third Edition (2006).

[265] Hearing on the matter of *Jessica Gonzales v. United States* at the 127th Ordinary Period of Sessions of the Inter-American Commission on Human Rights, March 2, 2007.

[266] U.S. Response to the Petition Alleging Violations of the Human Rights of Jessica Gonzales by the United States of America and the State of Colorado, September 22, 2006, Tab D: Investigator's Progress Report, Castle Rock Police Department, Castle Rock, Colorado, Cr #99-3226, Third Call at 21:57 hours.

Her pleas for police action became more disturbing as the evening progressed.[267] The Commission accentuates that this form of mistreatment results in a mistrust that the State structure can really protect women and girl-children from harm, which reproduces the social tolerance toward these acts.[268] The Commission also underscores the internationally-recognized principle that law enforcement officials "shall respect and protect human dignity and maintain and uphold the human rights of all persons in the performance of their duties."[269]

168. The Commission reiterates that State inaction towards cases of violence against women fosters an environment of impunity and promotes the repetition of violence "since society sees no evidence of willingness by the State, as the representative of the society, to take effective action to sanction such acts."[270]

169. The Commission also observes that the State's obligations to protect Jessica Lenahan and her daughters from domestic violence did not conclude that evening. They extended to offering Jessica Lenahan a remedy for these failures and to investigating the circumstances of Leslie, Katheryn and Rebecca Gonzales' death, as will be discussed in the following section.

170. Based on these considerations, the Commission holds that the systemic failure of the United States to offer a coordinated and effective response to protect Jessica Lenahan and her daughters from domestic violence, constituted an act of discrimination, a breach of their obligation not to discriminate, and a violation of their right to equality before the law under Article II of the American Declaration. The Commission also finds that the State failure to undertake reasonable measures to protect the life of Leslie, Katheryn and Rebecca Gonzales, and that this failure constituted a violation of their right to life established in Article I of the American Declaration, in relation to their right to special protection contained in Article VII of the American Declaration.

---

[267] During her first call, Jessica Lenahan described the situation to the dispatcher as "scary" and "that she did not know what to do." During her telephone conversation with Officer Brink, she communicated that she considered Simon Gonzales' taking of his daughters and their friend to the park, "unusual," "wrong" and "weird." During her third call at 9:57 p.m. that evening, Jessica Lenahan informed the dispatcher that she was a "little wigged out" because her daughters were still not home and that she "did not know what to do," that she was a "mess," and that she was "freaking out." During her last call to the CRPD at midnight, she reported that her daughters were still not home, that Simon Gonzales had run off with the girls, and that she was very worried about her children. When Jessica Lenahan visited the CRPD at 12:30 a.m., she was crying, and she informed Officer Ahlfinger that she still "didn't know what to do" and was "scared" for her children, that she was afraid Simon Gonzales had "lost it," and that he might be "suicidal." For a more detailed discussion, see paragraphs 71–79 of this report.
[268] IACHR, *Access to Justice for Women Victims of Violence in the Americas*, OEA/Ser. L/V/II. doc.68, January 20, 2007, paras. 172–180.
[269] IACHR, *Access to Justice for Women Victims of Violence in the Americas*, OEA/Ser. L/V/II. doc.68, January 20, 2007, para. 134.
[270] IACHR, Report N° 54/01, Case 12.051, *Maria Da Penha Fernandes* (Brazil), April 16, 2001, para. 56.

2. The right to judicial protection under Article XVIII

171. Article XVIII of the American Declaration provides:

> Every person may resort to the courts to ensure respect for his legal rights. There should likewise be available to him a simple, brief procedure whereby the courts will protect him from acts of authority that, to his prejudice, violate any fundamental constitutional rights.

172. Article XVIII of the American Declaration establishes that all persons are entitled to access judicial remedies when they have suffered human rights violations.[271] This right is similar in scope to the right to judicial protection and guarantees contained in Article 25 of the American Convention on Human Rights, which is understood to encompass: the right of every individual to go to a tribunal when any of his or her rights have been violated; to obtain a judicial investigation conducted by a competent, impartial and independent tribunal that establishes whether or not a violation has taken place; and the corresponding right to obtain reparations for the harm suffered.[272]

173. The inter-American system has affirmed for many years that it is not the formal existence of such remedies that demonstrates due diligence, but rather that they are available and effective.[273] Therefore, when the State apparatus leaves human rights violations unpunished and the victim's full enjoyment of human rights is not promptly restored, the State fails to comply with its positive duties under international human rights law.[274] The same principle applies when a State allows private persons to act freely and with impunity to the detriment of the rights recognized in the governing instruments of the inter-American system.

174. The petitioners raise several claims related to the scope of the right to judicial protection under Article XVIII of the American Declaration. They claim that Jessica Lenahan's rights were violated because she has not obtained: a remedy for the non-enforcement of her protection order; adequate access to the United States Courts; and a diligent investigation into her daughters' deaths. As part of their claims related to the investigation, the petitioners also allege that Jessica Lenahan's and her next-of-kin's right to truth has been violated due to the State's failure to provide them information surrounding the deaths of Leslie, Katheryn and Rebecca

---

[271] IACHR, Report N° 54/01, Case 12.051, *Maria Da Penha Maia Fernandes* (Brazil), April 16, 2001, para. 37.

[272] IACHR, Report N° 40/4, Case 12.053, *Maya Indigenous Community* (Belize), para. 174; IACHR, Report N° 54/01, Case 12.051, *Maria Da Penha Fernandes* (Brazil), April 16, 2001, para. 37.

[273] See, IACHR, Report N° 81/10, Case 12.562, *Wayne Smith, Hugo Armendatriz, et al.*, United States, July 12, 2010, para. 62; IACHR, ACHR, Report on Admissibility N° 52/07, Petition 1490-05, *Jessica Gonzales and Others (United States)*, July 24, 2007, para. 42; IACHR, *Access to Justice for Women Victims of Violence in the Americas*, OEA/Ser.L/V/II, Doc. 68 (January 20, 2007), para. 26; I/A Court H.R., *The "Street Children" Case (Villagrán Morales et al.)*. Judgment of November 19, 1999. Series C No. 63, para. 235.

[274] IACHR, *The Situation of the Rights of Women in Ciudad Juarez*, OEA/Ser. L/V/II.117. Doc. 44 (March 7, 2003), para. 51.

Gonzales. The petitioners also raise these claims under the right to petition established in Article XXIV of the American Declaration, and the right to freedom of investigation, opinion, expression and dissemination under Article IV of the American Declaration.

175. The State for its part claims that Article XVIII of the American Declaration does not comprehend a right to a remedy related to the non-enforcement of restraining orders; that the United States' judicial system was available to Jessica Lenahan since her case was seen by the United States Supreme Court; that Jessica Lenahan had other valid legal avenues available to adjudicate facts related to the death of her daughters which she failed to pursue; and that the State undertook two extensive investigations following the tragic deaths of Leslie, Katheryn and Rebecca Gonzales which conformed to existing human rights standards. Concerning the right to truth, the State claims that the Commission should not rule on this claim under Article IV of the American Declaration since it was not raised at the admissibility stage.

176. The Commission will discuss how the obligations under Article XVIII apply to the given case in the following order: i) claims related to remedies for the non-enforcement of the protection order; and ii) claims related to the investigation of Leslie, Katheryn and Rebecca Gonzales' deaths, including allegations pertaining to access to information and the right to truth.

i. Claims related to remedies for the non-enforcement of a protection order

177. The Commission has identified the duty of State parties to adopt legal measures to prevent imminent acts of violence, as one side of their obligation to ensure that victims can adequately and effectively access judicial protection mechanisms.[275] The Commission has identified restraining orders, and their adequate and effective enforcement, among these legal measures.[276] According to this principle, the failures of the State in this case to adequately and effectively organize its apparatus to ensure the implementation of the restraining order also violated the right to judicial protection of Jessica Lenahan and Leslie, Katheryn and Rebecca Gonzales.

178. The Commission also considers that when there are State failures, negligence and/or omissions to protect women from imminent acts of violence, the State also has the obligation to investigate systemic failures to prevent their repetition in the future. This involves an impartial, serious and exhaustive investigation of the State structures that were involved in the enforcement of a protection order, including a thorough inquiry into the individual actions of the public officials involved.[277]

---

[275] IACHR, *Access to Justice for Women Victims of Violence in the Americas*, OEA/Ser.L/V/II, Doc. 68 (January 20, 2007), para. 56.
[276] IACHR, *Access to Justice for Women Victims of Violence in the Americas*, OEA/Ser.L/V/II, Doc. 68 (January 20, 2007), para. 56.
[277] IACHR, Report Nº 28/07, Case 12, 496, *Claudia Ivette González and Others* (Mexico), March 9, 2007, para. 242, Recommendation 2.

States must hold public officials accountable—administratively, disciplinarily or criminally—when they do not act in accordance with the rule of law.[278]

179. The State should undertake this systemic inquiry on its own motion and promptly.[279] A delay in this inquiry constitutes a form of impunity in the face of acts of violence against women and promotes their repetition.[280]

180. The Commission does not have information indicating that the State authorities have undertaken any inquiry into the response actions of the Castle Rock police officers in their contacts with Jessica Lenahan throughout the evening of June 22nd and the morning of June 23rd. The Commission does not have information indicating either that any inquiry has been undertaken at the level of the Federal Bureau of Investigations for the approval of the gun-purchase. The two investigations before the Commission appear to have focused exclusively on clarifying the circumstances of the shooting death of Simon Gonzales, and not on determining individual responsibilities on the part of public officials for failures to act in accordance with the relevant state and federal laws. Therefore, the Commission notes that the State responsibilities in this case were not met by the United States Supreme Court decision regarding Jessica Lenahan's constitutional claims and extended to investigating the systemic failures which occurred during the evening of June 22nd and the morning of June 23rd in enforcing the restraining order at issue.

ii. The investigation of Leslie, Katheryn and Rebecca's deaths, access to information, and the right to truth

181. The Commission has emphasized the principle that the ability of victims of violence against women to access judicial protection and remedies includes ensuring clarification of the truth of what has happened.[281] Investigations must be serious, prompt, thorough, and impartial, and must be conducted in accordance with international standards in this area.[282] In addition, the IACHR has established that

---

[278]IACHR, *Access to Justice for Women Victims of Violence in the Americas*, OEA/Ser.L/V/II, Doc. 68 (January 20, 2007), para. 77; United Nations, *Crime Prevention and Criminal Justice Measures to Eliminate Violence against Women*, resolution approved by the United Nations General Assembly, A/RES/52/86, February 2, 1998, Annex, Section II.

[279]IACHR, *Access to Justice for Women Victims of Violence in the Americas*, OEA/Ser.L/V/II, Doc. 68 (January 20, 2007), para. 77; United Nations, *Crime Prevention and Criminal Justice Measures to Eliminate Violence against Women*, resolution approved by the United Nations General Assembly, A/RES/52/86, February 2, 1998, Annex, Section II.

[280]IACHR, *The Situation of the Rights of Women in Ciudad Juarez*, OEA/Ser. L/V/II.117. Doc. 44 (March 7, 2003), para. 142; IACHR, *Access to Justice for Women Victims of Violence in the Americas*, OEA/Ser.L/V/II, Doc. 68 (January 20, 2007), Recommendation 1.

[281]IACHR, Report N° 28/07, Case 12, 496, *Claudia Ivette González and Others* (Mexico), March 9, 2007, para. 206; IACHR, *Access to Justice for Women Victims of Violence in the Americas*, OEA/Ser.L/V/II, Doc. 68 (January 20, 2007), para. 40.

[282]IACHR, Report N° 53/01, *Ana, Beatriz and Celia González Pérez* (Mexico), Case 11.565, April 4, 2001, paras. 84-88; IACHR, *The Situation of the Rights of Women in Ciudad Juárez, Mexico: The Right to be Free from Violence and Discrimination*, OEA/Ser.L/V/II.117, Doc. 44, March 7, 2003, para. 132.

the State must show that the investigation "was not the product of a mechanical implementation of certain procedural formalities without the State genuinely seeking the truth."[283] The State is ultimately the one responsible for ascertaining the truth on its own initiative, and this does not depend on the efforts of the victim or her next-of-kin.[284] In accordance with its special protection obligation and the due diligence principle, this obligation is particularly critical in cases implicating the right to life of girl-children.[285]

182. The inter-American system has referred to the "Principles on the Effective Prevention and Investigation of Extra-legal, Arbitrary and Summary Executions," adopted by the Economic and Social Council of the United Nations by UN Resolution 1989/65, as guidelines that must be observed in the investigation of a violent death.[286] These principles require that in cases such as that of Leslie, Katheryn and Rebecca Gonzales, the investigation of every suspicious death must have the following objectives: to identify the victim; to recover and analyze all the material and documentary evidence; to identify possible witnesses and collect their testimony; to determine the cause, manner and time of death, as well as the procedure, practice, or instruments which may have caused the death; to distinguish between natural death, accidental death, suicide, and homicide; and to identify and apprehend the person or persons who may have participated in the execution.[287]

183. The regional system has also referred to the guidelines established in the United Nations Manual on the Effective Prevention and Investigation of Extra-Legal, Arbitrary and Summary Executions, noting that one of the most important aspects of a "full and impartial" investigation of an extralegal, arbitrary, or summary execution is gathering and analyzing the evidence for each suspicious death.[288] To this end, the manual establishes that in relation to the crime scene, that investigators must, at a minimum, photograph that scene, any other physical evidence, and the body as found and after being moved; all samples of blood, hair, fibers, threads, or other clues should be collected and conserved; examine the area in search of footprints of shoes or anything else in the nature of evidence; and make a report

---

[283]IACHR, Report N° 55/97, *Juan Carlos Abella et al.* (Argentina), November 18, 1997, para. 412.

[284]IACHR, *Access to Justice for Women Victims of Violence in the Americas*, OEA/Ser.L/V/II, Doc. 68 (January 20, 2007), para. 40; I/A Court H.R., *Godínez Cruz Case*. Judgment of January 20, 1989. Series C No. 5, para. 188.

[285]IACHR, Report N° 28/07, Cases 12.496-12.498, *Claudia Ivette González and Others* (Mexico), March 9, 2007, para. 247.

[286]IACHR, Report N° 28/07, Cases 12.496-12.498, *Claudia Ivette González and Others* (Mexico), March 9, 2007, paras. 216-217; IACHR, Report N° 10/95, Case 10.580, *Manuel Stalin Bolaños*, Ecuador, Annual Report of the IACHR 1995, OEA/Ser.L/V/II.91, Doc. 7, rev. 3, April 3, 1996, paras. 32-34.

[287]United Nations, Principles on the Effective Prevention and Investigation of Extra-legal, Arbitrary and Summary Executions, Recommended by Economic and Social Council Resolution 1989/65.

[288]United Nations Manual on the Effective Prevention and Investigation of Extralegal, Arbitrary and Summary Executions, Doc. E/ST/CSDHA/12 (1991).

detailing any observation of the scene, the actions of the investigators, and the disposition of all evidence collected.[289] In addition, it is necessary to investigate the crime scene exhaustively, autopsies should be performed, and human remains must be analyzed rigorously by competent professionals.

184. In light of these international standards, the United States had the duty to undertake, on its own initiative, a prompt, thorough and separate investigation aimed at clarifying the cause, time and place of the deaths of Leslie, Katheryn and Rebecca Gonzales.

185. The petitioners claim that the investigations conducted by the authorities solely related to the shooting death of Simon Gonzales. According to them, these documents raise many unanswered questions and demonstrate the inadequate nature of the investigation into the death of the three girls. They claim that the evidence in these documents is insufficient to determine which bullets killed Jessica Lenahan's daughters, those of the CRPD or those of Simon Gonzales. The State, for its part, claims that in the wake of the tragedy two investigations were undertaken by the Colorado Bureau of Investigations and by the Critical Incident Team of the 18th Judicial District which were prompt, extensive and thorough.[290] The State is surprised that the petitioners now argue that because there was no adequate investigation, the actual cause of the death of the Leslie, Katheryn and Rebecca Gonzales is unknown. The State considers that the petitioners' suggestion that the gunfire originating from the CRPD officers may have killed the children is contradictory to the evidence amassed in the investigative reports mentioned by the State, which suggests that Simon Gonzales murdered the girl-children.

186. The established facts before the Commission reveal that two investigations were undertaken by the State related to the case at hand,[291] one by the Colorado Bureau of Investigations and one by the Critical Incident Team of the 18th Judicial District, but these mainly focused on clarifying the facts surrounding the shooting

---

[289] IACHR, Report N° 28/07, Cases 12.496-12.498, *Claudia Ivette González and Others* (Mexico), March 9, 2007, paras. 218; I/A Court H.R., *Case of González et al. ("Cotton Field"). Preliminary Objection, Merits, Reparations and Costs.* Judgment of November 16, 2009. Series C No. 205, para. 301.

[290] Final Observations Regarding the Merits of the Case submitted by the petitioners, March 24, 2008, Ex. B: Colorado Bureau of Investigation: Report of Investigation, prepared by Agents J. Clayton Jr. & D. Sollars, July 19, 1999 and Ex. C: 18th Judicial Critical Incident Team Shooting of Simon Gonzales Castle Rock PD Case #99-3226.

[291] Investigation by the Colorado Bureau of Investigation (CBI) and Investigation by Critical Incident Team (CIT) of 18th Judicial District, Exhibits B and C respectively of Final Observations Regarding the Merits of the Case submitted by the petitioners, March 24, 2008. The State also presents a supplemental report related to the CIT investigation dated July 1, 1999 in Tab E of its U.S. Response to the Petition Alleging Violations of the Human Rights of Jessica Gonzales by the United States of America and the State of Colorado, September 22, 2006.

The Commission observes that on August 3, 2009, it requested from the United States the entire investigation file related to the death of Leslie, Katheryn and Rebecca Gonzales, but this request has not been met. Therefore, the Commission bases the analysis of these two investigations on the information that has been provided to date by the parties.

death of Simon Gonzales, and not the murder of Leslie, Katheryn and Rebecca Gonzales.[292] No investigation reports before the Commission indicate as their main objective the clarification of the circumstances related to the girl-children deaths. Documents related to the investigations conclude in summary fashion that Simon Gonzales murdered his daughters before the shooting at the CRPD station, and that they were not struck by any of the rounds fired by the police officers, but fail to provide any foundation for this premise.[293]

187. Available information regarding the circumstances of the shooting leave doubt as to the conclusion that Simon Gonzales's bullets were the ones that killed his daughters. Each girl was found to be shot in the head and chest from multiple angles.[294] The CIT investigation report reveals that several witness accounts mentioned hearing screams, two from female voices, at the time of the shooting in front of the Castle Rock Police Department.[295] However, there is no indication in the record that these aspects were investigated. The investigations before the Commission also reveal important omissions such as the quick disposal of Simon Gonzales' truck, even though it contained blood, clothing and other evidence related to the girl-children, making the truck an important piece of evidence in the clarification of the circumstances of the girl-children's deaths.[296]

188. An expert report prepared by Peter Diaczuk,[297] a forensic scientist, presented by the petitioners on July 16, 2009 and uncontested by the State, reviews in detail documentation related to these two investigations and identifies significant irregularities pertaining to the inquiry into Leslie, Katheryn and Rebecca's deaths. He notes that the "incomplete handling, documentation, and analysis of the evidence

---

[292] The documents related to these two investigations read in conjunction also show that their main objective was to investigate the exchange of gunfire between the police and Simon Gonzales. See, for example, Final Observations Regarding the Merits of the Case submitted by the petitioners, March 24, 2008, Exhibit H: Letter to Colorado Bureau of Investigations from Agents Contos and Vanecek, June 28, 1999; Reply by the Government of the United States of America to the Final Observations Regarding the Merits of the Case by the Petitioners, October 17, 2008, Tab I: Letter from the District Attorney, 18th Judicial District to Castle Rock Police Department, August 13, 1999.

[293] Final Observations Regarding the Merits of the Case submitted by the petitioners, March 24, 2008, Exhibit C: 18th Judicial Critical Incident Team Shooting of Simon Gonzales Castle Rock PD Case #99-3226, p. 38.

[294] Final Observations Regarding the Merits of the Case submitted by the petitioners, March 24, 2008, Exhibit E: Douglas County Coroner's Report: Rebecca Gonzales, Exhibit F: Douglas County Coroner's Report: Katheryn Gonzales, and Exhibit G: Douglas County Coroner's Report: Leslie Gonzales.

[295] See, December 11, 2006 Observations from Petitioners, Ex. I: Critical Incident Team Report, Dated June 23, 1999, R. E. Garrett, Detective.

[296] Final Observations Regarding the Merits of the Case submitted by the petitioners, March 24, 2008, Exhibit B: Colorado Bureau of Investigation: Report of Investigation, prepared by Agents J. Clayton, Jr. & D. Sollars, July 19, 1999.

[297] Expert Report by Peter Diaczuk, Forensic Scientist and the Director of Forensic Science Training at the Center for Modern Forensic Practice, John Jay College of Criminal Justice, City University of New York, presented by petitioners to the Commission on July 16, 2009 (hereinafter "Expert Report by Peter Diaczuk").

in this case resulted in unnecessary uncertainty surrounding the time, place, and circumstances of the three girls' deaths;" and that "while many answers appeared within reach, law enforcement officials simply did not take the steps necessary to fully uncover them." [298]

189. Professor Diaczuk in his report notes key differences between the quality of the investigation of elements found outside of Simon Gonzales' pick-up truck, and the evidence found inside the truck, where the three bodies of the girl-children were found. For example, he observes that even though law enforcement used care in photographing and documenting the outside crime scene and evidence found at the street level, near Simon Gonzales' body, the bodies of the girls and the interior of the truck were photographed hastily, without use of the proper lighting equipment or measurements. Even though important items of physical evidence at the crime scene were recognized, photographed, documented and collected, most of the items collected from inside of the truck were not routed to the laboratory for analysis, as opposed to the items collected outside the truck, which were properly analyzed. Professor Diaczuk highlights as a particularly troubling aspect the Colorado authorities' analysis and accounting of the firearm evidence found inside of Simon Gonzales' truck, noting that pursuant to investigatory procedures, a laboratory examination of all cases, projectiles and fragments—including those found inside and outside of the truck—was critical; but was not performed in this case. He furthermore notes that the truck in which the bodies of the girl-children were found was disposed of quickly, before time, location and circumstances surrounding the deaths of Jessica Lenahan's children were even recorded on their death certificates, even though inquiries into the girl-children's deaths were still pending.

190. Professor Diaczuk concludes overall that even if circumstantial evidence may have suggested to the authorities that Simon Gonzales was responsible for the deaths of the girl-children, the forensic analyses he reviewed do not sustain this conclusion, instead showing that the investigation of their deaths was prematurely concluded. He indicated that the death of each victim should have been treated as a separate occurrence, and investigated in its own right.

191. The Commission notes that the State has not challenged the expert report presented by Professor Peter Diaczuk. The State has responded overall to the petitioners' claims by stating that if the petitioners considered the investigation of the girl-children's deaths inappropriate and incomplete, they should have availed themselves of the Citizen Complaint Procedure of the Castle Rock Police Department. Regarding this State claim, the Commission established at the admissibility stage that the State had not indicated how the alternative administrative remedy it mentions could have provided Jessica Lenahan with a different judicial redress for her pretentions, or how this could have been adequate and effective in remedying the violations alleged.[299]

---

[298] Expert Report by Peter Diaczuk, para. 54.
[299] IACHR, Report on Admissibility N° 52/07, Petition 1490-05, *Jessica Gonzales and Others (United States)*, July 24, 2007, Annual Report of the IACHR 2007, para. 48.

192. Regarding this issue, the Commission finally underscores that the State had the obligation to investigate the death of Leslie, Katheryn and Rebecca Gonzales as separate occurrences, on its own motion and initiative, and in a prompt, exhaustive and impartial manner.

193. The Commission has also identified the right to access information in respect to existing investigations as a crucial component of a victim's adequate access to judicial remedies.[300] A critical component of the right to access information is the right of the victim, her family members and society as a whole to be informed of all happenings related to a serious human rights violation.[301] The inter-American system has established that this right—the right to truth—is not only a private right for relatives of the victims, affording them a form of reparation, but also a collective right that ensures that society has access to information essential for the workings of democratic systems.[302]

194. Eleven years have passed since the murders of Leslie, Katheryn and Rebecca Gonzales, and the State has not fully clarified the cause, time and place of their deaths. The State has not duly communicated this information to their family. The petitioners have presented information highlighting the challenges that Jessica Lenahan and her family members have faced to obtain basic information surrounding the circumstances of Leslie, Katheryn and Rebecca Gonzales' deaths.[303] They also indicate that Leslie, Katheryn and Rebecca Gonzales' gravestones still do not contain information about the time and place of their death. In regards to concrete efforts, Jessica Lenahan's mother, Tina Rivera, has declared the following before the Commission:

> Despite our repeated requests for information and documentation about the circumstances of the deaths of Rebecca, Katheryn and Leslie in the days following their shooting, the CRPD gave us nothing . . . . For several weeks, Jessica, Rosalie Ochoa, and I attempted to obtain information from the Castle Rock and Colorado officials. Jessica and Rosalie went to the Douglas County Court House several times to try to obtain the tapes of Jessica's 911 calls. They also made repeated in-person trips to the CRPD, requesting access to the police records from the night that my granddaughters were killed. They traveled to Denver General Hospital's mental health center and Simon Gonzales' employer to find more information about Simon Gonzales . . . . However, officials at the Douglas County Court House and CRPD were not cooperative and tried to dissuade us from our efforts. We were denied access to the files

---

[300] IACHR, *Access to Justice for Women Victims of Violence in the Americas*, OEA/Ser.L/V/II, Doc. 68 (January 20, 2007), paras. 54, 134, 139, 172 and 177.
[301] See, i.e., IACHR, Report on the Merits N 136/99, Case 10.488, *Ignacio Ellacuria and Others* (El Salvador), December 12, 1999, paras. 224–226.
[302] See, i.e., IACHR, Report on the Merits N° 136/99, Case 10.488, *Ignacio Ellacuria and Others* (El Salvador), December 12, 1999, para. 224.
[303] Hearing on the matter of *Jessica Gonzales v. United States* at the 133th Ordinary Period of Sessions of the Inter-American Commission on Human Rights, October 22, 2008; Final Observations Regarding the Merits of the Case submitted by the petitioners, March 24, 2008, Ex. A: Declaration of Tina Rivera, March 17, 2008.

and documents we sought. While denying our requests, the Police and Court House officials treated us in a dismissive and harassing manner. We felt treated as criminals, not victims.[304]

195. The Commission underscores that under the American Declaration, the State is obligated to investigate the circumstances surrounding Leslie, Katheryn and Rebecca Gonzales' deaths and to communicate the results of such an investigation to their family. Compliance with this State obligation is critical to sending a social message in the United States that violence against girl-children will not be tolerated, and will not remain in impunity, even when perpetrated by private actors.

196. In light of the considerations presented, the Commission finds that the United States violated the right to judicial protection of Jessica Lenahan and her next-of-kin under Article XVIII, for omissions at two levels. First, the State failed to undertake a proper inquiry into systemic failures and the individual responsibilities for the non-enforcement of the protection order. Second, the State did not perform a prompt, thorough, exhaustive and impartial investigation into the deaths of Leslie, Katheryn and Rebecca Gonzales, and failed to convey information to the family members related to the circumstances of their deaths.

197. The Commission considers that it does not have sufficient information to find the State internationally responsible for failures to grant Jessica Lenahan an adequate access to courts under Article XVIII. The Commission notes that Jessica Lenahan chose to raise her claims at the national level before federal courts. The undisputed facts show that her allegations reached the U.S. Supreme Court, the highest judicial instance and appellate court in the United States. The Supreme Court ruled on her claims on June 27, 2005. Even though this ruling was unfavorable to the victim, the record before the Commission does not display that this legal process was affected by any irregularities, omissions, delays, or any other due process violations that would contravene Article XVIII of the American Declaration.

198. Regarding Articles XXIV and IV of the American Declaration, the Commission considers that the claims related to these articles were addressed under Article XVIII of the American Declaration.

V. CONCLUSIONS

199. Based on the foregoing considerations of fact and law, and having examined the evidence and arguments presented by the parties during the proceedings, the Commission concludes that the State failed to act with due diligence to protect Jessica Lenahan and Leslie, Katheryn and Rebecca Gonzales from domestic violence, which violated the State's obligation not to discriminate and to provide for equal protection before the law under Article II of the American Declaration. The State also failed to undertake reasonable measures to prevent the death of Leslie,

---

[304]Final Observations Regarding the Merits of the Case submitted by the petitioners, March 24, 2008, Ex. A: Declaration of Tina Rivera, March 17, 2008.

Katheryn and Rebecca Gonzales in violation of their right to life under Article I of the American Declaration, in conjunction with their right to special protection as girl-children under Article VII of the American Declaration. Finally, the Commission concludes that the State violated the right to judicial protection of Jessica Lenahan and her next-of kin, under Article XVIII of the American Declaration.

200. The Commission does not find that it has sufficient information to find violations of articles V and VI. As to Articles XXIV and IV of the American Declaration, it considers the claims related to these articles to have been addressed under Article XVIII of the American Declaration.

VI. RECOMMENDATIONS

201. Based on the analysis and conclusions pertaining to the instant case, the Inter-American Commission on Human Rights recommends to the United States:

1. To undertake a serious, impartial and exhaustive investigation with the objective of ascertaining the cause, time and place of the deaths of Leslie, Katheryn and Rebecca Gonzales, and to duly inform their next-of-kin of the course of the investigation.

2. To conduct a serious, impartial and exhaustive investigation into systemic failures that took place related to the enforcement of Jessica Lenahan's protection order as a guarantee of their non-repetition, including performing an inquiry to determine the responsibilities of public officials for violating state and/or federal laws, and holding those responsible accountable.

3. To offer full reparations to Jessica Lenahan and her next-of-kin considering their perspective and specific needs.

4. To adopt multifaceted legislation at the federal and state levels, or to reform existing legislation, making mandatory the enforcement of protection orders and other precautionary measures to protect women from imminent acts of violence, and to create effective implementation mechanisms. These measures should be accompanied by adequate resources destined to foster their implementation; regulations to ensure their enforcement; training programs for the law enforcement and justice system officials who will participate in their execution; and the design of model protocols and directives that can be followed by police departments throughout the country.

5. To adopt multifaceted legislation at the federal and state levels, or reform existing legislation, including protection measures for children in the context of domestic violence. Such measures should be accompanied by adequate resources destined to foster their implementation; regulations to ensure their enforcement; training programs for the law enforcement and justice system officials who will participate in their execution; and the design of model protocols and directives that can be followed by police departments throughout the country.

6. To continue adopting public policies and institutional programs aimed at restructuring the stereotypes of domestic violence victims, and to promote the eradication of discriminatory socio-cultural patterns that impede women and children's full protection from domestic violence acts, including programs to train public officials in all branches of the administration of justice and police, and comprehensive prevention programs.

7. To design protocols at the federal and state levels specifying the proper components of the investigation by law enforcement officials of a report of missing children in the context of a report of a restraining order violation.

VII. ACTIONS SUBSEQUENT TO REPORT No. 114/10

202. On October 21, 2010, the IACHR adopted Report No. 114/10 on the merits of this case. This report was sent to the State on November 15, 2010, with a time period of two months to inform the Inter-American Commission on the measures adopted to comply with its recommendations. On the same date, the petitioners were notified of the adoption of the report.

203. On January 14, 2011, the State requested an extension to present its response to the merits report. The Commission granted an extension to the State until March 15, 2011 to present its observations, in accordance with Article 37(2) of the IACHR's Rules of Procedure.

204. The petitioners presented their observations regarding the report on January 28, 2011, which were forwarded to the State on February 15, 2011, with a one-month period to send its observations. The petitioners also forwarded additional information to the Commission on February 18, 2011, which was transmitted to the State for its information on March 11, 2011.

205. In the present case, the State requested an extension in which to present information, but did not do so within the time period provided. The petitioners, for their part, provided a series of observations with respect to the analysis and determinations made by the Commission in its merits report, concerning such issues as: ongoing violence against women in Castle Rock; the scope of the right to an adequate and effective remedy in United States courts; the reiteration of arguments concerning the applicability of Articles I, V, VI and VII of the American Declaration in the case; and the need for the United States to ensure compliance with its obligations under the American Declaration in a way that resolves the challenges of federalism. The petitioners also requested that the Commission adopt a number of more detailed recommendations and proposed measures of follow-up on compliance.

206. In accordance with the objectives of the individual case system and the applicable terms of the Commission's Rules of Procedure, in cases in which the IACHR has established a violation of the duties set forth in the American Declaration, it transmits the report to the State in question in order for the latter to report on compliance with the recommendations issued. The Commission notifies the petitioners

as well, with the same objective of receiving information with respect to compliance with its recommendations. This phase of the proceedings does not serve as an opportunity to reopen questions that have been analyzed and decided by the Commission.

207. Given the lack of information from the State, the Commission must conclude that the recommendations issued have not been implemented, and that their compliance thus remains pending. The Commission is accordingly required to reiterate those recommendations and continue monitoring compliance.

208. With respect to the submissions of the petitioners, the information presented goes not toward issues of compliance but toward questions of law that, for the most part, were analyzed by the Commission.

209. The petitioners make one observation, however, that suggests a need for clarification as to the scope of the Commission's findings with respect to judicial protection. In their submission, the petitioners take issue with what they consider to have been an overly narrow reading of the right to an adequate and effective remedy in the United States court system. They claim that: "In the Commission's view, Ms. Lenahan's right to a remedy was not violated because she was able to present her allegations to the country's highest court and the legal process she followed was unaffected 'by any irregularities, omissions, delays or any other due process violations . . . .'" [Citation omitted.] The petitioners also claim that this narrow view of the right to a remedy fails to take into consideration the long-standing jurisprudence of the inter-American human rights system, as well as guidance from other international authorities, recognizing that the right to a remedy must be effective, "not merely illusory or theoretical," and that it must be suitable to grant appropriate relief for the legal right that is alleged to have been infringed. They reiterate that taken together, three United States Supreme Court holdings—in the cases of *Castle Rock v. Gonzales, DeShaney v. Winnebago County Department of Social Services*, and *United States v. Morrison*—act as a categorical bar to victims and survivors of domestic violence initiating legal proceedings against government officials under the United States Constitution to vindicate their rights to be protected from such violence.

210. With respect to this point, the Commission considers it pertinent to reiterate certain aspects of its findings. On the one hand, the Commission was asked to pronounce upon the response that Jessica Lenahan encountered when she filed a federal suit under the due process clause of the Fourteenth Amendment. On this specific question, the Commission concluded that Ms. Lenahan was able to present her claims and be heard. This aspect of the Commission's analysis related to the claim that was in fact brought in the present case.

211. The petitioners have underlined concerns about limitations in the availability and scope of federal claims of action for victims of violence. These questions are important, and the Commission has taken due note of the restrictive approach employed by the Supreme Court in this regard. As the Special Rapporteur on

Violence against Women of the United Nations indicated at the close of a recent visit to the United States:

> Although VAWA's [Violence against Women's Act] intentions are laudable, there is little in terms of actual legally binding federal provisions which provide substantive protection or prevention for acts of domestic violence against women. This challenge has been further exacerbated by jurisprudence emanating from the Supreme Court. The effect of cases such as *DeShaney*, *Morrison* and *Castle Rock* is that even where local and state police are grossly negligent in their duties to protect women's right to physical security, and even where they fail to respond to an urgent call of assistance from victims of domestic violence, there is no constitutional or statutory remedy at the federal level.[305]

212. The Commission also underscores, as established in the present report, that the inter-American system has affirmed for many years that it is not the formal existence of judicial remedies that demonstrates due diligence, but rather that they are available and effective.[306] Therefore, when the State apparatus leaves human rights violations unpunished and the victim's full enjoyment of human rights is not promptly restored, the State fails to comply with its positive duties under international human rights law.[307] The same principle applies when a State allows private persons to act freely and with impunity to the detriment of the rights recognized in the governing instruments of the inter-American system.

213. The key aspect of the Commission's analysis in this case did not deal with the scope of federal claims of action under national law, but rather with the deficiencies in the judicial response of the State at all levels to the concrete events of the present case. This analysis was centered on the obligation of the state to provide judicial remedies to Ms. Lenahan with respect to the non-enforcement of the protection order and the subsequent deaths of her daughters. This obligation covers a range of required responses on the part of the State that were not provided, beginning first with the duty to respond to Ms. Lenahan's calls and complaints that her daughters were at risk due to the violation of the terms of the restraining order. That restraining order was the only means available to her at the state level to protect herself and her children in a context of domestic violence, and the police did not effectively enforce it. Given the failure to effectively enforce that restraining order, the

---

[305] Statement from Special Rapporteur on violence against women, its causes, and consequences, at the conclusion of her fact finding mission to the United States of America, February 8, 2011, *available at* http://www.ohchr.org.

[306] See, IACHR, Report N° 81/10, Case 12.562, *Wayne Smith, Hugo Armendatriz, et al.,* United States, July 12, 2010, para. 62; IACHR, Report on Admissibility N° 52/07, Petition 1490-05, *Jessica Gonzales and Others (United States),* July 24, 2007, para. 42; IACHR, *Access to Justice for Women Victims of Violence in the Americas,* OEA/Ser.L/V/II, Doc. 68 (January 20, 2007), para. 26; I/A Court H.R., *The "Street Children" Case (Villagrán Morales et al.). Judgment of November 19, 1999. Series C No. 63, para. 235.

[307] IACHR, *The Situation of the Rights of Women in Ciudad Juarez,* OEA/Ser. L/V/II.117. Doc. 44 (March 7, 2003), para. 51.

state is required to investigate the circumstances in order to identify the reasons, remedy them where required, and hold those responsible to account. Further, as established in the Commission's report, the state is obliged to investigate and clarify the circumstances of the deaths of Leslie, Katheryn and Rebecca Gonzales, and to provide Jessica Lenahan access to that information. That investigation must be prompt, thorough and effective, and undertaken by the state at its own initiative. The state's failure to comply with the foregoing obligations gives rise to the requirement to adopt concrete measures to remedy the violations.

214. On April 4, 2011, the Commission transmitted Report N° 62/11 to the parties and requested the State to present information on compliance with the recommendations within one month from the date of transmittal. No further submission on this matter was received from either party. Accordingly, based on the information available, the Commission decided to ratify its conclusions and to reiterate its recommendations in this case, as set forth below.

VIII. FINAL CONCLUSIONS AND RECOMMENDATIONS

215. On the basis of the facts and information provided, the IACHR finds that the State has not taken measures toward compliance with the recommendations in the merits report in this case. Accordingly,

THE INTER-AMERICAN COMMISSION ON HUMAN RIGHTS REITERATES ITS RECOMMENDATIONS THAT THE UNITED STATES:

1. Undertake a serious, impartial and exhaustive investigation with the objective of ascertaining the cause, time and place of the deaths of Leslie, Katheryn and Rebecca Gonzales, and to duly inform their next-of-kin of the course of the investigation.

2. Conduct a serious, impartial and exhaustive investigation into systemic failures that took place related to the enforcement of Jessica Lenahan's protection order as a guarantee of their non-repetition, including performing an inquiry to determine the responsibilities of public officials for violating state and/or federal laws, and holding those responsible accountable.

3. Offer full reparations to Jessica Lenahan and her next-of-kin considering their perspective and specific needs.

4. Adopt multifaceted legislation at the federal and state levels, or to reform existing legislation, making mandatory the enforcement of protection orders and other precautionary measures to protect women from imminent acts of violence, and to create effective implementation mechanisms. These measures should be accompanied by adequate resources destined to foster their implementation; regulations to ensure their enforcement; training programs for the law enforcement and justice system officials who will participate in their execution; and the design of model protocols and directives that can be followed by police departments throughout the country.

5. Adopt multifaceted legislation at the federal and state levels, or reform existing legislation, including protection measures for children in the context of domestic violence. Such measures should be accompanied by adequate resources destined to foster their implementation; regulations to ensure their enforcement; training programs for the law enforcement and justice system officials who will participate in their execution; and the design of model protocols and directives that can be followed by police departments throughout the country.

6. Continue adopting public policies and institutional programs aimed at restructuring the stereotypes of domestic violence victims, and to promote the eradication of discriminatory socio-cultural patterns that impede women and children's full protection from domestic violence acts, including programs to train public officials in all branches of the administration of justice and police, and comprehensive prevention programs.

7. Design protocols at the federal and state levels specifying the proper components of the investigation by law enforcement officials of a report of missing children in the context of a report of a restraining order violation.

IX. PUBLICATION

216. In light of the above and in accordance with Article 47 of its Rules of Procedure, the IACHR decides to make this report public, and to include it in its Annual Report to the General Assembly of the Organization of American States. The Inter-American Commission, according to the norms contained in the instruments which govern its mandate, will continue evaluating the measures adopted by the United States with respect to the above recommendations until it determines there has been full compliance.

Done and signed in the city of Washington, D.C., on the 21th day of July 2011.
(Signed): José de Jesús Orozco Henríquez, First Vice President; Paulo Sérgio Pinheiro, Felipe González, Luz Patricia Mejía Guerrero, and María Silvia Guillén, Commission Members.

Source: Organization of American States. Inter-American Commission on Human Rights. Report No. 80/11. "Case 12.626. Merits. Jessica Lenahan (Gonzales) et al. United States." July 21, 2011. Available at http://www.equalaccessadvocates.com/2011%20August%2008%20Petitioners%20-%20Report%20No%20%2080-11.pdf

3. Trafficking Victims Protection Act of 2000

In Brief:
The TVPA was a bipartisan effort by the U.S. Congress, resulting in an act passed in 2000 designed to combat and prevent trafficking of persons. In addition to providing training, awareness campaigns, services to victims, and resources for the apprehension and prosecution of traffickers, TVPA authorized the annual publishing of a report describing

other countries' efforts to address trafficking and assigning them to tiers, with Tier One referring to those countries making significant efforts and Tier Three referring to those countries doing little. For more information, see entry in encyclopedia on **Trafficking Victims Protection Act (TVPA).**

H.R.3244

One Hundred Sixth Congress of the United States of America

AT THE SECOND SESSION

Begun and held at the City of Washington on Monday,

the twenty-fourth day of January, two thousand

An Act

To combat trafficking in persons, especially into the sex trade, slavery, and involuntary servitude, to reauthorize certain Federal programs to prevent violence against women, and for other purposes.

Be it enacted by the Senate and House of Representatives of the United States of America in Congress assembled,

SECTION 1. SHORT TITLE.

This Act may be cited as the 'Victims of Trafficking and Violence Protection Act of 2000'.

SEC. 2. ORGANIZATION OF ACT INTO DIVISIONS; TABLE OF CONTENTS.

(a) DIVISIONS—This Act is organized into three divisions, as follows:
  (1) DIVISION A—Trafficking Victims Protection Act of 2000.
  (2) DIVISION B—Violence Against Women Act of 2000.
  (3) DIVISION C—Miscellaneous Provisions.
(b) TABLE OF CONTENTS—The table of contents for this Act is as follows:
  Sec.1.Short title.
  Sec.2.Organization of Act into divisions; table of contents.

DIVISION A—TRAFFICKING VICTIMS PROTECTION ACT OF 2000

Sec.101.Short title.
Sec.102.Purposes and findings.
Sec.103.Definitions.
Sec.104.Annual Country Reports on Human Rights Practices.
Sec.105.Interagency Task Force To Monitor and Combat Trafficking.
Sec.106.Prevention of trafficking.

Sec.107.Protection and assistance for victims of trafficking.
Sec.108.Minimum standards for the elimination of trafficking.
Sec.109.Assistance to foreign countries to meet minimum standards.
Sec.110.Actions against governments failing to meet minimum standards.
Sec.111.Actions against significant traffickers in persons.
Sec.112.Strengthening prosecution and punishment of traffickers.
Sec.113.Authorizations of appropriations.

DIVISION B—VIOLENCE AGAINST WOMEN ACT OF 2000

Sec.1001.Short title.
Sec.1002.Definitions.
Sec.1003.Accountability and oversight.

TITLE I—STRENGTHENING LAW ENFORCEMENT TO REDUCE VIOLENCE AGAINST WOMEN

Sec.1101.Full faith and credit enforcement of protection orders.
Sec.1102.Role of courts.
Sec.1103.Reauthorization of STOP grants.
Sec.1104.Reauthorization of grants to encourage arrest policies.
Sec.1105.Reauthorization of rural domestic violence and child abuse enforcement grants.
Sec.1106.National stalker and domestic violence reduction.
Sec.1107.Amendments to domestic violence and stalking offenses.
Sec.1108.School and campus security.
Sec.1109.Dating violence.

TITLE II—STRENGTHENING SERVICES TO VICTIMS OF VIOLENCE

Sec.1201.Legal assistance for victims.
Sec.1202.Shelter services for battered women and children.
Sec.1203.Transitional housing assistance for victims of domestic violence.
Sec.1204.National domestic violence hotline.
Sec.1205.Federal victims counselors.
Sec.1206.Study of State laws regarding insurance discrimination against victims of violence against women.
Sec.1207.Study of workplace effects from violence against women.
Sec.1208.Study of unemployment compensation for victims of violence against women.
Sec.1209.Enhancing protections for older and disabled women from domestic violence and sexual assault.

TITLE III—LIMITING THE EFFECTS OF VIOLENCE ON CHILDREN

Sec.1301.Safe havens for children pilot program.
Sec.1302.Reauthorization of victims of child abuse programs.
Sec.1303.Report on effects of parental kidnapping laws in domestic violence cases.

TITLE IV—STRENGTHENING EDUCATION AND TRAINING TO COMBAT VIOLENCE AGAINST WOMEN

Sec.1401.Rape prevention and education.
Sec.1402.Education and training to end violence against and abuse of women with disabilities.
Sec.1403.Community initiatives.
Sec.1404.Development of research agenda identified by the Violence Against Women Act of 1994.
Sec.1405.Standards, practice, and training for sexual assault forensic examinations.
Sec.1406.Education and training for judges and court personnel.
Sec.1407.Domestic Violence Task Force.

TITLE V—BATTERED IMMIGRANT WOMEN

Sec.1501.Short title.
Sec.1502.Findings and purposes.
Sec.1503.Improved access to immigration protections of the Violence Against Women Act of 1994 for battered immigrant women.
Sec.1504.Improved access to cancellation of removal and suspension of deportation under the Violence Against Women Act of 1994.
Sec.1505.Offering equal access to immigration protections of the Violence Against Women Act of 1994 for all qualified battered immigrant self-petitioners.
Sec.1506.Restoring immigration protections under the Violence Against Women Act of 1994.
Sec.1507.Remedying problems with implementation of the immigration provisions of the Violence Against Women Act of 1994.
Sec.1508.Technical correction to qualified alien definition for battered immigrants.
Sec.1509.Access to Cuban Adjustment Act for battered immigrant spouses and children.
Sec.1510.Access to the Nicaraguan Adjustment and Central American Relief Act for battered spouses and children.
Sec.1511.Access to the Haitian Refugee Fairness Act of 1998 for battered spouses and children.
Sec.1512.Access to services and legal representation for battered immigrants.
Sec.1513.Protection for certain crime victims including victims of crimes against women.

TITLE VI—MISCELLANEOUS

Sec.1601.Notice requirements for sexually violent offenders.
Sec.1602.Teen suicide prevention study.
Sec.1603.Decade of pain control and research.

DIVISION C—MISCELLANEOUS PROVISIONS

Sec.2001.Aimee's law.
Sec.2002.Payment of anti-terrorism judgments.
Sec.2003.Aid to victims of terrorism.
Sec.2004.Twenty-first amendment enforcement.

DIVISION A—TRAFFICKING VICTIMS PROTECTION ACT OF 2000

SEC. 101. SHORT TITLE.

This division may be cited as the 'Trafficking Victims Protection Act of 2000'.

SEC. 102. PURPOSES AND FINDINGS.

(a) PURPOSES—The purposes of this division are to combat trafficking in persons, a contemporary manifestation of slavery whose victims are predominantly women and children, to ensure just and effective punishment of traffickers, and to protect their victims.

(b) FINDINGS—Congress finds that:

(1) As the 21st century begins, the degrading institution of slavery continues throughout the world. Trafficking in persons is a modern form of slavery, and it is the largest manifestation of slavery today. At least 700,000 persons annually, primarily women and children, are trafficked within or across international borders. Approximately 50,000 women and children are trafficked into the United States each year.

(2) Many of these persons are trafficked into the international sex trade, often by force, fraud, or coercion. The sex industry has rapidly expanded over the past several decades. It involves sexual exploitation of persons, predominantly women and girls, involving activities related to prostitution, pornography, sex tourism, and other commercial sexual services. The low status of women in many parts of the world has contributed to a burgeoning of the trafficking industry.

(3) Trafficking in persons is not limited to the sex industry. This growing transnational crime also includes forced labor and involves significant violations of labor, public health, and human rights standards worldwide.

(4) Traffickers primarily target women and girls, who are disproportionately affected by poverty, the lack of access to education, chronic unemployment, discrimination, and the lack of economic opportunities in countries of origin. Traffickers lure women and girls into their networks through false promises of decent working conditions at relatively good pay as nannies, maids, dancers, factory workers, restaurant workers, sales clerks, or models. Traffickers also buy children from poor families and sell them into prostitution or into various types of forced or bonded labor.

(5) Traffickers often transport victims from their home communities to unfamiliar destinations, including foreign countries away from family and friends, religious institutions, and other sources of protection and support, leaving the victims defenseless and vulnerable.

(6) Victims are often forced through physical violence to engage in sex acts or perform slavery-like labor. Such force includes rape and other forms of sexual abuse, torture, starvation, imprisonment, threats, psychological abuse, and coercion.

(7) Traffickers often make representations to their victims that physical harm may occur to them or others should the victim escape or attempt to escape. Such representations can have the same coercive effects on victims as direct threats to inflict such harm.

(8) Trafficking in persons is increasingly perpetrated by organized, sophisticated criminal enterprises. Such trafficking is the fastest growing source of profits for organized criminal enterprises worldwide. Profits from the trafficking industry contribute to the expansion of organized crime in the United States and worldwide. Trafficking in persons is often aided by official corruption in countries of origin, transit, and destination, thereby threatening the rule of law.

(9) Trafficking includes all the elements of the crime of forcible rape when it involves the involuntary participation of another person in sex acts by means of fraud, force, or coercion.

(10) Trafficking also involves violations of other laws, including labor and immigration codes and laws against kidnapping, slavery, false imprisonment, assault, battery, pandering, fraud, and extortion.

(11) Trafficking exposes victims to serious health risks. Women and children trafficked in the sex industry are exposed to deadly diseases, including HIV and AIDS. Trafficking victims are sometimes worked or physically brutalized to death.

(12) Trafficking in persons substantially affects interstate and foreign commerce. Trafficking for such purposes as involuntary servitude, peonage, and other forms of forced labor has an impact on the nationwide employment network and labor market. Within the context of slavery, servitude, and labor or services which are obtained or maintained through coercive conduct that amounts to a condition of servitude, victims are subjected to a range of violations.

(13) Involuntary servitude statutes are intended to reach cases in which persons are held in a condition of servitude through nonviolent coercion. In United States v. Kozminski, 487 U.S. 931 (1988), the Supreme Court found that section 1584 of title 18, United States Code, should be narrowly interpreted, absent a definition of involuntary servitude by Congress. As a result, that section was interpreted to criminalize only servitude that is brought about through use or threatened use of physical or legal coercion, and to exclude other conduct that can have the same purpose and effect.

(14) Existing legislation and law enforcement in the United States and other countries are inadequate to deter trafficking and bring traffickers to justice, failing to reflect the gravity of the offenses involved. No

comprehensive law exists in the United States that penalizes the range of offenses involved in the trafficking scheme. Instead, even the most brutal instances of trafficking in the sex industry are often punished under laws that also apply to lesser offenses, so that traffickers typically escape deserved punishment.

(15) In the United States, the seriousness of this crime and its components is not reflected in current sentencing guidelines, resulting in weak penalties for convicted traffickers.

(16) In some countries, enforcement against traffickers is also hindered by official indifference, by corruption, and sometimes even by official participation in trafficking.

(17) Existing laws often fail to protect victims of trafficking, and because victims are often illegal immigrants in the destination country, they are repeatedly punished more harshly than the traffickers themselves.

(18) Additionally, adequate services and facilities do not exist to meet victims' needs regarding health care, housing, education, and legal assistance, which safely reintegrate trafficking victims into their home countries.

(19) Victims of severe forms of trafficking should not be inappropriately incarcerated, fined, or otherwise penalized solely for unlawful acts committed as a direct result of being trafficked, such as using false documents, entering the country without documentation, or working without documentation.

(20) Because victims of trafficking are frequently unfamiliar with the laws, cultures, and languages of the countries into which they have been trafficked, because they are often subjected to coercion and intimidation including physical detention and debt bondage, and because they often fear retribution and forcible removal to countries in which they will face retribution or other hardship, these victims often find it difficult or impossible to report the crimes committed against them or to assist in the investigation and prosecution of such crimes.

(21) Trafficking of persons is an evil requiring concerted and vigorous action by countries of origin, transit or destination, and by international organizations.

(22) One of the founding documents of the United States, the Declaration of Independence, recognizes the inherent dignity and worth of all people. It states that all men are created equal and that they are endowed by their Creator with certain unalienable rights. The right to be free from slavery and involuntary servitude is among those unalienable rights. Acknowledging this fact, the United States outlawed slavery and involuntary servitude in 1865, recognizing them as evil institutions that must be abolished. Current practices of sexual slavery and trafficking of women and children are similarly abhorrent to the principles upon which the United States was founded.

(23) The United States and the international community agree that trafficking in persons involves grave violations of human rights and is a matter of pressing international concern. The international community has repeatedly condemned slavery and involuntary servitude, violence against women, and other elements of trafficking, through declarations, treaties, and United Nations resolutions and reports, including the Universal Declaration of Human Rights; the 1956 Supplementary Convention on the Abolition of Slavery, the Slave Trade, and Institutions and Practices Similar to Slavery; the 1948 American Declaration on the Rights and Duties of Man; the 1957 Abolition of Forced Labor Convention; the International Covenant on Civil and Political Rights; the Convention Against Torture and Other Cruel, Inhuman or Degrading Treatment or Punishment; United Nations General Assembly Resolutions 50/167, 51/66, and 52/98;
the Final Report of the World Congress against Sexual Exploitation of Children (Stockholm, 1996); the Fourth World Conference on Women (Beijing, 1995); and the 1991 Moscow Document of the Organization for Security and Cooperation in Europe.

(24) Trafficking in persons is a transnational crime with national implications. To deter international trafficking and bring its perpetrators to justice, nations including the United States must recognize that trafficking is a serious offense. This is done by prescribing appropriate punishment, giving priority to the prosecution of trafficking offenses, and protecting rather than punishing the victims of such offenses. The United States must work bilaterally and multilaterally to abolish the trafficking industry by taking steps to promote cooperation among countries linked together by international trafficking routes. The United States must also urge the international community to take strong action in multilateral fora to engage recalcitrant countries in serious and sustained efforts to eliminate trafficking and protect trafficking victims.

SEC. 103. DEFINITIONS.

In this division:
(1) APPROPRIATE CONGRESSIONAL COMMITTEES—The term 'appropriate congressional committees' means the Committee on Foreign Relations and the Committee on the Judiciary of the Senate and the Committee on International Relations and the Committee on the Judiciary of the House of Representatives.
(2) COERCION—The term 'coercion' means—
    (A) threats of serious harm to or physical restraint against any person;
    (B) any scheme, plan, or pattern intended to cause a person to believe that failure to perform an act would result in serious harm to or physical restraint against any person; or
    (C) the abuse or threatened abuse of the legal process.

(3) COMMERCIAL SEX ACT—The term 'commercial sex act' means any sex act on account of which anything of value is given to or received by any person.
(4) DEBT BONDAGE—The term 'debt bondage' means the status or condition of a debtor arising from a pledge by the debtor of his or her personal services or of those of a person under his or her control as a security for debt, if the value of those services as reasonably assessed is not applied toward the liquidation of the debt or the length and nature of those services are not respectively limited and defined.
(5) INVOLUNTARY SERVITUDE—The term 'involuntary servitude' includes a condition of servitude induced by means of—
> (A) any scheme, plan, or pattern intended to cause a person to believe that, if the person did not enter into or continue in such condition, that person or another person would suffer serious harm or physical restraint; or
> (B) the abuse or threatened abuse of the legal process.

(6) MINIMUM STANDARDS FOR THE ELIMINATION OF TRAFFICKING—The term 'minimum standards for the elimination of trafficking' means the standards set forth in section 108.
(7) NONHUMANITARIAN, NONTRADE-RELATED FOREIGN ASSISTANCE—The term 'nonhumanitarian, nontrade-related foreign assistance' means—
> (A) any assistance under the Foreign Assistance Act of 1961, other than—
>> (i) assistance under chapter 4 of part II of that Act that is made available for any program, project, or activity eligible for assistance under chapter 1 of part I of that Act;
>> (ii) assistance under chapter 8 of part I of that Act;
>> (iii) any other narcotics-related assistance under part I of that Act or under chapter 4 or 5 part II of that Act, but any such assistance provided under this clause shall be subject to the prior notification procedures applicable to reprogrammings pursuant to section 634A of that Act;
>> (iv) disaster relief assistance, including any assistance under chapter 9 of part I of that Act;
>> (v) antiterrorism assistance under chapter 8 of part II of that Act;
>> (vi) assistance for refugees;
>> (vii) humanitarian and other development assistance in support of programs of nongovernmental organizations under chapters 1 and 10 of that Act;
>> (viii) programs under title IV of chapter 2 of part I of that Act, relating to the Overseas Private Investment Corporation; and
>> (ix) other programs involving trade-related or humanitarian assistance; and
> (B) sales, or financing on any terms, under the Arms Export Control Act, other than sales or financing provided for narcotics-related purposes following notification in accordance with the prior notification procedures applicable to reprogrammings pursuant to section 634A of the Foreign Assistance Act of 1961.

(8) SEVERE FORMS OF TRAFFICKING IN PERSONS—The term 'severe forms of trafficking in persons' means—
   (A) sex trafficking in which a commercial sex act is induced by force, fraud, or coercion, or in which the person induced to perform such act has not attained 18 years of age; or
   (B) the recruitment, harboring, transportation, provision, or obtaining of a person for labor or services, through the use of force, fraud, or coercion for the purpose of subjection to involuntary servitude, peonage, debt bondage, or slavery.
(9) SEX TRAFFICKING—The term 'sex trafficking' means the recruitment, harboring, transportation, provision, or obtaining of a person for the purpose of a commercial sex act.
(10) STATE—The term 'State' means each of the several States of the United States, the District of Columbia, the Commonwealth of Puerto Rico, the United States Virgin Islands, Guam, American Samoa, the Commonwealth of the Northern Mariana Islands, and territories and possessions of the United States.
(11) TASK FORCE—The term 'Task Force' means the Interagency Task Force to Monitor and Combat Trafficking established under section 105.
(12) UNITED STATES—The term 'United States' means the fifty States of the United States, the District of Columbia, the Commonwealth of Puerto Rico, the Virgin Islands, American Samoa, Guam, the Commonwealth of the Northern Mariana Islands, and the territories and possessions of the United States.
(13) VICTIM OF A SEVERE FORM OF TRAFFICKING—The term 'victim of a severe form of trafficking' means a person subject to an act or practice described in paragraph (8).
(14) VICTIM OF TRAFFICKING—The term 'victim of trafficking' means a person subjected to an act or practice described in paragraph (8) or (9).

SEC. 104. ANNUAL COUNTRY REPORTS ON HUMAN RIGHTS PRACTICES.

(a) COUNTRIES RECEIVING ECONOMIC ASSISTANCE—Section 116(f) of the Foreign Assistance Act of 1961 (22 U.S.C. 2151(f)) is amended to read as follows:
   '(f)(1) The report required by subsection (d) shall include the following:
      '(A) A description of the nature and extent of severe forms of trafficking in persons, as defined in section 103 of the Trafficking Victims Protection Act of 2000, in each foreign country.
      '(B) With respect to each country that is a country of origin, transit, or destination for victims of severe forms of trafficking in persons, an assessment of the efforts by the government of that country to combat such trafficking. The assessment shall address the following:
         '(i) Whether government authorities in that country participate in, facilitate, or condone such trafficking.

'(ii) Which government authorities in that country are involved in activities to combat such trafficking.
'(iii) What steps the government of that country has taken to prohibit government officials from participating in, facilitating, or condoning such trafficking, including the investigation, prosecution, and conviction of such officials.
'(iv) What steps the government of that country has taken to prohibit other individuals from participating in such trafficking, including the investigation, prosecution, and conviction of individuals involved in severe forms of trafficking in persons, the criminal and civil penalties for such trafficking, and the efficacy of those penalties in eliminating or reducing such trafficking.
'(v) What steps the government of that country has taken to assist victims of such trafficking, including efforts to prevent victims from being further victimized by traffickers, government officials, or others, grants of relief from deportation, and provision of humanitarian relief, including provision of mental and physical health care and shelter.
'(vi) Whether the government of that country is cooperating with governments of other countries to extradite traffickers when requested, or, to the extent that such cooperation would be inconsistent with the laws of such country or with extradition treaties to which such country is a party, whether the government of that country is taking all appropriate measures to modify or replace such laws and treaties so as to permit such cooperation.
'(vii) Whether the government of that country is assisting in international investigations of transnational trafficking networks and in other cooperative efforts to combat severe forms of trafficking in persons.
'(viii) Whether the government of that country refrains from prosecuting victims of severe forms of trafficking in persons due to such victims having been trafficked, and refrains from other discriminatory treatment of such victims.
'(ix) Whether the government of that country recognizes the rights of victims of severe forms of trafficking in persons and ensures their access to justice.
'(C) Such other information relating to trafficking in persons as the Secretary of State considers appropriate.
'(2) In compiling data and making assessments for the purposes of paragraph (1), United States diplomatic mission personnel shall consult with human rights organizations and other appropriate nongovernmental organizations.'.
(b) COUNTRIES RECEIVING SECURITY ASSISTANCE—Section 502B of the Foreign Assistance Act of 1961 (22 U.S.C. 2304) is amended by adding at the end the following new subsection:
'(h)(1) The report required by subsection (b) shall include the following:

'(A) A description of the nature and extent of severe forms of trafficking in persons, as defined in section 103 of the Trafficking Victims Protection Act of 2000, in each foreign country.

'(B) With respect to each country that is a country of origin, transit, or destination for victims of severe forms of trafficking in persons, an assessment of the efforts by the government of that country to combat such trafficking. The assessment shall address the following:

'(i) Whether government authorities in that country participate in, facilitate, or condone such trafficking.

'(ii) Which government authorities in that country are involved in activities to combat such trafficking.

'(iii) What steps the government of that country has taken to prohibit government officials from participating in, facilitating, or condoning such trafficking, including the investigation, prosecution, and conviction of such officials.

'(iv) What steps the government of that country has taken to prohibit other individuals from participating in such trafficking, including the investigation, prosecution, and conviction of individuals involved in severe forms of trafficking in persons, the criminal and civil penalties for such trafficking, and the efficacy of those penalties in eliminating or reducing such trafficking.

'(v) What steps the government of that country has taken to assist victims of such trafficking, including efforts to prevent victims from being further victimized by traffickers, government officials, or others, grants of relief from deportation, and provision of humanitarian relief, including provision of mental and physical health care and shelter.

'(vi) Whether the government of that country is cooperating with governments of other countries to extradite traffickers when requested, or, to the extent that such cooperation would be inconsistent with the laws of such country or with extradition treaties to which such country is a party, whether the government of that country is taking all appropriate measures to modify or replace such laws and treaties so as to permit such cooperation.

'(vii) Whether the government of that country is assisting in international investigations of transnational trafficking networks and in other cooperative efforts to combat severe forms of trafficking in persons.

'(viii) Whether the government of that country refrains from prosecuting victims of severe forms of trafficking in persons due to such victims having been trafficked, and refrains from other discriminatory treatment of such victims.

'(ix) Whether the government of that country recognizes the rights of victims of severe forms of trafficking in persons and ensures their access to justice.

'(C) Such other information relating to trafficking in persons as the Secretary of State considers appropriate.

'(2) In compiling data and making assessments for the purposes of paragraph (1), United States diplomatic mission personnel shall consult with human rights organizations and other appropriate nongovernmental organizations.'.

SEC. 105. INTERAGENCY TASK FORCE TO MONITOR AND COMBAT TRAFFICKING.

(a) ESTABLISHMENT—The President shall establish an Interagency Task Force to Monitor and Combat Trafficking.

(b) APPOINTMENT—The President shall appoint the members of the Task Force, which shall include the Secretary of State, the Administrator of the United States Agency for International Development, the Attorney General, the Secretary of Labor, the Secretary of Health and Human Services, the Director of Central Intelligence, and such other officials as may be designated by the President.

(c) CHAIRMAN—The Task Force shall be chaired by the Secretary of State.

(d) ACTIVITIES OF THE TASK FORCE—The Task Force shall carry out the following activities:

(1) Coordinate the implementation of this division.

(2) Measure and evaluate progress of the United States and other countries in the areas of trafficking prevention, protection, and assistance to victims of trafficking, and prosecution and enforcement against traffickers, including the role of public corruption in facilitating trafficking. The Task Force shall have primary responsibility for assisting the Secretary of State in the preparation of the reports described in section 110.

(3) Expand interagency procedures to collect and organize data, including significant research and resource information on domestic and international trafficking. Any data collection procedures established under this subsection shall respect the confidentiality of victims of trafficking.

(4) Engage in efforts to facilitate cooperation among countries of origin, transit, and destination. Such efforts shall aim to strengthen local and regional capacities to prevent trafficking, prosecute traffickers and assist trafficking victims, and shall include initiatives to enhance cooperative efforts between destination countries and countries of origin and assist in the appropriate reintegration of stateless victims of trafficking.

(5) Examine the role of the international 'sex tourism' industry in the trafficking of persons and in the sexual exploitation of women and children around the world.

(6) Engage in consultation and advocacy with governmental and nongovernmental organizations, among other entities, to advance the purposes of this division.

(e) SUPPORT FOR THE TASK FORCE—The Secretary of State is authorized to establish within the Department of State an Office to Monitor and Combat Trafficking, which shall provide assistance to the Task Force. Any such Office shall be headed by a Director. The Director shall have the primary responsibility for assisting the Secretary of State in carrying out the purposes of this division and may have additional responsibilities as determined by the Secretary. The Director shall consult with nongovernmental organizations and multilateral organizations, and with trafficking victims or other affected persons. The Director shall have the authority to take evidence in public hearings or by other means. The agencies represented on the Task Force are authorized to provide staff to the Office on a nonreimbursable basis.

SEC. 106. PREVENTION OF TRAFFICKING.

(a) ECONOMIC ALTERNATIVES TO PREVENT AND DETER TRAFFICKING—The President shall establish and carry out international initiatives to enhance economic opportunity for potential victims of trafficking as a method to deter trafficking. Such initiatives may include—
>   (1) microcredit lending programs, training in business development, skills training, and job counseling;
>   (2) programs to promote women's participation in economic decisionmaking;
>   (3) programs to keep children, especially girls, in elementary and secondary schools, and to educate persons who have been victims of trafficking;
>   (4) development of educational curricula regarding the dangers of trafficking; and
>   (5) grants to nongovernmental organizations to accelerate and advance the political, economic, social, and educational roles and capacities of women in their countries.

(b) PUBLIC AWARENESS AND INFORMATION—The President, acting through the Secretary of Labor, the Secretary of Health and Human Services, the Attorney General, and the Secretary of State, shall establish and carry out programs to increase public awareness, particularly among potential victims of trafficking, of the dangers of trafficking and the protections that are available for victims of trafficking.

(c) CONSULTATION REQUIREMENT—The President shall consult with appropriate nongovernmental organizations with respect to the establishment and conduct of initiatives described in subsections (a) and (b).

SEC. 107. PROTECTION AND ASSISTANCE FOR VICTIMS OF TRAFFICKING.

(a) Assistance for Victims in Other Countries—
>   (1) IN GENERAL—The Secretary of State and the Administrator of the United States Agency for International Development, in consultation with appropriate nongovernmental organizations, shall establish and carry out programs and initiatives in foreign countries to assist in the safe integration, reintegration, or resettlement, as appropriate, of victims of trafficking. Such

programs and initiatives shall be designed to meet the appropriate assistance needs of such persons and their children, as identified by the Task Force.
(2) ADDITIONAL REQUIREMENT—In establishing and conducting programs and initiatives described in paragraph (1), the Secretary of State and the Administrator of the United States Agency for International Development shall take all appropriate steps to enhance cooperative efforts among foreign countries, including countries of origin of victims of trafficking, to assist in the integration, reintegration, or resettlement, as appropriate, of victims of trafficking, including stateless victims.

(b) Victims in the United States—
  (1) ASSISTANCE—
    (A) ELIGIBILITY FOR BENEFITS AND SERVICES—Notwithstanding title IV of the Personal Responsibility and Work Opportunity Reconciliation Act of 1996, an alien who is a victim of a severe form of trafficking in persons shall be eligible for benefits and services under any Federal or State program or activity funded or administered by any official or agency described in subparagraph (B) to the same extent as an alien who is admitted to the United States as a refugee under section 207 of the Immigration and Nationality Act.
    (B) REQUIREMENT TO EXPAND BENEFITS AND SERVICES—Subject to subparagraph (C) and, in the case of nonentitlement programs, to the availability of appropriations, the Secretary of Health and Human Services, the Secretary of Labor, the Board of Directors of the Legal Services Corporation, and the heads of other Federal agencies shall expand benefits and services to victims of severe forms of trafficking in persons in the United States, without regard to the immigration status of such victims.
    (C) DEFINITION OF VICTIM OF A SEVERE FORM OF TRAFFICKING IN PERSONS—For the purposes of this paragraph, the term 'victim of a severe form of trafficking in persons' means only a person—
      (i) who has been subjected to an act or practice described in section 103(8) as in effect on the date of the enactment of this Act; and
      (ii)(I) who has not attained 18 years of age; or
      (II) who is the subject of a certification under subparagraph (E).
    (D) ANNUAL REPORT—Not later than December 31 of each year, the Secretary of Health and Human Services, in consultation with the Secretary of Labor, the Board of Directors of the Legal Services Corporation, and the heads of other appropriate Federal agencies shall submit a report, which includes information on the number of persons who received benefits or other services under this paragraph in connection with programs or activities funded or administered by such agencies or officials during the preceding fiscal year, to the

Committee on Ways and Means, the Committee on International Relations, and the Committee on the Judiciary of the House of Representatives and the Committee on Finance, the Committee on Foreign Relations, and the Committee on the Judiciary of the Senate.
(E) CERTIFICATION—
  (i) IN GENERAL—Subject to clause (ii), the certification referred to in subparagraph (C) is a certification by the Secretary of Health and Human Services, after consultation with the Attorney General, that the person referred to in subparagraph (C)(ii)(II)—
    (I) is willing to assist in every reasonable way in the investigation and prosecution of severe forms of trafficking in persons; and
    (II)(aa) has made a bona fide application for a visa under section 101(a)(15)(T) of the Immigration and Nationality Act, as added by subsection (e), that has not been denied; or
    (bb) is a person whose continued presence in the United States the Attorney General is ensuring in order to effectuate prosecution of traffickers in persons.
  (ii) PERIOD OF EFFECTIVENESS—A certification referred to in subparagraph (C), with respect to a person described in clause (i)(II)(bb), shall be effective only for so long as the Attorney General determines that the continued presence of such person is necessary to effectuate prosecution of traffickers in persons.
  (iii) INVESTIGATION AND PROSECUTION DEFINED—For the purpose of a certification under this subparagraph, the term 'investigation and prosecution' includes—
    (I) identification of a person or persons who have committed severe forms of trafficking in persons;
    (II) location and apprehension of such persons; and
    (III) testimony at proceedings against such persons.
(2) GRANTS—
  (A) IN GENERAL—Subject to the availability of appropriations, the Attorney General may make grants to States, Indian tribes, units of local government, and nonprofit, nongovernmental victims' service organizations to develop, expand, or strengthen victim service programs for victims of trafficking.
  (B) ALLOCATION OF GRANT FUNDS—Of amounts made available for grants under this paragraph, there shall be set aside—
    (i) three percent for research, evaluation, and statistics;
    (ii) two percent for training and technical assistance; and
    (iii) one percent for management and administration.
  (C) LIMITATION ON FEDERAL SHARE—The Federal share of a grant made under this paragraph may not exceed 75 percent of the total costs of the projects described in the application submitted.
(c) TRAFFICKING VICTIM REGULATIONS—Not later than 180 days after the date of the enactment of this Act, the Attorney General and the Secretary of State

shall promulgate regulations for law enforcement personnel, immigration officials, and Department of State officials to implement the following:

(1) PROTECTIONS WHILE IN CUSTODY—Victims of severe forms of trafficking, while in the custody of the Federal Government and to the extent practicable, shall—

(A) not be detained in facilities inappropriate to their status as crime victims;

(B) receive necessary medical care and other assistance; and

(C) be provided protection if a victim's safety is at risk or if there is danger of additional harm by recapture of the victim by a trafficker, including—

(i) taking measures to protect trafficked persons and their family members from intimidation and threats of reprisals and reprisals from traffickers and their associates; and

(ii) ensuring that the names and identifying information of trafficked persons and their family members are not disclosed to the public.

(2) ACCESS TO INFORMATION—Victims of severe forms of trafficking shall have access to information about their rights and translation services.

(3) AUTHORITY TO PERMIT CONTINUED PRESENCE IN THE UNITED STATES—Federal law enforcement officials may permit an alien individual's continued presence in the United States, if after an assessment, it is determined that such individual is a victim of a severe form of trafficking and a potential witness to such trafficking, in order to effectuate prosecution of those responsible, and such officials in investigating and prosecuting traffickers shall protect the safety of trafficking victims, including taking measures to protect trafficked persons and their family members from intimidation, threats of reprisals, and reprisals from traffickers and their associates.

(4) TRAINING OF GOVERNMENT PERSONNEL—Appropriate personnel of the Department of State and the Department of Justice shall be trained in identifying victims of severe forms of trafficking and providing for the protection of such victims.

(d) CONSTRUCTION—Nothing in subsection (c) shall be construed as creating any private cause of action against the United States or its officers or employees.

(e) PROTECTION FROM REMOVAL FOR CERTAIN CRIME VICTIMS—

(1) IN GENERAL—Section 101(a)(15) of the Immigration and Nationality Act (8 U.S.C. 1101(a)(15)) is amended—

(A) by striking 'or' at the end of subparagraph (R);

(B) by striking the period at the end of subparagraph (S) and inserting '; or'; and

(C) by adding at the end the following new subparagraph:

'(T)(i) subject to section 214(n), an alien who the Attorney General determines—

'(I) is or has been a victim of a severe form of trafficking in persons, as defined in section 103 of the Trafficking Victims Protection Act of 2000,

'(II) is physically present in the United States, American Samoa, or the Commonwealth of the Northern Mariana Islands, or at a port of entry thereto, on account of such trafficking,

'(III)(aa) has complied with any reasonable request for assistance in the investigation or prosecution of acts of trafficking, or

'(bb) has not attained 15 years of age, and

'(IV) the alien would suffer extreme hardship involving unusual and severe harm upon removal; and

'(ii) if the Attorney General considers it necessary to avoid extreme hardship—

'(I) in the case of an alien described in clause (i) who is under 21 years of age, the spouse, children, and parents of such alien; and

'(II) in the case of an alien described in clause (i) who is 21 years of age or older, the spouse and children of such alien,

if accompanying, or following to join, the alien described in clause (i).'.

(2) CONDITIONS OF NONIMMIGRANT STATUS—Section 214 of the Immigration and Nationality Act (8 U.S.C. 1184) is amended—

(A) by redesignating the subsection (l) added by section 625(a) of the Illegal Immigration Reform and Immigrant Responsibility Act of 1996 (Public Law 104-208; 110 Stat. 3009-1820) as subsection (m); and

(B) by adding at the end the following:

'(n)(1) No alien shall be eligible for admission to the United States under section 101(a)(15)(T) if there is substantial reason to believe that the alien has committed an act of a severe form of trafficking in persons (as defined in section 103 of the Trafficking Victims Protection Act of 2000).

'(2) The total number of aliens who may be issued visas or otherwise provided nonimmigrant status during any fiscal year under section 101(a)(15)(T) may not exceed 5,000.

'(3) The numerical limitation of paragraph (2) shall only apply to principal aliens and not to the spouses, sons, daughters, or parents of such aliens.'.

(3) WAIVER OF GROUNDS FOR INELIGIBILITY FOR ADMISSION—

Section 212(d) of the Immigration and Nationality Act (8 U.S.C. 1182(d)) is amended by adding at the end the following:

'(13)(A) The Attorney General shall determine whether a ground for inadmissibility exists with respect to a nonimmigrant described in section 101(a)(15)(T).

'(B) In addition to any other waiver that may be available under this section, in the case of a nonimmigrant described in section 101(a)(15)(T), if the Attorney General considers it to be in the national interest to do so, the Attorney General, in the Attorney General's discretion, may waive the application of—

'(i) paragraphs (1) and (4) of subsection (a); and
'(ii) any other provision of such subsection (excluding paragraphs (3), (10)(C), and (10)(E)) if the activities rendering the alien inadmissible under the provision were caused by, or were incident to, the victimization described in section 101(a)(15)(T)(i)(I).'.
(4) DUTIES OF THE ATTORNEY GENERAL WITH RESPECT TO 'T' VISA NONIMMIGRANTS—Section 101 of the Immigration and Nationality Act (8 U.S.C. 1101) is amended by adding at the end the following new subsection:
'(i) With respect to each nonimmigrant alien described in subsection (a)(15)(T)(i)—
'(1) the Attorney General and other Government officials, where appropriate, shall provide the alien with a referral to a nongovernmental organization that would advise the alien regarding the alien's options while in the United States and the resources available to the alien; and
'(2) the Attorney General shall, during the period the alien is in lawful temporary resident status under that subsection, grant the alien authorization to engage in employment in the United States and provide the alien with an 'employment authorized' endorsement or other appropriate work permit.'.
(5) STATUTORY CONSTRUCTION—Nothing in this section, or in the amendments made by this section, shall be construed as prohibiting the Attorney General from instituting removal proceedings under section 240 of the Immigration and Nationality Act (8 U.S.C. 1229a) against an alien admitted as a nonimmigrant under section 101(a)(15)(T)(i) of that Act, as added by subsection (e), for conduct committed after the alien's admission into the United States, or for conduct or a condition that was not disclosed to the Attorney General prior to the alien's admission as a nonimmigrant under such section 101(a)(15)(T)(i).
(f) ADJUSTMENT TO PERMANENT RESIDENT STATUS—Section 245 of such Act (8 U.S.C 1255) is amended by adding at the end the following new subsection:
'(l)(1) If, in the opinion of the Attorney General, a nonimmigrant admitted into the United States under section 101(a)(15)(T)(i)—
'(A) has been physically present in the United States for a continuous period of at least 3 years since the date of admission as a nonimmigrant under section 101(a)(15)(T)(i),
'(B) has, throughout such period, been a person of good moral character, and
'(C)(i) has, during such period, complied with any reasonable request for assistance in the investigation or prosecution of acts of trafficking, or
'(ii) the alien would suffer extreme hardship involving unusual and severe harm upon removal from the United States, the Attorney General may adjust the status of the alien (and any person admitted under that section as the spouse, parent, or child of the alien) to that of an alien lawfully admitted for permanent residence.
'(2) Paragraph (1) shall not apply to an alien admitted under section 101(a)(15)(T) who is inadmissible to the United States by reason of a ground that has not been waived under section 212, except that, if the Attorney General considers it

to be in the national interest to do so, the Attorney General, in the Attorney General's discretion, may waive the application of—
   '(A) paragraphs (1) and (4) of section 212(a); and
   '(B) any other provision of such section (excluding paragraphs (3), (10)(C), and (10)(E)), if the activities rendering the alien inadmissible under the provision were caused by, or were incident to, the victimization described in section 101(a)(15)(T)(i)(I).
'(2) An alien shall be considered to have failed to maintain continuous physical presence in the United States under paragraph (1)(A) if the alien has departed from the United States for any period in excess of 90 days or for any periods in the aggregate exceeding 180 days.
'(3)(A) The total number of aliens whose status may be adjusted under paragraph (1) during any fiscal year may not exceed 5,000.
'(B) The numerical limitation of subparagraph (A) shall only apply to principal aliens and not to the spouses, sons, daughters, or parents of such aliens.
'(4) Upon the approval of adjustment of status under paragraph (1), the Attorney General shall record the alien's lawful admission for permanent residence as of the date of such approval.'.
(g) ANNUAL REPORTS—On or before October 31 of each year, the Attorney General shall submit a report to the appropriate congressional committees setting forth, with respect to the preceding fiscal year, the number, if any, of otherwise eligible applicants who did not receive visas under section 101(a)(15)(T) of the Immigration and Nationality Act, as added by subsection (e), or who were unable to adjust their status under section 245(l) of such Act, solely on account of the unavailability of visas due to a limitation imposed by section 214(n)(1) or 245(l)(4)(A) of such Act.

SEC. 108. MINIMUM STANDARDS FOR THE ELIMINATION OF TRAFFICKING.

(a) MINIMUM STANDARDS—For purposes of this division, the minimum standards for the elimination of trafficking applicable to the government of a country of origin, transit, or destination for a significant number of victims of severe forms of trafficking are the following:
   (1) The government of the country should prohibit severe forms of trafficking in persons and punish acts of such trafficking.
   (2) For the knowing commission of any act of sex trafficking involving force, fraud, coercion, or in which the victim of sex trafficking is a child incapable of giving meaningful consent, or of trafficking which includes rape or kidnapping or which causes a death, the government of the country should prescribe punishment commensurate with that for grave crimes, such as forcible sexual assault.
   (3) For the knowing commission of any act of a severe form of trafficking in persons, the government of the country should prescribe punishment

that is sufficiently stringent to deter and that adequately reflects the heinous nature of the offense.

(4) The government of the country should make serious and sustained efforts to eliminate severe forms of trafficking in persons.

(b) CRITERIA—In determinations under subsection (a)(4), the following factors should be considered as indicia of serious and sustained efforts to eliminate severe forms of trafficking in persons:

(1) Whether the government of the country vigorously investigates and prosecutes acts of severe forms of trafficking in persons that take place wholly or partly within the territory of the country.

(2) Whether the government of the country protects victims of severe forms of trafficking in persons and encourages their assistance in the investigation and prosecution of such trafficking, including provisions for legal alternatives to their removal to countries in which they would face retribution or hardship, and ensures that victims are not inappropriately incarcerated, fined, or otherwise penalized solely for unlawful acts as a direct result of being trafficked.

(3) Whether the government of the country has adopted measures to prevent severe forms of trafficking in persons, such as measures to inform and educate the public, including potential victims, about the causes and consequences of severe forms of trafficking in persons.

(4) Whether the government of the country cooperates with other governments in the investigation and prosecution of severe forms of trafficking in persons.

(5) Whether the government of the country extradites persons charged with acts of severe forms of trafficking in persons on substantially the same terms and to substantially the same extent as persons charged with other serious crimes (or, to the extent such extradition would be inconsistent with the laws of such country or with international agreements to which the country is a party, whether the government is taking all appropriate measures to modify or replace such laws and treaties so as to permit such extradition).

(6) Whether the government of the country monitors immigration and emigration patterns for evidence of severe forms of trafficking in persons and whether law enforcement agencies of the country respond to any such evidence in a manner that is consistent with the vigorous investigation and prosecution of acts of such trafficking, as well as with the protection of human rights of victims and the internationally recognized human right to leave any country, including one's own, and to return to one's own country.

(7) Whether the government of the country vigorously investigates and prosecutes public officials who participate in or facilitate severe forms of trafficking in persons, and takes all appropriate measures against officials who condone such trafficking.

SEC. 109. ASSISTANCE TO FOREIGN COUNTRIES TO MEET MINIMUM STANDARDS.

Chapter 1 of part I of the Foreign Assistance Act of 1961 (22 U.S.C. 2151 et seq.) is amended by adding at the end the following new section:

'SEC. 134. ASSISTANCE TO FOREIGN COUNTRIES TO MEET MINIMUM STANDARDS FOR THE ELIMINATION OF TRAFFICKING.

'(a) AUTHORIZATION—The President is authorized to provide assistance to foreign countries directly, or through nongovernmental and multilateral organizations, for programs, projects, and activities designed to meet the minimum standards for the elimination of trafficking (as defined in section 103 of the Trafficking Victims Protection Act of 2000), including—
  '(1) the drafting of laws to prohibit and punish acts of trafficking;
  '(2) the investigation and prosecution of traffickers;
  '(3) the creation and maintenance of facilities, programs, projects, and activities for the protection of victims; and
  '(4) the expansion of exchange programs and international visitor programs for governmental and nongovernmental personnel to combat trafficking.
'(b) FUNDING—Amounts made available to carry out the other provisions of this part (including chapter 4 of part II of this Act) and the Support for East European Democracy (SEED) Act of 1989 shall be made available to carry out this section.'.

SEC. 110. ACTIONS AGAINST GOVERNMENTS FAILING TO MEET MINIMUM STANDARDS.

(a) STATEMENT OF POLICY—It is the policy of the United States not to provide nonhumanitarian, nontrade-related foreign assistance to any government that—
  (1) does not comply with minimum standards for the elimination of trafficking; and
  (2) is not making significant efforts to bring itself into compliance with such standards.
(b) REPORTS TO CONGRESS—
  (1) ANNUAL REPORT—Not later than June 1 of each year, the Secretary of State shall submit to the appropriate congressional committees a report with respect to the status of severe forms of trafficking in persons that shall include—
    (A) a list of those countries, if any, to which the minimum standards for the elimination of trafficking are applicable and whose governments fully comply with such standards;
    (B) a list of those countries, if any, to which the minimum standards for the elimination of trafficking are applicable and whose

governments do not yet fully comply with such standards but are making significant efforts to bring themselves into compliance; and
(C) a list of those countries, if any, to which the minimum standards for the elimination of trafficking are applicable and whose governments do not fully comply with such standards and are not making significant efforts to bring themselves into compliance.

(2) INTERIM REPORTS—In addition to the annual report under paragraph (1), the Secretary of State may submit to the appropriate congressional committees at any time one or more interim reports with respect to the status of severe forms of trafficking in persons, including information about countries whose governments—

(A) have come into or out of compliance with the minimum standards for the elimination of trafficking; or
(B) have begun or ceased to make significant efforts to bring themselves into compliance,
since the transmission of the last annual report.

(3) SIGNIFICANT EFFORTS—In determinations under paragraph (1) or (2) as to whether the government of a country is making significant efforts to bring itself into compliance with the minimum standards for the elimination of trafficking, the Secretary of State shall consider—

(A) the extent to which the country is a country of origin, transit, or destination for severe forms of trafficking;
(B) the extent of noncompliance with the minimum standards by the government and, particularly, the extent to which officials or employees of the government have participated in, facilitated, condoned, or are otherwise complicit in severe forms of trafficking; and
(C) what measures are reasonable to bring the government into compliance with the minimum standards in light of the resources and capabilities of the government.

(c) NOTIFICATION—Not less than 45 days or more than 90 days after the submission, on or after January 1, 2003, of an annual report under subsection (b)(1), or an interim report under subsection (b)(2), the President shall submit to the appropriate congressional committees a notification of one of the determinations listed in subsection (d) with respect to each foreign country whose government, according to such report—

(A) does not comply with the minimum standards for the elimination of trafficking; and
(B) is not making significant efforts to bring itself into compliance, as described in subsection (b)(1)(C).

(d) PRESIDENTIAL DETERMINATIONS—The determinations referred to in subsection (c) are the following:

(1) WITHHOLDING OF NONHUMANITARIAN, NONTRADE-RELATED ASSISTANCE—The President has determined that—

(A)(i) the United States will not provide nonhumanitarian, nontrade-related foreign assistance to the government of the country for the subsequent fiscal year until such government complies with the minimum standards or makes significant efforts to bring itself into compliance; or

(ii) in the case of a country whose government received no nonhumanitarian, nontrade-related foreign assistance from the United States during the previous fiscal year, the United States will not provide funding for participation by officials or employees of such governments in educational and cultural exchange programs for the subsequent fiscal year until such government complies with the minimum standards or makes significant efforts to bring itself into compliance; and

(B) the President will instruct the United States Executive Director of each multilateral development bank and of the International Monetary Fund to vote against, and to use the Executive Director's best efforts to deny, any loan or other utilization of the funds of the respective institution to that country (other than for humanitarian assistance, for trade-related assistance, or for development assistance which directly addresses basic human needs, is not administered by the government of the sanctioned country, and confers no benefit to that government) for the subsequent fiscal year until such government complies with the minimum standards or makes significant efforts to bring itself into compliance.

(2) ONGOING, MULTIPLE, BROAD-BASED RESTRICTIONS ON ASSISTANCE IN RESPONSE TO HUMAN RIGHTS VIOLATIONS—The President has determined that such country is already subject to multiple, broad-based restrictions on assistance imposed in significant part in response to human rights abuses and such restrictions are ongoing and are comparable to the restrictions provided in paragraph (1). Such determination shall be accompanied by a description of the specific restriction or restrictions that were the basis for making such determination.

(3) SUBSEQUENT COMPLIANCE—The Secretary of State has determined that the government of the country has come into compliance with the minimum standards or is making significant efforts to bring itself into compliance.

(4) CONTINUATION OF ASSISTANCE IN THE NATIONAL INTEREST—Notwithstanding the failure of the government of the country to comply with minimum standards for the elimination of trafficking and to make significant efforts to bring itself into compliance, the President has determined that the provision to the country of nonhumanitarian, nontrade-related foreign assistance, or the multilateral assistance described in paragraph (1)(B), or both, would promote the purposes of this division or is otherwise in the national interest of the United States.

(5) EXERCISE OF WAIVER AUTHORITY—
   (A) IN GENERAL—The President may exercise the authority under paragraph (4) with respect to—
      (i) all nonhumanitarian, nontrade-related foreign assistance to a country;
      (ii) all multilateral assistance described in paragraph (1)(B) to a country; or
      (iii) one or more programs, projects, or activities of such assistance.
   (B) AVOIDANCE OF SIGNIFICANT ADVERSE EFFECTS—The President shall exercise the authority under paragraph (4) when necessary to avoid significant adverse effects on vulnerable populations, including women and children.
(6) DEFINITION OF MULTILATERAL DEVELOPMENT BANK—In this subsection, the term 'multilateral development bank' refers to any of the following institutions: the International Bank for Reconstruction and Development, the International Development Association, the International Finance Corporation, the Inter-American Development Bank, the Asian Development Bank, the Inter-American Investment Corporation, the African Development Bank, the African Development Fund, the European Bank for Reconstruction and Development, and the Multilateral Investment Guaranty Agency.

(e) CERTIFICATION—Together with any notification under subsection (c), the President shall provide a certification by the Secretary of State that, with respect to any assistance described in clause (ii), (iii), or (v) of section 103(7)(A), or with respect to any assistance described in section 103(7)(B), no assistance is intended to be received or used by any agency or official who has participated in, facilitated, or condoned a severe form of trafficking in persons.

SEC. 111. ACTIONS AGAINST SIGNIFICANT TRAFFICKERS IN PERSONS.

(a) AUTHORITY TO SANCTION SIGNIFICANT TRAFFICKERS IN PERSONS—
   (1) IN GENERAL—The President may exercise the authorities set forth in section 203 of the International Emergency Economic Powers Act (50 U.S.C. 1701) without regard to section 202 of that Act (50 U.S.C. 1701) in the case of any of the following persons:
      (A) Any foreign person that plays a significant role in a severe form of trafficking in persons, directly or indirectly in the United States.
      (B) Foreign persons that materially assist in, or provide financial or technological support for or to, or provide goods or services in support of, activities of a significant foreign trafficker in persons identified pursuant to subparagraph (A).
      (C) Foreign persons that are owned, controlled, or directed by, or acting for or on behalf of, a significant foreign trafficker identified pursuant to subparagraph (A).

(2) PENALTIES—The penalties set forth in section 206 of the International Emergency Economic Powers Act (50 U.S.C. 1705) apply to violations of any license, order, or regulation issued under this section.

(b) REPORT TO CONGRESS ON IDENTIFICATION AND SANCTIONING OF SIGNIFICANT TRAFFICKERS IN PERSONS—

(1) IN GENERAL—Upon exercising the authority of subsection (a), the President shall report to the appropriate congressional committees—

(A) identifying publicly the foreign persons that the President determines are appropriate for sanctions pursuant to this section and the basis for such determination; and

(B) detailing publicly the sanctions imposed pursuant to this section.

(2) REMOVAL OF SANCTIONS—Upon suspending or terminating any action imposed under the authority of subsection (a), the President shall report to the committees described in paragraph (1) on such suspension or termination.

(3) SUBMISSION OF CLASSIFIED INFORMATION—Reports submitted under this subsection may include an annex with classified information regarding the basis for the determination made by the President under paragraph (1)(A).

(c) LAW ENFORCEMENT AND INTELLIGENCE ACTIVITIES NOT AFFECTED—Nothing in this section prohibits or otherwise limits the authorized law enforcement or intelligence activities of the United States, or the law enforcement activities of any State or subdivision thereof.

(d) EXCLUSION OF PERSONS WHO HAVE BENEFITED FROM ILLICIT ACTIVITIES OF TRAFFICKERS IN PERSONS—Section 212(a)(2) of the Immigration and Nationality Act (8 U.S.C. 1182(a)(2)) is amended by inserting at the end the following new subparagraph:

'(H) SIGNIFICANT TRAFFICKERS IN PERSONS—

'(i) IN GENERAL—Any alien who is listed in a report submitted pursuant to section 111(b) of the Trafficking Victims Protection Act of 2000, or who the consular officer or the Attorney General knows or has reason to believe is or has been a knowing aider, abettor, assister, conspirator, or colluder with such a trafficker in severe forms of trafficking in persons, as defined in the section 103 of such Act, is inadmissible.

'(ii) BENEFICIARIES OF TRAFFICKING—Except as provided in clause (iii), any alien who the consular officer or the Attorney General knows or has reason to believe is the spouse, son, or daughter of an alien inadmissible under clause (i), has, within the previous 5 years, obtained any financial or other benefit from the illicit activity of that alien, and knew or reasonably should have known that the financial or other benefit was the product of such illicit activity, is inadmissible.

'(iii) EXCEPTION FOR CERTAIN SONS AND DAUGHTERS—Clause (ii) shall not apply to a son or daughter who was a child at the time he or she received the benefit described in such clause.'.

(e) IMPLEMENTATION—
   (1) DELEGATION OF AUTHORITY—The President may delegate any authority granted by this section, including the authority to designate foreign persons under paragraphs (1)(B) and (1)(C) of subsection (a).
   (2) PROMULGATION OF RULES AND REGULATIONS—The head of any agency, including the Secretary of Treasury, is authorized to take such actions as may be necessary to carry out any authority delegated by the President pursuant to paragraph (1), including promulgating rules and regulations.
   (3) OPPORTUNITY FOR REVIEW—Such rules and regulations shall include procedures affording an opportunity for a person to be heard in an expeditious manner, either in person or through a representative, for the purpose of seeking changes to or termination of any determination, order, designation or other action associated with the exercise of the authority in subsection (a).
(f) DEFINITION OF FOREIGN PERSONS—In this section, the term 'foreign person' means any citizen or national of a foreign state or any entity not organized under the laws of the United States, including a foreign government official, but does not include a foreign state.
(g) CONSTRUCTION—Nothing in this section shall be construed as precluding judicial review of the exercise of the authority described in subsection (a).

SEC. 112. STRENGTHENING PROSECUTION AND PUNISHMENT OF TRAFFICKERS.

(a) TITLE 18 AMENDMENTS—Chapter 77 of title 18, United States Code, is amended—
   (1) in each of sections 1581(a), 1583, and 1584—
      (A) by striking '10 years' and inserting '20 years'; and
      (B) by adding at the end the following: 'If death results from the violation of this section, or if the violation includes kidnapping or an attempt to kidnap, aggravated sexual abuse or the attempt to commit aggravated sexual abuse, or an attempt to kill, the defendant shall be fined under this title or imprisoned for any term of years or life, or both.';
   (2) by inserting at the end the following:

'**Sec. 1589. Forced labor**

   'Whoever knowingly provides or obtains the labor or services of a person—
      '(1) by threats of serious harm to, or physical restraint against, that person or another person;

'(2) by means of any scheme, plan, or pattern intended to cause the person to believe that, if the person did not perform such labor or services, that person or another person would suffer serious harm or physical restraint; or
'(3) by means of the abuse or threatened abuse of law or the legal process, shall be fined under this title or imprisoned not more than 20 years, or both. If death results from the violation of this section, or if the violation includes kidnapping or an attempt to kidnap, aggravated sexual abuse or the attempt to commit aggravated sexual abuse, or an attempt to kill, the defendant shall be fined under this title or imprisoned for any term of years or life, or both.

'Sec. 1590. Trafficking with respect to peonage, slavery, involuntary servitude, or forced labor

'Whoever knowingly recruits, harbors, transports, provides, or obtains by any means, any person for labor or services in violation of this chapter shall be fined under this title or imprisoned not more than 20 years, or both. If death results from the violation of this section, or if the violation includes kidnapping or an attempt to kidnap, aggravated sexual abuse, or the attempt to commit aggravated sexual abuse, or an attempt to kill, the defendant shall be fined under this title or imprisoned for any term of years or life, or both.

'Sec. 1591. Sex trafficking of children or by force, fraud or coercion

'(a) Whoever knowingly—
'(1) in or affecting interstate commerce, recruits, entices, harbors, transports, provides, or obtains by any means a person; or
'(2) benefits, financially or by receiving anything of value, from participation in a venture which has engaged in an act described in violation of paragraph (1), knowing that force, fraud, or coercion described in subsection (c)(2) will be used to cause the person to engage in a commercial sex act, or that the person has not attained the age of 18 years and will be caused to engage in a commercial sex act, shall be punished as provided in subsection (b).
'(b) The punishment for an offense under subsection (a) is—
'(1) if the offense was effected by force, fraud, or coercion or if the person transported had not attained the age of 14 years at the time of such offense, by a fine under this title or imprisonment for any term of years or for life, or both; or
'(2) if the offense was not so effected, and the person transported had attained the age of 14 years but had not attained the age of 18 years at the time of such offense, by a fine under this title or imprisonment for not more than 20 years, or both.
'(c) In this section:
'(1) The term 'commercial sex act' means any sex act, on account of which anything of value is given to or received by any person.

'(2) The term 'coercion' means—
    '(A) threats of serious harm to or physical restraint against any person;
    '(B) any scheme, plan, or pattern intended to cause a person to believe that failure to perform an act would result in serious harm to or physical restraint against any person; or
    '(C) the abuse or threatened abuse of law or the legal process.
'(3) The term 'venture' means any group of two or more individuals associated in fact, whether or not a legal entity.

'Sec. 1592. Unlawful conduct with respect to documents in furtherance of trafficking, peonage, slavery, involuntary servitude, or forced labor

'(a) Whoever knowingly destroys, conceals, removes, confiscates, or possesses any actual or purported passport or other immigration document, or any other actual or purported government identification document, of another person—
    '(1) in the course of a violation of section 1581, 1583, 1584, 1589, 1590, 1591, or 1594(a);
    '(2) with intent to violate section 1581, 1583, 1584, 1589, 1590, or 1591; or
    '(3) to prevent or restrict or to attempt to prevent or restrict, without lawful authority, the person's liberty to move or travel, in order to maintain the labor or services of that person, when the person is or has been a victim of a severe form of trafficking in persons, as defined in section 103 of the Trafficking Victims Protection Act of 2000, shall be fined under this title or imprisoned for not more than 5 years, or both.
'(b) Subsection (a) does not apply to the conduct of a person who is or has been a victim of a severe form of trafficking in persons, as defined in section 103 of the Trafficking Victims Protection Act of 2000, if that conduct is caused by, or incident to, that trafficking.

'Sec. 1593. Mandatory restitution

'(a) Notwithstanding section 3663 or 3663A, and in addition to any other civil or criminal penalties authorized by law, the court shall order restitution for any offense under this chapter.
'(b)(1) The order of restitution under this section shall direct the defendant to pay the victim (through the appropriate court mechanism) the full amount of the victim's losses, as determined by the court under paragraph (3) of this subsection.
'(2) An order of restitution under this section shall be issued and enforced in accordance with section 3664 in the same manner as an order under section 3663A.
'(3) As used in this subsection, the term 'full amount of the victim's losses' has the same meaning as provided in section 2259(b)(3) and shall in addition include the greater of the gross income or value to the defendant of the victim's services or labor or the value of the victim's labor as guaranteed under the minimum wage and overtime guarantees of the Fair Labor Standards Act (29 U.S.C. 201 et seq.).

'(c) As used in this section, the term 'victim' means the individual harmed as a result of a crime under this chapter, including, in the case of a victim who is under 18 years of age, incompetent, incapacitated, or deceased, the legal guardian of the victim or a representative of the victim's estate, or another family member, or any other person appointed as suitable by the court, but in no event shall the defendant be named such representative or guardian.

'Sec. 1594. General provisions

'(a) Whoever attempts to violate section 1581, 1583, 1584, 1589, 1590, or 1591 shall be punishable in the same manner as a completed violation of that section.
'(b) The court, in imposing sentence on any person convicted of a violation of this chapter, shall order, in addition to any other sentence imposed and irrespective of any provision of State law, that such person shall forfeit to the United States—
    '(1) such person's interest in any property, real or personal, that was used or intended to be used to commit or to facilitate the commission of such violation; and
    '(2) any property, real or personal, constituting or derived from, any proceeds that such person obtained, directly or indirectly, as a result of such violation.
'(c)(1) The following shall be subject to forfeiture to the United States and no property right shall exist in them:
    '(A) Any property, real or personal, used or intended to be used to commit or to facilitate the commission of any violation of this chapter.
    '(B) Any property, real or personal, which constitutes or is derived from proceeds traceable to any violation of this chapter.
'(2) The provisions of chapter 46 of this title relating to civil forfeitures shall extend to any seizure or civil forfeiture under this subsection.
'(d) WITNESS PROTECTION—Any violation of this chapter shall be considered an organized criminal activity or other serious offense for the purposes of application of chapter 224 (relating to witness protection).'; and
    (3) by amending the table of sections at the beginning of chapter 77 by adding at the end the following new items:
    '1589. Forced labor.
    '1590. Trafficking with respect to peonage, slavery, involuntary servitude, or forced labor.
    '1591. Sex trafficking of children or by force, fraud, or coercion.
    '1592. Unlawful conduct with respect to documents in furtherance of trafficking, peonage, slavery, involuntary servitude, or forced labor.
    '1593. Mandatory restitution.
    '1594. General provisions.'.
(b) AMENDMENT TO THE SENTENCING GUIDELINES—
    (1) Pursuant to its authority under section 994 of title 28, United States Code, and in accordance with this section, the United States Sentencing Commission shall review and, if appropriate, amend the sentencing

guidelines and policy statements applicable to persons convicted of offenses involving the trafficking of persons including component or related crimes of peonage, involuntary servitude, slave trade offenses, and possession, transfer or sale of false immigration documents in furtherance of trafficking, and the Fair Labor Standards Act and the Migrant and Seasonal Agricultural Worker Protection Act.

(2) In carrying out this subsection, the Sentencing Commission shall—
    (A) take all appropriate measures to ensure that these sentencing guidelines and policy statements applicable to the offenses described in paragraph (1) of this subsection are sufficiently stringent to deter and adequately reflect the heinous nature of such offenses;
    (B) consider conforming the sentencing guidelines applicable to offenses involving trafficking in persons to the guidelines applicable to peonage, involuntary servitude, and slave trade offenses; and
    (C) consider providing sentencing enhancements for those convicted of the offenses described in paragraph (1) of this subsection that—
        (i) involve a large number of victims;
        (ii) involve a pattern of continued and flagrant violations;
        (iii) involve the use or threatened use of a dangerous weapon; or
        (iv) result in the death or bodily injury of any person.

(3) The Commission may promulgate the guidelines or amendments under this subsection in accordance with the procedures set forth in section 21(a) of the Sentencing Act of 1987, as though the authority under that Act had not expired.

SEC. 113. AUTHORIZATIONS OF APPROPRIATIONS.

(a) AUTHORIZATION OF APPROPRIATIONS IN SUPPORT OF THE TASK FORCE—To carry out the purposes of sections 104, 105, and 110, there are authorized to be appropriated to the Secretary of State $1,500,000 for fiscal year 2001 and $3,000,000 for fiscal year 2002.

(b) AUTHORIZATION OF APPROPRIATIONS TO THE SECRETARY OF HEALTH AND HUMAN SERVICES—To carry out the purposes of section 107 (b), there are authorized to be appropriated to the Secretary of Health and Human Services $5,000,000 for fiscal year 2001 and $10,000,000 for fiscal year 2002.

(c) AUTHORIZATION OF APPROPRIATIONS TO THE SECRETARY OF STATE—
    (1) ASSISTANCE FOR VICTIMS IN OTHER COUNTRIES—To carry out the purposes of section 107(a), there are authorized to be appropriated to the Secretary of State $5,000,000 for fiscal year 2001 and $10,000,000 for fiscal year 2002.
    (2) VOLUNTARY CONTRIBUTIONS TO OSCE—To carry out the purposes of section 109, there are authorized to be appropriated to the Secretary of State $300,000 for voluntary contributions to advance projects aimed at

preventing trafficking, promoting respect for human rights of trafficking victims, and assisting the Organization for Security and Cooperation in Europe participating states in related legal reform for fiscal year 2001.
(3) PREPARATION OF ANNUAL COUNTRY REPORTS ON HUMAN RIGHTS—To carry out the purposes of section 104, there are authorized to be appropriated to the Secretary of State such sums as may be necessary to include the additional information required by that section in the annual Country Reports on Human Rights Practices, including the preparation and publication of the list described in subsection (a)(1) of that section.

(d) AUTHORIZATION OF APPROPRIATIONS TO ATTORNEY GENERAL—To carry out the purposes of section 107(b), there are authorized to be appropriated to the Attorney General $5,000,000 for fiscal year 2001 and $10,000,000 for fiscal year 2002.

(e) Authorization of Appropriations to President—
(1) FOREIGN VICTIM ASSISTANCE—To carry out the purposes of section 106, there are authorized to be appropriated to the President $5,000,000 for fiscal year 2001 and $10,000,000 for fiscal year 2002.
(2) ASSISTANCE TO FOREIGN COUNTRIES TO MEET MINIMUM STANDARDS—To carry out the purposes of section 109, there are authorized to be appropriated to the President $5,000,000 for fiscal year 2001 and $10,000,000 for fiscal year 2002.

(f) AUTHORIZATION OF APPROPRIATIONS TO THE SECRETARY OF LABOR—To carry out the purposes of section 107(b), there are authorized to be appropriated to the Secretary of Labor $5,000,000 for fiscal year 2001 and $10,000,000 for fiscal year 2002.

DIVISION B—VIOLENCE AGAINST WOMEN ACT OF 2000

SEC. 1001. SHORT TITLE.

This division may be cited as the 'Violence Against Women Act of 2000'.

SEC. 1002. DEFINITIONS.

In this division—
(1) the term 'domestic violence' has the meaning given the term in section 2003 of title I of the Omnibus Crime Control and Safe Streets Act of 1968 (42 U.S.C. 3796gg-2); and
(2) the term 'sexual assault' has the meaning given the term in section 2003 of title I of the Omnibus Crime Control and Safe Streets Act of 1968 (42 U.S.C. 3796gg-2).

SEC. 1003. ACCOUNTABILITY AND OVERSIGHT.

(a) REPORT BY GRANT RECIPIENTS—The Attorney General or Secretary of Health and Human Services, as applicable, shall require grantees under any program authorized or reauthorized by this division or an amendment made by this division to report on the effectiveness of the activities carried out with amounts made available to carry out that program, including number of persons served, if applicable, numbers of persons seeking services who could not be served and such other information as the Attorney General or Secretary may prescribe.

(b) REPORT TO CONGRESS—The Attorney General or Secretary of Health and Human Services, as applicable, shall report biennially to the Committees on the Judiciary of the House of Representatives and the Senate on the grant programs described in subsection (a), including the information contained in any report under that subsection.

TITLE I—STRENGTHENING LAW ENFORCEMENT TO REDUCE VIOLENCE AGAINST WOMEN

SEC. 1101. FULL FAITH AND CREDIT ENFORCEMENT OF PROTECTION ORDERS.

(a) IN GENERAL—Part U of title I of the Omnibus Crime Control and Safe Streets Act of 1968 (42 U.S.C. 3796hh et seq.) is amended—
   (1) in the heading, by adding '**AND ENFORCEMENT OF PROTECTION ORDERS**' at the end;
   (2) in section 2101(b)—
       (A) in paragraph (6), by inserting '(including juvenile courts)' after 'courts'; and
       (B) by adding at the end the following:
   '(7) To provide technical assistance and computer and other equipment to police departments, prosecutors, courts, and tribal jurisdictions to facilitate the widespread enforcement of protection orders, including interstate enforcement, enforcement between States and tribal jurisdictions, and enforcement between tribal jurisdictions.'; and
   (3) in section 2102—
       (A) in subsection (b)—
           (i) in paragraph (1), by striking 'and' at the end;
           (ii) in paragraph (2), by striking the period at the end and inserting ', including the enforcement of protection orders from other States and jurisdictions (including tribal jurisdictions);'; and
           (iii) by adding at the end the following:
   '(3) have established cooperative agreements or can demonstrate effective ongoing collaborative arrangements with neighboring jurisdictions to facilitate the enforcement of protection orders from other States and jurisdictions (including tribal jurisdictions); and
   '(4) in applications describing plans to further the purposes stated in paragraph (4) or (7) of section 2101(b), will give priority to using the grant to develop and install data collection and communication systems, including computerized systems, and training on how to use these systems effectively to link police, prosecutors, courts, and tribal jurisdictions for the purpose of identifying and

tracking protection orders and violations of protection orders, in those jurisdictions where such systems do not exist or are not fully effective.'; and

  (B) by adding at the end the following:

'(c) DISSEMINATION OF INFORMATION—The Attorney General shall annually compile and broadly disseminate (including through electronic publication) information about successful data collection and communication systems that meet the purposes described in this section. Such dissemination shall target States, State and local courts, Indian tribal governments, and units of local government.'.

(b) PROTECTION ORDERS—

 (1) FILING COSTS—Section 2006 of part T of title I of the Omnibus Crime Control and Safe Streets Act of 1968 (42 U.S.C. 3796gg-5) is amended—

  (A) in the heading, by striking 'filing' and inserting 'and protection orders' after 'charges';

  (B) in subsection (a)—

   (i) by striking paragraph (1) and inserting the following:

'(1) certifies that its laws, policies, and practices do not require, in connection with the prosecution of any misdemeanor or felony domestic violence offense, or in connection with the filing, issuance, registration, or service of a protection order, or a petition for a protection order, to protect a victim of domestic violence, stalking, or sexual assault, that the victim bear the costs associated with the filing of criminal charges against the offender, or the costs associated with the filing, issuance, registration, or service of a warrant, protection order, petition for a protection order, or witness subpoena, whether issued inside or outside the State, tribal, or local jurisdiction; or'; and

   (ii) in paragraph (2)(B), by striking '2 years' and inserting '2 years after the date of the enactment of the Violence Against Women Act of 2000'; and

  (C) by adding at the end the following:

'(c) DEFINITION—In this section, the term 'protection order' has the meaning given the term in section 2266 of title 18, United States Code.'.

 (2) ELIGIBILITY FOR GRANTS TO ENCOURAGE ARREST POLICIES—Section 2101 of part U of title I of the Omnibus Crime Control and Safe Streets Act of 1968 (42 U.S.C. 3796hh) is amended—

  (A) in subsection (c), by striking paragraph (4) and inserting the following:

'(4) certify that their laws, policies, and practices do not require, in connection with the prosecution of any misdemeanor or felony domestic violence offense, or in connection with the filing, issuance, registration, or service of a protection order, or a petition for a protection order, to protect a victim of domestic violence, stalking, or sexual assault, that the victim bear the costs associated with the filing of criminal charges against the offender, or the costs associated with the filing, issuance, registration, or service of a warrant, protection order, petition for a protection order, or witness subpoena, whether issued inside or outside the State, tribal, or local jurisdiction.'; and

  (B) by adding at the end the following:

'(d) DEFINITION—In this section, the term 'protection order' has the meaning given the term in section 2266 of title 18, United States Code.'.

(3) APPLICATION FOR GRANTS TO ENCOURAGE ARREST POLICIES—Section 2102(a)(1)(B) of part U of title I of the Omnibus Crime Control and Safe Streets Act of 1968 (42 U.S.C. 3796hh-1(a)(1)(B)) is amended by inserting before the semicolon the following: 'or, in the case of the condition set forth in subsection 2101(c)(4), the expiration of the 2-year period beginning on the date the of the enactment of the Violence Against Women Act of 2000'.

(4) REGISTRATION FOR PROTECTION ORDERS—Section 2265 of title 18, United States Code, is amended by adding at the end the following:

'(d) NOTIFICATION AND REGISTRATION—

'(1) NOTIFICATION—A State or Indian tribe according full faith and credit to an order by a court of another State or Indian tribe shall not notify or require notification of the party against whom a protection order has been issued that the protection order has been registered or filed in that enforcing State or tribal jurisdiction unless requested to do so by the party protected under such order.

'(2) NO PRIOR REGISTRATION OR FILING AS PREREQUISITE FOR ENFORCEMENT—Any protection order that is otherwise consistent with this section shall be accorded full faith and credit, notwithstanding failure to comply with any requirement that the order be registered or filed in the enforcing State or tribal jurisdiction.

'(e) TRIBAL COURT JURISDICTION—For purposes of this section, a tribal court shall have full civil jurisdiction to enforce protection orders, including authority to enforce any orders through civil contempt proceedings, exclusion of violators from Indian lands, and other appropriate mechanisms, in matters arising within the authority of the tribe.'.

(c) TECHNICAL AMENDMENT—The table of contents for title I of the Omnibus Crime Control and Safe Streets Act of 1968 (42 U.S.C. 3711 et seq.) is amended in the item relating to part U, by adding 'AND ENFORCEMENT OF PROTECTION ORDERS' at the end.

SEC. 1102. ROLE OF COURTS.

(a) COURTS AS ELIGIBLE STOP SUBGRANTEES—Part T of title I of the Omnibus Crime Control and Safe Streets Act of 1968 (42 U.S.C. 3796gg et seq.) is amended—
  (1) in section 2001—
    (A) in subsection (a), by striking 'Indian tribal governments,' and inserting 'State and local courts (including juvenile courts), Indian tribal governments, tribal courts,'; and
    (B) in subsection (b)—
      (i) in paragraph (1), by inserting ', judges, other court personnel,' after 'law enforcement officers';

(ii) in paragraph (2), by inserting ', judges, other court personnel,' after 'law enforcement officers'; and

(iii) in paragraph (3), by inserting ', court,' after 'police'; and

(2) in section 2002—

(A) in subsection (a), by inserting 'State and local courts (including juvenile courts),' after 'States,' the second place it appears;

(B) in subsection (c), by striking paragraph (3) and inserting the following:

'(3) of the amount granted—

'(A) not less than 25 percent shall be allocated to police and not less than 25 percent shall be allocated to prosecutors;

'(B) not less than 30 percent shall be allocated to victim services; and

'(C) not less than 5 percent shall be allocated for State and local courts (including juvenile courts); and'; and

(C) in subsection (d)(1), by inserting 'court,' after 'law enforcement,'.

(b) ELIGIBLE GRANTEES; USE OF GRANTS FOR EDUCATION—Section 2101 of part U of title I of the Omnibus Crime Control and Safe Streets Act of 1968 (42 U.S.C. 3796hh) is amended—

(1) in subsection (a), by inserting 'State and local courts (including juvenile courts), tribal courts,' after 'Indian tribal governments,';

(2) in subsection (b)—

(A) by inserting 'State and local courts (including juvenile courts),' after 'Indian tribal governments';

(B) in paragraph (2), by striking 'policies and' and inserting 'policies, educational programs, and';

(C) in paragraph (3), by inserting 'parole and probation officers,' after 'prosecutors,'; and

(D) in paragraph (4), by inserting 'parole and probation officers,' after 'prosecutors,';

(3) in subsection (c), by inserting 'State and local courts (including juvenile courts),' after 'Indian tribal governments'; and

(4) by adding at the end the following:

'(e) ALLOTMENT FOR INDIAN TRIBES—Not less than 5 percent of the total amount made available for grants under this section for each fiscal year shall be available for grants to Indian tribal governments.'.

SEC. 1103. REAUTHORIZATION OF STOP GRANTS.

(a) REAUTHORIZATION—Section 1001(a) of title I of the Omnibus Crime Control and Safe Streets Act of 1968 (42 U.S.C. 3793(a)) is amended by striking paragraph (18) and inserting the following:

'(18) There is authorized to be appropriated to carry out part T $185,000,000 for each of fiscal years 2001 through 2005.'.

(b) GRANT PURPOSES—Part T of title I of the Omnibus Crime Control and Safe Streets Act of 1968 (42 U.S.C. 3796gg et seq.) is amended—

(1) in section 2001—
- (A) in subsection (b)—
  - (i) in paragraph (5), by striking 'racial, cultural, ethnic, and language minorities' and inserting 'underserved populations';
  - (ii) in paragraph (6), by striking 'and' at the end;
  - (iii) in paragraph (7), by striking the period at the end and inserting a semicolon; and
  - (iv) by adding at the end the following:

'(8) supporting formal and informal statewide, multidisciplinary efforts, to the extent not supported by State funds, to coordinate the response of State law enforcement agencies, prosecutors, courts, victim services agencies, and other State agencies and departments, to violent crimes against women, including the crimes of sexual assault, domestic violence, and dating violence;

'(9) training of sexual assault forensic medical personnel examiners in the collection and preservation of evidence, analysis, prevention, and providing expert testimony and treatment of trauma related to sexual assault;'; and

- (B) by adding at the end the following:

'(c) STATE COALITION GRANTS—

'(1) PURPOSE—The Attorney General shall award grants to each State domestic violence coalition and sexual assault coalition for the purposes of coordinating State victim services activities, and collaborating and coordinating with Federal, State, and local entities engaged in violence against women activities.

'(2) GRANTS TO STATE COALITIONS—The Attorney General shall award grants to—

   '(A) each State domestic violence coalition, as determined by the Secretary of Health and Human Services through the Family Violence Prevention and Services Act (42 U.S.C. 10410 et seq.); and
   '(B) each State sexual assault coalition, as determined by the Center for Injury Prevention and Control of the Centers for Disease Control and Prevention under the Public Health Service Act (42 U.S.C. 280b et seq.).

'(3) ELIGIBILITY FOR OTHER GRANTS—Receipt of an award under this subsection by each State domestic violence and sexual assault coalition shall not preclude the coalition from receiving additional grants under this part to carry out the purposes described in subsection (b).';

(2) in section 2002(b)—
- (A) by redesignating paragraphs (2) and (3) as paragraphs (5) and (6), respectively;
- (B) in paragraph (1), by striking '4 percent' and inserting '5 percent';
- (C) in paragraph (5), as redesignated, by striking '$500,000' and inserting '$600,000'; and
- (D) by inserting after paragraph (1) the following:

'(2) 2.5 percent shall be available for grants for State domestic violence coalitions under section 2001(c), with the coalition for each State, the coalition for the District of Columbia, the coalition for the Commonwealth of Puerto Rico, and the coalition for the combined Territories of the United States, each receiving an amount equal to 1/54 of the total amount made available under this paragraph for each fiscal year;

'(3) 2.5 percent shall be available for grants for State sexual assault coalitions under section 2001(c), with the coalition for each State, the coalition for the District of Columbia, the coalition for the Commonwealth of Puerto Rico, and the coalition for the combined Territories of the United States, each receiving an amount equal to 1/54 of the total amount made available under this paragraph for each fiscal year;

'(4) 1/54 shall be available for the development and operation of nonprofit tribal domestic violence and sexual assault coalitions in Indian country;';

(3) in section 2003, by striking paragraph (7) and inserting the following:

'(7) the term 'underserved populations' includes populations underserved because of geographic location (such as rural isolation), underserved racial and ethnic populations, populations underserved because of special needs (such as language barriers, disabilities, alienage status, or age), and any other population determined to be underserved by the State planning process in consultation with the Attorney General;'; and

(4) in section 2004(b)(3), by inserting ', and the membership of persons served in any underserved population' before the semicolon.

SEC. 1104. REAUTHORIZATION OF GRANTS TO ENCOURAGE ARREST POLICIES.

Section 1001(a) of title I of the Omnibus Crime Control and Safe Streets Act of 1968 (42 U.S.C. 3793(a)) is amended by striking paragraph (19) and inserting the following:

'(19) There is authorized to be appropriated to carry out part U $65,000,000 for each of fiscal years 2001 through 2005.'.

SEC. 1105. REAUTHORIZATION OF RURAL DOMESTIC VIOLENCE AND CHILD ABUSE ENFORCEMENT GRANTS.

Section 40295(c) of the Violence Against Women Act of 1994 (42 U.S.C. 13971(c)) is amended—

(1) by striking paragraph (1) and inserting the following:

'(1) IN GENERAL—There is authorized to be appropriated to carry out this section $40,000,000 for each of fiscal years 2001 through 2005.'; and

(2) by adding at the end the following:

'(3) ALLOTMENT FOR INDIAN TRIBES—Not less than 5 percent of the total amount made available to carry out this section for each fiscal year shall be available for grants to Indian tribal governments.'.

SEC. 1106. NATIONAL STALKER AND DOMESTIC VIOLENCE REDUCTION.

(a) REAUTHORIZATION—Section 40603 of the Violence Against Women Act of 1994 (42 U.S.C. 14032) is amended to read as follows:

'SEC. 40603. AUTHORIZATION OF APPROPRIATIONS.

'There is authorized to be appropriated to carry out this subtitle $3,000,000 for each of fiscal years 2001 through 2005.'.

(b) TECHNICAL AMENDMENT—Section 40602(a) of the Violence Against Women Act of 1994 (42 U.S.C. 14031 note) is amended by inserting 'and implement' after 'improve'.

SEC. 1107. AMENDMENTS TO DOMESTIC VIOLENCE AND STALKING OFFENSES.

(a) INTERSTATE DOMESTIC VIOLENCE—Section 2261 of title 18, United States Code, is amended by striking subsection (a) and inserting the following:
'(a) OFFENSES—
'(1) TRAVEL OR CONDUCT OF OFFENDER—A person who travels in interstate or foreign commerce or enters or leaves Indian country with the intent to kill, injure, harass, or intimidate a spouse or intimate partner, and who, in the course of or as a result of such travel, commits or attempts to commit a crime of violence against that spouse or intimate partner, shall be punished as provided in subsection (b).
'(2) CAUSING TRAVEL OF VICTIM—A person who causes a spouse or intimate partner to travel in interstate or foreign commerce or to enter or leave Indian country by force, coercion, duress, or fraud, and who, in the course of, as a result of, or to facilitate such conduct or travel, commits or attempts to commit a crime of violence against that spouse or intimate partner, shall be punished as provided in subsection (b).'.
(b) INTERSTATE STALKING—
(1) IN GENERAL—Section 2261A of title 18, United States Code, is amended to read as follows:

'Sec. 2261A. Interstate stalking

'Whoever—
'(1) travels in interstate or foreign commerce or within the special maritime and territorial jurisdiction of the United States, or enters or leaves Indian country, with the intent to kill, injure, harass, or intimidate another person, and in the course of, or as a result of, such travel places that person in reasonable fear of the death of, or serious bodily injury to, that person, a member of the immediate family (as defined in section 115) of that person, or the spouse or intimate partner of that person; or

'(2) with the intent—
'(A) to kill or injure a person in another State or tribal jurisdiction or within the special maritime and territorial jurisdiction of the United States; or
'(B) to place a person in another State or tribal jurisdiction, or within the special maritime and territorial jurisdiction of the United States, in reasonable fear of the death of, or serious bodily injury to—
'(i) that person;
'(ii) a member of the immediate family (as defined in section 115) of that person; or
'(iii) a spouse or intimate partner of that person, uses the mail or any facility of interstate or foreign commerce to engage in a course of conduct that places that person in reasonable fear of the death of, or serious bodily injury to, any of the persons described in clauses (i) through (iii), shall be punished as provided in section 2261(b).'.

(2) AMENDMENT OF FEDERAL SENTENCING GUIDELINES—
(A) IN GENERAL—Pursuant to its authority under section 994 of title 28, United States Code, the United States Sentencing Commission shall amend the Federal Sentencing Guidelines to reflect the amendment made by this subsection.
(B) FACTORS FOR CONSIDERATION—In carrying out subparagraph (A), the Commission shall consider—
(i) whether the Federal Sentencing Guidelines relating to stalking offenses should be modified in light of the amendment made by this subsection; and
(ii) whether any changes the Commission may make to the Federal Sentencing Guidelines pursuant to clause (i) should also be made with respect to offenses under chapter 110A of title 18, United States Code.

(c) INTERSTATE VIOLATION OF PROTECTION ORDER—Section 2262 of title 18, United States Code, is amended by striking subsection (a) and inserting the following:
'(a) OFFENSES—
'(1) TRAVEL OR CONDUCT OF OFFENDER—A person who travels in interstate or foreign commerce, or enters or leaves Indian country, with the intent to engage in conduct that violates the portion of a protection order that prohibits or provides protection against violence, threats, or harassment against, contact or communication with, or physical proximity to, another person, or that would violate such a portion of a protection order in the jurisdiction in which the order was issued, and subsequently engages in such conduct, shall be punished as provided in subsection (b).
'(2) CAUSING TRAVEL OF VICTIM—A person who causes another person to travel in interstate or foreign commerce or to enter or leave Indian country by force, coercion, duress, or fraud, and in the course of, as a result of, or to facilitate such conduct or travel engages in conduct that violates the portion of

a protection order that prohibits or provides protection against violence, threats, or harassment against, contact or communication with, or physical proximity to, another person, or that would violate such a portion of a protection order in the jurisdiction in which the order was issued, shall be punished as provided in subsection (b).'.

(d) DEFINITIONS—Section 2266 of title 18, United States Code, is amended to read as follows:

'Sec. 2266. Definitions

'In this chapter:

'(1) BODILY INJURY—The term 'bodily injury' means any act, except one done in self-defense, that results in physical injury or sexual abuse.

'(2) COURSE OF CONDUCT—The term 'course of conduct' means a pattern of conduct composed of 2 or more acts, evidencing a continuity of purpose.

'(3) ENTER OR LEAVE INDIAN COUNTRY—The term 'enter or leave Indian country' includes leaving the jurisdiction of 1 tribal government and entering the jurisdiction of another tribal government.

'(4) INDIAN COUNTRY—The term 'Indian country' has the meaning stated in section 1151 of this title.

'(5) PROTECTION ORDER—The term 'protection order' includes any injunction or other order issued for the purpose of preventing violent or threatening acts or harassment against, or contact or communication with or physical proximity to, another person, including any temporary or final order issued by a civil and criminal court (other than a support or child custody order issued pursuant to State divorce and child custody laws, except to the extent that such an order is entitled to full faith and credit under other Federal law) whether obtained by filing an independent action or as a pendente lite order in another proceeding so long as any civil order was issued in response to a complaint, petition, or motion filed by or on behalf of a person seeking protection.

'(6) SERIOUS BODILY INJURY—The term 'serious bodily injury' has the meaning stated in section 2119(2).

'(7) SPOUSE OR INTIMATE PARTNER—The term 'spouse or intimate partner' includes—

'(A) for purposes of—

'(i) sections other than 2261A, a spouse or former spouse of the abuser, a person who shares a child in common with the abuser, and a person who cohabits or has cohabited as a spouse with the abuser; and

'(ii) section 2261A, a spouse or former spouse of the target of the stalking, a person who shares a child in common with the target of the stalking, and a person who cohabits or has cohabited as a spouse with the target of the stalking; and

'(B) any other person similarly situated to a spouse who is protected by the domestic or family violence laws of the State or tribal jurisdiction in which the injury occurred or where the victim resides.

'(8) STATE—The term 'State' includes a State of the United States, the District of Columbia, and a commonwealth, territory, or possession of the United States.
'(9) TRAVEL IN INTERSTATE OR FOREIGN COMMERCE—The term 'travel in interstate or foreign commerce' does not include travel from 1 State to another by an individual who is a member of an Indian tribe and who remains at all times in the territory of the Indian tribe of which the individual is a member.'.

SEC. 1108. SCHOOL AND CAMPUS SECURITY.

(a) GRANTS TO REDUCE VIOLENT CRIMES AGAINST WOMEN ON CAMPUS—Section 826 of the Higher Education Amendments of 1998 (20 U.S.C. 1152) is amended—
    (1) in paragraphs (2), (6), (7), and (9) of subsection (b), by striking 'and domestic violence' and inserting 'domestic violence, and dating violence';
    (2) in subsection (c)(2)(B), by striking 'and domestic violence' and inserting ', domestic violence and dating violence';
    (3) in subsection (f)—
        (A) by redesignating paragraphs (1), (2), and (3) as paragraphs (2), (3), and (4), respectively;
        (B) by inserting before paragraph (2) (as redesignated by subparagraph (A)) the following:
'(1) the term 'dating violence' means violence committed by a person—
    '(A) who is or has been in a social relationship of a romantic or intimate nature with the victim; and
    '(B) where the existence of such a relationship shall be determined based on a consideration of the following factors:
        '(i) the length of the relationship;
        '(ii) the type of relationship; and
        '(iii) the frequency of interaction between the persons involved in the relationship.';
    (C) in paragraph (2) (as redesignated by subparagraph (A)), by inserting ', dating' after 'domestic' each place the term appears; and
    (D) in paragraph (4) (as redesignated by subparagraph (A))—
        (i) by inserting 'or a public, nonprofit organization acting in a nongovernmental capacity' after 'organization';
        (ii) by inserting ', dating violence' after 'assists domestic violence';
        (iii) by striking 'or domestic violence' and inserting ', domestic violence or dating violence'; and
        (iv) by inserting 'dating violence,' before 'stalking,'; and
    (4) in subsection (g), by striking 'fiscal year 1999 and such sums as may be necessary for each of the 4 succeeding fiscal years' and inserting 'each of fiscal years 2001 through 2005'.
(b) MATCHING GRANT PROGRAM FOR SCHOOL SECURITY—Title I of the Omnibus Crime Control and Safe Streets Act of 1968 is amended by inserting after part Z the following new part:

'PART AA—MATCHING GRANT PROGRAM FOR SCHOOL SECURITY

'SEC. 2701. PROGRAM AUTHORIZED.

'(a) IN GENERAL—The Attorney General is authorized to make grants to States, units of local government, and Indian tribes to provide improved security, including the placement and use of metal detectors and other deterrent measures, at schools and on school grounds.

'(b) USES OF FUNDS—Grants awarded under this section shall be distributed directly to the State, unit of local government, or Indian tribe, and shall be used to improve security at schools and on school grounds in the jurisdiction of the grantee through one or more of the following:

'(1) Placement and use of metal detectors, locks, lighting, and other deterrent measures.
'(2) Security assessments.
'(3) Security training of personnel and students.
'(4) Coordination with local law enforcement.
'(5) Any other measure that, in the determination of the Attorney General, may provide a significant improvement in security.

'(c) PREFERENTIAL CONSIDERATION—In awarding grants under this part, the Attorney General shall give preferential consideration, if feasible, to an application from a jurisdiction that has a demonstrated need for improved security, has a demonstrated need for financial assistance, and has evidenced the ability to make the improvements for which the grant amounts are sought.

'(d) MATCHING FUNDS—

'(1) The portion of the costs of a program provided by a grant under subsection (a) may not exceed 50 percent.
'(2) Any funds appropriated by Congress for the activities of any agency of an Indian tribal government or the Bureau of Indian Affairs performing law enforcement functions on any Indian lands may be used to provide the non-Federal share of a matching requirement funded under this subsection.
'(3) The Attorney General may provide, in the guidelines implementing this section, for the requirement of paragraph (1) to be waived or altered in the case of a recipient with a financial need for such a waiver or alteration.

'(e) EQUITABLE DISTRIBUTION—In awarding grants under this part, the Attorney General shall ensure, to the extent practicable, an equitable geographic distribution among the regions of the United States and among urban, suburban, and rural areas.

'(f) ADMINISTRATIVE COSTS—The Attorney General may reserve not more than 2 percent from amounts appropriated to carry out this part for administrative costs.

'SEC. 2702. APPLICATIONS.

'(a) IN GENERAL—To request a grant under this part, the chief executive of a State, unit of local government, or Indian tribe shall submit an application to the Attorney General at such time, in such manner, and accompanied by such information as the Attorney General may require. Each application shall—
    '(1) include a detailed explanation of—
        '(A) the intended uses of funds provided under the grant; and
        '(B) how the activities funded under the grant will meet the purpose of this part; and
    '(2) be accompanied by an assurance that the application was prepared after consultation with individuals not limited to law enforcement officers (such as school violence researchers, child psychologists, social workers, teachers, principals, and other school personnel) to ensure that the improvements to be funded under the grant are—
        '(A) consistent with a comprehensive approach to preventing school violence; and
        '(B) individualized to the needs of each school at which those improvements are to be made.
'(b) GUIDELINES—Not later than 90 days after the date of the enactment of this part, the Attorney General shall promulgate guidelines to implement this section (including the information that must be included and the requirements that the States, units of local government, and Indian tribes must meet) in submitting the applications required under this section.

'SEC. 2703. ANNUAL REPORT TO CONGRESS.

'Not later than November 30th of each year, the Attorney General shall submit a report to the Congress regarding the activities carried out under this part. Each such report shall include, for the preceding fiscal year, the number of grants funded under this part, the amount of funds provided under those grants, and the activities for which those funds were used.

'SEC. 2704. DEFINITIONS.

'For purposes of this part—
'(1) the term 'school' means a public elementary or secondary school;
'(2) the term 'unit of local government' means a county, municipality, town, township, village, parish, borough, or other unit of general government below the State level; and
'(3) the term 'Indian tribe' has the same meaning as in section 4(e) of the Indian Self-Determination and Education Assistance Act (25 U.S.C. 450b(e)).

'SEC. 2705. AUTHORIZATION OF APPROPRIATIONS.

'There are authorized to be appropriated to carry out this part $30,000,000 for each of fiscal years 2001 through 2003.'.

SEC. 1109. DATING VIOLENCE.

(a) DEFINITIONS—
  (1) SECTION 2003—Section 2003 of title I of the Omnibus Crime Control and Safe Streets Act of 1968 (42 U.S.C. 3996gg-2) is amended—
    (A) in paragraph (8), by striking the period at the end and inserting '; and'; and
    (B) by adding at the end the following:
  '(9) the term 'dating violence' means violence committed by a person—
    '(A) who is or has been in a social relationship of a romantic or intimate nature with the victim; and
    '(B) where the existence of such a relationship shall be determined based on a consideration of the following factors:
      '(i) the length of the relationship;
      '(ii) the type of relationship; and
      '(iii) the frequency of interaction between the persons involved in the relationship.'.
  (2) SECTION 2105—Section 2105 of title I of the Omnibus Crime Control and Safe Streets Act of 1968 (42 U.S.C. 3796hh-4) is amended—
    (A) in paragraph (1), by striking 'and' at the end;
    (B) in paragraph (2), by striking the period at the end and inserting '; and'; and
    (C) by adding at the end the following:
  '(3) the term 'dating violence' means violence committed by a person—
    '(A) who is or has been in a social relationship of a romantic or intimate nature with the victim; and
    '(B) where the existence of such a relationship shall be determined based on a consideration of the following factors:
      '(i) the length of the relationship;
      '(ii) the type of relationship; and
      '(iii) the frequency of interaction between the persons involved in the relationship.'.

(b) STOP GRANTS—Section 2001(b) of title I of the Omnibus Crime Control and Safe Streets Act of 1968 (42 U.S.C. 3796gg(b)) is amended—
  (1) in paragraph (1), by striking 'sexual assault and domestic violence' and inserting 'sexual assault, domestic violence, and dating violence'; and
  (2) in paragraph (5), by striking 'sexual assault and domestic violence' and inserting 'sexual assault, domestic violence, and dating violence'.

(c) GRANTS TO ENCOURAGE ARREST POLICIES—Section 2101(b) of title I of the Omnibus Crime Control and Safe Streets Act of 1968 (42 U.S.C. 3796hh(b)) is amended—
  (1) in paragraph (2), by inserting 'and dating violence' after 'domestic violence'; and
  (2) in paragraph (5), by inserting 'and dating violence' after 'domestic violence'.

(d) RURAL DOMESTIC VIOLENCE AND CHILD ABUSE ENFORCEMENT—Section 40295(a) of the Safe Homes for Women Act of 1994 (42 U.S.C. 13971 (a)) is amended—

(1) in paragraph (1), by inserting 'and dating violence (as defined in section 2003 of title I of the Omnibus Crime Control and Safe Streets Act of 1968 (42 U.S.C. 3996gg-2))' after 'domestic violence'; and

(2) in paragraph (2), by inserting 'and dating violence (as defined in section 2003 of title I of the Omnibus Crime Control and Safe Streets Act of 1968 (42 U.S.C. 3996gg-2))' after 'domestic violence'.

TITLE II—STRENGTHENING SERVICES TO VICTIMS OF VIOLENCE

SEC. 1201. LEGAL ASSISTANCE FOR VICTIMS.

(a) IN GENERAL—The purpose of this section is to enable the Attorney General to award grants to increase the availability of legal assistance necessary to provide effective aid to victims of domestic violence, stalking, or sexual assault who are seeking relief in legal matters arising as a consequence of that abuse or violence, at minimal or no cost to the victims.

(b) DEFINITIONS—In this section:

(1) DOMESTIC VIOLENCE—The term 'domestic violence' has the meaning given the term in section 2003 of title I of the Omnibus Crime Control and Safe Streets Act of 1968 (42 U.S.C. 3796gg-2).

(2) LEGAL ASSISTANCE FOR VICTIMS—The term 'legal assistance' includes assistance to victims of domestic violence, stalking, and sexual assault in family, immigration, administrative agency, or housing matters, protection or stay away order proceedings, and other similar matters. No funds made available under this section may be used to provide financial assistance in support of any litigation described in paragraph (14) of section 504 of Public Law 104-134.

(3) SEXUAL ASSAULT—The term 'sexual assault' has the meaning given the term in section 2003 of title I of the Omnibus Crime Control and Safe Streets Act of 1968 (42 U.S.C. 3796gg-2).

(c) LEGAL ASSISTANCE FOR VICTIMS GRANTS—The Attorney General may award grants under this subsection to private nonprofit entities, Indian tribal governments, and publicly funded organizations not acting in a governmental capacity such as law schools, and which shall be used—

(1) to implement, expand, and establish cooperative efforts and projects between domestic violence and sexual assault victim services organizations and legal assistance providers to provide legal assistance for victims of domestic violence, stalking, and sexual assault;

(2) to implement, expand, and establish efforts and projects to provide legal assistance for victims of domestic violence, stalking, and sexual assault by organizations with a demonstrated history of providing direct legal or advocacy services on behalf of these victims; and

(3) to provide training, technical assistance, and data collection to improve the capacity of grantees and other entities to offer legal assistance to victims of domestic violence, stalking, and sexual assault.

(d) ELIGIBILITY—To be eligible for a grant under subsection (c), applicants shall certify in writing that—

(1) any person providing legal assistance through a program funded under subsection (c) has completed or will complete training in connection with domestic violence or sexual assault and related legal issues;

(2) any training program conducted in satisfaction of the requirement of paragraph (1) has been or will be developed with input from and in collaboration with a State, local, or tribal domestic violence or sexual assault program or coalition, as well as appropriate State and local law enforcement officials;

(3) any person or organization providing legal assistance through a program funded under subsection (c) has informed and will continue to inform State, local, or tribal domestic violence or sexual assault programs and coalitions, as well as appropriate State and local law enforcement officials of their work; and

(4) the grantee's organizational policies do not require mediation or counseling involving offenders and victims physically together, in cases where sexual assault, domestic violence, or child sexual abuse is an issue.

(e) EVALUATION—The Attorney General may evaluate the grants funded under this section through contracts or other arrangements with entities expert on domestic violence, stalking, and sexual assault, and on evaluation research.

(f) AUTHORIZATION OF APPROPRIATIONS—

(1) IN GENERAL—There is authorized to be appropriated to carry out this section $40,000,000 for each of fiscal years 2001 through 2005.

(2) ALLOCATION OF FUNDS—

(A) TRIBAL PROGRAMS—Of the amount made available under this subsection in each fiscal year, not less than 5 percent shall be used for grants for programs that assist victims of domestic violence, stalking, and sexual assault on lands within the jurisdiction of an Indian tribe.

(B) VICTIMS OF SEXUAL ASSAULT—Of the amount made available under this subsection in each fiscal year, not less than 25 percent shall be used for direct services, training, and technical assistance to support projects focused solely or primarily on providing legal assistance to victims of sexual assault.

(3) NONSUPPLANTATION—Amounts made available under this section shall be used to supplement and not supplant other Federal, State, and local funds expended to further the purpose of this section.

SEC. 1202. SHELTER SERVICES FOR BATTERED WOMEN AND CHILDREN.

(a) REAUTHORIZATION—Section 310(a) of the Family Violence Prevention and Services Act (42 U.S.C. 10409(a)) is amended to read as follows:

'(a) IN GENERAL—There are authorized to be appropriated to carry out this title $175,000,000 for each of fiscal years 2001 through 2005.'.
(b) STATE MINIMUM; REALLOTMENT—Section 304 of the Family Violence Prevention and Services Act (42 U.S.C. 10403) is amended—
    (1) in subsection (a), by striking 'for grants to States for any fiscal year' and all that follows and inserting the following: 'and available for grants to States under this subsection for any fiscal year—
    '(1) Guam, American Samoa, the United States Virgin Islands, and the Commonwealth of the Northern Mariana Islands shall each be allotted not less than 1/8 of 1 percent of the amounts available for grants under section 303(a) for the fiscal year for which the allotment is made; and
    '(2) each State shall be allotted for payment in a grant authorized under section 303(a), $600,000, with the remaining funds to be allotted to each State in an amount that bears the same ratio to such remaining funds as the population of such State bears to the population of all States.';
    (2) in subsection (c), in the first sentence, by inserting 'and available' before 'for grants'; and
    (3) by adding at the end the following:
'(e) In subsection (a)(2), the term 'State' does not include any jurisdiction specified in subsection (a)(1).'.

SEC. 1203. TRANSITIONAL HOUSING ASSISTANCE FOR VICTIMS OF DOMESTIC VIOLENCE.

Title III of the Family Violence Prevention and Services Act (42 U.S.C. 10401 et seq.) is amended by adding at the end the following:

'SEC. 319. TRANSITIONAL HOUSING ASSISTANCE.

'(a) IN GENERAL—The Secretary shall award grants under this section to carry out programs to provide assistance to individuals, and their dependents—
    '(1) who are homeless or in need of transitional housing or other housing assistance, as a result of fleeing a situation of domestic violence; and
    '(2) for whom emergency shelter services are unavailable or insufficient.
'(b) ASSISTANCE DESCRIBED—Assistance provided under this section may include—
    '(1) short-term housing assistance, including rental or utilities payments assistance and assistance with related expenses, such as payment of security deposits and other costs incidental to relocation to transitional housing, in cases in which assistance described in this paragraph is necessary to prevent homelessness because an individual or dependent is fleeing a situation of domestic violence; and
    '(2) support services designed to enable an individual or dependent who is fleeing a situation of domestic violence to locate and secure permanent housing, and to integrate the individual or dependent into a community,

such as transportation, counseling, child care services, case management, employment counseling, and other assistance.

'(c) TERM OF ASSISTANCE—

'(1) IN GENERAL—Subject to paragraph (2), an individual or dependent assisted under this section may not receive assistance under this section for a total of more than 12 months.

'(2) WAIVER—The recipient of a grant under this section may waive the restrictions of paragraph (1) for up to an additional 6-month period with respect to any individual (and dependents of the individual) who has made a good-faith effort to acquire permanent housing and has been unable to acquire the housing.

'(d) REPORTS—

'(1) REPORT TO SECRETARY—

'(A) IN GENERAL—An entity that receives a grant under this section shall annually prepare and submit to the Secretary a report describing the number of individuals and dependents assisted, and the types of housing assistance and support services provided, under this section.

'(B) CONTENTS—Each report shall include information on—

'(i) the purpose and amount of housing assistance provided to each individual or dependent assisted under this section;

'(ii) the number of months each individual or dependent received the assistance;

'(iii) the number of individuals and dependents who were eligible to receive the assistance, and to whom the entity could not provide the assistance solely due to a lack of available housing; and

'(iv) the type of support services provided to each individual or dependent assisted under this section.

'(2) REPORT TO CONGRESS—The Secretary shall annually prepare and submit to the Committee on the Judiciary of the House of Representatives and the Committee on the Judiciary of the Senate a report that contains a compilation of the information contained in reports submitted under paragraph (1).

'(e) EVALUATION, MONITORING, AND ADMINISTRATION—Of the amount appropriated under subsection (f) for each fiscal year, not more than 1 percent shall be used by the Secretary for evaluation, monitoring, and administrative costs under this section.

'(f) AUTHORIZATION OF APPROPRIATIONS—There are authorized to be appropriated to carry out this section $25,000,000 for fiscal year 2001.'.

SEC. 1204. NATIONAL DOMESTIC VIOLENCE HOTLINE.

Section 316(f) of the Family Violence Prevention and Services Act (42 U.S.C. 10416 (f)) is amended by striking paragraph (1) and inserting the following:

'(1) IN GENERAL—There are authorized to be appropriated to carry out this section $2,000,000 for each of fiscal years 2001 through 2005.'.

SEC. 1205. FEDERAL VICTIMS COUNSELORS.

Section 40114 of the Violent Crime Control and Law Enforcement Act of 1994 (Public Law 103-322; 108 Stat. 1910) is amended by striking '(such as District of Columbia)—' and all that follows and inserting '(such as District of Columbia), $1,000,000 for each of fiscal years 2001 through 2005.'.

SEC. 1206. STUDY OF STATE LAWS REGARDING INSURANCE DISCRIMINATION AGAINST VICTIMS OF VIOLENCE AGAINST WOMEN.

(a) IN GENERAL—The Attorney General shall conduct a national study to identify State laws that address discrimination against victims of domestic violence and sexual assault related to issuance or administration of insurance policies.

(b) REPORT—Not later than 1 year after the date of the enactment of this Act, the Attorney General shall submit to Congress a report on the findings and recommendations of the study required by subsection (a).

SEC. 1207. STUDY OF WORKPLACE EFFECTS FROM VIOLENCE AGAINST WOMEN.

The Attorney General shall—

(1) conduct a national survey of plans, programs, and practices developed to assist employers and employees on appropriate responses in the workplace related to victims of domestic violence, stalking, or sexual assault; and

(2) not later than 18 months after the date of the enactment of this Act, submit to Congress a report describing the results of that survey, which report shall include the recommendations of the Attorney General to assist employers and employees affected in the workplace by incidents of domestic violence, stalking, and sexual assault.

SEC. 1208. STUDY OF UNEMPLOYMENT COMPENSATION FOR VICTIMS OF VIOLENCE AGAINST WOMEN.

The Secretary of Labor, in consultation with the Attorney General, shall—

(1) conduct a national study to identify State laws that address the separation from employment of an employee due to circumstances directly resulting from the experience of domestic violence by the employee and circumstances governing that receipt (or nonreceipt) by the employee of unemployment compensation based on such separation; and

(2) not later than 1 year after the date of the enactment of this Act, submit to Congress a report describing the results of that study, together with any recommendations based on that study.

SEC. 1209. ENHANCING PROTECTIONS FOR OLDER AND DISABLED WOMEN FROM DOMESTIC VIOLENCE AND SEXUAL ASSAULT.

(a) ELDER ABUSE, NEGLECT, AND EXPLOITATION—The Violence Against Women Act of 1994 (108 Stat. 1902 et seq.) is amended by adding at the end the following:

'Subtitle H—Elder Abuse, Neglect, and Exploitation, Including Domestic Violence and Sexual Assault Against Older or Disabled Individuals

'SEC. 40801. DEFINITIONS.

'In this subtitle:
'(1) IN GENERAL—The terms 'elder abuse, neglect, and exploitation', and 'older individual' have the meanings given the terms in section 102 of the Older Americans Act of 1965 (42 U.S.C. 3002).
'(2) DOMESTIC VIOLENCE—The term 'domestic violence' has the meaning given such term by section 2003 of title I of the Omnibus Crime Control and Safe Streets Act of 1968 (42 U.S.C. 3796gg-2).
'(3) SEXUAL ASSAULT—The term 'sexual assault' has the meaning given the term in section 2003 of title I of the Omnibus Crime Control and Safe Streets Act of 1968 (42 U.S.C. 3796gg-2).

'SEC. 40802. TRAINING PROGRAMS FOR LAW ENFORCEMENT OFFICERS.

'The Attorney General may make grants for training programs to assist law enforcement officers, prosecutors, and relevant officers of Federal, State, tribal, and local courts in recognizing, addressing, investigating, and prosecuting instances of elder abuse, neglect, and exploitation and violence against individuals with disabilities, including domestic violence and sexual assault, against older or disabled individuals.

'SEC. 40803. AUTHORIZATION OF APPROPRIATIONS.

'There are authorized to be appropriated to carry out this subtitle $5,000,000 for each of fiscal years 2001 through 2005.'.
(b) PROTECTIONS FOR OLDER AND DISABLED INDIVIDUALS FROM DOMESTIC VIOLENCE AND SEXUAL ASSAULT IN PRO-ARREST GRANTS— Section 2101(b) of part U of title I of the Omnibus Crime Control and Safe Streets Act of 1968 (42 U.S.C. 3796hh et seq.) is amended by adding at the end the following:
'(8) To develop or strengthen policies and training for police, prosecutors, and the judiciary in recognizing, investigating, and prosecuting instances of domestic violence and sexual assault against older individuals (as defined in section 102 of the Older Americans Act of 1965 (42 U.S.C. 3002)) and

individuals with disabilities (as defined in section 3(2) of the Americans with Disabilities Act of 1990 (42 U.S.C. 12102(2))).'.

(c) PROTECTIONS FOR OLDER AND DISABLED INDIVIDUALS FROM DOMESTIC VIOLENCE AND SEXUAL ASSAULT IN STOP GRANTS—Section 2001(b) of title I of the Omnibus Crime Control and Safe Streets Act of 1968 (42 U.S.C. 3796gg(b)) (as amended by section 1103(b) of this division) is amended by adding at the end the following:

'(10) developing, enlarging, or strengthening programs to assist law enforcement, prosecutors, courts, and others to address the needs and circumstances of older and disabled women who are victims of domestic violence or sexual assault, including recognizing, investigating, and prosecuting instances of such violence or assault and targeting outreach and support, counseling, and other victim services to such older and disabled individuals; and'.

TITLE III—LIMITING THE EFFECTS OF VIOLENCE ON CHILDREN

SEC. 1301. SAFE HAVENS FOR CHILDREN PILOT PROGRAM.

(a) IN GENERAL—The Attorney General may award grants to States, units of local government, and Indian tribal governments that propose to enter into or expand the scope of existing contracts and cooperative agreements with public or private nonprofit entities to provide supervised visitation and safe visitation exchange of children by and between parents in situations involving domestic violence, child abuse, sexual assault, or stalking.

(b) CONSIDERATIONS—In awarding grants under subsection (a), the Attorney General shall take into account—

(1) the number of families to be served by the proposed visitation programs and services;

(2) the extent to which the proposed supervised visitation programs and services serve underserved populations (as defined in section 2003 of title I of the Omnibus Crime Control and Safe Streets Act of 1968 (42 U.S.C. 3796gg-2));

(3) with respect to an applicant for a contract or cooperative agreement, the extent to which the applicant demonstrates cooperation and collaboration with nonprofit, nongovernmental entities in the local community served, including the State or tribal domestic violence coalition, State or tribal sexual assault coalition, local shelters, and programs for domestic violence and sexual assault victims; and

(4) the extent to which the applicant demonstrates coordination and collaboration with State and local court systems, including mechanisms for communication and referral.

(c) APPLICANT REQUIREMENTS—The Attorney General shall award grants for contracts and cooperative agreements to applicants that—

(1) demonstrate expertise in the area of family violence, including the areas of domestic violence or sexual assault, as appropriate;

(2) ensure that any fees charged to individuals for use of programs and services are based on the income of those individuals, unless otherwise provided by court order;

(3) demonstrate that adequate security measures, including adequate facilities, procedures, and personnel capable of preventing violence, are in place for the operation of supervised visitation programs and services or safe visitation exchange; and

(4) prescribe standards by which the supervised visitation or safe visitation exchange will occur.

(d) REPORTING—

(1) IN GENERAL—Not later than 1 year after the last day of the first fiscal year commencing on or after the date of the enactment of this Act, and not later than 180 days after the last day of each fiscal year thereafter, the Attorney General shall submit to Congress a report that includes information concerning—

> (A) the number of—
>> (i) individuals served and the number of individuals turned away from visitation programs and services and safe visitation exchange (categorized by State);
>> (ii) the number of individuals from underserved populations served and turned away from services; and
>> (iii) the type of problems that underlie the need for supervised visitation or safe visitation exchange, such as domestic violence, child abuse, sexual assault, other physical abuse, or a combination of such factors;
>
> (B) the numbers of supervised visitations or safe visitation exchanges ordered under this section during custody determinations under a separation or divorce decree or protection order, through child protection services or other social services agencies, or by any other order of a civil, criminal, juvenile, or family court;
>
> (C) the process by which children or abused partners are protected during visitations, temporary custody transfers, and other activities for which supervised visitation is established under this section;
>
> (D) safety and security problems occurring during the reporting period during supervised visitation under this section, including the number of parental abduction cases; and
>
> (E) the number of parental abduction cases in a judicial district using supervised visitation programs and services under this section, both as identified in criminal prosecution and custody violations.

(2) GUIDELINES—The Attorney General shall establish guidelines for the collection and reporting of data under this subsection.

(e) AUTHORIZATION OF APPROPRIATIONS—There is authorized to be appropriated to carry out this section $15,000,000 for each of fiscal years 2001 and 2002.

(f) ALLOTMENT FOR INDIAN TRIBES—Not less than 5 percent of the total amount made available for each fiscal year to carry out this section shall be available for grants to Indian tribal governments.

SEC. 1302. REAUTHORIZATION OF VICTIMS OF CHILD ABUSE PROGRAMS.

(a) COURT-APPOINTED SPECIAL ADVOCATE PROGRAM—Section 218 of the Victims of Child Abuse Act of 1990 (42 U.S.C. 13014) is amended by striking subsection (a) and inserting the following:

'(a) AUTHORIZATION—There is authorized to be appropriated to carry out this subtitle $12,000,000 for each of fiscal years 2001 through 2005.'.

(b) CHILD ABUSE TRAINING PROGRAMS FOR JUDICIAL PERSONNEL AND PRACTITIONERS—Section 224 of the Victims of Child Abuse Act of 1990 (42 U.S.C. 13024) is amended by striking subsection (a) and inserting the following:

'(a) AUTHORIZATION—There is authorized to be appropriated to carry out this subtitle $2,300,000 for each of fiscal years 2001 through 2005.'.

(c) GRANTS FOR TELEVISED TESTIMONY—Section 1001(a) of title I of the Omnibus Crime Control and Safe Streets Act of 1968 (42 U.S.C. 3793(a)) is amended by striking paragraph (7) and inserting the following:

'(7) There is authorized to be appropriated to carry out part N $1,000,000 for each of fiscal years 2001 through 2005.'.

(d) DISSEMINATION OF INFORMATION—The Attorney General shall—
  (1) annually compile and disseminate information (including through electronic publication) about the use of amounts expended and the projects funded under section 218(a) of the Victims of Child Abuse Act of 1990 (42 U.S.C. 13014(a)), section 224(a) of the Victims of Child Abuse Act of 1990 (42 U.S.C. 13024(a)), and section 1007(a)(7) of title I of the Omnibus Crime Control and Safe Streets Act of 1968 (42 U.S.C. 3793(a)(7)), including any evaluations of the projects and information to enable replication and adoption of the strategies identified in the projects; and
  (2) focus dissemination of the information described in paragraph (1) toward community-based programs, including domestic violence and sexual assault programs.

SEC. 1303. REPORT ON EFFECTS OF PARENTAL KIDNAPPING LAWS IN DOMESTIC VIOLENCE CASES.

(a) IN GENERAL—The Attorney General shall—
  (1) conduct a study of Federal and State laws relating to child custody, including custody provisions in protection orders, the Uniform Child

Custody Jurisdiction and Enforcement Act adopted by the National Conference of Commissioners on Uniform State Laws in July 1997, the Parental Kidnaping Prevention Act of 1980 and the amendments made by that Act, and the effect of those laws on child custody cases in which domestic violence is a factor; and

(2) submit to Congress a report describing the results of that study, including the effects of implementing or applying model State laws, and the recommendations of the Attorney General to reduce the incidence or pattern of violence against women or of sexual assault of the child.

(b) SUFFICIENCY OF DEFENSES—In carrying out subsection (a) with respect to the Parental Kidnaping Prevention Act of 1980 and the amendments made by that Act, the Attorney General shall examine the sufficiency of defenses to parental abduction charges available in cases involving domestic violence, and the burdens and risks encountered by victims of domestic violence arising from jurisdictional requirements of that Act and the amendments made by that Act.

(c) AUTHORIZATION OF APPROPRIATIONS—There is authorized to be appropriated to carry out this section $200,000 for fiscal year 2001.

(d) CONDITION FOR CUSTODY DETERMINATION—Section 1738A(c)(2)(C)(ii) of title 28, United States Code, is amended by striking 'he' and inserting 'the child, a sibling, or parent of the child'.

TITLE IV—STRENGTHENING EDUCATION AND TRAINING TO COMBAT VIOLENCE AGAINST WOMEN

SEC. 1401. RAPE PREVENTION AND EDUCATION.

(a) IN GENERAL—Part J of title III of the Public Health Service Act (42 U.S.C. 280b et seq.) is amended by inserting after section 393A the following:

'SEC. 393B. USE OF ALLOTMENTS FOR RAPE PREVENTION EDUCATION.

'(a) PERMITTED USE—The Secretary, acting through the National Center for Injury Prevention and Control at the Centers for Disease Control and Prevention, shall award targeted grants to States to be used for rape prevention and education programs conducted by rape crisis centers, State sexual assault coalitions, and other public and private nonprofit entities for—

'(1) educational seminars;
'(2) the operation of hotlines;
'(3) training programs for professionals;
'(4) the preparation of informational material;
'(5) education and training programs for students and campus personnel designed to reduce the incidence of sexual assault at colleges and universities;
'(6) education to increase awareness about drugs used to facilitate rapes or sexual assaults; and

'(7) other efforts to increase awareness of the facts about, or to help prevent, sexual assault, including efforts to increase awareness in underserved communities and awareness among individuals with disabilities (as defined in section 3 of the Americans with Disabilities Act of 1990 (42 U.S.C. 12102)).

'(b) COLLECTION AND DISSEMINATION OF INFORMATION ON SEXUAL ASSAULT—The Secretary shall, through the National Resource Center on Sexual Assault established under the National Center for Injury Prevention and Control at the Centers for Disease Control and Prevention, provide resource information, policy, training, and technical assistance to Federal, State, local, and Indian tribal agencies, as well as to State sexual assault coalitions and local sexual assault programs and to other professionals and interested parties on issues relating to sexual assault, including maintenance of a central resource library in order to collect, prepare, analyze, and disseminate information and statistics and analyses thereof relating to the incidence and prevention of sexual assault.

'(c) AUTHORIZATION OF APPROPRIATIONS—

'(1) IN GENERAL—There is authorized to be appropriated to carry out this section $80,000,000 for each of fiscal years 2001 through 2005.

'(2) NATIONAL RESOURCE CENTER ALLOTMENT—Of the total amount made available under this subsection in each fiscal year, not more than the greater of $1,000,000 or 2 percent of such amount shall be available for allotment under subsection (b).

'(d) LIMITATIONS—

'(1) SUPPLEMENT NOT SUPPLANT—Amounts provided to States under this section shall be used to supplement and not supplant other Federal, State, and local public funds expended to provide services of the type described in subsection (a).

'(2) STUDIES—A State may not use more than 2 percent of the amount received by the State under this section for each fiscal year for surveillance studies or prevalence studies.

'(3) ADMINISTRATION—A State may not use more than 5 percent of the amount received by the State under this section for each fiscal year for administrative expenses.'.

(b) REPEAL—Section 40151 of the Violence Against Women Act of 1994 (108 Stat. 1920), and the amendment made by such section, is repealed.

SEC. 1402. EDUCATION AND TRAINING TO END VIOLENCE AGAINST AND ABUSE OF WOMEN WITH DISABILITIES.

(a) IN GENERAL—The Attorney General, in consultation with the Secretary of Health and Human Services, may award grants to States, units of local government, Indian tribal governments, and nongovernmental private entities to provide education and technical assistance for the purpose of providing training, consultation, and information on domestic violence, stalking,

and sexual assault against women who are individuals with disabilities (as defined in section 3 of the Americans with Disabilities Act of 1990 (42 U.S.C. 12102)).
(b) PRIORITIES—In awarding grants under this section, the Attorney General shall give priority to applications designed to provide education and technical assistance on—
> (1) the nature, definition, and characteristics of domestic violence, stalking, and sexual assault experienced by women who are individuals with disabilities;
> (2) outreach activities to ensure that women who are individuals with disabilities who are victims of domestic violence, stalking, and sexual assault receive appropriate assistance;
> (3) the requirements of shelters and victim services organizations under Federal anti-discrimination laws, including the Americans with Disabilities Act of 1990 and section 504 of the Rehabilitation Act of 1973; and
> (4) cost-effective ways that shelters and victim services may accommodate the needs of individuals with disabilities in accordance with the Americans with Disabilities Act of 1990.

(c) USES OF GRANTS—Each recipient of a grant under this section shall provide information and training to organizations and programs that provide services to individuals with disabilities, including independent living centers, disability-related service organizations, and domestic violence programs providing shelter or related assistance.
(d) AUTHORIZATION OF APPROPRIATIONS—There is authorized to be appropriated to carry out this section $7,500,000 for each of fiscal years 2001 through 2005.

SEC. 1403. COMMUNITY INITIATIVES.

Section 318 of the Family Violence Prevention and Services Act (42 U.S.C. 10418) is amended by striking subsection (h) and inserting the following:
> '(h) AUTHORIZATION OF APPROPRIATIONS—There are authorized to be appropriated to carry out this section $6,000,000 for each of fiscal years 2001 through 2005.'.

SEC. 1404. DEVELOPMENT OF RESEARCH AGENDA IDENTIFIED BY THE VIOLENCE AGAINST WOMEN ACT OF 1994.

(a) IN GENERAL—The Attorney General shall—
> (1) direct the National Institute of Justice, in consultation and coordination with the Bureau of Justice Statistics and the National Academy of Sciences, through its National Research Council, to develop a research agenda based on the recommendations contained in the report entitled 'Understanding Violence Against Women' of the National Academy of Sciences; and

(2) not later than 1 year after the date of the enactment of this Act, in consultation with the Secretary of the Department of Health and Human Services, submit to Congress a report which shall include—
    (A) a description of the research agenda developed under paragraph (1) and a plan to implement that agenda; and
    (B) recommendations for priorities in carrying out that agenda to most effectively advance knowledge about and means by which to prevent or reduce violence against women.

(b) AUTHORIZATION OF APPROPRIATIONS—There are authorized to be appropriated such sums as may be necessary to carry out this section.

SEC. 1405. STANDARDS, PRACTICE, AND TRAINING FOR SEXUAL ASSAULT FORENSIC EXAMINATIONS.

(a) IN GENERAL—The Attorney General shall—
(1) evaluate existing standards of training and practice for licensed health care professionals performing sexual assault forensic examinations and develop a national recommended standard for training;
(2) recommend sexual assault forensic examination training for all health care students to improve the recognition of injuries suggestive of rape and sexual assault and baseline knowledge of appropriate referrals in victim treatment and evidence collection; and
(3) review existing national, State, tribal, and local protocols on sexual assault forensic examinations, and based on this review, develop a recommended national protocol and establish a mechanism for its nationwide dissemination.

(b) CONSULTATION—The Attorney General shall consult with national, State, tribal, and local experts in the area of rape and sexual assault, including rape crisis centers, State and tribal sexual assault and domestic violence coalitions and programs, and programs for criminal justice, forensic nursing, forensic science, emergency room medicine, law, social services, and sex crimes in underserved communities (as defined in section 2003(7) of title I of the Omnibus Crime Control and Safe Streets Act of 1968 (42 U.S.C. 3796gg-2(7)), as amended by this division).

(c) REPORT—The Attorney General shall ensure that not later than 1 year after the date of the enactment of this Act, a report of the actions taken pursuant to subsection (a) is submitted to Congress.

(d) AUTHORIZATION OF APPROPRIATIONS—There is authorized to be appropriated to carry out this section $200,000 for fiscal year 2001.

SEC. 1406. EDUCATION AND TRAINING FOR JUDGES AND COURT PERSONNEL.

(a) GRANTS FOR EDUCATION AND TRAINING FOR JUDGES AND COURT PERSONNEL IN STATE COURTS—

(1) SECTION 40412—Section 40412 of the Equal Justice for Women in the Courts Act of 1994 (42 U.S.C. 13992) is amended—
    (A) by striking 'and' at the end of paragraph (18);
    (B) by striking the period at the end of paragraph (19) and inserting a semicolon; and
    (C) by inserting after paragraph (19) the following:
'(20) the issues raised by domestic violence in determining custody and visitation, including how to protect the safety of the child and of a parent who is not a predominant aggressor of domestic violence, the legitimate reasons parents may report domestic violence, the ways domestic violence may relate to an abuser's desire to seek custody, and evaluating expert testimony in custody and visitation determinations involving domestic violence;

'(21) the issues raised by child sexual assault in determining custody and visitation, including how to protect the safety of the child, the legitimate reasons parents may report child sexual assault, and evaluating expert testimony in custody and visitation determinations involving child sexual assault, including the current scientifically-accepted and empirically valid research on child sexual assault;

'(22) the extent to which addressing domestic violence and victim safety contributes to the efficient administration of justice;'.

(2) SECTION 40414—Section 40414(a) of the Equal Justice for Women in the Courts Act of 1994 (42 U.S.C. 13994(a)) is amended by inserting 'and $1,500,000 for each of the fiscal years 2001 through 2005' after '1996'.

(b) GRANTS FOR EDUCATION AND TRAINING FOR JUDGES AND COURT PERSONNEL IN FEDERAL COURTS—
    (1) SECTION 40421—Section 40421(d) of the Equal Justice for Women in the Courts Act of 1994 (42 U.S.C. 14001(d)) is amended to read as follows:

'(d) CONTINUING EDUCATION AND TRAINING PROGRAMS—The Federal Judicial Center, in carrying out section 620(b)(3) of title 28, United States Code, shall include in the educational programs it prepares, including the training programs for newly appointed judges, information on the aspects of the topics listed in section 40412 that pertain to issues within the jurisdiction of the Federal courts, and shall prepare materials necessary to implement this subsection.'.

    (2) SECTION 40422—Section 40422(2) of the Equal Justice for Women in the Courts Act of 1994 (42 U.S.C. 14002(2)) is amended by inserting 'and $500,000 for each of the fiscal years 2001 through 2005' after '1996'.

(c) TECHNICAL AMENDMENTS TO THE EQUAL JUSTICE FOR WOMEN IN THE COURTS ACT OF 1994—
    (1) ENSURING COLLABORATION WITH DOMESTIC VIOLENCE AND SEXUAL ASSAULT PROGRAMS—Section 40413 of the Equal Justice for Women in the Courts Act of 1994 (42 U.S.C. 13993) is

amended by adding ', including national, State, tribal, and local domestic violence and sexual assault programs and coalitions' after 'victim advocates'.

(2) PARTICIPATION OF TRIBAL COURTS IN STATE TRAINING AND EDUCATION PROGRAMS—Section 40411 of the Equal Justice for Women in the Courts Act of 1994 (42 U.S.C. 13991) is amended by adding at the end the following: 'Nothing shall preclude the attendance of tribal judges and court personnel at programs funded under this section for States to train judges and court personnel on the laws of the States.'.

(3) USE OF FUNDS FOR DISSEMINATION OF MODEL PROGRAMS—Section 40414 of the Equal Justice for Women in the Courts Act of 1994 (42 U.S.C. 13994) is amended by adding at the end the following:

'(c) STATE JUSTICE INSTITUTE—The State Justice Institute may use up to 5 percent of the funds appropriated under this section for annually compiling and broadly disseminating (including through electronic publication) information about the use of funds and about the projects funded under this section, including any evaluations of the projects and information to enable the replication and adoption of the projects.'.

(d) DATING VIOLENCE—

(1) SECTION 40411—Section 40411 of the Equal Justice for Women in Courts Act of 1994 (42 U.S.C 13991) is amended by inserting 'dating violence,' after 'domestic violence,'.

(2) SECTION 40412—Section 40412 of such Act (42 U.S.C 13992) is amended—

(A) in paragraph (10), by inserting 'and dating violence (as defined in section 2003 of title I of the Omnibus Crime Control and Safe Streets Act of 1968 (42 U.S.C. 3996gg-2))' before the semicolon;

(B) in paragraph (11), by inserting 'and dating violence' after 'domestic violence';

(C) in paragraph (13), by inserting 'and dating violence' after 'domestic violence' in both places that it appears;

(D) in paragraph (17), by inserting 'or dating violence' after 'domestic violence' in both places that it appears; and

(E) in paragraph (18), by inserting 'and dating violence' after 'domestic violence'.

SEC. 1407. DOMESTIC VIOLENCE TASK FORCE

The Violence Against Women Act of 1994 (108 Stat. 1902 et seq.) (as amended by section 1209(a) of this division) is amended by adding at the end the following:

'**Subtitle I—Domestic Violence Task Force**

'SEC. 40901. TASK FORCE.

'(a) ESTABLISH—The Attorney General, in consultation with national nonprofit, nongovernmental organizations whose primary expertise is in domestic violence, shall establish a task force to coordinate research on domestic violence and to report to Congress on any overlapping or duplication of efforts on domestic violence issues. The task force shall be comprised of representatives from all Federal agencies that fund such research.

'(b) USES OF FUNDS—Funds appropriated under this section shall be used to—
'(1) develop a coordinated strategy to strengthen research focused on domestic violence education, prevention, and intervention strategies;
'(2) track and report all Federal research and expenditures on domestic violence; and
'(3) identify gaps and duplication of efforts in domestic violence research and governmental expenditures on domestic violence issues.

'(c) REPORT—The Task Force shall report to Congress annually on its work under subsection (b).

'(d) DEFINITION—For purposes of this section, the term 'domestic violence' has the meaning given such term by section 2003 of title I of the Omnibus Crime Control and Safe Streets Act of 1968 (42 U.S.C. 3796gg-2(1)).

'(e) AUTHORIZATION OF APPROPRIATIONS—There is authorized to be appropriated to carry out this section $500,000 for each of fiscal years 2001 through 2004.'.

TITLE V—BATTERED IMMIGRANT WOMEN

SEC. 1501. SHORT TITLE.

This title may be cited as the 'Battered Immigrant Women Protection Act of 2000'.

SEC. 1502. FINDINGS AND PURPOSES.

(a) FINDINGS—Congress finds that—
(1) the goal of the immigration protections for battered immigrants included in the Violence Against Women Act of 1994 was to remove immigration laws as a barrier that kept battered immigrant women and children locked in abusive relationships;
(2) providing battered immigrant women and children who were experiencing domestic violence at home with protection against deportation allows them to obtain protection orders against their abusers and frees them to cooperate with law enforcement and prosecutors in criminal cases brought against their abusers and the abusers of their children without fearing that the abuser will retaliate by withdrawing

or threatening withdrawal of access to an immigration benefit under the abuser's control; and

(3) there are several groups of battered immigrant women and children who do not have access to the immigration protections of the Violence Against Women Act of 1994 which means that their abusers are virtually immune from prosecution because their victims can be deported as a result of action by their abusers and the Immigration and Naturalization Service cannot offer them protection no matter how compelling their case under existing law.

(b) PURPOSES—The purposes of this title are—

(1) to remove barriers to criminal prosecutions of persons who commit acts of battery or extreme cruelty against immigrant women and children; and

(2) to offer protection against domestic violence occurring in family and intimate relationships that are covered in State and tribal protection orders, domestic violence, and family law statutes.

SEC. 1503. IMPROVED ACCESS TO IMMIGRATION PROTECTIONS OF THE VIOLENCE AGAINST WOMEN ACT OF 1994 FOR BATTERED IMMIGRANT WOMEN.

(a) INTENDED SPOUSE DEFINED—Section 101(a) of the Immigration and Nationality Act (8 U.S.C. 1101(a)) is amended by adding at the end the following:

'(50) The term 'intended spouse' means any alien who meets the criteria set forth in section 204(a)(1)(A)(iii)(II)(aa)(BB), 204(a)(1)(B)(ii)(II)(aa)(BB), or 240A(b)(2)(A)(i)(III).'.

(b) IMMEDIATE RELATIVE STATUS FOR SELF-PETITIONERS MARRIED TO U.S. CITIZENS—

(1) SELF-PETITIONING SPOUSES—

(A) BATTERY OR CRUELTY TO ALIEN OR ALIEN'S CHILD—
Section 204(a)(1)(A)(iii) of the Immigration and Nationality Act (8 U.S.C. 1154(a)(1)(A)(iii)) is amended to read as follows:

'(iii)(I) An alien who is described in subclause (II) may file a petition with the Attorney General under this clause for classification of the alien (and any child of the alien) if the alien demonstrates to the Attorney General that—

'(aa) the marriage or the intent to marry the United States citizen was entered into in good faith by the alien; and

'(bb) during the marriage or relationship intended by the alien to be legally a marriage, the alien or a child of the alien has been battered or has been the subject of extreme cruelty perpetrated by the alien's spouse or intended spouse.

'(II) For purposes of subclause (I), an alien described in this subclause is an alien—

'(aa)(AA) who is the spouse of a citizen of the United States;

'(BB) who believed that he or she had married a citizen of the United States and with whom a marriage ceremony was actually performed and who otherwise meets any applicable requirements under this Act to establish the existence of and bona fides of a marriage, but whose marriage is not legitimate solely because of the bigamy of such citizen of the United States; or

'(CC) who was a bona fide spouse of a United States citizen within the past 2 years and—

>'(aaa) whose spouse died within the past 2 years;
>
>'(bbb) whose spouse lost or renounced citizenship status within the past 2 years related to an incident of domestic violence; or
>
>'(ccc) who demonstrates a connection between the legal termination of the marriage within the past 2 years and battering or extreme cruelty by the United States citizen spouse;

'(bb) who is a person of good moral character;

'(cc) who is eligible to be classified as an immediate relative under section 201(b)(2)(A)(i) or who would have been so classified but for the bigamy of the citizen of the United States that the alien intended to marry; and

'(dd) who has resided with the alien's spouse or intended spouse.'.

(2) SELF-PETITIONING CHILDREN—Section 204(a)(1)(A)(iv) of the Immigration and Nationality Act (8 U.S.C. 1154(a)(1)(A)(iv)) is amended to read as follows:

'(iv) An alien who is the child of a citizen of the United States, or who was a child of a United States citizen parent who within the past 2 years lost or renounced citizenship status related to an incident of domestic violence, and who is a person of good moral character, who is eligible to be classified as an immediate relative under section 201(b)(2)(A)(i), and who resides, or has resided in the past, with the citizen parent may file a petition with the Attorney General under this subparagraph for classification of the alien (and any child of the alien) under such section if the alien demonstrates to the Attorney General that the alien has been battered by or has been the subject of extreme cruelty perpetrated by the alien's citizen parent. For purposes of this clause, residence includes any period of visitation.'.

(3) FILING OF PETITIONS—Section 204(a)(1)(A) of the Immigration and Nationality Act (8 U.S.C. 1154(a)(1)(A)) is amended by adding at the end the following:

'(v) An alien who—

>'(I) is the spouse, intended spouse, or child living abroad of a citizen who—
>
>>'(aa) is an employee of the United States Government;
>>
>>'(bb) is a member of the uniformed services (as defined in section 101(a) of title 10, United States Code); or
>>
>>'(cc) has subjected the alien or the alien's child to battery or extreme cruelty in the United States; and
>
>'(II) is eligible to file a petition under clause (iii) or (iv),
>
>shall file such petition with the Attorney General under the procedures that apply to self-petitioners under clause (iii) or (iv), as applicable.'.

(c) SECOND PREFERENCE IMMIGRATION STATUS FOR SELF-PETITIONERS MARRIED TO LAWFUL PERMANENT RESIDENTS—

(1) SELF-PETITIONING SPOUSES—Section 204(a)(1)(B)(ii) of the Immigration and Nationality Act (8 U.S.C. 1154(a)(1)(B)(ii)) is amended to read as follows:

'(ii)(I) An alien who is described in subclause (II) may file a petition with the Attorney General under this clause for classification of the alien (and any child of the alien) if such a child has not been classified under clause (iii) of section 203(a)(2)(A) and if the alien demonstrates to the Attorney General that—

'(aa) the marriage or the intent to marry the lawful permanent resident was entered into in good faith by the alien; and

'(bb) during the marriage or relationship intended by the alien to be legally a marriage, the alien or a child of the alien has been battered or has been the subject of extreme cruelty perpetrated by the alien's spouse or intended spouse.

'(II) For purposes of subclause (I), an alien described in this paragraph is an alien—

'(aa)(AA) who is the spouse of a lawful permanent resident of the United States; or

'(BB) who believed that he or she had married a lawful permanent resident of the United States and with whom a marriage ceremony was actually performed and who otherwise meets any applicable requirements under this Act to establish the existence of and bona fides of a marriage, but whose marriage is not legitimate solely because of the bigamy of such lawful permanent resident of the United States; or

'(CC) who was a bona fide spouse of a lawful permanent resident within the past 2 years and—

'(aaa) whose spouse lost status within the past 2 years due to an incident of domestic violence; or

'(bbb) who demonstrates a connection between the legal termination of the marriage within the past 2 years and battering or extreme cruelty by the lawful permanent resident spouse;

'(bb) who is a person of good moral character;

'(cc) who is eligible to be classified as a spouse of an alien lawfully admitted for permanent residence under section 203(a)(2)(A) or who would have been so classified but for the bigamy of the lawful permanent resident of the United States that the alien intended to marry; and

'(dd) who has resided with the alien's spouse or intended spouse.'.

(2) SELF-PETITIONING CHILDREN—Section 204(a)(1)(B)(iii) of the Immigration and Nationality Act (8 U.S.C. 1154(a)(1)(B)(iii)) is amended to read as follows:

'(iii) An alien who is the child of an alien lawfully admitted for permanent residence, or who was the child of a lawful permanent resident who within the past 2 years lost lawful permanent resident status due to an incident of domestic violence, and who is a person of good moral character, who is eligible for classification under section 203(a)(2)(A), and who resides, or has resided in the past, with the alien's permanent resident alien parent may file a petition with the

Attorney General under this subparagraph for classification of the alien (and any child of the alien) under such section if the alien demonstrates to the Attorney General that the alien has been battered by or has been the subject of extreme cruelty perpetrated by the alien's permanent resident parent.'.

(3) FILING OF PETITIONS—Section 204(a)(1)(B) of the Immigration and Nationality Act (8 U.S.C. 1154(a)(1)(B)) is amended by adding at the end the following:

'(iv) An alien who—

'(I) is the spouse, intended spouse, or child living abroad of a lawful permanent resident who—

'(aa) is an employee of the United States Government;

'(bb) is a member of the uniformed services (as defined in section 101(a) of title 10, United States Code); or

'(cc) has subjected the alien or the alien's child to battery or extreme cruelty in the United States; and

'(II) is eligible to file a petition under clause (ii) or (iii), shall file such petition with the Attorney General under the procedures that apply to self-petitioners under clause (ii) or (iii), as applicable.'.

(d) GOOD MORAL CHARACTER DETERMINATIONS FOR SELF-PETITIONERS AND TREATMENT OF CHILD SELF-PETITIONERS AND PETITIONS INCLUDING DERIVATIVE CHILDREN ATTAINING 21 YEARS OF AGE—Section 204(a)(1) of the Immigration and Nationality Act (8 U.S.C. 1154(a)(1)) is amended—

(1) by redesignating subparagraphs (C) through (H) as subparagraphs (E) through (J), respectively;

(2) by inserting after subparagraph (B) the following:

'(C) Notwithstanding section 101(f), an act or conviction that is waivable with respect to the petitioner for purposes of a determination of the petitioner's admissibility under section 212(a) or deportability under section 237(a) shall not bar the Attorney General from finding the petitioner to be of good moral character under subparagraph (A)(iii), (A)(iv), (B)(ii), or (B)(iii) if the Attorney General finds that the act or conviction was connected to the alien's having been battered or subjected to extreme cruelty.

'(D)(i)(I) Any child who attains 21 years of age who has filed a petition under clause (iv) of section 204(a)(1)(A) that was filed or approved before the date on which the child attained 21 years of age shall be considered (if the child has not been admitted or approved for lawful permanent residence by the date the child attained 21 years of age) a petitioner for preference status under paragraph (1), (2), or (3) of section 203(a), whichever paragraph is applicable, with the same priority date assigned to the self-petition filed under clause (iv) of section 204(a)(1)(A). No new petition shall be required to be filed.

'(II) Any individual described in subclause (I) is eligible for deferred action and work authorization.

'(III) Any derivative child who attains 21 years of age who is included in a petition described in clause (ii) that was filed or approved before the date on which the child attained 21 years of age shall be considered (if the child has not been admitted or approved for lawful permanent residence by the date the child attained 21 years of age) a petitioner for preference status under paragraph (1), (2), or (3) of section 203(a), whichever paragraph is applicable, with the same priority date as that assigned to the petitioner in any petition described in clause (ii). No new petition shall be required to be filed.

'(IV) Any individual described in subclause (III) and any derivative child of a petition described in clause (ii) is eligible for deferred action and work authorization.

'(ii) The petition referred to in clause (i)(III) is a petition filed by an alien under subparagraph (A)(iii), (A)(iv), (B)(ii) or (B)(iii) in which the child is included as a derivative beneficiary.'; and

> (3) in subparagraph (J) (as so redesignated), by inserting 'or in making determinations under subparagraphs (C) and (D),' after 'subparagraph (B),'.

(e) ACCESS TO NATURALIZATION FOR DIVORCED VICTIMS OF ABUSE—Section 319(a) of the Immigration and Nationality Act (8 U.S.C. 1430(a)) is amended—

> (1) by inserting ', or any person who obtained status as a lawful permanent resident by reason of his or her status as a spouse or child of a United States citizen who battered him or her or subjected him or her to extreme cruelty,' after 'United States' the first place such term appears; and
> (2) by inserting '(except in the case of a person who has been battered or subjected to extreme cruelty by a United States citizen spouse or parent)' after 'has been living in marital union with the citizen spouse'.

SEC. 1504. IMPROVED ACCESS TO CANCELLATION OF REMOVAL AND SUSPENSION OF DEPORTATION UNDER THE VIOLENCE AGAINST WOMEN ACT OF 1994.

(a) CANCELLATION OF REMOVAL AND ADJUSTMENT OF STATUS FOR CERTAIN NONPERMANENT RESIDENTS—Section 240A(b)(2) of the Immigration and Nationality Act (8 U.S.C. 1229b(b)(2)) is amended to read as follows:

> '(2) SPECIAL RULE FOR BATTERED SPOUSE OR CHILD—
>> '(A) AUTHORITY—The Attorney General may cancel removal of, and adjust to the status of an alien lawfully admitted for permanent residence, an alien who is inadmissible or deportable from the United States if the alien demonstrates that—
>>> '(i)(I) the alien has been battered or subjected to extreme cruelty by a spouse or parent who is or was a United States citizen (or is the parent of a child of a United States citizen and the child has been battered or subjected to extreme cruelty by such citizen parent);
>>> '(II) the alien has been battered or subjected to extreme cruelty by a spouse or parent who is or was a lawful permanent resident (or is

the parent of a child of an alien who is or was a lawful permanent resident and the child has been battered or subjected to extreme cruelty by such permanent resident parent); or

'(III) the alien has been battered or subjected to extreme cruelty by a United States citizen or lawful permanent resident whom the alien intended to marry, but whose marriage is not legitimate because of that United States citizen's or lawful permanent resident's bigamy;

'(ii) the alien has been physically present in the United States for a continuous period of not less than 3 years immediately preceding the date of such application, and the issuance of a charging document for removal proceedings shall not toll the 3-year period of continuous physical presence in the United States;

'(iii) the alien has been a person of good moral character during such period, subject to the provisions of subparagraph (C);

'(iv) the alien is not inadmissible under paragraph (2) or (3) of section 212(a), is not deportable under paragraphs (1)(G) or (2) through (4) of section 237(a) (except in a case described in section 237(a)(7) where the Attorney General exercises discretion to grant a waiver), and has not been convicted of an aggravated felony; and

'(v) the removal would result in extreme hardship to the alien, the alien's child, or the alien's parent.

'(B) PHYSICAL PRESENCE—Notwithstanding subsection (d)(2), for purposes of subparagraph (A)(i)(II) or for purposes of section 244(a)(3) (as in effect before the title III-A effective date in section 309 of the Illegal Immigration Reform and Immigrant Responsibility Act of 1996), an alien shall not be considered to have failed to maintain continuous physical presence by reason of an absence if the alien demonstrates a connection between the absence and the battering or extreme cruelty perpetrated against the alien. No absence or portion of an absence connected to the battering or extreme cruelty shall count toward the 90-day or 180-day limits established in subsection (d)(2). If any absence or aggregate absences exceed 180 days, the absences or portions of the absences will not be considered to break the period of continuous presence. Any such period of time excluded from the 180-day limit shall be excluded in computing the time during which the alien has been physically present for purposes of the 3-year requirement set forth in section 240A(b)(2)(B) and section 244(a)(3) (as in effect before the title III-A effective date in section 309 of the Illegal Immigration Reform and Immigrant Responsibility Act of 1996).

'(C) GOOD MORAL CHARACTER—Notwithstanding section 101(f), an act or conviction that does not bar the Attorney General from granting relief under this paragraph by reason of subparagraph (A)(iv) shall not bar the Attorney General from finding the alien to be of good moral character under subparagraph (A)(i)(III) or section 244(a)(3) (as in effect before the title III-A effective date in section 309 of the Illegal

Immigration Reform and Immigrant Responsibility Act of 1996), if the Attorney General finds that the act or conviction was connected to the alien's having been battered or subjected to extreme cruelty and determines that a waiver is otherwise warranted.

'(D) CREDIBLE EVIDENCE CONSIDERED—In acting on applications under this paragraph, the Attorney General shall consider any credible evidence relevant to the application. The determination of what evidence is credible and the weight to be given that evidence shall be within the sole discretion of the Attorney General.'.

(b) CHILDREN OF BATTERED ALIENS AND PARENTS OF BATTERED ALIEN CHILDREN—Section 240A(b) of the Immigration and Nationality Act (8 U.S.C. 1229b(b)) is amended by adding at the end the following:

'(4) CHILDREN OF BATTERED ALIENS AND PARENTS OF BATTERED ALIEN CHILDREN—

'(A) IN GENERAL—The Attorney General shall grant parole under section 212(d)(5) to any alien who is a—

'(i) child of an alien granted relief under section 240A(b)(2) or 244(a)(3) (as in effect before the title III-A effective date in section 309 of the Illegal Immigration Reform and Immigrant Responsibility Act of 1996); or

'(ii) parent of a child alien granted relief under section 240A(b)(2) or 244(a)(3) (as in effect before the title III-A effective date in section 309 of the Illegal Immigration Reform and Immigrant Responsibility Act of 1996).

'(B) DURATION OF PAROLE—The grant of parole shall extend from the time of the grant of relief under section 240A(b)(2) or section 244(a)(3) (as in effect before the title III-A effective date in section 309 of the Illegal Immigration Reform and Immigrant Responsibility Act of 1996) to the time the application for adjustment of status filed by aliens covered under this paragraph has been finally adjudicated. Applications for adjustment of status filed by aliens covered under this paragraph shall be treated as if they were applications filed under section 204(a)(1)(A)(iii), (A)(iv), (B)(ii), or (B)(iii) for purposes of section 245 (a) and (c). Failure by the alien granted relief under section 240A(b)(2) or section 244(a)(3) (as in effect before the title III-A effective date in section 309 of the Illegal Immigration Reform and Immigrant Responsibility Act of 1996) to exercise due diligence in filing a visa petition on behalf of an alien described in clause (i) or (ii) may result in revocation of parole.'.

(c) EFFECTIVE DATE—Any individual who becomes eligible for relief by reason of the enactment of the amendments made by subsections (a) and (b), shall be eligible to file a motion to reopen pursuant to section 240(c)(6)(C)(iv). The amendments made by subsections (a) and (b) shall take effect as if included in the enactment of section 304 of the Illegal Immigration Reform and Immigrant Responsibility Act of 1996 (Public Law 104-208; 110 Stat. 587). Such portions of the amendments made by subsection (b) that relate to section 244(a)(3) (as in effect before the title III-A effective date in section 309 of the Illegal Immigration Reform and Immigrant Responsibility Act of 1996) shall take effect as if included in subtitle G of title IV of the Violent Crime Control and Law Enforcement Act of 1994 (Public Law 103-322; 108 Stat. 1953 et seq.).

SEC. 1505. OFFERING EQUAL ACCESS TO IMMIGRATION PROTECTIONS OF THE VIOLENCE AGAINST WOMEN ACT OF 1994 FOR ALL QUALIFIED BATTERED IMMIGRANT SELF-PETITIONERS.

(a) BATTERED IMMIGRANT WAIVER—Section 212(a)(9)(C)(ii) of the Immigration and Nationality Act (8 U.S.C. 1182(a)(9)(C)(ii)) is amended by adding at the end the following: 'The Attorney General in the Attorney General's discretion may waive the provisions of section 212(a)(9)(C)(i) in the case of an alien to whom the Attorney General has granted classification under clause (iii), (iv), or (v) of section 204(a)(1)(A), or classification under clause (ii), (iii), or (iv) of section 204(a)(1)(B), in any case in which there is a connection between—

'(1) the alien's having been battered or subjected to extreme cruelty; and
'(2) the alien's—
　'(A) removal;
　'(B) departure from the United States;
　'(C) reentry or reentries into the United States; or
　'(D) attempted reentry into the United States.'.

(b) DOMESTIC VIOLENCE VICTIM WAIVER—
(1) WAIVER FOR VICTIMS OF DOMESTIC VIOLENCE—Section 237(a) of the Immigration and Nationality Act (8 U.S.C. 1227(a)) is amended by inserting at the end the following:
'(7) WAIVER FOR VICTIMS OF DOMESTIC VIOLENCE—
　'(A) IN GENERAL—The Attorney General is not limited by the criminal court record and may waive the application of paragraph (2)(E)(i) (with respect to crimes of domestic violence and crimes of stalking) and (ii) in the case of an alien who has been battered or subjected to extreme cruelty and who is not and was not the primary perpetrator of violence in the relationship—
　　'(i) upon a determination that—
　　　'(I) the alien was acting is self-defense;
　　　'(II) the alien was found to have violated a protection order intended to protect the alien; or
　　　'(III) the alien committed, was arrested for, was convicted of, or pled guilty to committing a crime—
'(aa) that did not result in serious bodily injury; and
'(bb) where there was a connection between the crime and the alien's having been battered or subjected to extreme cruelty.

'(B) CREDIBLE EVIDENCE CONSIDERED—In acting on applications under this paragraph, the Attorney General shall consider any credible evidence relevant to the application. The determination of what evidence is credible and the weight to be given that evidence shall be within the sole discretion of the Attorney General.'.

(2) CONFORMING AMENDMENT—Section 240A(b)(1)(C) of the Immigration and Nationality Act (8 U.S.C. 1229b(b)(1)(C)) is amended by inserting '(except in a case described in section 237(a)(7) where the Attorney General exercises discretion to grant a waiver)' after '237(a)(3)'.

(c) MISREPRESENTATION WAIVERS FOR BATTERED SPOUSES OF UNITED STATES CITIZENS AND LAWFUL PERMANENT RESIDENTS—

(1) WAIVER OF INADMISSIBILITY—Section 212(i)(1) of the Immigration and Nationality Act (8 U.S.C. 1182(i)(1)) is amended by inserting before the period at the end the following: 'or, in the case of an alien granted classification under clause (iii) or (iv) of section 204(a)(1)(A) or clause (ii) or (iii) of section 204(a)(1)(B), the alien demonstrates extreme hardship to the alien or the alien's United States citizen, lawful permanent resident, or qualified alien parent or child'.

(2) WAIVER OF DEPORTABILITY—Section 237(a)(1)(H) of the Immigration and Nationality Act (8 U.S.C. 1227(a)(1)(H)) is amended—

(A) in clause (i), by inserting '(I)' after '(i)';
(B) by redesignating clause (ii) as subclause (II); and
(C) by adding after clause (i) the following:
'(ii) is an alien who qualifies for classification under clause (iii) or (iv) of section 204(a)(1)(A) or clause (ii) or (iii) of section 204(a)(1)(B).'.

(d) BATTERED IMMIGRANT WAIVER—Section 212(g)(1) of the Immigration and Nationality Act (8 U.S.C. 1182(g)(1)) is amended—

(1) in subparagraph (A), by striking 'or' at the end;
(2) in subparagraph (B), by adding 'or' at the end; and
(3) by inserting after subparagraph (B) the following:
'(C) qualifies for classification under clause (iii) or (iv) of section 204(a)(1)(A) or classification under clause (ii) or (iii) of section 204(a)(1)(B);'.

(e) WAIVERS FOR VAWA ELIGIBLE BATTERED IMMIGRANTS—Section 212(h)(1) of the Immigration and Nationality Act (8 U.S.C. 1182(h)(1)) is amended—

(1) in subparagraph (B), by striking 'and' and inserting 'or'; and
(2) by adding at the end the following:
'(C) the alien qualifies for classification under clause (iii) or (iv) of section 204(a)(1)(A) or classification under clause (ii) or (iii) of section 204(a)(1)(B); and'.

(f) PUBLIC CHARGE—Section 212 of the Immigration and Nationality Act (8 U.S.C. 1182) is amended by adding at the end the following:

'(p) In determining whether an alien described in subsection (a)(4)(C)(i) is inadmissible under subsection (a)(4) or ineligible to receive an immigrant visa or otherwise to adjust to the status of permanent resident by reason of subsection (a)(4), the consular officer or the Attorney General shall not consider any benefits the alien may have received that were authorized under section 501 of the Illegal Immigration Reform and Immigrant Responsibility Act of 1996 (8 U.S.C. 1641(c)).'.

(g) REPORT—Not later than 6 months after the date of the enactment of this Act, the Attorney General shall submit a report to the Committees on the Judiciary of the Senate and the House of Representatives covering, with respect to fiscal year 1997 and each fiscal year thereafter—

> (1) the policy and procedures of the Immigration and Naturalization Service under which an alien who has been battered or subjected to extreme cruelty who is eligible for suspension of deportation or cancellation of removal can request to be placed, and be placed, in deportation or removal proceedings so that such alien may apply for suspension of deportation or cancellation of removal;
> (2) the number of requests filed at each district office under this policy;
> (3) the number of these requests granted reported separately for each district; and
> (4) the average length of time at each Immigration and Naturalization office between the date that an alien who has been subject to battering or extreme cruelty eligible for suspension of deportation or cancellation of removal requests to be placed in deportation or removal proceedings and the date that the immigrant appears before an immigration judge to file an application for suspension of deportation or cancellation of removal.

SEC. 1506. RESTORING IMMIGRATION PROTECTIONS UNDER THE VIOLENCE AGAINST WOMEN ACT OF 1994.

> (a) REMOVING BARRIERS TO ADJUSTMENT OF STATUS FOR VICTIMS OF DOMESTIC VIOLENCE—
>> (1) IMMIGRATION AMENDMENTS—Section 245 of the Immigration and Nationality Act (8 U.S.C. 1255) is amended—
>>> (A) in subsection (a), by inserting 'or the status of any other alien having an approved petition for classification under subparagraph (A)(iii), (A)(iv), (B)(ii), or (B)(iii) of section 204(a)(1) or' after 'into the United States.'; and
>>> (B) in subsection (c), by striking 'Subsection (a) shall not be applicable to' and inserting the following: 'Other than an alien having an approved petition for classification under subparagraph (A)(iii), (A)(iv), (A)(v), (A)(vi), (B)(ii), (B)(iii), or (B)(iv) of section 204(a)(1), subsection (a) shall not be applicable to'.

(2) EFFECTIVE DATE—The amendments made by paragraph (1) shall apply to applications for adjustment of status pending on or made on or after January 14, 1998.

(b) REMOVING BARRIERS TO CANCELLATION OF REMOVAL AND SUSPENSION OF DEPORTATION FOR VICTIMS OF DOMESTIC VIOLENCE—

(1) NOT TREATING SERVICE OF NOTICE AS TERMINATING CONTINUOUS PERIOD—Section 240A(d)(1) of the Immigration and Nationality Act (8 U.S.C. 1229b(d)(1)) is amended by striking 'when the alien is served a notice to appear under section 239(a) or' and inserting '(A) except in the case of an alien who applies for cancellation of removal under subsection (b)(2), when the alien is served a notice to appear under section 239(a), or (B)'.

(2) EFFECTIVE DATE—The amendment made by paragraph (1) shall take effect as if included in the enactment of section 304 of the Illegal Immigration Reform and Immigrant Responsibility Act of 1996 (Public Law 104-208; 110 Stat. 587).

(3) MODIFICATION OF CERTAIN TRANSITION RULES FOR BATTERED SPOUSE OR CHILD—Section 309(c)(5)(C) of the Illegal Immigration Reform and Immigrant Responsibility Act of 1996 (8 U.S.C. 1101 note) is amended—

(A) by striking the subparagraph heading and inserting the following:

'(C) SPECIAL RULE FOR CERTAIN ALIENS GRANTED TEMPORARY PROTECTION FROM DEPORTATION AND FOR BATTERED SPOUSES AND CHILDREN—'; and

(B) in clause (i)—

(i) in subclause (IV), by striking 'or' at the end;

(ii) in subclause (V), by striking the period at the end and inserting '; or'; and

(iii) by adding at the end the following:

'(VI) is an alien who was issued an order to show cause or was in deportation proceedings before April 1, 1997, and who applied for suspension of deportation under section 244(a)(3) of the Immigration and Nationality Act (as in effect before the date of the enactment of this Act).'.

(4) EFFECTIVE DATE—The amendments made by paragraph (3) shall take effect as if included in the enactment of section 309 of the Illegal Immigration Reform and Immigrant Responsibility Act of 1996 (8 U.S.C. 1101 note).

(c) ELIMINATING TIME LIMITATIONS ON MOTIONS TO REOPEN REMOVAL AND DEPORTATION PROCEEDINGS FOR VICTIMS OF DOMESTIC VIOLENCE—

(1) REMOVAL PROCEEDINGS—

(A) IN GENERAL—Section 240(c)(6)(C) of the Immigration and Nationality Act (8 U.S.C. 1229a(c)(6)(C)) is amended by adding at the end the following:

'(iv) SPECIAL RULE FOR BATTERED SPOUSES AND CHILDREN—The deadline specified in subsection (b)(5)(C) for filing a motion to reopen does not apply—

'(I) if the basis for the motion is to apply for relief under clause (iii) or (iv) of section 204(a)(1)(A), clause (ii) or (iii) of section 204(a)(1)(B), or section 240A(b)(2);

'(II) if the motion is accompanied by a cancellation of removal application to be filed with the Attorney General or by a copy of the self-petition that has been or will be filed with the Immigration and Naturalization Service upon the granting of the motion to reopen; and

'(III) if the motion to reopen is filed within 1 year of the entry of the final order of removal, except that the Attorney General may, in the Attorney General's discretion, waive this time limitation in the case of an alien who demonstrates extraordinary circumstances or extreme hardship to the alien's child.'.

(B) EFFECTIVE DATE—The amendment made by subparagraph (A) shall take effect as if included in the enactment of section 304 of the Illegal Immigration Reform and Immigrant Responsibility Act of 1996 (8 U.S.C. 1229-1229c).

(2) DEPORTATION PROCEEDINGS—

(A) IN GENERAL—Notwithstanding any limitation imposed by law on motions to reopen or rescind deportation proceedings under the Immigration and Nationality Act (as in effect before the title III-A effective date in section 309 of the Illegal Immigration Reform and Immigrant Responsibility Act of 1996 (8 U.S.C. 1101 note)), there is no time limit on the filing of a motion to reopen such proceedings, and the deadline specified in section 242B(c)(3) of the Immigration and Nationality Act (as so in effect) (8 U.S.C. 1252b(c)(3)) does not apply—

(i) if the basis of the motion is to apply for relief under clause (iii) or (iv) of section 204(a)(1)(A) of the Immigration and Nationality Act (8 U.S.C. 1154(a)(1)(A)), clause (ii) or (iii) of section 204(a)(1)(B) of such Act (8 U.S.C. 1154(a)(1)(B)), or section 244(a)(3) of such Act (as so in effect) (8 U.S.C. 1254(a)(3)); and

(ii) if the motion is accompanied by a suspension of deportation application to be filed with the Attorney General or by a copy of the self-petition that will be filed with the Immigration and Naturalization Service upon the granting of the motion to reopen.

(B) APPLICABILITY—Subparagraph (A) shall apply to motions filed by aliens who—

(i) are, or were, in deportation proceedings under the Immigration and Nationality Act (as in effect before the title III-A effective date in section 309 of the Illegal Immigration Reform and Immigrant Responsibility Act of 1996 (8 U.S.C. 1101 note)); and

(ii) have become eligible to apply for relief under clause (iii) or (iv) of section 204(a)(1)(A) of the Immigration and Nationality Act (8 U.S.C. 1154(a)(1)(A)), clause (ii) or (iii) of section 204(a)(1)(B) of such Act (8 U.S.C. 1154(a)(1)(B)), or section 244(a)(3) of such Act (as in effect before the title III-A effective date in section 309 of the Illegal Immigration Reform and Immigrant Responsibility Act of 1996 (8 U.S.C. 1101 note)) as a result of the amendments made by—

(I) subtitle G of title IV of the Violent Crime Control and Law Enforcement Act of 1994 (Public Law 103-322; 108 Stat. 1953 et seq.); or

(II) this title.

SEC. 1507. REMEDYING PROBLEMS WITH IMPLEMENTATION OF THE IMMIGRATION PROVISIONS OF THE VIOLENCE AGAINST WOMEN ACT OF 1994.

(a) EFFECT OF CHANGES IN ABUSERS' CITIZENSHIP STATUS ON SELF-PETITION—

(1) RECLASSIFICATION—Section 204(a)(1)(A) of the Immigration and Nationality Act (8 U.S.C. 1154(a)(1)(A)) (as amended by section 1503(b)(3) of this title) is amended by adding at the end the following:

'(vi) For the purposes of any petition filed under clause (iii) or (iv), the denaturalization, loss or renunciation of citizenship, death of the abuser, divorce, or changes to the abuser's citizenship status after filing of the petition shall not adversely affect the approval of the petition, and for approved petitions shall not preclude the classification of the eligible self-petitioning spouse or child as an immediate relative or affect the alien's ability to adjust status under subsections (a) and (c) of section 245 or obtain status as a lawful permanent resident based on the approved self-petition under such clauses.'.

(2) LOSS OF STATUS—Section 204(a)(1)(B) of the Immigration and Nationality Act (8 U.S.C. 1154(a)(1)(B)) (as amended by section 1503(c)(3) of this title) is amended by adding at the end the following:

'(v)(I) For the purposes of any petition filed or approved under clause (ii) or (iii), divorce, or the loss of lawful permanent resident status by a spouse or parent after the filing of a petition under that clause shall not adversely affect approval of the petition, and, for an approved petition, shall not affect the alien's ability to adjust status under subsections (a) and (c) of section 245 or obtain status as a lawful permanent resident based on an approved self-petition under clause (ii) or (iii).

'(II) Upon the lawful permanent resident spouse or parent becoming or establishing the existence of United States citizenship through naturalization, acquisition of citizenship, or other means, any petition filed with the Immigration and Naturalization Service and pending or approved under clause (ii) or (iii) on behalf of an alien who has been battered or subjected to extreme cruelty shall be deemed reclassified as a petition filed under subparagraph (A) even if the acquisition of citizenship occurs after divorce or termination of parental rights.'.

(3) DEFINITION OF IMMEDIATE RELATIVES—Section 201(b)(2)(A)(i) of the Immigration and Nationality Act (8 U.S.C. 1154(b)(2)(A)(i)) is amended by adding at the end the following: 'For purposes of this clause, an alien who has filed a petition under clause (iii) or (iv) of section 204(a)(1)(A) of this Act remains an immediate relative in the event that the United States citizen spouse or parent loses United States citizenship on account of the abuse.'.

(b) ALLOWING REMARRIAGE OF BATTERED IMMIGRANTS—Section 204(h) of the Immigration and Nationality Act (8 U.S.C. 1154(h)) is amended by adding at the end the following: 'Remarriage of an alien whose petition was approved under section 204(a)(1)(B)(ii) or 204(a)(1)(A)(iii) or marriage of an alien described in clause (iv) or (vi) of section 204(a)(1)(A) or in section 204(a)(1)(B)(iii) shall not be the basis for revocation of a petition approval under section 205.'.

SEC. 1508. TECHNICAL CORRECTION TO QUALIFIED ALIEN DEFINITION FOR BATTERED IMMIGRANTS.

Section 431(c)(1)(B)(iii) of the Personal Responsibility and Work Opportunity Reconciliation Act of 1996 (8 U.S.C. 1641(c)(1)(B)(iii)) is amended to read as follows:

'(iii) suspension of deportation under section 244(a)(3) of the Immigration and Nationality Act (as in effect before the title III-A effective date in section 309 of the Illegal Immigration Reform and Immigrant Responsibility Act of 1996).'.

SEC. 1509. ACCESS TO CUBAN ADJUSTMENT ACT FOR BATTERED IMMIGRANT SPOUSES AND CHILDREN.

(a) IN GENERAL—The last sentence of the first section of Public Law 89-732 (November 2, 1966; 8 U.S.C. 1255 note) is amended by striking the period at the end and inserting the following: ', except that such spouse or child who has been battered or subjected to extreme cruelty may adjust to permanent resident status under this Act without demonstrating that he or she is residing with the Cuban spouse or parent in the United States. In acting on applications under this section with respect to spouses or children who have been battered or subjected to extreme cruelty, the Attorney General shall apply the provisions of section 204(a)(1)(H).'.

(b) EFFECTIVE DATE—The amendment made by subsection (a) shall be effective as if included in subtitle G of title IV of the Violent Crime Control and Law Enforcement Act of 1994 (Public Law 103-322; 108 Stat. 1953 et seq.).

SEC. 1510. ACCESS TO THE NICARAGUAN ADJUSTMENT AND CENTRAL AMERICAN RELIEF ACT FOR BATTERED SPOUSES AND CHILDREN.

(a) ADJUSTMENT OF STATUS OF CERTAIN NICARAGUAN AND CUBAN BATTERED SPOUSES—Section 202(d) of the Nicaraguan Adjustment and Central American Relief Act (8 U.S.C. 1255 note; Public Law 105-100, as amended) is amended—

(1) in paragraph (1), by striking subparagraph (B) and inserting the following:

'(B) the alien—

'(i) is the spouse, child, or unmarried son or daughter of an alien whose status is adjusted to that of an alien lawfully admitted for permanent residence under subsection (a), except that in the case of such an unmarried son or daughter, the son or daughter shall be required to establish that the son or daughter has been physically present in the United States for a continuous period beginning not later than December 1, 1995, and ending not earlier than the date on which the application for adjustment under this subsection is filed; or

'(ii) was, at the time at which an alien filed for adjustment under subsection (a), the spouse or child of an alien whose status is adjusted to that of an alien lawfully admitted for permanent residence under subsection (a), and the spouse, child, or child of the spouse has been battered or subjected to extreme cruelty by the alien that filed for adjustment under subsection (a);'; and

(2) by adding at the end the following:

'(3) PROCEDURE—In acting on an application under this section with respect to a spouse or child who has been battered or subjected to extreme cruelty, the Attorney General shall apply section 204(a)(1)(H).'.

(b) CANCELLATION OF REMOVAL AND SUSPENSION OF DEPORTATION TRANSITION RULES FOR CERTAIN BATTERED SPOUSES—Section 309(c)(5)(C) of the Illegal Immigration and Reform and Immigrant Responsibility Act of 1996 (division C of Public Law 104-208; 8 U.S.C. 1101 note) (as amended by section 1506(b)(3) of this title) is amended—

(1) in clause (i)—

(A) by striking the period at the end of subclause (VI) (as added by section 1506(b)(3) of this title) and inserting '; or'; and

(B) by adding at the end the following:

'(VII)(aa) was the spouse or child of an alien described in subclause (I), (II), or (V)—

'(AA) at the time at which a decision is rendered to suspend the deportation or cancel the removal of the alien;
'(BB) at the time at which the alien filed an application for suspension of deportation or cancellation of removal; or
'(CC) at the time at which the alien registered for benefits under the settlement agreement in American Baptist Churches, et. al. v. Thornburgh (ABC), applied for temporary protected status, or applied for asylum; and
> '(bb) the spouse, child, or child of the spouse has been battered or subjected to extreme cruelty by the alien described in subclause (I), (II), or (V).'; and

(2) by adding at the end the following:
> '(iii) CONSIDERATION OF PETITIONS—In acting on a petition filed under subclause (VII) of clause (i) the provisions set forth in section 204(a)(1)(H) shall apply.
> '(iv) RESIDENCE WITH SPOUSE OR PARENT NOT REQUIRED—For purposes of the application of clause (i)(VII), a spouse or child shall not be required to demonstrate that he or she is residing with the spouse or parent in the United States.'.

(c) EFFECTIVE DATE—The amendments made by subsections (a) and (b) shall be effective as if included in the Nicaraguan Adjustment and Central American Relief Act (8 U.S.C. 1255 note; Public Law 105-100, as amended).

SEC. 1511. ACCESS TO THE HAITIAN REFUGEE FAIRNESS ACT OF 1998 FOR BATTERED SPOUSES AND CHILDREN.

(a) IN GENERAL—Section 902(d)(1)(B) of the Haitian Refugee Immigration Fairness Act of 1998 (division A of section 101(h) of Public Law 105-277; 112 Stat. 2681-538) is amended to read as follows:
> '(B)(i) the alien is the spouse, child, or unmarried son or daughter of an alien whose status is adjusted to that of an alien lawfully admitted for permanent residence under subsection (a), except that, in the case of such an unmarried son or daughter, the son or daughter shall be required to establish that the son or daughter has been physically present in the United States for a continuous period beginning not later than December 1, 1995, and ending not earlier than the date on which the application for such adjustment is filed;
> '(ii) at the time of filing of the application for adjustment under subsection (a), the alien is the spouse or child of an alien whose status is adjusted to that of an alien lawfully admitted for permanent residence under subsection (a) and the spouse, child, or child of the spouse has been battered or subjected to extreme cruelty by the individual described in subsection (a); and

'(iii) in acting on applications under this section with respect to spouses or children who have been battered or subjected to extreme cruelty, the Attorney General shall apply the provisions of section 204(a)(1)(H).'.

(b) EFFECTIVE DATE—The amendment made by subsection (a) shall be effective as if included in the Haitian Refugee Immigration Fairness Act of 1998 (division A of section 101(h) of Public Law 105-277; 112 Stat. 2681-538).

SEC. 1512. ACCESS TO SERVICES AND LEGAL REPRESENTATION FOR BATTERED IMMIGRANTS.

(a) LAW ENFORCEMENT AND PROSECUTION GRANTS—Section 2001(b) of part T of title I of the Omnibus Crime Control and Safe Streets Act of 1968 (42 U.S.C. 3796gg(b)) (as amended by section 1209(c) of this division) is amended by adding at the end the following:

'(11) providing assistance to victims of domestic violence and sexual assault in immigration matters.'.

(b) GRANTS TO ENCOURAGE ARRESTS—Section 2101(b)(5) of part U of title I of the Omnibus Crime Control and Safe Streets Act of 1968 (42 U.S.C. 3796hh(b)(5)) is amended by inserting before the period the following: ', including strengthening assistance to such victims in immigration matters'.

(c) RURAL DOMESTIC VIOLENCE AND CHILD ABUSE ENFORCEMENT GRANTS—Section 40295(a)(2) of the Violent Crime Control and Law Enforcement Act of 1994 (Public Law 103-322; 108 Stat. 1953; 42 U.S.C. 13971(a)(2)) is amended to read as follows:

'(2) to provide treatment, counseling, and assistance to victims of domestic violence and child abuse, including in immigration matters; and'.

(d) CAMPUS DOMESTIC VIOLENCE GRANTS—Section 826(b)(5) of the Higher Education Amendments of 1998 (Public Law 105-244; 20 U.S.C. 1152) is amended by inserting before the period at the end the following: ', including assistance to victims in immigration matters'.

SEC. 1513. PROTECTION FOR CERTAIN CRIME VICTIMS INCLUDING VICTIMS OF CRIMES AGAINST WOMEN.

(a) FINDINGS AND PURPOSE—

(1) FINDINGS—Congress makes the following findings:

(A) Immigrant women and children are often targeted to be victims of crimes committed against them in the United States, including rape, torture, kidnaping, trafficking, incest, domestic violence, sexual assault, female genital mutilation, forced prostitution, involuntary servitude, being held hostage or being criminally restrained.

(B) All women and children who are victims of these crimes committed against them in the United States must be able to report these crimes to law enforcement and fully participate in the investigation of the crimes committed against them and the prosecution of the perpetrators of such crimes.

(2) PURPOSE—

(A) The purpose of this section is to create a new nonimmigrant visa classification that will strengthen the ability of law enforcement agencies to detect, investigate, and prosecute cases of domestic violence, sexual assault, trafficking of aliens, and other crimes described in section 101(a)(15)(U)(iii) of the Immigration and Nationality Act committed against aliens, while offering protection to victims of such offenses in keeping with the humanitarian interests of the United States. This visa will encourage law enforcement officials to better serve immigrant crime victims and to prosecute crimes committed against aliens.

(B) Creating a new nonimmigrant visa classification will facilitate the reporting of crimes to law enforcement officials by trafficked, exploited, victimized, and abused aliens who are not in lawful immigration status. It also gives law enforcement officials a means to regularize the status of cooperating individuals during investigations or prosecutions. Providing temporary legal status to aliens who have been severely victimized by criminal activity also comports with the humanitarian interests of the United States.

(C) Finally, this section gives the Attorney General discretion to convert the status of such nonimmigrants to that of permanent residents when doing so is justified on humanitarian grounds, for family unity, or is otherwise in the public interest.

(b) ESTABLISHMENT OF HUMANITARIAN/MATERIAL WITNESS NONIMMIGRANT CLASSIFICATION—Section 101(a)(15) of the Immigration and Nationality Act (8 U.S.C. 1101(a)(15)) (as amended by section 107 of this Act) is amended—

(1) by striking 'or' at the end of subparagraph (S);

(2) by striking the period at the end of subparagraph (T) and inserting '; or'; and

(3) by adding at the end the following new subparagraph:

'(U)(i) subject to section 214(o), an alien who files a petition for status under this subparagraph, if the Attorney General determines that—

'(I) the alien has suffered substantial physical or mental abuse as a result of having been a victim of criminal activity described in clause (iii);

'(II) the alien (or in the case of an alien child under the age of 16, the parent, guardian, or next friend of the alien) possesses information concerning criminal activity described in clause (iii);

'(III) the alien (or in the case of an alien child under the age of 16, the parent, guardian, or next friend of the alien) has been helpful, is being helpful, or is likely to be helpful to a Federal, State, or local law enforcement official, to a Federal, State, or local prosecutor, to a Federal or State judge, to the Service, or to other Federal, State, or local authorities investigating or prosecuting criminal activity described in clause (iii); and

'(IV) the criminal activity described in clause (iii) violated the laws of the United States or occurred in the United States (including in Indian country and military installations) or the territories and possessions of the United States;

'(ii) if the Attorney General considers it necessary to avoid extreme hardship to the spouse, the child, or, in the case of an alien child, the parent of the alien described in clause (i), the Attorney General may also grant status under this paragraph based upon certification of a government official listed in clause (i)(III) that an investigation or prosecution would be harmed without the assistance of the spouse, the child, or, in the case of an alien child, the parent of the alien; and

'(iii) the criminal activity referred to in this clause is that involving one or more of the following or any similar activity in violation of Federal, State, or local criminal law: rape; torture; trafficking; incest; domestic violence; sexual assault; abusive sexual contact; prostitution; sexual exploitation; female genital mutilation; being held hostage; peonage; involuntary servitude; slave trade; kidnapping; abduction; unlawful criminal restraint; false imprisonment; blackmail; extortion; manslaughter; murder; felonious assault; witness tampering; obstruction of justice; perjury; or attempt, conspiracy, or solicitation to commit any of the above mentioned crimes.'.

(c) CONDITIONS FOR ADMISSION AND DUTIES OF THE ATTORNEY GENERAL—Section 214 of such Act (8 U.S.C. 1184) (as amended by section 107 of this Act) is amended by adding at the end the following new subsection:

'(o) REQUIREMENTS APPLICABLE TO SECTION 101(a)(15)(U) VISAS—

'(1) PETITIONING PROCEDURES FOR SECTION 101(a)(15)(U) VISAS—The petition filed by an alien under section 101(a)(15)(U)(i) shall contain a certification from a Federal, State, or local law enforcement official, prosecutor, judge, or other Federal, State, or local authority investigating criminal activity described in section 101(a)(15)(U)(iii). This certification may also be provided by an official of the Service whose ability to provide such certification is not limited to information concerning immigration violations. This certification shall state that the alien 'has been helpful, is being helpful, or is likely to be helpful' in the investigation or prosecution of criminal activity described in section 101(a)(15)(U)(iii).

'(2) NUMERICAL LIMITATIONS—

'(A) The number of aliens who may be issued visas or otherwise provided status as nonimmigrants under section 101(a)(15)(U) in any fiscal year shall not exceed 10,000.

'(B) The numerical limitations in subparagraph (A) shall only apply to principal aliens described in section 101(a)(15)(U)(i), and not to spouses, children, or, in the case of alien children, the alien parents of such children.

'(3) DUTIES OF THE ATTORNEY GENERAL WITH RESPECT TO 'U' VISA NONIMMIGRANTS—With respect to nonimmigrant aliens described in subsection (a)(15)(U)—

'(A) the Attorney General and other government officials, where appropriate, shall provide those aliens with referrals to nongovernmental organizations to advise the aliens regarding their options while in the United States and the resources available to them; and

'(B) the Attorney General shall, during the period those aliens are in lawful temporary resident status under that subsection, provide the aliens with employment authorization.

'(4) CREDIBLE EVIDENCE CONSIDERED—In acting on any petition filed under this subsection, the consular officer or the Attorney General, as appropriate, shall consider any credible evidence relevant to the petition.

'(5) NONEXCLUSIVE RELIEF—Nothing in this subsection limits the ability of aliens who qualify for status under section 101(a)(15)(U) to seek any other immigration benefit or status for which the alien may be eligible.'.

(d) PROHIBITION ON ADVERSE DETERMINATIONS OF ADMISSIBILITY OR DEPORTABILITY—Section 384(a) of the Illegal Immigration Reform and Immigrant Responsibility Act of 1996 is amended—

(1) by striking 'or' at the end of paragraph (1)(C);

(2) by striking the comma at the end of paragraph (1)(D) and inserting ', or'; and

(3) by inserting after paragraph (1)(D) the following new subparagraph:

'(E) in the case of an alien applying for status under section 101(a)(15)(U) of the Immigration and Nationality Act, the perpetrator of the substantial physical or mental abuse and the criminal activity,'; and

(4) in paragraph (2), by inserting 'section 101(a)(15)(U),' after 'section 216(c)(4)(C),'.

(e) WAIVER OF GROUNDS OF INELIGIBILITY FOR ADMISSION—Section 212(d) of the Immigration and Nationality Act (8 U.S.C. 1182(d)) is amended by adding at the end the following new paragraph:

'(13) The Attorney General shall determine whether a ground of inadmissibility exists with respect to a nonimmigrant described in section 101(a)(15)(U). The Attorney General, in the Attorney General's discretion, may waive the application of subsection (a) (other than paragraph (3)(E)) in the case of a nonimmigrant described in section 101(a)(15)(U), if the Attorney General considers it to be in the public or national interest to do so.'.

(f) ADJUSTMENT TO PERMANENT RESIDENT STATUS—Section 245 of such Act (8 U.S.C. 1255) is amended by adding at the end the following new subsection:

'(l)(1) The Attorney General may adjust the status of an alien admitted into the United States (or otherwise provided nonimmigrant status) under section 101(a)(15)(U) to that of an alien lawfully admitted for permanent residence if the alien is not described in section 212(a)(3)(E), unless the Attorney General determines based on affirmative evidence that the alien unreasonably refused to provide assistance in a criminal investigation or prosecution, if—

'(A) the alien has been physically present in the United States for a continuous period of at least 3 years since the date of admission as a nonimmigrant under clause (i) or (ii) of section 101(a)(15)(U); and

'(B) in the opinion of the Attorney General, the alien's continued presence in the United States is justified on humanitarian grounds, to ensure family unity, or is otherwise in the public interest.

'(2) An alien shall be considered to have failed to maintain continuous physical presence in the United States under paragraph (1)(A) if the alien has departed from the United States for any period in excess of 90 days or for any periods in the aggregate exceeding 180 days unless the absence is in order to assist in the investigation or prosecution or unless an official involved in the investigation or prosecution certifies that the absence was otherwise justified.

'(3) Upon approval of adjustment of status under paragraph (1) of an alien described in section 101(a)(15)(U)(i) the Attorney General may adjust the status of or issue an immigrant visa to a spouse, a child, or, in the case of an alien child, a parent who did not receive a nonimmigrant visa under section 101(a)(15)(U)(ii) if the Attorney General considers the grant of such status or visa necessary to avoid extreme hardship.

'(4) Upon the approval of adjustment of status under paragraph (1) or (3), the Attorney General shall record the alien's lawful admission for permanent residence as of the date of such approval.'.

TITLE VI—MISCELLANEOUS

SEC. 1601. NOTICE REQUIREMENTS FOR SEXUALLY VIOLENT OFFENDERS.

(a) SHORT TITLE—This section may be cited as the 'Campus Sex Crimes Prevention Act'.

(b) NOTICE WITH RESPECT TO INSTITUTIONS OF HIGHER EDUCATION—

(1) IN GENERAL—Section 170101 of the Violent Crime Control and Law Enforcement Act of 1994 (42 U.S.C. 14071) is amended by adding at the end the following:

'(j) NOTICE OF ENROLLMENT AT OR EMPLOYMENT BY INSTITUTIONS OF HIGHER EDUCATION—

'(1) NOTICE BY OFFENDERS—

'(A) IN GENERAL—In addition to any other requirements of this section, any person who is required to register in a State shall provide notice as required under State law—

'(i) of each institution of higher education in that State at which the person is employed, carries on a vocation, or is a student; and

'(ii) of each change in enrollment or employment status of such person at an institution of higher education in that State.

'(B) CHANGE IN STATUS—A change in status under subparagraph (A)(ii) shall be reported by the person in the manner provided by State law. State procedures shall ensure that the updated information is promptly made available to a law enforcement agency having jurisdiction where such institution is located and entered into the appropriate State records or data system.

'(2) STATE REPORTING—State procedures shall ensure that the registration information collected under paragraph (1)—

'(A) is promptly made available to a law enforcement agency having jurisdiction where such institution is located; and

'(B) entered into the appropriate State records or data system.

'(3) REQUEST—Nothing in this subsection shall require an educational institution to request such information from any State.'.

(2) EFFECTIVE DATE—The amendment made by this subsection shall take effect 2 years after the date of the enactment of this Act.

(c) DISCLOSURES BY INSTITUTIONS OF HIGHER EDUCATION—

(1) IN GENERAL—Section 485(f)(1) of the Higher Education Act of 1965 (20 U.S.C. 1092(f)(1)) is amended by adding at the end the following:

'(I) A statement advising the campus community where law enforcement agency information provided by a State under section 170101(j) of the Violent Crime Control and Law Enforcement Act of 1994 (42 U.S.C. 14071(j)), concerning registered sex offenders may be obtained, such as the law enforcement office of the institution, a local law enforcement agency with jurisdiction for the campus, or a computer network address.'.

(2) EFFECTIVE DATE—The amendment made by this subsection shall take effect 2 years after the date of the enactment of this Act.

(d) AMENDMENT TO FAMILY EDUCATIONAL RIGHTS AND PRIVACY ACT OF 1974—Section 444(b) of the General Education Provisions Act (20 U.S.C. 1232g(b)), also known as the Family Educational Rights and Privacy Act of 1974, is amended by adding at the end the following:

'(7)(A) Nothing in this section may be construed to prohibit an educational institution from disclosing information provided to the institution under section 170101 of the Violent Crime Control and Law Enforcement Act of 1994 (42 U.S.C. 14071) concerning registered sex offenders who are required to register under such section.

'(B) The Secretary shall take appropriate steps to notify educational institutions that disclosure of information described in subparagraph (A) is permitted.'.

SEC. 1602. TEEN SUICIDE PREVENTION STUDY.

(a) SHORT TITLE—This section may be cited as the 'Teen Suicide Prevention Act of 2000'.

(b) FINDINGS—Congress finds that—

(1) measures that increase public awareness of suicide as a preventable public health problem, and target parents and youth so that suicide risks and warning signs can be recognized, will help to eliminate the ignorance and stigma of suicide as barriers to youth and families seeking preventive care;

(2) suicide prevention efforts in the year 2000 should—

(A) target at-risk youth, particularly youth with mental health problems, substance abuse problems, or contact with the juvenile justice system;

(B) involve—

(i) the identification of the characteristics of the at-risk youth and other youth who are contemplating suicide, and barriers to treatment of the youth; and

(ii) the development of model treatment programs for the youth;

(C) include a pilot study of the outcomes of treatment for juvenile delinquents with mental health or substance abuse problems;

(D) include a public education approach to combat the negative effects of the stigma of, and discrimination against individuals with, mental health and substance abuse problems; and

(E) include a nationwide effort to develop, implement, and evaluate a mental health awareness program for schools, communities, and families;

(3) although numerous symptoms, diagnoses, traits, characteristics, and psychosocial stressors of suicide have been investigated, no single factor or set of factors has ever come close to predicting suicide with accuracy;

(4) research of United States youth, such as a 1994 study by Lewinsohn, Rohde, and Seeley, has shown predictors of suicide, such as a history of suicide attempts, current suicidal ideation and depression, a recent attempt or completed suicide by a friend, and low self-esteem; and

(5) epidemiological data illustrate—

    (A) the trend of suicide at younger ages as well as increases in suicidal ideation among youth in the United States; and

    (B) distinct differences in approaches to suicide by gender, with—

        (i) 3 to 5 times as many females as males attempting suicide; and

        (ii) 3 to 5 times as many males as females completing suicide.

(c) PURPOSE—The purpose of this section is to provide for a study of predictors of suicide among at-risk and other youth, and barriers that prevent the youth from receiving treatment, to facilitate the development of model treatment programs and public education and awareness efforts.

(d) STUDY—Not later than 1 year after the date of the enactment of this Act, the Secretary of Health and Human Services shall carry out, directly or by grant or contract, a study that is designed to identify—

(1) the characteristics of at-risk and other youth age 13 through 21 who are contemplating suicide;

(2) the characteristics of at-risk and other youth who are younger than age 13 and are contemplating suicide; and

(3) the barriers that prevent youth described in paragraphs (1) and (2) from receiving treatment.

(e) AUTHORIZATION OF APPROPRIATIONS—There are authorized to be appropriated to carry out this section such sums as may be necessary.

SEC. 1603. DECADE OF PAIN CONTROL AND RESEARCH.

The calendar decade beginning January 1, 2001, is designated as the 'Decade of Pain Control and Research'.

DIVISION C—MISCELLANEOUS PROVISIONS

SEC. 2001. AIMEE'S LAW.

(a) SHORT TITLE—This section may be cited as 'Aimee's Law'.

(b) DEFINITIONS—In this section:

(1) DANGEROUS SEXUAL OFFENSE—The term 'dangerous sexual offense' means any offense under State law for conduct that would constitute an offense under chapter 109A of title 18, United States

Code, had the conduct occurred in the special maritime and territorial jurisdiction of the United States or in a Federal prison.

(2) MURDER—The term 'murder' has the meaning given the term in part I of the Uniform Crime Reports of the Federal Bureau of Investigation.

(3) RAPE—The term 'rape' has the meaning given the term in part I of the Uniform Crime Reports of the Federal Bureau of Investigation.

(c) PENALTY—

(1) SINGLE STATE—In any case in which a State convicts an individual of murder, rape, or a dangerous sexual offense, who has a prior conviction for any one of those offenses in a State described in paragraph (3), the Attorney General shall transfer an amount equal to the costs of incarceration, prosecution, and apprehension of that individual, from Federal law enforcement assistance funds that have been allocated to but not distributed to the State that convicted the individual of the prior offense, to the State account that collects Federal law enforcement assistance funds of the State that convicted that individual of the subsequent offense.

(2) MULTIPLE STATES—In any case in which a State convicts an individual of murder, rape, or a dangerous sexual offense, who has a prior conviction for any one or more of those offenses in more than one other State described in paragraph (3), the Attorney General shall transfer an amount equal to the costs of incarceration, prosecution, and apprehension of that individual, from Federal law enforcement assistance funds that have been allocated to but not distributed to each State that convicted such individual of the prior offense, to the State account that collects Federal law enforcement assistance funds of the State that convicted that individual of the subsequent offense.

(3) STATE DESCRIBED—A State is described in this paragraph if—

(A) the average term of imprisonment imposed by the State on individuals convicted of the offense for which the individual described in paragraph (1) or (2), as applicable, was convicted by the State is less than the average term of imprisonment imposed for that offense in all States; or

(B) with respect to the individual described in paragraph (1) or (2), as applicable, the individual had served less than 85 percent of the term of imprisonment to which that individual was sentenced for the prior offense.

For purposes of subparagraph (B), in a State that has indeterminate sentencing, the term of imprisonment to which that individual was sentenced for the prior offense shall be based on the lower of the range of sentences.

(d) STATE APPLICATIONS—In order to receive an amount transferred under subsection (c), the chief executive of a State shall submit to the Attorney General an application, in such form and containing such information as the Attorney General may reasonably require, which shall include a certification that the State has convicted an individual of murder, rape, or a dangerous sexual offense, who has a prior conviction for one of those offenses in another State.

(e) SOURCE OF FUNDS—
> (1) IN GENERAL—Any amount transferred under subsection (c) shall be derived by reducing the amount of Federal law enforcement assistance funds received by the State that convicted such individual of the prior offense before the distribution of the funds to the State. The Attorney General shall provide the State with an opportunity to select the specific Federal law enforcement assistance funds to be so reduced (other than Federal crime victim assistance funds).
> (2) PAYMENT SCHEDULE—The Attorney General, in consultation with the chief executive of the State that convicted such individual of the prior offense, shall establish a payment schedule.

(f) CONSTRUCTION—Nothing in this section may be construed to diminish or otherwise affect any court ordered restitution.

(g) EXCEPTION—This section does not apply if the individual convicted of murder, rape, or a dangerous sexual offense has been released from prison upon the reversal of a conviction for an offense described in subsection (c) and subsequently been convicted for an offense described in subsection (c).

(h) REPORT—The Attorney General shall—
> (1) conduct a study evaluating the implementation of this section; and
> (2) not later than October 1, 2006, submit to Congress a report on the results of that study.

(i) COLLECTION OF RECIDIVISM DATA—
> (1) IN GENERAL—Beginning with calendar year 2002, and each calendar year thereafter, the Attorney General shall collect and maintain information relating to, with respect to each State—
>> (A) the number of convictions during that calendar year for—
>>> (i) any dangerous sexual offense;
>>> (ii) rape; and
>>> (iii) murder; and
>> (B) the number of convictions described in subparagraph (A) that constitute second or subsequent convictions of the defendant of an offense described in that subparagraph.
>
> (2) REPORT—Not later than March 1, 2003, and on March 1 of each year thereafter, the Attorney General shall submit to Congress a report, which shall include—
>> (A) the information collected under paragraph (1) with respect to each State during the preceding calendar year; and
>> (B) the percentage of cases in each State in which an individual convicted of an offense described in paragraph (1)(A) was

previously convicted of another such offense in another State during the preceding calendar year.

(j) EFFECTIVE DATE—This section shall take effect on January 1, 2002.

SEC. 2002. PAYMENT OF CERTAIN ANTI-TERRORISM JUDGMENTS.

(a) PAYMENTS—

(1) IN GENERAL—Subject to subsections (b) and (c), the Secretary of the Treasury shall pay each person described in paragraph (2), at the person's election—

(A) 110 percent of compensatory damages awarded by judgment of a court on a claim or claims brought by the person under section 1605 (a)(7) of title 28, United States Code, plus amounts necessary to pay post-judgment interest under section 1961 of such title, and, in the case of a claim or claims against Cuba, amounts awarded as sanctions by judicial order on April 18, 2000 (as corrected on June 2, 2000), subject to final appellate review of that order; or

(B) 100 percent of the compensatory damages awarded by judgment of a court on a claim or claims brought by the person under section 1605(a)(7) of title 28, United States Code, plus amounts necessary to pay post-judgment interest, as provided in section 1961 of such title, and, in the case of a claim or claims against Cuba, amounts awarded as sanctions by judicial order on April 18, 2000 (as corrected June 2, 2000), subject to final appellate review of that order.

Payments under this subsection shall be made promptly upon request.

(2) PERSONS COVERED—A person described in this paragraph is a person who—

(A)(i) as of July 20, 2000, held a final judgment for a claim or claims brought under section 1605(a)(7) of title 28, United States Code, against Iran or Cuba, or the right to payment of an amount awarded as a judicial sanction with respect to such claim or claims; or

(ii) filed a suit under such section 1605(a)(7) on February 17, 1999, December 13, 1999, January 28, 2000, March 15, 2000, or July 27, 2000;

(B) relinquishes all claims and rights to compensatory damages and amounts awarded as judicial sanctions under such judgments;

(C) in the case of payment under paragraph (1)(A), relinquishes all rights and claims to punitive damages awarded in connection with such claim or claims; and

(D) in the case of payment under paragraph (1)(B), relinquishes all rights to execute against or attach property that is at issue in claims against the United States before an international tribunal, that is the subject of awards rendered by such tribunal, or that is subject to section 1610(f)(1)(A) of title 28, United States Code.

(b) FUNDING OF AMOUNTS—

(1) JUDGMENTS AGAINST CUBA—For purposes of funding the payments under subsection (a) in the case of judgments and sanctions entered against the Government of Cuba or Cuban entities, the President shall vest and liquidate up to and not exceeding the amount of property of the Government of Cuba and sanctioned entities in the United States or any commonwealth, territory, or possession thereof that has been blocked pursuant to section 5(b) of the Trading with the Enemy Act (50 U.S.C. App. 5(b)), sections 202 and 203 of the International Emergency Economic Powers Act (50 U.S.C. 1701-1702), or any other proclamation, order, or regulation issued thereunder. For the purposes of paying amounts for judicial sanctions, payment shall be made from funds or accounts subject to sanctions as of April 18, 2000, or from blocked assets of the Government of Cuba.

(2) JUDGMENTS AGAINST IRAN—For purposes of funding payments under subsection (a) in the case of judgments against Iran, the Secretary of the Treasury shall make such payments from amounts paid and liquidated from—

(A) rental proceeds accrued on the date of the enactment of this Act from Iranian diplomatic and consular property located in the United States; and

(B) funds not otherwise made available in an amount not to exceed the total of the amount in the Iran Foreign Military Sales Program account within the Foreign Military Sales Fund on the date of the enactment of this Act.

(c) SUBROGATION—Upon payment under subsection (a) with respect to payments in connection with a Foreign Military Sales Program account, the United States shall be fully subrogated, to the extent of the payments, to all rights of the person paid under that subsection against the debtor foreign state. The President shall pursue these subrogated rights as claims or offsets of the United States in appropriate ways, including any negotiation process which precedes the normalization of relations between the foreign state designated as a state sponsor of terrorism and the United States, except that no funds shall be paid to Iran, or released to Iran, from property blocked under the International Emergency Economic Powers Act or from the Foreign Military Sales Fund, until such subrogated claims have been dealt with to the satisfaction of the United States.

(d) SENSE OF THE CONGRESS—It is the sense of the Congress that the President should not normalize relations between the United States and Iran until the claims subrogated have been dealt with to the satisfaction of the United States.

(e) REAFFIRMATION OF AUTHORITY—Congress reaffirms the President's statutory authority to manage and, where appropriate and consistent with the national interest, vest foreign assets located in the United States for the purposes, among other things, of assisting and, where appropriate, making payments to victims of terrorism.
(f) AMENDMENTS—(1) Section 1610(f) of title 28, United States Code, is amended—
> (A) in paragraphs (2)(A) and (2)(B)(ii), by striking 'shall' each place it appears and inserting 'should make every effort to'; and
> (B) by adding at the end the following new paragraph:
> '(3) WAIVER—The President may waive any provision of paragraph (1) in the interest of national security.'.

(2) Subsections (b) and (d) of section 117 of the Treasury Department Appropriations Act, 1999 (as contained in section 101(h) of Public Law 105-277) are repealed.

SEC. 2003. AID FOR VICTIMS OF TERRORISM.

(a) MEETING THE NEEDS OF VICTIMS OF TERRORISM OUTSIDE THE UNITED STATES—
> (1) IN GENERAL—Section 1404B(a) of the Victims of Crime Act of 1984 (42 U.S.C. 10603b(a)) is amended as follows:

'(a) VICTIMS OF ACTS OF TERRORISM OUTSIDE UNITED STATES—
> '(1) IN GENERAL—The Director may make supplemental grants as provided in 1402(d)(5) to States, victim service organizations, and public agencies (including Federal, State, or local governments) and nongovernmental organizations that provide assistance to victims of crime, which shall be used to provide emergency relief, including crisis response efforts, assistance, training, and technical assistance, and ongoing assistance, including during any investigation or prosecution, to victims of terrorist acts or mass violence occurring outside the United States who are not persons eligible for compensation under title VIII of the Omnibus Diplomatic Security and Antiterrorism Act of 1986.
> '(2) VICTIM DEFINED—In this subsection, the term 'victim'—
>> '(A) means a person who is a national of the United States or an officer or employee of the United States Government who is injured or killed as a result of a terrorist act or mass violence occurring outside the United States; and
>> '(B) in the case of a person described in subparagraph (A) who is less than 18 years of age, incompetent, incapacitated, or deceased, includes a family member or legal guardian of that person.

'(3) RULE OF CONSTRUCTION—Nothing in this subsection shall be construed to allow the Director to make grants to any foreign power (as defined by section 101(a) of the Foreign Intelligence Surveillance Act of 1978 (50 U.S.C. 1801(a)) or to any domestic or foreign organization operated for the purpose of engaging in any significant political or lobbying activities.'.

(2) APPLICABILITY—The amendment made by this subsection shall apply to any terrorist act or mass violence occurring on or after December 21, 1988, with respect to which an investigation or prosecution was ongoing after April 24, 1996.

(3) ADMINISTRATIVE PROVISION—Not later than 90 days after the date of the enactment of this Act, the Director shall establish guidelines under section 1407(a) of the Victims of Crime Act of 1984 (42 U.S.C. 10604(a)) to specify the categories of organizations and agencies to which the Director may make grants under this subsection.

(4) TECHNICAL AMENDMENT—Section 1404B(b) of the Victims of Crime Act of 1984 (42 U.S.C. 10603b(b)) is amended by striking '1404(d)(4)(B)' and inserting '1402(d)(5)'.

(b) AMENDMENTS TO EMERGENCY RESERVE FUND—

(1) CAP INCREASE—Section 1402(d)(5)(A) of the Victims of Crime Act of 1984 (42 U.S.C. 10601(d)(5)(A)) is amended by striking '$50,000,000' and inserting '$100,000,000'.

(2) TRANSFER—Section 1402(e) of the Victims of Crime Act of 1984 (42 U.S.C 10601(e)) is amended by striking 'in excess of $500,000' and all that follows through 'than $500,000' and inserting 'shall be available for deposit into the emergency reserve fund referred to in subsection (d)(5) at the discretion of the Director. Any remaining unobligated sums'.

(c) COMPENSATION TO VICTIMS OF INTERNATIONAL TERRORISM—

(1) IN GENERAL—The Victims of Crime Act of 1984 (42 U.S.C. 10601 et seq.) is amended by inserting after section 1404B the following:

'SEC. 1404C. COMPENSATION TO VICTIMS OF INTERNATIONAL TERRORISM.

'(a) DEFINITIONS—In this section:

'(1) INTERNATIONAL TERRORISM—The term 'international terrorism' has the meaning given the term in section 2331 of title 18, United States Code.

'(2) NATIONAL OF THE UNITED STATES—The term 'national of the United States' has the meaning given the term in section 101(a) of the Immigration and Nationality Act (8 U.S.C. 1101(a)).

'(3) VICTIM—

'(A) IN GENERAL—The term 'victim' means a person who—
'(i) suffered direct physical or emotional injury or death as a result of international terrorism occurring on or after December 21, 1988 with respect to which an investigation or prosecution was ongoing after April 24, 1996; and
'(ii) as of the date on which the international terrorism occurred, was a national of the United States or an officer or employee of the United States Government.
'(B) INCOMPETENT, INCAPACITATED, OR DECEASED VICTIMS—In the case of a victim who is less than 18 years of age, incompetent, incapacitated, or deceased, a family member or legal guardian of the victim may receive the compensation under this section on behalf of the victim.
'(C) EXCEPTION—Notwithstanding any other provision of this section, in no event shall an individual who is criminally culpable for the terrorist act or mass violence receive any compensation under this section, either directly or on behalf of a victim.
'(b) AWARD OF COMPENSATION—The Director may use the emergency reserve referred to in section 1402(d)(5)(A) to carry out a program to compensate victims of acts of international terrorism that occur outside the United States for expenses associated with that victimization.
'(c) ANNUAL REPORT—The Director shall annually submit to Congress a report on the status and activities of the program under this section, which report shall include—
'(1) an explanation of the procedures for filing and processing of applications for compensation;
'(2) a description of the procedures and policies instituted to promote public awareness about the program;
'(3) a complete statistical analysis of the victims assisted under the program, including—
'(A) the number of applications for compensation submitted;
'(B) the number of applications approved and the amount of each award;
'(C) the number of applications denied and the reasons for the denial;
'(D) the average length of time to process an application for compensation; and
'(E) the number of applications for compensation pending and the estimated future liability of the program; and
'(4) an analysis of future program needs and suggested program improvements.'.
(2) CONFORMING AMENDMENT—Section 1402(d)(5)(B) of the Victims of Crime Act of 1984 (42 U.S.C. 10601(d)(5)(B)) is amended by inserting ', to provide compensation to victims of international terrorism under the program under section 1404C,' after 'section 1404B'.

(d) AMENDMENTS TO VICTIMS OF CRIME FUND—Section 1402(c) of the Victims of Crime Act 1984 (42 U.S.C. 10601(c)) is amended by adding at the end the following: 'Notwithstanding section 1402(d)(5), all sums deposited in the Fund in any fiscal year that are not made available for obligation by Congress in the subsequent fiscal year shall remain in the Fund for obligation in future fiscal years, without fiscal year limitation.'.

SEC. 2004. TWENTY-FIRST AMENDMENT ENFORCEMENT.

(a) SHIPMENT OF INTOXICATING LIQUOR IN VIOLATION OF STATE LAW—The Act entitled 'An Act divesting intoxicating liquors of their interstate character in certain cases', approved March 1, 1913 (commonly known as the 'Webb-Kenyon Act') (27 U.S.C. 122) is amended by adding at the end the following:

'SEC. 2. INJUNCTIVE RELIEF IN FEDERAL DISTRICT COURT.

'(a) DEFINITIONS—In this section—
'(1) the term 'attorney general' means the attorney general or other chief law enforcement officer of a State or the designee thereof;
'(2) the term 'intoxicating liquor' means any spirituous, vinous, malted, fermented, or other intoxicating liquor of any kind;
'(3) the term 'person' means any individual and any partnership, corporation, company, firm, society, association, joint stock company, trust, or other entity capable of holding a legal or beneficial interest in property, but does not include a State or agency thereof; and
'(4) the term 'State' means any State of the United States, the District of Columbia, the Commonwealth of Puerto Rico, or any territory or possession of the United States.
'(b) ACTION BY STATE ATTORNEY GENERAL—If the attorney general has reasonable cause to believe that a person is engaged in, or has engaged in, any act that would constitute a violation of a State law regulating the importation or transportation of any intoxicating liquor, the attorney general may bring a civil action in accordance with this section for injunctive relief (including a preliminary or permanent injunction) against the person, as the attorney general determines to be necessary to—
'(1) restrain the person from engaging, or continuing to engage, in the violation; and
'(2) enforce compliance with the State law.
'(c) FEDERAL JURISDICTION—
'(1) IN GENERAL—The district courts of the United States shall have jurisdiction over any action brought under this section by an attorney general against any person, except one licensed or otherwise authorized to produce, sell, or store intoxicating liquor in such State.

'(2) VENUE—An action under this section may be brought only in accordance with section 1391 of title 28, United States Code, or in the district in which the recipient of the intoxicating liquor resides or is found.

'(3) FORM OF RELIEF—An action under this section is limited to actions seeking injunctive relief (a preliminary and/or permanent injunction).

'(4) NO RIGHT TO JURY TRIAL—An action under this section shall be tried before the court.

'(d) REQUIREMENTS FOR INJUNCTIONS AND ORDERS—

'(1) IN GENERAL—In any action brought under this section, upon a proper showing by the attorney general of the State, the court may issue a preliminary or permanent injunction to restrain a violation of this section. A proper showing under this paragraph shall require that a State prove by a preponderance of the evidence that a violation of State law as described in subsection (b) has taken place or is taking place.

'(2) ADDITIONAL SHOWING FOR PRELIMINARY INJUNCTION—No preliminary injunction may be granted except upon—

'(A) evidence demonstrating the probability of irreparable injury if injunctive relief is not granted; and

'(B) evidence supporting the probability of success on the merits.

'(3) NOTICE—No preliminary or permanent injunction may be issued under paragraph (1) without notice to the adverse party and an opportunity for a hearing.

'(4) FORM AND SCOPE OF ORDER—Any preliminary or permanent injunction entered in an action brought under this section shall—

'(A) set forth the reasons for the issuance of the order;

'(B) be specific in terms;

'(C) describe in reasonable detail, and not by reference to the complaint or other document, the act or acts sought to be restrained; and

'(D) be binding upon—

'(i) the parties to the action and the officers, agents, employees, and attorneys of those parties; and

'(ii) persons in active concert or participation with the parties to the action who receive actual notice of the order by personal service or otherwise.

'(5) ADMISSIBILITY OF EVIDENCE—In a hearing on an application for a permanent injunction, any evidence previously received on an application for a preliminary injunction in connection with the same civil action and that would otherwise be admissible, may be made a part of the record of the hearing on the permanent injunction.

'(e) RULES OF CONSTRUCTION—This section shall be construed only to extend the jurisdiction of Federal courts in connection with State law that is a valid exercise of power vested in the States—

'(1) under the twenty-first article of amendment to the Constitution of the United States as such article of amendment is interpreted by the Supreme Court of the United States including interpretations in conjunction with other provisions of the Constitution of the United States; and

'(2) under the first section herein as such section is interpreted by the Supreme Court of the United States; but shall not be construed to grant to States any additional power.

'(f) ADDITIONAL REMEDIES—

'(1) IN GENERAL—A remedy under this section is in addition to any other remedies provided by law.

'(2) STATE COURT PROCEEDINGS—Nothing in this section may be construed to prohibit an authorized State official from proceeding in State court on the basis of an alleged violation of any State law.

'SEC. 3. GENERAL PROVISIONS.

'(a) EFFECT ON INTERNET TAX FREEDOM ACT—Nothing in this section may be construed to modify or supersede the operation of the Internet Tax Freedom Act (47 U.S.C. 151 note).

'(b) INAPPLICABILITY TO SERVICE PROVIDERS—Nothing in this section may be construed to—

'(1) authorize any injunction against an interactive computer service (as defined in section 230(f) of the Communications Act of 1934 (47 U.S.C. 230(f)) used by another person to engage in any activity that is subject to this Act;

'(2) authorize any injunction against an electronic communication service (as defined in section 2510(15) of title 18, United States Code) used by another person to engage in any activity that is subject to this Act; or

'(3) authorize an injunction prohibiting the advertising or marketing of any intoxicating liquor by any person in any case in which such advertising or marketing is lawful in the jurisdiction from which the importation, transportation or other conduct to which this Act applies originates.'.

(b) EFFECTIVE DATE—This section and the amendments made by this section shall become effective 90 days after the date of the enactment of this Act.

(c) STUDY—The Attorney General shall carry out the study to determine the impact of this section and shall submit the results of such study not later than 180 days after the enactment of this Act.

Speaker of the House of Representatives.

Vice President of the United States and

President of the Senate.

Source: U.S. Congress. Victims of Trafficking and Violence Protection Act of 2000. Public Law 106-386. 106th Congress. (January 24, 2000). H.R. 3244. Available at http://www.state.gov/documents/organization/10492.pdf

4. Violence Against Women Act

In Brief:

The 1994 Violent Crime Control and Law Enforcement Act included what is commonly referred to as the Violence Against Women Act (VAWA). The text of Title IV below outlines the provisions of the original VAWA. The law originally included civil remedy for victims, allowing them to sue their attackers in court. This part of VAWA was struck down by the Supreme Court in 2005. VAWA was reauthorized in 2000 and 2005. Reauthorization is being debated in 2012. For more information, see entry in the encyclopedia on **Violence against Women Act (VAWA).**

Bill Text
103rd Congress (1993-1994)
H.R.3355.ENR

H.R.3355

Violent Crime Control and Law Enforcement Act of 1994 (Enrolled Bill [Final as Passed Both House and Senate] —ENR)

TITLE IV—VIOLENCE AGAINST WOMEN

SEC. 40001. SHORT TITLE.

This title may be cited as the 'Violence Against Women Act of 1994'.

Subtitle A—Safe Streets for Women

SEC. 40101. SHORT TITLE.

This subtitle may be cited as the 'Safe Streets for Women Act of 1994'.

CHAPTER 1—FEDERAL PENALTIES FOR SEX CRIMES

SEC. 40111. REPEAT OFFENDERS.

(a) IN GENERAL—Chapter 109A of title 18, United States Code, is amended by adding at the end the following new section:

'Sec. 2247. Repeat offenders

'Any person who violates a provision of this chapter, after one or more prior convictions for an offense punishable under this chapter, or after one or more prior convictions under the laws of any State relating to aggravated sexual abuse, sexual abuse, or abusive sexual contact have become final, is punishable by a term of imprisonment up to twice that otherwise authorized.'.

(b) AMENDMENT OF SENTENCING GUIDELINES—The Sentencing Commission shall implement the amendment made by subsection (a) by promulgating amendments, if appropriate, in the sentencing guidelines applicable to chapter 109A offenses.

(c) CHAPTER ANALYSIS—The chapter analysis for chapter 109A of title 18, United States Code, is amended by adding at the end the following new item:
'2247. Repeat offenders.'.

SEC. 40112. FEDERAL PENALTIES.

(a) AMENDMENT OF SENTENCING GUIDELINES—Pursuant to its authority under section 994(p) of title 28, United States Code, the United States Sentencing Commission shall review and amend, where necessary, its sentencing guidelines on aggravated sexual abuse under section 2241 of title 18, United States Code, or sexual abuse under section 2242 of title 18, United States Code, as follows:

(1) The Commission shall review and promulgate amendments to the guidelines, if appropriate, to enhance penalties if more than 1 offender is involved in the offense.

(2) The Commission shall review and promulgate amendments to the guidelines, if appropriate, to reduce unwarranted disparities between the sentences for sex offenders who are known to the victim and sentences for sex offenders who are not known to the victim.

(3) The Commission shall review and promulgate amendments to the guidelines to enhance penalties, if appropriate, to render Federal penalties on Federal territory commensurate with penalties for similar offenses in the States.

(4) The Commission shall review and promulgate amendments to the guidelines, if appropriate, to account for the general problem of recidivism in cases of sex offenses, the severity of the offense, and its devastating effects on survivors.

(b) REPORT—Not later than 180 days after the date of enactment of this Act, the United States Sentencing Commission shall review and submit to Congress a report containing an analysis of Federal rape sentencing, accompanied by comment from independent experts in the field, describing—

(1) comparative Federal sentences for cases in which the rape victim is known to the defendant and cases in which the rape victim is not known to the defendant;

(2) comparative Federal sentences for cases on Federal territory and sentences in surrounding States; and

(3) an analysis of the effect of rape sentences on populations residing primarily on Federal territory relative to the impact of other Federal offenses in which the existence of Federal jurisdiction depends upon the offense's being committed on Federal territory.

SEC. 40113. MANDATORY RESTITUTION FOR SEX CRIMES.

(a) SEXUAL ABUSE—
(1) IN GENERAL—Chapter 109A of title 18, United States Code, is amended by adding at the end the following new section:

'Sec. 2248. Mandatory restitution

'(a) IN GENERAL—Notwithstanding section 3663, and in addition to any other civil or criminal penalty authorized by law, the court shall order restitution for any offense under this chapter.

'(b) SCOPE AND NATURE OF ORDER—
'(1) DIRECTIONS—The order of restitution under this section shall direct that—
'(A) the defendant pay to the victim (through the appropriate court mechanism) the full amount of the victim's losses as determined by the court, pursuant to paragraph (3); and
'(B) the United States Attorney enforce the restitution order by all available and reasonable means.
'(2) ENFORCEMENT BY VICTIM—An order of restitution also may be enforced by a victim named in the order to receive the restitution in the same manner as a judgment in a civil action.
'(3) DEFINITION—For purposes of this subsection, the term 'full amount of the victim's losses' includes any costs incurred by the victim for—
'(A) medical services relating to physical, psychiatric, or psychological care;
'(B) physical and occupational therapy or rehabilitation;
'(C) necessary transportation, temporary housing, and child care expenses;
'(D) lost income;
'(E) attorneys' fees, plus any costs incurred in obtaining a civil protection order; and
'(F) any other losses suffered by the victim as a proximate result of the offense.
'(4) ORDER MANDATORY—(A) The issuance of a restitution order under this section is mandatory.

'(B) A court may not decline to issue an order under this section because of—
>'(i) the economic circumstances of the defendant; or
>'(ii) the fact that a victim has, or is entitled to, receive compensation for his or her injuries from the proceeds of insurance or any other source.

'(C)(i) Notwithstanding subparagraph (A), the court may take into account the economic circumstances of the defendant in determining the manner in which and the schedule according to which the restitution is to be paid.

'(ii) For purposes of this subparagraph, the term 'economic circumstances' includes—
>'(I) the financial resources and other assets of the defendant;
>'(II) projected earnings, earning capacity, and other income of the defendant; and
>'(III) any financial obligations of the defendant, including obligations to dependents.

'(D) Subparagraph (A) does not apply if—
>'(i) the court finds on the record that the economic circumstances of the defendant do not allow for the payment of any amount of a restitution order, and do not allow for the payment of any or some portion of the amount of a restitution order in the foreseeable future (under any reasonable schedule of payments); and
>'(ii) the court enters in its order the amount of the victim's losses, and provides a nominal restitution award.

'(5) MORE THAN 1 OFFENDER—When the court finds that more than 1 offender has contributed to the loss of a victim, the court may make each offender liable for payment of the full amount of restitution or may apportion liability among the offenders to reflect the level of contribution and economic circumstances of each offender.

'(6) MORE THAN 1 VICTIM—When the court finds that more than 1 victim has sustained a loss requiring restitution by an offender, the court shall order full restitution of each victim but may provide for different payment schedules to reflect the economic circumstances of each victim.

'(7) PAYMENT SCHEDULE—An order under this section may direct the defendant to make a single lump-sum payment or partial payments at specified intervals.

'(8) SETOFF—Any amount paid to a victim under this section shall be set off against any amount later recovered as compensatory damages by the victim from the defendant in—
>'(A) any Federal civil proceeding; and
>'(B) any State civil proceeding, to the extent provided by the law of the State.

'(9) EFFECT ON OTHER SOURCES OF COMPENSATION—The issuance of a restitution order shall not affect the entitlement of a victim to receive compensation with respect to a loss from insurance or any other source until the payments actually received by the victim under the restitution order fully compensate the victim for the loss.

'(10) CONDITION OF PROBATION OR SUPERVISED RELEASE—Compliance with a restitution order issued under this section shall be a condition of any probation or supervised release of a defendant. If an offender fails to comply with a restitution order, the court may, after a hearing, revoke probation or a term of supervised release, modify the terms or conditions of probation or a term of supervised release, or hold the defendant in contempt pursuant to section 3583(e). In determining whether to revoke probation or a term of supervised release, modify the terms or conditions of probation or supervised release or hold a defendant serving a term of supervised release in contempt, the court shall consider the defendant's employment status, earning ability and financial resources, the willfulness of the defendant's failure to comply, and any other circumstances that may have a bearing on the defendant's ability to comply.

'(c) PROOF OF CLAIM—

'(1) AFFIDAVIT—Within 60 days after conviction and, in any event, not later than 10 days prior to sentencing, the United States Attorney (or the United States Attorney's delegee), after consulting with the victim, shall prepare and file an affidavit with the court listing the amounts subject to restitution under this section. The affidavit shall be signed by the United States Attorney (or the United States Attorney's delegee) and the victim. Should the victim object to any of the information included in the affidavit, the United States Attorney (or the United States Attorney's delegee) shall advise the victim that the victim may file a separate affidavit and shall provide the victim with an affidavit form which may be used to do so.

'(2) OBJECTION—If, after the defendant has been notified of the affidavit, no objection is raised by the defendant, the amounts attested to in the affidavit filed pursuant to paragraph (1) shall be entered in the court's restitution order. If objection is raised, the court may require the victim or the United States Attorney (or the United States Attorney's delegee) to submit further affidavits or other supporting documents, demonstrating the victim's losses.

'(3) ADDITIONAL DOCUMENTATION AND TESTIMONY—If the court concludes, after reviewing the supporting documentation and considering the defendant's objections, that there is a substantial reason for doubting the authenticity or veracity of the records submitted, the court may require additional documentation or hear testimony on those questions. The privacy of any records filed, or testimony heard, pursuant to this section shall be maintained to the greatest extent possible, and such records may be filed or testimony heard in camera.

'(4) FINAL DETERMINATION OF LOSSES—If the victim's losses are not ascertainable by the date that is 10 days prior to sentencing as provided in paragraph (1), the United States Attorney (or the United States Attorney's delegee) shall so inform the court, and the court shall set a date for the final determination of the victim's losses, not to exceed 90 days after sentencing. If the victim subsequently discovers further losses, the victim shall have 60 days after discovery of those losses in which to petition the court for an amended restitution order. Such order may be granted only upon a showing of good cause for the failure to include such losses in the initial claim for restitutionary relief.

'(d) MODIFICATION OF ORDER—A victim or the offender may petition the court at any time to modify a restitution order as appropriate in view of a change in the economic circumstances of the offender.

'(e) REFERENCE TO MAGISTRATE OR SPECIAL MASTER—The court may refer any issue arising in connection with a proposed order of restitution to a magistrate or special master for proposed findings of fact and recommendations as to disposition, subject to a de novo determination of the issue by the court.

'(f) DEFINITION—For purposes of this section, the term 'victim' means the individual harmed as a result of a commission of a crime under this chapter, including, in the case of a victim who is under 18 years of age, incompetent, incapacitated, or deceased, the legal guardian of the victim or representative of the victim's estate, another family member, or any other person appointed as suitable by the court, but in no event shall the defendant be named as such representative or guardian.'.

(2) TECHNICAL AMENDMENT—The chapter analysis for chapter 109A of title 18, United States Code, is amended by adding at the end the following new item:

'2248. Mandatory restitution.'.

(b) SEXUAL EXPLOITATION AND OTHER ABUSE OF CHILDREN—

(1) IN GENERAL—Chapter 110 of title 18, United States Code, is amended by adding at the end the following new section:

'Sec. 2259. Mandatory restitution

'(a) IN GENERAL—Notwithstanding section 3663, and in addition to any other civil or criminal penalty authorized by law, the court shall order restitution for any offense under this chapter.

'(b) SCOPE AND NATURE OF ORDER—

'(1) DIRECTIONS—The order of restitution under this section shall direct that—

'(A) the defendant pay to the victim (through the appropriate court mechanism) the full amount of the victim's losses as determined by the court, pursuant to paragraph (3); and

'(B) the United States Attorney enforce the restitution order by all available and reasonable means.

'(2) ENFORCEMENT BY VICTIM—An order of restitution may also be enforced by a victim named in the order to receive the restitution in the same manner as a judgment in a civil action.

'(3) DEFINITION—For purposes of this subsection, the term 'full amount of the victim's losses' includes any costs incurred by the victim for—
    '(A) medical services relating to physical, psychiatric, or psychological care;
    '(B) physical and occupational therapy or rehabilitation;
    '(C) necessary transportation, temporary housing, and child care expenses;
    '(D) lost income;
    '(E) attorneys' fees, as well as other costs incurred; and
    '(F) any other losses suffered by the victim as a proximate result of the offense.
'(4) ORDER MANDATORY—(A) The issuance of a restitution order under this section is mandatory.
'(B) A court may not decline to issue an order under this section because of—
    '(i) the economic circumstances of the defendant; or
    '(ii) the fact that a victim has, or is entitled to, receive compensation for his or her injuries from the proceeds of insurance or any other source.
'(C)(i) Notwithstanding subparagraph (A), the court may take into account the economic circumstances of the defendant in determining the manner in which and the schedule according to which the restitution is to be paid.
'(ii) For purposes of this subparagraph, the term 'economic circumstances' includes—
    '(I) the financial resources and other assets of the defendant;
    '(II) projected earnings, earning capacity, and other income of the defendant; and
    '(III) any financial obligations of the defendant, including obligations to dependents.
'(D) Subparagraph (A) does not apply if—
    '(i) the court finds on the record that the economic circumstances of the defendant do not allow for the payment of any amount of a restitution order, and do not allow for the payment of any or some portion of the amount of a restitution order in the foreseeable future (under any reasonable schedule of payments); and
    '(ii) the court enters in its order the amount of the victim's losses, and provides a nominal restitution award.
'(5) MORE THAN 1 OFFENDER—When the court finds that more than 1 offender has contributed to the loss of a victim, the court may make each offender liable for payment of the full amount of restitution or may apportion liability among the offenders to reflect the level of contribution and economic circumstances of each offender.
'(6) MORE THAN 1 VICTIM—When the court finds that more than 1 victim has sustained a loss requiring restitution by an offender, the court shall order full restitution of each victim but may provide for different payment schedules to reflect the economic circumstances of each victim.

'(7) PAYMENT SCHEDULE—An order under this section may direct the defendant to make a single lump-sum payment or partial payments at specified intervals.

'(8) SETOFF—Any amount paid to a victim under this section shall be set off against any amount later recovered as compensatory damages by the victim from the defendant in—

'(A) any Federal civil proceeding; and

'(B) any State civil proceeding, to the extent provided by the law of the State.

'(9) EFFECT ON OTHER SOURCES OF COMPENSATION—The issuance of a restitution order shall not affect the entitlement of a victim to receive compensation with respect to a loss from insurance or any other source until the payments actually received by the victim under the restitution order fully compensate the victim for the loss.

'(10) CONDITION OF PROBATION OR SUPERVISED RELEASE— Compliance with a restitution order issued under this section shall be a condition of any probation or supervised release of a defendant. If an offender fails to comply with a restitution order, the court may, after a hearing, revoke probation or a term of supervised release, modify the terms or conditions of probation or a term of supervised release, or hold the defendant in contempt pursuant to section 3583(e). In determining whether to revoke probation or a term of supervised release, modify the terms or conditions of probation or supervised release or hold a defendant serving a term of supervised release in contempt, the court shall consider the defendant's employment status, earning ability and financial resources, the willfulness of the defendant's failure to comply, and any other circumstances that may have a bearing on the defendant's ability to comply.

'(c) PROOF OF CLAIM—

'(1) AFFIDAVIT—Within 60 days after conviction and, in any event, not later than 10 days prior to sentencing, the United States Attorney (or the United States Attorney's delegee), after consulting with the victim, shall prepare and file an affidavit with the court listing the amounts subject to restitution under this section. The affidavit shall be signed by the United States Attorney (or the United States Attorney's delegee) and the victim. Should the victim object to any of the information included in the affidavit, the United States Attorney (or the United States Attorney's delegee) shall advise the victim that the victim may file a separate affidavit and shall provide the victim with an affidavit form which may be used to do so.

'(2) OBJECTION—If, after the defendant has been notified of the affidavit, no objection is raised by the defendant, the amounts attested to in the affidavit filed pursuant to paragraph (1) shall be entered in the court's restitution order. If objection is raised, the court may require the victim or the United States Attorney (or the United States Attorney's delegee) to submit further affidavits or other supporting documents, demonstrating the victim's losses.

'(3) ADDITIONAL DOCUMENTATION AND TESTIMONY—If the court concludes, after reviewing the supporting documentation and considering the defendant's objections, that there is a substantial reason for doubting the authenticity or veracity of the records submitted, the court may require additional documentation or hear testimony on those questions.

CHAPTER 2—LAW ENFORCEMENT AND PROSECUTION GRANTS TO REDUCE VIOLENT CRIMES AGAINST WOMEN

SEC. 40121. GRANTS TO COMBAT VIOLENT CRIMES AGAINST WOMEN.

(a) IN GENERAL—Title I of the Omnibus Crime Control and Safe Streets Act of 1968 (42 U.S.C. 3711 et seq.), as amended by section 32101(a), is amended—
    (1) by redesignating part T as part U;
    (2) by redesignating section 2001 as section 2101; and
    (3) by inserting after part S the following new part:

'Part T—Grants To Combat Violent Crimes Against Women

'SEC. 2001. PURPOSE OF THE PROGRAM AND GRANTS.

'(a) GENERAL PROGRAM PURPOSE—The purpose of this part is to assist States, Indian tribal governments, and units of local government to develop and strengthen effective law enforcement and prosecution strategies to combat violent crimes against women, and to develop and strengthen victim services in cases involving violent crimes against women.

'(b) PURPOSES FOR WHICH GRANTS MAY BE USED—Grants under this part shall provide personnel, training, technical assistance, data collection and other equipment for the more widespread apprehension, prosecution, and adjudication of persons committing violent crimes against women, and specifically, for the purposes of—

    '(1) training law enforcement officers and prosecutors to more effectively identify and respond to violent crimes against women, including the crimes of sexual assault and domestic violence;

    '(2) developing, training, or expanding units of law enforcement officers and prosecutors specifically targeting violent crimes against women, including the crimes of sexual assault and domestic violence;

    '(3) developing and implementing more effective police and prosecution policies, protocols, orders, and services specifically devoted to preventing, identifying, and responding to violent crimes against women, including the crimes of sexual assault and domestic violence;

'(4) developing, installing, or expanding data collection and communication systems, including computerized systems, linking police, prosecutors, and courts or for the purpose of identifying and tracking arrests, protection orders, violations of protection orders, prosecutions, and convictions for violent crimes against women, including the crimes of sexual assault and domestic violence;

'(5) developing, enlarging, or strengthening victim services programs, including sexual assault and domestic violence programs, developing or improving delivery of victim services to racial, cultural, ethnic, and language minorities, providing specialized domestic violence court advocates in courts where a significant number of protection orders are granted, and increasing reporting and reducing attrition rates for cases involving violent crimes against women, including crimes of sexual assault and domestic violence;

'(6) developing, enlarging, or strengthening programs addressing stalking; and

'(7) developing, enlarging, or strengthening programs addressing the needs and circumstances of Indian tribes in dealing with violent crimes against women, including the crimes of sexual assault and domestic violence.

'SEC. 2002. STATE GRANTS.

'(a) GENERAL GRANTS—The Attorney General may make grants to States, for use by States, units of local government, nonprofit nongovernmental victim services programs, and Indian tribal governments for the purposes described in section 2001(b).

'(b) AMOUNTS—Of the amounts appropriated for the purposes of this part—

'(1) 4 percent shall be available for grants to Indian tribal governments;

'(2) $500,000 shall be available for grants to applicants in each State; and

'(3) the remaining funds shall be available for grants to applicants in each State in an amount that bears the same ratio to the amount of remaining funds as the population of the State bears to the population of all of the States that results from a distribution among the States on the basis of each State's population in relation to the population of all States (not including populations of Indian tribes).

'(c) QUALIFICATION—Upon satisfying the terms of subsection (d), any State shall be qualified for funds provided under this part upon certification that—

'(1) the funds shall be used for any of the purposes described in section 2001(b);

'(2) grantees and subgrantees shall develop a plan for implementation and shall consult and coordinate with nonprofit, nongovernmental victim services programs, including sexual assault and domestic violence victim services programs;

'(3) at least 25 percent of the amount granted shall be allocated, without duplication, to each of the following 3 areas: prosecution, law enforcement, and victim services; and

'(4) any Federal funds received under this part shall be used to supplement, not supplant, non-Federal funds that would otherwise be available for activities funded under this subtitle.

'(d) APPLICATION REQUIREMENTS—The application requirements provided in section 513 shall apply to grants made under this part. In addition, each application shall include the certifications of qualification required by subsection (c), including documentation from nonprofit, nongovernmental victim services programs, describing their participation in developing the plan required by subsection (c)(2). An application shall include—

'(1) documentation from the prosecution, law enforcement, and victim services programs to be assisted, demonstrating—

'(A) need for the grant funds;
'(B) intended use of the grant funds;
'(C) expected results from the use of grant funds; and
'(D) demographic characteristics of the populations to be served, including age, marital status, disability, race, ethnicity and language background;

'(2) proof of compliance with the requirements for the payment of forensic medical exams provided in section 2005; and

'(3) proof of compliance with the requirements for paying filing and service fees for domestic violence cases provided in section 2006.

'(e) DISBURSEMENT—

'(1) IN GENERAL—Not later than 60 days after the receipt of an application under this part, the Attorney General shall—

'(A) disburse the appropriate sums provided for under this part; or
'(B) inform the applicant why the application does not conform to the terms of section 513 or to the requirements of this section.

'(2) REGULATIONS—In disbursing monies under this part, the Attorney General shall issue regulations to ensure that States will—

'(A) give priority to areas of varying geographic size with the greatest showing of need based on the availability of existing domestic violence and sexual assault programs in the population and geographic area to be served in relation to the availability of such programs in other such populations and geographic areas;
'(B) determine the amount of subgrants based on the population and geographic area to be served;
'(C) equitably distribute monies on a geographic basis including nonurban and rural areas of various geographic sizes; and
'(D) recognize and address the needs of underserved populations.

'(f) FEDERAL SHARE—The Federal share of a grant made under this subtitle may not exceed 75 percent of the total costs of the projects described in the application submitted.

'(g) INDIAN TRIBES—Funds appropriated by the Congress for the activities of any agency of an Indian tribal government or of the Bureau of Indian Affairs performing law enforcement functions on any Indian lands may be used to provide the non-Federal share of the cost of programs or projects funded under this part.

'(h) GRANTEE REPORTING—

'(1) IN GENERAL—Upon completion of the grant period under this part, a State or Indian tribal grantee shall file a performance report with the Attorney General explaining the activities carried out, which report shall include an assessment of the effectiveness of those activities in achieving the purposes of this part.

'(2) CERTIFICATION BY GRANTEE AND SUBGRANTEES—A section of the performance report shall be completed by each grantee and subgrantee that performed the direct services contemplated in the application, certifying performance of direct services under the grant.

'(3) SUSPENSION OF FUNDING—The Attorney General shall suspend funding for an approved application if—

'(A) an applicant fails to submit an annual performance report;
'(B) funds are expended for purposes other than those described in this part; or
'(C) a report under paragraph (1) or accompanying assessments demonstrate to the Attorney General that the program is ineffective or financially unsound.

'SEC. 2003. DEFINITIONS.

'In this part—

'(1) the term 'domestic violence' includes felony or misdemeanor crimes of violence committed by a current or former spouse of the victim, by a person with whom the victim shares a child in common, by a person who is cohabitating with or has cohabitated with the victim as a spouse, by a person similarly situated to a spouse of the victim under the domestic or family violence laws of the jurisdiction receiving grant monies, or by any other adult person against a victim who is protected from that person's acts under the domestic or family violence laws of the jurisdiction receiving grant monies;

'(2) the term 'Indian country' has the meaning stated in section 1151 of title 18, United States Code;

'(3) the term 'Indian tribe' means a tribe, band, pueblo, nation, or other organized group or community of Indians, including any Alaska Native village or regional or village corporation (as defined in, or established pursuant to, the Alaska Native Claims Settlement Act (43 U.S.C. 1601 et seq.)), that is recognized as eligible for the special programs and services provided by the United States to Indians because of their status as Indians;

'(4) the term 'law enforcement' means a public agency charged with policing functions, including any of its component bureaus (such as governmental victim services programs);

'(5) the term 'prosecution' means any public agency charged with direct responsibility for prosecuting criminal offenders, including such agency's component bureaus (such as governmental victim services programs);

'(6) the term 'sexual assault' means any conduct proscribed by chapter 109A of title 18, United States Code, whether or not the conduct occurs in the special maritime and territorial jurisdiction of the United States or in a Federal prison and includes both assaults committed by offenders who are strangers to the victim and assaults committed by offenders who are known or related by blood or marriage to the victim;

'(7) the term 'underserved populations' includes populations underserved because of geographic location (such as rural isolation), underserved racial or ethnic populations, and populations underserved because of special needs, such as language barriers or physical disabilities; and

'(8) the term 'victim services' means a nonprofit, nongovernmental organization that assists domestic violence or sexual assault victims, including rape crisis centers, battered women's shelters, and other sexual assault or domestic violence programs, including nonprofit, nongovernmental organizations assisting domestic violence or sexual assault victims through the legal process.

'SEC. 2004. GENERAL TERMS AND CONDITIONS.

'(a) NONMONETARY ASSISTANCE—In addition to the assistance provided under this part, the Attorney General may request any Federal agency to use its authorities and the resources granted to it under Federal law (including personnel, equipment, supplies, facilities, and managerial, technical, and advisory services) in support of State, tribal, and local assistance efforts.

'(b) REPORTING—Not later than 180 days after the end of each fiscal year for which grants are made under this part, the Attorney General shall submit to the Committee on the Judiciary of the House of Representatives and the Committee on the Judiciary of the Senate a report that includes, for each State and for each grantee Indian tribe—

'(1) the number of grants made and funds distributed under this part;

'(2) a summary of the purposes for which those grants were provided and an evaluation of their progress;

'(3) a statistical summary of persons served, detailing the nature of victimization, and providing data on age, sex, relationship of victim to offender, geographic distribution, race, ethnicity, language, and disability; and

'(4) an evaluation of the effectiveness of programs funded under this part.

'(c) REGULATIONS OR GUIDELINES—Not later than 120 days after the date of enactment of this part, the Attorney General shall publish proposed regulations or guidelines implementing this part. Not later than 180 days after the date of enactment, the Attorney General shall publish final regulations or guidelines implementing this part.

'SEC. 2005. RAPE EXAM PAYMENTS.

'(a) RESTRICTION OF FUNDS—
'(1) IN GENERAL—A State, Indian tribal government, or unit of local government, shall not be entitled to funds under this part unless the State, Indian tribal government, unit of local government, or another governmental entity incurs the full out-of-pocket cost of forensic medical exams described in subsection (b) for victims of sexual assault.
'(2) REDISTRIBUTION—Funds withheld from a State or unit of local government under paragraph (1) shall be distributed to other States or units of local government pro rata. Funds withheld from an Indian tribal government under paragraph (1) shall be distributed to other Indian tribal governments pro rata.
'(b) MEDICAL COSTS—A State, Indian tribal government, or unit of local government shall be deemed to incur the full out-of-pocket cost of forensic medical exams for victims of sexual assault if any government entity—
'(1) provides such exams to victims free of charge to the victim;
'(2) arranges for victims to obtain such exams free of charge to the victims; or
'(3) reimburses victims for the cost of such exams if—
'(A) the reimbursement covers the full cost of such exams, without any deductible requirement or limit on the amount of a reimbursement;
'(B) the reimbursing governmental entity permits victims to apply for reimbursement for not less than one year from the date of the exam;
'(C) the reimbursing governmental entity provides reimbursement not later than 90 days after written notification of the victim's expense; and
'(D) the State, Indian tribal government, unit of local government, or reimbursing governmental entity provides information at the time of the exam to all victims, including victims with limited or no English proficiency, regarding how to obtain reimbursement.

'SEC. 2006. FILING COSTS FOR CRIMINAL CHARGES.

'(a) IN GENERAL—A State, Indian tribal government, or unit of local government, shall not be entitled to funds under this part unless the State, Indian tribal government, or unit of local government—
'(1) certifies that its laws, policies, and practices do not require, in connection with the prosecution of any misdemeanor or felony domestic violence offense, that the abused bear the costs associated with the filing of criminal charges against the domestic violence offender, or the costs associated with the issuance or service of a warrant, protection order, or witness subpoena; or
'(2) gives the Attorney General assurances that its laws, policies and practices will be in compliance with the requirements of paragraph (1) within the later of—

'(A) the period ending on the date on which the next session of the State legislature ends; or

'(B) 2 years.

'(b) REDISTRIBUTION—Funds withheld from a State, unit of local government, or Indian tribal government under subsection (a) shall be distributed to other States, units of local government, and Indian tribal government, respectively, pro rata.'.

(b) TECHNICAL AMENDMENT—The table of contents of title I of the Omnibus Crime Control and Safe Streets Act of 1968 (42 U.S.C. 3711 et seq.), as amended by section 32101(b), is amended by striking the matter relating to part T and inserting the following:

'Part T—Grants To Combat Violent Crimes Against Women

'Sec. 2001. Purpose of the program and grants.
'Sec. 2002. State grants.
'Sec. 2003. General definitions.
'Sec. 2004. General terms and conditions.
'Sec. 2005. Rape exam payments.
'Sec. 2006. Filing costs for criminal charges.

'Part U—Transition—Effective Date—Repealer

'Sec. 2101. Continuation of rules, authorities, and proceedings.'.

(c) AUTHORIZATION OF APPROPRIATIONS—Section 1001(a) of title I of the Omnibus Crime Control and Safe Streets Act of 1968 (42 U.S.C. 3793), as amended by section 32101(d), is amended—

(1) in paragraph (3) by striking 'and S' and inserting 'S, and T'; and

(2) by adding at the end the following new paragraph:

'(18) There are authorized to be appropriated to carry out part T—

'(A) $26,000,000 for fiscal year 1995;
'(B) $130,000,000 for fiscal year 1996;
'(C) $145,000,000 for fiscal year 1997;
'(D) $160,000,000 for fiscal year 1998;
'(E) $165,000,000 for fiscal year 1999; and
'(F) $174,000,000 for fiscal year 2000.'.

CHAPTER 3—SAFETY FOR WOMEN IN PUBLIC TRANSIT AND PUBLIC PARKS

SEC. 40131. GRANTS FOR CAPITAL IMPROVEMENTS TO PREVENT CRIME IN PUBLIC TRANSPORTATION.

(a) GENERAL PURPOSE—There is authorized to be appropriated not to exceed $10,000,000, for the Secretary of Transportation (referred to in this section as the 'Secretary') to make capital grants for the prevention of crime and to increase security in existing and future public transportation systems. None of the provisions of this Act may be construed to prohibit the financing of projects under this section where law enforcement responsibilities are vested in a local public body other than the grant applicant.

(b) GRANTS FOR LIGHTING, CAMERA SURVEILLANCE, AND SECURITY PHONES—

(1) From the sums authorized for expenditure under this section for crime prevention, the Secretary is authorized to make grants and loans to States and local public bodies or agencies for the purpose of increasing the safety of public transportation by—

(A) increasing lighting within or adjacent to public transportation systems, including bus stops, subway stations, parking lots, or garages;

(B) increasing camera surveillance of areas within and adjacent to public transportation systems, including bus stops, subway stations, parking lots, or garages;

(C) providing emergency phone lines to contact law enforcement or security personnel in areas within or adjacent to public transportation systems, including bus stops, subway stations, parking lots, or garages; or

(D) any other project intended to increase the security and safety of existing or planned public transportation systems.

(2) From the sums authorized under this section, at least 75 percent shall be expended on projects of the type described in subsection (b)(1) (A) and (B).

(c) REPORTING—All grants under this section are contingent upon the filing of a report with the Secretary and the Department of Justice, Office of Victims of Crime, showing crime rates in or adjacent to public transportation before, and for a 1-year period after, the capital improvement. Statistics shall be compiled on the basis of the type of crime, sex, race, ethnicity, language, and relationship of victim to the offender.

(d) INCREASED FEDERAL SHARE—Notwithstanding any other provision of law, the Federal share under this section for each capital improvement project that enhances the safety and security of public transportation systems and that is not required by law (including any other provision of this Act) shall be 90 percent of the net project cost of the project.

(e) SPECIAL GRANTS FOR PROJECTS TO STUDY INCREASING SECURITY FOR WOMEN—From the sums authorized under this section, the Secretary shall provide grants and loans for the purpose of studying ways to reduce violent crimes against women in public transit through better design or operation of public transit systems.

(f) GENERAL REQUIREMENTS—All grants or loans provided under this section shall be subject to the same terms, conditions, requirements, and provisions applicable to grants and loans as specified in section 5321 of title 49, United States Code.

SEC. 40132. GRANTS FOR CAPITAL IMPROVEMENTS TO PREVENT CRIME IN NATIONAL PARKS.

Public Law 91-383 (16 U.S.C. 1a-1 et seq.) is amended by adding at the end the following new section:

'SEC. 13. NATIONAL PARK SYSTEM CRIME PREVENTION ASSISTANCE.

'(a) AVAILABILITY OF FUNDS—There are authorized to be appropriated out of the Violent Crime Reduction Trust Fund, not to exceed $10,000,000, for the Secretary of the Interior to take all necessary actions to seek to reduce the incidence of violent crime in the National Park System.

'(b) RECOMMENDATIONS FOR IMPROVEMENT—The Secretary shall direct the chief official responsible for law enforcement within the National Park Service to—

'(1) compile a list of areas within the National Park System with the highest rates of violent crime;

'(2) make recommendations concerning capital improvements, and other measures, needed within the National Park System to reduce the rates of violent crime, including the rate of sexual assault; and

'(3) publish the information required by paragraphs (1) and (2) in the Federal Register.

'(c) DISTRIBUTION OF FUNDS—Based on the recommendations and list issued pursuant to subsection (b), the Secretary shall distribute the funds authorized by subsection (a) throughout the National Park System. Priority shall be given to those areas with the highest rates of sexual assault.

'(d) USE OF FUNDS—Funds provided under this section may be used—

'(1) to increase lighting within or adjacent to National Park System units;

'(2) to provide emergency phone lines to contact law enforcement or security personnel in areas within or adjacent to National Park System units;

'(3) to increase security or law enforcement personnel within or adjacent to National Park System units; or

'(4) for any other project intended to increase the security and safety of National Park System units.'.

SEC. 40133. GRANTS FOR CAPITAL IMPROVEMENTS TO PREVENT CRIME IN PUBLIC PARKS.

Section 6 of the Land and Water Conservation Fund Act of 1965 (16 U.S.C. 460l-8) is amended by adding at the end the following new subsection:

'(h) CAPITAL IMPROVEMENT AND OTHER PROJECTS TO REDUCE CRIME—

'(1) AVAILABILITY OF FUNDS—In addition to assistance for planning projects, and in addition to the projects identified in subsection (e), and from amounts appropriated out of the Violent Crime Reduction Trust Fund, the Secretary may provide financial assistance to the States, not to

exceed $15,000,000, for projects or combinations thereof for the purpose of making capital improvements and other measures to increase safety in urban parks and recreation areas, including funds to—
>   '(A) increase lighting within or adjacent to public parks and recreation areas;
>   '(B) provide emergency phone lines to contact law enforcement or security personnel in areas within or adjacent to public parks and recreation areas;
>   '(C) increase security personnel within or adjacent to public parks and recreation areas; and
>   '(D) fund any other project intended to increase the security and safety of public parks and recreation areas.
'(2) ELIGIBILITY—In addition to the requirements for project approval imposed by this section, eligibility for assistance under this subsection shall be dependent upon a showing of need. In providing funds under this subsection, the Secretary shall give priority to projects proposed for urban parks and recreation areas with the highest rates of crime and, in particular, to urban parks and recreation areas with the highest rates of sexual assault.
'(3) FEDERAL SHARE—Notwithstanding subsection (c), the Secretary may provide 70 percent improvement grants for projects undertaken by any State for the purposes described in this subsection, and the remaining share of the cost shall be borne by the State.'.

CHAPTER 4—NEW EVIDENTIARY RULES

SEC. 40141. SEXUAL HISTORY IN CRIMINAL AND CIVIL CASES.

(a) MODIFICATION OF PROPOSED AMENDMENT—The proposed amendments to the Federal Rules of Evidence that are embraced by an order entered by the Supreme Court of the United States on April 29, 1994, shall take effect on December 1, 1994, as otherwise provided by law, but with the amendment made by subsection (b).
(b) RULE—Rule 412 of the Federal Rules of Evidence is amended to read as follows:

'**Rule 412. Sex Offense Cases; Relevance of Alleged Victim's Past Sexual Behavior or Alleged Sexual Predisposition**

'(a) EVIDENCE GENERALLY INADMISSIBLE—The following evidence is not admissible in any civil or criminal proceeding involving alleged sexual misconduct except as provided in subdivisions (b) and (c):
   '(1) Evidence offered to prove that any alleged victim engaged in other sexual behavior.
   '(2) Evidence offered to prove any alleged victim's sexual predisposition.
'(b) EXCEPTIONS—
   '(1) In a criminal case, the following evidence is admissible, if otherwise admissible under these rules:

'(A) evidence of specific instances of sexual behavior by the alleged victim offered to prove that a person other than the accused was the source of semen, injury or other physical evidence;
'(B) evidence of specific instances of sexual behavior by the alleged victim with respect to the person accused of the sexual misconduct offered by the accused to prove consent or by the prosecution; and
'(C) evidence the exclusion of which would violate the constitutional rights of the defendant.
'(2) In a civil case, evidence offered to prove the sexual behavior or sexual predisposition of any alleged victim is admissible if it is otherwise admissible under these rules and its probative value substantially outweighs the danger of harm to any victim and of unfair prejudice to any party.

SEC. 40151. EDUCATION AND PREVENTION GRANTS TO REDUCE SEXUAL ASSAULTS AGAINST WOMEN.

Part A of title XIX of the Public Health and Human Services Act (42 U.S.C. 300w et seq.) is amended by adding at the end the following new section:

'SEC. 1910A. USE OF ALLOTMENTS FOR RAPE PREVENTION EDUCATION.

'(a) PERMITTED USE—Notwithstanding section 1904(a)(1), amounts transferred by the State for use under this part may be used for rape prevention and education programs conducted by rape crisis centers or similar nongovernmental nonprofit entities for—
  '(1) educational seminars;
  '(2) the operation of hotlines;
  '(3) training programs for professionals;
  '(4) the preparation of informational materials; and
  '(5) other efforts to increase awareness of the facts about, or to help prevent, sexual assault, including efforts to increase awareness in underserved racial, ethnic, and language minority communities.
'(b) TARGETING OF EDUCATION PROGRAMS—States providing grant monies must ensure that at least 25 percent of the monies are devoted to education programs targeted for middle school, junior high school, and high school students.
'(c) AUTHORIZATION OF APPROPRIATIONS—There are authorized to be appropriated to carry out this section—
  '(1) $35,000,000 for fiscal year 1996;
  '(2) $35,000,000 for fiscal year 1997;
  '(3) $45,000,000 for fiscal year 1998;
  '(4) $45,000,000 for fiscal year 1999; and
  '(5) $45,000,000 for fiscal year 2000.

'(d) LIMITATION—Funds authorized under this section may only be used for providing rape prevention and education programs.

'(e) DEFINITION—For purposes of this section, the term 'rape prevention and education' includes education and prevention efforts directed at offenses committed by offenders who are not known to the victim as well as offenders who are known to the victim.

'(f) TERMS—The Secretary shall make allotments to each State on the basis of the population of the State, and subject to the conditions provided in this section and sections 1904 through 1909.'.

SEC. 40152. TRAINING PROGRAMS.

(a) IN GENERAL—The Attorney General, after consultation with victim advocates and individuals who have expertise in treating sex offenders, shall establish criteria and develop training programs to assist probation and parole officers and other personnel who work with released sex offenders in the areas of—
    (1) case management;
    (2) supervision; and
    (3) relapse prevention.

(b) TRAINING PROGRAMS—The Attorney General shall ensure, to the extent practicable, that training programs developed under subsection (a) are available in geographically diverse locations throughout the country.

(c) AUTHORIZATION OF APPROPRIATIONS—There are authorized to be appropriated to carry out this section—
    (1) $1,000,000 for fiscal year 1996; and
    (2) $1,000,000 for fiscal year 1997.

SEC. 40153. CONFIDENTIALITY OF COMMUNICATIONS BETWEEN SEXUAL ASSAULT OR DOMESTIC VIOLENCE VICTIMS AND THEIR COUNSELORS.

(a) STUDY AND DEVELOPMENT OF MODEL LEGISLATION—The Attorney General shall—
    (1) study and evaluate the manner in which the States have taken measures to protect the confidentiality of communications between sexual assault or domestic violence victims and their therapists or trained counselors;
    (2) develop model legislation that will provide the maximum protection possible for the confidentiality of such communications, within any applicable constitutional limits, taking into account the following factors:
        (A) the danger that counseling programs for victims of sexual assault and domestic violence will be unable to achieve their goal of helping victims recover from the trauma associated with these crimes if there is no assurance that the records of the counseling sessions will be kept confidential;

(B) consideration of the appropriateness of an absolute privilege for communications between victims of sexual assault or domestic violence and their therapists or trained counselors, in light of the likelihood that such an absolute privilege will provide the maximum guarantee of confidentiality but also in light of the possibility that such an absolute privilege may be held to violate the rights of criminal defendants under the Federal or State constitutions by denying them the opportunity to obtain exculpatory evidence and present it at trial; and

(C) consideration of what limitations on the disclosure of confidential communications between victims of these crimes and their counselors, short of an absolute privilege, are most likely to ensure that the counseling programs will not be undermined, and specifically whether no such disclosure should be allowed unless, at a minimum, there has been a particularized showing by a criminal defendant of a compelling need for records of such communications, and adequate procedural safeguards are in place to prevent unnecessary or damaging disclosures; and

(3) prepare and disseminate to State authorities the findings made and model legislation developed as a result of the study and evaluation.

(b) REPORT AND RECOMMENDATIONS—Not later than the date that is 1 year after the date of enactment of this Act, the Attorney General shall report to the Congress—

(1) the findings of the study and the model legislation required by this section; and

(2) recommendations based on the findings on the need for and appropriateness of further action by the Federal Government.

(c) REVIEW OF FEDERAL EVIDENTIARY RULES—The Judicial Conference of the United States shall evaluate and report to Congress its views on whether the Federal Rules of Evidence should be amended, and if so, how they should be amended, to guarantee that the confidentiality of communications between sexual assault victims and their therapists or trained counselors will be adequately protected in Federal court proceedings.

SEC. 40154. INFORMATION PROGRAMS.

The Attorney General shall compile information regarding sex offender treatment programs and ensure that information regarding community treatment programs in the community into which a convicted sex offender is released is made available to each person serving a sentence of imprisonment in a Federal penal or correctional institution for a commission of an offense under chapter 109A of title 18, United States Code, or for the commission of a similar offense, including halfway houses and psychiatric institutions.

SEC. 40155. EDUCATION AND PREVENTION GRANTS TO REDUCE SEXUAL ABUSE OF RUNAWAY, HOMELESS, AND STREET YOUTH.

Part A of the Runaway and Homeless Youth Act (42 U.S.C. 5711 et seq.) is amended—

(1) by redesignating sections 316 and 317 as sections 317 and 318, respectively; and

(2) by inserting after section 315 the following new section:

'GRANTS FOR PREVENTION OF SEXUAL ABUSE AND EXPLOITATION

'SEC. 316. (a) IN GENERAL—The Secretary shall make grants under this section to private, nonprofit agencies for street-based outreach and education, including treatment, counseling, provision of information, and referral for runaway, homeless, and street youth who have been subjected to or are at risk of being subjected to sexual abuse.

'(b) PRIORITY—In selecting among applicants for grants under subsection (a), the Secretary shall give priority to agencies that have experience in providing services to runaway, homeless, and street youth.

'(c) AUTHORIZATION OF APPROPRIATIONS—There are authorized to be appropriated to carry out this section—

'(1) $7,000,000 for fiscal year 1996;

'(2) $8,000,000 for fiscal year 1997; and

'(3) $15,000,000 for fiscal year 1998.

'(d) DEFINITIONS—For the purposes of this section—

'(1) the term 'street-based outreach and education' includes education and prevention efforts directed at offenses committed by offenders who are not known to the victim as well as offenders who are known to the victim; and

'(2) the term 'street youth' means a juvenile who spends a significant amount of time on the street or in other areas of exposure to encounters that may lead to sexual abuse.'.

SEC. 40156. VICTIMS OF CHILD ABUSE PROGRAMS.

(a) COURT-APPOINTED SPECIAL ADVOCATE PROGRAM—

(1) REAUTHORIZATION—Section 218(a) of the Victims of Child Abuse Act of 1990 (42 U.S.C. 13014(a)) is amended to read as follows:

'(a) AUTHORIZATION—There are authorized to be appropriated to carry out this subtitle—

'(1) $6,000,000 for fiscal year 1996;

'(2) $6,000,000 for fiscal year 1997;

'(3) $7,000,000 for fiscal year 1998;

'(4) $9,000,000 for fiscal year 1999; and

'(5) $10,000,000 for fiscal year 2000.'.

(2) TECHNICAL AMENDMENT—Section 216 of the Victims of Child Abuse Act of 1990 (42 U.S.C. 13012) is amended by striking 'this chapter' and inserting 'this subtitle'.

(b) CHILD ABUSE TRAINING PROGRAMS FOR JUDICIAL PERSONNEL AND PRACTITIONERS—

(1) REAUTHORIZATION—Section 224(a) of the Victims of Child Abuse Act of 1990 (42 U.S.C. 13024(a)) is amended to read as follows:

'(a) AUTHORIZATION—There are authorized to be appropriated to carry out this subtitle—

'(1) $750,000 for fiscal year 1996;

'(2) $1,000,000 for fiscal year 1997;

'(3) $2,000,000 for fiscal year 1998;

'(4) $2,000,000 for fiscal year 1999; and

'(5) $2,300,000 for fiscal year 2000.'.

(2) TECHNICAL AMENDMENT—Section 221(b) of the Victims of Child Abuse Act of 1990 (42 U.S.C. 13021(b)) is amended by striking 'this chapter' and inserting 'this subtitle'.

(c) GRANTS FOR TELEVISED TESTIMONY—Title I of the Omnibus Crime Control and Safe Streets Act of 1968 is amended—

(1) by amending section 1001(a)(7) (42 U.S.C. 3793(a)(7)) to read as follows:

'(7) There are authorized to be appropriated to carry out part N—

'(A) $250,000 for fiscal year 1996;

'(B) $1,000,000 for fiscal year 1997;

'(C) $1,000,000 for fiscal year 1998;

'(D) $1,000,000 for fiscal year 1999; and

'(E) $1,000,000 for fiscal year 2000.';

(2) in section 1402 (42 U.S.C. 3796aa-1) by striking 'to States, for the use of States and units of local government in the States';

(3) in section 1403 (42 U.S.C. 3796aa-2)—

    (A) by inserting 'or unit of local government' after 'of a State';

    (B) by inserting 'and' after paragraph (1);

    (C) in paragraph (2) by striking the semicolon at the end and inserting a period; and

    (D) by striking paragraphs (3) and (4);

(4) in section 1404 (42 U.S.C. 3796aa-3)—

    (A) in subsection (a)—

        (i) by striking 'The Bureau' and all that follows through 'determining that' and inserting 'An applicant is eligible to receive a grant under this part if—';

        (ii) in paragraph (1) by striking 'there is in effect in such State' and inserting 'the applicant certifies and the Director determines that there is in effect in the State';

(iii) in paragraph (2) by striking 'such State law shall meet' and inserting 'the applicant certifies and the Director determines that State law meets';

(iv) by inserting 'and' after subparagraph (E);

(v) in paragraph (3)—

(I) by inserting 'the Director determines that' before 'the application'; and

(II) by striking '; and' and inserting a period;

(vi) by striking paragraph (4);

(vii) by striking 'Each application' and inserting the following: '(b) Each application'; and

(viii) by striking 'the Bureau' each place it appears and inserting 'the Director'; and

(B) by redesignating subsection (b) as subsection (c) and by striking 'The Bureau' and inserting 'The Director';

(5) by striking section 1405 (42 U.S.C. 3796aa-4);

(6) in section 1406 (42 U.S.C. 3796aa-5)—

(A) in subsection (a)—

(i) by striking 'State which' and inserting 'State or unit of local government that';

(ii) by striking 'title' and inserting 'part'; and

(iii) in paragraph (1) by striking 'State'; and

(B) in subsection (b)(1) by striking 'such State' and inserting 'the State and units of local government in the State';

(7) in section 1407 (42 U.S.C. 3796aa-6)—

(A) in subsection (c)—

(i) by striking 'Each State' and all that follows through 'effective audit' and inserting 'Grant recipients (or private organizations with which grant recipients have contracted to provide equipment or training using grant funds) shall keep such records as the Director may require by rule to facilitate such an audit.'; and

(ii) in paragraph (2) by striking 'States which receive grants, and of units of local government which receive any part of a grant made under this part' and inserting 'grant recipients (or private organizations with which grant recipients have contracted to provide equipment or training using grant funds)'; and

(B) by adding at the end the following new subsection:

'(d) UTILIZATION OF PRIVATE SECTOR—Nothing in this part shall prohibit the utilization of any grant funds to contract with a private organization to provide equipment or training for the televising of testimony as contemplated by the application submitted by an applicant.';

(8) by striking section 1408 (42 U.S.C. 3796aa-7); and

(9) in the table of contents—

(A) in the item relating to section 1405 by striking 'Allocation and distribution of funds under formula grants' and inserting '(Repealed)'; and
(B) in the item relating to section 1408 by striking 'State office' and inserting '(Repealed)'.

Subtitle B—Safe Homes for Women

SEC. 40201. SHORT TITLE.

This title may be cited as the 'Safe Homes for Women Act of 1994'.

CHAPTER 1—NATIONAL DOMESTIC VIOLENCE HOTLINE

SEC. 40211. GRANT FOR A NATIONAL DOMESTIC VIOLENCE HOTLINE.

The Family Violence Prevention and Services Act (42 U.S.C. 10401 et seq.) is amended by adding at the end the following new section:

'SEC. 316. NATIONAL DOMESTIC VIOLENCE HOTLINE GRANT.

'(a) IN GENERAL—The Secretary may award a grant to a private, nonprofit entity to provide for the operation of a national, toll-free telephone hotline to provide information and assistance to victims of domestic violence.
'(b) DURATION—A grant under this section may extend over a period of not more than 5 years.
'(c) ANNUAL APPROVAL—The provision of payments under a grant under this section shall be subject to annual approval by the Secretary and subject to the availability of appropriations for each fiscal year to make the payments.
'(d) ACTIVITIES—Funds received by an entity under this section shall be used to establish and operate a national, toll-free telephone hotline to provide information and assistance to victims of domestic violence. In establishing and operating the hotline, a private, nonprofit entity shall—
    '(1) contract with a carrier for the use of a toll-free telephone line;
    '(2) employ, train, and supervise personnel to answer incoming calls and provide counseling and referral services to callers on a 24-hour-a-day basis;
    '(3) assemble and maintain a current database of information relating to services for victims of domestic violence to which callers may be referred throughout the United States, including information on the availability of shelters that serve battered women; and
    '(4) publicize the hotline to potential users throughout the United States.
'(e) APPLICATION—A grant may not be made under this section unless an application for such grant has been approved by the Secretary. To be approved by the Secretary under this subsection an application shall—
    '(1) contain such agreements, assurances, and information, be in such form and be submitted in such manner as the Secretary shall prescribe through notice in the Federal Register;

'(2) include a complete description of the applicant's plan for the operation of a national domestic violence hotline, including descriptions of—
  '(A) the training program for hotline personnel;
  '(B) the hiring criteria for hotline personnel;
  '(C) the methods for the creation, maintenance and updating of a resource database;
  '(D) a plan for publicizing the availability of the hotline;
  '(E) a plan for providing service to non-English speaking callers, including hotline personnel who speak Spanish; and
  '(F) a plan for facilitating access to the hotline by persons with hearing impairments;
'(3) demonstrate that the applicant has nationally recognized expertise in the area of domestic violence and a record of high quality service to victims of domestic violence, including a demonstration of support from advocacy groups, such as domestic violence State coalitions or recognized national domestic violence groups;
'(4) demonstrates that the applicant has a commitment to diversity, and to the provision of services to ethnic, racial, and non-English speaking minorities, in addition to older individuals and individuals with disabilities; and
'(5) contain such other information as the Secretary may require.
'(f) AUTHORIZATION OF APPROPRIATIONS—
  '(1) IN GENERAL—There are authorized to be appropriated to carry out this section—
    '(A) $1,000,000 for fiscal year 1995;
    '(B) $400,000 for fiscal year 1996;
    '(C) $400,000 for fiscal year 1997;
    '(D) $400,000 for fiscal year 1998;
    '(E) $400,000 for fiscal year 1999; and
    '(F) $400,000 for fiscal year 2000.
  '(2) AVAILABILITY—Funds authorized to be appropriated under paragraph (1) shall remain available until expended.'.

CHAPTER 2—INTERSTATE ENFORCEMENT

SEC. 40221. INTERSTATE ENFORCEMENT.

(a) IN GENERAL—Part 1 of title 18, United States Code, is amended by inserting after chapter 110 the following new chapter:

'CHAPTER 110A—DOMESTIC VIOLENCE

'Sec. 2261. Interstate domestic violence.
'Sec. 2262. Interstate violation of protection order.
'Sec. 2263. Pretrial release of defendant.
'Sec. 2264. Restitution.

'Sec. 2265. Full faith and credit given to protection orders.
'Sec. 2266. Definitions.

'Sec. 2261. Interstate domestic violence

'(a) OFFENSES—
'(1) CROSSING A STATE LINE—A person who travels across a State line or enters or leaves Indian country with the intent to injure, harass, or intimidate that person's spouse or intimate partner, and who, in the course of or as a result of such travel, intentionally commits a crime of violence and thereby causes bodily injury to such spouse or intimate partner, shall be punished as provided in subsection (b).
'(2) CAUSING THE CROSSING OF A STATE LINE—A person who causes a spouse or intimate partner to cross a State line or to enter or leave Indian country by force, coercion, duress, or fraud and, in the course or as a result of that conduct, intentionally commits a crime of violence and thereby causes bodily injury to the person's spouse or intimate partner, shall be punished as provided in subsection (b).
'(b) PENALTIES—A person who violates this section shall be fined under this title, imprisoned—
'(1) for life or any term of years, if death of the offender's spouse or intimate partner results;
'(2) for not more than 20 years if permanent disfigurement or life threatening bodily injury to the offender's spouse or intimate partner results;
'(3) for not more than 10 years, if serious bodily injury to the offender's spouse or intimate partner results or if the offender uses a dangerous weapon during the offense;
'(4) as provided for the applicable conduct under chapter 109A if the offense would constitute an offense under chapter 109A (without regard to whether the offense was committed in the special maritime and territorial jurisdiction of the United States or in a Federal prison); and
'(5) for not more than 5 years, in any other case,
or both fined and imprisoned.

'Sec. 2262. Interstate violation of protection order

'(a) OFFENSES—
'(1) CROSSING A STATE LINE—A person who travels across a State line or enters or leaves Indian country with the intent to engage in conduct that—
'(A)(i) violates the portion of a protection order that involves protection against credible threats of violence, repeated harassment, or bodily injury to the person or persons for whom the protection order was issued; or
'(ii) would violate subparagraph (A) if the conduct occurred in the jurisdiction in which the order was issued; and

'(B) subsequently engages in such conduct, shall be punished as provided in subsection (b).

'(2) CAUSING THE CROSSING OF A STATE LINE—A person who causes a spouse or intimate partner to cross a State line or to enter or leave Indian country by force, coercion, duress, or fraud, and, in the course or as a result of that conduct, intentionally commits an act that injures the person's spouse or intimate partner in violation of a valid protection order issued by a State shall be punished as provided in subsection (b).

'(b) PENALTIES—A person who violates this section shall be fined under this title, imprisoned—

'(1) for life or any term of years, if death of the offender's spouse or intimate partner results;

'(2) for not more than 20 years if permanent disfigurement or life threatening bodily injury to the offender's spouse or intimate partner results;

'(3) for not more than 10 years, if serious bodily injury to the offender's spouse or intimate partner results or if the offender uses a dangerous weapon during the offense;

'(4) as provided for the applicable conduct under chapter 109A if the offense would constitute an offense under chapter 109A (without regard to whether the offense was committed in the special maritime and territorial jurisdiction of the United States or in a Federal prison); and

'(5) for not more than 5 years, in any other case, or both fined and imprisoned.

'Sec. 2263. Pretrial release of defendant

'In any proceeding pursuant to section 3142 for the purpose of determining whether a defendant charged under this chapter shall be released pending trial, or for the purpose of determining conditions of such release, the alleged victim shall be given an opportunity to be heard regarding the danger posed by the defendant.

'Sec. 2264. Restitution

'(a) IN GENERAL—Notwithstanding section 3663, and in addition to any other civil or criminal penalty authorized by law, the court shall order restitution for any offense under this chapter.

'(b) SCOPE AND NATURE OF ORDER—

'(1) DIRECTIONS—The order of restitution under this section shall direct that—

'(A) the defendant pay to the victim (through the appropriate court mechanism) the full amount of the victim's losses as determined by the court, pursuant to paragraph (3); and

'(B) the United States Attorney enforce the restitution order by all available and reasonable means.

'(2) ENFORCEMENT BY VICTIM—An order of restitution also may be enforced by a victim named in the order to receive the restitution in the same manner as a judgment in a civil action.

'(3) DEFINITION—For purposes of this subsection, the term 'full amount of the victim's losses' includes any costs incurred by the victim for—
>'(A) medical services relating to physical, psychiatric, or psychological care;
>'(B) physical and occupational therapy or rehabilitation;
>'(C) necessary transportation, temporary housing, and child care expenses;
>'(D) lost income;
>'(E) attorneys' fees, plus any costs incurred in obtaining a civil protection order; and
>'(F) any other losses suffered by the victim as a proximate result of the offense.

'(4) ORDER MANDATORY—(A) The issuance of a restitution order under this section is mandatory.

'(B) A court may not decline to issue an order under this section because of—
>'(i) the economic circumstances of the defendant; or
>'(ii) the fact that a victim has, or is entitled to, receive compensation for his or her injuries from the proceeds of insurance or any other source.

'(C)(i) Notwithstanding subparagraph (A), the court may take into account the economic circumstances of the defendant in determining the manner in which and the schedule according to which the restitution is to be paid.

'(ii) For purposes of this subparagraph, the term 'economic circumstances' includes—
>'(I) the financial resources and other assets of the defendant;
>'(II) projected earnings, earning capacity, and other income of the defendant; and
>'(III) any financial obligations of the defendant, including obligations to dependents.

'(D) Subparagraph (A) does not apply if—
>'(i) the court finds on the record that the economic circumstances of the defendant do not allow for the payment of any amount of a restitution order, and do not allow for the payment of any or some portion of the amount of a restitution order in the foreseeable future (under any reasonable schedule of payments); and
>'(ii) the court enters in its order the amount of the victim's losses, and provides a nominal restitution award.

'(5) MORE THAN 1 OFFENDER—When the court finds that more than 1 offender has contributed to the loss of a victim, the court may make each offender liable for payment of the full amount of restitution or may apportion liability among the offenders to reflect the level of contribution and economic circumstances of each offender.

'(6) MORE THAN 1 VICTIM—When the court finds that more than 1 victim has sustained a loss requiring restitution by an offender, the court shall order full restitution of each victim but may provide for different payment schedules to reflect the economic circumstances of each victim.

'(7) PAYMENT SCHEDULE—An order under this section may direct the defendant to make a single lump-sum payment or partial payments at specified intervals.

'(8) SETOFF—Any amount paid to a victim under this section shall be set off against any amount later recovered as compensatory damages by the victim from the defendant in—

'(A) any Federal civil proceeding; and

'(B) any State civil proceeding, to the extent provided by the law of the State.

'(9) EFFECT ON OTHER SOURCES OF COMPENSATION—The issuance of a restitution order shall not affect the entitlement of a victim to receive compensation with respect to a loss from insurance or any other source until the payments actually received by the victim under the restitution order fully compensate the victim for the loss.

'(10) CONDITION OF PROBATION OR SUPERVISED RELEASE—Compliance with a restitution order issued under this section shall be a condition of any probation or supervised release of a defendant. If an offender fails to comply with a restitution order, the court may, after a hearing, revoke probation or a term of supervised release, modify the terms or conditions of probation or a term of supervised release, or hold the defendant in contempt pursuant to section 3583(e). In determining whether to revoke probation or a term of supervised release, modify the terms or conditions of probation or supervised release or hold a defendant serving a term of supervised release in contempt, the court shall consider the defendant's employment status, earning ability and financial resources, the willfulness of the defendant's failure to comply, and any other circumstances that may have a bearing on the defendant's ability to comply.

'(c) AFFIDAVIT—Within 60 days after conviction and, in any event, not later than 10 days before sentencing, the United States Attorney (or such Attorney's delegate), after consulting with the victim, shall prepare and file an affidavit with the court listing the amounts subject to restitution under this section. The affidavit shall be signed by the United States Attorney (or the delegate) and the victim. Should the victim object to any of the information included in the affidavit, the United States Attorney (or the delegate) shall advise the victim that the victim may file a separate affidavit and assist the victim in the preparation of the affidavit.

'(d) OBJECTION—If, after the defendant has been notified of the affidavit, no objection is raised by the defendant, the amounts attested to in the affidavit filed pursuant to subsection (a) shall be entered in the court's restitution order. If objection is raised, the court may require the victim or the United States Attorney (or the United States Attorney's delegate) to submit further affidavits or other supporting documents, demonstrating the victim's losses.

'(e) ADDITIONAL DOCUMENTATION AND TESTIMONY—If the court concludes, after reviewing the supporting documentation and considering the defendant's objections, that there is a substantial reason for doubting the authenticity or veracity of the records submitted, the court may require additional documentation or hear testimony on those questions. The privacy of any records filed, or testimony heard, pursuant to this section, shall be maintained to the greatest extent possible, and such records may be filed or testimony heard in camera.

'(f) FINAL DETERMINATION OF LOSSES—If the victim's losses are not ascertainable 10 days before sentencing as provided in subsection (c), the United States Attorney (or the United States Attorney's delegate) shall so inform the court, and the court shall set a date for the final determination of the victim's losses, not to exceed 90 days after sentencing. If the victim subsequently discovers further losses, the victim shall have 90 days after discovery of those losses in which to petition the court for an amended restitution order. Such order may be granted only upon a showing of good cause for the failure to include such losses in the initial claim for restitutionary relief.

'(g) RESTITUTION IN ADDITION TO PUNISHMENT—An award of restitution to the victim of an offense under this chapter is not a substitute for imposition of punishment under this chapter.

'Sec. 2265. Full faith and credit given to protection orders

'(a) FULL FAITH AND CREDIT—Any protection order issued that is consistent with subsection (b) of this section by the court of one State or Indian tribe (the issuing State or Indian tribe) shall be accorded full faith and credit by the court of another State or Indian tribe (the enforcing State or Indian tribe) and enforced as if it were the order of the enforcing State or tribe.

'(b) PROTECTION ORDER—A protection order issued by a State or tribal court is consistent with this subsection if—

'(1) such court has jurisdiction over the parties and matter under the law of such State or Indian tribe; and

'(2) reasonable notice and opportunity to be heard is given to the person against whom the order is sought sufficient to protect that person's right to due process. In the case of ex parte orders, notice and opportunity to be heard must be provided within the time required by State or tribal law, and in any event within a reasonable time after the order is issued, sufficient to protect the respondent's due process rights.

'(c) CROSS OR COUNTER PETITION—A protection order issued by a State or tribal court against one who has petitioned, filed a complaint, or otherwise filed a written pleading for protection against abuse by a spouse or intimate partner is not entitled to full faith and credit if—

'(1) no cross or counter petition, complaint, or other written pleading was filed seeking such a protection order; or

'(2) a cross or counter petition has been filed and the court did not make specific findings that each party was entitled to such an order.

'Sec. 2266. Definitions

'In this chapter—
'bodily injury' means any act, except one done in self-defense, that results in physical injury or sexual abuse.
'Indian country' has the meaning stated in section 1151.
'protection order' includes any injunction or other order issued for the purpose of preventing violent or threatening acts or harassment against, or contact or communication with or physical proximity to, another person, including temporary and final orders issued by civil and criminal courts (other than support or child custody orders) whether obtained by filing an independent action or as a pendente lite order in another proceeding so long as any civil order was issued in response to a complaint, petition or motion filed by or on behalf of a person seeking protection.
'spouse or intimate partner' includes—
'(A) a spouse, a former spouse, a person who shares a child in common with the abuser, and a person who cohabits or has cohabited with the abuser as a spouse; and
'(B) any other person similarly situated to a spouse who is protected by the domestic or family violence laws of the State in which the injury occurred or where the victim resides.
'State' includes a State of the United States, the District of Columbia, a commonwealth, territory, or possession of the United States.
'travel across State lines' does not include travel across State lines by an individual who is a member of an Indian tribe when such individual remains at all times in the territory of the Indian tribe of which the individual is a member.'.
(b) TECHNICAL AMENDMENT—The part analysis for part I of title 18, United States Code, is amended by inserting after the item for chapter 110 the following new item:

2261.'.

CHAPTER 3—ARREST POLICIES IN DOMESTIC VIOLENCE CASES

SEC. 40231. ENCOURAGING ARREST POLICIES.

(a) IN GENERAL—Title I of the Omnibus Crime Control and Safe Streets Act of 1968 (42 U.S.C. 3711 et seq.), as amended by section 40121(a), is amended—
(1) by redesignating part U as part V;
(2) by redesignating section 2101 as section 2201; and
(3) by inserting after part T the following new part:

'PART U—GRANTS TO ENCOURAGE ARREST POLICIES

'SEC. 2101. GRANTS.

'(a) PURPOSE—The purpose of this part is to encourage States, Indian tribal governments, and units of local government to treat domestic violence as a serious violation of criminal law.

'(b) GRANT AUTHORITY—The Attorney General may make grants to eligible States, Indian tribal governments, or units of local government for the following purposes:

'(1) To implement mandatory arrest or proarrest programs and policies in police departments, including mandatory arrest programs and policies for protection order violations.

'(2) To develop policies and training in police departments to improve tracking of cases involving domestic violence.

'(3) To centralize and coordinate police enforcement, prosecution, or judicial responsibility for domestic violence cases in groups or units of police officers, prosecutors, or judges.

'(4) To coordinate computer tracking systems to ensure communication between police, prosecutors, and both criminal and family courts.

'(5) To strengthen legal advocacy service programs for victims of domestic violence.

'(6) To educate judges in criminal and other courts about domestic violence and to improve judicial handling of such cases.

'(c) ELIGIBILITY—Eligible grantees are States, Indian tribal governments, or units of local government that—

'(1) certify that their laws or official policies—

'(A) encourage or mandate arrests of domestic violence offenders based on probable cause that an offense has been committed; and

'(B) encourage or mandate arrest of domestic violence offenders who violate the terms of a valid and outstanding protection order;

'(2) demonstrate that their laws, policies, or practices and their training programs discourage dual arrests of offender and victim;

'(3) certify that their laws, policies, or practices prohibit issuance of mutual restraining orders of protection except in cases where both spouses file a claim and the court makes detailed findings of fact indicating that both spouses acted primarily as aggressors and that neither spouse acted primarily in self-defense; and

'(4) certify that their laws, policies, or practices do not require, in connection with the prosecution of any misdemeanor or felony domestic violence offense, that the abused bear the costs associated with the filing of criminal charges or the service of such charges on an abuser, or that the abused bear the costs associated with the issuance or service of a warrant, protection order, or witness subpoena.

'SEC. 2102. APPLICATIONS.

'(a) APPLICATION—An eligible grantee shall submit an application to the Attorney General that—
> '(1) contains a certification by the chief executive officer of the State, Indian tribal government, or local government entity that the conditions of section 2101(c) are met or will be met within the later of—
>> '(A) the period ending on the date on which the next session of the State or Indian tribal legislature ends; or
>> '(B) 2 years of the date of enactment of this part;
>
> '(2) describes plans to further the purposes stated in section 2101(a);
> '(3) identifies the agency or office or groups of agencies or offices responsible for carrying out the program; and
> '(4) includes documentation from nonprofit, private sexual assault and domestic violence programs demonstrating their participation in developing the application, and identifying such programs in which such groups will be consulted for development and implementation.

'(b) PRIORITY—In awarding grants under this part, the Attorney General shall give priority to applicants that—
> '(1) do not currently provide for centralized handling of cases involving domestic violence by police, prosecutors, and courts; and
> '(2) demonstrate a commitment to strong enforcement of laws, and prosecution of cases, involving domestic violence.

'SEC. 2103. REPORTS.

'Each grantee receiving funds under this part shall submit a report to the Attorney General evaluating the effectiveness of projects developed with funds provided under this part and containing such additional information as the Attorney General may prescribe.

'SEC. 2104. REGULATIONS OR GUIDELINES.

'Not later than 120 days after the date of enactment of this part, the Attorney General shall publish proposed regulations or guidelines implementing this part. Not later than 180 days after the date of enactment of this part, the Attorney General shall publish final regulations or guidelines implementing this part.

'SEC. 2105. DEFINITIONS.

'For purposes of this part—
> '(1) the term 'domestic violence' includes felony or misdemeanor crimes of violence committed by a current or former spouse of the victim, by a person with whom the victim shares a child in common, by a person who is cohabitating with or has cohabitated with the victim as a spouse, by a person

similarly situated to a spouse of the victim under the domestic or family violence laws of the jurisdiction receiving grant monies, or by any other adult person against a victim who is protected from that person's acts under the domestic or family violence laws of the eligible State, Indian tribal government, or unit of local government that receives a grant under this part; and

'(2) the term 'protection order' includes any injunction issued for the purpose of preventing violent or threatening acts of domestic violence, including temporary and final orders issued by civil or criminal courts (other than support or child custody orders or provisions) whether obtained by filing an independent action or as a pendente lite order in another proceeding.'.

(b) TECHNICAL AMENDMENT—The table of contents of title I of the Omnibus Crime Control and Safe Streets Act of 1968 (42 U.S.C. 3711 et seq.), as amended by section 40121(b), is amended by striking the matter relating to part U and inserting the following:

'Part U—Grants to Encourage Arrest Policies

'Sec. 2101. Grants.
'Sec. 2102. Applications.
'Sec. 2103. Reports.
'Sec. 2104. Regulations or guidelines.
'Sec. 2105. Definitions.

'Part V—Transition—Effective Date—Repealer

'Sec. 2201. Continuation of rules, authorities, and proceedings.'.

(c) AUTHORIZATION OF APPROPRIATIONS—Section 1001(a) of title I of the Omnibus Crime Control and Safe Streets Act of 1968 (42 U.S.C. 3793), as amended by section 40121(c), is amended—
    (1) in paragraph (3) by striking 'and T' and inserting 'T, and U'; and
    (2) by adding at the end the following new paragraph:
'(19) There are authorized to be appropriated to carry out part U—
    '(A) $28,000,000 for fiscal year 1996;
    '(B) $33,000,000 for fiscal year 1997; and
    '(C) $59,000,000 for fiscal year 1998.
(d) ADMINISTRATIVE PROVISIONS—
    (1) REGULATIONS—Section 801(b) of title I of the Omnibus Crime Control and Safe Streets Act of 1968 (42 U.S.C. 3782(b)), is amended by striking 'and O' and inserting 'O, and U'.
    (2) DENIAL OF APPLICATION—Section 802(b) of title I of the Omnibus Crime Control and Safe Streets Act of 1968 (42 U.S.C. 3783 (b))

is amended in the first sentence by striking 'or O' and inserting 'O, or U'.

CHAPTER 4—SHELTER GRANTS

SEC. 40241. GRANTS FOR BATTERED WOMEN'S SHELTERS.

Section 310(a) of the Family Violence Prevention and Services Act (42 U.S.C. 10409(a)) is amended to read as follows:

'(a) IN GENERAL—There are authorized to be appropriated to carry out this title—
'(1) $50,000,000 for fiscal year 1996;
'(2) $60,000,000 for fiscal year 1997;
'(3) $70,000,000 for fiscal year 1998;
'(4) $72,500,000 for fiscal year 1999; and
'(5) $72,500,000 for fiscal year 2000.'.

CHAPTER 5—YOUTH EDUCATION

SEC. 40251. YOUTH EDUCATION AND DOMESTIC VIOLENCE.

The Family Violence Prevention and Services Act (42 U.S.C. 10401 et seq.), as amended by section 40211, is amended by adding at the end the following new section:

'SEC. 317. YOUTH EDUCATION AND DOMESTIC VIOLENCE.

'(a) GENERAL PURPOSE—For purposes of this section, the Secretary may, in consultation with the Secretary of Education, select, implement and evaluate 4 model programs for education of young people about domestic violence and violence among intimate partners.

'(b) NATURE OF PROGRAM—The Secretary shall select, implement and evaluate separate model programs for 4 different audiences: primary schools, middle schools, secondary schools, and institutions of higher education. The model programs shall be selected, implemented, and evaluated in consultation with educational experts, legal and psychological experts on battering, and victim advocate organizations such as battered women's shelters, State coalitions and resource centers.

'(c) REVIEW AND DISSEMINATION—Not later than 2 years after the date of enactment of this section, the Secretary shall transmit the design and evaluation of the model programs, along with a plan and cost estimate for nationwide distribution, to the relevant committees of Congress for review.

'(d) AUTHORIZATION OF APPROPRIATIONS—There are authorized to be appropriated to carry out this section $400,000 for fiscal year 1996.'.

CHAPTER 6—COMMUNITY PROGRAMS ON DOMESTIC VIOLENCE

SEC. 40261. ESTABLISHMENT OF COMMUNITY PROGRAMS ON DOMESTIC VIOLENCE.

The Family Violence Prevention and Services Act (42 U.S.C. 10401 et seq.), as amended by section 40251, is amended by adding at the end the following new section:

'SEC. 318. DEMONSTRATION GRANTS FOR COMMUNITY INITIATIVES.

'(a) IN GENERAL—The Secretary shall provide grants to nonprofit private organizations to establish projects in local communities involving many sectors of each community to coordinate intervention and prevention of domestic violence.

'(b) ELIGIBILITY—To be eligible for a grant under this section, an entity—
'(1) shall be a nonprofit organization organized for the purpose of coordinating community projects for the intervention in and prevention of domestic violence; and
'(2) shall include representatives of pertinent sectors of the local community, which may include—
'(A) health care providers;
'(B) the education community;
'(C) the religious community;
'(D) the justice system;
'(E) domestic violence program advocates;
'(F) human service entities such as State child services divisions;
'(G) business and civic leaders; and
'(H) other pertinent sectors.

'(c) APPLICATIONS—An organization that desires to receive a grant under this section shall submit to the Secretary an application, in such form and in such manner as the Secretary shall prescribe through notice in the Federal Register, that—
'(1) demonstrates that the applicant will serve a community leadership function, bringing together opinion leaders from each sector of the community to develop a coordinated community consensus opposing domestic violence;
'(2) demonstrates a community action component to improve and expand current intervention and prevention strategies through increased communication and coordination among all affected sectors;
'(3) includes a complete description of the applicant's plan for the establishment and operation of the community project, including a description of—
'(A) the method for identification and selection of an administrative committee made up of persons knowledgeable in domestic violence to

oversee the project, hire staff, assure compliance with the project outline, and secure annual evaluation of the project;

'(B) the method for identification and selection of project staff and a project evaluator;

'(C) the method for identification and selection of a project council consisting of representatives of the community sectors listed in subsection (b)(2);

'(D) the method for identification and selection of a steering committee consisting of representatives of the various community sectors who will chair subcommittees of the project council focusing on each of the sectors; and

'(E) a plan for developing outreach and public education campaigns regarding domestic violence; and

'(4) contains such other information, agreements, and assurances as the Secretary may require.

'(d) TERM—A grant provided under this section may extend over a period of not more than 3 fiscal years.

'(e) CONDITIONS ON PAYMENT—Payments under a grant under this section shall be subject to—

'(1) annual approval by the Secretary; and

'(2) availability of appropriations.

'(f) GEOGRAPHICAL DISPERSION—The Secretary shall award grants under this section to organizations in communities geographically dispersed throughout the country.

'(g) USE OF GRANT MONIES—

'(1) IN GENERAL—A grant made under subsection (a) shall be used to establish and operate a community project to coordinate intervention and prevention of domestic violence.

'(2) REQUIREMENTS—In establishing and operating a project, a nonprofit private organization shall—

'(A) establish protocols to improve and expand domestic violence intervention and prevention strategies among all affected sectors;

'(B) develop action plans to direct responses within each community sector that are in conjunction with development in all other sectors; and

'(C) provide for periodic evaluation of the project with a written report and analysis to assist application of this concept in other communities.

'(h) AUTHORIZATION OF APPROPRIATIONS—There are authorized to be appropriated to carry out this section—

'(1) $4,000,000 for fiscal year 1996; and

'(2) $6,000,000 for fiscal year 1997.

'(i) REGULATIONS—Not later than 60 days after the date of enactment of this section, the Secretary shall publish proposed regulations implementing this section. Not later than 120 days after the date of enactment, the Secretary shall publish final regulations implementing this section.'.

CHAPTER 7—FAMILY VIOLENCE PREVENTION AND SERVICES ACT AMENDMENTS

SEC. 40271. GRANTEE REPORTING.

(a) SUBMISSION OF APPLICATION—Section 303(a)(2)(C) of the Family Violence Prevention and Services Act (42 U.S.C. 10402(a)(2)(C)) is amended by inserting 'and a plan to address the needs of underserved populations, including populations underserved because of ethnic, racial, cultural, language diversity or geographic isolation' after 'such State'.

(b) APPROVAL OF APPLICATION—Section 303(a) of the Family Violence Prevention and Services Act (42 U.S.C. 10402(a)) is amended by adding at the end the following new paragraph:

> '(4) Upon completion of the activities funded by a grant under this subpart, the State grantee shall file a performance report with the Director explaining the activities carried out together with an assessment of the effectiveness of those activities in achieving the purposes of this subpart. A section of this performance report shall be completed by each grantee or subgrantee that performed the direct services contemplated in the application certifying performance of direct services under the grant. The Director shall suspend funding for an approved application if an applicant fails to submit an annual performance report or if the funds are expended for purposes other than those set forth under this subpart, after following the procedures set forth in paragraph (3). Federal funds may be used only to supplement, not supplant, State funds.'.

SEC. 40272. TECHNICAL AMENDMENTS.

(a) DEFINITIONS—Section 309(5)(B) of the Family Violence Prevention and Services Act (42 U.S.C. 10408(5)(B)) is amended by inserting 'or other supportive services' before 'by peers individually or in groups,'.

(b) SPECIAL ISSUE RESOURCE CENTERS—

> (1) GRANTS—Section 308(a)(2) of the Family Violence Prevention and Services Act (42 U.S.C. 10407(a)(2)) is amended by striking 'six' and inserting 'seven'.
>
> (2) FUNCTIONS—Section 308(c) of the Family Violence Prevention and Services Act (42 U.S.C. 10407(c)) is amended—
>> (A) by striking the period at the end of paragraph (6) and inserting ', including the issuance and enforcement of protection orders.'; and
>> (B) by adding at the end the following new paragraph:
>
> '(7) Providing technical assistance and training to State domestic violence coalitions.'.

(c) STATE DOMESTIC VIOLENCE COALITIONS—Section 311(a) of the Family Violence Prevention and Services Act (42 U.S.C. 10410(a)) is amended—

> (1) by redesignating paragraphs (1), (2), (3), and (4) as paragraphs (2), (3), (4), and (5);

(2) by inserting before paragraph (2), as redesignated by paragraph (1), the following new paragraph:

'(1) working with local domestic violence programs and providers of direct services to encourage appropriate responses to domestic violence within the State, including—

>'(A) training and technical assistance for local programs and professionals working with victims of domestic violence;
>
>'(B) planning and conducting State needs assessments and planning for comprehensive services;
>
>'(C) serving as an information clearinghouse and resource center for the State; and
>
>'(D) collaborating with other governmental systems which affect battered women;';

(3) in paragraph (2)(K), as redesignated by paragraph (1), by striking 'and court officials and other professionals' and inserting ', judges, court officers and other criminal justice professionals,';

(4) in paragraph (3), as redesignated by paragraph (1)—

>(A) by inserting ', criminal court judges,' after 'family law judges,' each place it appears;
>
>(B) in subparagraph (F), by inserting 'custody' after 'temporary'; and
>
>(C) in subparagraph (H), by striking 'supervised visitations that do not endanger victims and their children,' and inserting 'supervised visitations or denial of visitation to protect against danger to victims or their children'; and

(5) in paragraph (4), as redesignated by paragraph (1), by inserting ', including information aimed at underserved racial, ethnic or language-minority populations' before the semicolon.

CHAPTER 8—CONFIDENTIALITY FOR ABUSED PERSONS

SEC. 40281. CONFIDENTIALITY OF ABUSED PERSON'S ADDRESS.

(a) REGULATIONS—Not later than 90 days after the date of enactment of this Act, the United States Postal Service shall promulgate regulations to secure the confidentiality of domestic violence shelters and abused persons' addresses.

(b) REQUIREMENTS—The regulations under subsection (a) shall require—

>(1) in the case of an individual, the presentation to an appropriate postal official of a valid, outstanding protection order; and
>
>(2) in the case of a domestic violence shelter, the presentation to an appropriate postal authority of proof from a State domestic violence coalition that meets the requirements of section 311 of the Family Violence Prevention and Services Act (42 U.S.C. 10410)) verifying that the organization is a domestic violence shelter.

(c) DISCLOSURE FOR CERTAIN PURPOSES—The regulations under subsection (a) shall not prohibit the disclosure of addresses to State or Federal agencies for legitimate law enforcement or other governmental purposes.

(d) EXISTING COMPILATIONS—Compilations of addresses existing at the time at which order is presented to an appropriate postal official shall be excluded from the scope of the regulations under subsection (a).

CHAPTER 9—DATA AND RESEARCH

SEC. 40291. RESEARCH AGENDA.

(a) REQUEST FOR CONTRACT—The Attorney General shall request the National Academy of Sciences, through its National Research Council, to enter into a contract to develop a research agenda to increase the understanding and control of violence against women, including rape and domestic violence. In furtherance of the contract, the National Academy shall convene a panel of nationally recognized experts on violence against women, in the fields of law, medicine, criminal justice, and direct services to victims and experts on domestic violence in diverse, ethnic, social, and language minority communities and the social sciences. In setting the agenda, the Academy shall focus primarily on preventive, educative, social, and legal strategies, including addressing the needs of underserved populations.

(b) DECLINATION OF REQUEST—If the National Academy of Sciences declines to conduct the study and develop a research agenda, it shall recommend a nonprofit private entity that is qualified to conduct such a study. In that case, the Attorney General shall carry out subsection (a) through the nonprofit private entity recommended by the Academy. In either case, whether the study is conducted by the National Academy of Sciences or by the nonprofit group it recommends, the funds for the contract shall be made available from sums appropriated for the conduct of research by the National Institute of Justice.

(c) REPORT—The Attorney General shall ensure that no later than 1 year after the date of enactment of this Act, the study required under subsection (a) is completed and a report describing the findings made is submitted to the Committee on the Judiciary of the Senate and the Committee on the Judiciary of the House of Representatives.

SEC. 40292. STATE DATABASES.

(a) IN GENERAL—The Attorney General shall study and report to the States and to Congress on how the States may collect centralized databases on the incidence of sexual and domestic violence offenses within a State.

(b) CONSULTATION—In conducting its study, the Attorney General shall consult persons expert in the collection of criminal justice data, State statistical administrators, law enforcement personnel, and nonprofit nongovernmental agencies that provide direct services to victims of domestic violence. The final report shall set forth the views of the persons consulted on the recommendations.

(c) REPORT—The Attorney General shall ensure that no later than 1 year after the date of enactment of this Act, the study required under subsection (a) is completed and a report describing the findings made is submitted to the Committees on the Judiciary of the Senate and the House of Representatives.

(d) AUTHORIZATION OF APPROPRIATIONS—There are authorized to be appropriated to carry out this section $200,000 for fiscal year 1996.

SEC. 40293. NUMBER AND COST OF INJURIES.

(a) STUDY—The Secretary of Health and Human Services, acting through the Centers for Disease Control Injury Control Division, shall conduct a study to obtain a national projection of the incidence of injuries resulting from domestic violence, the cost of injuries to health care facilities, and recommend health care strategies for reducing the incidence and cost of such injuries.

(b) AUTHORIZATION OF APPROPRIATIONS—There are authorized to be appropriated to carry out this section—$100,000 for fiscal year 1996.

CHAPTER 10—RURAL DOMESTIC VIOLENCE AND CHILD ABUSE ENFORCEMENT

SEC. 40295. RURAL DOMESTIC VIOLENCE AND CHILD ABUSE ENFORCEMENT ASSISTANCE.

(a) GRANTS—The Attorney General may make grants to States, Indian tribal governments, and local governments of rural States, and to other public or private entities of rural States—

(1) to implement, expand, and establish cooperative efforts and projects between law enforcement officers, prosecutors, victim advocacy groups, and other related parties to investigate and prosecute incidents of domestic violence and child abuse;

(2) to provide treatment and counseling to victims of domestic violence and child abuse; and

(3) to work in cooperation with the community to develop education and prevention strategies directed toward such issues.

(b) DEFINITIONS—In this section—

'Indian tribe' means a tribe, band, pueblo, nation, or other organized group or community of Indians, including an Alaska Native village (as defined in or established under the Alaska Native Claims Settlement Act (43 U.S.C. 1601 et seq.), that is recognized as eligible for the special programs and services provided by the United States to Indians because of their status as Indians. 'rural State' has the meaning stated in section 1501(b) of title I of the Omnibus Crime Control and Safe Streets Act of 1968 (42 U.S.C. 3796bb(B)).

(c) AUTHORIZATION OF APPROPRIATIONS—

(1) IN GENERAL—There are authorized to be appropriated to carry out this section—
    (A) $7,000,000 for fiscal year 1996;
    (B) $8,000,000 for fiscal year 1997; and
    (C) $15,000,000 for fiscal year 1998.
(2) ADDITIONAL FUNDING—In addition to funds received under a grant under subsection (a), a law enforcement agency may use funds received under a grant under section 103 to accomplish the objectives of this section.

Subtitle C—Civil Rights for Women

SEC. 40301. SHORT TITLE.

This subtitle may be cited as the 'Civil Rights Remedies for Gender-Motivated Violence Act'.

SEC. 40302. CIVIL RIGHTS.

(a) PURPOSE—Pursuant to the affirmative power of Congress to enact this subtitle under section 5 of the Fourteenth Amendment to the Constitution, as well as under section 8 of Article I of the Constitution, it is the purpose of this subtitle to protect the civil rights of victims of gender motivated violence and to promote public safety, health, and activities affecting interstate commerce by establishing a Federal civil rights cause of action for victims of crimes of violence motivated by gender.
(b) RIGHT TO BE FREE FROM CRIMES OF VIOLENCE—All persons within the United States shall have the right to be free from crimes of violence motivated by gender (as defined in subsection (d)).
(c) CAUSE OF ACTION—A person (including a person who acts under color of any statute, ordinance, regulation, custom, or usage of any State) who commits a crime of violence motivated by gender and thus deprives another of the right declared in subsection (b) shall be liable to the party injured, in an action for the recovery of compensatory and punitive damages, injunctive and declaratory relief, and such other relief as a court may deem appropriate.
(d) DEFINITIONS—For purposes of this section—
    (1) the term 'crime of violence motivated by gender' means a crime of violence committed because of gender or on the basis of gender, and due, at least in part, to an animus based on the victim's gender; and
    (2) the term 'crime of violence' means—
        (A) an act or series of acts that would constitute a felony against the person or that would constitute a felony against property if the conduct presents a serious risk of physical injury to another, and that would come within the meaning of State or Federal offenses described in section 16 of title 18, United States Code, whether or not those acts have actually resulted in criminal charges, prosecution, or conviction

and whether or not those acts were committed in the special maritime, territorial, or prison jurisdiction of the United States; and

(B) includes an act or series of acts that would constitute a felony described in subparagraph (A) but for the relationship between the person who takes such action and the individual against whom such action is taken.

(e) Limitation and Procedures—

(1) LIMITATION—Nothing in this section entitles a person to a cause of action under subsection (c) for random acts of violence unrelated to gender or for acts that cannot be demonstrated, by a preponderance of the evidence, to be motivated by gender (within the meaning of subsection (d)).

(2) NO PRIOR CRIMINAL ACTION—Nothing in this section requires a prior criminal complaint, prosecution, or conviction to establish the elements of a cause of action under subsection (c).

(3) CONCURRENT JURISDICTION—The Federal and State courts shall have concurrent jurisdiction over actions brought pursuant to this subtitle.

(4) SUPPLEMENTAL JURISDICTION—Neither section 1367 of title 28, United States Code, nor subsection (c) of this section shall be construed, by reason of a claim arising under such subsection, to confer on the courts of the United States jurisdiction over any State law claim seeking the establishment of a divorce, alimony, equitable distribution of marital property, or child custody decree.

(5) LIMITATION ON REMOVAL—Section 1445 of title 28, United States Code, is amended by adding at the end the following new subsection:

'(d) A civil action in any State court arising under section 40302 of the Violence Against Women Act of 1994 may not be removed to any district court of the United States.'.

SEC. 40303. ATTORNEY'S FEES.

Section 722 of the Revised Statutes (42 U.S.C. 1988) is amended in the last sentence—

(1) by striking 'or' after 'Public Law 92-318,'; and

(2) by inserting ', or section 40302 of the Violence Against Women Act of 1994,' after '1964'.

SEC. 40304. SENSE OF THE SENATE CONCERNING PROTECTION OF THE PRIVACY OF RAPE VICTIMS.

It is the sense of the Senate that news media, law enforcement officers, and other persons should exercise restraint and respect a rape victim's privacy by not disclosing the victim's identity to the general public or facilitating such disclosure without the consent of the victim.

Subtitle D—Equal Justice for Women in the Courts Act

SEC. 40401. SHORT TITLE.

This subtitle may be cited as the 'Equal Justice for Women in the Courts Act of 1994'.

CHAPTER 1—EDUCATION AND TRAINING FOR JUDGES AND COURT PERSONNEL IN STATE COURTS

SEC. 40411. GRANTS AUTHORIZED.

The State Justice Institute may award grants for the purpose of developing, testing, presenting, and disseminating model programs to be used by States (as defined in section 202 of the State Justice Institute Act of 1984 (42 U.S.C. 10701)) in training judges and court personnel in the laws of the States and by Indian tribes in training tribal judges and court personnel in the laws of the tribes on rape, sexual assault, domestic violence, and other crimes of violence motivated by the victim's gender.

SEC. 40412. TRAINING PROVIDED BY GRANTS.

Training provided pursuant to grants made under this subtitle may include current information, existing studies, or current data on—
   (1) the nature and incidence of rape and sexual assault by strangers and nonstrangers, marital rape, and incest;
   (2) the underreporting of rape, sexual assault, and child sexual abuse;
   (3) the physical, psychological, and economic impact of rape and sexual assault on the victim, the costs to society, and the implications for sentencing;
   (4) the psychology of sex offenders, their high rate of recidivism, and the implications for sentencing;
   (5) the historical evolution of laws and attitudes on rape and sexual assault;
   (6) sex stereotyping of female and male victims of rape and sexual assault, racial stereotyping of rape victims and defendants, and the impact of such stereotypes on credibility of witnesses, sentencing, and other aspects of the administration of justice;
   (7) application of rape shield laws and other limits on introduction of evidence that may subject victims to improper sex stereotyping and harassment in both rape and nonrape cases, including the need for sua sponte judicial intervention in inappropriate cross-examination;
   (8) the use of expert witness testimony on rape trauma syndrome, child sexual abuse accommodation syndrome, post-traumatic stress syndrome, and similar issues;
   (9) the legitimate reasons why victims of rape, sexual assault, and incest may refuse to testify against a defendant;
   (10) the nature and incidence of domestic violence;

(11) the physical, psychological, and economic impact of domestic violence on the victim, the costs to society, and the implications for court procedures and sentencing;

(12) the psychology and self-presentation of batterers and victims and the implications for court proceedings and credibility of witnesses;

(13) sex stereotyping of female and male victims of domestic violence, myths about presence or absence of domestic violence in certain racial, ethnic, religious, or socioeconomic groups, and their impact on the administration of justice;

(14) historical evolution of laws and attitudes on domestic violence;

(15) proper and improper interpretations of the defenses of self-defense and provocation, and the use of expert witness testimony on battered woman syndrome;

(16) the likelihood of retaliation, recidivism, and escalation of violence by batterers, and the potential impact of incarceration and other meaningful sanctions for acts of domestic violence including violations of orders of protection;

(17) economic, psychological, social and institutional reasons for victims' inability to leave the batterer, to report domestic violence or to follow through on complaints, including the influence of lack of support from police, judges, and court personnel, and the legitimate reasons why victims of domestic violence may refuse to testify against a defendant;

(18) the need for orders of protection, and the implications of mutual orders of protection, dual arrest policies, and mediation in domestic violence cases; and

(19) recognition of and response to gender-motivated crimes of violence other than rape, sexual assault and domestic violence, such as mass or serial murder motivated by the gender of the victims.

SEC. 40413. COOPERATION IN DEVELOPING PROGRAMS IN MAKING GRANTS UNDER THIS TITLE.

The State Justice Institute shall ensure that model programs carried out pursuant to grants made under this subtitle are developed with the participation of law enforcement officials, public and private nonprofit victim advocates, legal experts, prosecutors, defense attorneys, and recognized experts on gender bias in the courts.

SEC. 40414. AUTHORIZATION OF APPROPRIATIONS.

(a) IN GENERAL—There are authorized to be appropriated to carry out this chapter $600,000 for fiscal year 1996.

(b) MODEL PROGRAMS—Of amounts appropriated under this section, the State Justice Institute shall expend not less than 40 percent on model programs regarding domestic violence and not less than 40 percent on model programs regarding rape and sexual assault.

CHAPTER 2—EDUCATION AND TRAINING FOR JUDGES AND COURT PERSONNEL IN FEDERAL COURTS

SEC. 40421. AUTHORIZATIONS OF CIRCUIT STUDIES; EDUCATION AND TRAINING GRANTS.

(a) STUDIES—In order to gain a better understanding of the nature and the extent of gender bias in the Federal courts, the circuit judicial councils are encouraged to conduct studies of the instances, if any, of gender bias in their respective circuits and to implement recommended reforms.
(b) MATTERS FOR EXAMINATION—The studies under subsection (a) may include an examination of the effects of gender on—
 (1) the treatment of litigants, witnesses, attorneys, jurors, and judges in the courts, including before magistrate and bankruptcy judges;
 (2) the interpretation and application of the law, both civil and criminal;
 (3) treatment of defendants in criminal cases;
 (4) treatment of victims of violent crimes in judicial proceedings;
 (5) sentencing;
 (6) sentencing alternatives and the nature of supervision of probation and parole;
 (7) appointments to committees of the Judicial Conference and the courts;
 (8) case management and court sponsored alternative dispute resolution programs;
 (9) the selection, retention, promotion, and treatment of employees;
 (10) appointment of arbitrators, experts, and special masters;
 (11) the admissibility of the victim's past sexual history in civil and criminal cases; and
 (12) the aspects of the topics listed in section 40412 that pertain to issues within the jurisdiction of the Federal courts.
(c) CLEARINGHOUSE—The Administrative Office of the United States Courts shall act as a clearinghouse to disseminate any reports and materials issued by the gender bias task forces under subsection (a) and to respond to requests for such reports and materials. The gender bias task forces shall provide the Administrative Office of the Courts of the United States with their reports and related material.
(d) MODEL PROGRAMS—The Federal Judicial Center, in carrying out section 620(b)(3) of title 28, United States Code, may—
 (1) include in the educational programs it presents and prepares, including the training programs for newly appointed judges, information on issues related to gender bias in the courts including such areas as are listed in subsection (a) along with such other topics as the Federal Judicial Center deems appropriate;
 (2) prepare materials necessary to implement this subsection; and

(3) take into consideration the findings and recommendations of the studies conducted pursuant to subsection (a), and to consult with individuals and groups with relevant expertise in gender bias issues as it prepares or revises such materials.

SEC. 40422. AUTHORIZATION OF APPROPRIATIONS.

There are authorized to be appropriated—
(1) to the Salaries and Expenses Account of the Courts of Appeals, District Courts, and other Judicial Services to carry out section 40421(a) $500,000 for fiscal year 1996;
(2) to the Federal Judicial Center to carry out section 40421(d) $100,000 for fiscal year 1996; and
(3) to the Administrative Office of the United States Courts to carry out section 40421(c) $100,000 for fiscal year 1996.

Subtitle E—Violence Against Women Act Improvements

SEC. 40501. PRE-TRIAL DETENTION IN SEX OFFENSE CASES.

Section 3156(a)(4) of title 18, United States Code, is amended—
(1) by striking 'or' at the end of subparagraph (A);
(2) by striking the period at the end of subparagraph (B) and inserting '; or'; and
(3) by adding after subparagraph (B) the following new subparagraph:
'(C) any felony under chapter 109A or chapter 110.'.

SEC. 40502. INCREASED PENALTIES FOR SEX OFFENSES AGAINST VICTIMS BELOW THE AGE OF 16.

Section 2245(2) of title 18, United States Code, is amended—
(1) by striking 'or' at the end of subparagraph (B);
(2) by striking '; and' at the end of subparagraph (C) and inserting '; or'; and
(3) by inserting after subparagraph (C) the following new subparagraph:
'(D) the intentional touching, not through the clothing, of the genitalia of another person who has not attained the age of 16 years with an intent to abuse, humiliate, harass, degrade, or arouse or gratify the sexual desire of any person;'.

SEC. 40503. PAYMENT OF COST OF TESTING FOR SEXUALLY TRANSMITTED DISEASES.

(a) FOR VICTIMS IN SEX OFFENSE CASES—Section 503(c)(7) of the Victims' Rights and Restitution Act of 1990 (42 U.S.C. 10607(c)(7)) is amended by adding at the end the following: 'The Attorney General shall provide for the payment of the cost of up to 2 anonymous and confidential tests of the victim for sexually transmitted diseases, including HIV, gonorrhea, herpes, chlamydia, and syphilis, during the 12 months following sexual assaults that pose a risk of transmission, and the cost of a counseling session by a medically trained professional on the accuracy of such tests and the risk of transmission of sexually transmitted diseases to the victim as the result of the assault. A victim may waive anonymity and confidentiality of any tests paid for under this section.'.

(b) Limited Testing of Defendants—

    (1) COURT ORDER—The victim of an offense of the type referred to in subsection (a) may obtain an order in the district court of the United States for the district in which charges are brought against the defendant charged with the offense, after notice to the defendant and an opportunity to be heard, requiring that the defendant be tested for the presence of the etiologic agent for acquired immune deficiency syndrome, and that the results of the test be communicated to the victim and the defendant. Any test result of the defendant given to the victim or the defendant must be accompanied by appropriate counseling.

    (2) SHOWING REQUIRED—To obtain an order under paragraph (1), the victim must demonstrate that—

        (A) the defendant has been charged with the offense in a State or Federal court, and if the defendant has been arrested without a warrant, a probable cause determination has been made;

        (B) the test for the etiologic agent for acquired immune deficiency syndrome is requested by the victim after appropriate counseling; and

        (C) the test would provide information necessary for the health of the victim of the alleged offense and the court determines that the alleged conduct of the defendant created a risk of transmission, as determined by the Centers for Disease Control, of the etiologic agent for acquired immune deficiency syndrome to the victim.

    (3) FOLLOW-UP TESTING—The court may order follow-up tests and counseling under paragraph (b)(1) if the initial test was negative. Such follow-up tests and counseling shall be performed at the request of the victim on dates that occur six months and twelve months following the initial test.

    (4) TERMINATION OF TESTING REQUIREMENTS—An order for follow-up testing under paragraph (3) shall be terminated if the person obtains an acquittal on, or dismissal of, all charges of the type referred to in subsection (a).

    (5) CONFIDENTIALITY OF TEST—The results of any test ordered under this subsection shall be disclosed only to the victim or, where the court deems appropriate, to the parent or legal guardian of the victim, and to the person tested. The victim may disclose the test results only to any medical professional, counselor, family member or sexual partner(s) the victim may have had since the attack. Any such individual to whom the test results are disclosed by the victim shall maintain the confidentiality of such information.

(6) DISCLOSURE OF TEST RESULTS—The court shall issue an order to prohibit the disclosure by the victim of the results of any test performed under this subsection to anyone other than those mentioned in paragraph (5). The contents of the court proceedings and test results pursuant to this section shall be sealed. The results of such test performed on the defendant under this section shall not be used as evidence in any criminal trial.

(7) CONTEMPT FOR DISCLOSURE—Any person who discloses the results of a test in violation of this subsection may be held in contempt of court.

(c) PENALTIES FOR INTENTIONAL TRANSMISSION OF HIV—Not later than 6 months after the date of enactment of this Act, the United States Sentencing Commission shall conduct a study and prepare and submit to the committees on the Judiciary of the Senate and the House of Representatives a report concerning recommendations for the revision of sentencing guidelines that relate to offenses in which an HIV infected individual engages in sexual activity if the individual knows that he or she is infected with HIV and intends, through such sexual activity, to expose another to HIV.

SEC. 40504. EXTENSION AND STRENGTHENING OF RESTITUTION.

Section 3663(b) of title 18, United States Code, is amended—
(1) in paragraph (2) by inserting 'including an offense under chapter 109A or chapter 110' after 'an offense resulting in bodily injury to a victim';
(2) by striking 'and' at the end of paragraph (3);
(3) by redesignating paragraph (4) as paragraph (5); and
(4) by inserting after paragraph (3) the following new paragraph:
'(4) in any case, reimburse the victim for lost income and necessary child care, transportation, and other expenses related to participation in the investigation or prosecution of the offense or attendance at proceedings related to the offense; and'.

SEC. 40505. ENFORCEMENT OF RESTITUTION ORDERS THROUGH SUSPENSION OF FEDERAL BENEFITS.

Section 3663 of title 18, United States Code, is amended by adding at the end the following new subsection:
'(i)(1) A Federal agency shall immediately suspend all Federal benefits provided by the agency to the defendant, and shall terminate the defendant's eligibility for Federal benefits administered by that agency, upon receipt of a certified copy of a written judicial finding that the defendant is delinquent in making restitution in accordance with any schedule of payments or any requirement of immediate payment imposed under this section.
'(2) Any written finding of delinquency described in paragraph (1) shall be made by a court, after a hearing, upon motion of the victim named in the order to receive the restitution or upon motion of the United States.

'(3) A defendant found to be delinquent may subsequently seek a written finding from the court that the defendant has rectified the delinquency or that the defendant has made and will make good faith efforts to rectify the delinquency. The defendant's eligibility for Federal benefits shall be reinstated upon receipt by the agency of a certified copy of such a finding.
'(4) In this subsection, 'Federal benefit' means a grant, contract, loan, professional license, or commercial license provided by an agency of the United States.'.

SEC. 40506. NATIONAL BASELINE STUDY ON CAMPUS SEXUAL ASSAULT.

(a) STUDY—The Attorney General, in consultation with the Secretary of Education, shall provide for a national baseline study to examine the scope of the problem of campus sexual assaults and the effectiveness of institutional and legal policies in addressing such crimes and protecting victims.

SEC. 40507. REPORT ON BATTERED WOMEN'S SYNDROME.

(a) REPORT—Not less than 1 year after the date of enactment of this Act, the Attorney General and the Secretary of Health and Human Services shall transmit to the House Committee on Energy and Commerce, the Senate Committee on Labor and Human Resources, and the Committees on the Judiciary of the Senate and the House of Representatives a report on the medical and psychological basis of 'battered women's syndrome' and on the extent to which evidence of the syndrome has been considered in criminal trials.
(b) COMPONENTS—The report under subsection (a) shall include—
(1) medical and psychological testimony on the validity of battered women's syndrome as a psychological condition;
(2) a compilation of State, tribal, and Federal court cases in which evidence of battered women's syndrome was offered in criminal trials; and
(3) an assessment by State, tribal, and Federal judges, prosecutors, and defense attorneys of the effects that evidence of battered women's syndrome may have in criminal trials.

SEC. 40508. REPORT ON CONFIDENTIALITY OF ADDRESSES FOR VICTIMS OF DOMESTIC VIOLENCE.

(a) REPORT—The Attorney General shall conduct a study of the means by which abusive spouses may obtain information concerning the addresses or locations of estranged or former spouses, notwithstanding the desire of the victims to have such information withheld to avoid further exposure to abuse. Based on the study, the Attorney General shall transmit a report to Congress including—

(1) the findings of the study concerning the means by which information concerning the addresses or locations of abused spouses may be obtained by abusers; and

(2) analysis of the feasibility of creating effective means of protecting the confidentiality of information concerning the addresses and locations of abused spouses to protect such persons from exposure to further abuse while preserving access to such information for legitimate purposes.

(b) USE OF COMPONENTS—The Attorney General may use the National Institute of Justice and the Office for Victims of Crime in carrying out this section.

SEC. 40509. REPORT ON RECORDKEEPING RELATING TO DOMESTIC VIOLENCE.

Not later than 1 year after the date of enactment of this Act, the Attorney General shall complete a study of, and shall submit to Congress a report and recommendations on, problems of recordkeeping of criminal complaints involving domestic violence. The study and report shall examine—

(1) the efforts that have been made by the Department of Justice, including the Federal Bureau of Investigation, to collect statistics on domestic violence; and

(2) the feasibility of requiring that the relationship between an offender and victim be reported in Federal records of crimes of aggravated assault, rape, and other violent crimes.

Subtitle F—National Stalker and Domestic Violence Reduction

SEC. 40601. AUTHORIZING ACCESS TO FEDERAL CRIMINAL INFORMATION DATABASES.

(a) ACCESS AND ENTRY—Section 534 of title 28, United States Code, is amended by adding at the end the following:

'(e)(1) Information from national crime information databases consisting of identification records, criminal history records, protection orders, and wanted person records may be disseminated to civil or criminal courts for use in domestic violence or stalking cases. Nothing in this subsection shall be construed to permit access to such records for any other purpose.

'(2) Federal and State criminal justice agencies authorized to enter information into criminal information databases may include—

'(A) arrests, convictions, and arrest warrants for stalking or domestic violence or for violations of protection orders for the protection of parties from stalking or domestic violence; and

'(B) protection orders for the protection of persons from stalking or domestic violence, provided such orders are subject to periodic verification.

'(3) As used in this subsection—
'(A) the term 'national crime information databases' means the National Crime Information Center and its incorporated criminal history databases, including the Interstate Identification Index; and
'(B) the term 'protection order' includes an injunction or any other order issued for the purpose of preventing violent or threatening acts or harassment against, or contact or communication with or physical proximity to, another person, including temporary and final orders issued by civil or criminal courts (other than support or child custody orders) whether obtained by filing an independent action or as a pendente lite order in another proceeding so long as any civil order was issued in response to a complaint, petition, or motion filed by or on behalf of a person seeking protection.'.

(b) RULEMAKING—The Attorney General may make rules to carry out the subsection added to section 534 of title 28, United States Code, by subsection (a), after consultation with the officials charged with managing the National Crime Information Center and the Criminal Justice Information Services Advisory Policy Board.

SEC. 40602. GRANT PROGRAM.

(a) IN GENERAL—The Attorney General is authorized to provide grants to States and units of local government to improve processes for entering data regarding stalking and domestic violence into local, State, and national crime information databases.

(b) ELIGIBILITY—To be eligible to receive a grant under subsection (a), a State or unit of local government shall certify that it has or intends to establish a program that enters into the National Crime Information Center records of—
(1) warrants for the arrest of persons violating protection orders intended to protect victims from stalking or domestic violence;
(2) arrests or convictions of persons violating protection or domestic violence; and
(3) protection orders for the protection of persons from stalking or domestic violence.

SEC. 40603. AUTHORIZATION OF APPROPRIATIONS.

There are authorized to be appropriated to carry out this subtitle—
(1) $1,500,000 for fiscal year 1996;
(2) $1,750,000 for fiscal year 1997; and
(3) $2,750,000 for fiscal year 1998.

SEC. 40604. APPLICATION REQUIREMENTS.

An application for a grant under this subtitle shall be submitted in such form and manner, and contain such information, as the Attorney General may prescribe. In addition, applications shall include documentation showing—
   (1) the need for grant funds and that State or local funding, as the case may be, does not already cover these operations;
   (2) intended use of the grant funds, including a plan of action to increase record input; and
   (3) an estimate of expected results from the use of the grant funds.

SEC. 40605. DISBURSEMENT.

Not later than 90 days after the receipt of an application under this subtitle, the Attorney General shall either provide grant funds or shall inform the applicant why grant funds are not being provided.

SEC. 40606. TECHNICAL ASSISTANCE, TRAINING, AND EVALUATIONS.

The Attorney General may provide technical assistance and training in furtherance of the purposes of this subtitle, and may provide for the evaluation of programs that receive funds under this subtitle, in addition to any evaluation requirements that the Attorney General may prescribe for grantees. The technical assistance, training, and evaluations authorized by this section may be carried out directly by the Attorney General, or through contracts or other arrangements with other entities.

SEC. 40607. TRAINING PROGRAMS FOR JUDGES.

The State Justice Institute, after consultation with nationally recognized nonprofit organizations with expertise in stalking and domestic violence cases, shall conduct training programs for State (as defined in section 202 of the State Justice Institute Authorization Act of 1984 (42 U.S.C. 10701)) and Indian tribal judges to ensure that a judge issuing an order in a stalking or domestic violence case has all available criminal history and other information, whether from State or Federal sources.

SEC. 40608. RECOMMENDATIONS ON INTRASTATE COMMUNICATION.

The State Justice Institute, after consultation with nationally recognized nonprofit associations with expertise in data sharing among criminal justice agencies and familiarity with the issues raised in stalking and domestic violence cases, shall recommend proposals regarding how State courts may increase intrastate communication between civil and criminal courts.

SEC. 40609. INCLUSION IN NATIONAL INCIDENT-BASED REPORTING SYSTEM.

Not later than 2 years after the date of enactment of this Act, the Attorney General, in accordance with the States, shall compile data regarding domestic violence and intimidation (including stalking) as part of the National Incident-Based Reporting System (NIBRS).

SEC. 40610. REPORT TO CONGRESS.

The Attorney General shall submit to the Congress an annual report, beginning one year after the date of the enactment of this Act, that provides information concerning the incidence of stalking and domestic violence, and evaluates the effectiveness of State antistalking efforts and legislation.

SEC. 40611. DEFINITIONS.

As used in this subtitle—

(1) the term 'national crime information databases' refers to the National Crime Information Center and its incorporated criminal history databases, including the Interstate Identification Index; and

(2) the term 'protection order' includes an injunction or any other order issued for the purpose of preventing violent or threatening acts or harassment against, or contact or communication with or physical proximity to, another person, including temporary and final orders issued by civil or criminal courts (other than support or child custody orders) whether obtained by filing an independent action or as a pendente lite order in another proceeding so long as any civil order was issued in response to a complaint, petition, or motion filed by or on behalf of a person seeking protection.

Subtitle G—Protections for Battered Immigrant Women and Children

SEC. 40701. ALIEN PETITIONING RIGHTS FOR IMMEDIATE RELATIVE OR SECOND PREFERENCE STATUS.

(a) IN GENERAL—Section 204(a)(1) of the Immigration and Nationality Act (8 U.S.C. 1154(a)(1)) is amended—

(1) in subparagraph (A)—

(A) by inserting '(i)' after '(A)',

(B) by redesignating the second sentence as clause (ii), and

(C) by adding at the end the following new clauses:

'(iii) An alien who is the spouse of a citizen of the United States, who is a person of good moral character, who is eligible to be classified as an immediate relative under section 201(b)(2)(A)(i), and who has resided in the United States with the alien's spouse may file a petition with the Attorney General under this subparagraph for classification of the alien (and any child of the alien if such a child has not been classified under clause (iv)) under such section if the alien demonstrates to the Attorney General that—

'(I) the alien is residing in the United States, the marriage between the alien and the spouse was entered into in good faith by the alien, and during the marriage the alien or a child of the alien has been battered by or has been the subject of extreme cruelty perpetrated by the alien's spouse; and

'(II) the alien is a person whose deportation, in the opinion of the Attorney General, would result in extreme hardship to the alien or a child of the alien.

'(iv) An alien who is the child of a citizen of the United States, who is a person of good moral character, who is eligible to be classified as an immediate relative under section 201(b)(2)(A)(i), and who has resided in the United States with the citizen parent may file a petition with the Attorney General under this subparagraph for classification of the alien under such section if the alien demonstrates to the Attorney General that—

'(I) the alien is residing in the United States and during the period of residence with the citizen parent the alien has been battered by or has been the subject of extreme cruelty perpetrated by the alien's citizen parent; and

'(II) the alien is a person whose deportation, in the opinion of the Attorney General, would result in extreme hardship to the alien.';

(2) in subparagraph (B)—

    (A) by inserting '(i)' after '(B)'; and

    (B) by adding at the end the following new clauses:

'(ii) An alien who is the spouse of an alien lawfully admitted for permanent residence, who is a person of good moral character, who is eligible for classification under section 203(a)(2)(A), and who has resided in the United States with the alien's legal permanent resident spouse may file a petition with the Attorney General under this subparagraph for classification of the alien (and any child of the alien if such a child has not been classified under clause (iii)) under such section if the alien demonstrates to the Attorney General that the conditions described in subclauses (I) and (II) of subparagraph (A)(iii) are met with respect to the alien.

'(iii) An alien who is the child of an alien lawfully admitted for permanent residence, who is a person of good moral character, who is eligible for classification under section 203(a)(2)(A), and who has resided in the United States with the alien's permanent resident alien parent may file a petition with the Attorney General under this subparagraph for classification of the alien under such section if the alien demonstrates to the Attorney General that—

'(I) the alien is residing in the United States and during the period of residence with the permanent resident parent the alien has been battered by or has been the subject of extreme cruelty perpetrated by the alien's permanent resident parent; and

'(II) the alien is a person whose deportation, in the opinion of the Attorney General, would result in extreme hardship to the alien.'; and

(3) by adding at the end the following new subparagraph:

'(H) In acting on petitions filed under clause (iii) or (iv) of subparagraph (A) or clause (ii) or (iii) of subparagraph (B), the Attorney General shall consider any credible evidence relevant to the petition. The determination of what evidence is credible and the weight to be given that evidence shall be within the sole discretion of the Attorney General.'.

(b) CONFORMING AMENDMENTS—(1) Section 204(a)(2) of the Immigration and Nationality Act (8 U.S.C. 1154(a)(2)) is amended—

    (A) in subparagraph (A) by striking 'filed by an alien who,' and inserting 'for the classification of the spouse of an alien if the alien,'; and

    (B) in subparagraph (B) by striking 'by an alien whose prior marriage' and inserting 'for the classification of the spouse of an alien if the prior marriage of the alien'.

(2) Section 201(b)(2)(A)(i) of the Immigration and Nationality Act (8 U.S.C. 1151(b)(2)(A)(i)) is amended by striking '204(a)(1)(A)' and inserting '204(a)(1)(A)(ii)'.

(c) SURVIVAL RIGHTS TO PETITION—Section 204 of the Immigration and Nationality Act (8 U.S.C. 1154) is amended by adding at the end the following new subsection:

'(h) The legal termination of a marriage may not be the sole basis for revocation under section 205 of a petition filed under subsection (a)(1)(A)(iii) or a petition filed under subsection (a)(1)(B)(ii) pursuant to conditions described in subsection (a)(1)(A)(iii)(I).'.

(d) EFFECTIVE DATE—The amendments made by this section shall take effect January 1, 1995.

SEC. 40702. USE OF CREDIBLE EVIDENCE IN SPOUSAL WAIVER APPLICATIONS.

(a) IN GENERAL—Section 216(c)(4) of the Immigration and Nationality Act (8 U.S.C. 1186a(c)(4)) is amended by inserting after the second sentence the following: 'In acting on applications under this paragraph, the Attorney General shall consider any credible evidence relevant to the application. The determination of what evidence is credible and the weight to be given that evidence shall be within the sole discretion of the Attorney General.'.

(b) EFFECTIVE DATE—The amendment made by subsection (a) shall take effect on the date of enactment of this Act and shall apply to applications made before, on, or after such date.

SEC. 40703. SUSPENSION OF DEPORTATION.

(a) BATTERED SPOUSE OR CHILD—Section 244(a) of the Immigration and Nationality Act (8 U.S.C. 1254(a)) is amended—

    (1) by striking 'or' at the end of paragraph (1);

    (2) by striking the period at the end of paragraph (2) and inserting '; or'; and

(3) by inserting after paragraph (2) the following:

'(3) is deportable under any law of the United States except section 241(a)(1)(G) and the provisions specified in paragraph (2); has been physically present in the United States for a continuous period of not less than 3 years immediately preceding the date of such application; has been battered or subjected to extreme cruelty in the United States by a spouse or parent who is a United States citizen or lawful permanent resident (or is the parent of a child of a United States citizen or lawful permanent resident and the child has been battered or subjected to extreme cruelty in the United States by such citizen or permanent resident parent); and proves that during all of such time in the United States the alien was and is a person of good moral character; and is a person whose deportation would, in the opinion of the Attorney General, result in extreme hardship to the alien or the alien's parent or child.'.

(b) CONSIDERATION OF EVIDENCE—Section 244 of the Immigration and Nationality Act (8 U.S.C. 1254) is amended by adding at the end the following new subsection:

'(g) In acting on applications under subsection (a)(3), the Attorney General shall consider any credible evidence relevant to the application. The determination of what evidence is credible and the weight to be given that evidence shall be within the sole discretion of the Attorney General.'

Source: U.S. Congress. *Violent Crime Control and Law Enforcement Act* 103rd Congress (1993-1994). H.R.3355.ENR. Available at http://thomas.loc.gov/cgi-bin/query/z?c103:H.R.3355.ENR:

Appendix 2: State, National, and International Organizations Related to Domestic Abuse

State Coalition List

Alabama Coalition Against Domestic Violence
P.O. Box 4762
Montgomery, AL 36101
(334) 832-4842 Fax: (334) 832-4803
(800) 650-6522 Hotline
Website: http://www.acadv.org
E-mail: info@acadv.org

Alaska Network on Domestic and Sexual Violence
130 Seward Street, Room 209
Juneau, AK 99801
(907) 586-3650 Fax: (907) 463-4493
Website: http://www.andvsa.org
E-mail: info@andvsa.org

Arizona Coalition Against Domestic Violence
301 East Bethany Home Road, Suite C194
Phoenix, AZ 85012
(602) 279-2900 Fax: (602) 279-2980
(800) 782-6400 Nationwide
Website: http://www.azcadv.org
E-mail: acadv@azcadv.org

Arkansas Coalition Against Domestic Violence
1401 West Capitol Avenue, Suite 170
Little Rock, AR 72201
(501) 907-5612 Fax: (501) 907-5618
(800) 269-4668 Nationwide
Website: http://www.domesticpeace.com
E-mail: kbangert@domesticpeace.com

California Partnership to End Domestic Violence
P.O. Box 1798
Sacramento, CA 95812
(916) 444-7163 Fax: (916) 444-7165
(800) 524-4765 Nationwide
Website: http://www.cpedv.org
E-mail: info@cpedv.org

Colorado Coalition Against Domestic Violence
1120 Lincoln Street, Suite 900
Denver, CO 80203
(303) 831-9632 Fax: (303) 832-7067
(888) 778-7091
Website: http://www.ccadv.org

Connecticut Coalition Against Domestic Violence
90 Pitkin Street
East Hartford, CT 06108
(860) 282-7899 Fax: (860) 282-7892
(888) 774-2900 In State DV Hotline
Website: http://www.ctcadv.org
E-mail: info@ctcadv.org

Delaware Coalition Against Domestic Violence
100 West 10th Street, #703
Wilmington, DE 19801
(302) 658-2958 Fax: (302) 658-5049
(800) 701-0456 Statewide
Website: http://www.dcadv.org
E-mail: dcadvadmin@dcadv.org

DC Coalition Against Domestic Violence
5 Thomas Circle Northwest
Washington, DC 20005
(202) 299-1181 Fax: (202) 299-1193
Website: http://www.dccadv.org
E-mail: info@dccadv.org

Florida Coalition Against Domestic Violence
425 Office Plaza
Tallahassee, FL 32301
(850) 425-2749 Fax: (850) 425-3091
(850) 621-4202 TDD
(800) 500-1119 In State
Website: http://www.fcadv.org

APPENDIX 2: STATE, NATIONAL, AND INTERNATIONAL ORGANIZATIONS

Georgia Coalition Against Domestic Violence
114 New Street, Suite B
Decatur, GA 30030
(404) 209-0280 Fax: (404) 766-3800
(800) 334-2836 Crisis Line
Website: http://www.gcadv.org
E-mail: info@gcadv.org

Hawaii State Coalition Against Domestic Violence
810 Richards Street
Suite 960
Honolulu, HI 96813
(808) 832-9316 Fax: (808) 841-6028
Website: http://www.hscadv.org
E-mail: admin@hscadv.org

Idaho Coalition Against Sexual and Domestic Violence
300 Mallard Drive, Suite 130
Boise, ID 83706
(208) 384-0419 Fax: (208) 331-0687
(888) 293-6118 Nationwide
Website: http://www.idvsa.org
E-mail: thecoalition@idvsa.org

Illinois Coalition Against Domestic Violence
801 South 11th Street
Springfield, IL 62703
(217) 789-2830 Fax: (217) 789-1939
(217) 242-0376 TTY
Website: http://www.ilcadv.org
E-mail: ilcadv@ilcadv.org

Indiana Coalition Against Domestic Violence
1915 West 18th Street
Indianapolis, IN 46202
(317) 917-3685 Fax: (317) 917-3695
(800) 332-7385 In State
Website: http://www.violenceresource.org
E-mail: icadv@violenceresource.org

Iowa Coalition Against Domestic Violence
515 - 28th Street, Suite 104
Des Moines, IA 50312
(515) 244-8028 Fax: (515) 244-7417
(800) 942-0333 In State Hotline

Website: http://www.icadv.org
E-mail: admin@icadv.org
Kansas Coalition Against Sexual and Domestic Violence
634 Southwest Harrison Street
Topeka, KS 66603
(785) 232-9784 Fax: (785) 266-1874
Website: http://www.kcsdv.org
E-mail: coalition@kcsdv.org

Kentucky Domestic Violence Association
P.O. Box 356
Frankfort, KY 40602
(502) 695-5382 Phone/Fax
Website: http://www.kdva.org
E-mail:kdvasac@aol.com

Louisiana Coalition Against Domestic Violence
P.O. Box 77308
Baton Rouge, LA 70879
(225) 752-1296 Fax: (225) 751-8927
Website: http://www.lcadv.org
E-mail:sheila@lcadv.org

Maine Coalition to End Domestic Violence
104 Sewall Street
Augusta, ME 04330
(207) 430-8334 Fax: (207) 430-8348
Website: http://www.mcedv.org
E-mail: info@mcedv.org

Maryland Network Against Domestic Violence
6911 Laurel-Bowie Road, Suite 309
Bowie, MD 20715
(301) 352-4574 Fax: (301) 809-0422
(800) 634-3577 Nationwide
Website: http://www.mnadv.org
E-mail: info@mnadv.org

Jane Doe, Inc./Massachusetts Coalition Against Sexual Assault
and Domestic Violence
14 Beacon Street, Suite 507
Boston, MA 02108
(617) 248-0922 Fax: (617) 248-0902
(617) 263-2200 TTY/TDD

Website: http://www.janedoe.org
E-mail: info@janedoe.org

Michigan Coalition Against Domestic and Sexual Violence
3893 Okemos Road, Suite B-2
Okemos, MI 48864
(517) 347-7000 Phone/TTY Fax: (517) 248-0902
Website: http://www.mcadsv.org
E-mail: general@mcadsv.org

Minnesota Coalition for Battered Women
60 E. Plato Boulevard, Suite 130
St. Paul, MN 55107
(651) 646-6177 Fax: (651) 646-1527
(651) 646-0994 Crisis Line
(800) 289-6177 Nationwide
Website: http://www.mcbw.org
E-mail: mcbw@mcbw.org

Mississippi Coalition Against Domestic Violence
P.O. Box 4703
Jackson, MS 39296
(601) 981-9196 Fax: (601) 981-2501
(800) 898-3234
Website: http://www.mcadv.org
E-mail: dvpolicy@mcadv.org

Missouri Coalition Against Domestic and Sexual Violence
718 East Capitol Avenue
Jefferson City, MO 65101
(573) 634-4161 Fax: (573) 636-3728
Website: http://www.mocadsv.org
E-mail: mocadsv@mocadsv.org

Montana Coalition Against Domestic and Sexual Violence
P.O. Box 818
Helena, MT 59624
(406) 443-7794 Fax: (406) 443-7818
(888) 404-7794 Nationwide
Website: http://www.mcadsv.com
E-mail: mcadsv@mt.net

Nebraska Domestic Violence Sexual Assault Coalition
1000 "O" Street, Suite 102
Lincoln, NE 68508

(402) 476-6256 Fax: (402) 476-6806
(800) 876-6238 In State Hotline
(877) 215-0167 Spanish Hotline
Website: http://www.ndvsac.org
E-mail: help@ndvsac.org

Nevada Network Against Domestic Violence
220 South Rock Boulevard
Reno, NV 89502
(775) 828-1115 Fax: (775) 828-9911
(800) 500-1556 In State Hotline
Website: http://www.nnadv.org
E-mail: nnadv@powernet.net

New Hampshire Coalition Against Domestic and Sexual Violence
P.O. Box 353
Concord, NH 03302
(603) 224-8893 Fax: (603) 228-6096
(866) 644-3574 In State
Website: http://www.nhcadsv.org
E-mail: director@nhcadsv.org

New Jersey Coalition for Battered Women
1670 Whitehorse Hamilton Square
Trenton, NJ 08690
(609) 584-8107 Fax: (609) 584-9750
(800) 572-7233 In State
Website: http://www.njcbw.org
E-mail: info@njcbw.org

New Mexico Coalition Against Domestic Violence
201 Coal Avenue Southwest
Albuquerque, NM 87102
(505) 246-9240 Fax: (505) 246-9434
(800) 773-3645 In State
Website: http://www.nmcadv.org
E-mail: info@nmcadv.org

New York State Coalition Against Domestic Violence
350 New Scotland Avenue
Albany, NY 12054
(518) 482-5464 Fax: (518) 482-3807
(800) 942-6906 English-In State
(800) 942-6908 Spanish-In State

Website: http://www.nyscadv.org
E-mail: nyscadv@nyscadv.org

North Carolina Coalition Against Domestic Violence
123 West Main Street, Suite 700
Durham, NC 27701
(919) 956-9124 Fax: (919) 682-1449
(888) 232-9124 Nation wide
Website: http://www.nccadv.org

North Dakota Council on Abused Women's Services
418 East Rosser Avenue, Suite 320
Bismarck, ND 58501
(701) 255-6240 Fax: (701) 255-1904
(888) 255-6240 Nationwide
Website: http://www.ndcaws.org
E-mail: ndcaws@ndcaws.org

Action Ohio Coalition For Battered Women
5900 Roche Drive, Suite 445
Columbus, OH 43229
(614) 825-0551 Fax: (614) 825-0673
(888) 622-9315 In State
Website: http://www.actionohio.org
E-mail: actionohio@sbcglobal.net

Ohio Domestic Violence Network
4807 Evanswood Drive, Suite 201
Columbus, OH 43229
(614) 781-9651 Fax: (614) 781-9652
(614) 781-9654 TTY
(800) 934-9840
Website: http://www.odvn.org
E-mail: info@odvn.org

Oklahoma Coalition Against Domestic Violence and Sexual Assault
3815 North Santa Fe Avenue, Suite 124
Oklahoma City, OK 73118
(405) 524-0700 Fax: (405) 524-0711
Website: http://www.ocadvsa.org

Oregon Coalition Against Domestic and Sexual Violence
380 Southeast Spokane Street, Suite 100
Portland, OR 97202
(503) 230-1951 Fax: (503) 230-1973

(877) 230-1951
Website: http://www.ocadsv.com
E-mail: adminasst@ocadsv.com

Pennsylvania Coalition Against Domestic Violence
6400 Flank Drive, Suite 1300
Harrisburg, PA 17112
(717) 545-6400 Fax: (717) 545-9456
(800) 932-4632 Nationwide
Website: http://www.pcadv.org

The Office of Women Advocates
Box 11382
Fernandez Juancus Station
Santurce, PR 00910
(787) 721-7676 Fax: (787) 725-9248

Rhode Island Coalition Against Domestic Violence
422 Post Road, Suite 202
Warwick, RI 02888
(401) 467-9940 Fax: (401) 467-9943
(800) 494-8100 In State
Website: http://www.ricadv.org
E-mail: ricadv@ricadv.org

South Carolina Coalition Against Domestic Violence
and Sexual Assault
P.O. Box 7776
Columbia, SC 29202
(803) 256-2900 Fax: (803) 256-1030
(800) 260-9293 Nationwide
Website: http://www.sccadvasa.org

South Dakota Coalition Against Domestic Violence
and Sexual Assault
P.O. Box 141
Pierre, SD 57501
(605) 945-0869 Fax: (605) 945-0870
(800) 572-9196 Nationwide
Website: http://www.southdakotacoalition.org
E-mail: pierre@sdcadvsa.org

Tennessee Coalition Against Domestic and Sexual Violence
2 International Plaza Drive, Suite 425
Nashville, TN 37217

APPENDIX 2: STATE, NATIONAL, AND INTERNATIONAL ORGANIZATIONS

(615) 386-9406 Fax: (615) 383-2967
(800) 289-9018 In State
Website: http://www.tcadsv.org
E-mail: tcadsv@tcadsv.org

Texas Council on Family Violence
P.O. Box 161810
Austin, TX 78716
(512) 794-1133 Fax: (512) 794-1199
Website: http://www.tcfv.org

Utah Domestic Violence Council
205 North 400 West
Salt Lake City, UT 84103
(801) 521-5544 Fax: (801) 521-5548
Website: http://www.udvac.org

Vermont Network Against Domestic Violence and Sexual Assault
P.O. Box 405
Montpelier, VT 05601
(802) 223-1302 Fax: (802) 223-6943
(802) 223-1115 TTY
Website: http://www.vtnetwork.org
E-mail: info@vtnetwork.org

Women's Coalition of St. Croix
Box 2734
Christiansted
St. Croix, VI 00822
(340) 773-9272 Fax: (340) 773-9062
Website: http://www.wcstx.com
E-mail: wcsc@pennswoods.net

Virginians Against Domestic Violence
2850 Sandy Bay Road, Suite 101
Williamsburg, VA 23185
(757) 221-0990 Fax: (757) 229-1553
(800) 838-8238 Nationwide
Website: http://www.vadv.org
E-mail: vadv@tni.net

Washington State Coalition Against Domestic Violence
711 Capitol Way, Suite 702
Olympia, WA 98501
(360) 586-1022 Fax: (360) 586-1024

(360) 586-1029 TTY
1402 Third Avenue, Suite 406
Seattle, WA 98101
(206) 389-2515 Fax: (206) 389-2520
(800) 886-2880 Nationwide
(206) 389-2900 TTY
Website: http://www.wscadv.org
E-mail: wscadv@wscadv.org

Washington State Native American Coalition Against Domestic and Sexual Assault
P.O. Box 13260
Olympia, WA 98508
(360) 352-3120 Fax: (360) 357-3858
(888) 352-3120
Website: http://www.womenspiritcoalition.org

West Virginia Coalition Against Domestic Violence
5004 Elk River Road South
Elkview, WV 25071
(304) 965-3552 Fax: (304) 965-3572
Website: http://www.wvcadv.org

Wisconsin Coalition Against Domestic Violence
307 South Paterson Street, Suite 1
Madison, WI 53703
(608) 255-0539 Fax: (608) 255-3560
Website: http://www.wcadv.org
E-mail: wcadv@wcadv.org

Wyoming Coalition Against Domestic Violence and Sexual Assault
P.O. Box 236
409 South Fourth Street
Laramie, WY 82073
(307) 755-5481 Fax: (307) 755-5482
(800) 990-3877 Nationwide
Website: http://www.wyomingdvsa.org
E-mail: info@mail.wyomingdvsa.org

Other Resources in the United States

Alianza: National Latino Alliance for the Elimination of Domestic Violence:
http://www.dvalianza.org/
Addresses the needs of Latino/a victims of abuse.

American Bar Association Commission on Domestic Violence: http://www.abanet.org/domviol
Legal resources and information related to abuse.

American Civil Liberties Union (ACLU): http://www.aclu.org
Advocating for civil rights broadly.

American Domestic Violence Crisis Line: http://www.866uswomen.org
Crisis line and resources for civilian and enlisted Americans living overseas.

American Humane Association: http://www.americanhumane.org
Information about pet abuse and domestic violence.

American Institute on Domestic Violence: http://www.aidv-usa.com
Focuses on workplace violence.

American Medical Association: http://www.ama-assn.org/ama/pub/physician-resources/public-health/promoting-healthy-lifestyles/violence-prevention.page
Provides information and resources regarding health care and domestic violence.

Amnesty International USA: http://www.amnestyusa.org
Human rights group includes work on violence against women.

Asian and Pacific Islander Institute on Domestic Violence: http://www.apiahf.org/apidvinstitute
"Works to eliminate domestic violence in Asian and Pacific Islander communities."

Asian Task Force Against Domestic Violence: http://www.atask.org
Helping end abuse in Asian communities.

The Audre Lorde Project: http://www.alp.org
Promotes community wellness and economic and social justice.

Ayuda: http://www.ayudainc.org
Resources and information about the rights of battered immigrant women.

Bureau of Justice Statistics Clearinghouse: http://www.ojp.usdoj.gov/bjs
Provides statistics and research on a variety of topics.

Childhelp USA: http://www.childhelpusa.org
Addressing the prevention and treatment of child abuse.

Children's Defense Fund: http://www.childrensdefense.org
A voice for the health and safety of children.

Child Welfare League of America: http://www.cwla.org
Focuses on the welfare of children.

Code Pink For Peace: http://www.codepink4peace.org
Female-led initiative to stop war and promote peace.

College Brides Walk: http://www.collegebrideswalk.org
Coordinates annual walk to raise awareness and end abuse.

Communities Against Violence Network (CAVNET):
http://www.cavnet.blogspot.org
Wealth of resources on all topics related to abuse.

Corporate Alliance to End Partner Violence: http://www.caepv.org/
Information and resource primarily about domestic violence in the workplace.

Do Something: http://www.dosomething.org
Teen-focused website providing information and support to empower young people to be agents of change.

Faith Trust Institute: http://www.cpsdv.org
Largely focused on abuse in faith communities.

The Feminist Majority and the Feminist Majority Foundation:
http://www.feminist.org
Promotes gender equality.

Futures Without Violence: http://www.futureswithoutviolence.org
Wealth of information and resources related to abuse.

Human Rights Watch: http://www.hrw.org
Global human rights watchdog.

INCITE! Women of Color Against Violence: http://www.incite-national.org
Grassroots organization addressing violence against women of color.

Indigenous Women's Network: http://www.indigenouswomen.org
Provides information and support for indigenous women.

Institute on Domestic Violence in the African American Community:
http://www.dvinstitute.org
Promoting research and resources related to abuse in the African American community.

APPENDIX 2: STATE, NATIONAL, AND INTERNATIONAL ORGANIZATIONS

Jewish Women International: http://www.jewishwomen.org
Addresses abuse involving the Jewish community.
The Joyful Heart Foundation: http://www.joyfulheart.org
Founded in 2002 by actress Mariska Hargitay with the aim of helping survivors heal.

LAMBDA GLBT Community Services: http://www.lambda.org
Legal resources for LGBT persons.

Legal Momentum: http://www.nowldef.org
Focuses on legal resources for victims.

Love Is Not Abuse: http://loveisnotabuse.com
Provides resources and information related to teen dating violence.

Love Is Respect: http://www.loveisrespect.org
Focuses on promoting healthy teen relationships.

Men Can Stop Rape: http://www.mencanstoprape.org
Advocates for men to address societal sexism and stop sexual harassment and assault.

Mending the Sacred Hoop: http://www.mshoop.org
"Working to End Violence Against Native American Women"

Men Stopping Violence: http://www.menstoppingviolence.org
"Works to dismantle belief systems, social structures, and institutional practices that oppress women and children and dehumanize men."

Ms. Foundation for Women: http://www.ms.foundation.org
Grants and support for domestic violence shelters.

National Center for Elder Abuse: http://www.elderabusecenter.org
Clearinghouse of information related to elder abuse.

National Center for Victims of Crime: http://www.ncvc.org
Information and advocacy for domestic violence victims and other crime victims.

National Center on Domestic and Sexual Violence: http://www.ncdsv.org
Provides information on all forms of abuse.

National Center on Elder Abuse: http://www.ncea.aoa.gov
Clearinghouse of information and resources related to elder abuse.

National Clearinghouse for the Defense of Battered Women:
http://www.ncdbw.org/
"Working for justice for battered women charged with crimes."

National Clearinghouse on Abuse in Later Life: http://www.ncall.us
Focuses on elder abuse.

National Coalition for the Homeless: http://www.nationalhomeless.org
Advocacy for the homeless.

National Coalition of Anti-Violence Programs: http://www.ncavp.org
Brings together numerous antiviolence efforts.

National Domestic Violence Hotline: http://www.ndvh.org
Information and hotline for victims.

National Gay and Lesbian Task Force: http://www.ngltf.org
Advocacy and empowerment for LGBT persons.

National Immigration Forum: http://www.immigrationforum.org
Promoting immigrants' rights.

National Latino Alliance for the Elimination of Domestic Violence (ALIANZA):
http://www.dvalianza.org
Focuses on domestic violence in Latino/a communities.

National Network for Immigrant and Refugee Rights: http://www.nnirr.org
"Works to defend and expand the rights of all immigrants and refugees, regardless of immigration status."

National Network to End Domestic Violence: http://www.nnedv.org
Coordinates annual 24-hour census on domestic violence, among other things.

National Organization for Men Against Sexism: http://www.nomas.org
Male-led feminist organization devoted to ending sexism and violence against women.

National Organization for Victim Assistance: http://www.try-nova.org
Promotes dignity and compassion for victims of crime.

National Resource Center on Domestic Violence: http://www.nrcdv.org
Information and research on all forms of abuse.

National Runaway Switchboard: http://www.nrscrisisline.org
Resources for preventing and responding to runaways.

National Sexual Violence Resource Center: http://www.nsvrc.org
Provides information and resources related to sexual violence.

National Women's Political Caucus: http://www.nwpc.org
Promoting women's issues and women's involvement in the political system.

No More Tears: http://www.nmtproject.org
Grassroots nonprofit assisting victims.

Office for Victims of Crime: http://www.ovc.gov
U.S. governmental office for crime victims resources and support.

Planned Parenthood Federation of America: http://www.plannedparenthood.org
"The nation's leading sexual and reproductive health care provider and advocate."

Rape, Abuse and Incest National Network (RAINN): http://www.rainn.org
Statistics, research, and resources related to sexual violence and abuse.

Rural Assistance Center: http://www.raconline.org
"Health and human service information for rural America."

The Sister Fund: http://www.sisterfund.org
"Private foundation that supports and gives voice to women working for justice from a religious framework."

Soroptimist International of the Americas: http://www.soroptimist.org
"International organization for business and professional women who work to improve the lives of women and girls."

Stop Abuse for Everyone: http://www.safe4all.org
"A human rights organization that provides services, publications, and training to serve those who typically fall between the cracks of domestic violence services: straight men, GLBT victims, teens, and the elderly."

Students Active for Ending Rape: http://www.safer.org
"Empowers students to hold their universities accountable for having strong campus sexual assault policies and programming."

Third Wave Foundation: http://www.thirdwavefoundation.org
Supports third-wave feminists in their efforts to promote gender equality.

Violence Against Women Office, U.S. Department of Justice:
http://www.ojp.usdoj.gov/vaw
Information and grant funding for domestic violence services.

Women's e-news: http://www.womensenews.org
Compilation of news articles related to women's issues or of interest to women.

Women's Independence Scholarship Program, The Sunshine Lady Foundation: http://www.sunshineladyfdn.org
Scholarship for domestic violence victims.

WomensLaw.org: http://www.womenslaw.org
"Providing legal information and support to victims of domestic violence and sexual assault.

International Resources

Afghan Institute of Learning: http://www.creatinghope.org
Operates schools and programs for women and girls in Afghanistan and in the border areas of Pakistan.

American Assistance for Cambodia: http://www.cambodiaschools.com
Fights trafficking and helps subsidize poor girls so they can remain in school.

Americans for United Nations Population Fund (UNFPA): http://www.americansforunfpa.org
Helps support the work of the UN Population Fund in addressing reproductive issues and family planning across the globe.

Apne Aap: http://www.apneap.org
NGO helping to address sex slavery in India.

Ashoka: http://www.ashoka.org
Helps identify and support social entrepreneurs who can assist people across the globe.

Averting Maternal Death and Disability: http://www.amdprogram.org
Organization devoted to promoting maternal health.

BC Institute Against Domestic Violence: http://www.bcifv.org
Supports, coordinates, and initiates research and educational programs related to domestic violence in British Columbia, Canada.

Campaign for Female Education: http://www.camfed.org
Organization supporting the schooling of girls in Africa.

CARE: http://www.care.org
Large NGO focused on helping people struggling with poverty or other human needs.

APPENDIX 2: STATE, NATIONAL, AND INTERNATIONAL ORGANIZATIONS

Center for Development and Population Activities: http://www.cedpa.org
Works on a variety of issues related to women and development.

Center for Reproductive Rights: http://www.reproductiverights.org
New York–based NGO focusing on reproductive rights and health worldwide.

Domestic Violence and Incest Resource Center: http://home.vicnet.net.au/~dvirc/
Provides information and referral to domestic violence victims, to child victims, and to incest survivors in Australia.

ECPAT: http://www.ecpat.net
Focused largely on Southeast Asia; addresses child prostitution.

Engender Health: http://www.engenderhealth.org
NGO focusing on global reproductive health.

Equality Now: http://www.equalitynow.org
U.S.-based organization promoting all forms of equality, in particular, the rights of LGBT persons.

Family Care International: http://www.familycareintl.org
Addresses maternal health in Africa, Latin America, and the Caribbean.

Global Fund for Women: http://www.globalfundforwomen.org
A venture-capital group for women's organizations in poor countries.

Global Grassroots: http://www.globalgrassroots.org
Helps women in poor countries, in particular, Sudan.

Grameen Bank: http://www.grameen-infp.org
Microfinance organization originating in Bangladesh but now involved in other countries and involved in diverse projects.

Heal Africa: http://www.healafrica.org
Operates a hospital in Goma, Congo, that helps repair fistulas and assists rape victims.

Hot Peach Pages: http://www.hotpeachpages.net
Worldwide list of agencies against domestic violence.

Human Rights Watch: http://www.hrw.org
Multiple worldwide offices devoted to documenting human rights atrocities.

Hunger Project: http://www.thp.org
Empowers women and girls to end hunger.

International Center for Research on Women: http://www.icrw.org
Focuses on gender equality as key to improving economic development.

International Justice Mission: http://www.ijm.org
Christian organization that focuses on sex trafficking.

International Women's Health Coalition: http://www.iwhc.org
New York–based NGO that promotes reproductive health worldwide.

Marie Stopes International: http://www.mariestopes.org
UK-based NGO that promotes reproductive health worldwide.

National Clearinghouse on Family Violence (NCFV):
http://www.hc-sc.gc.ca/hppb/familyviolence
National resource center for Canadians regarding partner abuse, child abuse, and elder abuse.

New Light: http://www.newlightindia.org
Helps prostitutes and their children in Kolkata, India.

Northern Ireland Women's Aid Federation: http://www.niwaf.org
24-hour hotline, support services, and referral for victims, children, and refugees in Northern Ireland.

Pathfinder International: http://www.pathfind.org
Operating in more than 25 countries, an NGO focusing on reproductive health.

Pro Mujer: http://www.promujer.org
Provides microfinancing and business training to women in Latin America.

Provincial Association of Transition Houses and Services of Saskatchewan (PATHS): http://www.abusehelplines.org
Nonprofit organization providing shelter and transitional housing for victims in Saskatchewan.

Scottish Women's Aid: http://www.scottishwomensaid.co.uk
Provides information, support, and referrals for victims.

Self-Employed Women's Association: http://www.sewa.org
Large union for self-employed women in India.

APPENDIX 2: STATE, NATIONAL, AND INTERNATIONAL ORGANIZATIONS

Shared Hope International: http://www.sharedhope.org
Global NGO fighting sex trafficking.

Shelternet: http://www.shelternet.ca
Canadian resource center.

Somaly Mam Foundation: http://www.somaly.org
Founded by victim of child trafficking, fights sex slavery in Cambodia.

Stop Honour Killings: http://www.stophonourkillings.com/
Organization devoted to awareness and lobbying for legislation to end honor killings.

Tostan: http://www.tostan.org
Focuses on ending female genital cutting in Africa.

UNICEF: http://www.unicef.org
Mandated by the UN General Assembly and guided by the UN Convention on the Rights of the Child, a global advocate for children's human rights.

United Nations Women (UN Women): http://www.unwomen.org
The United Nations' only group devoted specifically to addressing gender inequalities.

V-Day: http://www.vday.org
Eve Ensler's organization focused on ending gender violence.

Violence Against Women Network: http://www.vaw-net.org
Provides a wealth of information on all types of abuse, victims and offenders, interventions and prevention strategies.

Vital Voices: http://www.vitalvoices.org
Addresses numerous gender inequalities globally.

White Ribbon Alliance for Safe Motherhood: http://www.whiteribbonalliance.org
Advocacy group to address maternal mortality worldwide.

White Ribbon Campaign: http://www.whiteribbon.ca
Male-led campaign based in Canada. Focus is on awareness and education.

Women Against Violence Europe (WAVE): http://www.wave-network.org
Provides shelters, counseling, education, and hotlines throughout Europe.

Women for Women International: http://www.womenforwomen.org
Helps connect female sponsors with needy women in conflict-ridden or post-conflict countries.

Women's Aid Federation of England: http://www.womensaid.org.uk
National domestic violence charity in England.

Women's Campaign International: http://www.womenscampaignnternational.org
Focuses on increasing women's political involvement across the globe.

Women's Dignity Project: http://www.womensdignity.org
Provides medical services and repairs fistulas in Tanzania.

Women's Learning Project: http://www.learningpartnership.org
Focuses on empowering women to be leaders in the developing world.

Women's Link Worldwide: http://www.womenslinkworldwide.org
Wealth of information relevant to women's issues in Western Europe and Latin America

Women's Refugee Commission: http://www.womensrefugeecommission.org
Assists refugees and their children.

Women's Resource Information and Support Centre: http://wrisc.ballart.net.au
Offers information, outreach, and support throughout Australia.

Women's World Banking: http://www.womensworldbanking.org
Supports microfinance groups for women.

Women Thrive Worldwide: http://www.womenthrive.org
International advocacy group for poor women.

World Pulse: http://www.worldpulse.org
Media outlet focusing on women's empowerment.

Worldwide Fistula Fund: http://www.worldwidefistulafund.org
Helps raise awareness about fistulas as well as funds to repair them.

Glossary

Abusive personality: Coined by Donald Dutton, a term used to describe batterers. Proposes that men become violent because they fear abandonment. Characteristics include a tendency to blame, attachment anxiety, and sustained rageful outbursts.

Acid attack: The throwing of acid onto the body, often the face, by one family member against another, typically a female, with the goal of disfiguring or killing that person.

Adjudicatory hearings: Juvenile and Family Court hearings intended to determine whether a child has been maltreated or whether another legal basis exists for the State to intervene to protect the child.

Aggravated assault: An unlawful attack by one person on another involving the use or display of a weapon in a threatening manner, or when the victim suffers obvious severe or aggravated bodily injury, such as broken bones, loss of teeth, severe lacerations, loss of consciousness, or other noticeable injuries.

Anger management programs: Courses, often but not always court-mandated, that help attendees understand what triggers their anger and work on managing anger in healthy, constructive ways.

Animal abuse: Violence toward a family pet or other wildlife intended as a means of demonstrating or acquiring power and control over a victim and/or children.

Antisocial behaviors: Behaviors that involve violating social norms and suggest a disregard for the feelings of others.

Antisocial personality disorder: A personality disorder that is characterized by impulsivity, inability to follow societal customs and laws, and lack of anxiety and guilt.

Battered woman: A women who bas been the victim of physical abuse from an intimate partner.

Battered woman syndrome: Developed by psychologist Lenore Walker, the syndrome is said to include feelings of learned helplessness and the cycle of violence that are the result of trauma experienced through domestic abuse. Typically used as a defense for battered women who kill their abusers.

Batterer: The perpetrator of physical intimate partner violence.

Batterer's intervention program: Coursework, typically court-mandated, to help abusers take responsibility for their behavior and identify ways to change it so as not to reoffend.

Battering: A pattern of physical abuse against an intimate partner used to obtain and maintain power and control in the relationship.

Beijing Platform: An agenda for women's empowerment that emerged out of the 1995 United Nations Fourth World Conference on Women.

Biological theories: A category of theories explaining abuse as the result of heredity, childhood trauma, or head injuries.

Borderline personality disorder: A personality disorder that features various manifestations, including impulsivity, mood instability, and perhaps even functional psychosis. Patients typically experience periods of normalcy as well.

Bullying: Physical, sexual, verbal, emotional, and other forms of harmful or violent behavior perpetrated by one person against another. Typically associated with youth but shares the same power-control dynamic as in dating and domestic violence.

Bystander intervention programs: Educational programs focused on informing participants about a phenomena and providing them with skills to intervene safely to disrupt harmful behavior like bullying and abuse.

Case management: The arrangement, coordination, and monitoring of services to assist victims and their families.

Child Protective Services (CPS): In most states, the designated social services agency to receive reports, investigate, and provide intervention and treatment services to children and families in which child maltreatment has allegedly occurred.

Child victim: A child for whom an incident of abuse or neglect has been substantiated or indicated by an investigation or assessment by authorities.

Child witness: Refers to a child who is present when abuse occurs, regardless of whether s/he sees the abuse.

Compassion fatigue: Occurs when advocates experience a state of exhaustion, often accompanied by depression and hopelessness due to the challenging nature of working with traumatized populations.

Convention on the Elimination of All Forms of Violence Against Women (CEDAW): UN treaty now ratified by 189 nations, designed to address global gender inequalities, including a variety of forms of violence against women.

Coordinated community response: A community effort that includes key representatives from politics, law enforcement, courts, education, social services, medical professions, faith leaders and more, with the goal of changing social norms that lead to abuse, providing services for those who have been harmed, and holding abusers accountable.

Counseling services: Application of therapeutic assistance to persons who have been victimized or affected by abuse. May be provided by staff at a domestic violence center or a private practitioner.

Court-appointed representative: A person appointed by a judge or court official to represent a person in neglect or abuse proceedings.

Crime Victims Compensation Program (CVC): Government fund established to assist qualifying victims of violent crime and their families with crime-related expenses, including, but not limited to, costs related to counseling, funeral and burial, medical and mental health, emergency/temporary shelter, and other costs as permitted by statute.

Cultural competence: Attitudes, behaviors, and policies ensure that persons of all cultural backgrounds are served fairly and humanely.

Cycle of violence: First described by Lenore Walker, the idea that some abusive relationships demonstrate a specific cycle involving a building of tensions, a violent outburst, and then a honeymoon period in which the abuser apologizes and promises to change.

Dating violence: Violence in a dating relationship involving people ages 14 to 22.

Domestic violence: A pattern of coercive behavior used by one person to control another in an intimate relationship. May include physical, sexual, emotional, financial, spiritual, or other means.

Domestic violence victims advocates: Individuals, both professional and volunteer, who advocate for the rights and safety of adult victims and children and helps connect them to appropriate resources.

Dowry killings: Killing of a family member, typically a female, by members of her own family or the family into which she is to wed over some dispute related to the payment of a dowry or bride price.

Dual arrest: Arrest of both parties in a domestic violence situation because the officer is unable to determine the predominant aggressor or believes both parties have committed an arrestable offense.

Economic/financial abuse: Batterers' use of finances to establish and maintain power and control over a victim, including but not limited to, controlling a partner's finances, taking the victim's money without permission, giving the victim an allowance, prohibiting/limiting a victim's access to bank accounts or credit card, denying the victim the right to work, and/or sabotaging a victim's credit.

Elder abuse: Includes physical, sexual, financial, emotional, and verbal maltreatment as well as neglectful treatment of a person over the age of 60.

Emotional abuse: Refers to a type of abuse that causes emotional pain. May include withholding approval, constant insults, yelling, humiliation, belittling, demanding exclusive attention, destruction of property, accusations, and other tactics. Typically used in conjunction with other types of abuse.

Failure to protect: Used by some Child Protective Services workers, a claim that victims have failed to protect their child from harm in the home.

Family systems theory: A model that addresses the whole family in assessing the cause and forms of abuse. Critics contend this blames victims.

Family violence: Typically refers to any type of violence occurring between family members, such as domestic violence, child abuse, and elder abuse.

Female genital mutilation (FGM): Painful procedure involving the removal of some or all of a female's genitalia. Still practiced in many cultures but considered by women's rights advocates to be a human rights violation.

Feminism: The belief that men and women are of inherently equal worth.

Help-seeking: The act of seeking help to end or escape from abuse.

Heterosexism: An ideological system that promotes heterosexuality as the norm and denies or even denigrates and stigmatizes nonheterosexual identity, behavior, relationships, or communities.

Homophobia: Fear of homosexuality, typically manifested in a dislike or dread of being near those who are or are perceived to be homosexual.

Honor killing: Murder perpetrated by a family member against a fellow member, typically a female, who is perceived to have dishonored the family.

Human rights: Fundamental and inalienable rights that each person in the world is guaranteed. First laid out in the Universal Declaration of Human Rights and since delineated in numerous international treaties and agreements.

Human trafficking: Taking someone by force or deception for the purposes of sexual or commercial labor.

International Violence Against Women Act (I-VAWA): Proposed legislation that would help provide funding and support to address violence against women domestically and globally.

Intervention: Societal responses to domestic violence, including shelters, arrest and prosecution, counseling, medical attention, and more.

Keeping Children and Families Safe Act: Enacted in 2003 (P.L. 108-36), this legislation included the reauthorization of the Child Abuse Prevention and Treatment Act (CAPTA). CAPTA provides minimum standards for defining child physical abuse and neglect and sexual abuse that states must incorporate into their statutory definitions in order to receive federal funds.

Learned helplessness: A condition in which a person does not escape from a painful or dangerous situation after learning from previous experience that such escape is impossible.

Level of lethality (or dangerousness): Assessing both the number and types of indicators (e.g., use of weapons, stalking, threats of homicide, sexual abuse, mental illness) that help determine the risk of a batterer severely harming or killing the adult victim or the children.

Mandatory arrest laws: Laws requiring police arrest perpetrators of domestic violence when they have probable cause.

Mandatory report laws: Laws requiring specific professionals to report certain types of abuse to designated authorities. All 50 states require health-care professionals and educators to report child abuse and elder abuse. Some states require health-care professionals to report domestic violence.

Mediation: The process in which a neutral third party attempts to guide conflict partners in the search for a mutually agreeable and beneficial solution through open and honest communication.

Minnesota Domestic Violence Experiment: Eighteen-month scientific experiment conducted in 1981–82 by researchers Lawrence Sherman and Richard Berk to determine the police response most effective at reducing reoffense. Results showed arresting perpetrators to be most effective, leading to the wide-scale enactment of mandatory arrest policies and laws.

Patriarchy: A society that is male dominated, male identified, and male centered. Argued by feminists to be the root cause of domestic violence.

Perpetrator: Person committing the abuse.

Physical abuse: May include any variety of assaults, ranging from pinching, shoving, slapping, and punching to actual murder.

Post-traumatic stress disorder (PTSD): An anxiety disorder produced by an extremely stressful event. Victims may reexperience the trauma; become numb, disinterested, or detached; demonstrate exaggerated responses; disturbed sleep; difficulty concentrating; or a variety of other effects.

Prevalence: In this regard, the number of people in the population who are affected by domestic violence.

Primary prevention: Efforts to prevent domestic violence from occurring. Typically includes efforts to reduce gender inequalities and address gender role stereotypes, decrease violent media, educate young people about healthy relationships, and more.

Protective factor: A variable that decreases the chance that a phenomenon will occur.

Psychopathology: Mental disorders. Some theorists maintain that batterers suffer from various psychopathologies.

Reproductive coercion: Form of abuse in which abusers control access to or use of birth control.

Resiliency: Qualities that allow individuals to adapt and remain strong despite risk and adversity.

Restraining orders: Sometimes called personal protection orders, a legal document that mandates a person who has been determined by a judge to be a threat stay a designated distance away from and make no contact with their victim.

Risk factor: A variable that increases the chance that a phenomenon will occur.

Safety plan: A document developed by victims, typically with the support of an advocate, that outlines how the victim intends to remain safe when threat is imminent.

Secondary prevention: Targeting of at-risk populations for services in order to decease risk factors, thereby decreasing domestic violence.

Secondary trauma: A risk we incur when we engage compassionately or empathically with a traumatized adult or child.

Self-defense: Legal right to defend oneself when facing an imminent threat.

Sexual abuse: Sexual acts completed against a victim's will or when the victim is unable to consent due to age, illness, disability, or the influence of drugs or alcohol. May include actual or threatened physical force, use of weapons, coercion, intimidation, or pressure.

Shelter: A short-term, undisclosed safe space for victims of intimate partner violence.

Simple assault: An unlawful physical attack by one person on another where the offender does not display a weapon nor does the victim suffer obvious physical injury.

Social learning theories: Theories that assert that deviant or criminal behavior such as battering is learned behavior.

Spiritual/religious abuse: Batterer's use of spirituality or religion, including, but not limited to, controlling the partner's ability to practice her/his own religion or attend services, forcing the partner to convert or practice another religion against her/his will and/or using the spiritual or religious environment, leader, and/or congregation to influence a victim's behavior.

Spousal abuse: Abuse occurring in a marital relationship.

Stalking: Unwanted and repeated visual or physical proximity or nonconsensual communication resulting in fear for the targeted person.

Tertiary prevention: Attempts to minimize the effects of domestic violence by identifying and holding abusers accountable and providing resources to victims.

Trafficking Victims Protection Act: Legislation enacted in 2000 to raise awareness about trafficking and to provide funding and support for victims' services and prosecution of traffickers.

Transitional housing: Housing that typically lasts up to two years, serving as a bridge between receiving emergency services and finding permanent housing.

Tribal Law and Justice Act: Legislation enacted in 2009 to address violence against women in Indian country.

Violence Against Women Act: First authorized in 1994 and reauthorized in 2000 and 2005, legislation that provided for services and support for victims of abuse. Being debated for reauthorization in 2012.

Recommended Resources: Books, Journals, Articles, and Videos

Books

Aldarondo, E., & Mederos, F. (Eds.). (2002). *Programs for men who batter.* Kingston, NJ: Civic Research Institute.

Bales. K. (2007). *Ending slavery: How we free today's slaves.* Berkeley, CA: University of California Press.

Bales, K., & Soodalter, R. (2010). *The slave next door: Human trafficking and slavery in America today.* Berkeley, CA: University of California Press.

Banaszak, L. (2005). *The U.S. women's movement in global perspective.* Lanham, MD: Rowman and Littlefield.

Bancroft, L. (2003). *Why does he do that? Inside the minds of angry and controlling men.* New York, NY: Berkley Trade.

Barnett, O., Miller-Perrin, C., & Perrin, R. (2011). *Family violence across the lifespan: An introduction* (3rd ed.). Thousand Oaks, CA: Sage

Batstone, D. (2007). *Not for sale.* New York, NY: HarperCollins.

Baumgardner, J., & Richards, A. (2005). *Grassroots: A field guide for feminist activism.* New York, NY: Farrar, Straus, & Giroux.

Benedict, J. (1997). *Public heroes, private felons.* Boston, MA: Northeastern University Press.

Benedict, J. (1998). *Athletes and acquaintance rape.* Thousand Oaks, CA: Sage.

Benedict, J. (1998). *Pros and cons: The criminals who play in the NFL.* New York: Grand Central Press.

Benedict, J. (2004). *Out of bounds: Inside the NBA's culture of rape, violence & crime.* New York, NY: HarperCollins.

Berns, N. (2004). *Framing the victim: Domestic violence, media, and social problems.* Piscataway, NJ: Aldine.

Boyle, K. (2005). *Media violence: Gendering the debates.* London, England: Sage.

Brown, L. (2000). *Sex slaves: The trafficking of women in Asia.* New York, NY: Vintage.

Brown, L. (2005). *The dancing girls of Lahore.* New York, NY: HarperCollins.

Buzawa, E., & Buzawa, C. (2002). *Domestic violence: The criminal justice response.* Thousand Oaks, CA: Sage.

Ching-In, C., Dulani, J., & Piepzna-Samarasinha, L. (Eds.). (2011). *The revolution starts at home: Confronting intimate violence within activist communities.* Boston, MA: South End Press.

Collins, G. (2003). *American women.* New York, NY: Harper Perennial.

Cook, P. (2009). *Abused men: The hidden side of domestic violence.* Westport, CT: Praeger.

Cose, E. (1995). *A man's world: How real is male privilege—and how high is its price?* New York, NY: HarperCollins.

Daniel, O., & Erica, M. (Eds.). (2009). *Psychological and physical aggression in couples: Causes and interventions*. Washington, DC: American Psychological Association Press.

Davies, J., Lyon, E., & Monti-Cantania, D. (1998). *Safety planning with battered women: Complex lives, different choices*. Thousand Oaks, CA: Sage.

Dostrovsky, N., Cook, R. J., & Gagnon, M. (2007). *Annotated bibliography on comparative and international law relating to forced marriage*. Ottawa, ON: Department of Justice Canada.

Douglas, E. M., & Straus, M. A. (2003). *Corporal punishment experienced by university students in 17 countries and its relation to assault and injury of dating partners*. Helsinki, Finland: European Society of Criminology.

Dutton. D. (2007). *Rethinking domestic violence*. Vancouver, Canada: UBC Press.

Faludi, S. (1991). *Backlash: The undeclared war against American women*. New York, NY: Doubleday.

Finley, L., & Stringer, E. (Eds.). (2010). *Beyond burning bras: Feminist activism for everyone*. Santa Barbara, CA: Praeger.

Freedman, E. (2002). *No turning back: The history of feminism and the future of women*. New York, NY: Ballantine.

Gaon, I., & Forbord, N. (2005). *For sale: Women and children*. Victoria, BC: Trafford.

Goodwin, J. (2003). *Price of honor: Muslim women lift the veil of silence on the Islamic world*. New York, NY: Penguin.

Gordon, L. (2002). *Heroes of their own lives: The politics and history of family violence*. Champaign, IL: University of Illinois Press.

Haaken, J. (2010). *What does storytelling tell us about domestic violence? Hard knocks: Domestic violence and the psychology of storytelling*. London, England: Routledge.

Hamel, J. (2005). *Gender-inclusive treatment of intimate partner abuse: A comprehensive approach*. New York, NY: Springer.

Hansen, M., & Harway, M. (Eds.). (2002). *Battering and family therapy: A feminist perspective*. Thousand Oaks, CA: Sage.

Healey, K., Smith, C., & O'Sullivan, C. (2009). *Batterer intervention: program approaches and criminal justice strategies*. Washington, DC: U.S. Department of Justice.

Herz, B., & Sperling, G. (2004). *What works in girls' education: Evidence and policies from the developing world*. New York, NY: Council on Foreign Relations.

Hines, D., & Malley-Morrison, K. (2005). *Family violence in the United States: Defining, understanding, and combating abuse*. Thousand Oaks, CA: Sage.

Holland, J. (2006). *Misogyny: the world's oldest prejudice*. New York, NY: Carroll & Graf.

Incite! Women of Color Against Violence. (2007). *The revolution will not be funded: Beyond the non-profit industrial complex*. Boston, MA: South End Press.

Jones, A. (2000). *Next time, she'll be dead: Battering and how to stop it*. Boston, MA: Beacon.

Katz, J. (2006). *The macho paradox*. Naperville, IL: Sourcebooks.

Kelly, S., & Breslin, J. (Eds.). (2010). *Women's rights in the Middle East and North Africa: Progress amid resistance*. New York, NY: Freedom House.

Kilbourne, J. (2000). *Can't buy my love: How advertising changes the way we think and feel*. New York, NY: Free Press.

Kimmel, M. (2006). *Manhood in America* (2nd ed.). New York, NY: Oxford University Press.

Kimmel, M. (2008). *Guyland: The perilous world where boys become men*. New York, NY: Harper.

Kimmel, M., & Messner, M. (Eds.). (2001). *Men's Lives*. Boston, MA: Allyn & Bacon.

Kirk, G., & Okazawa-Rey, M. (2007). *Women's lives, multicultural perspectives* (4th ed.). Boston, MA: McGraw-Hill.

Kristof, N., & WuDunn, S. (2009). *Half the sky: Turning oppression into opportunity for women worldwide.* New York, NY: Alfred A. Knopf.
La Violette, A., & Barnett, O. (2000). *It could happen to anyone: Why battered women stay* (2nd ed.). Thousand Oaks, CA: Sage.
Laughlin, K., & Castledine, J. (2010) *Breaking the wave: Women, their organizations, and feminism 1945–1985.* New York, NY: Routledge.
Leonard. E. (2002). *Convicted survivors: The imprisonment of battered women who kill.* New York, NY: SUNY Press.
Levy, B. (1998). *Dating violence: Young women in danger* (2nd ed.). Seattle, WA: Seal Press.
Levy, B. (Ed.). (1998). *In love and danger: A teen's guide to breaking free of abusive relationships* (2nd ed.). Seattle, WA: Seal Press.
Lobel, K. (Ed.). (1986). *Naming the violence: Speaking out about lesbian battering.* Seattle, WA: Seal Press.
Logan, T. K., Cole, J., Shannon, L., & Walker, R. (2006). *Partner stalking: How women respond, cope, and survive (Springer Series on Family Violence).* New York, NY: Springer.
Loseke, D., & Gelles, R., & Cavanaugh, M. (Eds.). (2004). *Current controversies on family violence* (2nd ed.). Newbury Park, CA: Sage.
Mai, M. (2006). *In the name of honor.* New York, NY: Atria.
McNulty, F. (1989). *The burning bed.* New York, NY: Avon.
Miedzian, M. (2002). *Boys will be boys: Breaking the link between masculinity and violence.* New York, NY: Lantern Books.
Muhammad, M. (2009). *Scared silent: The Mildred Muhammad story.* New York, NY: Strebor Books.
Murray, A. (2008). *From outrage to courage: Women taking action for health and justice.* Monroe, ME: Common Courage.
Pinals, D. (2007). *Stalking: Psychiatric perspectives and practical approaches.* New York, NY: Oxford University Press.
Pleck, E. (1989). *Domestic tyranny: The making of American social policy against family violence from colonial times to the present.* New York, NY: Oxford.
Quindlen. A. (1999). *Black and blue.* New York, NY: Dell.
Renzetti, C. (1992). *Violent betrayal: Partner abuse in lesbian relationships.* Thousand Oaks, CA: Sage.
Rowland, D. (2004). *The boundaries of her body: The troubling history of women's rights in America.* Naperville, IL: Sphinx.
Russell, B. (2010). *Battered woman syndrome as a legal defense: History, effectiveness, and implications.* Jefferson, NC: McFarland.
Sage, J., & Kasten, L. (Eds.). (2006). *Enslaved: True stories of modern day slavery.* New York, NY: Palgrave Macmillan.
Salbi, Z., & Becklund, L. (2005). *Between two worlds: Escape from tyranny, growing up in the shadow of Saddam.* New York, NY: Gotham.
Schechter, S. (1982). *Women and male violence: The visions and struggles of the battered women's movement.* Cambridge, MA: South End Press.
Shaw, S., & Lee, J. (2007). *Women's voices, feminist visions* (3rd ed.). Boston, MA: McGraw-Hill.
Shelley, L. (2010). *Human trafficking: A global perspective.* New York: Cambridge University Press.
Smith A. (2005). *Conquest: Sexual violence and American Indian genocide.* Boston, MA: South End Press.
Smith, P., & Thurman, E. (2007). *A billion bootstraps: Microcredit, barefoot banking, and the business solution for ending poverty.* New York, NY: McGraw-Hill.

Sokoloff, N., Smith. B., West, C., & Dupont, I. (2005). *Domestic violence at the margins: Readings on race, class, gender and culture.* New Brunswick, NJ: Rutgers University Press.

Stark, E. (2009). *Coercive control: How men entrap women in personal life.* New York: Oxford University Press.

Stith, S., McCollum, E., & Rosen, K. (2011). *Couples therapy for domestic violence: Finding safe solutions.* Washington, DC: American Psychological Association.

Straus, M., Gelles, R., & Steinmetz, S. (2009). *Behind closed doors: Violence in the American family.* New Brunswick, NJ: Transaction.

Tifft, L. (1993). *Battering of women: The failure of intervention and the case for prevention.* Boulder, CO: Westview.

Vlachova, M., & Biason, L. (Eds.). (2005). *Women in an insecure world: Violence against women facts, figures, and analysis.* Geneva, Switzerland: Centre for the Democratic Control of Armed Forces.

Walker, L. (1980). *The battered woman.* New York, NY: Harper.

Walker, L. (2000). *The battered woman syndrome* (2nd ed.). New York, NY: Springer.

Weatherholt, A. (2008). *Breaking the silence: The church responds to domestic violence.* New York, NY: Morehouse.

Welchman, L., & Houssain, S. (Eds.). (2005). *Honour: Crimes, paradigms, and violence against women.* London, England: Zed Press.

Yunus, M. (2003). *Banker to the poor: Microlending and the battle against world poverty.* New York, NY: Public Affairs.

Journals That May Cover Domestic Abuse and Violence

Contemporary Justice Review
Gender & Society
Journal of Interpersonal Violence
Violence against Women: An International and Interdisciplinary Journal
Violence and Victims
The Voice: A Journal of the Battered Women's Movement

Selected Journal Articles, 2000–2012

Ahmed-Ghosh, H. (2004). Chattels of society: Domestic violence in India. *Violence Against Women, 10*(1), 94–118.

Anastasio, P., & Costa, D. (2004). Twice hurt: How newspaper coverage may reduce empathy and engender blame for female victims of crime. *Sex Roles, 51,* 535–542.

Anderson, D., & Saunders, D. (2003). Leaving an abusive partner: An empirical review of predictors, the process of leaving, and psychological well-being. *Trauma Violence Abuse, 4*(2),163–191.

Ascione, F., Weber, C., Thompson, T., Heath, J., Maruyama, M., & Hayashi. K. (2007). Battered pets and domestic violence: Animal abuse reported by women experiencing intimate violence and by non-abused women. *Violence Against Women, 13*(4), 354–373.

Babcock, J., Green, C., & Robie, C. (2004). Does batterers' treatment work? A meta-analytic review of domestic violence treatment. *Clinical Psychological Review, 23,* 1023–1053.

Banyard, V., Moynihan, M., & Crossman, M. (2009). Reducing sexual violence on campus: The role of student leaders as empowered bystanders. *Journal of College Student Development, 50*(4), 446–457.

Bennett, L., & Williams, O. (2003). Substance abuse and men who batter: Issues in therapy and practice. *Violence Against Women, 9,* 558–575.

Betancourt, G., Breitbart, V., & Colarossi, L. (2010). Barriers to screening for intimate partner violence: A mixed-methods study of providers in family planning clinics. *Perspectives on Sexual and Reproductive Health, 42*(4), 236.

Black, B., & Weisz, A. (2003). Dating violence: Help-seeking behaviors of African American middle schoolers. *Violence Against Women, 9*(2), 187–206.

Bui, H. (2003). Help-seeking behavior among abused immigrant women: A case of Vietnamese American Women. *Violence Against Women, 9*(2), 207–239.

Bhuyan, R., Mell, M., Senturia, K., Sullivan, M., & Shiu-Thornton, S. (2005). "Women must endure according to their karma": Cambodian immigrant women talk about domestic violence. *Journal of Interpersonal Violence, 20*(8), 902–921.

Bhuyan, R., & Senturia, K. (2005). Understanding domestic violence resource utilization and survivor solutions among immigrant and refugee women. *Journal of Interpersonal Violence, 20*(8), 895–901.

Boy, A., & Kulczycki, A. (2008). What we know about intimate partner violence in the Middle East and North Africa. *Violence Against Women, 14*(1), 53–70.

Bui, H.N. (2003). Help-Seeking behavior among abused immigrant women. *Violence Against Women, 9*(2), 207–239.

Burke, J., Thieman, L., Gielen, A., O'Campo, P., & McDonnell, K. (2005). Intimate partner violence, substance abuse, and HIV among low-income women: Taking a closer look. *Violence Against Women, 11*(9), 1140–1161.

Burn, S. (2009). A situational model of sexual assault prevention through bystander intervention. *Sex Roles, 60,* 779–792.

Carlson, B., & Worden, A. (2005). Attitudes and beliefs about domestic violence: Results of a public opinion survey: I. Definitions of domestic violence, criminal domestic violence, and prevalence. *Journal of Interpersonal Violence, 20*(10), 1197–1218.

Carlson, M. (2008). I'd rather go along and be considered a man: Masculinity and bystander intervention. *Journal of Men's Studies, 16*(1), 3–17.

Carlyle, K. E., Slater, M. D., & Chakroff, J. L. (2008). Newspaper coverage of intimate partner violence: Skewing representation of risk. *Journal of Communication, 58,* 168–186.

Chapell, M., Casey, D., De la Cruz, C., Ferrell, J., Forman, J., Lipkin, R., et al. (2004). Bullying in college by students and teachers. *Adolescence, 39*(153), 54–64.

Chapell, M., Hasselman, S., Kitchin, T., Lomon, S., MacIver, K., & Sarullo, P. (2006). Bullying in elementary school, high school, and college. *Adolescence, 41*(164), 633–648.

Chiu, E. (2010). That guy's a batterer! A scarlet letter approach to domestic violence in the information age. *Family Law Quarterly, 44*(2), 255.

Cismaru, M., & Lavack, A. M. (2011). Campaigns targeting perpetrators of intimate partner violence. *Trauma, Violence, & Abuse, 12,* 183–197.

Clark, B., & Richards, C. (2008). The prevention and prohibition of forced marriages: A comparative approach. *International and Comparative Law Quarterly, 57,* 501–528.

Coker, D. (2006). Restorative justice, Navajo peacemaking, and domestic violence. *Theoretical Criminology, 10*(1), 67–85.

Danis, F. (2003). Domestic violence and crime victim compensation: A research agenda. *Violence Against Women, 9*(3), 374–390.

Dick, A., & McMahon, S. (2011). "Being in a room with like-minded men": An exploratory study of men's participation in a bystander intervention program to prevent intimate partner violence. *Journal of Men's Studies, 19*(1), 3.

Edleson, J., Mbilinyi, L., Beeman, S., & Hagemesiter, A. (2003). How children are involved in adult domestic violence: Results from a four-city telephone survey. *Journal of Interpersonal Violence, 18*(1), 18–32.

Fabiano, P., Perkins, H. W., Berkowitz, A., Linkenbach, J., & Stark, C. (2004). Engaging men as social justice allies in ending violence against women: Evidence for a social norms approach. *Journal of American College Health, 52*(3), 105–112.

Faver, C., & Strand, E. (2003). Domestic violence and animal cruelty: Untangling the web of abuse. *Journal of Social Work Education, 39*(2), 237–253.

Feder, L., & Wilson, D.B. (2005). A meta-analytic review of court-mandated batterer intervention programs: Can courts affect abusers' behavior? *Journal of Experimental Criminology, 1*, 239–262.

Fischer, P., Greitemeyer, T., Pollozek, F., & Frey, D. (2006). The unresponsive bystander: Are bystanders more responsive in dangerous emergencies? *European Journal of Social Psychology, 36*(2), 267–278.

Foubert, J., & Perry, B. (2007). Creating lasting attitude and behavior changes in fraternity members and male student athletes. *Violence Against Women, 13*(1), 70–86.

Fox, J., & Tierney, S. (2011). Trapped in a toxic relationship: Comparing the views of women living with anorexia nervosa to those experiencing domestic violence. *Journal of Gender Studies, 20*(1), 31–41.

Frohmann, L. (2005). The framing safety project: Photographs and narratives by battered women. *Violence Against Women, 11*(11), 1396–1419.

Gondolf, E., & Beeman, A. (2003). Women's accounts of domestic violence versus tactics-based outcome categories. *Violence Against Women, 9*(3), 278–301.

Goodkind, J., Gillum, T., Bybee, D., & Sullivan, C. (2003). The impact of family and friends' reactions on the well-being of women with abusive partners. *Violence Against Women, 9*(3), 347–373.

Hampton, R., Oliver, W., & Maragan, L. (2003). Domestic violence in the African American community: An analysis of social and structural factors. *Violence Against Women, 9*(5), 533–557.

Hernandez-Ruiz, E. (2005). Effect of music therapy on the anxiety levels and sleep patterns of abused women in shelters. *Journal of Music Therapy, XLII*(2), 140–158.

Kantor, G., & Little, L. (2003). Defining the boundaries of child neglect: When does domestic violence equate with parental failure to protect? *Journal of Interpersonal Violence, 18*, 338–354.

Kennedy, A. (2005). Resilience among urban adolescent mothers living with violence: Listening to their stories. *Violence Against Women, 11*(12), 1490–1514.

Kocot, T., & Goodman, L. (2003). The roles of coping and social support in battered women's mental health. *Violence Against Women, 9*(3), 323–346.

Lehrner, A., & Allen, N. E. (2009). Still a movement after all these years? Current tensions in the domestic violence movement. *Violence Against Women, 15*, 656–677.

Lippy, C., Perilla, J., Vasquez-Serrata, J., & Wienberg, J. (2012). Integrating women's voices and theory: A comprehensive domestic violence intervention for Latinas. *Women and Therapy, 93*.

McMahon, M., & Pence, E. (2003). Making social change reflections on individual and institutional advocacy with women arrested for domestic violence. *Violence Against Women, 9*(10), 47–74.

McMahon, S., Postmus, J. L., & Koenick, R. A. (2011). Conceptualizing the engaging bystander approach to sexual violence prevention on college campuses. *Journal of College Student Development, 52*(1), 115–130.

Mears, D. (2003). Research and interventions to reduce domestic violence revictimization. *Trauma Violence Abuse, 4*(2), 127–147.

Menjívar, C., & Salcido, O. (2002). Immigrant women and domestic violence: Common experiences in different countries. *Gender & Society, 16*(6), 898–920.

Moynihan, N., Banyard, V., Arnold, J., Eckstein, R., & Stapleton, J. (2010). Engaging intercollegiate athletes in preventing and intervening in sexual and intimate partner violence *Journal of American College Health, 59*(3), 197–204.

Murphy, J. C., & Rubinson, R. (2005). Domestic violence and mediation: Responding to the challenges of crafting effective screens. *Family Law Quarterly, 39*(1), 53–85.

Nash, S. (2005). Through black eyes: African American women's constructions of their experiences with intimate male partner violence. *Violence Against Women, 11*(11), 1420–1440.

Neighbors, C., Walker, D. D., Mbilinyi, L. F., O'Rourke, A., Edeison, J., Zegree, J., et al. (2010). Normative misperceptions of abuse among perpetrators of intimate partner violence. *Violence Against Women, 16*(4), 370–386.

Ockleford, E., Barnes-Holmes, Y., Morichelli, R., Morjaria, A., Scocchera, F., Furniss, F., Sdogatti, C., & Barnes-Holmes, D. (2003). Mistreatment of older women in three European counties. *Violence Against Women, 9*(12), 1453–1464.

Patterson, N., & Sears, C. (2011). Letting men off the hook? Domestic violence and postfeminist celebrity culture. *Genders, 53*.

Raj, A., & Silverman, J. (2007). Domestic violence help-seeking behaviors of South Asian battered women residing in the United States. *International Review of Victimology, 14*, 143–170.

Rogers, B., McGee, G., Vann, A., Thompson, N., & Williams, O. (2003). Substance abuse and domestic violence: Stories of practitioners that address the co-occurrence among battered women. *Violence Against Women, 9*(5), 590–598.

Rosenberg, J. (2010). Intimate partner violence and infant death in India. *International Perspectives on Sexual and Reproductive Health, 36*(3), 121.

Russell, B., & Melillo, L. (2006). Attitudes toward battered women who kill: Defendant typicality and judgments of culpability. *Criminal Justice and Behavior, 33*(2), 219–241.

Sagot, M. (2005). The critical path of women affected by family violence in Latin America: Case studies from 10 countries. *Violence Against Women, 11*(10), 1292–1318.

Shetty, S., & Edleson, J. (2005). Adult domestic violence in cases of international parental child abduction. *Violence Against Women, 11*(1), 115–138.

Shetty, S., & Kaguyutan, J. (2002, February). Immigrant victims of domestic violence: Cultural challenges and available legal protections. Harrisburg, PA: VAWnet. Retrieved from http://www.vawnet.org/applied-research-papers/print-document.php?doc_id=384

Shiu-Thornton, S., Senturia, K., & Sullivan, M. (2005). "Like a bird in a cage": Vietnamese women survivors talk about domestic violence. *Journal of Interpersonal Violence, 20*(8), 959–976.

Slote, K., Cuthbert, C., Mesh, C., Driggers, M., Bancroft, L., & Silverman, J. (2005). Battered mothers speak out: Participatory human rights documentation as a model for research and activism in the United States. *Violence Against Women, 11*(11), 1367–1395.

Stayton, C., & Duncan, M. (2005). Mutable influences on intimate partner abuse screening in health care settings: A synthesis of the literature. *Trauma Violence Abuse, 6*(4), 271–285.

Stuart, G. I., Temple, J. R., & Moore, T. M. (2007). Improving batterer intervention programs through theory-based research. *Journal of the American Medical Association, 2*(5), 560–562.

Swanberg, J., Logan, T., & Macke, C. (2005). Intimate partner violence, employment, and the workplace: Consequences and future directions. *Trauma Violence Abuse, 6*(4), 286–312.

Taylor, J. (2005). No resting place: African American women at the crossroads of violence. *Violence Against Women, 11*(12), 1473–1489.

Tower, L. E. (2006). Barriers in screening women for domestic violence: A survey of social workers, family practitioners, and obstetrician-gynecologists. *Journal of Family Violence, 21,* 245–257.

Tyler, K. A., Brownridge, D. A., & Melander, L.A. (2011). The effect of poor parenting on the male and female dating violence perpetration and victimization. *Violence and Victims 26*(2), 218–230.

Ventura, L., & Davis, G. (2005). Domestic violence: Court case conviction and recidivism. *Violence Against Women, 11*(2), 255–277.

Wahab, S., & Olson, L. (2004). Intimate partner violence and sexual assault in Native American communities. *Trauma Violence Abuse, 5,* 353–366.

Worden, A., & Carlson, B. (2005). Attitudes and beliefs about domestic violence: Results of a public opinion survey: ii. Beliefs about causes. *Journal of Interpersonal Violence, 20*(10), 1219–1243.

Curricula, Manuals and Handbooks

Creighton, A., & Kivel, P. (1993). *Helping teens stop violence: A practical guide for counselors, educators, and parents* (2nd ed.). Alameda, CA: Hunter House.

Creighton, A., & Kivel, P. (1998). *Young men's work: Stopping violence and building community: A multi-session group program.* Center City, MN: Hazelden.

Fortune, M. (1991). *Violence in the family: A workshop curriculum for clergy and other helpers.* Cleveland, OH: Pilgrim Press.

Goodman, M., & Fallon, B. (1995). *Pattern changing for abused women: An educational program.* Thousand Oaks, CA: Sage.

Kivel, P. (1993). *Men's work: Comprehensive violence treatment.* Center City, MN: Hazelden.

Kivel, P., & Creighton, A. (2002). *Making the peace: A 15-session violence prevention curriculum for young people.* Alameda, CA: Hunter House.

Patterson, S. (2002). *I wish the hitting would stop.* Fargo, ND: Red Flag, Green Flag.

Vasquez, H., Myhand, N., & Creighton, A., (2003). *Making allies, making friends: A curriculum for making the peace in middle school communities.* Alameda, CA: Hunter House.

Video

The Bro Code: How Contemporary Culture Creates Sexist Men
2011, Media Education Foundation
Available for purchase from http://www.mediaed.org
Addresses multiple forms of contemporary popular culture that glorify misogyny and promote men's control and subordination of women.

RECOMMENDED RESOURCES: BOOKS, JOURNALS, ARTICLES, AND VIDEOS 849

City of Shelter: A Coordinated Community Response to Domestic Violence
2006, Global Village Communications
Available for purchase at http://www.cityofshelter.org
This 11-part series includes interviews with leaders in the field, including police, prosecutors, judges, scholars, and advocates. Designed to assist professionals who work with domestic violence victims, the series helps viewers not only understand the dynamics of abuse but begin to put together a response for their particular communities. There is also a two-hour version that is appropriate for the general public.

Domestic Violence: What Churches Can Do
2002, Faith Trust Institute
Available for purchase at http://www.faithtrustinstitute.org
Designed for use in Christian education, this program highlights the ways that churches can help victims and can become involved in efforts to end abuse.

Generation M: Misogyny in Media and Culture
2008, Media Education Foundation
Available for purchase at http://www.mediaed.org
An assessment of misogyny and sexism in mainstream American media.

Half the Sky: Turning Oppression into Opportunity for Women
2012. Show of Force and Half the Sky Foundation. Available for purchase from PBS http://www.shoppbs.org/product/index.jsp?productId=13358537#Details
This video, shown on PBS's *Independent Lens* television program in 2012, is based on Nicholas Kristof and Sheryl WuDunn's 2009 book of the same title about the trafficking of children and women, the sexual and domestic violence toward women and girls worldwide, as well as continued poverty, lack of education, and poor health care.

Hip Hop: Beyond Beats and Rhymes
2006, Media Education Foundation
Available for purchase at http://www.mediaed.org
Shows how hip-hop and the culture surrounding it promote destructive gender stereotypes. Also highlights hip-hop artists who have and are challenging this culture of exploitation.

Killing Us Softly 4
2010, Media Education Foundation
Available for purchase at http://www.mediaed.org
The latest update from Jean Kilbourne exploring how advertisements promote dangerous conceptions about females' bodies.

Not Just a Game: Power, Politics & American Sports
2010, Media Education Foundation
Available for purchase at http://www.mediaed.org
Explores how American sports have glamorized militarism, racism, sexism, and homophobia. It also profiles the many athletes who have fought for social justice, both on and off the field of play.

Something My Father Would Do: Overcoming Legacies of Family Violence
No date, Futures Without Violence
Available for purchase from http://www.futureswithoutviolence.com
This film focuses on men who grew up with abusive fathers, stressing how they grapple with their own intimate relationships.

There's No Place Like Home: Growing Up with Family Violence
No date, Intermedia
Available from http://www.intermedia-inc.com
Four-part film focusing on the impact of abuse on children.

Toxic Relationships: The Next Generation Speaks Out about Dating Violence
2000, Insight Media
Available for purchase at http://www.insight-media.com
High school students discuss their experiences with abuse and how to develop healthy relationships.

Voices of Survivors
No date, Futures Without Violence
Available for purchase from http://www.futureswithoutviolence.com
Through interviews with survivors, this film helps health-care providers understand the importance of and how to screen for abuse.

When Injuries Speak, Who Will Listen? A Healthcare Response to Domestic Violence
No date, Intermedia
Available from http://www.intermedia-inc.com
Valuable resource for health-care providers regarding scope and extent of abuse, screening, documenting, and response protocols.

Wrestling with Manhood: Boys, Bullying, and Battering
2002, Media Education Foundation
Available for purchase from http://www.mediaed.org
An in-depth analysis of sexism, homophobia, and violence presented in professional wrestling.

About the Editor and Contributors

The Editor

Laura L. Finley earned her PhD in sociology from Western Michigan University in 2002. She is assistant professor of sociology and criminology at Barry University in Miami Shores, Florida. Dr. Finley is the author/coauthor/editor of 11 books and numerous book chapters and journal articles, including the *Encyclopedia of School Crime and Violence* (Greenwood, 2011). She is actively involved in serving domestic violence victims and in raising awareness about abuse.

The Contributors

Natasha A. Abdin is a history and sociology major with a minor in philosophy at Florida Atlantic University. She is a community activist who has a passion for helping others and fighting for civil rights. She is currently forming her own organization to help empower women through raising self-esteem, confidence, and promoting self-love.

Nathan Andrews is a doctoral student in the Department of Political Science at the University of Alberta with specialization in international relations and comparative politics. His broad research interests include globalization and global governance, critical theory, poverty and social justice, and politics of the global South.

Megan H. Bair-Merritt, MD, MSCE, is affiliated with the Division of General Pediatrics and Adolescent Medicine at Johns Hopkins University, Baltimore, Maryland.

Kristin A. Bell is a doctoral student in the School of Criminology and Criminal Justice at Northeastern University, Boston. After receiving her BA in criminology and BS in psychology, she completed her master's degree in criminology, law, & society at the University of Florida. Kristin is currently a project manager at the Center for Criminal Justice Policy Research and the Institute on Race and Justice at Northeastern University, where she assists in examining trends in hate crime against immigrants and Hispanic Americans.

Kimberly Bellon, BSW, is a clinical research assistant at Santa Clara Valley Medical Center's Rehabilitation Research Center in San Jose, California. She is a certified brain injury specialist and has given numerous presentations on outcomes following traumatic brain injury and spinal cord injury.

Elizabeth Biebel is an assistant professor of criminology at Morehead State University, Morehead, Kentucky. Dr. Biebel's research interests include policing, compassion fatigue, the association of post-traumatic stress disorder with substance use, victimization, and criminal justice organizations.

About the Editor and Contributors

Allison Brimmer is assistant professor in the Division of Humanities at Nova Southeastern University, Fort Lauderdale, Florida, where she focuses on composition studies, rhetorics of white privilege, feminist and antiracist pedagogy, writing in the community, and cultural studies.

Sade Brooks earned a bachelor's degree in criminology from Barry University, Miami Shores, Florida, in 2012. She began attending law school at the University of Maryland in fall, 2012.

Samuel L. Browning, MS, is a clinical psychology doctoral candidate at Nova Southeastern University, Center for Psychological Studies, Fort Lauderdale, Florida. He was a certified police officer for the state of Georgia and is currently the program coordinator for the Family Violence Program at Nova Southeastern University.

Eduin Caceres-Ortiz, PhD, is a clinical psychologist and a member of the PTSD Research Team at the Psychology Clinic at the University Complutense of Madrid.

Stephanie Chaban is a consultant with and the former project manager of the Women and Security' Project at the Ramallah office of the Geneva Centre for the Democratic Control of Armed Forces (DCAF). She has an MA in women's studies from San Diego State University.

AnneMarie Conlon is assistant professor at the Virginia Commonwealth University School of Social Work, Richmond. She has more than eight years' experience with vulnerable adult populations and has served as adjunct faculty at New York University and the University of Houston.

Jennifer Cote is assistant professor of History at Saint Joseph College, West Hartford, Connecticut. Her work focuses on American women, with a particular focus on reform.

Tatyana Cottle, MA, trained as a mental health and school counselor, works at Fairfax County Public Schools, Virginia, and is a doctoral student at Virginia Tech University. She has experience working both in public schools and various mental health settings.

Peter F. Cronholm, MD, MSCE, is affiliated with the Department of Family Medicine and Community Health, the Center for Public Health Initiatives, the Leonard Davis Institute of Health Economics, and the Firearm and Injury Center at Penn, University of Pennsylvania, Philadelphia.

Antje Deckert studied law and criminology and has practiced law in Germany, specializing in criminal defense. The completion of her PhD in 2009 was followed by a move to Auckland/New Zealand, where she is a permanent staff member in the Social Sciences department at AUT University.

Andrea J. Dickens is assistant professor of church history at United Theological Seminary, New York City. Her teaching and research interests include medieval theology and church history, medieval women's history, mysticism, monastic traditions, vernacular theology and literature, religion and the arts, Augustine and Augustinianisms, and Dante.

ABOUT THE EDITOR AND CONTRIBUTORS

Jessica J. Eckstein, PhD, is an assistant professor of communication at Western Connecticut State University. Her research foci include gender communication, family relationships, and abusive romantic relationships.

Maria F. Espinola, MS, is a clinical psychology doctoral candidate at Nova Southeastern University, Center for Psychological Studies, Fort Lauderdale, Florida. She is the community research coordinator for Dr. Lenore Walker's Battered Women Syndrome Questionnaire Validation Study and the founder of the Student Coalition for Human Rights.

Renee Fillette is the executive director of Grace Smith House, a domestic violence program serving the Hudson Valley region of New York State. She is currently writing her dissertation for the completion of a doctoral degree in Public Service: Leadership and Management of Nonprofit Organizations. She lives in upstate New York with her husband and children.

Kristin Franklin (who writes about her own experiences with domestic violence and past troubled relationships) has finally won her prize in husband Bobby. Kris and Bobby hope to collaborate soon on a screenplay about overcoming addiction. They live in Denver, Colorado.

Brandon Fryman graduated with his master's degree in anthropology in 2011, conducting a program evaluation on an NGO focusing on development among orphans and their female caretakers in Uganda. He has worked for Amnesty International and the UN Association of the United States of America focusing on human rights. He has published a book on female genital mutilation and several articles on rituals/rites of passage and heroes and heroines among Burmese Americans.

Dr. Tony Gaskew is associate professor of criminal justice and coordinator of criminal forensics at the University of Pittsburgh-Bradford. He has over 25 years of experience in the field of criminal justice, including as a police detective assigned to the U.S. Department of Justice Organized Crime Drug Enforcement Task.

Lynn Geurin is an assistant professor of social work at Morehead State University, Morehead, Kentucky. Dr. Geurin's teaching and research interests involve law and social work and intimate partner violence. She has extensive clinical practice experience in working with domestic violence victims and offenders.

Chuck Goesel is a PhD candidate in conflict analysis and resolution at Nova Southeastern University in Fort Lauderdale, Florida. He has conducted research for the Florida Center for Survivors of Torture. He is also the Middle East Committee Leader for the Student Coalition for the Defense of Human Rights. He has a master's degree in liberal studies with a concentration in history from Valparaiso University and is currently teaching English as a Second Language in Miami, Florida.

Kathryn Goesel is a doctoral student in the clinical psychology program at the Center for Psychological Studies at Nova Southeastern University (NSU) in Fort Lauderdale, FL. She is a research assistant for the Battered Woman Syndrome Questionnaire study and head of the Women's Committee for the Student Coalition for Human Rights at NSU. She attended the UN University for Peace program for Gender and Peace Studies and worked on the

Amnesty International Stop Violence Against Women Campaign. She is also an organizing member for the College Brides Walk, a campaign that promotes education and violence prevention of abuse in intimate relationships.

Lynsay Gott is a graduate of University of Cincinnati College of Law and was the program director at Human Rights USA. She has written on human trafficking and T and U visas.

Kori A. Hakala, MA, MS, is a clinical psychology doctoral candidate at Nova Southeastern University, Center for Psychological Studies, Fort Lauderdale, Florida. She is currently the research coordinator for the Family Violence Program at Nova Southeastern University.

KaaVonia Hinton-Johnson is the coauthor (with Katherine T. Bucher) of *Young Adult Literature: Exploration, Evaluation, and Appreciation* (2009) and (with Sueanne McKinney) *Mathematics Literature in the Classroom and Library* (Linworth Publishing, 2010). She can be reached on her blog, http://kaavoniahinton.blogspot.com/.

Andrew Hund is a recent PhD graduate (2010) from Case Western Reserve University, Cleveland, in medical sociology and gerontology. Andrew has taught sociology at four campuses. He is presently an independent academic and working on a book investigating epidemics in the circumpolar North.

Mark Ikeke is affiliated with the Department of Religious Studies and Philosophy at Delta State University in Abraka, Nigeria.

Njoki Kinyatti is an associate professor and the chief librarian at York College/City University of New York.

Denice Knight-Slater received her MA degree from Prescott College in Arizona. She explores issues of subjugation and gender roles in women's literature.

Stephanie A. Kolakowsky-Hayner, PhD, CBIST, is the director of rehabilitation research at the Santa Clara Valley Medical Center in San Jose, California. Dr. Kolakowsky-Hayner holds an appointment as a clinical assistant professor affiliated in the Department of Orthopaedic Surgery, Stanford University School of Medicine, and is also a member of the Brain Injury Association of California Board of Directors, the Academy of Certified Brain Injury Specialists Board of Governors, the Bay Area Brain Injury Task Force, and the American Spinal Injury Association Prevention Committee.

Carol Lenhart, PhD, received her bachelor's degree from SUNY Brockport, and earned her master's and doctorate degrees from the University of Delaware. She is currently assistant professor of criminal justice at Elmira College.

Kera Lovell is a recent graduate from Purdue University's master's program in American studies. Her research examines gender, identity, and social activism in post-WWII America. She currently works at Harrison College in Indiana and will pursue her PhD in August 2012.

Alison Marganski, PhD, is assistant professor of sociology and criminal justice at Virginia Wesleyan College, where she focuses on family violence (exposure to intimate partner violence, intimate partner violence, parent-to-child violence, sibling violence); social relationships; gender and crime.

Mark Marquez has been a licensed clinical social worker for over 25 years and is president and owner of eSocialWorker LLC as well as adjunct assistant professor with the Department of Social Work at Fayetteville State University, North Carolina.

Vanessa Marquez holds a bachelor's degree in criminology from Barry University, Miami Shores, Florida. Her present goal is to further her education and obtain her master's in sociology and to become a professor.

Alison Mulcahy is a doctoral student and Graduate Assistant to the Provost and Vice President of Academic Affairs at Nova Southeastern University.

Shondrah Tarrezz Nash is an associate professor of sociology at Morehead State University, Morehead, Kentucky. Dr. Nash's primary research involves spousal violence and religious coping.

Catherine Ekwe (Kate) Ngozi holds an MS in theology from Auxilium in Rome, Italy, and an MS in counseling from Franciscan University in Steubenville, Ohio. She earned a doctoral degree in counseling from Barry University in 2012.

Cheryl O'Brien, EdM, MA, is a PhD candidate in political science at Purdue University, West Lafayette, Indiana, focusing on policies to fight violence against women. She has been volunteering with or working for agencies opposing violence against women since 1992 in the United States and abroad.

Patricia (author of a personal narrative about abuse) was born in Jamaica. She is currently living in South Florida with her two boys.

Marla Perkins, PhD, is affiliated with the Rassias Center for World Languages and Cultures at Dartmouth College, Hanover, New Hampshire.

Lauren Pilnick is project coordinator, NE Victim Assistance Academy at Creighton University, Omaha, Nebraska. She was formerly executive director of Crime Victim Services, a nonprofit agency in Minnesota that provides sexual assault and domestic violence advocacy.

William Plouffe Jr. is an independent scholar.

Jennifer Rey is violence prevention coordinator at Aid to Victims of Domestic Abuse (AVDA) in West Palm Beach, Florida.

Sabrina (author of a personal narrative about abuse) was born in Brazil. She lives and works as a personal trainer in South Florida. She has one daughter.

About the Editor and Contributors

Robin C. Sager is currently a dissertation fellow and PhD candidate in history at Rice University, Houston. Her dissertation is a multistate comparative study of martial cruelty in antebellum America.

Jeff Shantz is professor of criminology at Kwantlen Polytechnic University in Vancouver, British Columbia. His work focuses on elite crime and radical criminology.

Amanda Mathisen Stylianou, MSW, LCSW, is a doctoral research assistant at the Center for Violence against Women and Children at Rutgers University, School of Social Work. Ms. Stylianou focuses her research on the intersection of trauma and mental health and runs a private practice in Pennington, New Jersey.

Sharon Thiel graduated from Florida Atlantic University, Boca Raton, with a master's degree in sociology. She is a freelance health writer, focusing on the areas of natural health and nutrition.

Vincent B. Van Hasselt, PhD, is a professor of psychology and criminal justice at Nova Southeastern University, Fort Lauderdale, Florida, and the director of the Family Violence Program at Nova Southeastern University. He is also a certified police officer in the state of Florida.

Stephanie Van Hook is executive director of the Metta Center for Nonviolence Education in Petaluma, California.

W. Jesse Weins is assistant professor of criminal justice at Dakota Wesleyan University, Mitchell, South Dakota. His journal articles on constitutional and criminal law have been recognized by a U.S. federal district court, *USA Today*, and the *New York Times*.

Ashley Wiegand is finishing her undergraduate degree at Central Michigan University, Mount Pleasant. She has a double major in psychology and sociology with a concentration on criminal justice, and will begin pursuing graduate studies in criminology in the fall semester of 2012.

Jackie Wiersma earned her PhD from Texas Tech University. She is a professor at the University of Arkansas. Her research focuses on alcohol us and misuse in relationships as well as interpersonal violence.

Hakim Mohandas Amani Williams is a doctoral candidate at Columbia University, New York, New York, in international educational development, focusing on peace education. He is the research coordinator for the Advanced Consortium on Cooperation, Conflict and Complexity (AC^4) at the Earth Institute, and teaches peace education online at Drexel University.

Fatima Zimichi is a graduate of Barry University, Miami Shores, Florida, where she was a reporter for the student newspaper. Currently working as a financial analyst, Fatima dreams of a writing career.

Index

Page numbers in **bold** indicate main entries in the encyclopedia

Abolition movement, 557
Abstinence, Be Faithful, and Condom Use (ABC), 10
An Abuse, Rape, and Domestic Violence Aid and Resource Collection (AARDVARC), 163, 287
Abused Women and Survivor Therapy (Walker), 541
Abused Women's Coalition, 443
Abusive person, warning signs of, 548
"Abusive personality," xxv
Abusive principle, 289
Academy of Family Mediators, 313
Accusing, 290
Achebe, Chinua, 7
Acid Control Law of 2002, 2
Acid Crimes Law, 2
Acid Survivors Foundation Bangladesh, 2
Acid Survivors Foundation Uganda (ASF), 3
Acid throwing, xxiv, **1–5**, 119
Active bystanders, 62. *See also* Bystander approach
Act on the Prevention of Spousal Violence Law, 29
Acute Battering Incident, 447
Addressing Intimate Partner Violence, Reproductive and Sexual Coercion, 419
Adler, Freda, 187
Adolescent Girls' Legal Defense Fund, 143
Adverse Childhood Experiences (ACEs), 196
Advocacy, 383
Advocacy for Women & Kids in Emergencies (AWAKE), 443
Affirmative action, 557

Affliction, 170
Affordable Care Act. *See* Patient Protection and Affordable Healthcare Act
Afghanistan, 281–82
Africa and domestic abuse, xxiii, **6–8**, 158–62
African Americans, 157, 211
African American women, 199, 207, 376, 417, 423, 477, 486
Age, support groups and, 487
Agir Pour les Femmes en Situation Precaire (AFESIP), 302
Aguilera, Christina, 72
AIDS and domestic violence, **9–11**, 231
Aid to Families with Dependent Children (AFDC), 551
Akan people of Ghana, 7
Alabama, 535
Alaska Natives and domestic abuse, **11–15**
  demographics, 357–58
  intimate partner violence, 358–59
  micro-level predictors, 157
  vs. Native Americans, 12, 13, 14, 358
Al Baz, Rania, 323
Albright, Madeleine, 501, 538
Alcohol and domestic abuse, xxv, **15–17**, 165–66, 196
Alexander, Marissa, 423–24
Alfonso, Michael, 480
Algeria, 325–26
Ali, Nojoud Mohammed, 324
Ali, Somy, **17–20**, 297
All China Women's Federation, 28
Allstate Foundation, 180–81, 350, 567
Allstate Insurance Company, 567
American Assistance for Cambodia, 234

American Association of Family Physicians (AAFP), 404
American Association of Pediatrics (AAP), 404
American Bar Association (ABA), 313, 425, 531
American Civil Liberties Union (ACLU), 69, 307
American College of Emergency Physicians, 435
American College of Obstetrics and Gynecology (ACOG), 404
American Journal of Public Health, 418
American Medical Association (AMA), **20–22**, 404
American Society for the Prevention of Cruelty to Animals (ASPCA), 26
Americans Overseas Domestic Violence Crisis Center, 96–97
America's Health Futures Act, 419
Amnesty International, xix–xx, **22–23**, 246, 285–86
Amy's Courage Fund, 309–10
Anarchists, 193
Anarchist theories, 466
Anderson, Jocelyn, 85
Androcentrism, 187
Anger management and domestic abuse, **23–25**, 42
Animal abuse and domestic abuse, **25–28**
Anthony, Susan B., 199
Antisocial personality disorder, 52, 77
Antistalking laws, 209, 210, 479–80
Apne Aap Women Worldwide, 234
Archambault, Joanne, 141
Argentina, 275, 320, 471
Arizona, 566
Arkansas, 566
Armed Forces Domestic Security Act, 327–28
Armenia, 287
Army 2020: Generating Health and Discipline in the Force Ahead of the Strategic Reset: Report 2012, 544
Army Times, 544
Arranged marriage, 153, 175. *See also* Forced marriage and domestic abuse
Artspring, 425

Ashton, Myhosi "Josie," 59–60, 66
Asia and domestic abuse, **28–31**. *See also* South and southeast Asia and domestic abuse
Asian & Pacific Islander Institute on Domestic Violence, 30–31
Asian and Pacific Islander Institute (API Institute), 30
Asian Institute on Domestic Violence, 212
Asian Legal Resource Center, 121
Asian/Pacific Islanders, 157
Asian Task Force Against Domestic Violence, 30
Asian women, 487
Association of Family and Conciliation Courts (AFCC), 313
Assortative pairing, 103
Assumptions, communication and, 288–89
Astra Network, 145
Atherton-Zeman, Ben, 214
Athletes and Acquaintance Rape (Benedict), 317
Athletes and domestic abuse, **31–36**
Atkins, Rodney, 70
Atlanta Long Term Care Ombudsman program, 138
Attachment, children and, 83
Australia, 159, 519
Australian Capital Territory Family Violence Intervention Programme, 282
Austria, 213, 282
Avery, Margaret, 168
Avoidance behaviors, 39
Avon Corporation, **36–37**
Avon Foundation, 180–81, 456
Avon Global Center for Women and Justice, 423, 424
Avon Products Inc., 36
Azerbaijan, 287

Bachelet, Michelle, 274
Backlash against women's rights, 207–8
Bahrain, 323, 325, 326
Bailey, Christopher, 210
Bailey, Sonya, 210
Balkans, 146
Bangladesh, 2–3, 114, 121

Ban Ki Moon, 214, 522, 523
Barriers to leaving abusers, xxvii–xxviii, 473–74. *See also* Battered woman syndrome (BWS)
Barrymore, Drew, 169
Barry University, 132
Bashir, Shaykh, 250
Bassett, Angela, 169
Bates, Kathy, 168
The Battered Woman (Walker), 541, 559
Battered woman syndrome (BWS), xxvii, **39–41**, 52, 200, 427, 449–50, 453–54, 541–42, 559
The Battered Woman Syndrome (Walker), 541
Battered Woman Syndrome Questionnaire (BWSQ), 39, 40
Battered Women's Justice Project, 211
Battered women's movement, 197–98, 201, 204, 207
Batterer intervention programs, **41–46**
   court mandate, 93
   ethnic and cultural differences, 44
   group therapy, 498
   intervention modalities, 42–43
   intervention procedures, 43–44
   introduction to, 42–43
   program effectiveness, 45
Batterer Intervention Programs: Where Do We Go from Here? 125
Bay Area Women Against Rape, 559
Beauty That Counts campaign, 309
Beck, Aaron, 42
Bedford Hills Correctional Facility, 423
Behavioral problems, children and, 82
Beijing +5, 48
Beijing Conference, 519
Beijing Declaration and Platform for Action, xxxi, **46–49**, 519
Belgium, 179
Benedict, Jeff, 31, 33, 316–17
Bentley, Judy, 500
Bergin, Patrick, 168
Berk, Richard, 205, 304, 329, 331, 560
Berman, Howard, 246
Bernsen, Corbin, 169
Be the Change (Hunter), 234
Better Business Bureau, 308

Beyond Title IX, 183
Bhopal disaster, 114
Bible, 85, 477
Biden, Joseph, xxxi, 96, 246, 524, 527, 533
Bijlani, Sangeeta, 18
Biological and psychological theories about domestic abuse, xxv–xxvi, **49–54**
   biological theories, 50–51
   introduction to, 49–50
   psychological theories, 51–53
Birth control sabotage, 431–33. *See also* Reproductive coercion
Bisexual victims. *See* Lesbian, gay, bisexual, and transgendered victims
Blackmum, Harry, 110
Blaming, 290
Blocking, 290
Bobbit, John Wayne, 300
Body of Liberties, 198
The Body Shop, **54–56**
Bolivia, 271, 470
Bollywood films, 18
Bonasarro, Carole, 204
Booklist, 303
Borderline personality disorder, 52
Boston Strangler, 25
Boulding, Kenneth, 374
Bowe, Riddick, 33
Bowers, Paul, 268
Boxer, Barbara, 246, 533
Boys on the Side, 169
Brazil, 273, 275, 469–70, 471
Breaking the Rules (Harden and Hill), 425
Breaking the Silence, 310
Break the Cycle, **56–58**, 130–31, 215, 277, 279, 356, 436, 493
Break the Silence award, 37
Breakthrough India, 37
Brennan, William, 110
Bride kidnapping, 176, 178
Bride price, 177–78
Brides Walk, **58–60**, 66
Bride trafficking, 178. *See also* Human trafficking
Bridges TV, 249–50
Britain. *See* United Kingdom
British Crime Survey (BCS), 146

Brooklyn Felony Domestic Violence
  Court, 93
Brother, 352
Brother Peace: An International Day
  of Men Taking Action to End Men's
  Violence, 352
Broward Community College, 88
Brown, Bobby, 71
Brown, Chris, 66–67, 72, 215
Brown, Denise, 460
Brown, Helen Gurley, 558
Brown, Jim, 33
Brown, Sarah, 556
Brundige, Elizabeth, 424
Bruno v. Codd, 203, 304, 559–60
Brzonkala, Christy, 527–28
Bublick, Ellen, 527
Building Comprehensive Solutions to Domestic Violence, 445
Bulgaria, 179
Bullock, Anna Mae, 169
Bullying and domestic abuse, **61–62**
Bureau of Justice Statistics, 423, 431, 480–81, 507
Bureau of Labor Statistics, 564, 565
The Burning Bed, 41, 52, 168, 228
Bush, George W., 296, 524–25
Bush, Laura, 296
Buttar, Amna, 297
Bystander approach, 35, 62, 132, 261, 317
Bystander intervention programs, **62–64**, 132

Cadiz Declaration, 146
Cain, Herman, 262
California, 42, 210, 479, 493, 566
Cambodia, xix–xx, 3, 107, 302–3
Cambodian Acid Survivors Charity (CASC), 3
Cameroon, 521
Campaign to End Homophobia, 352
Campbell, Billy, 170
Campbell, Jacquelyn, 382
Canada, 159, 193, 305, 318, 375–78, 519, 553
Canadian Centre for Justice Statistics, 375
Canadian Women's Foundation, 56
Capitalism, 166, 389

Carbon, Susan, 535–36
CARE, xxxi
Caregivers, abuse by, 491–92
Caribbean American Domestic Violence Awareness, 66
Caribbean and domestic abuse, **65–67**
Carney, Cyril, 409
Carney, Pat, 409
Carter, Jimmy, xxxi, 204, 208, 378, 524, 526, 559
Castle doctrine, 452–53
Castle Rock v. Gonzales case, **67–70**, 110, 213. *See also* Lenahan (Gonzales), Jessica
CAVNET, 112
CBS News, 543
CDC. *See* Centers for Disease Control and Prevention (CDC)
CDC Division of Violence Prevention (CDC/DVP), 74–75
CEDAW. *See* Convention on the Elimination of All Forms of Discrimination against Women (CEDAW)
Celebrities and domestic abuse, **70–74**
Cellini v. Sterling Heights, 306
Cell phones, 489–90
Center for Gender and Development Studies (CGDS), 66
Center for Health and Gender Equity, 375
Center for Research on Women, 242
Center for Substance Abuse Treatment, 123
Centers for Disease Control and Prevention (CDC), **74–76**
  community-based prevention efforts, 211
  on dating violence, 376
  on economic impact of domestic violence, 462–63, 519
  education programs, 130, 131
  on intimate partner violence, 358–59
  on male victims, 298
  on Native American alcohol deaths, 507
  on physical abuse, 510
  on workplace violence, 564. *See also* Domestic Violence Prevention

Enhancements and Leadership Through Alliances (DELTA) program
Centre for Social Research (CSR), 321
Centro Reina Sofia (CRS), 272
Chad, 158
Chain, Chain Change (White), 207
Chan, Margaret, 569
Changing Men, 352
Charity Navigator, 182
Charlie Rose, 268
Chbab Srey, xix
Chernobyl disaster, 113–14
Cheswick Women's Aid, 408, 410–11
Chicago magazine, 567
Child, Lydia Maria, 557
Child abuse and domestic abuse, 75, **76–80**, 123. *See also* Children, impact of domestic abuse on; Child sex tourism (CST); *DeShaney v. Winnebago Department of Social Services* case
Child Abuse Prevention and Treatment Act (CAPTA), 76, 149, 204, 456
Childbirth, xxii
Child custody. *See* Joint custody arrangements; Parental custody
Childhood experiences, 52–53
Child Protective Services, 455–56, 505
Children, financial abuse of, 172
Children, impact of domestic abuse on, **80–84**
    attachment and interpersonal relationships, 83
    behavioral problems, 82
    counseling and therapy, 497
    disruption of school lives, 462
    introduction to, 80
    parental custody, 83
    physical symptoms, 81–82
    psychological symptoms, 81, 134–35
    role reversal, 81
    treatment, 83–84
    witnessing domestic violence, 150–52, 156, 427–28, 495. *See also* Child abuse and domestic abuse
Children's Hospital, 443
Child sex tourism (CST), 232
Child Soldiers Prevention Act (CSPA), 234

Child Welfare Information Gateway, 79, 100
Chile, 271, 272, 275, 470, 471
China, xx, xxii, 28–29, 121, 178, 231–32, 519. *See also* Beijing Declaration and Platform for Action
China Law Institute, 28
China Wakes (Kristof and WuDunn), 269
Chisholm, Shirley, 353
Choose Respect, 131, 279
Christian Coalition Against Domestic Abuse (CCADA), 478
Christian hegemony, 267
Christianity and domestic abuse, **84–87**, 477
Christy-McMullin, Kameri, 320
Civil law, 276
Civil remedies, 527–28
Civil rights movement, 558
Claiborne, Liz, 292
Class. *See* Middle and upper classes and domestic abuse
Classism, impact on victims' ability to receive help, xx–xxi
Clinton, Bill, xxviii, 209, 210, 345, 417, 524, 533
Clinton, Hillary, 46, 501, 538
Clitoridectomy, 159
CNN, 302
Coaching Boys Into Men, 35, 183, 317
Coalition Capacity Project, 350
Coalition for Assisting Tsunami Affected Women (CATAW), 115
Cochran, Johnnie, 458
Coercion, 512
Cognitive behavioral therapy (CBT), 42
The Colbert Report, 268
Coleman, Monieque, 73
College-aged victims, **87–90**
College Brides Walk, 60, 66, 131–32
Collins, Susan, 246
Colombia, 105, 107, 271, 272, 273, 469, 470, 521
Colonialism, 241
Color of Violence, 242
The Color Purple, 73, 168
Commerce Clause, 527

Commission on Crime, 343
Commission on the Status of Women (CSW), 91, 519
Common couple violence, 299, 301, 446
Common law, 451
Communication, 288–90
Community Oriented Policing Services (COPS), 239
Community Partnerships for Protecting Children (CPPC), 443–44
Comstock Laws, 557
Conflict Resolution Education Network, 313
Conflict Tactics Scale (CTS), 52, 106, 347–49, 483
Congo, xxiii, 121, 542
Conjoint couple therapy, 498–99
Connecticut, 281, 499, 560
Connolly, Noreen, 268
Consciousness-raising groups, 42, 192, 200, 351, 498
Contraception, 557
Controlling person, warning signs of, 547
Convention Against Torture (CAT), 160, 286
Convention on the Civil Aspects of Child Abduction, 94
Convention on the Elimination of All Forms of Discrimination against Women (CEDAW), xxx–xxxi, **90–92**
  China and, 28–29
  drafting of, 519
  European Union, 146
  events leading up to, 46
  female genital mutilation and, 160
  honor killings, 220
  Obama and, 23
  signatories to, 281
  text of, 571–85
  UNIFEM and, 515
  United States and, 378, 526
Convergence Partnership, 422
Conyers, John, 534
Cook, Emily, 303–4
Cooperative principle, 289
Coordinated community responses (CCRs), xxx, 118, 214, 463

Corporate Alliance to End Partner Violence, 565, 567
Corporate foundations, 180–81
Corrales, Diego, 33
"Corrective rapes," 287
Cosmetic and Reconstructive Support Program (CRS), 342
Costa Rica, 271, 272, 273
Council of Europe, 145
Council on Ethical and Judicial Affairs, 20, 21
Council on Science and Public Health, 20, 21
Counseling services. See Therapy and counseling for domestic abuse
Countering, 290
Couples therapy, 43, 498
Courts and domestic abuse, **92–95**
Covenant House, 440, 441
Craig, Daniel, 72
Crawford, James, 527
Created to Be His Help Meet (Pearl), 85
Crime rates, 187
Crime reports. See Uniform Crime Reports
Criminal Code (Canada), 377
Criminal law, 276
Criminologists, 467–68
Crisis intervention, 428
Crisis lines, **95–98**, 275, 310, 455, 550. See also National Domestic Violence Hotline; National Runaway Switchboard (NRS); National Teen Dating Abuse Helpline
Criticizing, 290–91
Cross systems collaboration, 383–84
Crow Dog, 359–60
Cruise, Tricia, 441
A Cry for Help, 168, 206, 501
Cult of Domesticity, 199
Cult of True Womanhood, 199
Cult of virginity, xxiv
Cultural background, support groups and, 486–87, 495–96
Cultural barriers, 237–38
Culturally competent services, **98–101**
Cultural norms, 155
Culture Handbook for the Family Violence Prevention Fund, 100

Cyberbullying, 489
Cyberstalking, 481, 489
Cycle of violence, 51–53, **101–4**, 156, 406, 427
Cyclones, 114

Dads & Daughters, 317
Dahmer, Jeffrey, 25
Danger Assessment tool, 382
Dangerous Intentions, 169
Danis, Fran S., 445
Darwin, Charles, 50
Dating Matters, 131
Dating violence, xxi, 61, 103, 215, 281, 376, 492–93. See also College-aged victims; Legislation and policies, dating violence
Dave, Saumya, 268
Davies, Jill, 445
DAYA, 473
Dead by Sunset, 169
Deadly Delivery (Amnesty International), 22
Deadly force, 452
Declaration of Sentiments, 355, 557
Defending Childhood Initiative, 183, 525
Defense, Department of, 327, 543–44
Defense Task Force on Domestic Violence, 328
Delahunt, Bill, 247
Demographic and health surveys, **105–8**, 272, 470
Denial, 290, 291
De Niro, Robert, 168, 169
Denmark, 179
Department of Defense Advocacy Program, 543
DeSalvo, Albert, 25
DeShaney, Joshua, 109–10
DeShaney, Melody, 109
DeShaney, Randy, 109
DeShaney v. Winnebago Department of Social Services case, **108–11**
Desperation, crimes of, 172
Detailed Assessment of Postraumatic Stress (DAPS), 40
DiCaprio, Leonardo, 169
Dirie, Waris, 73

Disabilities and domestic abuse, **111–13**
Disasters and domestic violence, **113–17**
Discounting, 290
Discourtesy, maxim of, 289
Disinformation, maxim of, 289
Disney, Abby, 190
Diverting, 290
Division for the Advancement of Women (DAW), 520
Divorce, 462, 474
Dobson, Kevin, 169
Doherty, Shannen, 170
Domestic Abuse Intervention Programs (DAIP), 42
Domestic Violence (Schechter and Ganley), 444
Domestic Violence Act (Trinidad and Tobago), 65, 282
Domestic Violence and Matrimonial Proceedings Act (UK), 408, 555
Domestic Violence Awareness Month, 132, 342, 560
Domestic Violence Coalition on Public Policy, 211. See also National Network to End Domestic Violence (NNEDV)
Domestic Violence Counts 2011, 455
Domestic violence-focused couple therapy (DVFCT), 498
Domestic Violence Hotline, 544
Domestic Violence Prevention Enhancement and Leadership Through Alliances (DELTA) program, 75, **117–19**, 214, 280
Domestic Violence Resource Network, 211
Domestic Violence Survivors Justice Act, 425
Dominican Republic, 107, 271, 272
Dove, 531
Dowry killings, **119–22**, 154, 243
Dowry Prohibition Act, 120, 243
Draft Law on the Protection of Women from Family Violence (Lebanon), 324–25
Dreamworlds, 260
Dress for Success Worldwide, 531
Dressler, Joshua, 230
Drugs and domestic abuse, xxv, **122–24**

Duluth Domestic Abuse Intervention Project, 125
Duluth Model, 42, **124–26**, 166, 282, 389, 447, 510, 512
Dunne, Dominick, 457

Early Childhood, Domestic Violence, and Poverty (Schechter and Knitzer), 444–45
Earthquakes, 114
Economic abuse in intimate partner relationships, 173–74
Economic Commission for Latin America and the Caribbean (ECLAC), 273, 274, 468
Economic dependence, 9, 238, 466
Economic development, women and, xxiv–xxv
Economic impact of domestic violence, 462–63, 519
Economic Justice Project, 350
Economic recession and domestic abuse, **127–30**, 200
The Economist, 321
Ecuador, 275, 521
Edleson, Jeff L., 444, 445
Edna McConnell Clark Foundation, 443
Education, as a risk factor, 273
Education, Department of, 281
Education, in Pakistan, 295–96
Educational programs, **130–33**
Edwards, Donna, 211
Effective Intervention in Domestic Violence and Child Maltreatment (Schechter and Edleson), 444
Effects of domestic violence, **133–36**
Egypt, 105, 107, 158, 159, 219, 323, 325
Eisenhower, Dwight D., 369
Elder abuse, xxi, 75, **136–40**, 155, 511. *See also* Financial abuse
Elder Abuse Victims Act of 2011, 172
Elder Financial Protection Network, 174
Elder Just Act, 172
El Salvador, 273
Emergency Assistance (EA) program, 551
Emergency plan, 549–50
Emergency rooms. *See* Hospital and medical records and domestic abuse; Physicians, health-care providers, and domestic abuse
Emerging Pacific Women's Leadership Program, 540
Eminem, 67, 72, 215, 336
Emotional abuse, 76, 288, 510–11, 547
Emotional health, effects of domestic abuse on, 195, 300
Emotional numbing, 39
Employee Assistance Program, at Liz Claiborne, 292–93
Ending Men's Violence, 352
Ending Violence, 130–31
"Ending Violence against Women: From Words to Action," 521
End Violence Against Women (EVAW) International, **141–42**
Engaging Men program, 183
England, 146
Enlightenment programs, 8
Enough, 170
Ensler, Eve, 72
Entrepreneurs in Handcrafts, 540
Equal Employment Opportunity Commission, 353, 557
Equality Now (EN), **143–45**
Equal Justice Foundation Newsletter, 164
Equal Pay Act of 1963, 557
Equal Protection Clause, 527
Equal Rights Amendment (ERA), 353, 558
Erdas, Naile, 146
Esperanza, Casa de, 206
Estate of Bailey v. County of York, 109
Ethiopia, 159, 519
Ethnic and cultural differences, in batterer intervention programs, 44
Europe and domestic abuse, **145–47**
European Parliament, 161
European Union, human trafficking in, 232
EuroPRO-Fem, 318
Evaluative mediation, 312
Evans, Patricia, 289
Evans, Sara, 204
Everywoman's Shelter, 454
"Evil tongue," 253
Evolution, 50
Excision, 159

Expanding Solutions for Domestic Violence and Poverty (Schechter), 443
Ex parte Crow Dog, 359–60
Expect Respect, 130
Extended family structure, 153
Extrajudicial, Summary, and Arbitrary Executions report, 219
Exxon Valdez oil spill, 115
Eye Movement Desensitization and Reprocessing (EMDR), 498

Facilitative mediation, 312
Failure to protect, **149–53**
Faith Trust Institute, 251, 478
Falsehood, maxim of, 289
Faludi, Susan, 207–8
Family Act (UK), 555
Family Advocacy Program, 327
Family and Adolescent Well-Being, 153
Family Consultation Centre, 325
Family Court, 203
Family ideal, 197–98, 204
Family Justice Center Initiative, 525
Family of origin, 156
Family Protection Law (Jordan), 326
Family Protection Law (Palestine), 325
Family Reconciliation House, 325
Family Research Laboratory, 483
Family structure and domestic abuse, **153–54**
Family systems theory, xxvi
Family violence, risk factors for, **154–58**
Family Violence Court, 193
Family Violence Initiative, 376
Family violence perspectives, 483–84
Family Violence Prevention and Health Practice, 184
Family Violence Prevention and Services Act (FVPSA), 75, 117–18, 280, 351
Family Violence Prevention Fund, 35, 434, 445, 531. *See also* Futures Without Violence
Family Violence Protection Act (Australia), 174
Farentino, James, 169
Fawcett, Farrah, 41, 52, 168, 228
Fear, 169
Fedders, Charlotte, 320

Fedders, John, 320
Federal Bureau of Investigation (FBI), 343, 517–18
Federal Housing and Domestic Violence Study, 226
Federal housing programs, 225–27
Female genital mutilation (FGM), xxi, xxiii, 143, 155, **158–62**, 325
Female infanticide, xxi
Female perpetrators, **162–65**
Female self-defense, 300
Femicide, 221, 272–73, 324, 470, 472
"Femicide: The Politics of Women Killing," 210
The Feminine Mystique (Freidan), 558
Feminism and domestic abuse, **165–67**
    criminologists, 467–68
    first-wave, 556–57
    in Latin America, 272–73
    on patriarchy, 389
    prostitution, 232–33
    second-wave, 197–98, 352, 557–58
    social change movements, 463–64
    sociological theories about domestic abuse, 466–67
    third-wave, 166, 209, 558
    victimology, 467. *See also* National Organization for Women (NOW); Women's Rights Movement
Feministe, 321
Feminist Majority Foundation, 88, 528
Feminist-oriented therapy, 498
Field, Sally, 168
FIFA World Cup, 522
Fillion, Nathan, 170
Films and domestic abuse, **167–71**
Financial abuse, **171–75**
Financial dependence, 177
Financial Education Project, 342
Financial literacy, 526
Financial stress. *See* Economic recession and domestic abuse
Finley, Chuck, 299
"The First National Conference on Men and Masculinity," 351
First-wave feminism, 556–57
Fishburne, Laurence, 169
Fistulas, xxii–xxiii, xxiii

Fletcher, Geoffrey, 171
Florida, 280, 281, 423–24, 456
Forbes magazine, 216
Forced Marriage (Civil Protection) Act (United Kingdom), 179
Forced marriage and domestic abuse, **175–80**
　effects of, 176–77
　factors in, 177–78
　family structure and, 153–54
　introduction to, 175–76
　legal responses, 178–79
Ford, Gerald, 203
Ford Foundation, 214
Forgetting, 290
Forms of domestic abuse, xxvi
Fort Bragg, 327
Fort Campbell, Kentucky, 326
Foster care, 151, 440
Fourteenth Amendment, 108, 109, 527
Fourth R, 130
France, 179
Franklin, Kristin. *See* Personal narrative: Kristin Franklin
Frederick County, Maryland, 333–34
Freedom House, 325
Freel, Gary, 85
Freire, Paulo, 125
French, Jonta, 33
Freud, Sigmund, 187
Friedan, Betty, 353–54, 558
Fried Green Tomatoes, 168–69
Fuhrman, Mark, 458
Funding for domestic violence services, 45, **180–81**, 206
Furlong, Eddie, 70
Futures Without Violence, **182–85**, 239, 246–47, 279, 419

Gabriel, Peter, 73
Gandhi, 371–73
Ganley, Anne, 444
Garcia, Agustin, 59, 66
Garrison, Lane, 70
Gates, Bill and Melinda, 268
Gay activism, 558
Gayford, John, 409
Gay Men's Domestic Violence Project, 435
Gay victims. *See* Lesbian, gay, bisexual, and transgendered victims
Gaza Strip, 454, 544
Gelles, Richard J., 347–48
Gemelli, Neil, 500
Gender, Women and Health (GWH), Department of, 569–70
Gender and Natural Disasters Fact Sheet, 114
Gender equality, 515–17, 521
Gender inequalities, xxi–xxv, 9, 53, 150, 387, 558
Gender-related theories, **187–89**
Gender roles, xxv, 34, 155, 188, 231, 254, 274, 316, 389, 466
Gender-specific therapy groups, 498
Gender symmetry, 263–64
"Gender Symmetry" (Kimmel), 263
Gene-environment correlations, 102–3
General Provisions of the Marriage Law, 28
General Social Survey on Victimization, 375
Georgia (state), 334–35
Georgia, Republic of, 287
Georgia Annual Report, 334
Germany, 179, 282
Getting Together, 267
Gibson, Mel, 71
Girls Be Ambitious, 234
Girl Scouts, 57
Givens, Robin, 32, 70
Glamour magazine, 296, 302
GLBT National Help Center, 97
Global Believe Fund, 37
Global Fund for Women (GFW), 181, **189–91**
Global gender inequalities, xxi–xxv
Global Peace Index, 389
"Global Strategy to Stop Health Care Providers from Performing Female Genital Mutilation" (WHO), 161
Global Virtual Knowledge Centre to End Violence against Women and Girls, 521
Global Women's Leadership and Public Policy Program, 540
Global Women's Mentoring Partnership, 540
Goldberg, Whoopi, 168, 169

Goldman, Emma, 466
Goldman, Ron, xxviii, 32, 71, 209, 320, 457
Gonzales, Pam, 115
Gonzales, Simon, 67–69, 213
Goodsearch.com, 309
Gordon, Linda, 198
Gore, Al, 212
Grandiose narcissistic personality disorder, 53
Grassroots movements, **192–94**
Gray, Rico, 424
Great Britain. *See* United Kingdom
Great Depression, 200
Greater London Council (GLC), 410–11
Great Recession, 127–29
Greene, Ashley, 36
Greenwald, Robert, 168
Grice, H. Paul, 289
Grigorieva, Oksiana, 71
Grimke, Sarah, 557
Group therapy, 428, 498–99
Guangdong Municipal Women's Federation, 28
Guatemala, 273
Gulabi gang, 245
Guyland (Kimmel), 263, 264–65

Hagan, John, 188
Hague Convention, 94
Haiti, 22–23, 271, 272
Half the Sky (Kristof and WuDunn), 269, 304, 317
Half the Sky movement, 269
Handbook for Legislation on Violence against Women, 521
Harne, Lynne, 6
Harris, Eric, 25
Harvard International Law Journal, 91
Hassan, Aasiya Zubair, 249–50
Haven House, 202
Hayek, Salma, 73
Hazing, 265
HBV (Honor-based violence). *See* Honor killings
Head injuries, 50
HEAL Africa, xxxi

Health and Human Services, Department of, 74, 100, 180, 211, 216, 405, 438, 502, 504, 506
Health-care providers. *See* Emergency rooms; Hospital and medical records and domestic abuse; Physicians, health-care providers, and domestic abuse
Health Cares About Domestic Violence Day, 184
Health effects of domestic abuse, **195–97**
Health Resource Center on Domestic Violence, 211
Healthy Places Coalition, 422
Hegemonic masculinity, 63
Helping Teens Stop Violence (Kivel), 266
HELPS tool, 506
Heritage Foundation, 153
Hernandez, Aileen, 353
Hill, Jeffrey, 230
History of U.S. domestic violence before 1970, **197–201**
History of U.S. domestic violence developments, 1970s, **201–5**
History of U.S. domestic violence developments, 1980s, **205–8**
History of U.S. domestic violence developments, 1990s, **209–12**
History of U.S. domestic violence developments, 2000s, **212–16**
HIV/AIDS. *See* AIDS and domestic violence
HIV/AIDS & Domestic Violence Project, 350
Hoffman, Isabella, 170
Holder, Eric, 183
Hollabaugh, Sheila, 207
Holmes, Michael, 88
Homeland Security, Department of, 234
Homeless youth. *See* Runaway and homeless youth
Home visits, 526
Homicides. *See* Self-defense, homicides, and domestic abuse
Homophobia, 260
Homosexuality, forced marriage and, 178. *See also* Lesbian, gay, bisexual, and transgendered victims

Honduras, 271, 273
Honeymoon Phase, 447
Hong Kong, 287
Honor-based violence (HBV). See Honor killings
Honor killings, xxiv, **216–21**
  appellation, 221
  in Brazil, 273
  vs. domestic violence, 218–19
  dowry killings, 119
  honor and shame cultures, 217–18
  introduction to, 216–17
  locations, 220
  male victims, 220
  in the Middle East, 324
  perpetrators, 219–20
  reasons for, 220–21
  South and southeast Asia and, 473
  statistics, 219
  in Turkey, 146
Honor Our Voices, 37
Honor rapes, xxiv
hooks, bell, 353
Hope Street Shelter, 439
Hospital and medical records and domestic abuse, **221–24**
The Hotline. See National Domestic Violence Hotline
Hotlines. See Crisis lines
Hot Peach Pages, 66, 97, 147
House of Peace, 250
Housing Act (UK), 555
Housing and domestic abuse, **224–28**
Housing and Urban Development, Department of, 225–26, 526
Housing assistance, 526
Houston, Whitney, 71
Huffington Post, 259, 261, 317
Hughes, Francine, 41, 52, 168, **228–31**
Hughes, Mickey, 168, 228–29
Humane Society of the United States, 25–26
Humanity Project, 62
Human rights issues, 160, 175. See also Amnesty International
Human Rights Watch, 218
Human trafficking, 144, 178, **231–35**, 493–94. See also Mam, Somaly; Trafficking Victims Protection Act (TVPA)
Hunter, Zach, 234
Hurricane Andrew, 114–15
Hurricane Floyd, 115
Hurricane Katrina, 115–16
Hurricane Rita, 116
Hydrochloric acid, 1

I Can Make My World a Safer Place (Kivel), 266
"Iceberg theory," 364
If Someone Had Known, 169
Illiteracy, 273
Immigrant victims of domestic abuse, xxi, **237–40**
  Ali and, 18–20
  from Asia, 30–31
  from the Caribbean, 66
  from Central America, 99
  legal services and outreach, 382–83
  provisions for in VAWA, 215
  from South and Southeast Asia, 472
  from Southeast Asia, 99
Imminence of a threat, 452–53
Incite! **241–42**, 306, 370
Incite! Women of Color Against Violence, 214
India and domestic abuse, xx, **242–46**
  abuse during pregnancy, 417, 418
  dowry killings, 119–21
  female genital mutilation in, 159
  homicide, 448
  human trafficking, 231–32
  intimate partner violence, 107
  middle- and upper-class victims, 320–21
  sex ratio imbalance, xxii
Indiana, 280
Indian Andhra Pradesh Public Model, 282
Indian Civil Rights Act of 1968, 359, 360
Indian "Dilassa" Model, 282
Indian Health Service, 508
Indian Law and Order Commission, 508–9
Indian Ocean tsunami, 114, 115
Indian Penal Code, 244
Indigenous communities, 193, 274. See also Alaska Natives and domestic abuse; Native Americans and domestic abuse

Individual counseling and therapy, 497–98
Indonesia, 159
Infanticide, female, xxi, 119
Infernal Child (Pizzey), 408, 409
Infibulation, 159
Institute for Leadership in Education Development (I-LED) program, 184
Institute for Solution-Focused Therapy, 498
Institute of Medicine (IOM), 405
Institute on Domestic Violence in the African American Community, 211
Integrated Domestic Court, 93
Integrated Protection Measures against Gender Violence (Spain), 282
Inter-agency Network on Women and Gender Equality (IANWGE), 522
Inter-American Commission on Human Rights (IACHR), 67, 69–70, 110, 213, 378, 436–37
Inter-American Commission on Human Rights, report of, 585–661
Inter-American Convention of Belém do Pará, 468
INTERCEPT, 35, 318
Intergenerational violence, 409. *See also* Cycle of violence
Intergovernmental organizations (IGOs), 367
Interim DHS Surveys, 105
Intermediate-level predictors of family violence, 155–57
International Association of Chiefs of Police, 517
International Child Abduction Remedies Act, 94
International Convention on the Elimination of All Forms of Racial Discrimination (CERD), 286
International Covenant on Civil and Political Rights (ICCPR), 160, 286
International Covenant on Economic, Social, and Cultural Rights (ICESCR), xxx, 160
International Dating Violence Study, 88
International Day Against Violence Against Women, 183
International Day for the Elimination of Violence against Women, 569
International Health Conference, 568
International Herald Tribune, 286–87
International Human Rights Day, 183
International Labour Organization, 231
International Research and Training Institute for the Advancement of Women (INSTRAW), 520
International Violence Against Women Act (I-VAWA), xxxi, 23, 161, 183, 213, **246–49**, 378
International Violence Against Women Survey, 272, 321
International Women's Day, 36
International Women's Year (IWY), 46, 203
Internet, 216, 487–88, 490. *See also* Technology and abuse
Interpersonal relationships, children and, 83
Intimate partner violence (IPV):
    in Alaska, 13
    Alaska Natives and, 358–59
    battered woman syndrome and, 39
    CDC and, 75
    failure to protect and, 150–52
    as a form of family violence, 155
    gender disparity in, 150
    health impact of, 196
    identification of in health-care settings, 404–5
    increase in, 334
    in India, 107
    intervention, 405–6
    Native Americans and, 358–59
    prevalence of, 403
    prevention, 406
    as a public health issue, 402–3
    reproductive coercion and, 431
    South Asian immigrants, 472–73
    teenagers and, 491–93
Intimate terrorism, 299–300
Intimidation, 512
Iraq, 325
Irrelevance, maxim of, 289

Islam and domestic abuse, **249–52**, 474, 476–77
Israel, 323, 324, 325, 519
Israeli Law for Prevention of Family Violence, 324
Iverson, Allen, 33
Iverson, Tawanna, 33

Jamaica, 521
Jamelia, 73
Japan, 29, 282
Jarrett, Valerie, 525
Jessica Lenahan (Gonzales) et al v. United States, 585–661. *See also Castle Rock v. Gonzales* case; Lenahan (Gonzales), Jessica
Jewish Coalition Against Domestic Abuse (JCADA), 255, 256
Jewish Women International (JWI), 254, 256, 478
Jhally, Sut, 260
Job Opportunities and Basic Skills Training (JOBS) program, 551
Joe Torre Safe at Home Foundation, 35, 72, 317
John Chafee Foster Care Independence Program (CFCIP), 441–42
Johnson, Lyndon, 343, 353
Joint custody arrangements, 78. *See also* Parental custody
Joint Use Statewide Taskforce (JUST), 422
Jones, Mary Harris, 557
Jordan, 219, 324, 325, 326
Jouriles, Ernest N., 497
Journal of Family Issues, 483
Journal of Family Violence, 210
Journal of Sex Research, 439–40
Journal of the American Medical Association (JAMA), 15, 20–21, 200
The Joy Luck Club, 169
Judaism and domestic abuse, **253–57**, 476, 477
Judging, 290–91
Judicial continuing education, 184
Jung, Andrea, 36–37
Justice, Department of, 112, 123, 172, 180, 184, 212, 355, 479, 491, 525

Katz, Jackson, 63, 166, 188, 214, **259–62**, 316, 317
Kaufman, Michael, 554
Keeping Children and Families Safe Act, 76
Keeton, Cheryl, 169
Kelly, Lisa Robin, 70
Kemmeter, Ann, 109
Kentucky, 493
Kenya, 159, 521
Kerry, John, 246–47
Khaliq, Abdul, 297
Khan, Salman, 18, 19
Kid & Teen SAFE, 131
Kidd, Jason, 33
Kidd, Joumana, 33
Kidman, Nicole, 73, 516
Kilbourne, Jean, 261
Kimmel, Michael, 165, 166, 215, **263–66**, 316, 317
King, Martin Luther, Jr., 373
Kinkel, Kip, 25
Kissling, Frances, 189
Kitaen, Tawny, 299
"Kitchen fires," 448
Kivel, Paul, 166, 214, **266–67**, 316, 317
Klebold, Dylan, 25
Kneir, Thomas J., 480
Knightley, Keira, 37
Knitzer, Jane, 444–45
Knowmoresaymore.org, 183
Kobe earthquake, 114
Koenig, Michael, 418
Koop, C. Everett, 208, 561
Korea, 29, 121
Korean immigrants, 239
Kravitz, Lenny, 171
Kristof, Nicholas and Sheryl WuDunn, xxii, xxiii–xxiv, xxxi, 231–33, **267–69**, 295–97, 304, 316–17, 473
Kyrgyzstan, 146

Lambert, Adam, 70, 71
Language, disabilities and, 112
Language barriers, 30, 99, 107, 237–38
Language skill development, 135
Laos, 303
Lapidus, Lenora, 69

Latin America and domestic abuse, xxx, **271–76**
  achievements and initiatives, 274–75
  characteristics, 272
  culturally competent services, 99
  femicide, 272–73
  indigenous groups, 274
  introduction to, 271–72
  risk factors, 273–74
Latino Americans, 211–12, 239
Law Enforcement Officers Killed and Assaulted (LEOKA), 412
Law on Elimination of Violence Against Women (Afghanistan), 281–82
Lawyers Collective, 244
Layton, Jack, 554
Leadership Conference (Mary Kay Corp.), 309
Leadership role models, 388
Learned helplessness, 40, 51, 467
Learning is of Value to Everyone (LOVE), 55
Lebanon, 323, 324–25, 521
Lederer, Laura, 189
Lee, Michelle, 169
Lee, Spike, 33
Legal access, 525, 531
Legal discrimination, 143
Leghorn, Lisa, 559
Legislation and policies, dating violence, **276–79**
Legislation and policies, domestic abuse, **279–84**, 412–13
Le Mat, Paul, 168, 228
Lenahan (Gonzales), Jessica, 67–70, 110, 213, 378, 436–37. *See also* Castle Rock v. Gonzales case; *Jessica Lenahan (Gonzales) et al v. United States*
Lennox, Annie, 72
Lepine, Marc, 377–78
Lesbian, gay, bisexual, and transgendered victims, xx, **284–88**
  Break the Cycle and, 58
  crisis hotlines, 97
  dating violence, 61
  education campaigns, 215
  gay activism, 558
  grassroots movements, 192
  policing domestic violence and, 413–14
  runaway and homeless youth, 439–40
Liberal feminism, 166
Liberation hypothesis, 187
Liberia, 143
Lifetime network, 72
Likert Scale, 336
Linguistic analysis of verbal abuse, **288–92**
Lithuania, 145
Liz Claiborne Foundation, 180–81
Liz Claiborne Inc., 262, **292–93**, 355, 565
Lloyd, Rachel, 502
London Domestic Violence Forum, 282
Loose Change to Loosen Chains (LC2LC), 234
Lopez, Jennifer, 170
L'Oréal, 54
Los Angeles Unified School District, 130
Love Is Not Abuse, 215, 279, 292
Love Is Respect, 97
Loveisrespect.org, 356–57
"Love the Way You Lie" (Rihanna and Eminem), 66–67, 72, 215
Lugar, Richard, xxxi, 246
Lutheran Disaster Response of New York, 114

Macedonia, 179
The Macho Paradox (Katz), 259, 317
Macro-level predictors of family violence, 155
Macro-level systems, 388
Maffin, Neil, 170
Mahmoody, Betty, 168
Mahmoody, Sayed, 168
Mai, Mukhtar, 18, 268, **295–98**
Mail-order brides, 237–38
Maimonides, 253, 477
Major Crimes Act of 1885, 359, 360
Making a Difference (MAD) program, 142
Making the Peace (Kivel), 266
Malaria Control in War Areas, 74
Malaysia, 159
Male Reproductive Control of Women, Who Have Experienced Intimate Partner Violence in the United States, 432
Male sexual aggression, 88

Male victims of domestic abuse, 215, 220, **298–302**, 364–65, 455
Mali, 143
Mam, Somaly, **302–4**
Mandated clients, 43, 45
Mandatory arrest policies, 193, 203, 206, **304–8**, 412–13, 414–15, 560. *See also* Pro-arrest policies
Manner, maxim of, 289
Manu, 242
Marital rape, 213
Marshall, Thurgood, 110
Martin, Kellie, 169
Martin, Trayvon, 424
Marxist feminism, 166, 466
Mary Kay Corporation, 57, **308–11**
Mary Kay Foundation, 180, 456
"Mary Kay Truth About Abuse" survey, 308–9
Massachusetts, 435
Massachusetts Bay Colony, 198
Matheson, Tim, 170
McAfee, Robert, 211
McConaughey, Matthew, 169
McDonald, Renee, 497
McGraw, Tim, 73
McKeon, Nancy, 168, 501
McNulty, Faith, 228
Mean jokes, 290
Media Advocacy Project, 350
Media Education Foundation, 317
Mediation and domestic violence, **311–16**, 326
Medicare and Medicaid fraud, 171, 172
Meeting Survivor's Needs study, 225
Men & Masculinity Conference, 351–52
Men Can Stop Rape, 131
Men for Change, 318
Men's efforts against domestic abuse, **316–19**
The Men's Program, 63
Men's Studies Review, 352
Men Stopping Violence, 317
Men's Work (Kivel), 266
Mentors in Violence Prevention (MVP), 35, 63, 132, 259, 261, 317
Mercy Corps, 296

Messner, Michael, 262
Metta Center for Nonviolence, 374
Metzgar, Eric Daniel, 268
Mexico, 275
Michigan Coalition Against Domestic Violence, 425
Michigan Women's Justice & Clemency Project, 423
Micro-level predictors of family violence, 157
Micro-level systems, 388
Middle and upper classes and domestic abuse, **319–22**
Middle East and domestic abuse, xxx, 159, **322–26**
Migiro, Asha-Rose, 523
Military and domestic violence, 261, **326–28**, 543–44
Mill, John Stuart, 557
Millennium Development Goals (MDGs), 214, 569–70
Millon Clinical Multiaxial Inventory (MCMI) Borderline Personality Organization, xxv, 52
Mills, Donna, 169
Mindfulness practice, 497–98
Minneapolis Domestic Violence Experiment (MDVE), 205, 304, 306, **329–33**
Minnesota Multiphasic Personality Inventory, 52
Mission creep, 369
Missouri, 493
Mobile apps, 216
Model Code of the Family Violence Project, 83
Model Code Statute, 78
Modeling, 101–2
Model legislation, 282
Model Standards of Practice for Family and Divorce Mediation, 313
Modern-day slavery. *See* Human trafficking
Modernizing Foreign Assistance Network (MFAN), 562
Moldova, 145–46
Molina, Alfred, 168
Momm, Srey, 232
Money Smart curriculum, 526

Mo'Nique, 171
Monopolizing, 291
"Monsters," 532
Montreal Massacre of 1989, 318
Moon, Felicia, 32
Moon, Warren, 32
Moore, Gwen, 534
Moriarty, Cathy, 168
Morocco, 325
Morrison, Antonio, 527
Mortality review boards (MRBs) and domestic abuse, **333–35**
MOST Clubs, 131
Mother Jones, 557
Mount St. Helens volcano eruption, 115
Movement to end abuse, xxviii–xxxi
Ms. magazine, 203, 342, 559
Mukhtar Mai Women's Welfare Organization, 296
Murray, Anne Firth, 189
Murray, Jenni, 556
Murray, Pauli, 353, 355
Musharraf, Pervez, 295–96
Music and domestic abuse, **335–39**
Music therapy, 338
Muslim Women's League, 251

Nagler, Michael, 372
Nairobi Forward-looking Strategies for the Advancement of Women, 46
Name-calling, 289–90
Narcissistic injury, 53
Narcissistic personality, 77
National Advisory Council on Violence Against Women, 445
National Advisory Council on Violence and Abuse (NACVA), 20, 21
National Association for Community Mediation, 313
National Association of Female Executives (NAFE), 567
National Basketball Association (NBA), 31
National Census of Domestic Violence Services, 454–55
National Center for Cultural Competence (NCCC), 98–100
National Center for Injury Prevention and Control (NCIPC), 74, 211
National Center for Victims of Crime (NCVC), 506, 507–8
National Center on Domestic and Sexual Violence, 366
National Center on Elder Abuse (NCEA), 136–39
National Center on Elder Abuse: Nursing Home Abuse Risk Prevention Profile and Checklist, 138
National Clearinghouse for the Defense of Battered Women, 425
National Clearinghouse on Family Violence, 376
National Coalition Against Domestic Violence (NCADV), **341–43**
  on alcohol, 123
  on animal abuse, 26
  The Body Shop and, 55
  conferences, 207
  crisis hotlines, 206, 561
  formation of, 204, 559
  housing, 224
  legislation, 174
  National Day of Unity, 560
  shelters and, 41, 116
  U.S. statistics, 376
National Coalition Against Violent Athletes (NCAVA), 35, 318
National Coalition of Physicians Against Family Violence, 211
National Collegiate Athletic Association (NCAA), 34
National Commission for the Prevention of Infant Mortality, 133
National Commission on the Observance of International Women's Year, 203
National Committee for the Prevention of Elder Abuse, 174
National Compadres Network, 317
National Conference on Peacemaking and Conflict Resolution, 313
National Council of Dispute Resolution Organizations, 313
National Council of Juvenile and Family Court Judges, 78, 83, 209, 210, 444
National Council on Family Violence, 355

National Council on Independent Living, 112
National Crime Survey, 343
National Crime Victimization Survey (NCVS), 320, **343–45**, 518
National Dating Abuse Helpline, 57
National Day of Remembrance and Action on Violence Against Women, 378
National Day of Unity, 207, 560
National Defense Authorization Act, 328
National Demographic and Health Survey, 470
National Domestic Violence Hotline, xxix, 96, 210, 280, **345–47**, 455, 524, 532, 544
National Domestic Violence Pro Bono Directory, 531
National Domestic Violence Summit, 532
National Family Health Survey, 242, 321
National Family Violence Survey, 150, 298, **347–49**
National Football League (NFL), 34
National Forum against Domestic Violence, 66
National Gay and Lesbian Task Force, 440
National Human Trafficking Resource Center (NHTRC), 97
National Incident Based Reporting System (NIBRS), 413
National Institute for Occupational Safety (NIOSH), 564
National Institute of Justice (NIJ), 125, 205, 210, 304, 307, 329, 332, 360, 551
National Institute of Mental Health, 39, 542
National Institute on Alcohol Abuse and Alcoholism, 15
National Institute on Fatherhood and Domestic Violence, 184
National Intimate Partner and Sexual Violence Survey, 164
National Latino Alliance, 212
National Law Center on Homelessness and Poverty, 224
National Longitudinal Study of Adolescent Health, 491

National Network to End Domestic Violence (NNEDV), 57, 96, 180, 211, 216, 239, **349–51**, 454–55, 533, 567
National Organization for Changing Men (NOCM), 351–52
National Organization for Men Against Sexism (NOMAS), 317, **351–53**
National Organization for Women (NOW), **353–55**, 527, 528, 533, 558
National Police Agency of Japan, 29
National Public Radio, 268
National Research Council, 136
National Resource Center on Domestic Violence, 211, 224–25, 445
National Runaway Switchboard (NRS), 97, 441
National Taskforce to End Domestic and Sexual Violence, 341, 533
National Teen Dating Abuse Helpline, 292, **355–57**
National Violence Against Women Survey, 298
National Women's Aid Federation, 408
Native Americans and domestic abuse, **357–61**
  vs. Alaskan Natives, 12, 13, 14
  crime statistics, 507–8
  increased risk of, xxi
  micro-level predictors, 157
  rates of violence, 376
  tribal criminal law and jurisprudence, 508
  Violence Against Women Act and, 537. *See also* Tribal Law and Justice Act
Natural disasters. *See* Disasters and domestic violence
Nature Explore Classrooms, 310
NCADV. *See* National Coalition Against Domestic Violence (NCADV)
Nepal, 213, 521
Netherlands, 233
Network/LA Red, 287
Network of Men Leaders, 523
Network Women's Program, 146
Neutralization, techniques of, 188
Nevada, 566

New Right, 197, 204
News media and domestic abuse, **361–66**
   female victims and male perpetrators, 363–64
   framing domestic abuse, 365
   introduction to, 361–62
   male victims and female perpetrators, 364–65
   under- and overreporting, 362–63, 364
   summary, 365–66
Newsweek, 269, 388–89
New York, 93, 151, 305, 424–25
New York City Administration for Children's Services, 151
New York City Police Department, 330
New York State Coalition Against Domestic Violence, 505–6
New York Times, 24, 267–68, 305, 317, 327
New Zealand, 159, 179, 299
Nicaragua, 107, 272, 275
Nicholson v. Williams, 151
Nicole Brown Charitable Foundation, 460
Nigeria, 7–8
Nineteenth Amendment, 557
Nitric acid, 1
No-drop prosecutions, 92–93
Nolte, Nick, 170
No More awareness campaign, 37
No More Tears (NMT), 19–20, 370–71, 473
Nonconfrontational homicide, 230
Nongovernmental organizations (NGOs) and domestic abuse, xxxi, 46, 48, 49, 234, **366–69**, 468–69. *See also specific organizations*
Nonprofit-industrial complex, 369
Nonprofit organizations and domestic abuse, xxxi, 213–14, 234, **369–71**. *See also specific organizations*
Nonviolence theories and domestic abuse, **371–75**
Norman, Judy, xxvii
North America and domestic abuse, **375–79**
North Carolina, 566
Norway, 179

Not to People Like Us (Weitzman), 319–20
Not Under Bondage (Roberts), 85
Not without My Daughter, 168
Nouri, Michael, 168
Nova Southeastern University, 88
Nuclear family structure, 153
Nursing homes, 138–39
Nussbaum, Hedda, 207, 320

Oakland Men's Project, 266, 317
Oakland Police Department, 330
Obama, Barack, 23, 184, 280, 378, 507, 525–26, 567
Occupational Safety and Health Administration (OSHA), 564
Occupy Wall Street movement, 128, 370
O'Dell, Anne, 33
Office for the High Commissioner for Human Rights (OHCHR), 522
Office for Victims of Crime (OVC), 180
Office of Domestic Violence, 524
Office of Global Women's Development, 248
Office of Global Women's Issues, 247–48
Office of Juvenile Justice and Delinquency Prevention, 438
Office of the Special Adviser on Gender Issues and Advancement of Women (OSAGI), 520
Office of Women's Global Initiatives, xxxi
Office on Domestic Violence, 204, 208, 559
Office on Violence Against Women (OVW), 24, 112, 180, 184, 276, 278, 456, 525, 534
Office on Women's Health, 180
Okun, Will, 268
Olin, Ken, 169
Oliphant, Mark, 360
Oliphant v. Suquamish Indian Tribe, 359, 360
100 Steps to Equality campaign, 144
On-Line Training Institute (OLTI), 141–42
Operant conditioning, 102
Opportunity, crimes of, 172

Ordering, 291
Oregon, 559
Organizations related to domestic abuse, 815–34
O'Toole, Annette, 169
Out of Bounds (Benedict), 31, 316
Outreach services, **381–85**
Over-parentified children, 81
Overreporting, 362–63, 364

Pakistan, xxii, 119–22, 159, 179, 219, 295–97
Palermo Protocol, 233–34
Palestine, 323, 324, 325
Palestine Central Bureau for Statistics, 324
Palmer v. State, 149
Pan American Health Organization, 114
Papua New Guinea, 521
Paraguay, 470
Parental custody, 83, 94. *See also DeShaney v. Winnebago Department of Social Services* case; Joint custody arrangements
Parent-Child version of the CTS (CTSPC), 484
Parenting skills, 156
A Parent's Handbook, 292
Park, Allan, 458
Parker, Mary-Louise, 169
Parks, Casey, 268
Parrish, Nancy, 34
Parrish, Robert, 34
Partners for Prevention, 521
Passive bystanders, 62
Passive genotype-environment correlations, 102–3
Passive language, 363
Paternity fraud, 162
Patient Protection and Affordable Healthcare Act, 281, 419, 526
Patriarchal terrorism, 446
Patriarchy and domestic abuse, xxii, **387–90**
    Christianity and, 84–85
    definition of, 387–89
    economic abuse and, 173
    family structure and, 153
    feminism and, 166, 210
    forced marriage and, 177–78
    honor killings, 221
    in India, 243
    macro-level predictors, 155
    male victims and, 162–63
    religion and, 253
    sociological theories about domestic abuse, 466
Patricia. *See* Personal narrative: Patricia
Peaceful Families Project, 250, 251, 478
Peal, Ruth Berry, 143
Pearl, Debi, 85
Penn, Robin Wright, 73
Pennsylvania, 559
People power, 374
The People v. Francine Hughes, 230
Pepper, Claude, 136
Perry, Tyler, 72
Personal narratives
    Kristin Franklin, **390–91**
    Lauren Pilnick, **391–94**
    Patricia, **394–97**
    Sabrina, **397–402**
Personal protection orders (PPOs). *See* Restraining orders and personal protection orders
Peru, 107, 271, 469–70, 519
Pesci, Joe, 168
Peterson, William, 169
Phelps v. State, 150
Philippines, 282
Physical abuse, 510
Physical health, effects of domestic abuse on, 195
Physical symptoms, children and, 81–82
Physicians, health-care providers, and domestic abuse, **402–7**
    health-care settings, IVP in, 402–3
    health outcomes and IVP, 403
    identification of IVP, 404–5, 419
    insurance discrimination, 281
    intervention, 405–6
    prevention of IVP, 406
    reproductive coercion and, 433–34
Pierce, Moriah, 88
Pilnick, Lauren. *See* Personal narrative: Lauren Pilnick
Piper, John, 85
Pixel Project, 72
Pizzey, Cleo, 409

Pizzey, Erin, **408–11**, 454, 555, 558–59
Pizzey, Jack, 409
A Place to Go, 561
Planned Parenthood Federation of America, 434
Pleck, Elizabeth, 197–98, 199–200
Plymouth Colony, 198
Poe, Red, 247
Polaris Project, 97
Policing domestic abuse, xxviii, **411–16**
   diversity and, 413–14
   history of, 200, 202–3
   in India, 244
   legislation, 412–13
   officer-level factors, 414–15
   risk to officers, 412
   same-sex couples and, 284–86. *See also* Mandatory arrest policies; Minneapolis Domestic Violence Experiment (MDVE)
Port Madison Indian Reservation, 360
Post-traumatic stress disorder (PTSD), xxvii
   battered woman syndrome and, 39, 427
   checklist, 40
   college-age victims, 89
   military and, 327, 543–44
   music therapy, 338
   natural disasters, 115–16
   psychological harm, 134
   sexual violence, 143
   social and societal effects, 462
   treatment of, 498
Poverty, 7, 273. *See also* Welfare and domestic abuse; Women Thrive Worldwide
Power and Control Wheel, 42, 125, 447, 510, 512
Power-control theory, 188
Power imbalance, and mediation, 312, 314, 315
PPOs (Personal protection orders). *See* Restraining orders and personal protection orders
Pray the Devil Back to Hell, 190
Precious, 170–71
Precursors of aggression, 337
Predatory crimes, 172
Preferred arrest policies. *See* Pro-arrest policies
Pregnancy and domestic abuse, **416–20**
Pregnancy coercion, 431–33
Pregnancy Coercion, Intimate Partner Violence and Unintended Pregnancy, 432
Prevention, levels of, xxx
Prevention and Early Intervention Task Force, 445
Prevention Institute, **420–23**
Prevention of Domestic Violence and Victim Protection Act, 29
Primary prevention, xxx, 118
Prisons and domestic abuse, **423–26**
Pro-arrest policies, 306, 412–13, 414–15. *See also* Mandatory arrest policies
Profamilia, 470
Profeminist men's movement, 352–53
Progressive Era, 200
Progressive muscle relaxation (PMR), 338
Progress of the World's Women report, 214
Project SUPPORT, 497
The Promise, 170
Prone to Violence (Pizzey), 408–9
Propaganda, 291
Prostitution. *See* Human trafficking
Protection from Family Violence Law (Jordan), 324
Prothrow-Stith, Deborah, 187
Protocols for domestic violence in hospitals, 222–23
Psychological effects of domestic abuse, 81, 134, 300, **426–29**
Psychological theories about domestic abuse. *See* Biological and psychological theories about domestic abuse
PTSD. *See* Post-traumatic stress disorder (PTDS)
Public Health Agency of Canada, 376
Public Heroes, Private Felons, Pros and Cons (Benedict), 316
Public housing authorities (PHAs), 225–26
Public Law 83-280 of 1953, 359, 360

Public service announcements (PSA), 35, 58
Public sphere vs. private sphere, 198–99
Puerto Rico, 307
Puerto Rico Police Department, 307
Pulitzer Prize, 267–68
Puritans, 198
Push (Sapphire), 170

Qatar, 325
Quality, maxim of, 289
Quantity, maxim of, 289
Quran, 250, 474, 476–77, 478

Racism, impact on victims' ability to receive help, xx. *See also* African American women
Radford, Jill, 6
Radical feminism, 166, 202, 203, 204, 466–67, 558. *See also* Incite!
Raging Bull, 168
Rai, Aishwarya, 18
Rainbow Retreat, 202
Rajadhyaksha, Gautam, 18
Ramirez, Manny, 70
Ramsay, Tana and Gordon, 556
Rape, xxiii–xxiv, 32, 175–76, 213, 542. *See also* Mai, Mukhtar
Rational choice theory, 188, 467
Reagan, Ronald, 204, 208, 524
Real Men, 262
Recidivism of batterers, 92–93
Red River floods, 115
Regional Committee for Europe, 145
Rehnquist, William, 109
Reinelt, Claire, 203
Relevance, maxim of, 289
Religion. *See* Christianity and domestic abuse; Islam and domestic abuse; Judaism and domestic abuse; Spiritual abuse
Religious freedom, denial of, 477
Religious leaders, 477
"Remember My Name" Project, 342
Reno, Janet, 211, 445, 501
Reporter, 268
Reproductive coercion, 418, **431–34**
Request for proposals, 180

Resiliency, 104
Resource 4 the People, 435
Resource Center on Domestic Violence, 211
Restitution order, 435
Restorative justice, 125, 193
Restraining orders and personal protection orders, 67–68, 276–77, 280, **434–38**, 449, 493, 500, 566
Retreat, duty to, 452
Reuss, Pat, 533
Revised Conflict Tactics Scales (CTS2), 347–48
Ricart, Gladys, 58–60, 66
Rice, Condoleezza, 296
Rihanna, 66–67, 71, 72, 215
Risk factors for domestic abuse, xx–xxi
Ritter, Bruce, 441
Rivera, Marco, 35
Rivera, Michelle, 35
The Road to Lost Innocence (Mam), 303–4
Roberts, Barbara, 85
Roberts, Jane, 161
Roberts, Julia, 168
Robertson, Deidre, 458
Robert Wood Johnson Foundation, 180
Robinson, Glenn, 33
Roddick, Anita, 54–55
Roethlisberger, Ben, 261–62
Role reversal, 81
Romania, 145
Rose, Mary, 441
Rule, Ann, 169
"Rule of thumb," 198
Runaway and homeless youth, 97, **438–42**
Rush, Benjamin, 557
Russell, Brenda L., 230
Russell, Keri, 170
Russian Federation, xix, 145, 178, 448, 454, 521
Russian Mafia, 231
Rwanda, 521
Rwanda Women Network, 37
Ryan, Kevin, 441

Sabo, Mahlon, 501
Sabrina. *See* Personal narrative: Sabrina
Safe Dates, 130–31

SAFE HANDS program, 567
Safe Horizon, 565
SAFE Teen Act, 278–79
Safety Net:
    National Safe & Strategic Technology Project, 350
Safety Net Project, 532
Safety plan, 381–82
Safety Siren app, 37
Sakhi for South Asian Women, 473
Salma Hayek Foundation, 73
Salvation Army, 410
Sanders, Deion, 71
Sanders, Pilar, 71
Sandusky, Jerry, 262
Sanger, Margaret, 557
Sapphire, 170
Sati, 119
Save the Children-Sweden, 324
"Say No to Violence against Women" campaign, 516
Schaeffer, Rebecca, 479
Schakowsky, Jan, 247
Schechter, Susan, 204, **443–46**
Schlafly, Phyllis, 204
Schwimmer, David, 72–73
Scope and extent of domestic abuse, xix–xx
Scotland, 284, 299
Scott v. Hart, 203, 304, 559–60
Scream Quietly or the Neighbors Will Hear (Pizzey), 408, 558
Screening for domestic violence, 222–23, 404–5, 419
Secondary prevention, xxx
Second-wave feminism, 197–98, 352, 557–58
Seiden, Anne, 229
Select Committee on Aging, 136
Self-defense, homicides, and domestic abuse, xxvii, **446–50**
    female victimization, types of, 446–47
    homicide, 448
    legal system, 448–50
    prisons and, 423–25
    theories, 447–48
Self-defense, legal issues, **451–54**
Self-image, 461–62, 496
Sen, Amartya, xxii

Separate spheres, 198–99, 200
September 11, 2001, terrorist attacks, 215
Sergei, Ivan, 169
Sex, entitlement and, 265
Sex and the Single Girl (Brown), 558
Sex discrimination, 353
Sex ratio imbalances, xxii
Sex-selective abortions, xxi, xxii
Sex slavery, 302
Sexual abuse, 276, 511
Sexual assault forums, 525
Sexual Assault Training and Investigations Inc., 141
Sexual bullying, 61
Sexual honor, codes of, xxiv
Sexual jealousy, 50
Sexually transmitted diseases (STDs), 9
Shadow state, nonprofits as, 369
Shalala, Donna, 211, 445
Shalom Bayit, 256
Shame, 125, 221, 255–56. *See also* Honor killings
Shapiro, Francine, 498
Shapiro, Robert, 457
Sharia law, 250
Sharp, Gene, 373–74
Shattered Dreams, 168
Sheen, Charlie, 70
Shelters and domestic abuse, **454–57**
    child abuse and, 79
    establishment of, 201–2
    feminism and, 166
    funding, 180–81, 456
    grassroots movements, 192
    growth of, 206
    homeless shelters, 438–40
    lesbian, gay, bisexual, and transgendered victims, 286
    Mary Kay Foundation and, 308–10
    Mary Kay Truth About Abuse survey, 308–9
    in the Middle East, 325
    pet abuse and, 26–27
    A Place to Go, 561
    staff training, 455–56
    therapy and counseling, 495. *See also* Pizzey, Erin

Sherman, Lawrence, 205, 304, 306, 329, 331, 560
Sherrill, Patrick, 25
Shields, Brooke, 296
Sibling violence, 155, 156
Sidibe, Gabourey, 170
Sierra Leone, 521
Silent Veil, 121
Simon, Rita, 187
Simpson, Nicole Brown, xxviii, 32–33, 71, 72, 207, 209, 320, 457–60
Simpson, O. J., case, xxviii, **457–61**
  athletes and domestic abuse, 32–33
  awareness of domestic violence, 209
  celebrities and domestic abuse, 71, 72
  community resources, 460
  middle- and upper-class victims, 320
  news media and, 363
  overview of, 457–58
  police and judges, responses of, 459–60
  power and control, 459
  societal reaction, 458–59
Sin and redemption narrative, 363
Singapore, 299, 321
Single-parent homes, 156–57
Sisto, Jeremy, 170
16 Days of Activism, 182–83
60 Minutes, 207, 326, 560–61
Skopp, Nancy, 497
Slaughter, Candice, 417
Sleeping with the Devil, 170
Sleeping with the Enemy, 168
Sling Blade, 170
Smith, Mitch, 268
Snowe, Olympia, 246
So-called honor killings, 221
Social and societal effects of domestic violence, **461–63**
Social change movements, **463–65**
Socialist feminism, 166, 558
Socialization, 263–64
Social justice, 266
Social learning theories, xxv, 81, 101–2, 427
Social networking, 216
Social norms theory, 62–63, 132
Social Security Act, 136
Social welfare movement, 200

Society of Professionals in Dispute Resolution, 313
Socioeconomic status, risk for abuse during pregnancy and, 417
Sociological theories about domestic abuse, **465–68**
Sojourner House, 460
Soler, Esta, 247
Somalia, 158, 159
Somaly Mam Foundation, 302–3
So-Me Designs, 19
Somerhalder, Ian, 73
Sorichetti v. City of New York, 330
Sorority members, 88
Sotoudeh, Nasrin, 22
South Africa, xx, 287, 521
South America and domestic abuse, **468–72**
South and southeast Asia and domestic abuse, xix–xx, 99, 218, **472–76**. See also Dowry killings
South Asian Women's Network, 475
Southwest Center for Law and Poverty, 507
Spacek, Sissy, 170
Spain, 282
Spanking, 79, 102
Speak.Act.Change, 130
Speaking Out about Violence against Women awards, 37
Speak Out against Domestic Violence campaign, 36
Special Act on Domestic Violence, 29
Spin the Bottle, 261
Spiritual abuse, **476–79**, 511–12
Spousal Assault Replication Program (SARP), 332
Sri Lanka, 521
Stalking, 12, 210, 264, **479–83**, 511
Standard DHS Surveys, 105
Standards of Practice for Lawyer Mediators in Family Law Disputes, 313
Standing Together Against Rape (STAR), 13
"Stand Your Ground" law, 424, 452. See also Castle doctrine
Stanton, Elizabeth Cady, 199
Stark, Evan, 320
State-by-State Teen Dating Violence Report, 277

State Department, 231, 247–48, 502, 524–25
State Law Report Card, 57
Statement on Gender Violence and the Prison Industrial Complex, 306
"Stay Away Agreements," 277–78
Steinberg, Joel, 320
Steinberg, Lisa, 320
Steinem, Gloria, 72, 352–53, 355
Stereotypical gender roles, xxv
St. Hilaire, Richard, 500
Stills, Susan, 566–67
"Stitch rule," 200
Stockholm Syndrome, xxvii
Stonewalled (Amnesty International), 285–86
Stop Abuse for Every Teen Act, 278–79
Stophonourkillings.com, 219, 220
Stop Rape Now, 521
STOP Recovery Act, 535
Stop Violence Against Women global campaign, 22
Stop Violence Against Women organization, 226
Stop Violence in the Home campaign, 54, 55
The Story of a Shelter, 202
Stowe, Harriet Beecher, 557
Strategic Alliance for Healthy Food and Activity Environments, 422
Straus, Murray, 76, 88, 347–49, **483–84**
Strauss-Kahn, Dominique, 262
Street survival behaviors, 440
Stuart-Masterson, Mary, 169
Study on Violence against Children, 56
Substance Abuse and Mental Health Administration (SAMHSA), 130
Suffrage movement, 557
Suicide, in China, 28
Sulfuric acid, 1
Support groups for victims of domestic abuse, 383, **484–88**
Supporting Organizations Sustainability Institute (SOS Institute), 184
Support system, importance of, 549
Supreme Court, U.S., 436–37. See also *Castle Rock v. Gonzales* case; *DeShaney v. Winnebago Department of Social Services* case; *United States v. Morrison* case
Suquamish Tribe, 360
Survival of the fittest, 50
Survivor Therapy Empowerment Program, 542
Sweden, 233
Symposium on Standards of Practice, 313
Syria, 323, 324, 325, 521

Taiwan, 29–30
Tandy, Jessica, 168
Tanzania, 521
Task Force on Domestic Violence, 262
Taylor, Harriet, 557
Teaching Sociology, 483
Technology and abuse, **489–90**
Ted Global Conference, 268
Teenage Research Unlimited (TRU), 293
Teen Dating Violence Awareness Month, 36, 58, 278, 494, 526
Teen pregnancy, 438
Teen victims of domestic abuse, **491–95**
  abuse by caregivers, 491–92
  bullying, 61
  crisis hotlines, 97
  domestic violence, 491
  human trafficking, 493–94
  protective factors and prevention efforts, 494
  teen dating violence, 492–93
  Teen Dating Violence Awareness Month, 494
Television, violence on, 337
Temperance movement, 166, 557
Temporary Assistance to Needy Families (TANF), 224, 551–52
Tension-Building Stage, 447
Terrifying Love (Walker), 541
Tertiary prevention, xxx
Testosterone, 51
Texas Council on Family Violence, 203
Thailand, 303
That's Not Cool website, 183
The Handbook for National Action Plans on Violence against Women, 521

Therapy and counseling for domestic abuse, 83–84, 383, 484–88, **495–99**
Theron, Charlize, 72
Things Fall Apart (Achebe), 7
Third-wave feminism, 166, 209, 558
This Boy's Life, 169
This Way to the Revolution (Pizzey), 409
Thomas, Linda Johnson, 310
Thomson Reuters, 153
Thornton, Billy Bob, 170
Threatening, 289–90
Thunder from the East (Kristof and WuDunn), 269
Thurman, Charles J. "Buck," Jr., 499–501
Thurman, C. J., 501
Thurman, Tracey, case, 168, 205–6, **499–501**, 560
"Thurman Law," 499
Thurman v. City of Torrington, 330, 560
Tidal Wave (Evans), 204
Tierney, Kathleen, 206
Time magazine, 302, 320
The Times, 120, 121
Times of India, 121
Title IX of the Education Act of 1972, 557
Title VII of the Civil Rights Act, 557
Tone Loc, 70
Torre, Joe, 35, 72, 317
Torrington Police Department, 499–501
Tough Guise, 63, 259–60
Trafficking. *See* Human trafficking
Trafficking in Persons (TIP) report, 233
Trafficking Victims Protection Act (TVPA), 212–13, 232–33, 280, 378, 493, **501–4**, 524–25, 661–756
Transformative mediation, 312
Transgendered victims. *See* Lesbian, gay, bisexual, and transgendered victims
Trauma Symptom Inventory (TSI), 40
Traumatic brain injury (TBI) and domestic abuse, 50, 196, **504–7**
Treatment, of children of domestic violence, 83–84
Tribal Law and Justice Act, 213, 378, **507–10**, 525
Tribal Law and Order Act, 280
Trinidad and Tobago, 65, 282
Trivializing, 291

True Women, 199
Trust, 72–73
Trust Fund on Violence Against Women, 247
TrustLaw, 153
Tsunami, Indian Ocean, 114, 115
Tunisia, 323, 325
Turkey, 146–47, 324, 417
Turner, Ike, 169
Turner, Tina, 169
Turning Point for Women and Families, 250
T visa, 502
Tween and Teen Dating Violence and Abuse Study of 2008, 215
Types of domestic abuse, **510–13**
The Tyra Banks Show, 72
Tyson, Mike, 32, 70

U Care, 115
Uganda, 3, 121, 213, 287
Ukraine, 145
Ultra Orthodox Judaism, 254
Uncle Tom's Cabin (Stowe), 557
UN Commission on Human Rights, xxx–xxxi
Undermining, 291
Under-reporting, 362–63
UN Economic and Social Council (ECOSOC), 519
Unemployment, 551
UNICEF, 56, 321, 522
UNIFEM and UN Women, **515–17**, 520–21, 544–45
Uniform Crime Reports, 343, 412, 434–35, **517–18**
UNiTE, 214, 517, 522–23
United Arab Emirates, 325, 326
United Kingdom, 146, 147, 158, 179, 206, 320, 417, 455. *See also* Women's Aid Federation of England
United Nations Action Against Sexual Violence (UN Action), 522
United Nations and domestic abuse, **519–23**
  on honor killings, 219
  Latin America and, 274
  on natural disasters, 115

INDEX

NGOs and, 367
Palermo Protocol, 233–34
in South America, 468
UNiTE, 214. *See also* Convention on the Elimination of All Forms of Discrimination against Women (CEDAW); UNIFEM and UN Women; World Health Organization (WHO)
United Nations Children's Fund. *See* UNICEF
United Nations Decade for Women, 46
United Nations Development Fund for Women. *See* UNIFEM and UN Women
United Nations Development Programme (UNDP), 522
United Nations High Commission for Refugees (UNHCR), 522
United Nations Population Fund (UNPF), 219, 522
United States, 159, 376, 378–79, 388–89. *See also specific topics*
United States v. Morrison case, 524, **527–29**
Unite to End Violence Against Women, 274
UNITY, 422
Universal Declaration of Human Rights, 160
University of Miami Human Rights Law Clinic, 70
University of Tennessee, 351
UN Non-Governmental Liaison Service (UN-NGLS), 367
UN Population Fund, xxiv
UN Trust Fund, 181
UN UNiTE to End Violence against Women, 66
UN Women, xxxi, 214, 271, 274, 282–83, 470–71, 515–17, 520–21, 522
Uprooting Racism (Kivel), 266
Urban vs. rural domestic abuse, 6–7
Uruguay, 471
U.S. Agency for International Development (USAID), 105, 248
U.S. Attorney General, 208
U.S. Census Bureau, 137, 343, 507
U.S. Civil Rights Commission, 204
U.S. Commission on Civil Rights, 341, 559
U.S. Conference of Catholic Bishops, 503
U.S. Conference of Mayors, 224, 551
U.S. government responses to domestic violence, **524–26**
U.S. National Census of Domestic Violence Services, 350
U.S. National Comorbidity Survey (NCS), 299
U.S. National Youth Survey, 298
U.S. Preventive Services Task Force (USPSTF), 404–5
U.S. Surgeon General, 74
U-visa, 474
Uzbekistan, 179

Vacate order, 435, 436
VAWA. *See* Violence Against Women Act (VAWA)
Venezuela, 284, 469
Vera Institute of Justice, 112
Verbal abuse. *See* Linguistic analysis of verbal abuse
Verizon Communications, Inc., 531
Verizon Foundation, 180–81, 355, **531–33**
Verizon Wireless, 35
Verizon Wireless Hope Line, 532
Vermont, 305
Veterans Affairs, 327
Victimology, 467
Victims of Crime Act, 209, 351, 456
Vietnam, 303, 521
Vimochana, 122
Violence & Crime (Benedict), 317
Violence Against Women (Schechter), 444
Violence Against Women Act (VAWA), xxviii–xxix, **533–38**
  challenge to, 527–28
  crisis hotlines, 96
  housing, 225
  immigrants and, 20, 215, 239, 286, 474
  lesbian, gay, bisexual, and transgendered victims, 286
  National Domestic Violence Hotline, 345
  Native Americans and, 286, 359, 360, 537
  passage of, 209–10, 524, 533

provisions of, 278, 279–80, 378, 449, 520, 524, 533–36
reauthorization of, 23, 183, 212, 279–80, 351, 524, 536–37
shelters and, 456
support for, 309, 341–42, 349, 478
text of, 756–813
Violence Against Women Network (VAWnet), 180, 456, 506
Violent Crime Control and Law Enforcement Act, 345, 360
Violent music. *See* Music and domestic abuse
Virginia, 334
Virginia Tech University, 527
Vital Voices, **538–40**
Vital Voices Democracy Initiative (VVDI), 538
Vital Voices Global Businesswomen's Network, 540
Vital Voices Global Partnership (VVGP), 538
Voices Against Violence, 342
The Voices and Faces Project (TVFP), 142
Voices for Change (VFC), 303
Von Brenner, Karin, 94
Vulnerable persons, financial abuse of, 171–72

Wagner, Lindsay, 168
Wahlberg, Mark, 169
Waitress, 170
Wales, 146
Walker, Alice, 168
Walker, Lenore, 39–41, 51–53, 427, 447, 449, **541–42**, 559
Wall Street Journal, 268
War and domestic violence, **542–46**
Ware, Bruce, 85
Warning signs of abuse, **546–50**
Washington, D.C., 285
Washington, Desiree, 32
Webinars, 142
Webster, Charlie, 556
Weitzman, Susan, 319–20
Welfare and domestic abuse, **551–53**
Wen, Leana, 268

West Virginia, 334
What's Love Got to Do with It? 169
When Love Goes Wrong (Schechter), 444
When No One Would Listen, 169
"Where Did the Movement Go?" (Esperanza), 206
White, Deborah Gray, 199
White, Evelyn, 207
Whitefield-Madrano, Autumn, 321
White House Council on Women and Girls, 525
White Ribbon Campaign, 31, 318, 378, **553–54**
White v. Beasley, 307
Widow inheritance, 175
Wilder Research Center, 224
Williams, Oliver J., 211
Win a Trip with Nick Kristof contest, 268
Winfrey, Oprah, 73, 168
Wireless Foundation, 55
Witherspoon, Reese, 36–37, 73, 169
Withholding, 290
Witness, 73
Witnessing domestic violence, 150–52, 156, 427–28, 491, 495
Witness Protection Program, 502
Wolff, Tobias, 169
Wollstonecraft, Mary, 557
Women, Faith, and Development Alliance (WFDA), 562
Women against Violence Europe, 147
Women and Male Violence (Schechter), 204, 444
Women and Male Violence in Violence Against Women (Schechter), 444
Women in Prison Project, 423
Women of All Red Nations, 370
Women of Color Leadership Project, 350
Women of Color Network, 78
Women's Action Coalition, 32
Women's Action Network (WAN), 143, 144
Women's Advocates, 200, 201–2, 203, 559
Women's Aid, 56
Women's Aid Federation of England, 147, **554–56**, 559
Women's Aid of the UK, 37

Women's Center & Shelter of Greater Pittsburgh, 72
Women's Edge Coalition, 561
Women's Institute for Housing and Economic Development, 224
Women's Law Initiative, 450
WomensLaw.org, 350
Women's Law Project, 350
Women's Rights Movement, xxviii, 207–8, **556–61**
Women's Rights Project, ACLU, 69
Women's Work campaign, 262, 292
Women Thrive Worldwide, 213, 246–47, **561–64**
Woodham, Luke, 25
Working Mother magazine, 567
Workplaces Respond to Domestic and Sexual Violence, 184, 567
Workplace violence and domestic abuse, **564–68**
World Bank, 65, 469
World Conference of Women's Shelters, 351, 456
World Health Organization (WHO), xix–xx, 61, 105, 106, 113, 114, 116, 118, 159, 160–61, 469, 522, **568–70**

World Health Report, 569
Worldsafe Study, 470
World Sage Study, 272
Worth magazine, 182
Wrestling with Manhood, 63, 260–61
WuDunn, Sheryl. *See* Kristof, Nicholas and Sheryl WuDunn

Yashodhara, 115
Yemen, 158, 324
Yoakam, Dwight, 170
Yoga, 497–98
You Call This a Democracy? (Kivel), 266
Young, Rosemary, 69
Young, Will, 73
Young Women's Lives (Kivel), 266
Youthful offenders, 440–41
Youth Risk Surveillance Study, 416
YWCA Canada, 37

Zaire, 159
Zambia, 107, 519
Zero tolerance policies, 193
Zimbabwe, 521
Zimmerman, George, 424